# your
# gap
# year

Everything you need
for an adventure of
a lifetime

Susan Griffith

This edition first published in Great Britain 2010 by
Crimson Publishing, a division of Crimson Business Ltd
Westminster House
Kew Road
Richmond
Surrey
TW9 2ND

First published 1999 as *Taking a Gap Year*. Revised every other year. Sixth edition 2010.

A catalogue record for this book is available from the British Library.

ISBN 978 1 85458 491 5

Printed and bound by LegoPrint SpA, Trento

# ACKNOWLEDGEMENTS

This sixth edition of *Your Gap Year* would not have been possible without the help of scores of gap year students, year out organisations and an army of travel informants who have generously shared their information and stories by email, telephone and, in quite a few cases, down the pub. My warmest thanks are owed to the following gap travellers and volunteers who shared their stories so generously since the last edition:

Rob Ashpole – *Canada*
Afton Blight – *Peru*
Julia Bowler – *Thailand*
Rachael Brown – *Ghana*
Sadie Brown – *Borneo*
Ryan Conroy – *USA*
Nadia Daer – *Guyana*
Ashleigh Davey – *Thailand*
Ellena D'Silva – *Thailand*
Melissa Evans – *Nepal*
Richard Ferguson – *Portugal, Argentina*
Sam Forbes – *France, Thailand*
Samantha Fuller – *Morocco*
Caroline Gosney – *Madagascar, Europe*
Rob Harris – *Bolivia*
Andy Hicks – *USA*
Catherine Howard – *USA*
Louisa Ingham – *Italy*
Charlotte Kane – *Galapagos, Ecuador*

Emily Kidson – *South Africa*
Anna Ling – *Morocco, France, Guatemala*
Emily Logie – *South Africa, Botswana*
Charlie Macdonald – *Tobago*
Claire Mullineaux – *India*
Mark Nash – *Africa*
Jen Newby – *On choosing agencies*
James Pengelley – *Thailand*
Sarah Phillips – *Arctic Svalbard (Norway)*
Simon Preddy – *Uganda*
Dominic Samuels – *USA*
Lauren Smith – *Thailand*
Jonny Stephens – *Ghana*
Alice Stueck – *UK, Spain*
Holly Tate – *Australia*
Samantha Thornley – *Vietnam*
Lizzie Walker – *Tobago*
Becky Warden-Brown – *South Africa, Thailand*
Katie Yewdall – *Madagascar*

I am especially indebted to Laura Parker for the section on Travel in Latin America which she wrote while on her gap year travelling from Argentina to Bolivia, Peru, Honduras, Belize, Mexico and Cuba. Warm thanks are due to Hannah Adcock who has lived in Paris, the Greek islands and Scandinavia, and wrote the chapter on Travel in Europe. Gregory Deacon did a splendid job of writing about travel in Africa where he has spent long periods travelling while researching a PhD thesis about slum churches in Kenya. A vivid first-hand account of InterRailing was contributed by Jenny Hardie. For all these I am most appreciative.

While every effort has been made to ensure that the information contained in this book was accurate at the time of going to press, some details are bound to change within the lifetime of this edition. Addresses, phone numbers and prices are particularly susceptible to fluctuations, so the ones quoted here are intended merely as a guide.

If in the course of your gap year travels you come across something which might be of interest to readers of the next edition, please contact Susan Griffith at s.griffith@ntlworld.com. Future editions will depend on up-to-date reports from gap travellers who have been inspired to take a year out before or after university. The best contributions will be rewarded with a free copy of the next edition or any other Crimson/Vacation-Work title (see inside back cover).

**Note:** *Any organisation mentioned in the text without an accompanying address or cross-reference can be found in the Contact Details of Organisations at the end of the book.*

# PREFACE

The gap year is a once-in-a-lifetime opportunity, which should not be squandered. As you approach the end of school or university, you will be bombarded with choices. Remember, this year out is *your* gap year, not your parents' or your friends', and you can create whatever combination of experiences you want. Most gap years comprise a medley of activities which complement one another, home and abroad, work and play, earning and spending, challenge and self-indulgence.

Since I researched the last edition of this book two years ago, the world's economy has suffered a grievous blow. The global recession has bitten hard into the UK economy, causing panic and alarm on all fronts. Last year's graduates faced one of the most difficult job markets ever. In these troubled times, the idea of flitting off to a distant corner of the world on a gap year might sound irresponsible. On the contrary, it could be exactly the right approach to the problem, and one that the British government has been promoting, by funding various schemes for new graduates to volunteer abroad and to gain work experience at home.

With demand for university places outstripping supply, some school leavers will have had a gap year thrust upon them. Rather than twiddle thumbs and feel hard done by, why not turn an unplanned year out to advantage and go off to work in a Rocky Mountain ski resort, volunteer to teach at a school in Thailand, or join a marine research project in Tobago – all of which will enhance a future CV. In the wake of the Copenhagen Climate Change Conference, many young people will be spurred on to investigate the myriad environmental projects available. The new graduate discouraged by the prospect of impending joblessness can think of broadening horizons and skills by travelling, working, volunteering or interning abroad.

The continuing popularity of gap years has given rise to an ever-increasing number of programmes and schemes targeted at young people. The range of choices can be overwhelming – studying lemurs in Madagascar, teaching English to Ecuadorian children, doing work experience with an engineering firm, picking fruit in New Zealand to fund some adventure travel, surveying coral reefs in the Philippines, spending the summer at an American summer camp, learning Spanish in Argentina. The possibility of arranging a DIY gap year without the shelter of a fee-charging company is also covered. Sifting the responsible wheat from the profit-mongering chaff is no easy task when faced with the welter of schemes vying for attention. Here you will find solid advice on how to avoid disappointment and rip-offs.

Many gappers will simply want to go backpacking and this new edition includes a whole continent-by-continent section on how to maximise your travelling fun while keeping to a realistic budget. This book has grown up with the travel industry and takes account of all the shortcuts that now exist to fixing up an unforgettable gap year. The inclusion in its pages of hundreds if not thousands of possibilities sometimes makes me feel like a walking database. Amongst all the specific agency details, websites and realistic practical advice, the first-hand stories told by gap year students (pre- and post-university) are interwoven to inspire and encourage. This book is written to renew optimism and spark the imagination of all potential gappers.

Susan Griffith
Cambridge
January 2010

# Part I
# Planning your gap year

## ONCE IN A LIFETIME
## BEFORE YOU GO

# ONCE IN A LIFETIME

As James Bond failed to notice, you only live once. Superlatives such as 'amazing', 'incredible' and even 'blissful' pepper the travel reminiscences of people who have had adventurous gap years, even the ones who have spent the first six months working behind the till at their local supermarket in order to save enough funds. A once-in-a-lifetime experience need not require any derring-do. Cycling through Patagonia or tracking the endangered black rhino is not for everyone. It could simply be breaking away from your friendship group to work in a ski resort in the Canadian Rockies or leaving home for the first time to go InterRailing or surviving the uncomfortable bus journey from Bangkok to Siem Reap.

Nothing can compare with the joy of the open road. Certainly not overdue term papers and a late student loan payment. The sense of possibility and adventure while travelling brings feelings of exhilaration, long submerged in the everyday routines of school and home. Cheap air travel has opened up parts of the globe once reserved for the sons and daughters of the seriously affluent. When travelling in far-flung corners of the world, you suddenly escape the deadlines, the chores, the clutter, the feeling of stagnation when you have been doing the same old thing for a long time. Even 18 year olds can get into ruts.

Travelling spontaneously means you have the freedom to choose from an infinite spectrum of possibilities. Those who have experienced independent travel usually catch the bug and long to visit more places, see more wonders and spend a longer time abroad. Today trekking in the hinterland of Rio de Janeiro or diving in the Philippines can be within the grasp of ordinary school leavers and college graduates. The longing might stem from a fascination left over from childhood with an exotic destination such as Madagascar or Spitsbergen. The motivation might come from a friend's reminiscences or a television travelogue or a personal passion for a certain culture or natural habitat or sport. At some point in your schooling a vague idea begins to crystallise into an actual possibility.

That is the point at which the purple prose of brochure-speak must be interrupted by hard-headed planning. The first question is always: how can I afford such a trip? How can ordinary people possibly move their dreams on to reality? The conventional means to an exciting end is to work and save hard. A grim spell of working overtime and denying yourself a social life is one route to being able to join an overland expedition through East Africa, a dive instructor's course on a Greek island or a bungee-jump in New Zealand. Picking up bits and pieces of work and volunteering along the way can go some way to reducing the cost. Informal ways can be found of offsetting the cost of travel. Work-for-keep arrangements on a Canadian farm or Costa Rican eco-lodge will mean that you have to save far less than if you booked a long-haul package holiday to those destinations – in some cases little more than the cost of the flight and onward transport.

Volunteering or working abroad makes it possible to stay overseas for an extended period, to have a chance to get below the surface of another culture, to meet foreign people on their own terms and to gain a better perspective on your own culture and habits. Those who go down this route often relish being able to do something completely unfamiliar in an alien setting. The hundreds of pages that follow will help you to discover the means of doing just that.

> **TRAVEL TIP**
> *The only essentials for having a great time on your gap year are motivation and money (and without the former you are unlikely to be able to save or fundraise the latter).*

## WHY TAKE A GAP YEAR?

For many young people approaching the end of school, the decision whether or not to take a gap year can be a fraught one. The first question to ask yourself is: Does the idea have a strong appeal? If you close your eyes and imagine yourself in the student union bar at university and then transport yourself in your imagination to an Amazonian rainforest or a Tanzanian village school or an Italian language class – what gives you more of a buzz? Think of the bad bits. Think of yourself sitting in a college library swotting for yet another exam and then picture yourself swatting mosquitoes doing some manual job in the broiling sun of the tropics. If the idea of striking off to some remote corner of the world, far away from family and (most likely) friends, gives you the heebie-jeebies, then perhaps that kind of gap year is not for you. You can always come back to the idea after college (discussed below). What you want to avoid is spending a year hanging around passively waiting for something to turn up.

Deciding whether to take a year off and then how to spend it may not be as momentous as some other life decisions such as which university course to choose, but it is as individual. No parent or adviser or guidebook or even friend can make the decision for you. All that outsiders can do is set out the possibilities and see if any of them takes your fancy enough to pursue. Do as much research as possible, let the ideas swill around in your head and see what floats up.

There is no doubt that it is easier to stay on the funicular that leads directly from the sixth form to higher education. After all, the majority of school leavers still do just that. Yet the number of people deferring is much higher than it used to be and an increasing number of students from a variety of backgrounds are at least giving the idea some serious thought. In many circles, taking a gap year is still considered something that only the rich and privileged do; but the explosion in the number of specialist organisations helping students to set up gap years is the result of a democratisation of the concept. Of course there are still plenty of people from top public schools and privileged backgrounds who take gap years (famously both the royal princes did) but anybody who is determined and enthusiastic enough can do it.

Try not to get too worried by all the emphasis on taking a 'constructive' and 'structured' gap year, if all you want to do is spread your wings, travel and see what turns up. Teachers, parents and organisations sometimes go overboard in insisting that everything has to count for the future, and may fall prey to a near-obsession with what looks good on a CV. This is an aspect of culture in the highly developed West that might be usefully challenged on a backpacking trip in Cambodia and Laos or a volunteer school-building scheme in Madagascar. The much maligned phrase 'university of life' contains an important truth: that life experiences and getting to know yourself better may be hard to measure on any league table but are just as educationally valuable as writing waffly essays about the semiotics of film.

Many 17 year olds are simply too young to make the choices expected of them regarding university and careers. If you are in this category, an extra year of exposing yourself to different experiences might provide some answers or at least whittle down some preferences. Otherwise there is a danger that you will drift along to university with the crowd and find that your heart just isn't in it. This is what happened to **Ross Fairgrieve:**

> *As I got towards the end of my A-Levels, I knew I wanted to get away for a bit. The degree course I was hoping to study, however, was a four-year course with the third year being in Australasia so I didn't really want to take another whole year out beforehand. I therefore decided that I'd finish my exams, jet off somewhere nice for the summer, and then come straight back and go to university. While I'm sure this works for some people, it didn't really happen for me. I spent my summer on Koh Tao, a little island in the Gulf of Thailand that's almost singularly dedicated to scuba diving. After two and a half months I came back to England and headed straight off to a grey, autumnal East Anglia. Unfortunately my heart was still in Thailand and after a month I had thrown in the towel and was working full-time to get back out there. So much for my cunning, time-saving plan! Anyway, I now had a gap year to fill. Leaving university was actually the best thing that could have happened. I then had a much clearer picture of what I wanted from university and applied for a slightly different course (I changed from Oceanography and Meteorology at UEA to Oceanography single honours at Southampton). Reapplication was no problem; I was just applying with the next year of school leavers. It's worth remembering though, that applying for university during your gap year rather than deferring your entry does mean that you might have to go to interviews so you will lose some flexibility in the planning of your year.*

For some, a gap year serves the same purpose as Dorothy's trip to the Land of Oz, which is to make them appreciate home. **Afton Blight's** nine months in Peru persuaded her that T S Eliot hit the nail on the head when he wrote in *Four Quartets*, '*We shall not cease from exploration, and the end of all our exploring will be to arrive where we started and know the place for the first time*':

*Living in Peru allowed me time apart from everything I knew in my farming background in the Midwest. Although I enjoyed my time volunteering with SKIP (Supporting Kids in Peru), I realised I truly missed working in agriculture. I love being outside, the variation of tasks, and working with big machines. Upon my return I knew I wanted to attend Michigan State University to further my knowledge in animal and crop science. I wasn't choosing this career because it was convenient, I chose it because it is something I see myself doing and liking for many years. SKIP did not directly result in me discovering my passion for farming, but it allowed me to discover who I am and my interests. It also revealed to me things that I am not cut out for, like teaching English for more than a short time!*

At the opposite end of the spectrum from those who don't have a clue what they want to do, **Marcus Starling** knew exactly what he wanted when he left school and used both a pre- and post-university gap year to impressive effect. Before uni he spent a month assisting an MEP in Brussels, six months as an ancillary teacher in a school in Leicester to earn money, two months on a study scholarship in Germany, and three months working on a kibbutz in Israel. After university he was not accepted on to the Civil Service Fast Stream so decided to gain some work experience abroad by joining the JET teaching programme in Japan (see *Asia* chapter) before re-applying. He got through the process second time round and is now working for the Training and Development Agency for Schools.

## PROS AND CONS

If major doubts remain about what the next step in your life should be, there is nothing better than taking a year out to do something completely different, to give yourself time and space to decide, away from all the pressures of home and school. Students repeatedly say that travelling or working/volunteering abroad helps to focus their minds on what they want to do next. But how might future employers view this pause? The majority of employers have been shown to value gap years. Some company application forms even include a question about the gap year. A report commissioned by the national volunteering organisation CSV (Community Service Volunteers) showed that of members questioned from the Association of Graduate Recruiters, 100% believed a constructive gap year helps young people to prepare for the workplace. In total, 88% thought that a well-structured gap year helped to furnish graduates with skills such as communication skills, decision-making and relationship building.

According to the most recent statistics from UCAS (the Universities & Colleges Admissions Service) for 2008/2009, a record 33,171 accepted applicants deferred entry to the following year, an overall increase of nearly 15% from the previous year, although the total number of university entrants increased by only 10%. Taken as a percentage of university acceptances overall the deferral rate has changed little since 2002 with approximately 7.3% of university entrants taking up a place a year late.

The culture is changing; education is no longer seen as a linear progression without interruption. Fifteen months is a miraculous period of time in which to pursue dreams and create memories. There will of course be opportunities later in life to take a break from routine – after university, between jobs, after having a child, sabbatical leave, after retirement, etc. But the combination of freedom from responsibility and leisure time is much harder to manage later on.

The standard objections raised by the doubting Thomases of the academic and parental world go as follows:

- You'll be a year behind your friends.
- You'll lose the impetus to study (though you may lose that over the four months between A-Levels and university anyway).
- You'll be seduced by travel and find it difficult to settle back into a comparatively boring routine on your return.
- You'll be seduced by the things that money can buy if you spend your year out earning enough money to save and spend and then will find it difficult to contemplate reverting to the poverty of studenthood.
- You'll be seduced full stop and abandon everything for love.

Parents will be relieved to learn that the vast majority of gap year students do not lose their way. Some are changed enormously but very few bring grief to their families by cashing in their return ticket to settle in Koh Samui or Goa. The experience of working hard at a local job in order to fund a gap year experience is usually enough to persuade even those who are lukewarm about the benefits of higher education to stay on as a student for a few more years.

There is a general and growing perception that we live in dangerous times. To take just one illustration, a generation ago hitchhiking was considered a perfectly normal activity, whereas now it has all but disappeared. With heightened alarm worldwide about personal security and some high-profile tragedies (e.g. the murder of the English teacher Lindsay Ann Hawker in Japan in 2007), some potential gappers and certainly their parents see gap years abroad as full of risk and danger. This anxiety probably afflicts young women more than young men, though the statistics show that this fear is irrational.

Another oft-touted objection is financial. The introduction of top-up fees has made it more difficult to justify taking a year off before university. If your poor parents are contributing to your university education, it seems too much to expect them to contribute large wads of money for a gap year jolly, and you will not want to add to your own burden of debt. As is well known, university debts do not have to be paid back until graduates are earning more than £15,000 a year. The levels of debt with which many students now leave university are so horrendous (typically £20,000+) that to delay the paying back for one more year may strike you as trivial in the scheme of things.

**KATIE WHITE** from New England had the determination to take a year off. Since the practice is less common in the USA, young Americans have to be more determined than their British counterparts:

*I knew I would have to deal with friends and family thinking something obviously must be wrong if I was not going straight to college. But on the positive side, my gap year would take pressure off my getting into the perfect college, knowing that I could reapply if I crashed and burned in my applications. Secondly, I wouldn't be going to college burnt out and unenthusiastic (as several of my friends ended up doing freshman year). I hoped to return refreshed and inspired and with a clearer idea of what I wanted to study. This has proved true since I've returned. I recently opened the course catalogue for pre-registration and had a much more informed sense of what I wanted to pursue, such as Spanish, Latin American Studies, Art, and Environmental Studies, based on my gap year experiences in Costa Rica and Italy. I didn't feel any pressure to take certain courses for graduate school or to get ahead in my major; I just registered for classes I was passionate about or intrigued by.*

*After saving money over the summer by working at a summer camp, I spent from the end of August through mid-December volunteering at the Monteverde Friends School in Costa Rica where I worked with students in 5th to 8th grades, teaching English literature and language, and World History. I lived with a local host family whose children attended the school. After returning home for a few months to earn money, I left for Tuscany in March after being accepted as a Farm Intern at a medium-sized farm and agriturismo called Spannocchia. I worked with seven other interns that spring, with each of us specialising in a certain part of the farm, mine being the vegetable garden. Now I am home for the summer, working and getting ready for college this fall.*

*My gap year included so many exquisite moments that I really don't think I can pick one out. I remember lying on the roof of our hotel in Panama with my fellow teachers, looking up at the stars for hours, and feeling so relaxed and free and independent. I skied a lot this winter along trails in Massachusetts and Vermont, and I will hold forever in my memory one evening when I came out of the woods and the sun was shining on the snow, and smoke was wisping out from the chimney of the lodge, and everything was just so brilliant, I couldn't believe I was a part of it. In retrospect, these small wonders and moments of overwhelming gratitude for and pride in my decision to take a gap year stand out.*

*My low points revolved around learning to balance my own health and safety with my adventures. I was eighteen when I left for Costa Rica and had no idea how little I knew about living on my own. Little by little, however, I learned to change my sheets, do my laundry, eat well-rounded meals, seek out advice, and thank people for their help. So my low points of feeling messy or sick or lonely shuffled me along to becoming more self-sufficient. I learned how to make tortillas and tamales, bake bread, start a vegetable garden from scratch, fix doors that have fallen off their hinges, use a power wrench, speak a bit of Spanish and Italian, and keep track of my own finances.*

*One of the greatest rewards of this gap year was the realisation that I didn't have to be funnelled through life; nothing should hold me back from doing what I love. I now feel that even if I get sucked into my workaholic mode again, I can sit myself down and say that there was a time when it wasn't like this and it doesn't have to be like this now. I know a simpler and more rewarding – albeit temporary – lifestyle that I can use to ground myself as I go through life. I know how to take a step back now.'*

## SOLO OR IN COMPANY?

You have to be fairly lucky to have a friend who has the time, money and motivation to join you on your chosen gap year travels or project. This is probably the single most common deterrent for school leavers contemplating a gap year, that they lack the self-confidence to strike off on their own. Joining an organised gap year scheme should allay these fears because this will introduce you to a ready-made group of peers at a pre-departure orientation, group travel or on arrival. Similarly you can simply join a backpacking tour group (see 'Travel' below).

If you don't have a suitable companion and are convinced you need one, you can search on appropriate internet forums such as Lonely Planet's thorntree, www.backpackers.com with a 'Travel Buddies' forum, www.travelchums.com (American), www.companions2travel.co.uk (membership £5) or www.gapyear.com's 'Find a Travel Mate', any of which might turn up a like-minded companion. An application on Facebook called 'Hostels' allows you to find out who is staying at hostels you're heading for, message them and possibly fix up onward travel together.

But there is no guarantee you will connect instantly with strangers found this way. Many travellers emphasise the benefits of travelling alone, especially the chance to make friends with the locals more easily. Most are surprised that loneliness is hardly an issue, since there is always congenial company to be met in hostels, harbourside pubs, overnight trains, etc. some of whom even team up with each other if they happen to be heading in the same direction. Of course, if you are working in a remote rural area and don't speak the language fluently, you will inevitably miss having a companion and may steer away from this kind of situation if it bothers you. If you are anxious about the trials and traumas of being on your own, try a short trip to see how you like it.

Women can travel solo just as enjoyably as men, though they may need some convincing of this. Travelling with friends is usually more fun but removes the perilous sense of possibility and adventure that some people love most about travelling. As one young solo woman traveller described it, '*the glorious moments, the stick-out-your-thumb-and-be-glad-for-whatever-is-going-to-happen-next moments, the feelings of triumph and absolute freedom, are uniquely yours.*'

Travelling can put a strain on the best of friendships. **Alice Stueck** comes from the small town of Abernethy (which has a population of 140) in the Canadian Prairies of Saskatchewan. Barely 18, she and a school friend hatched a plan to save money and see Europe. They arrived in England in the hostile month of November and stayed with some relations of Alice's travelling companion... and stayed and stayed. It seemed easier to remain in a comfortable house in the Home Counties than head off to who knows where. On a short trip to Paris, Alice began to suspect that she and her friend should have organised a trial trip together before committing themselves to the big adventure because their travelling styles were completely at odds. While the friend was keen to tick off the major tourist sites and spend a lot of money, Alice wanted to take things more slowly and give herself quiet periods to absorb what she was seeing. She also didn't want to blow her budget in the first few weeks. Things reached a crisis point back in England and she fled to the home of a friend of a friend of her mother's who happened to live not far away. She was tempted to go straight home but knew she would regret that later so decided to pause and catch her breath. Persuaded by her new hosts to leave 90% of her luggage behind and to join the Youth Hostel Association (YHA), she set off, albeit a little timidly, on her first solo trip, to Oxford, Bath and London. Gaining confidence she booked a no-frills flight to Valencia, where she had a wonderful time.

A further layer of complication is added if you are in a relationship with someone who is not keen on joining you in your adventures. Frequent contact by telephone, email or (dare I suggest it?) letters will help keep things on course. Compromise is one answer, for example to organise a trip that might be shorter than otherwise or plan to rendezvous with your partner part way through the gap year. What most people hope is that their relationship will survive a serious separation though at age 18 this is probably less likely than couples of more mature years. It would be a shame to have your decisions dictated by someone who might not be all that important to you once you get to university. **Camilla Burgess's** story is typical: her boyfriend tried to dissuade her from going to volunteer for three months in Ghana during her gap year and then put pressure on her to cut her stay short, which she did do (thereby incurring a financial penalty). They split up almost as soon as she got home. **Becky Warden-Brown's** relationship also didn't survive her 2009 gap year:

> *My lowest point was flying out to Thailand to meet my boyfriend of the time and then discovering he was cheating on me. I felt so alone in a foreign country and just wanted to go home. But I'm so happy I stayed and I had the best time of my life. It forced me to be independent, which I had never been able to do before.*

When choosing a volunteer programme, one important consideration is whether you will be 'alone' in your placement or with other gappers. After **Laura Parker** spent three months of her gap year in a town in northern Cambodia through *Outreach International*, she was persuaded of the benefits of solo placements:

> *Living and working with volunteers of the same age from home could make the transition less frightening, and you'd probably build some lifelong friendships. But for others that may defeat the point of travelling to a foreign country and integrating with the people you are helping, or who live there. Equally, being based in a small rural town with few Western comforts and no other English speakers around could seem terrifying. But the likelihood is that you'd be taken in by the local community far more readily, you'd pick up more of the language, and could have a much more unique experience.*

## WILL A GAP YEAR CHANGE YOUR LIFE?

The short answer is probably not – but maybe. In the first place six months of slogging at a local chain store or pizza restaurant usually works wonders to persuade you of the value of continuing your education. Six months spent overseas doing something completely different does have the potential for prompting a radical change of direction. For example **Joe Keely's** six months in Tanzania steered him in a completely new direction:

> *Not only did I achieve a fantastic feeling of well being, great friends and great memories from this six months, but I have (excuse the cliché) found myself. Before I left for Tanzania I was going to follow the electronic and electrical engineering line. I have now changed course and wish to become a journalist and have looked into working for Oxfam on completion of university. I wouldn't have dreamt of such a change before I left, a change I am very grateful for now. This year gave me the break and the sense to choose what I really wanted to do in life and to see my life from a different angle. In fact the only problem with the gap year is it makes life back here seem so much more dull.*

Parents worry that a gap year will derail plans for higher education. It is certainly not unknown for a young person to change their mind about university after a gap year. **Anja Ludgrove** expected to return to Britain to do a law conversion course after her snowboarding course but was so enamoured of the lifestyle that she has stayed on for several seasons as an instructor. The parents have to ask themselves where the tragedy lies in this. In these enlightened times of flexibility in education, the possibility always exists of resuming studies at a later stage.

**Faye Mold** is yet another student whose gap year – doing a divemaster course in Thailand – helped to shape and clarify her priorities:

> *At school we were not really given that much advice. We did have talks from major gap year companies which made me very excited but I already knew what I wanted to do (scuba diving) and the school never let us forget that it was all heading for university, which weighed me down somewhat. I didn't go to uni in the end (originally I was going to study Criminology) but saved up and went travelling again and I feel this was the best education I could get. I now realise I was only going to uni because the schools pressurised me into thinking I would be a nobody if I didn't have a degree which I now know is not true after meeting so many people abroad. My family are very supportive and have always said they just want their children to be happy so they were not disappointed about my decision not to go to uni (although for a while I could not help thinking they were). I have not regretted my decision at all. I am currently applying to join the Met Police and after my probationary period (if I pass) I want to specialise. So who knows – I may try to join the police underwater search and recovery team, so my diving would be put to use.*

**Simon Preddy's** gap year had exactly the opposite effect: '*It was taking a gap year that made me realise that I needed to go to university if I wanted to achieve my passions in life. That turned out to be teaching and also having a voice in the world (i.e. journalism), as seeing some shocking things in Uganda made me question why none of it would be reported in the UK.*'

One experienced observer of the effect that structured gap years have on school leavers is quoted as saying, '*These kids don't get lost in a gap year, they get found.*'

## DECIDING WHEN TO TAKE YOUR GAP YEAR

There are good arguments for taking a gap year before university and after university – and a few lucky people take both. After A-Levels many students are utterly sick of exams and books and timetables. They want to experience Life with a capital L and freedom and independence. University can satisfy these cravings up to a point, but heading off to work in a New Zealand ski resort or study Spanish in Ecuador or backpack round India or pick apples in Tasmania or volunteer at a village school in Tanzania, all of these guarantee a complete break from anything that has gone before.

## STRAIGHT OUT OF SCHOOL

It is not at all unusual for young people in their A-Level years to feel fairly unfocused about their futures. A huge number follow the unexamined assumption of family and peers that they will go to university but may not have a clear idea what to study or where to study it. At a basic level, many 18 year olds simply do not feel ready for university, and when they do drift off to a place of higher learning, possibly having chosen according to the pin-in-a-map technique, they may not have the motivation to last the distance. The obvious answer to this quandary is to take some time out, to give yourself time to mature and a chance for preferences and interests to develop. Most fresh-behind-the-ears school leavers have very limited horizons and a year of travel, volunteering and work is sure to expand them. A wider acquaintance of the world can be academically beneficial and arguably almost essential for lots of courses such as politics, media and communications, modern languages, art history, and so on.

A specially targeted gap year project will always impress, such as living and doing a course in a country whose language you want to study, or touring the ancient sites of the eastern Mediterranean if you want to study classical civilizations. But even a 'bog standard' gap year of working and travelling can do wonders for enhancing self-confidence and independence of thought. Anyone who has managed to rub along with a group of strangers on an Arctic expedition or engaged in drinking games with some Slovenian students met while backpacking in Europe is bound to feel less timid about tackling their university's freshers' week. Entering the canteen at uni for the first time can hold few terrors for someone who has stepped out of Bangkok or Delhi Airport and found their way around an alien city. Anyone who has experienced a homestay with a Mexican or Thai family will have learned a great deal about tolerance and respect for difference. Those who have backpacked on a shoestring and stayed in a few dives will not be too shocked by the declining standards of hygiene in their hall of residence.

Just as an average 18-year-old may not have a well-worked out pathway to the future, so they may not have much of a clue about what they want to do or where to go in their gap year. Their tastes are unformed. As a result many are attracted to the whirlwind kind of travel, to give them a snapshot of many different places so they can sort out where they would like to spend more time on a future trip. InterRailing is a classic gap year choice, and almost everybody wishes that they had spent longer in a few places rather than dashing from station to station, hostel to hostel. On the whole no one goes InterRailing twice, but it serves a valuable function in giving first-time travellers a taste of what the world holds.

**SUSANNAH KERR** took a gap year after A-Levels and then had another one after graduating in History from Nottingham. The difference between the two years is typical:

Out of the 15 months between finishing school and starting at university, Susannah Kerr spent from January to Easter travelling round the world with a friend, and the rest of the year earning money in her hometown. She invested £1,000 in a round-the-world (RTW) six-stopover ticket with STA Travel and chose to visit Cape Town, Singapore, Sydney, Auckland, Fiji and Los Angeles, with the longest period (six weeks) being spent in Australia and the shortest (a few days) in LA. She and her friend had pre-booked several organised tours with STA Travel, including the Oz Experience party bus in both directions along 'The Route' (Sydney–Cairns–Sydney) and a boat trip among the islands of Fiji. Altogether she had a great trip (apart from the bout of food poisoning in Fiji) but wouldn't be tempted by another 'it's Tuesday so it must be Kuala Lumpur' style of trip. Covering so much ground in a short time is wearing and stressful. When attempting such an ambitious trip, there are bound to be disagreements with your travelling companion about destinations, budget, allocation of logistical responsibilities, etc.

But this gap year trip definitely gave her the travel bug and she spent most of the summer before her final year of university volunteering at a school in Thailand. Not feeling ready to apply for a proper job straight after university, she was attracted to the idea of teaching English in Japan, partly because she had enjoyed visiting Japan when her older brother had been living there for a year. Also one of her university history courses had touched on some contemporary Japanese social history which had whetted her interest. So in her final year, she applied to teach English in Japan, was accepted and moved to a suburb of Japan in the October after graduating. Working and living abroad is a completely different experience from being on the road. She began studying Japanese fairly seriously, made friends with Japanese people her own age, acquired a Japanese boyfriend and really got to know Tokyo.

## STRAIGHT OUT OF UNIVERSITY

If the student who has just finished A-Levels feels in dire need of a major break, how much more has the university graduate deserved it. They may have partied in their first year, but the final year is usually an intense scramble to finish dissertations or complete scientific projects and of course to sit final exams. Many feel that they have really earned a break from all this pressure and obligation, and the idea of subjecting themselves to a round of job interviews fills them with dismay.

Because they are three years older and wiser, and have been exposed to many more ideas and possibilities, they may have a clearer idea of what aspects of the world they want to explore (see case study below). Their choice of gap year destination and/or activity might grow organically out of subjects that have grabbed their attention at university. They have already learned the art of fending for themselves, and will not worry as much about suffering from homesickness as they might have done when they were 18. Solo travel may not hold the terrors it would have when they were younger; on the other hand they might be in a relationship that they are reluctant to jeopardise. All these contingencies are very personal and there is no right or wrong time to fly the coop.

**Samantha Thornley** found that in her last year of college she became less interested in the business world and more interested in the *actual* world. She was aware of how much of the world she *hadn't* seen and how much she didn't know, and felt an urgency to remedy this. '*I knew that if I didn't take the chance now (after graduating from college) I never would*,' so she went off to teach in Vietnam.

One of the disadvantages of the post-university gap year is that many new graduates are oppressed by student debt, and find it difficult to justify to themselves jetting off to spend yet more money. Unlike the young gapper who has a deferred place at university already sorted, the graduate gapper has no such fixed structure and may feel uneasy at the prospect of returning to the job market after a long break after uni. With the recession biting, they may feel it is irresponsible to jet away from the troubled job market at home as **Holly Tate** did in 2009:

> With the credit crunch I felt like I should stick around and try to get my foot on the career ladder. But with the state of the economy, the job prospects in England weren't that great, so taking a year out to do what I fancied wasn't that big a deal. I've always wanted to travel, and Australia was pretty high on the list which is why I decided to do an internship with a video production company in Sydney fixed up by Intern Options in London. Doing a gap year after Uni meant I was more mature and independent so coming to a country half way round the world on my own wasn't nearly as daunting as it would have been when I was 18. It also meant I had loads more experience on my CV to get a good internship that would build on what I had already learnt rather than spending my days making tea and coffee and doing odd jobs.

**Richard Griffiths** left university with a vague interest in the environment, an interest that his gap years eventually crystallised into a life choice. In fact his gap year travels and interning were instrumental in his eventually finding a proper job in this field:

*After uni I went travelling in India and South East Asia for a year, and on to Australia where I worked in Sydney as a charity fundraiser/campaigner for the Wilderness Society. That experience, previous inclinations, and the environmental wonders/destruction I had seen on my travels cemented in my mind that I wanted to work in the environmental sector. Thus, after another nine months (during which I continued to work in campaigning, and also worked as a Padi Divemaster intern with the University of New South Wales), I headed home and looked for work in the environmental sector. Jobs were hard to come by given demand and supply (and my only having enthusiasm and a BA, with little direct experience), and thus I looked for internships. I found one in the Earthwatch office in Oxford. After working as their marketing intern for four months, I was offered a permanent (training) post, then a full-on post. Working as an intern at Earthwatch was a brilliant way to spend 3 months of a gap year, and with hindsight it's definitely something I'd like to have done earlier. It's a great first step on a very hard-to-reach ladder. Since September I have been working for DEFRA as a policy adviser on UK climate change (having first gone back to university to do a Masters in Environmental Change and Policy).*

## CLASSIC GAP YEAR CHOICES

Googling 'Planning a Gap Year' will give more than 75,000 results, and the book in your hand describes hundreds of specific gap year options as well as providing an enticing taste of travelling on the five continents of the world. The year has been freed up – now what? Many people feel overwhelmed by the welter of choices, knowing that as soon as they plump for one, all other options are closed down.

After the stress of A-Levels, most students want to cut loose with some mates, whether wild camping in Scotland or clubbing in Majorca. A large number kick off their gap year with an InterRail trip (see 'Getting Around' in the Europe section). Many plan to get back home in time for results day in mid-August in case the envelope contains any surprises that need follow-up action. Next comes the hard graft at a local pub or store or temping to save up for a more ambitious trip. A favourite departure time is in the new year, though some gappers work through until Easter to save enough for a long haul flight or an expensive gap year programme. Of course there is an infinite number of variations on this basic outline. For example participants in a gap year programme with a September start date might spend the summer earning money.

The first crucial decision to make is whether just to travel or to join a voluntary project, expedition or course. If pure travel is your choice, turn to the Travel chapter and the continent-by-continent chapters. Most gap years involve a combination of working locally to save money, travelling and possibly signing up with an organisation that makes placements overseas. The mainstream volunteering choices are conservation, community work (often teaching or working with children) and construction.

One advantage of joining a scheme is that it makes you stay put for an extended period instead of drifting from place to place in what can end up giving a superficial view of the countries visited. The great travel writer Dervla Murphy expressed her views on this subject in an essay in *The Traveller's Handbook*:

*The past decade or so has seen the emergence of another, hybrid category: youngsters who spend a year or more wandering around the world in a holidaymaking spirit, occasionally taking temporary jobs. Some gain enormously from this experience but many seem to cover too much ground too quickly, sampling everywhere and becoming familiar with nowhere. They have been from Alaska to Adelaide, Berlin to Bali, Calcutta to Cuzco, Lhasa to London. They tend to wander in couples or small packs, swapping yarns about the benefits – or otherwise – of staying here, doing that, buying this. They make a considerable impact where they happen to perch for a week or so, often bringing with them standards (sometimes too low) and expectations (sometimes too high) which unsettle their local contemporaries.*

*Of course one rejoices that the young are free to roam as never before, yet such rapid 'round-the-worlding' is, for many, more confusing than enlightening. It would be good if this fashion soon changed, if the young became more discriminating, allowing themselves time to travel seriously in a limited area that they had chosen because of its particular appeal to them, as individuals.*

The chapters that make up this book survey the range of possibilities and provide lots of concrete information to help you decide whether to earn a salary in a high-tech industry in Britain or join an expedition to Patagonia (or both). Details are provided on volunteering in residential situations in the UK and abroad, work experience, courses and homestays, seasonal jobs such as working in ski resorts, au pairing, English teaching, pure travelling: all are covered.

A traveller wrote in 1899: '*We took this trip around the world on bicycles because we are more or less conceited – like to be talked about and see our names in the newspapers.*' In some sixth forms a certain amount of one-upmanship prevails about who can do the most adventurous and exotic trip (though most end up going to Thailand or India or Australia where there are whole colonies of gap year students). Paraguay and Outer Mongolia are great if you have a particular interest in those regions but if you would be happier working on an American summer camp or a Scottish sailing school or attending a language school in Barcelona, so be it. It is possibly a mistake to think of the Himalayan gap year as vastly superior to the one spent closer to home. Trekking in northern Thailand does not necessarily trump working in a Swiss ski resort or volunteering to teach Gypsy children in Spain. Do not fall into the trap of making plans to impress. Find the route that suits you.

**ELLA HICKSON** was not as tempted as her peers by the attractions of Thai beaches and the Australian outback, having come to the conclusion that the more popular gap years have become, the less variety in the choices young people were making.

'My gap year was a little different. Yesterday I was perched on a wall in Vienna. My co-percher was a Geordie lad by the name of Elliott. With the facade of St Peter's Church in front of us, I started talking about why keys were associated with St Peter's. All very interesting I'm sure to an art enthusiast or history buff, but neither are really Elliott's scene – his Great Masters come from the Champions League. In spite of that the questions kept coming: How can you tell it's a saint? Why was Da Vinci such a good guy? And so forth. It was bizarre, he was genuinely intrigued and an hour later all four lads had got involved. All my resources, gathered a year previously on an Art History Abroad [AHA] course, were being seriously stretched.

When I explained what I had done on my gap year I knew it was a million miles from anything those lads would ever think of doing, and yet here they were, now round a table with pints in hand, still plying me for information about columns and the Vatican, I was answering to 'Miss, why isn't England Catholic now?' and 'Why is the Pope so rich?' I pondered their enthusiasm a little cynically; they did already have my number, so what was this about? Suddenly the 'Miss…' jokes stopped and four football lads all agreed that they had learnt more in the past few hours than they had in the last year, and all agreed they wished they had done something similar. It was so good to get someone else excited about art. It's an unstoppable infectious buzz that defies my generation's outdated maxim that learning just isn't cool. It's that same buzz that AHA gives its students and that those students then go on to spread wherever they go. AHA provides gappies with an unimaginable wealth of knowledge, a grounding in art and architecture that exceeds simple facts; AHA teaches students how to look, to get the back story and most importantly it starts a passion for learning which is fundamental in all areas of post gap year life. So when my Geordie friend and I are sat opposite St Peter's he sees a building that holds probably not much more than the memories of hours of boredom on Christmas Eve. I did my best to show him how to see stories, histories, *people and passions – money and politics, I'm sure I went on a bit but I knew that if I could get him to be even half as interested as my tutors made me, I'd be doing a good thing.*

*AHA still gives students the chance to dance till dawn and sample local drinks but it also teaches you to wax lyrical on Titian. Not only can I tell someone where the best bars are in Naples but also where the best Caravaggios are. Personally, I gained a passion and enthusiasm about art that has helped me decide where to head in life. I have changed my university course to Art History, I've done work experience at the Tate and have set up my own small company dealing in non-professional art works in my university city of Edinburgh.*

*As I waved goodbye to the lads at Vienna station, they had decided to go to Venice, Florence, Naples and Rome. As I'm writing down where they have to go to find good limoncello and prosecco, where the best clubs are and where to stagger home to, I hear a voice from the back 'Where was that Tintoretto guy? Which one was the dome that they can't work out how it was built? How do you spell the name of the murderer who painted grubby people?' So if anyone sees a bunch of boys, pints in hand, looking for Caravaggio could you show them the way!'*

## USING A GAP YEAR AGENCY

The ambition of many gap year students is simply to travel with a mate. However, if you have set your sights on volunteering or doing work experience or joining an expedition, it will be more difficult to fix this up independently. Although some 18 year olds fresh from school have the confidence and maturity to set off without anything set up (perhaps with a working holiday visa for Australia or a return ticket to Lima) many will prefer to enlist the help of a mediating organisation or agency to set up a placement and provide a back-up service if things go wrong.

Assuming you want to do something other than just travel, you must decide whether to throw in your lot with a sending organisation or arrange something independently. Many of the advantages of going on an organised scheme are self-evident but it is worth canvassing a few here:

- Makes the choice available less overwhelming since placement agencies have a finite number of destinations and opportunities.
- Saves you the time of contacting many organisations abroad and the anxiety of liaising with them assuming they do express interest. Pre-departure orientation will be provided. Even just a briefing booklet can be helpful and reassuring. Agencies are usually in a position to give reliable advice on necessary health precautions, insurance and flights.

- Back-up is available if you have an accident, become ill or the placement is unacceptable in some way.
- Reassurance for anxious parents. The agency often provides a conduit of communication between the gap year student and their family.
- Placement is usually in groups or pairs, so moral support is always available from gap year or volunteer partners.

**Angela Clegg** sums up why she was happy to use an agency for her trip to Africa, in her case *Cross-Cultural Solutions*:

> *After A-Levels I was looking for something that had variation and I discovered that a nursery project in Tanzania offered by Cross-Cultural Solutions [CCS] included formal lectures, Swahili lessons, free evenings and weekends and most importantly a compound to live in with fellow volunteers from all over the world. For my first big trip away I needed to feel safe. CCS matched up volunteers who would be in Amsterdam airport at the same time en route to Africa, which was brilliant because it meant we were less nervous about arriving in Africa without knowing anyone. My advice for anyone doing the same thing is that if you have any reservations about doing it alone, use a company like CCS. Throughout all of my preparation they were right there with help from reassuring phone calls, to a participants' handbook to putting you in touch with previous volunteers. They also gave me advice on fundraising, and sent me a letter to prove I was fundraising for my trip.*

The majority of students coming home from a gap year are grateful for the help and back-up given to them by their agency, claiming that they considered the fee they paid well spent. On the other hand, some find that their agency's local representative is not easy to contact and therefore not of much use. Others who end up not needing to make use of the support network begrudge the fee. The fee paid to a sending agency can be viewed as an insurance policy which many students and their parents are more than happy to pay. However, problems can arise when clients are paying Western prices, because it leads them to expect a Western standard of service that may not be possible in remote parts of developing countries. You should try to research the company and the project as thoroughly as you can, to avoid the ones that put profit above everything else. For a list of searching questions to put to a provider, see the introduction to the chapter *Specialist Gap Year Programmes*. You should try to find out what the company offers to justify the expense, and whether they make any financial contribution to the worthy projects to which they send volunteers.

Only you know whether you have the stamina and initiative to create a constructive gap year without the shelter of an umbrella in the form of a placement organisation. Bear in mind that locally run non-governmental organisations (NGOs) may profess to need your help but may have little experience of dealing with the kinds of problem faced by homesick 18 year olds. Without contact with a like-minded person, you can feel lonely and isolated. On the other hand, some gap year students do arrange their own job/placement, with or without contacts, and find the experience immensely gratifying. Arranging something independently shows great initiative (always something worth boasting about on future CVs) and of course saves the money that would otherwise go to a middle man.

**EMMA SEAGER** came to realise the pros and cons of agencies once she was well into her volunteer placement at a school for the deaf in South India, arranged though a Canadian gap year agency. The old proverb, 'It is easy to be wise after the event' may be apt here:

'The programme was quite costly, which seemed fine when I first signed up. However, once I got to India I realised how easy it would have been to find an organisation myself while actually there. Still, I think for the first time in India it was important to have someone meet us at the airport and put us on the bus to the school as otherwise it would have been extremely overwhelming. It did seem odd though that when we were visited by our placement manager on a visit from England, we were paying for her and a friend's trip in nice air-conditioned taxis and fancy hotels when we were slumming around in rickshaws and flea-infested places.'

As for the orientation and back-up she had received, it was of mixed benefit: 'We had a day-long orientation in Toronto the summer before we left where we went over basic GAP policies concerning insurance and logistical details. We were supposed to be able to talk to people who had volunteered in India before. Unfortunately, this was the first year that the programme had been introduced so we ended up talking to a very nice 11-year-old Indian boy who reassured us that we had absolutely nothing to worry about. We also had an orientation in India which was much more useful. The support we received during the orientation was wonderful but once we got to the school there was very little. This was challenging at the beginning but really forced us to go out and learn things on our own. The teachers provided very little supervision in the classes, which was all right most of the time as it meant we could do whatever we wanted. The teachers did not always agree with our teaching methods, as children there did not seem to learn in a creative way, but purely by memorisation, which we tried to change a bit.'

## GOING IT ALONE

Arranging your own placement can be hard work. **Rick Padfield** had seen his older sister Eleanor arrange her own volunteer placements in South America on her gap year, and was even more ferociously determined to do it on his own. He wanted to spend 12 months in Africa, which he did, and ended up spending a total of £3,800 over the whole period, including travel. He sent off a blizzard of emails to family friends, schools, charities and organisations in Africa and, impressively, arranged three-month placements in Kenya, Uganda and Ghana. The school in Kenya asked him to arrange to come in a pair so he even persuaded a friend to join him. After they had been in their Kenyan placement for a month, 24 trainee Kenyan teachers were suddenly assigned to the school, so he and his fellow volunteer were 'fired'. If something doesn't work out with an arrangement made privately, there is no one in the background to put alternative arrangements into place. Rick and Tom were lucky though, as the farm on which they were staying then offered them a GPS mapping project which filled several weeks.

## OVERCOMING ANXIETY

Often the hardest step is committing yourself to a decision, i.e. fixing a departure date and destination. Once you have booked a place on a scheme or bought a ticket and explained to your friends and family that you are off to see the world, the rest seems to fall into place. Inevitably first-time travellers suffer pre-departure anxieties as they contemplate leaving behind the comfortable routines of home. But these are usually much worse in anticipation than in retrospect.

Prepare yourself for a horrid 48 hours after saying good-bye at the airport (tip: don't look back after going through Passport Control). **Jake Lee** who went to Sri Lanka in his gap year puts it rather brutally:

> *Let me just state for the record. It doesn't matter who you are, but if you are travelling alone to a faraway place for a relatively long time, you will cack yourself on the plane. The excitement you previously had turns to fear, and you are desperate for the plane to turn around. I don't think there is anything you can do about this. Just ride it out. As a Buddhist monk at my school always said, 'There is never anything to worry about – Nothing.' This is true.*

**EMMA HOARE** did lots of research on a gap year but couldn't find an approach that suited her at first:

'For years I had always been saying 'yes, I really want to travel… maybe after A-Levels, maybe after my degree, maybe when I retire' and all my friends would go 'yeah, me too, definitely' and all my family, teachers, elders and betters would smile and nod in that way they do when a young person starts talking vaguely about the Big Things, that there is really no fear of them actually doing.

On results day I found that I had managed to get four A grades. At some point in all the celebrations I decided that, no, I didn't want to go straight to university. I wanted to go backpacking, see the world, have a spiritual epiphany, etc. To say this did not please my mother, teachers, etc. is an understatement. When I started talking about cancelling my place at York University and reapplying the next year, every adult I knew (except my Dad) was 100% against it. They did have a small point, I suppose. I didn't have any plans, though I had about £1,000, not even enough for a ticket to New Zealand as it turned out.

So I had about four days before I had to accept or decline my place at York. By the end of the third day, I had been pretty much convinced that it would be a stupid thing to go gallivanting around the world. I went into my local careers advisory centre and was sat down with a pile of leaflets dealing with gap years. Every single one of these dealt with either a structured voluntary course abroad or how to arrange work experience. 'On the road' it wasn't. Then – portentous roll of thunder, sudden bright light – one of the receptionists gave me a book that had just come in, Work Your Way Around the World. No exaggeration, I promise you. I sat there and read it until they closed the centre. Then I went straight to Waterstone's and bought a copy. Then I went home and wrote to York University declining my place. Three months later I was off to New Zealand… As you can probably surmise from my gushing tone, I had an amazing time. I crewed on a yacht, helped with haymaking, went to a sheep-shearers' reunion, did a 12,000ft skydive, saw sperm whales, etc.…. And now I'm off to start my degree (at Oxford!). I can assure you the transformation is nothing short of miraculous.'

# BEFORE YOU GO

Every successful gap year combines periodic flights of fancy with methodical planning; any homework you do ahead of time will benefit you later, if only because it will give you more confidence. Your first task in the planning stages is to consider some of the programmes and organisations described in this book and to make contact with the ones that tempt you to find out more. If an organisation offers a project that appeals, the next step is to find out whether you are eligible. Usually the hardest part is not being accepted to join but raising enough money to fund it. But before you get to that stage, you must sort out what you are going to do about further or higher education.

## UNIVERSITY APPLICATION

Applying to university is a stressful and complicated business, on which your school should offer detailed advice. The worst aspect of it is the uncertainty of outcome. Conditional offers are the bugbear of prospective students because it means it is difficult to make definite plans until you know your A-Level results. Of course the specialist placement organisations are used to coping with the problem and can offer support throughout. Many school leavers feel forced to make up their minds about university courses too early. More mature students make better decisions about what they want to study and are statistically less likely to drop out.

Taking a lead from UCAS and the Year Out Group, organisations involved in gap year travel always urge students to sort out their university applications before taking off if possible. It is also important to ascertain what line the department or university you're applying to takes on gap years. The vast majority will be more than tolerant of them, and may not even expect you to demonstrate that you will do something constructive with your year out.

### TIMING

Wherever possible, students should begin preparations for a gap year well in advance. There are so many plans to make and problems to sort out that the best way to avoid panics and disappointments is not to leave things to the last minute. University application forms have to be submitted to UCAS by 15 January of your A-Level year at the latest (earlier for Oxbridge and some courses such as medicine). This leaves just over five months until exams finish, which may seem plenty of time to decide how to spend your gap year until you realise that some of the schemes are already filling up or that you'll have to raise several thousand pounds in order to join your preferred programme. Similarly, many *Year in Industry* jobs require early application to ensure the chosen company and placement have places left.

Whatever decision is made about your gap year, it is important to keep the university informed. They are unlikely to look favourably on someone asking for deferred entry at the last minute, although even then they might permit it.

## PRE A-LEVEL APPLICATION

Students need to crystallise their reasons for taking a gap year before writing their personal statement or before being interviewed. It may be beneficial to stress the fact that time spent in the 'real world' will encourage a more mature outlook. Tutors are fully aware of the fact that many students who defer for a year go on to do comparatively better at university. According to a survey carried out on behalf of the Year Out Group, nine out of 10 university vice-chancellors agreed that a structured year out benefits the personal development of the typical undergraduate.

All but the most competitive universities indicate that they are perfectly happy to of-fer deferred places. However, there is evidence of hostility to deferring entry to certain courses such as maths, engineering and possibly music. **Ollie Perkins** was convinced that he was discriminated against by Edinburgh University because of his gap year plans (working with vulnerable people in Cape Town), although in the end he got his first choice place at Bristol University to read English. Students pursuing a particularly long course such as veterinary studies and architecture may choose not to delay embarking on the long haul of the course. **Jonny Stephens** and **Rachael Brown** from the same school in Cornwall knew that they wanted to pursue medicine so did not want to delay starting the training by a year. So they investigated medical projects offered by gap year agencies and did a summer hospital placement in Ghana between the upper and lower sixth (see *Africa* chapter). Those doing four-year modern languages courses who have a year abroad built into their course might also be inclined not to take a gap year, but all these choices are completely personal.

Attitudes to the gap year vary from tutor to tutor, subject to subject. If you are aim-ing for a top university, it makes sense to speak personally to the admissions tutor of your course. Certainly a high proportion of first-year students at the best universities have arrived after a year out, dispelling the anxiety that there is vestigial distrust of people who take a year out. To take just one example of the level of acceptance, Church-ill College in Cambridge even has a dedicated gap year adviser. The received wisdom on the subject of gap years and medical studies is that a year out will be tolerated only if it is spent in some way related to medicine. Many medical schools are reluc-tant to accept people straight out of school and prefer older students who will have more chance of sticking the course. Students need to impress on the university that they really want to have a place on that particular course and that come hell or high water they will return to take it. Universities have been made uneasy in the past by too many students provisionally accepting courses and then changing their minds. Having a coherent plan and focusing on the potential benefits will make the univer-sity realise that you are serious about spending the year in a responsible manner.

Questions about gap years often form a large part of an interview and can potentially be impressive.

Once it has been decided that a gap year is the best plan, this needs to be indicated on the UCAS form. To offer a deferred-entry place is then at the university's discretion and they will send their conditions to UCAS, who in turn send this to the student. Provided the student fulfils the requirements, their place is assured for the September following the gap year. All relevant information can be found on the UCAS site and on individual university websites.

It is certainly easier to apply to university while you are still at school and have the momentum and infrastructure in place all around you. On the other hand, the fact that the whole UCAS process must now be conducted online, means that all you really need the school for is your tutor's accompanying letter which you can request after leaving.

## POST A-LEVEL APPLICATION

If you haven't applied for deferred entry in the upper sixth, then you can apply during your gap year. Applying for university during your gap year means that you might have to go to open days and/or interviews in the winter, so you will lose some flexibility in the planning of your year. For example, **Pascale Hunter** had to interrupt her six-month gap year in Australia and South East Asia, at great expense, to fly back to England for a few weeks in January to attend interviews for the midwifery courses she was applying to.

Come results day, some students inevitably find that they have not done as well as anticipated and have not met their conditional offer. Several options are now possible:

- Carry on with your gap year plans and apply again the following year with the same exam results, probably to different courses.
- Contact your first choice university to see if they will take you despite missing your grades.
- Proceed to early entry in Clearing, bearing in mind that places gained through Clearing will be for that year and not for the year after. Courses with vacancies are published in the *Independent* and on the UCAS website (www.ucas.com) – and there were far fewer in 2009 than previously because of the sharp increase in the number of university applications overall. Speed of reaction and decisiveness are essential at this stage because lots of people are competing for remaining places. You must communicate directly with the institutions, which is easier said than done since the phone lines are often jammed in the days following results day.
- Plan to re-sit and reapply to your preferred university.

Even at this stage, a gap year might help your cause. An article about gap years in the *Guardian* quoted the admissions tutor for English and drama at Loughborough University who said that he might give a student who misses their grades another chance if they have taken a gap year: '*Students who have taken gap years have gone through the jolly japes of puberty when they start university. They understand that the world is different in different places and they appreciate things more because of that.*'

If your first choice university will not offer a place, you need to ask yourself some hard questions. Was the original choice of course suitable anyway? Would it be better to apply for something else? If your first choice course was vocational, it could be worthwhile having a serious chat with the careers service to reassess the situation, particularly if the grades fell a long way short. Reapplying post A-Level for the following year is straightforward; universities will either make an unconditional offer or reject your application.

**CAROLINE GOSNEY** felt compelled to take a gap year when she discovered in August that she had not met her conditional offer. In other words, some people choose to have a gap year and some have one thrust upon them:

'Last year on results day I was devastated. I hadn't done enough work during my final year at school and had missed my grades for my first choice university. Rather than take my insurance choice I decided to take a year out, re-take the necessary modules to get my grades and reapply. The restaurant where I was working kept me on and I worked for 5½ months to afford to travel. That was a learning curve in itself, as it requires immense discipline to get up at 8am every day through horrid weather and days when travelling seems so far away. All my friends were either heading off to uni or had planned their gap years months in advance so I felt rather alone. The possibilities for gap year travel are endless and deciding where to go and who with is a nightmare if it's all done very last minute!

I had always wanted to go to Africa and decided Blue Ventures based in Madagascar looked perfect for me. Leaving your family and friends for two months to go somewhere that has no mobile phone reception and an emailing facility only once a week is terrifying but is a truly valuable experience as you learn pretty quickly to fend for yourself. The whole experience is something I will never forget. I have never felt as happy as when I was living in a leaky hut, infested with cockroaches and getting up at 5.30am to head out into the Indian Ocean and dive with species of flora and fauna seen nowhere else in the world.

The other part of my gap year was spending 5 weeks InterRailing around Europe with a close friend who had done the complete opposite and done *far better in his A-Levels than he had expected to. We had a riot, visiting nine cities. Of course Europe was a completely different experience from Madagascar but equally valuable.*

*My gap year has been fantastic. Ironically, I can't imagine not taking one now and if I had fulfilled my offer requirements last August I wouldn't have met the people I have, done the things I've done and grown so much. Part of me thinks that if you plan it too carefully you build your expectations up too high and it's never as good as you imagine it will be. Gap years are all about spontaneity and broadening your horizons, so if you do worse than you expected it isn't the end of the world and I really urge you to consider taking a year out. However, if you aced your A-Levels you have nothing to lose, except the experience of a lifetime.'*

## TIMETABLE FOR UNIVERSITY APPLICATION

| Plan A | | |
|--------|--|--|
| Lower sixth | Autumn/spring | Begin to think about university courses and the possibility of taking a gap year |
| | Spring/summer | Visit university open days. Speak to Admissions tutors about taking gap years. Students should try to visit as many universities as possible to get a feel for the place. |
| Upper sixth | September to December | Fill in UCAS forms and clearly mark preference for deferred entry. Hand in no later than 15 January (or 15 October for Medicine and Oxbridge applications) |
| | October to April | Make plans for gap year (apply to placement scheme/s, volunteer organisations, consider travel options, etc.). Save as much money as possible to fund your gap year |
| | January to March | Receive conditional offers from universities |
| | Around April | Submit final decision for first and second (insurance) choice university courses |
| | May/June | Sit A2 Exams |
| | August (third Thur) | Results Day |
| | | ▓ Sufficient grades: accept the place and enjoy the gap year |
| | | ▓ Insufficient grades: implement Plan B |

| Plan B | | |
|---|---|---|
| Upper sixth | Late August | Phone universities to see if they will still offer a place. Be prepared to stay on the phone for a week. Clearing has been going on since mid-July |
| | | If yes, take the place offered and proceed with original gap year plans |
| | | If no, reapply the next year for alternative courses and proceed with original plans |
| | | Find a tutorial college and proceed as below |
| | 15th September | Closing date for clearing |
| Gap year | September to May | Study at tutorial college and spend spare time working, doing voluntary work, taking a skills course, etc. |
| | September to December | Reapply to universities via UCAS (presumably no deferred entry this time) |
| | January to March | Receive offers |
| | May/June | Re-sit examinations |
| | June to September | Free time for travelling, work, etc. |
| | August | Results Day (again) |
| First year | September to October | Freshers' Week at university |

# FUNDRAISING

For many gap year students, a shortage of money is the main obstacle. The most straightforward way of gathering together some cash for travels is to work locally and save like mad. Many gappers find that their parents are more willing to help them financially if they want to pursue a worthwhile ambition such as spending a month in Spain to learn the language or joining a voluntary scheme in the developing world. Of course many 18 year olds baulk at the idea of accepting hand-outs from parents. **Becky Warden-Brown** made a deal with her parents that they would match whatever she earned. Another possible compromise is the one arrived at by **Alice Mundy** whose ski instructor course in Canada cost a cool £6,000 before insurance or spending money. To finance her gap year she worked for around seven months over the year but the majority was covered by a loan from her parents which she will pay back once she is earning enough (possibly as a snowboard instructor in her vacations). Funding a trip or a project yourself will impress future employers more than taking a hand-out, and will also cause less envy if you happen to be travelling with a friend who has not been given money by his or her parents.

As we have seen, many of the most attractive gap year schemes are expensive (£3,000+), so fundraising becomes a major issue for those sixth formers and others who have decided on this kind of gap year. Others who simply want to travel will also have to save a substantial sum that should include a contingency fund as well as the minimum for airfares and living expenses.

**Jo Beker** found it rewarding to raise the funds herself for her *BSES* expedition to Amazonia:

*The fact that you have to fundraise for this expedition yourself makes the whole experience way more exciting! You know that you're going on this brilliant adventure because you found the money and you paid for it yourself and somehow that makes it feel more worthwhile! Having said that, the fundraising is not easy. We each had to raise just over £3,000 which is pretty daunting. I organised a range of events at school in order to help me fundraise including a second-hand book sale and stalls at a Christmas bazaar. On top of that I was sponsored to run the Brussels half marathon which not only was a great way to raise money but it also helped me to make sure that I was physically fit for the expedition. I also found that because BSES is very highly regarded many organisations were willing to donate and be supportive. As BSES aims to promote equal opportunities for all, there is a mentoring and bursary scheme that Young Explorers can apply for.*

Anyone undertaking a marathon, cycle ride or any sponsored event for a charitable purpose might want to register with JustGiving.com, one of the easiest ways for your supporters to donate money online. Also consider setting up a Facebook group and urging your 542 Facebook friends to support you.

Sometimes there isn't enough lead-up time for this, in which case you might follow a few tips from **Jonny Stephens**. Although the Chair of Governors at his school had warned him that it was going to be very difficult to raise £2,000+ in three months for a medical project in Ghana, Jonny and his friend **Rachael** were undaunted. They enlisted the readers of their local newspaper *The Cornish & Devon Post* and set about carrying out fundraising activities, culminating in a memorable wine & wisdom evening and auction at Bude Rugby Club just before they set off, which cleared over £1,600, thanks to support from friends, families and local businesses.

Once you have resolved to meet a particular target, it is surprising how single-mindedly you can pursue it. Most sending agencies provide extensive advice and support on fundraising, and a lot of useful tips and tricks can be found on the web. For example www.gapyear.com/fundraising carries plenty of information and links to real-life examples. For example **Tori Oram** from Kent who was 'binge-saving' to join a wildlife project in South Africa got sponsored to sit in a bath of (donated) cat food for an hour on the forecourt of a petrol station and raised £1,200 in an hour. Other non-squeamish fundraisers have undertaken to eat maggots and slugs in exchange for sponsorship money. A surprising number have made a sizeable profit by selling unwanted items on eBay.

If you have signed up for an organised placement, you will probably have been sent a timetable for paying the placement fee in instalments. Estimate how long it will take you to reach your target and stick to the deadline come what may. It might help to break the saving down into smaller amounts, so that you aim to save £X per week. Dedicated savers consider a 70-hour week at a local job quite tolerable (which will have the additional advantage of leaving you too tired to conduct an expensive social life). Bear in mind that saving over a long period, especially from a job which doesn't pay well, can be depressing since you will have to deny yourself all those expensive little treats. **Kitty Hill** is just one of the many gap year students who spent six months working 60-hour weeks and the valuable thing she learned from that experience was that '*it is a million times nicer to be in a job you enjoy than a job you hate but pays a bit better*'.

## LETTER WRITING

Some year out organisations provide a template of a letter seeking sponsorship and a list of suggested trusts to try. It helps to include a photo and make the letter succinct. Although time-consuming, hand-written letters are thought to attract more attention than slick computer-generated ones. The more obvious care you have taken, the better your chances of success so, for example, you should try to find out the name and job title of the person to whom your request will be referred, and enclose a letter of endorsement from your head teacher. Be aware that a great many businesses and charities have a policy of not funding individuals.

**CLARE COOPER,** in writing a report about her very successful post-university gap year in Ghana, describes the trepidation she felt at the prospect of raising the necessary funds to join an AfricaTrust Networks team:

*I accepted the offer (against the better judgement of some friends and family) and, armed with positivity, I began the mammoth task of raising £2,500. Already working as a care assistant to cover living costs, I took on two extra jobs in a bar and cinema to begin saving. I wrote literally hundreds of letters to local shops, businesses, schools, charities and churches explaining what I was doing and appealing for sponsorship. To raise awareness of my fundraising, the local newspaper ran a story on me explaining that I would be working with orphans in West Africa and any help with my fundraising would be much appreciated. I followed up this article by visiting local businesses in person asking them if they had received my letter and if not could I leave them another one. I found that using the local paper and visiting people in person really effective.*

*Still a fair distance from my financial target I had exactly six weeks left to raise the money or I couldn't go. As I worked in a cinema in a thriving local arts centre I decided to organise a fundraising art exhibition. After a couple of weeks of manic organisation and with the invaluable help of friends, family and local artists we held an exhibition of local arts, craft and textiles. The day was a real success, with lots of visitors and many of the artists selling work. With less than a month to go, I was closer to my financial target, but still not there, and running out of time and ideas. With the priceless help and support from the managers, staff and locals in the bar I worked in we organised an African-themed fundraising day. We had a BBQ, bring-and-buy stall, face painting, children's games, art and craft and traditional story telling followed by an evening of music from a number of local bands, a raffle with great prizes provided by local shops, restaurants and businesses and a fantastic African fire sculpture and fireworks display. As well as raising the rest of the money, the night was a great way of saying thank you and good-bye to all my friends and people who had been fundamental to my fundraising.'*

Target organisations, companies, schools and clubs with which you or your family have links, or which might have some connection with your project. The skill of fundraising is itself impressive when it appears on a CV. Local businesses are usually inundated with requests for donations and raffle prizes and are unlikely to give cash but some might donate some useful items of equipment. Keep track of all the individuals and businesses that have contributed and be sure to send them a thank you note mentioning your fundraising target and progress and then another letter describing the success of your gap year venture.

If you want to go down the route of applying to trusts and charitable bodies, consult a library copy of the *Directory of Grant Making Trusts* (new edition published each April) or contact the Association of Charitable Foundations (www.acf.org.uk), which can offer advice on how to approach grant-giving trusts. Also check the National Charities Database on www.charitiesdirect.com. Local service clubs such as Rotary, Lions Club and Round Table comprising business people might be willing to consider a well presented application for support, especially if you offer to give a presentation on your return.

If your gap year is being organised by a registered charity, always include the charity reference number in your letter of request since this may be needed by their accounts department. In fact the policy of a great many grant bodies is not to support individuals and so you may meet mostly with rejections. (One enterprising fundraiser got his friends and family to sponsor him for every rejection.) One potential source of benefactors can be found not in the library or on the internet but in your parents' address book. **Kitty Hill** hit upon a more painless way to raise money than her 60 hour-a-week job:

*For sponsorship I wrote to everyone on my parents' Christmas card list asking them to sponsor me for a day of my trip, at about £30 a day. Then I promised to send them a postcard on that day. I raised about £2,500 with this method.*

Impressive world traveller **Tom Grundy** has one further recommendation; he suggests writing to millionaires, particularly recent lottery winners.

## FUNDRAISING IDEAS

The ingenuity which sixth-formers have demonstrated in organising money-making events is impressive. If you happen to recall ideas that worked for Comic Relief, think of ways of adapting these. For example one fundraiser got everybody he knew to sponsor him to stay up a tree for a week. You may choose to shave your head, jump out of an aeroplane, organise a fancy dress pub crawl or a thousand other ways to raise money. Try to organise events that will be fun as well as expensive for your well-wishers. For example if you organise a fundraising quiz in your local pub, give away a few prizes such as glitter nail polish. If you have been sponsored to do a bungee jump or swim a mile, hand out sweets when you go round to collect the pledges. If you are seeking sponsorship from businesses, think of ways in which they might benefit, e.g. promise to wear the company T-shirt in a publicity photo on the top of Kilimanjaro or down the Amazon. Other ideas include holding a sweepstake on a big sporting event, hosting a garden fete with stalls and raffles, charging admission to a ceilidh or a salsa evening. One gap-year student who went to Mexico organised a huge fashion show which cost £5,000 to put on but raised a massive £11,000.

Publicise your plans and your need of funds wherever you can. Local papers and radio stations may be willing to carry details of your planned expedition, which may prompt a few local readers/listeners to support you. Try to make a specific request such as **Ollie Perkins** had published in the free *Cambridge Weekly News* in which his email and street addresses were included: '*Ollie is off to South Africa to work with orphans and young offenders. He is asking for donations of old recorders and piano music because he wants to teach music when he goes off with the Africa Inland Mission for 6 months (City Mission in Cape Town). He is a keen jazz pianist and ex-King's chorister, and wants to help with the church choir.*'

Ask family and friends to give cash instead of birthday and Christmas presents. Consider possibilities for organising a fundraising event such as a concert or a barn dance, a quiz night, wine tasting or an auction of promises. (If your mum or dad was ever on the PTA ask them for advice but don't expect them to run your campaign for you.)

## SOURCES OF FUNDING

A small percentage of schemes operate as scholarships and bring with them their own funding, e.g. the Youth for Understanding exchanges (www.yfu.org) for people aged 15–18. *European Voluntary Service* (see entry in the 'Directory of Specialist Gap Year Programmes') provides full funding for a 6–12-month stint as a volunteer on socially beneficial projects in Europe and beyond. Also the EU's *Leonardo* programme does not require any outlay from participants.

Most gap year agencies are commercial; however, *Lattitude Global Volunteering* is a registered charity that offers a range of bursary schemes allowing those who would not normally be able to afford a gap year to participate.

Some schools (not exclusively fee-paying schools) have odd bursaries and travel scholarships which the careers teachers will be able to tell you about. Various scholarships and grants are available to those who fulfil the necessary requirements. To take just a couple of examples: the Caley Gap Scholarship of up to £1,000 is offered by the Royal Caledonian Schools Trust (http://rcst.org.uk) to the children of Scottish past or current servicemen and women or people with a Scottish parent living in Greater London on a low income. Applicants must submit a proposal for a worthwhile project abroad which will be of at least six months' duration.

The Peter Kirk Memorial Scholarship (www.kirkfund.org.uk) funds 10–12 young people aged 18–26 to investigate and write about some aspect of modern Europe. Awards of up to £1,500 are made to those carrying out research over 6–12 weeks. The deadline for applications is early in November, interviews in London in December. Half a dozen school leavers were awarded £1,500 in 2009, one to look at contemporary European cabaret culture and another in France to look at how young people view their country's past in the second world war.

The Winston Churchill Memorial Trust (www.wcmt.org.uk) awards about 100 four to 12-week travelling fellowships to UK citizens of any age or background who wish to undertake a specific project or study related to their personal interests, job or community. The deadline for applications falls in early October. Past winners are listed on the website with their topic of study; most are older than school/college leaving age. Sixth formers at one of the 240 independent boys' and co-ed schools that belong to the Headmasters' and Headmistresses' Conference (HMC) may apply for one of the 30 annual Bulkeley-Evans gap year scholarships worth between £300 and £500 and a couple worth up to £1,000 for those with financial need. Full details of eligibility can be found on the website www.gapyear-bulkeley-evans-hmc.co.uk or can be requested from the Administrator (tonybeadles@freeuk.com). Applications should be in by the beginning of April.

The London livery companies can be worth investigating. For example the Worshipful Company of Cutlers offers at least three Captain F G Boot scholarships per year valued at £500–£1,000 depending on the financial need of the successful students. Applicants must be aged 17–25 and planning to spend at least six consecutive months in a foreign country to increase their understanding of the language and culture of that country. The closing date for applications is 12 June; details from the Clerk to the Cutlers' Company (www.cutlerslondon.co.uk).

The Royal Society for Asian Affairs (www.rsaa.org.uk) invites potential gappers planning to go to Asia to apply for a Peter Holmes Memorial Award towards a project of purposeful travel. Applications should be made by 31 October; email sec@rsaa.org.uk for more information.

*Archaeology Abroad* (www.britarch.ac.uk/archabroad; with an entry in the 'Directory of Volunteering Abroad') makes Fieldwork Awards of £100–£200 to selected subscribers to *Archaeology Abroad* to enable them to join an archaeological excavation.

## INSURANCE

Any student heading abroad should have travel insurance. Within Europe private insurance is not absolutely essential because European nationals are eligible for reciprocal emergency healthcare in the EEA. The European Health Insurance Card (EHIC) entitles EU nationals to emergency healthcare in any member state.

Outside Europe, a solid travel insurance policy is essential. Research carried out by the Foreign & Commonwealth Office (FCO) revealed that more than a quarter of young travellers aged 16–34 do not purchase travel insurance, which means that about three million people are taking a serious risk. Most students and backpackers shop around to find the cheapest policy. But if you are going outside the developed world or considering doing any kind of adventure sport, give some thought to what the policy covers, for example look closely at whether the policy will repatriate you or fly out a parent in an emergency. Check the exclusions carefully and the amount of excess you'll have to pay if you claim.

In situations where you might be two days from civilisation, it is imperative that you (or your sending agency) have water-tight insurance. During **Tom Watkins'** expedition with *BSES*, one of the members of the expedition had a fit. He was picked up by helicopter in less than half an hour (and was subsequently fine). At that point Tom was very glad that his expedition organisers had the best insurance policy that money could buy, even though earlier he had felt disappointed that he had not been allowed to go rock-climbing for reasons of insurance.

Most insurance companies offer a standard rate that covers medical emergencies and a premium rate that in addition covers personal baggage, cancellation, etc. Always read the fine print. Sometimes activities like bungee-jumping or scuba diving (now quite commonplace in parts of the world) are excluded. Some travel policies list as one of their exclusions: 'any claims which arise while the Insured is engaged in any manual employment'. If you are not planning to visit North America, the premiums will be significantly less expensive. Most insurance companies operate 24-hour helplines in the UK, which can be dialled from anywhere in the world. Quite a few of the gap year expedition and volunteer agencies offer bespoke policies drawn up by the long-established brokers Campbell Irvine (www.campbellirvine.com), which are not the cheapest but provide automatic cover for many extras.

Some basic companies to consider are listed here with an estimate of their premiums for 12 months of worldwide cover (including the USA). Expect to pay roughly £25 per month for basic cover and £30–£40 for more extensive cover.

**Ace Travel Insurance** (www.acetravellerinsurance.com). Strap line on website 'For backpackers, gap years, work and study abroad'. Gap year policy for people up to age 44. Budget cover for 12 months £165; standard cover £203.

**Boots Insurance Services** (0845 840 2020; www.bootsinsurance.com). Dedicated Gap Year travel cover which costs £199 for one year. Available to anyone up to 34 years of age.

**Club Direct**, West Sussex (0800 083 2466; www.clubdirect.com). Work abroad is included provided it does not involve using heavy machinery.

**Columbus Direct** (0870 033 9988; www.columbusdirect.com). One of the giants in the field of travel insurance. From £220 for 12 months worldwide cover.

**Coverworks Direct**, Cheshire (01270 625431). Policy specially designed for working holidays in Australia and New Zealand.

**Direct Travel Insurance**, (0845 605 2700). Consistently among the cheapest, e.g. 12 months worldwide minimalist cover starting at £131.

**Downunder Worldwide Travel Insurance**, London W2 (0800 393908; www.duin-sure.com). Can be extended while you're on the road.

**Endsleigh Insurance** (0800 028 3571; www.endsleigh.co.uk). 12 months of back-packer basic cover costs £335, £402 for comprehensive cover. Maximum age 35.

**FYI** (00 353 1 874 8458; www.fyi.ie). Irish backpacker specialist insurer which sells policies in sterling as well to clients under 35. Price for 12 months is £215 plus £9 for excess waiver.

**gosure.com** (0845 222 0020; www.gosure.com). Explorer one-year policies for 18–34 year olds cost £216 with no baggage cover, £240 with baggage cover.

**Mind the Gap Year** (www.mindthegapyear.com). Specialists in Gap Year and Back-packer Insurance, offering an online preparation and planning gap year service. £200 economy, £300 standard.

**MRL Insurance**, Surrey (0845 676 0691; www.mrlinsurance.co.uk).

**Navigator Travel Insurance Services**, Manchester (0161 973 6435; www.navigatortravel.co.uk).

## HEALTH AND SAFETY

### RISKS

Anyone with a vivid imagination will be able to think of many things that might go wrong with a gap year. Several young women and men who have been on gap year projects have had fatal accidents or worst of all, as in the case of the British backpacker Caroline Stuttle, have been murdered. A much less remote possibility is being mugged, losing your passport or having your backpack stolen. You may get sick or lonely or fed up. You may make a fool of yourself by allowing yourself to be tricked by a con-man who sells you some fake gems or rips you off in a currency transaction. You may feel desperately homesick for a situation in which you do not have to behave like an adult when you have only had an adolescent's experiences.

While some identify the initial decision to go abroad as the hardest part, others find the inevitable troughs more difficult to cope with, such as finding yourself alone in a cheap hotel room on your birthday, running out of money faster than anticipated, or getting travellers' diarrhoea. But if travelling requires a much greater investment of energy than staying at home, it will reward the effort many times over.

Friends and family are seldom reluctant to offer advice, and normally the perceived risks are far greater than the actual ones. When **Cathleen Graham** from Canada announced that she was bound for rural South Africa with the charity *SCORE* (see *Africa* chapter), many came forward to express grave concerns for her safety as a young woman:

> *People's reactions to my choice of destination were determined by what they saw portrayed about South Africa in the media. Of course, people who knew me best knew this was an opportunity that suited me. You really need to develop a strong filter about listening to people's opinions before you go: are they sound and balanced, or more reflecting the person's own fears and anxieties if they were the one going?*

Some gap year travellers undergo a process of disillusionment, which is not a bad thing in itself, since no one wants to live in a world of illusions. You harbour a desire to see some famous monument and find it surrounded by touts or chintzy boutiques. The reality of seeing the Taj Mahal or walking down the Gorge of Samaria in Crete or meeting an Amazonian Indian may be less romantic than you had imagined. (See Alain de Botton's elegant *The Art of Travel* for an in-depth study of the conflict between dreams of travel and the reality.)

In rare cases, students can be traumatised by what they experience in a gap year. According to the senior tutor of a Cambridge college who regularly meets students before and after their gap year, most come back much more changed than the students who have not deferred for a year. Some benefit enormously, but not all. He recalls one in particular who had gone to work in a Romanian orphanage with young children with AIDS. She came back so traumatised that she suffered from nightmares for a long time afterwards. But usually the changes are not so dire.

Several short courses specialise in preparing young people for potential danger and unpredictable situations abroad; see entries in the 'Gap Year Safety and Preparation'.

## DO's AND DON'Ts FOR YOUR GAP YEAR

*According to Anthony Lunch, managing director of non-profit volunteer-sending agency* **MondoChallenge,** *the following practical considerations will help to ensure a smooth and rewarding gap year.*

### Plan early

- *Look at the advice concerning personal safety given by the FCO (www.fco.gov.uk).*
- *Be aware of the laws, customs and dress code for the country. Guidebooks should provide all this information.*

- *Online banking is a great way to manage your finances while you are away. But many internet cafés are slow and access may not always be easy so don't leave important transactions until the last minute.*
- *Calculate how much money you will need for your trip and make sure you have some extra. Find out if you can use a credit or debit card to withdraw money at your destination.*
- *Visit your doctor for advice on vaccinations and medication needed.*
- *Contact the relevant embassy or consulate for advice on obtaining a visa. Many have online forms and often visas can be obtained on arrival although having one in your passport ahead of time can be comforting. Make sure your passport has enough blank pages, or get a new one well before you leave.*
- *Shop around for travel insurance and make sure you are covered for everything you intend to do e.g. trekking.*
- *Make sure your family or friends at home are aware of your travel itinerary.*
- *If you are volunteering through an organisation, ask for the contact details of the most recent volunteers on your project. They will be able to give you advice about the project.*

**On Arrival**
- *Register your details and itinerary on the FCO's LOCATE service (www.fco.gov.uk/locate) in countries where embassy officials may need to track you down in the event of an emergency.*
- *Keep photocopies of important documents (passport, insurance info, plane tickets) in separate bags from the original copies or send scanned images to your email account for ready access.*
- *Take advice from your local manager about your personal safety and your belongings.*
- *If you are staying in one country for several weeks, consider getting a cheap local mobile phone or a local SIM card for your UK mobile. Local texts and calls tend to be cheaper and incoming calls from abroad are free, which avoids the massive charges when using your UK mobile.*

## TRAVEL WARNINGS

Travel inevitably involves balancing risks and navigating through hazards real or imagined. The FCO runs a regular and updated service; you can ring the Travel Advice Unit on 0845 850 2829 (£0.04 per minute) or check their website (www.fco.gov.uk/travel), which gives frequently updated and detailed risk assessments of any trouble spots, including civil unrest, terrorism and crime.

Some believe that the FCO's travel warnings err on the side of caution to the detriment of NGOs struggling to attract volunteers, so try to balance the official warnings with a first-hand account from someone who lives in the place you are considering. The director of the charity *Sudan Volunteers Programme* describes what he sees as the FCO bias:

> *We continue to be dogged by the negative and, I believe, misleadingly indiscriminate travel advice issued by the FCO which puts off potential volunteers, or more particularly their families. It stems it seems to me from the alarming experiences of embassy staff which induces them to put up ever higher fences to guard their premises and of course this siege mentality brings about an ever greater ignorance of the actual conditions. There was one threat to embassy security about two years ago and one murder of an American official in Khartoum in January 2008. There were otherwise no attacks in the recent years on foreigners in Khartoum or smaller northern towns. I do not belittle these outrages but they cannot be described as 'indiscriminate' as used in the FCO warning.*

Several years ago the FCO launched a 'Know Before You Go' campaign to raise awareness among backpackers and independent travellers of potential risks and dangers and how to guard against them, principally by taking out a water-tight insurance policy. The same emphasis can be detected on the FCO website www.gogapyear.co.uk. However no insurance policy can help you if you are caught breaking the law, as happened to two British law graduates in 2009 who were arrested in Brazil for attempting insurance fraud, admitted their guilt and were sentenced to 16 months' community service. It might seem an easy wheeze to pretend that you've been robbed in order to claim on your insurance policy, but it is risky as well as immoral.

## BRITISH CONSUL HELP

**A British Consul can:**
- Issue an emergency passport.
- Contact relatives and friends to ask them for help with money or tickets.
- Tell you how to transfer money.
- Cash a sterling cheque worth up to £100 if supported by a valid banker's card.
- As a last resort give you a loan to return to the UK.
- Put you in touch with local lawyers, interpreters or doctors.
- Arrange for next of kin to be told of an accident or death.
- Visit you in case of arrest or imprisonment and arrange for a message to be sent to relatives or friends.
- Give guidance on organisations who can help trace missing persons.
- Speak to the local authorities for you.

**A British Consul cannot:**
- Intervene in court cases.
- Get you out of prison.
- Give legal advice or start court proceedings for you.

- ■ *Obtain better treatment in hospital or prison than is given to local nationals.*
- ■ *Investigate a crime.*
- ■ *Pay your hotel, legal, medical, or any other bills.*
- ■ *Pay your travel costs, except in rare circumstances.*
- ■ *Perform work normally done by travel agents, airlines, banks or motoring organisations.*
- ■ *Find you somewhere to live or a job or work permit.*
- ■ *Formally help you if you are a dual national in the country of your second nationality.*

The hard truth is that nothing can guarantee immunity from random accidents, whether tsunamis, landslides or motor accidents. Almost every year, at least one gap year traveller dies, filling the hearts of parents everywhere with dread. In a couple of cases the parents involved in tragedies have been prompted to become involved with promoting gap year safety. For example the parents of Caroline Stuttle, the British backpacker who was pushed off a bridge to her death in Queensland by a drug addict, have set up Caroline's Rainbow Foundation. This charity works to raise awareness of the importance of safe travel to young people, by means of its website (www.carolines rainbowfoundation.org), podcasts and travel stories with travel tips. Similarly Ian French, whose daughter Georgia died in a bus crash just two weeks into her gap year adventure in Peru in 2007, founded GapAid (www.gapaid.org), a charity to promote safer travel for young people. They endorse Mind the Gap Year Insurance (listed above).

 **EMILY LOGIE**, when writing at the end of a very successful gap year which took her to an animal project in South Africa and travelling in South America, reflected on how a family tragedy had affected her gap year:

'Walking my dog this morning I passed the spot by the roadside where I stood when my parents told me that my sister had been killed in a bus crash on her own gap year travels in Ecuador back in April 2008. Having spent much of the last year travelling myself, this morning was the first time I had visited this spot again and I found myself welling up with emotion. No one can ever know how they will react to such news but all I remember was doubling over with searing pain in my stomach and fighting the urge to run away.

Just over a year later I have returned from my own gap year, visiting Southern Africa (South Africa and Botswana), South America (Ecuador and

*Galapagos Islands), and North Africa. I had always planned to take a gap year as both my parents had enjoyed travelling and working abroad during years out before and after university. Going on to study a degree in veterinary medicine I have always been keen to gain work experience and work with animals. I have to admit that some people were more than shocked that I was going ahead with my gap year plans after my sister's accident, but my parents had made numerous statements to the press stating that others shouldn't be put off and I only wanted to strengthen that by going ahead. I was more than happy to do this publicly and was interviewed for various newspapers as well as appearing on radio and television. I felt that keeping a low profile wasn't going to help anyone, especially myself and I had huge amounts of support from friends and family.*

*At Easter I was in Ecuador with my parents and the families of the other four girls killed in the same bus accident. Again we had a lot of media attention and made it clear that other young people shouldn't let this put them off travelling. I have just enjoyed the best six months of my life and couldn't talk more enthusiastically about my travels. My gap year has been a rollercoaster of emotions and experiences. I have loved and hated it, cried, laughed and enjoyed some of the most memorable days of my life!'*

The father of Becci Logie has bravely said in public that he hopes the tragedy would not stop other young people travelling and following their dreams, which is exactly what his other daughter has done.

## HEALTH PRECAUTIONS

No matter what country you are heading for, you should obtain the Department of Health leaflet T7.1 *Health Advice for Travellers* (updated May 2006). This leaflet should be available from any post office or doctor's surgery. Alternatively you can request a free copy on the Health Literature Line 0300 123 1002 or read it online at www.dh. gov.uk, which also has country-by-country details. Increasingly, people are carrying out their own health research on the internet; check for example at www.fitfortravel. scot.nhs.uk and www.travelhealth.co.uk. The website of the World Health Organization (www.who.int/ith) has some information including a listing of the very few countries in which certain vaccinations are a requirement of entry. The BBC's health travel website (www.bbc.co.uk/health/travel) is a solid source of information about travel health ranging from tummy trouble to water quality and snake bites.

A company that has become one of the most authoritative sources of travellers' health information in Britain is *MASTA* (enquiries@masta.com; www.masta.com). It maintains a database of the latest information on the disease situation for all countries and the latest recommendations on the prevention of tropical and other diseases. This advice is provided via a personalised health brief based on your destinations and the nature of your trip which is emailed to you from their website, for a charge of £3.99. Along with vaccination recommendations it also provides practical advice such as protection against malaria, information on disease outbreaks and other non-vaccine preventable health risks for travellers. MASTA's network of travel clinics (which has taken over British Airways travel clinics) administers inoculations and sells medical kits and other specialist equipment such as water purifiers, mosquito nets and repellents.

Private specialist clinics abound in London but are thin on the ground elsewhere. A worldwide searchable listing of specialist travel clinics is maintained by the International Society of Travel Medicine (www.istm.org) although many countries are not included.

The Hospital for Tropical Diseases in central London (Mortimer Market Building, Capper Street, Tottenham Court Road, WC1E 6AU) offers appointments at its Travel Clinic (020 7388 9600) and operates an automated Travellers Healthline Advisory Service (020 7950 7799; www.thehtd.org) which charges 50p a minute (average phone call lasts about seven minutes). Other travel clinics include Nomad Travel Clinics, which have several branches in London including in Victoria (020 7823 5823; www.nomadtravel.co.uk) and also in Bristol, Manchester and Southampton. They offer walk-in appointments though you may have to wait at busy times. The Royal Free Travel Health Centre at the Royal Free Hospital (Pond Street, London; 020 7830 2885; www.travelclinicroyalfree.com) is a well-regarded private clinic, and the Trailfinders Travel Clinic (194 Kensington High Street; 020 7983 3999; www.trailfinders.com) is long-established. Several online shops compete for travellers' custom, among them Travelpharm (01395 233771; www.travelpharm.com) which carries an extensive range of mosquito nets, anti-malaria drugs, water purification equipment and travel accessories. The website carries lots of health information.

For advice on protecting your sexual health, Marie Stopes International (0845 300 8090; www.mariestopes.org.uk) is helpful. The government's free booklet *Drugs Abroad* and the National Drugs Helpline (0800 776600) can give information on drugs laws abroad. For routine travellers' complaints, it is worth looking at a general guide to travel medicine such as *Bugs, Bites and Bowels* by Dr Jane Wilson Howarth (Cadogan, £9.99). Travel health books all emphasise the necessity of avoiding tap water in developing countries and can recommend ways to purify your drinking water by filtering, boiling or chemical additives (iodine is more reliable than chlorine). Tap water throughout western Europe is safe to drink.

## MALARIA

Malaria is undoubtedly the greatest danger posed by visits to many tropical areas. The disease has been making a comeback in many parts of the world, due to the resistance of certain strains of mosquito to the pesticides and the preventive medications which have been so extensively relied on in the past. Because of increasing resistance, it is important to consult a specialist service as above. You can become better informed by looking at specialist websites such as www.malariahotspots.co.uk, www.hpa.org.uk/infections/topics_az/malaria/default.htm or www.preventingmalaria.info. You need to obtain the best information available to help you devise the most appropriate strategy for protection in the areas you intend to visit. Research indicates for example that the statistical chance of being bitten by a malarial mosquito in Thailand is once a year, but in Sierra Leone it rises to once a night. Start your research early since some courses of malaria prophylaxis need to be started up to three weeks before departure. It is always a good idea to find out in advance if there are any side effects you may suffer as well.

Falciparum malaria is potentially fatal. On average 1,600 travellers return to the UK with malaria every year (a decrease from a decade ago), and between five and 12 of those infected will die. The two main drugs can be obtained over the counter: chloroquine and proguanil (brand name Paludrine). In regions resistant to these drugs, you will have to take both or a third line of defence such as maloprim or mefloquine (or Lariam), which are available only on prescription. Because of possible side effects it is important that your doctor can vary the level of toxicity to match the risks prevalent in your destination. A relatively new (and expensive) drug called Malarone is used as an alternative to mefloquine or doxycycline, and is recommended for short trips to highly chloroquine-resistant areas. New drugs are being developed all the time and sometimes there is a time lag before they are licensed in the UK or USA. For example in her gap year in Madagascar, **Karen Hedges** twice contracted malaria but was quickly treated with an effective drug called Coartem (an artemisinin-based combination therapy), expensive by local standards, and only recently licensed in the UK for people over 12.

Unfortunately these prophylactic medications are not foolproof, and even those who have scrupulously swallowed their pills before and after their trip as well as during it have been known to contract the disease. For example **Tom Grundy** virtuously took his Lariam on a gap year placement in Uganda – enduring the discomfort of taking this powerful drug on an empty stomach and anxiety about possible side effects such as brain damage and depression – and also used repellent coil burners, impregnated mosquito nets, 'Doom' room spray and repellent gel. And he still succumbed to the disease 10 months after getting back to Britain.

It is essential to take mechanical precautions against mosquitoes. If possible, screen the windows and sleep under a permethrin-impregnated mosquito net since the offending mosquitoes feed between dusk and dawn. (Practise putting your mosquito net up before leaving home since some are tricky to assemble.) Some travellers have improvised with some netting intended for prams which takes up virtually no luggage space. If you don't have a net, cover your limbs at nightfall with light-coloured garments, apply insect repellent with the active ingredient DEET and sleep with a fan on to keep the air moving. Try to keep your room free of the insects too by using mosquito coils, vaporisers, etc.

DEET is strong (not to say toxic) enough to last many hours. Wrist and ankle bands impregnated with the chemical are available and easy to use. Cover your limbs as night falls (6pm on the equator). Wearing fine silk clothes discourages bites and keep the repellent topped up.

Prevention is vastly preferable to cure. It is a difficult disease to treat, particularly in its advanced stages. If you suffer a fever up to 12 months after returning home from a malarial zone, visit your doctor and mention your travels, even if you suspect it might just be flu.

## REASSURANCE FOR PARENTS

*The departure of a child from the family home is traumatic enough when they're merely going to university, but is made much more frightening if he or she is travelling to the ends of the earth on a year out adventure. When you were 18, you probably hadn't even heard of, let alone considered visiting, some of the destinations that gap travellers now visit, from Vientiane to Antananarivo, Patagonia to Sulawesi. The relative cheapness of long-distance flights, the range of gap year providers offering remote destinations and the raised expectations of the new generation account for these heightened travel ambitions. How you as a parent react will have a lot to do with what you did when you were 18. The parents who motorcycled through Afghanistan to India or hitchhiked round Greece with no money may be more sympathetic than the ones who carried straight through from school to university or a job.*

*The parental imagination is bound to dwell on the possible disasters (and the actual ones such as the Queensland hostel fire a few years ago). Feelings of helplessness when a child is far away fuel these anxieties. But a calm assessment of the risks will result in a startling realisation, that staying at home is just as risky. Clubbing in a city centre or driving on a British road poses risks, too, though parents don't tend to focus on those. According to an article in* The Times *headed 'Gap year away safer than rock festival at home,' research published in the* Journal of the Royal Society of Medicine *showed that taking part in a structured expedition brought with it less risk of death or injury than attending a music festival in Britain or going to a scout camp.*

*As the number of young people taking gap years abroad increases, it is inevitable that more accidents will occur. The raised profile of young people travelling abroad on their gap year means that these accidents tend to be widely reported. So if a young man slips down a waterfall in Costa Rica or a bus slips off the road on an Ecuadorian mountain pass, the world hears about it. By the same token some reported tragedies take place in Britain, as in the case of a young woman working at a Plymouth supermarket in her gap year who was murdered by the store manager. But mostly, if an 18-year-old dies of a drug overdose or is killed on his bicycle in his hometown, this is not reported nationally.*

*It is arguable that children nowadays are overprotected and should be given more not less freedom so that from an early age they learn to be streetwise and how to navigate dangers outside the home. Some say that adventures are now too easy. Young people are lulled into a false sense of security by the number of people doing likewise. A trek round Annapurna can be arranged in an instant, but that does not mean that a blizzard won't reduce visibility to nil inside 20 minutes.*

*A parent will want to take every reasonable precaution on his or her child's behalf, knowing that all 18 year olds believe themselves immortal. They should check with the Foreign & Commonwealth Office on world trouble spots (www.www.fco.gov.uk/travel). They should consider giving their son or daughter a gold-plated travel insurance policy as a birthday present or urge their child not to skimp on insurance. If you have resisted going on email, now is the time to relent, because your child is almost guaranteed to spend time in internet cafés and will be able to let you know that all is well at more frequent intervals. Investigate global roaming SIM cards and think about treating your child to one. Try not to be too prescriptive about how often your son or daughter contacts you because if they are out of contact for some reason, you will worry unnecessarily. A few causes of tragedy are avoidable, such as in the case of a girl who died of heat stroke and dehydration on an expedition in Borneo. Urging your child to take sensible precautions such as dressing modestly in countries where it is expected, not flaunting valuables, not falling prey to smooth-tongued con men, may have some beneficial effect. Those who can't rein in their anxiety might investigate enrolling their progeny on a gap year preparation course (see entries for Objective Gap Safety, Safetrek and Ultimate Gap Year in the Directory of Courses). The British Safety Council (www.britsafe.org) now offers gap year courses on basic health and safety, and works in partnership with some sending agencies such as VESL.*

*But really the hard truth is that it is time to let go. Try to give your child lots of credit for their initiative, enterprise and courage and remind yourself daily that they are now grown up. It is amazing how anxieties vanish once your child has actually left home. As the mother of a son who went to Togo for part of his gap year put it:* 'It's curious how my high anxiety lasted for about 24 hours after I waved him off. Since then it's been pretty much uninterrupted envy and bile.'

An innovative company, *Your Safe Planet* (www.yoursafeplanet.com), provides introductions to trusted locals in your destination who will share their inside travel knowledge and who may also have links to local community-run volunteering projects that are free to join, if that is what you are after. The cost of joining is £45. Any parents considering investing in one of the gap preparation courses might wonder how useful they are. Most of what they try to impart is basic common sense, something that can be in short supply at 18. One of the companies describes a case in which their training came in handy:

*One of our ex-students was on a bus in Ecuador that was held up. He was fine, having been taught that nothing is worth your life, but he had everything he owned taken. Thanks to the fact that he had taken scans of his passport and all other relevant documents which he had emailed to himself, he got a new passport in a record-breaking two days.*

Supporting your offspring can be hard work, especially for the 'helicopter parent' who likes to hover. A Canadian mother describes the key role she played when her daughter (aged 17½) was in the planning stages of a gap year placement at a school for the deaf in south India:

> *One of the recent low points was when I was waiting for my daughter and her friend to show up at the travel agent and they came in (late) asking whether they should put money in the parking meter! I tried to remain calm while I suggested they read the instructions and then make an executive decision. I try not to think about all the practical skills they will have to acquire very quickly when they are off on their own. I have got her a fantastic (cheap and very flexible) flight from Halifax to India at the end of August and back from Kuala Lumpur to Toronto at the end of April. I have confirmed all her insurance coverage. I have acquired signing authority on her bank account, I have photocopied all the relevant documents, and I have supplied her with an extra card on my VISA account. She has managed to do much less, although she is spending a fair bit of time making CDs for her friends and dreaming about what she will do next summer.*

# RED TAPE

## PASSPORTS

A 10-year UK passport costs £77.50 for 32 pages and £90.50 for 48 pages, and should be processed by the Identity and Passport Service within three weeks. The one-week fast track application procedure costs £30–£35 extra and an existing passport can be renewed within one day if it is done in person at a passport office but only if you have made a prior appointment by ringing 0300 222 0000 and will pay the premium fee of £129.50. Passport office addresses are listed on passport application forms available from main post offices. All relevant information can be found on the website (www.ips.gov.uk).

Most countries will want to see that your passport has at least 90 days to run beyond your proposed stay. If your passport is lost or stolen while travelling, contact first the police then your nearest Consulate. Obtaining replacement travel documents is easier if you have a record of the passport number and its date and place of issue, so keep these in a separate place, preferably a photocopy of the title page, which can be scanned and emailed to yourself.

## TRAVEL VISAS

Outside the Schengen Area of Europe in which border controls have been largely abolished for EU nationals, you can't continue in one direction for very long before you are impeded by border guards demanding to see your papers. Embassy websites are the best source of information or you can check online information posted by visa agencies. For example, *CIBT* (www.uk.cibt.com) allows you to search visa requirements and costs for any nationality visiting any country.

Getting visas is a headache anywhere, and most travellers feel happier obtaining them in their home country. Set aside a chunk of your travel budget to cover the costs; to give just a few examples of charges for tourist visas for UK citizens applying in London: £39 for India, £64.50 for China, £11 for Jordan, £38 for Vietnam. Last-minute applications often incur a higher fee, for example a Russian visa costs £75 if applied for a week in advance, but £133 for short notice processing. If you do not want to pin yourself down to entry dates, you may decide to apply for visas as you travel for example from a neighbouring country, which in many cases is cheaper, though may cause delays and hassle. If you are short of time or live a long way from the embassies in London, private visa agencies will undertake the footwork for you, at a price, in the region of £40–£45 per visa.

If you intend to cross a great many borders, especially on an overland trip through Africa, ensure that you have all the relevant documentation and that your passport contains as many blank pages as frontiers which you intend to cross.

Always reply simply and politely to any questions asked by immigration or customs officials. **Roger Blake** has a word of warning: '*Arriving in New Zealand was not really a problem other than a strange encounter with a customs officer: "Are you bringing drugs into the country?" "No!" "Do you take drugs?" "NO!" I reply. She asks "Why not?" This is the kind of carefully planned (and corrupt) trap for would-bes that you occasionally come across. Anyway, no worries on my part.*'

## STUDENT CARDS

With an International Student Identity Card (ISIC; www.isiccard.com) it is often possible to obtain reduced fares on trains, planes and buses, and discounts on hostels, museums, theatres, and so on. The ISIC is available to all students in full-time education and those who can show a letter of acceptance from UCAS. There is no age limit though some flight carriers do not apply discounts for students over 31. To obtain a card (which is valid for 15 months from September) you will need to complete the ISIC application form, provide a passport photo, proof of full-time student status (NUS card or official letter) and the fee of £9. Details are available from any branch of STA Travel. The card entitles you to get in touch with the ISIC helpline, a special service for travelling students who need advice in an emergency. However, this does not in any way replace the need for insurance.

## MONEY

The average budget of a travelling student is at least £25 a day, although many survive on less in cheap countries. Whatever the size of your travelling fund, you should give some thought to how and in what form to carry your money. Travellers' cheques are safer than cash, though they cost an extra 1% and banks able to cash them are not always near to hand, even in Europe. It is advisable also to carry cash and a debit or credit card. Sterling is fine for most countries but US dollars are preferred in much of the world such as Latin America. The easiest way to look up the exchange rate of any world currency is to check on the internet (e.g. www.oanda.com or www.xe.com/ucc) or to look at the Monday edition of the *Financial Times*. The travel chapters include some snapshots of exchange rates for countries of most interest to gappers.

The most straightforward way to access money abroad is by using your bank debit card in hole-in-the-wall ATMs. There is usually a minimum fee for a withdrawal so you should get larger amounts out at one time than you would at home. Read the fine print on those boring leaflets that come with your debit card because it may be that your bank will gouge you with various loading fees, withdrawal fees and transaction fees. For example the transaction fee for withdrawing foreign currency abroad or paying at point-of-sale with a standard Maestro card is 2.65% in addition to the ordinary exchange rate disadvantage plus cash machine withdrawals cost 2.25% of the sterling transaction. In everyday language this means that a withdrawal from a hole-in-the-wall can cost £4–£5. The Point of Sale charge is a more reasonable 75 pence. If you are going to be abroad for a considerable period drawing on funds in your home account, it would be worth shopping around for the best deal which is at present offered in the UK by the Nationwide Building Society. Until June 2009, their FlexAccount debit card permitted free withdrawals. However that now applies only to Europe, and outside Europe there is a 1% charge, which is still cheaper than most.

Remember that hole-in-the-wall cash dispensers abroad will not show your bank balance, so be sure to set up online banking before you go so that you can track your balance wherever you have internet access. The Post Office sells a Travel Money Card which is a prepaid, reloadable card that can be used like a debit card at ATMs and most shops but is not linked to your bank account. You can purchase it online and load it with sterling, euros or US dollars. Be aware that the exchange rate and transaction fees may not be better than the rival methods. Similarly the Travellers Cashcard (www.iceplc.com) part of MasterCard and Travelex's Cash Passport (www.travelex.co.uk) operate the same way, but charge steep exchange rates. The Tuxedo card (www.tuxedo-eccount.co.uk) works like a debit card in ATMs and anywhere that accepts Maestro. The card can be remotely loaded with money (for example by parents) and the site provides 24-hour online access to statements. The card costs £9.95 to buy, then there's a transaction fee of just under 3% (minimum 50 pence, maximum £1.50).

Theft takes many forms, from the highly trained gangs of gypsy children who artfully pick pockets in European railway stations to violent attacks on the streets of American cities to spiked drinks in Russia. Risks can be reduced by carrying your wealth in several places including a comfortable money belt worn inside your clothing, steering clear of seedy or crowded areas and moderating your intake of alcohol. If you are robbed, you must obtain a police report (sometimes for a fee) to stand any chance of recouping part of your loss from your insurer (assuming the loss of cash is covered in your policy) or from your travellers' cheque company. Usually insurance policies impose an excess of £50 or £100 so it is often not worth claiming for stolen cash.

# 1st Contact

### You Could Be In For A Tax Refund

Though it's been said there are only two things guaranteed in life - death and taxes - those in for a rebate following their work periods in the UK, whether it is a gap year travel stint or a firm period of employment, are often pleasantly surprised that some extra money in the bank is well within reach.

Jennifer Welzel a tax refund manager at 1st Contact notes that many individuals working and travelling in the UK, find extra money available to pay off debts, take a holiday or even invest, as a result of claiming a tax refund.

So how exactly can one see if they are eligible for a tax refund? 'It's a simple process and it really costs nothing to check. You can call a sales representative at 1st Contact who will run through all your employment information for the tax year to determine if you are eligible for that extra bit of cash.'

Welzel notes that the extra pounds can be transferred anywhere in the world. 'Once you have left the UK you can claim the money through 1st Contact. The average tax refund is generally around £850 pounds.'

Four to 10 weeks is realistically the time one will wait for a refund. To date Welzel records the highest amount paid standing at £18,000 pounds for an individual who had been working in the UK for five or six tax years.' It was certainly by far the biggest rebate, with our client absolutely over the moon.'

'We've had clients who have sent us chocolates and flowers in celebration,' she laughs, 'as well as offers for dinner and drinks.'

For more information on how to claim your tax refund visit www.1stcontact-taxrefunds.com.

Haggling is a topic of endless fascination among world travellers. Try to avoid boasting about how hard a bargain you are able to drive. Remember that in some countries, the rickshaw driver or temple guide could feed his family that day with the 50p you saved. But spreading largesse randomly is not advisable either. It is not uncommon for children to skip school in order to frequent tourist haunts where they stand a chance of being given a few coins.

## TRANSFERRING MONEY

Assuming your account at home remains in credit and you don't lose your cash/debit card, it shouldn't be necessary to have money wired to you urgently. If you run out of money abroad, whether through mismanagement, loss or theft, you will probably contact your parents who may be willing to top up your account (probably as a loan). If you cannot use a hole-in-the-wall money machine for some reason and need to contact your bank, it is much easier if you have set up a telephone or internet bank account before leaving home since they will then have the correct security checks in place to authorise a transfer without having to receive something from you in writing with your signature. You can request that the necessary sum be transferred from your bank to a named bank in the town you are in – something you have to arrange with your own bank, so you know where to pick the money up.

Western Union offers an international money transfer service whereby cash deposited at one branch can be withdrawn by you from any other branch or agency, which your benefactor need not specify. Western Union agents – there are 90,000 of them in 200 countries – come in all shapes and sizes, e.g. travel agencies, stationers, chemists. Unfortunately it is not well represented outside the developed world. The person sending money to you simply turns up at a Western Union counter, pays in the desired sum plus the fee, which is £14 for up to £100 transferred, £21 for £101–200, £37 for £500 and so on. For an extra £7 your benefactor can do this over the phone with a credit card. In the UK, ring 0800 833833 for further details, a list of outlets and a complete rate schedule. The website www.ukmoneytransfer.com allows you to search for the nearest outlet.

Thomas Cook and the UK Post Office offer a similar service called Moneygram. Cash deposited at one of their foreign exchange counters is available within 10 minutes at the named destination or can be collected up to 45 days later at one of 176,000 cooperating agents in 190 countries. The fees are very slightly lower than Western Union's. The Post Office website (www.postoffice.co.uk) explains how it works.

## ACCOMMODATION

Bookings at hostels worldwide can be made on www.hostelbookers.com, www.hostels. com, www.hostels.net and www.hostelworld.com. The original youth hostels federation is called Hostelling International (www.hihostels.com) and consists of 4,000 hostels in

80 countries. Membership costs only £9.95 for those under 26 (01629 592700 in the UK; www.yha.org.uk).

A congenial chain of hostels, mainly in the UK but also in Paris, Berlin and Amsterdam, were recently advertising for part-time travel writers who would be unpaid but would receive free nights in exchange for work done – contact travelwriters @st-christophers.co.uk.

## MAKING CONTACTS

The importance of knowing people, not necessarily in high places but on the spot, is stressed by many gap year travellers. Some people are lucky enough to have family and friends scattered around the world in positions to offer advice or even accommodation and employment. Others must create their own contacts by exploiting less obvious connections.

**Dick Bird**, who spent over a year travelling around South America, light-heartedly anticipates how this works:

> *In Bolivia we are practising another survival technique known as 'having some addresses'. The procedure is quite simple. Before leaving one's country of origin, inform everyone you know from your immediate family to the most casual acquaintance, that you are about to leave for South America. With only a little cajoling they might volunteer the address of somebody they once met on the platform of Clapham Junction or some other tenuous connection who went out to South America to seek their fortunes. You then present your worthy self on the unsuspecting emigré's doorstep and announce that you have been in close and recent communication with their nearest and dearest. Although you won't necessarily be welcomed with open arms, the chances are they will be eager for your company and conversation. Furthermore these contacts are often useful for finding work: doing odd jobs, farming, tutoring people they know, etc.*

If you or your travel companion has a relative or family friend willing to offer accommodation, think carefully about whether it is worth accepting. If you are looking forward to joining the 'travelling scene' but are stuck in a remote suburb struggling to be a good guest, you may regret saving a few nights hostel expenses. On the other hand living with the locals might prove a highlight.

Hospitality exchange organisations can make travel both interesting and cheap (and induce a panic attack in parents). When you register with the Hospitality Club, Global Freeloaders, place2stay.net or the Couchsurfing Project, all of which are completely free, you agree to host the occasional visitor in your home in order to earn the right to stay with other members worldwide. The one with the highest profile is www.couchsurfing. com. Like so many internet-based projects, the system depends on users' feedback, which means that you can check on a potential host's profile in advance and be fairly sure that dodgy hosts will be ousted straightaway. Couchsurfing is so mainstream that a *Sunday Times* journalist (Fleur Brittan) has written a whole book about it called *On the Couch*.

# WHAT TO TAKE...

Packing for travelling as a backpacker will always entail compromises because you will be limited in the amount of clothes and equipment you can take with you. When you're buying a backpack/rucksack, try to place a significant weight in it in the shop so you can feel how comfortable it might be to carry on your back, otherwise you'll be misled by lifting something usually filled with foam.

Any number of specialist stores and websites peddling travel gear are fun to browse but try to be discerning about what is really necessary. The Gap Year Travel Store (0871 918 2007; www.gapyeartravelstore.com) specialises in selling backpacking equipment to gappers and independent travellers. Another long-established supplier with a huge range is Nomad's online store (www.nomadtravel.co.uk). These ranges are tailored to budget travellers and offer travel products and accessories of all descriptions at keen prices.

If you plan to camp in a hot country, you might think about taking a tropical quilt rather than a sleeping bag. Either you can spread out the quilt as a bed to sleep on or it can be folded to create a lightweight sleeping bag. The other advantage is that it is much lighter to carry and takes up less room in your luggage. Alternatively, it can be wrapped around your shoulders for warmth in an air-conditioned space or on a chilly evening in the mountains. However, it will not provide enough warmth if you're planning to travel at high altitudes. A down vest might be a solution for travelling at altitude and can also double as a comfortable pillow. Another consideration for those going to high altitudes, such as Cusco Peru at nearly 10,000ft, is altitude sickness; the prescription drug Diamox has been recommended to alleviate the symptoms.

Now a seasoned traveller, **Tom Grundy** reminisces about his preparations for going to Uganda in his gap year: '*Two days of packing later, I was set to go. My nervous inexperience was reflected in the 40kg suitcase I packed containing "just the essentials" (including 8 bottles of shower gel, 30 packs of polo mints, 6 tubes of toothpaste, washing up gloves, thesaurus and washing line).*' While aiming to travel as lightly as possible, you should consider the advantage of taking certain extra pieces of equipment such as comfortable walking boots or a tent if you will have the chance to travel independently. If travelling in a part of the world where theft is rife, invest a few pennies in a padlock which will act as a deterrent if nothing else. One travelling tip is to carry dental floss, useful not only for your teeth but as strong twine for mending backpacks, hanging up laundry, etc.

In the tropics you must carry water, in order to prevent dehydration. Belts with zips worn under a shirt are very handy for carrying money unobtrusively. A bandana is also advisable in the tropics to mop up sweat or to put round your face in windy desert conditions. Some even have backgammon and chess sets printed on them to provide portable entertainment.

If you have plumped for a placement scheme where you'll stay put for a while, you might allow yourself the odd (lightweight) luxury, such as iPod speakers, short-wave radio or jar of peanut butter. **Camilla Burgess** who spent three months in Ghana recommends taking a bar of Vanish laundry soap; hers was in huge demand, since clothes become very dirty in big cities in the tropics.

## HANDY TRAVEL TIPS FOR BACKPACKERS FROM *VENTURE CO*

- *Keep a record of travel documents such as passport number, driving licence, travellers' cheque serial numbers, insurance policy, tickets, emergency number for cancelling credit cards, etc. Make two copies: stow one away in luggage and give the other to a friend or relative at home. Email this information to yourself so that you can access it at any time from an internet café.*
- *Make sure your passport will remain valid for at least six months beyond the expected duration of your trip.*
- *Carry valuable items (like passport, essential medicines and of course money) on your person rather than relegating them to a piece of luggage which might be lost or stolen.*
- *Only pack items you are prepared to be lost or stolen.*
- *Remember to ask permission before taking photographs of individuals or groups. In some cultures it can be insulting.*
- *Take advantage of loos in expensive hotels and fastfood chains.*
- *Learn a few key words and phrases in the local language, so as not to seem arrogant in assuming everyone communicates in English.*
- *Read up on a country before you arrive or during your travels to help avoid problems and enhance understanding.*
- *Make sure your equipment and clothes don't look brand new so that you will be less likely to attract attention to yourself.*
- *Most importantly make sure you get that perfect balance between travelling safely and enjoying yourself. Any problems during your trip could ruin it, but equally if you are over cautious you might miss out on something amazing.*

Good maps and guides always enhance one's enjoyment of a trip. Most people you will meet on the road will probably be carrying a Rough Guide or a Lonely Planet. These are both excellent series, though try not to become enslaved by their advice and preferences. Rough Guides has a series of First Time titles which could be of interest to gap year students including *Around the World*, *Europe*, *Africa*, *Asia* and *Latin America*. Even though so much advance information is available over the internet (web recommendations are given at the end of travel chapters), nothing can compete with a proper guide book to pore over and take away with you. If you are going to be based in a major city, buy a map ahead of time. Visit the famous travel book shop Edward Stanford, with branches in Bristol and Manchester as well as the mother-store in Covent Garden, London; their searchable catalogue is online at www.stanfords.co.uk.

# Pacsafe

Outpac Designs launched the original 'Pacsafe™' product in 1997. Shortly after, this product won the coveted Backpacker's Editor's Choice Award. One gapper, Jonathan Dorn, remembers how great his Pacsafe was on his travels:

'As I approached the ticket counter for my flight to Montana, the agent gave me the same skeptical look my mother used to when I'd ask for an advance on my pocket money. After poking at the steel mesh encircling my backpack, the ticket lady said, "You'll have to put your pack in a plastic bag so that thing doesn't damage our conveyor belts." Such sweet irony – a pack that might damage the airlines' property instead of the other way around. My pack was safely ensconced in the Pacsafe, a protective cover that thwarts not only airport goblins but also knife-wielding thieves.

The Pacsafe has travelled with me across three continents, delivering my gear unscathed to a dozen distant trailheads. Using the security cable and padlock, I've chained my load to trees and lampposts and ducked into stores for supplies. I've even used it to bear-bag my food.

The Pacsafe fits like a standard rain cover and either wraps around your pack's hip-belt and harness so they don't catch on conveyor belts, or lets them hang free so you can shoulder the pack. It cinches closed with a tug on a steel cable and locks with a small brass padlock. When not in use, the Pacsafe folds into a grapefruit-size pouch. But best of all, it's nearly indestructible. Despite my best efforts with hammer and hacksaw, I couldn't dent the stainless steel mesh or plastic components.

The consensus: The Pacsafe... a wise investment.'

The Map Shop in Worcestershire (0800 085 4080/01684 593146; www.themap shop.co.uk) and Maps Worldwide in Wiltshire (01225 707004; www.mapsworldwide. co.uk) both do an extensive mail order business in specialised maps and guide books.

If you are going to a country to learn or improve a language, you might take a good dictionary and a language course at a suitable level, for example the *Take Off In...* series from Oxford University Press (www.askoxford.com/languages) for £25 including mp3 downloads, the BBC (bbc.co.uk/languages), Linguaphone (0800 136973; linguaphone. co.uk) and Audioforum (audioforum.com). For more information about language learning, see the *Courses* chapter.

Preparation is half the fun but choose like-minded company before discussing your intended anti-malarial regimen and your water sterilising equipment since you don't want to turn into a pub bore.

On top of all these practical preparations, you will want to prepare yourself mentally, to try to imagine what it will be like in some distant corner of the world, doing things completely outside your past experience. **Angela Clegg** concentrated her efforts on researching Africa:

> *Before you go you spend so long trying to prepare yourself mentally but when you get there you just adjust instantly. I think the hardest thing for me was not preparing for living with 15 other volunteers. I researched culture shock in preparation for African culture but neglected to think about the different people I would be living with day in day out. I found myself in a kind of 'Big Brother/Real World' scenario. Again, once I had adjusted to it, I wouldn't have changed a thing, as I feel like those people will be friends for life after what we went through, experienced and saw together.*

Give yourself time to get excited about your plans, so try to avoid a last-minute scramble and not be working and partying flat out up until the moment of departure.

## ... AND WHAT TO LEAVE BEHIND

Make sure you leave a record of all-important documents with your parents plus at least four signed passport photos which are needed for university loan applications and by some university admissions departments. Whereas forms can be emailed, faxed or posted to you abroad for your attention, it is difficult to arrange for photos to be sent and impossible if you are on a placement teaching at a village school in Tanzania or Nepal.

Depending on your destination, don't take your trendy clothes and trainers. For tropical countries, leave behind anything that isn't made of natural fibres. Some travellers can't live without their iPods though gadgetry of this kind marks you out in many parts of the world as extremely affluent. If you do take one, you will need to invest in a universal charger (e.g. Callpod) that will fit into any shape of socket around the world.

## STAYING IN TOUCH

The revolution in communication technology means that you are never far from home. Internet cafés can be found in almost every corner of the world where, for a small fee, you can access your email, keep in touch with your friends via Facebook, check relevant information on the web or upload and distribute digital photos. Many gap year travellers also set up a free blog so that interested friends (and mothers) can check; try for example www.blogger.com/start, www.travelpod.com, http://realtravel.com and the well-named www.getjealous.com. The photo and video sharing site http://community. webshots.com is designed for people to upload their photos (free for storing up to 1,000 photos). Another recommended site for starting your own blog or following the travel blogs of others is http://blogs.bootsnall.com. Mytravelcompanion.com is another place that provides tools to travellers for sharing photos and travel diaries. Travellers Connected (www.travellersconnected.com) is an online community site for gap year travellers that is free to use. You can register your profile and contact travellers around the world to seek insider tips. It also allows you to set up a free travel blog with photos.

### MOBILE PHONES

Roaming charges for mobiles can cost an arm and a leg. Contact your mobile phone company to check on coverage; if not you may need to take it into a shop to have the phone 'unlocked'. Also check what deals your provider offers, which can be spectacularly complex. Vodafone's 'Passport' is a free tariff option available with any handset (abroad.vodafone.co.uk), which allows you to make calls at your home tariff after paying a 75p connection fee. It is available in most of Europe, Australia, New Zealand and Japan but not North America.

If you are going to be on the move a lot, you might want to investigate a gadget that can charge your mobile and iPod using solar power: the Solio charger (www.solio.com) retails from about £50.

A plethora of companies in the UK and US sell pre-paid calling cards intended to simplify international phoning. You credit your card account with an amount of your choice (normally starting at £10 or £20), or buy a card for $10 or $20. You are given an access code that can be used from any phone. Lonely Planet, the travel publisher, has an easy-to-use communications card called eKit (lonelyplanet.ekit.com), which offers low cost calls, voice mail and email. A company called 0044 (0044.co.uk) sells foreign SIM cards which allow you to take your mobile with you and call at local rates while you're away. Its global SIM card costs £20 compared with £30 from GO-SIM (www.gosim.com).

Warn friends not to call your UK mobile while you are away; you will be paying for all incoming calls from abroad. If you are staying in one country for more than a few weeks and use your phone a lot, consider getting either a cheap local mobile phone or a local SIM card for your UK mobile. Even better, ensure your UK contacts have the special access codes available for low cost dialling from landlines to your destination. One of the most often recommended discount companies (for people phoning abroad from the UK) is www.telediscount.co.uk in the UK, which offers unbeatable prices: in many cases you can make international calls at local rates.

For very anxious gappers and/or parents, there is a back-up system on the market called SafetyText (www.safetytext.com), which was launched by the father of the British woman Lucie Blackman who was murdered when she was working as a hostess in Japan. SafetyText is a delayed text messaging system, which depends on the user remembering to cancel the text once he or she has arrived safely.

## VISITS FROM PARENTS

Many gappers are lucky (or unlucky) enough to have parents who want to visit (and can afford to do so). After months of teaching in a Tanzanian village or backpacking in Laos or assisting at a New Zealand adventure sports centre, suddenly there are the dear old things from home. Whereas flying the coop might have been a major attraction at the outset, most students welcome the chance to turn back temporarily into being somebody's child. Often parental visits coincide with time off and may mean a sudden rise in your standard of living. Whereas some luxury-starved students will embrace this temporary change of fortune with glee, others may find that it jars on their grow- ing sense of what is appropriate in certain countries. You are bound to take pleasure in having the shoe on the other foot. This is your chance to guide your parents round and allay their anxieties; it is now you who is expert in the best cafés in Granada or the *tro-tro* timetable in Ghana. No doubt you will catch beaming smiles of pride on their faces as you navigate with confidence. Enthusiastic fledglings might be tempted to rave about all the things that are superior about the place they are living (which could be a little hurtful to visitors from home) whereas others take the opportunity to share their catalogue of moans. Try to avoid both.

Parents' plans can sometimes come unstuck when overtaken by events. Eighteen- year-old **Dan Hanfling** baked a creditable cake for his interview in the autumn for a job in a ski chalet in a French ski resort. But on arriving in the Alps, he learned that he was expected to service a number of chalets by carrying supplies, cleaning toilets, etc. This job was a lot less glamorous than he had imagined, and he returned to England after just a few weeks. Unfortunately, his parents (avid skiers) had already booked a holiday in the same resort so that they could all be together at Christmas.

**CHRIS MILNER**, a recent graduate, spent eight months in the Sudan through the Sudan Volunteer Programme and describes how his parents' visit made him realise how far he had travelled:

'My parents were arriving in Sudan for a visit. For me, this was to be a fantastic personal experience but it was also an opportunity to discover how much I had learned since walking up the jetty towards Wadi Halfa three months earlier. Their visit represented a chance to sit in the markets, drink the gingered coffee, suffer the insufferable heat, and queue for buses with a beginner's mind. I had now lived in Omdurman for three months and had become somewhat accustomed to life in Sudan. The rush of colours, faces, smells and sounds that had at first merged into a single overwhelming sensory experience had each disassociated into their constituent parts, and were now reaching the appropriate senses. At first, seemingly random events led me to Uud concerts, Sufi ritual, and river boat trips. Certainly large amounts of cake were consumed… and other activities such as evenings watching Celine Dion videos could be avoided without causing too much offence.

My parents arrived late and we took a taxi back to Shuhadda from the airport. Immediately and for the first time, I realised how familiar the city had become, how easy it was to predict the conversation with the driver, and how comfortable I felt… In short, Sudan was not what it once was. It had become for me a real place in which people lived, including me, and this gave me the freedom to both praise and criticise it. I took them along to meet my group of students at the Abdel Karim Centre. The 'AK' is a community-led organisation that believes in creating an environment in which young people can learn, take control of their lives, and use the skills they develop to move Sudan forward. I liked it there very much.

The parents were an instant hit and the lesson plan went out the window (actually we always studied on the roof) and for two hours we all took part in conversations on many topics; from love to taxation. I really can't describe how proud these young people should be of themselves – not because of the hardship in which some of them live (although that is another story). Their generosity of spirit, willingness to give, willingness to accept, willingness to welcome, and enthusiasm for life was quite inspiring.

*My parents and I were lucky enough to visit Juba together. However, for me, the highlight of their stay in Sudan was the party organised by the students at Abdel Karim to celebrate their visit. The amazing and some-times tiring fact about being a volunteer is that in Sudan, everything is Sudan. Through my students and friends, I could learn about it. Through my parents I realised I was a part of it.'*

## COMING HOME

Coming home and experiencing reverse culture shock is a problem for some. Settling back will take time especially if you have not been able to set aside some money for 'The Return'. It can be a wretched feeling after some glorious adventures to find yourself with nothing to start over on. Life at home may seem dull and routine at first, while the outlook of your friends and family can strike you as narrow and limited. If you have been round the world between school and further study, you may find it difficult to bridge the gulf between you and your stay-at-home peers who may feel a little threatened or belittled by your experiences. After a brilliant gap year divided between volunteer teaching at an international school in Costa Rica, skiing in the Appalachians and working on a farm in Tuscany, **Katie White** observed, '*My high school friends have not been very supportive of my decision to take a year off. I still can't tell if it was/is jealousy or resentment of my opportunity or that I seemed arrogant because I was step-ping out of the box. High school social dynamics are dicey at best, and for some reason I generated some not-so-warm-and-fuzzy feelings with my decisions.*'

**Peta Miller** came back to the same grey airport she'd left six months before to go to Ghana with a classic case of reverse culture shock:

*I had thought it would be relatively easy to slot back into my life seeing friends, socialis-ing and in the end looking for my first proper job. But my soul was true to Ghana. I scru-tinised those around me and found the way they behaved rude, selfish and pretentious. They looked sallow, pale and unhealthy as they shuttled back and forth between home and the office, compressed into tube compartments, breathing black air. Nobody smiled or communicated. Train tickets, bars of chocolate, cinema tickets could all be purchased without uttering a word. Even my own friends seemed changed into frivolous consum-ers intent on image and appearance. There was no colour, no sincerity and no content. People seemed to be wasting the working week doing jobs that made rich men richer so that at the weekends they could go on frenzied shopping trips. From such a perspective the world seemed to have gone mad. Five months later I'm better acclimatised. But the fact remains that Ghanaians smile and laugh more than we do because their pleasures are simpler, more easily and more often fulfilled.*

The restlessness passes, the reverse culture shock wears off soon enough and you will begin to feel reintegrated. Gap year experiences are great conversation openers when you're meeting new people at university. You may find yourself gravitating to other first-year students who have taken a year off before uni.

As has been noted, what you did in your gap year provides an easy topic of conversation for future interviews so in official contexts you should be prepared to put as positive a spin on it as possible. Any evidence of initiative and organisational abilities will help. If you travelled alone you can boast of your independence; if you travelled with friends you can claim to have learned about cooperation and teamwork.

# Part II
# Gap year travel

## TRAVEL TO THE FOUR CORNERS

# TRAVEL TO THE FOUR CORNERS

It would be a pretty sad gap year that didn't include at least some pure and unadulterated travel. If you have one or more friends who want to go with you, many happy sessions can be spent in the pub poring over maps and planning the itinerary. If your friends are all disappearing in different directions, do not be put off the idea of going on your own or finding a travel companion elsewhere (see earlier section on travelling 'Solo or in company'). Cost is usually the crucial factor for gap students wondering where to go or how to get there. Those who go through a sending agency will either have their travel arranged for them or be offered plenty of guidance. But for those students who want to organise their trip independently, here is some general advice.

The purest form of travelling is on public transport cheek by jowl with the local people. By creating your own route and using your wits to find your way, you'll find yourself obliged to interact with local people rather than being cocooned in a foreign-run tour. When engaging with local people, always follow the golden rule of trusting your instincts. It may be stating the obvious, but you should never accept an invitation to go somewhere or participate in an activity that makes you feel uncomfortable or threatened. Even if you run the risk of offending a 'host', you need to keep your internal compass functioning. Bear in mind that foreigners may be viewed as easy targets for some form of exploitation, principally financial. If you feel that an offer sounds too good to be true then it almost certainly is.

While juggling bus or train timetables and the need to find suitable accommodation, try not to rush. The slow pace of life as a traveller, especially in the developing world, is something to be savoured not bemoaned. Even with an entire year at your disposal, you cannot possibly 'do' all of a country let alone a continent. Little can be gained from racing through an area, ticking off sights, which is both exhausting and unrewarding and will leave you with very superficial impressions of a culture and its people. Taking your time and getting to know a smaller number of places to a deeper level cannot fail to reward. It is by doing this that you will meet more local people and really come to appreciate the essence of a country, soaking up the atmosphere beneath the tourist façade.

Once you have been carrying your pack for a couple of weeks, caught the right buses, met a few other travellers, you will probably laugh at your pre-travelling misconceptions of danger and risk. In the developing world you will have encountered the warm welcome and endless curiosity with which ordinary people greet travellers from a far land. Remember to carry photos of your family or postcards of your home country, as these can spark off much discussion.

For practical tips on what to pack and how to stay safe, see the chapter *Before You Go*.

# THE BEATEN TRACK

A report by an academic was published a few years ago lambasting the negative impact that backpackers have on places where they congregate (Sinai, Kathmandu, Goa, Kho Pha-Ngan, Machu Picchu, etc). The organisation for responsible tourism, Tourism Concern (www.tourismconcern.org.uk), is also worried by the number of young people who travel to places they are not really interested in just to meet up with other travellers, to eat, drink and socialise in exactly the way they would at home but without as many inhibitions. There is even a novel about it. For a satirical account of the wrong way to go about being a gap year traveller, read William Sutcliffe's novel *Are You Experienced?* based on his own gap year experiences. In this extract, the anti-hero Dave is being lectured by an old-India hand:

> *Hippies coming for spiritual enlightenment have been replaced by morons on a poverty-tourism adventure holiday. Going to India is no longer an act of rebellion but an act of conformity for ambitious middle-class kids who believe that a trip to the Third World shows the kind of initiative which companies are looking for. You come here and cling to each other as if you're on some kind of extended management-bonding exercise in Epping Forest... It's a modern circumcision ritual, a badge of suffering you have to wear to be welcomed into the tribe of Britain's future elite. Your kind of travel is all about low horizons dressed up as open-mindedness. You have no interest in India and no sensitivity for the problems this country is trying to face up to. You treat Indians with a mixture of contempt and suspicion reminiscent of the Victorian colonials. Your presence here in my opinion is offensive and you should all go home to Surrey.*

Hard-hitting stuff but worth pondering.

# SPECIALIST TOUR OPERATORS

One solution to the problem of having no available travel companions is to join a group of like-minded people on an overland expedition. There are distinct advantages to having your travel arrangements organised for you en route. For a start you can hand over most concerns about personal security to someone else. Travelling with an overland company saves time and stress usually expended on things such as the bureaucratic snags of border crossings and provides help with food, accommodation, activities and excursions. Taking advantage of such insider knowledge removes all the hassle of solitary independent travel. For example *Oasis Overland* (www.oasisoverland.co.uk) specialises in adventure travel for young travellers with truck-based overland expeditions in South America, Africa, the Silk Road and the Middle East lasting 15 days to 40 weeks. Some trips attract more mature travellers while others (such as the 'Egypt Encompassed' trip) run on local transport, stay at simple hostels and are suited to partying young people.

## Oasis Overland

Karen Jones joined Oasis Overland's 23 week Trans Africa Expedition to Cape Town:

'The Trans Africa has been one of the most fantastic, awesome experiences of my life. I didn't really know what to expect and was a little apprehensive about travelling across Africa in the back of a truck with 23 strangers for 23 weeks!

We all met at Luton airport on a cold November evening, weighed down with massive backpacks and all wondering what the coming months would bring. On arrival in Gibraltar, we were met by our Oasis crew, Andi and Grant and a huge yellow truck - our new home! The truck was great, fitted with coach seats, lockers for our gear and a stereo, as well as carrying food, water and cooking equipment. Andi and Grant were organised and friendly and really made the trip.

Our journey took us from Morocco across the Sahara to the Dogon tribe of Mali and the beaches of the West African coast. We travelled through the rainforests of Nigeria and Cameroon as well as Gabon, Congo and Angola where we saw no other travellers and in Namibia we walked up Africa's highest sand dunes and watched amazing wildlife. We arrived into the city of Cape Town after 23 weeks of camping in the bush, sandmatting through the desert, pushing the truck out of enormous, muddy pot holes, getting bitten by mosquitoes, cooking over the camp fire and drinking warm beer as well as seeing incredible wildlife, experiencing new cultures, meeting amazing people, travelling through stunning landscapes and making friends for life. I still think I had good reason to be a little apprehensive, it was hard going at times, but these turned out to be the best memories and what made the trip such an adventure!'

Most overland companies cater for the backpacking market and keep prices down by providing basic accommodation, often camping, and expecting participants to share the cooking and other chores. Overland trips include optional adventurous excursions, such as mountain trekking, white water rafting or adrenaline sports. An average trip would cost between £100 and £150 a week plus £40–£50 a week for the food kitty. The longer the trip the lower the weekly cost, for example, Oasis Overland trips start at £92 per week plus £37 a week local payment (for food and camping fees) on 40-week trips in Africa and go up to around £140 a week for shorter South American trips (see 'Directory of Expeditions').

One of the most exciting trips on the market is available on the Oz-Bus which travels between London and Sydney, visiting 17 countries en route. From February 2010, it will operate as a hop-on, hop-off service, though the sectors must be booked in advance. The cost of the 92-day trip is £3,999 (0800 731 9427; www.oz-bus.com).

Agencies that specialise in trips for backpackers can be just what a solo gap year traveller needs to overcome a reluctance to strike off into the unknown. Small-group tours can allow you to experience a country at closer range and avoid the beaten path of larger groups. For example Intrepid Travel with a retail store in London (76 Upper Street, Islington N1 0NU; www.intrepidtravel.com) is a leading operator of adventure holidays to Asia, Latin America, Africa, Australasia, Middle East and Europe. The company runs more than 400 trips a year in 35 countries. Their 'Basix' trips are no-frills small-group trips suitable for first-time backpackers, lasting from six days in Northern Thailand to 39-day trips from Cairo to Casablanca.

Here is a selected list of overland operators whose websites provide detailed information about their trips. The average age on most of these would be 20–30 with a higher ratio of women to men. For more companies, see the directory of tour operators maintained by Overland Expedition Resources (www.go-overland.com). Specialist companies that operate only in one region (e.g. Africa) are mentioned later in this book.

*The Adventure Company*, www.adventurecompany.co.uk.

*Dragoman*, www.dragoman.co.uk.

*Encounter*, www.encounter.co.uk.

*Exodus*, www.exodus.co.uk.

*First 48*, www.first48.com.

*GAP Adventures*, www.gapadventures.com. Originally a Canadian company; acronym stands for 'Great Adventure People' so not specifically for gap years.

*Guerba*, www.guerba.co.uk. Africa specialists for three decades (now joined forces with Intrepid Travel to offer worldwide trips).

*Imaginative Traveller*, www.imaginative-traveller.com.

*Kumuka Expeditions*, www.kumuka.co.uk.

*Oasis Overland*, www.oasisoverland.co.uk. Africa, Middle East, Egypt and Latin America.

# AIR TRAVEL

Air travel has changed beyond recognition with no-frills airlines forcing national carriers to drop their fares in order to be competitive. A few low-cost airlines have tried to break into the long haul market but it is a lion's den. The Canadian Zoom Airlines failed last year as did the Hong Kong airline Oasis which had been flying passengers between London and Hong Kong for £150. Meanwhile there has been a surge in regional discount carriers on the Ryanair model, including Kingfisher Red and SpiceJet in India, AirAsia in Malaysia and Southeast Asia, Jetstar which links many Australian cities plus South and East Asia, West-Jet in Canada, Taca in Central America, GOL in Brazil and so on. All these airlines have their own websites and many allow online bookings, some at remarkably low prices.

For long-haul flights, especially to Asia, Australasia and more recently Latin America, discounted tickets are available in plenty. The major student travel agency STA Travel is one of the best starting places. STA Travel are specialists in student and youth travel offering low cost flights, accommodation, insurance, car hire, RTW tickets, overland travel, adventure tours, ski, and gap year travel. STA Travel have about 40 branches in the UK and hundreds more worldwide staffed by experienced travellers. 'Gap Year' is one of the icons on the STA homepage and the company estimates that it deals with about 14,000 enquiries per year from young people about gap year travel. For bookings and enquiries call STA Travel on 0871 230 0040 or log on at www.statravel.co.uk to find fares and check availability. You can also request a quote by email or make an appointment at your nearest branch.

Other reliable agencies specialising in long-haul travel including for student and budget travellers are:

*Flight Centre*, (0870 499 0040; www.flightcentre.co.uk). Branches around the UK.

*Marco Polo Travel*, Bristol (0117 929 4123; www.marcopolotravel.co.uk). Discounted airfares worldwide.

*North South Travel*, Chelmsford (01245 608291; www.northsouthtravel.co.uk). Discount travel agency that donates its profits to projects in the developing world.

*Trailfinders*, London W8 and other branches (0845 058 5858 worldwide; 0845 050 5940 Europe; www.trailfinders.com). 22 branches in UK cities plus Ireland and Australia.

*Travelbag*, Alton, Hampshire (0871 703 4700; www.travelbag.co.uk). Originally Australia and New Zealand specialist, owned by ebookers.

*Travelmood*, London (0800 011 1945; www.travelmood.com). Now part of TUI.

*Travel Nation*, Hove (0845 344 4225; www.travel-nation.co.uk). Staffed by real experts who specialise in finding the best deals on RTW flights, discounted long-haul flights and multi-stop tickets.

*Student Flights*, (www.studentflights.co.uk).

*Western Air*, Totnes, Devon (01548 821665). Good on rail and coach passes as well as RTW itineraries and long-haul flights.

**THINKING ABOUT YOUR CARBON FOOTPRINT?**

*Anyone who has followed developments at the 2009 Copenhagen Climate Conference or seen Al Gore's film* An Inconvenient Truth *will want to give some thought to minimising their carbon footprint. Of course it is best for the planet if you don't fly at all, but if you do, consider offsetting your emissions with a donation to fund tree-planting or other mechanisms to reduce the impact of air travel on the environment, which is offered by many companies including Climate Care (www.climatecare.org) and Carbon Neutral (www.carbonneutral.com).*

Other discount agents advertise in the travel pages of newspapers like the *Independent*. Phone a few outfits and pick the best price. General websites such as www.cheapflights.co.uk, www.travelocity.com, www.expedia.com and www.opodo.com are good starting points though comparison shopping this way can be time-consuming and frustrating. Even after long hours of surfing, the lowest internet fares can often be undercut by a good agent, particularly if your proposed route is complicated. For example an agent is more likely than the internet to come up with an offbeat route downunder using Emirates and SriLankan Airways to travel via Dubai to Mumbai, overland to Trivandrum in Kerala, on to Colombo, Singapore, Sydney (or Melbourne or Perth) then back to London via Dubai for less than £1,200.

When purchasing a discounted fare, you should be aware of whether or not the ticket is refundable, whether the date can be changed and if so at what cost, whether taxes are included, and so on. **Roger Blake** was pleased with the RTW ticket he bought from STA Travel that took in Johannesburg, Australia and South America. But once he embarked he wanted to stay in Africa longer than he had anticipated and wanted to alter the onward flight dates:

> *That is the biggest problem of having an air ticket. I had planned for six months in Africa but I've already spent five months in only three countries. I have been into the British Airways office here in Kampala to try my verbal skills but have been told the 12-month period of validity is non-negotiable. How stupid I was to presume I would get a refund when it states clearly on the back of the ticket that they may be able to offer refunds/credit. A lesson for me and a warning to future world travellers, to check before they buy whether or not the ticket is refundable/extendable.*

## ROUND-THE-WORLD FLIGHTS

The idea of going all the way around the world holds more than a touch of romance. From the early heroic navigators such as Ferdinand Magellan to the fictional traveller Phileas Fogg, circumnavigators of our planet have always captured the imagination of adventurous souls. The first question is always: how can I keep the cost of such a trip down to a manageable level? Magellan had the backing of the King and Queen of Spain, Phileas Fogg was a gentleman of independent means. The first step to achieving this goal is to understand how RTW fares are calculated.

The price of RTW tickets has remained fairly consistent over the past few years, though taxes and fuel surcharges have leapt up. You shouldn't count on getting much change from £1,000 even for the most limited route. Check www.roundtheworldflights. com (0844 844 2540) or Travel Nation in Hove, Sussex (01273 718025; www.travel-nation.co.uk) for ideas. RTW fares start at about £600 for four stops departing London between April and June (plus taxes of £350–£650 depending on stops) and have a maximum validity of one year. The cheapest fares involve one or more gaps which you must cover overland. The most amazing RTW fare on offer at the time of writing was all with Air New Zealand (available through Travelmood, 0800 0111 945; www.travelmood. com): London – Los Angeles – Auckland – Hong Kong – London for less than £700 including tax.

The most common RTW itineraries are ones that have been specially marketed by groups of airlines that cooperate and have formed various 'alliances'. A good travel agent will quickly tell you which alliance of airlines (if any) is best suited to your needs. Fare levels change according to how many stops and what distances you want to cover, so you will need to make some careful calculations about your route, and whether you want to travel 26,000 miles or up to 39,000 miles (which might mean a £700 difference in price). Note that If you don't particularly want to include North America on your itinerary, you may not really need an RTW ticket.

Generally speaking RTW itineraries must continue in one direction with no backtracking and invariably must be completed within 12 months with no possibility of extending. Fares that differ between low, shoulder and peak season depend on your date of departure from home. If possible try to start your RTW trip between September and November or April and June. The cheapest fares involve one or more gaps which you must cover overland, though be aware that the land mileage still counts towards the maximum.

The standard RTW stopovers are Singapore/Bangkok, Sydney/Auckland and Los Angeles/New York with a free stopover in the Pacific such as Fiji or the Cook Islands thrown in. Most fares will be quoted without tax so keep reminding yourself to add on at least £200 and for a complicated routing as much as £500. The main alliances are:

*One World*, www.oneworld.com. Member airlines includes British Airways, Qantas, Cathay Pacific, American, Finnair, Iberia, Japan (JAL), Lan Chile, Malev and Royal Jordanian. The OneWorld Explorer RTW fares are calculated according to season of travel and number of continents included. A three-continent itinerary starting in the low season costs £1,239 plus tax and a five-continent trip in a high season is well over £2,000.

*Star Alliance*, www.staralliance.com. 17 international airlines including Air New Zealand, Singapore Airlines, Air Canada, Lufthansa, United, Lot (Polish), TAP Portugal, SAS and South African Airways. The special RTW fare allows five stops and up to 26,000 miles. The website has a downloadable RTW mileage calculator tool.

*Skyteam*, www.skyteam.com. Member airlines are Aeroflot, AeroMexico, Air France, Alitalia, Continental, Czech Airlines, Delta, KLM, Korean and Northwest. Choices range from the basic 29,000 mile maximum with up to five stops to 39,000 miles with 15 stops.

Other options to consider include the *World Discovery Plus* available from BA, Qantas and Cathay Pacific. The restriction here is 29,000 miles and seven stopovers. Departures in the low season (mid-April to mid-June) are good value but a third more expensive in the peak summer or Christmas season. The excellent travel agent Western Air in Devon (www.westernair.co.uk/roundtheworld.html) provides some sample mileages on its website: London – Santiago – Sydney – Perth – Tokyo – London comes in at 28,033 miles.

The *Great Escapade* (www.thegreatescapade.com) can be booked using Virgin Atlantic, Singapore Airlines, Silkair and Air New Zealand. It is possible to stay inside the 29,000 mile limit and still visit eight or more countries, for a fare starting at £1,039 before tax.

Travel agents such as the ones listed above can piece together various sector flights to create a bespoke route that can incorporate as few or as many stops as you like. Before contacting them, spend some time poring over an atlas and deciding where you are sure you want to go and on what approximate dates. A specialist agent will quickly be able to tell you whether one of the alliance promotions is better than a DIY itinerary. It is possible to include almost anywhere on a RTW itinerary – at a price. For example it is usually disproportionately expensive to zigzag between hemispheres, so flying London – Johannesburg – Bombay – Sydney – Tokyo – Santiago could end up being astronomically expensive. Be prepared to compromise on your wish list of destinations. Console yourself that this might be just your first gap year over your lifetime and there will be other occasions in which to fit in the highlands of Papua New Guinea or the Galapagos.

## SAMPLE BUDGETS

**With next to nothing:**
*A couple of EU-funded programmes provide full funding. For example participants pay nothing to join the European Voluntary Service (EVS) scheme in which they will spend 6–12 months as a volunteer on socially beneficial projects in Europe.*

- *Summer camp counselling programmes in the USA run by BUNAC, Camp America and CCUSA advance you your transatlantic fare and later deduct this from your wages. The placement agencies charge varying fees but your end-of-summer wages will cover this.*

- *The Leonardo programme is a fully funded 9-week vocational training and language learning programme that operates in Portugal and Spain (see www.workand volunteer.com).*

■ *Although the kibbutz movement in Israel is in steep decline, it is still possible to spend three to six months for a modest joining fee, provided you can afford to get to Tel Aviv (www.kibbutz.org.il/eng/welcome.htm).*

■ *Exchanging your labour for free accommodation and food works very well with the international WWOOF (World Wide Opportunities on Organic Farms) exchange (www.wwoofinternational.org).*

**With £1,000:**

■ *A month-long InterRail trip around Europe will cost £367 for the pass plus £25–£30 a day for living costs. If you stick mainly to the eastern countries (Turkey, Bosnia Herzegovina, Bulgaria, Romania, Slovakia) and cook for yourself in hostels some of the time, your budget will stretch much further than if you spend your time in Switzerland, France and Scandinavia.*

■ *Backpack in the developing world and concentrate on countries where your savings will stretch for many months. Assume you will have to spend at least half your budget on a return airfare. Ideas for the cheapest destinations are Nepal (especially trekking), India, Laos, Nicaragua, Bolivia and Syria. (Tim Leffel's little book* The World's Cheapest Destinations *is full of useful suggestions.)*

■ *Buy the cheapest return to New Zealand you can find in early February, hitchhike from Auckland and get a job picking apples in the Hawkes Bay area where there is a perennial shortage of harvest workers (see www.picknz.co.nz) who earn at least the weekly minimum wage of NZ $450. Afterwards, blow your savings in Queenstown, adventure capital of the South Island.*

■ *£1,000 won't last long travelling conventionally in North America, though with a J-1 visa from BUNAC (020 7251 3472; www.bunac.org) you can look for a seasonal job to cover your travel and leisure expenses.*

**With £2,000**

■ *Basic round-the-world fares start at £750 via Asia, though most end up costing well over £1,000 with extra stopovers and taxes for Australia/New Zealand. With your left over budget you could backpack for months around South East Asia and/or have a shorter time in the more expensive Antipodes.*

■ *An open-jaw ticket to Latin America allows you plenty of latitude to explore on the ground. For example, fares from London to Mexico City and out of Buenos Aires start at £700. If average daily spends are less than US$10 in Bolivia, US$15 in Chile and US$20 in Honduras and Guatemala, you could easily spend your whole gap year roaming the southern Americas.*

■ *Book a language course in a romantic European location like Sorrento on the Bay of Naples or Granada in Spain. A sample four-week course through CESA in southern Italy would cost £750 plus £625 for homestay accommodation with breakfast. By booking a cheap Easyjet flight to Naples, plenty of money would be left over for exploring the Mediterranean.*

■ *Various sending agencies such as The Leap and Madventurer offer five- or six-week travel/volunteer programmes in Africa which cost less than £2,000.*

## With £3,000

■ *The majority of conservation specialists run exciting gap year trips and projects in farflung corners of the world for on average £1,000 a month, so you can choose from helping to protect orangutans in Borneo, study lemurs in Madagascar or carry out a reef survey in the Bahamas.*

■ *Incorporate an Everest Expedition (£2,200 for 35 days with Realgap) into a trip around the Indian subcontinent.*

■ *Obtain a catering certificate in four weeks from the famous Leiths School of Food and Wine (£2,650) and then enlist their help to find you a job on a luxury yacht or in a ski chalet.*

■ *Learn to dive or even qualify as a PADI Divemaster on a Thai island with, for example, Personal Overseas Development.*

## With £4,000+

■ *Join an expedition to the Norwegian Arctic with BSES.*

■ *Work with big game on a South African game reserve.*

■ *Train to become a snowboard instructor in New Zealand, Patagonia, the Canadian Rockies or the Alps.*

■ *Spend a year living it up in a beachside house in the South Pacific or the Caribbean.*

# EUROPE

Europe has always punched above its weight in terms of global influence. Although relatively modest in size, it boasts more than 30 national cultures, vastly different climates and landscapes and one of the most ambitious peacetime organisations in history, the European Union. Added to all this, it has a quite amazing past. Greek ruins, Roman forts, and Gothic cathedrals all trace the story of Western civilisation, providing a kind of living history through which the interested gapper can wander and wonder, one foot in the past, the other in the present. And hot on the heels of the EU expansion into eastern Europe have galloped budget airlines and youth hostel entrepreneurs; so budget conscious gappers can balance more expensive Western destinations such as Sweden and Switzerland with cheaper chill out periods in Estonia and Slovenia.

Europe's sheer variety can seem to border on the unmanageable, but it can easily be broken down into bite-size chunks that share certain borders or traditions (e.g. northern Europe, Scandinavia, Central Europe, the Mediterranean, Alpine, Balkans, and Russia, the Baltic Countries and the Ukraine). So with trains, plains and boats willing to whisk you away and few problems with border controls, why not develop a taste for the continent on our doorstep?

## THE LURE OF EUROPE

A gap year in Europe offers unrivalled access to some of the world's most famous cities, scenery, cultures and languages. After all, it is pretty darn good to sit in Rome, the 'Eternal City', sipping an espresso while eavesdropping on the world's most sensual language. Or leave the well-trodden track to meander down a country lane in Romania, shadowed by a dramatic castle far above. Europe has a seemingly endless capacity to surprise, to flaunt its fashionable modernity, while clinging to slow-paced traditions. Its people can be intimidatingly chic, reassuringly generous or depressingly impoverished; even its most famous monuments have a way of differing from their postcard faces. Somehow they are larger or smaller than expected, their surfaces surprising or their air of authority humbling.

You can follow tried and tested touring routes through the continent, or branch off and create your own. It is easy to follow the crowd to the Mediterranean for some indolent sun worshipping, then grab a cheap flight to party-capital Barcelona, before continuing the fun in Eastern Europe, where cities such as Riga are fast developing a reputation as party meccas. Should you wish to learn a language, then you will be spoilt for choice by the variety of courses on offer (see 'Directories of Courses' later in this book). But if you're no linguist, don't worry too much – many Europeans, particularly the younger generation, have a fair grasp of English. It is, however, polite to make at least some effort with the local language. Learning to order a beer is a good start, but a premature conclusion.

Then there is cost – gappers and their money are soon parted in Europe, but there is a chance you can pick up casual work, thanks to the blessed absence of red tape within the EU. The ability to play a musical instrument soulfully on a street corner might replace some of your funds, although you will need to check the busking conventions for each place you visit.

Overall, Europe does benefit from some planning as a gap year destination, but a canny gapper can save enough by tight budgeting to allow for the occasional splurge – perhaps an adrenaline-charged whitewater rafting trip in Austria, a music festival or that exhilarating dog-sled ride in snowy Lapland.

## UNMISSABLE HIGHLIGHTS

- Sample the delights of Paris, the city of romance, full of twisting streets, chic cafés and cheap wine and cheese.
- Find that Lapland, the land of the Midnight Sun, is warmer than expected in summer.
- Explore the island of Santorini, with its famous volcanic caldera and gravity-defying villages.
- Join pilgrims from all over Europe as they gather in the dazzling medieval city of Santiago de Compostela in Galicia.
- Chill out in Berlin, a place both exquisitely trendy and reassuringly relaxed.
- Visit the world's smallest State, Vatican City in Rome.
- Walk around Dubrovnik's city walls.
- Ski in the lofty Alps in summer or winter or, for an alternative range, try the Carpathian Mountains, curving through eastern Europe.

## GETTING THERE

Most gap year students these days turn to the internet for travel advice and information. No frills flights have exploded over the last decade, opening up all corners of Europe to adventurous gappers as well as to less adventurous stag and hen parties. You will have to do quite a bit of clicking to establish that the wonderful £10 flight advertised actually costs £85 after taxes, fuel surcharges and a fee per bag have been added. With unavoidable extras, the cheapest flights start at about £70 return and usually, the earlier you book on off-peak no-frills flights out of Stansted, Luton or regional airports, the cheaper the fare (though not invariably). Bookings should be made online because telephone bookings are more expensive; if you don't have your own debit or credit card, borrow one from a cooperative parent.

Make sure that you factor in the cost – and time – of getting from the airport to your city of choice. Cheap airlines often use small airfields some way from the city (or indeed from anywhere). If France or Belgium is your first destination, it can be easier to take Eurostar, costing from as little as £59 return (London St Pancras to Paris; cheapest fare must be bought in advance). Check out the cheap airlines' websites: www.ryanair. com, www.easyjet.com, www.bmibaby.com, www.flybe.com, www.jet2.com (Leeds-based) and www.thomsonfly.com (Coventry-based). This style of flying has spread to the continent and discount airlines have proliferated including clickair.com (Spanish), airberlin.com, germanwings.com (both German), transavia.com (Dutch), wizzair.com (Polish), smartwings.com (Czech), SkyEurope.com (Central Europe), blue1.com (Finnish), norwegian.no and so on. Central sources of information include flycheapo.com and whichbudget.com. Scheduled airlines like BA and Aer Lingus have had to drop fares to compete and are always worth comparing. After saying all this, you may wish to consider the environmental impact of flying. Gappers heading for Europe (unlike their counterparts going to New York or Thailand) can choose to avoid those nasty polluting flights. Visit ferries.co.uk as a starting point for your maritime ambitions.

Before the era of cheap flights, budget travellers' transport of choice was the long-distance coach. Eurolines is the group name for 32 independent coach operators serving 500 destinations in all European countries from Ireland to Romania. Return fares start at £45 for London–Amsterdam if booked a week in advance. Bookings can be made online at eurolines.co.uk or by phoning 08717 818181. So called 'funfares' mean that some off-season fares from the UK are even lower, e.g. £15 one way to Brussels, Amsterdam and Dublin.

For smaller independent coach operators, check advertisements in London-based magazines such as *TNT*. For example Poltours (020 8810 5625) links the UK with many cities in Poland; one-way fares start at around £50, return £75, but discount coach trips have been made almost redundant by cheap airlines such as Wizz Air for Poland.

## GETTING AROUND

InterRail is still one of the most popular ways to enjoy a variety of experiences and sights within a short time span and tight budget. The Global pass covering the whole of

Europe for one calendar month costs approximately £367 for those under 26 and £550 for those 26 and over. A shorter duration of 22 days is also available for £284/£431. If you plan to make a few long journeys in a certain number of days, investigate Flexi-passes; they permit five days of travel within 10 days, or 10 days of travel within 22 days. A number of specialised agencies sell InterRail products and add slightly different mark-ups. Passes can be bought online (in which case you will probably have to pay an extra £5 or £10 or so for Special Delivery) or in person at branches of STA Travel and similar outlets. Websites to check include www.raileurope.co.uk, www.trainseurope.co.uk (0871 700 7722), www.railpassshop.com or the marvellous site for train travellers everywhere www.seat61.com.

Even in the furthest corner of eastern Europe, clean, efficient, well-staffed trains run on time. InterRail gives you the freedom to travel at a reduced rate, it usually represents a saving compared to the cost of paying for the individual journeys and it means that you can go somewhere 'just because you like the sound of it'. Every experience will be different. Before you buy InterRail tickets, you need to know what you're getting for your money.

Alongside the usual travel books such as a Lonely Planet or Rough Guide, you're likely to need your own train information: the *Thomas Cook Rail Map* (£8.99) can prove invaluable for all the routes where direct trains are unavailable and alongside this, Thomas Cook's *European Rail Timetable* (£13.99).

Very often in high season (June/July/August), you will find the trains you need are booked up for days in advance. This can mean either losing the spontaneity and booking a week in advance, staying in one place a few more days than planned, or taking shorter regional journeys. If you are travelling outside high season, bear in mind that some train services will be unavailable and some attractions will be shut, although this means you can avoid crowds at the most popular destinations. Whatever happens, leave in the direction of home a good couple of days before your pass runs out.

Night trains are particularly useful, because you don't lose a day travelling. It isn't always easy to work out costs in advance as seat reservations are almost always compulsory and can cost anywhere between €3 and €30, requiring a budget of around an extra £150 per person.

Couchettes and sleepers are available, but at a far higher price than ordinary seats, even with the InterRail reduction; a couchette can cost up to €70 on the 'Trenhotels'. If you're travelling as a couple, couchettes (at least in the Catholic countries) mean you will be in separate carriages altogether as they don't allow mixed sleeping accommodation and for two it can be far more economical to sleep in the seating carriages. This is also a great way to meet fellow backpackers and to pick up tips on what to see and where to avoid.

It pays to know about the discounts available on InterRail, for example the P&O ferry from Dover to Calais, the Hellenic Mediterranean ferries between Italy and Greece

(25%), or the Eurostar discount. Some of these are listed in the back of the ticket book, but a little research goes a long way.

Stations are very often the hub of a small town and often families wait on the platform to offer rooms in their homes to tourists in order to supplement their income. This can be much cheaper than the hostels and the families are prepared to help you with timetables and translations. As well as making you feel at home, this offers the chance to see how real people live rather than just the inside of another chain hostel.

**JENNY HARDIE** went InterRailing and wrote about her Voyage of Discovery.

'After a month of train travel with InterRail I am bronzed, toned and still in one piece. I had a fantastic time, following a route that defied all logic and convention, and involved endless laughter, confusion and foreign officials. Even if things don't always go perfectly – well, that's a story to tell when you get back.

My boyfriend and I made the rather dangerous assumption that once we had our InterRail tickets, we'd have our travel expenses covered, apart from a few negligible charges for seat reservations on long-distance trains. Not quite! We found that reservations are almost always compulsory and we ended up spending at least £150 each on seat reservations alone. Nothing fancy, just the standard second class seats that the InterRail ticket covers. I wouldn't try and get away without paying these either. There are endless ticket inspections and some trains where they won't even let you on without checking your tickets and passports.

Waking up in a new country is a magical experience and I wouldn't hesitate to recommend the night trains, with the added advantage that you don't lose a day travelling. Normally we just booked seats when we slept on trains and made ourselves comfortable. If you make an effort to get on, people don't mind waking up with your foot in their face.

We had no planned route and when western Europe started to diminish our rather small savings, we headed east. Eastern Europe is one of those places that cause backpackers to cling together for safety. The frequent searches, passport checks and questioning are a bonding experience and we made some great friends. One piece of advice is never tell them you've just come from Amsterdam. One night, on the Czech border, seven young men burst into our carriage. They were dressed in hooded jumpers and rucksacks and were demanding our passports. They turned out to be German customs officials but naturally we all thought we were being robbed. If you question their authority, they empty your bag. Another time, on the train from Budapest, we were evicted from our seats by the police and had to stand for 17 hours. In both cases, there was a real sense of community and a party atmosphere as we helped people out and were in turn helped by fellow travellers.

The majority of countries have no problem with InterRail tickets, but in Spain they don't cover first class travel and there is no second class option. Eventually we found that you could pay €15 for an upgrade. In Romania, InterRail marks you out as foreign and we met a few unscrupulous ticket inspectors. On the train out of Bucharest, one such inspector chased us along the train to levy his imaginary fine of around £50 (it varied as he tried to bargain the bribe, but it had to be cash). He told us if we wouldn't pay the fine (and we wouldn't – we had legitimate tickets and no money) then we would have to get off the train at a remote station at 3am. We hid from him in the toilet and as soon as we made it over the border, the Hungarian ticket inspector had no problem with our tickets. But set against that bad Romanian experience, we were really lucky in Transylvania and found a kind lady who couldn't do enough for us – she even did all our washing. Her concern when we drunkenly wanted to use the gas cooker at 1am was more for our safety than that of her house.

Seeing the sunset in Madrid and exploring Roman ruins under palm trees in Croatia were fantastic experiences, which I hope to repeat some day. The advice we were given and the help we received in so many places have given me a renewed faith in human nature. Lastly, I hope you have a loving family to come back to – you can't use InterRail in your home country and the only time we were genuinely stranded was when no one would pick us up from the ferry port at Dover.'

Train travel throughout continental Europe is subsidised and therefore reasonably cheap in many countries, especially Italy, so buying point-to-point tickets is a good idea for those not covering too much distance. Often there is a huge differential in price between the elite high-speed services and the slower local trains. The coach equivalent of InterRail is the Eurolines Pass which is available for 15 or 30 days. A 30-day youth pass in high season will set you back about £245. An attractive alternative is a hop-on, hop-off backpacker bus. The main contender is Busabout (www.busabout.com), which offers a Flexitrip pass for £289 that allows six stops within the whole operating season between May and October; many other permutations are available.

For fixed coach itineraries designed for gap year students, investigate the 18, 27 or 33 day tours offered by London-based Topdeck Travel (www.gaptraveleurope.com/itineraries). These all-inclusive packages covering between nine and 17 countries cost from £1,235 to £2,185.The European landmass is one of the most expensive areas of the world to traverse. One of the cheapest ways is to pre-arrange a shared lift. Ride-sharing can be fixed up via websites such as Allostop in France (www.allostop.net), Taxistop/ Eurostop in Belgium (www.taxistop.be) and Citynetz-Mitzfahrzentrale in Germany (www. citynetz-mitfahrzentrale.de). The normal practice is that passengers make a contribution to the driver's expenses, e.g. €50 for Amsterdam to Warsaw. There are dozens of lift-sharing outlets across Europe, especially in Germany, where there are Citynetz offices in Berlin, Düsseldorf, Freiburg, Hamburg, Munich, etc. Most require you to register, which is free in some cases or costs €10–€20 in others. In most cases you will have to pay 3c–4c (3–4 eurocents) per kilometre you want to travel. Matches can seldom be made straightaway, so this system is of interest to those who can plan ahead.

## BUDGETING

Although parents will concern themselves unduly with this aspect of your trip (are you *sure* you have enough money? or are you *sure* you want to blow that much?), it is very wise to give it at least more than a passing thought. After all, your meals, accommodation, beer rations and transport options depend wholly on you possessing the requisite amount of hard cash – at the right time. Carrying some cash in Euros is a good idea, but try not to carry more than €100–€150 in case you are robbed. Easily spent, easily lost – such is the life cycle of cash. If it is hard to get to an ATM (say in rural Estonia) then at least the cost of living will be cheaper. A budget starting at €40 a day should suffice in western Europe, transport excluded. Eastern Europe is much cheaper, although Russia is more expensive.

When you arrive in a city it is a good idea to think what paying attractions you really want to see and to intersperse these with general ambling around. These meanderings, away from tourist hot spots, can often be the most rewarding, leading you to hidden architectural gems or kooky local hang-outs. European café culture gives you licence to while away afternoon hours while nursing a small coffee or beer. Look for cheap supermarkets of which Europe has plenty and buy picnic essentials. Eating bread and cheese and drinking wine on the banks of the Seine is an excellent and very cheap way to pass a Parisian evening. Also, look out for food stalls, which will save you the expense of a sit down meal. Falafel, for example, is a good bet – it has nutritional value, the good places let you pile your plate high with salad, and chickpeas are pretty filling. If you're keen to eat out, then lunch menus can offer unexpectedly good deals. It is often a good plan to ask locals or the expat community for advice on the best deals in terms of accommodation/food/free museum entry/free concerts. Good places to ask are English language bookshops and youth hostels.

## ACCOMMODATION

Hostels offer the cheapest beds in Europe, ranging from about €8 to €25 per night, depending on location. In cities such as Berlin, Barcelona and Milan, you are looking at at least €15 for a hostel bed away from the centre, and up to €25 for a central hostel. Hostels are a great way to meet people and find out about the area, but you will not have much privacy.

Hostels fall into two categories – 'official' and independent. The original Youth Hostels Federation is now called Hostelling International (www.hihostels.com) and consists of 4,000 hostels in 80 countries. Membership costs only £9.95 for those under 26 (01629 592700 in the UK; www.yha.org.uk). Rules and guidelines apply, often including curfews (good if you don't want to be woken up in the early hours by drunk party animals, bad if you want to be a drunk party animal) and dorms are usually single sex. You know what you'll get, but they can be a teeny bit boring. Technically you need to be a member, but you can pay a supplement. If you buy an International Guest Card and get it stamped every night (for a few euros extra) you can become a member after six nights. Private hostels are unpredictable, but often have fewer rules and more colour. Good hostel websites include www.hostelbookers.com, www.hostelworld.com and www.hostels.com, all of which allow online bookings; www.famoushostels.com lists a select few.

Hostels come in all shapes and sizes, including a sailing ship in Stockholm (www.stfturist.se; search for Af Chapman) and a former prison in Ljubljana (www.hostelcelica.com). These speciality hostels can get booked up very early, although in high season it is probably best to book ahead for any hostel especially if you plan to arrive in the evening. Some hostels charge extra for bedding and it is worth considering making/taking a sleep sack. Key deposits might also set you back €15, to be refunded when you check out. On the plus side, breakfast is often included in the price and some hostels offer other free services such as internet and railway/bus station pick-up.

Although hostels are popular with young people they are often open to all ages so not always party centrals. Similarly, they can be packed to the rafters with school parties. Practise tolerance/buy ear plugs/pay out a bit more for a single or double room. Keep your valuables on you as far as possible because theft can be an issue. If all the hostels are booked out, then ask for advice. Staff might know of another place or local families with vacancies. Alternatively, head back to the station and ask at the tourist information office or, in extremis, hop on a bus or train to a less well-known town where a bed will be easier to find. Sleeping in public places (i.e. train stations and parks) is a last resort and usually tolerated rather than encouraged. If you're stuck, sharing a hotel room may not be prohibitive. Visit www.hotels.com or www.laterooms.com.

In some cities it is almost as cheap to book an apartment if you are travelling in a group of at least four. Tourist offices and the internet can be helpful, but the real steals are achieved by asking around when you arrive. This will allow you to tap into the 'informal' letting market. For example, it is possible to rent a small house on a Greek island for only €60 a night in high season. The trick is to ask locals, starting with the manager of the café. It probably also helps if you are a group of girls, and you will need to head out to the less touristy areas.

Also, think how much you could save by camping. The latter does not need to remind you of soggy holidays in Cornwall. Try wild camping on the Swedish archipelago where there are no cars, pure water and the spicy smell of cinnamon buns wafting over the pine trees from the local bakery. The downside, of course, is that you have to lug your stuff around and camping grounds are usually some way from the centre of town. Cycling and camping make a good combination. Most campsites will keep your passport from the time you check in until you leave. Some countries are fine about wild camping, others much less so. Sweden is probably best of all since it has the law of *Allemansrätten* which gives everyone the right of public access to private land for recreational purposes. It is best to check and if you are in rural areas then ask the landowner's permission. You'll be surprised how chilled most of them will be – they might even offer you breakfast!

## CULTURE SHOCK

Although not such a vital topic as in developing countries, culture shock is still an issue, particularly in areas of eastern Europe. Traditional gender roles tend to be preserved in countries such as Romania, where many women work because of economic necessity rather than because there is any serious commitment to equality. Subsequently, Western women may be a little perturbed by flagrant examples of male chauvinism. Being hassled, however, can happen in any big Western city, particularly those with substantial immigrant populations and in southern Italy, rural Spain and parts of Turkey. The best way to tackle unwanted attention is not to break step if you are walking, and to learn a few choice phrases if you are reading in a park. One young female traveller found that speaking Welsh was an effective deterrent. On the whole, this attention is never a real problem – just annoying. If you don't want to talk to anyone/go for a drink with them simply tell them that you are not interested. Or buy a ring and tell them you're married. Visit www.journeywoman.com for advice.

Gay travellers should probably act discreetly in Central and eastern Europe – Poland is staunchly Catholic, with a distinctly intolerant right-wing government, and Belarus is known to treat homosexuality with contempt. The Czech Republic, however, was the first former communist country to grant legal recognition to same sex partnerships. Sunbathing topless is best reserved for liberal Western European destinations. Depending on your background you might at first be taken aback by the readiness with which Germans and Scandinavians strip off. Being rowdy in public will probably not be noticed in most big European cities, especially in lively Spain and Italy, but east European cities

# EXCITING WAYS TO GET INVOLVED

- Teach English at a children's summer camp on the Baltic coast of Poland (www.escs.pl).
- Do a three-month internship at a company in Munich or Berlin (www.astur-gmbh.de).
- Get paid work at a club in Ibiza (www.balearic-jobs.com).
- Pick strawberries on a Danish island (www.samsobaer.dk/summerjob.html).
- Study art history in Florence or Spanish in Salamanca (www.arthistoryabroad.com and www.mester.com).
- Go on horse patrols on the Greek island of Kefalonia to guard against forest fires (www.fnec.gr).
- Learn to surf on the Basque coast of France (www.gap.surf.france.free.fr).
- Live and volunteer with orphans at a children's village in Russia (www.ecologia.org.uk).
- Work a season at a Swiss ski resort (www.jobs-in-the-alps.com).
- Stay for free at a hostel in Amsterdam in exchange for doing some duties (www.flyingpig.nl).

For details of these and many other ideas for jobs, volunteering and courses, see the country-by-country chapters.

such as Prague and Riga are attracting more than their fair share of stag and hen parties, and as a result are getting a little sour about drunken British 'savages' (to quote a Latvian MP). In 2009, the mayor of Tallinn was reported to be wracking his brains to find ways of discouraging unruly Britons from relieving themselves on the national Monument of Freedom.

## WHAT TO EXPECT

What should you expect as you tour Europe? Decent transport, accessible culture and plenty of other travellers to exchange stories with. On the whole, it is very easy moving between countries, the obvious exception being Russia where you must organise a visa well before you go. On the whole Europe is pretty safe and violent crime is thankfully rare. Common sense will get you through most minor annoyances. Beware of pickpockets e.g. jostling gangs of children around stations or on crowded metros. Thieves can also target hostels and overnight trains, but camping sites tend to be fairly safe. Also, watch out for dodgy taxis that charge astronomical rates: make sure taxis are licensed, the meter is switched on and ask how much the journey will cost before you get in. There are also certain scams running in eastern Europe, involving a fake policeman. If anyone asks to see your passport/money make sure that they are legitimate (i.e. have identification) before handing anything over. If they become difficult, insist that they take you to the local police station. Also, make sure that you get the right amount of money when you get your currency converted – some blackboards advertising cut price rates may muddily suggest 0 when they mean 9. Again, check the rate before agreeing to the transaction, or better still, use a local ATM.

# SCANDINAVIA
## Sweden, Iceland, Finland, Norway, Denmark

### CURRENCY

Finland uses the euro (£1 = €1.08)

| | |
|---|---|
| £1 = 8 Danish kroner | US$1 = 5 Danish kroner |
| £1 = 9 Norwegian kroner | US$1 = 5.6 Norwegian kroner |
| £1 = 11 Swedish kronor | US$1 = 7 Swedish kronor |
| £1 = 199 Icelandic krona | US$1 = 125 Icelandic krona |

### BUDGET

€50–€75 per day excluding transport. Iceland is more expensive, although Scandinavia's big cities, such as Stockholm, will also knock your budget.

## HIGHLIGHTS

Blonde women, glistening blankets of snow and the intoxicating glory of the Northern Lights and the Midnight Sun – this is the picture conjured by most gap year travellers considering a trip to Scandinavia. You might also like to add Santa Claus, marauding Vikings, and ABBA. Many gappers are unfairly put off by high prices, but there are plenty of ways to save money in Scandinavia while enjoying some of the most stylish cities and spectacular wilderness areas in Europe.

Scandinavians have style, lots of it. After all, they came up with Ikea, which is practically a small nation in its own right. Stockholm, Helsinki and Oslo are fast-paced and trendy, while Copenhagen and Reykjavik have well-deserved reputations as weekend party centrals. Urban centres such as Gothenburg, in southern Sweden, Aarhus in Denmark and Tromsø in Norway, have a more edgy, youthful vibe. Alcohol can be ruinously expensive (£6 for a beer in Norway, £4.25 in Denmark), so hitting the town is definitely a 'splurge' activity.

For a cheaper and cheerful holiday, head for the hills, islands or beaches. The key to keeping costs down is to camp, preferably in the wilderness. Yes, there can be the odd (shy) bear and wolf, but on the whole it is very safe and Scandinavians have elevated camping into an art form, erecting fabric palaces with minimum fuss. Popular places include the island of Gotland, off the coast of Sweden, and the Stockholm and Åland archipelagos. These places offer crystal clear water (let's call it 'refreshing'), sandy beaches and a relaxed pace of life – although Gotland's ancient capital, Visby, is packed with partying Swedes in summer.

Head north on a sleeper train, and wake up in the Arctic Circle. Other northerly highlights are the Ice Hotel in Kiruna in Sweden and the Santa Claus Village, near Rovaniemi, Finland. Norway is justly famous for its fjords, the longest and deepest of which is Sognefjorden. Another highlight is the Lofoten Wall comprising spectacular glacier-carved mountains soaring straight out of the sea. It is worth taking a couple of ferry rides to really appreciate their spectacular height and shapes. The Hurtigruten's fleet of ships pulls into every sizable port and passes some of the best coastal scenes in Scandinavia (though prices are high, e.g. £520+ for the voyage south from the Arctic Circle to Bergen).

Iceland's scenery is out of this world, quite literally: US astronauts rehearsed for walking on the moon in its inhospitable interior. The 'land of fire and ice' seems to change and re-form before your eyes. Huge rivers, geysers and geothermal springs are often accessible by public transport or tours and some have been harnessed for the public good – the world-famous Blue Lagoon is a weird blue spa in the middle of a lava field. Scandinavia is also unusually good at producing talented musicians and then throwing large music festivals to show them off. Look out for the Iceland Airwaves festival (www. icelandairwaves.com), held in Reykjavik in October, the Roskilde Rock Festival, held in the last weekend of June, the Copenhagen Jazz Festival held in early July and, 'Yran', which also takes place in July in Östersund (look out for the lake monster). For a quirky non-music festival you couldn't do better than Finland's Wife Carrying Championships, held in Sonkajärvi.

**USEFUL SOURCES OF INFORMATION**
*Use It Oslo (Ungdomsinformasjonen), Møllergata 3, 0179 Oslo (+47 24 14 98 20; use-it@ung.info). Its English language online guide to Norway can be found at http://use-it. unginfo.oslo.no.*

# NORTHERN EUROPE
## Germany, France, Benelux

**CURRENCY**
Euro (£1 = €1.08)

**BUDGET**
€30–€60 per day excluding transport. Germany can be at the cheaper end, particularly outside the major cities, and Amsterdam is at the higher end, depending on how many coffee shops you frequent.

## HIGHLIGHTS
Northern Europe is the continent's powerhouse, a place of confident and prosperous countries with rich cultures, mediocre weather and a rather trying habit of throwing their weight around. Over the centuries they have begun world wars, laid the foundations of the EU, legalised prostitution and grown some of the most powerful business empires in the world. Northern Europe's past will continue to draw visitors, whether it's the beer drinking traditions of Bavaria or the fairy tale castles of Luxembourg, and its quite spectacular nature, from snow-capped mountains to luxurious beaches, will continue to be enjoyed.

France has always been a place where you can enjoy the finer things in life, whether you prefer world-class museums, haute cuisine or meandering around elegant streets, admiring chic people. The French are fiercely proud of their country, prioritising national identity above, say, monarchy (beheaded) or religion. Local cheese, bread and wine is lovingly made, exhibited and consumed. The French people have attracted more stereotypes than any other country: stubborn, rude, unbearably chic. Most of these are really aimed at Parisians, quite often by French 'provincials' who talk about their city cousins in less than respectful tones. Paris is the 'must visit' city of romance with wide boulevards, stylish cafés, ornate parks and wonderful shops. For more than 1,000 years it has been a trend-setter, creating the cancan and the cinematograph, publishing James

Joyce's *Ulysses* when no other city dared. But if you really want to find out about the French people, then leave Paris.

If you prefer hot weather and beaches head to the south. The Côte d'Azur is still the most popular beach spot, but seaside resorts along the Atlantic such as Biarritz are fast catching up. For a city that combines beaches and a chilled vibe, you couldn't do better than the stylish southern city of Montpellier. The Dordogne offers quintessentially French countryside, sparkling rivers and quaint châteaux, while the more industrial north is the place for second world war buffs, Camembert devotees and fans of Joan of Arc. In winter, do as the French do, and head for the French Alps. You can either blow your budget at resorts such as Chamonix or base yourself in attractive Grenoble, and catch the ski buses at slightly painful hours in the morning.

Germany is the most populous country in Europe, after Russia, and has always been a driving force in Europe, for worse when it came to Nazism and the holocaust, and for better when it comes to diverting money to the less wealthy (to East Germany for a start) and taking their past on the chin. They have a slightly scary reputation as polite, formal and efficient, but although this might be true on the institutional level, Germans you meet are often warm, relaxed and fun. They can also be generous, especially when it comes to the size of the sausage/lump of cheese/cake on offer.

Just two decades ago Berlin was a divided city, split between the communist East and the capitalist West. Today, it is cosmopolitan and relaxed, with a buzzing nightlife, a great modern art scene and an ambitious approach to modern architecture. Amazingly, it is still reasonably cheap compared with other major European capitals, so sampling its legendary nightlife won't break the bank. If you have only time for one part of Germany outside Berlin, try Bavaria. It has a definite national character, which includes a strong affiliation to lederhosen and beer. Go to Munich in the latter half of September for Oktoberfest, when vast beer tents fill to capacity with bacchanalian crowds. If you have time for a little more exploration, try the former GDR (East Germany).

Until at least the 16th century, Belgium, the Netherlands and Luxembourg were called the Low Countries. Amsterdam is justly famous for its liberal attitudes, beautiful canals and excellent art galleries. Or so you may tell yourself – most people still come to Amsterdam for dope and the Red Light District, and only later discover its multiple charms. For real edge head to Rotterdam, Europe's largest port. Belgium, by comparison, can seem a trifle dull, but it offers excellent beer, chocolate, and mussels and chips, and can soon grow on you. Luxembourg is Europe's third smallest country and a lovely little place, by all accounts, if you don't simply blink and miss it.

---

**TRAVEL TIP**

*The* Wochenendticket *('Happy Weekend ticket') in Germany is valid for the whole country on Saturdays and Sundays but only on regional trains. It costs €37 for up to five people which means that in theory you can get from the Austrian to the Danish border for less than £7 each.*

# CENTRAL EUROPE

## Romania, Hungary, Slovakia, Czech Republic, Poland

### CURRENCY

Slovakia uses the euro (£1 = €1.08)

| | |
|---|---|
| £1 = 28 Czech koruna | US$1 = 17.5 Czech koruna |
| £1 = 4.6 Romanian new lei | US$1 = 2.9 Romanian lei |
| £1 = 4.6 Polish zloty | US$1 = 2.88 Polish zloty |
| £1 = 292 Hungarian forint | US$1 = 184 Hungarian forint |

### BUDGET

€18–€40 per day excluding transport.

### HIGHLIGHTS

Just over 20 years ago these countries were cut off from western Europe by the Cold War and Soviet-sponsored communism. Now they are paid-up EU members, busy embracing their European identity while hanging on to their traditions, history and beliefs. As Brussels' bureaucrats have turned their attention eastward, so too have travellers, spurred on by cheap airfares and the promise of something a little different. Meanwhile, young Poles, Romanians, Hungarians, Czechs and Slovaks have turned their attention west, coming to Britain in their thousands. Central Europe headily mixes the old and the new, the cosmopolitan and the nationalistic. Its big cities have rapidly become lively 'must see' destinations, while rural areas tend to maintain their folk traditions and in some cases primitive and picturesque way of life. Although there are a number of overweening and ugly concrete buildings on show, they are often eclipsed by the grandeur of Roman ruins, Gothic cathedrals and Art Nouveau galleries, which have managed to escape destruction. Budapest is one of Europe's most exciting capitals, nicknamed 'The Paris of Central Europe', with a rich and varied cultural heritage. Summer sees a surge in visitors keen on the café culture, nightlife or just strolling down broad avenues while the sun shines. Prague is another unmissable destination with a stunning and ancient cityscape, cheap beer and an intoxicating mixture of traditional eateries and gourmet restaurants. Both cities suffer armies of tourists. Bucharest, Warsaw and Bratislava are not nearly as inundated, although still engaging. Bucharest, in particular, is a city in transition.

Prices are still reasonably low in terms of accommodation, particularly outside the major cities. You can still find a dorm bed in central Prague for £7 a night. To say goodbye to the city crowds head to Brasov in Romania, a beautiful base for appreciating some quite spectacular Royal castles, some with scary Dracula links, or head to the university town of Timisoara, nicknamed the 'city of students'.

Although the Czech Republic comprises the ancient lands of Bohemia and Moravia, it has only been around as a country since 1993 when Czechoslovakia split. History lovers will find plenty to amaze in the Czech Republic, but it is probably more famous among younger travellers for its beer. If you would like to raise a glass to the creators of lager, head to Plzen, where the golden nectar was invented in 1842. Neighbouring Slovakia has a thriving outdoors scene, including a number of very good ski resorts, while Hungary boasts Europe's most incomprehensible language (related to Finnish), some excellent open-air thermal spas and a love of paprika. Grappling with war, invasion and occupation for centuries, Poland has a strong national identity as well as much cause for sorrow. While lively towns such as Gdansk and Wroclaw are forward looking, places such as Auschwitz remain a horrific reminder of Poland's – and Europe's – tragic past. Krakow is arguably the most beautiful city in Poland.

Nature enthusiasts or adrenaline junkies should also make the most of Central Europe's beautiful countryside, particularly the Carpathian mountain chain, which offers excellent hiking and skiing opportunities. Slovakia has the highest peaks called the High Tatras, which dwarf most of central Europe. The Slovak Paradise mountain range is famous for its huge system of caves and cascading waterfalls. Romania and Poland also boast magnificent peaks. For the opposite experience, namely endless flat plains, visit Hungary's mysterious Alföld (Great Plain), where cowboys still ride.

# MEDITERRANEAN

## Spain, Italy, Portugal, Malta

### CURRENCY
All use the euro (£1 = €1.08)

### BUDGET
€40–€70 a day excluding transport. Italy and Spain tend to be at the higher end, Portugal and Malta at the lower end.

It's hard to plan any European trip without factoring in at least a couple of lazy days on the Mediterranean, glass of local wine in one hand, fork in the other, plate piled high with a delicious speciality of the region. Meals are carefully prepared, enthusiastically eaten and calmly digested.

Italy leads the field with *la dolce vita* (the good life), based on good food, wine, and company. Fashionable clothes are also popular, particularly in Milan, and young people often gather in the central square at night to preen, drink (usually very moderately) and generally show off. They are often typecast as volatile and sexy, which is true to a point, but many have a streak of old-fashioned conventionality, thanks to family loyalty, religion or a plain old attachment to their roots.

Italy has a lot to live up to with its great legacy of painters, popes and past democratic greatness, but its sheer vibrancy, which in Naples borders on chaos, means that it never feels like a museum. This is certainly true of Rome's Forum where hordes of tourists can't dim the excitement of exploring a site that is literally on top of centuries of history, while Fiats and mopeds rush past barely missing each other. Just let your senses soak up the magnificent sites and the furious sounds – and then head to the stately Vatican, regal Pantheon or iconic Coliseum. Art lovers tend to make a beeline for popular Florence, whose cultural and artistic richness under the powerful Medici family culminated in the Renaissance. Romantics might prefer Venice, a surreal and beautiful city where you should get lost and thereby escape the tourist hordes admiring the Grand Canal and Piazza San Marco. Only in relative isolation can you really appreciate the city's mysterious fading grandeur. It's not cheap though, so base yourself in neighbouring Mestre, Treviso or Padua, buy picnic food from its excellent markets, and then make a day trip (or two) into Venice by train. In winter, follow the Italians north to the Dolomites for some excellent skiing. The south feels like a very different country. Naples is the birthplace of pizza, rough and ready, while the Amalfi Coast is dramatically beautiful. The south is a great jumping off point for Malta, which has absorbed North African, Arabic and Italian influences but has a national character quite its own.

Spain is equally committed to the good life, perfecting tapas as both a style of food and a distinct way of dining. Often lively and sociable, the Spanish are a complex people and Spain's landscape is equally diverse. Even if you are a nighthawk, it will take time to adjust to Spanish time. No Spaniard goes out to a restaurant for dinner before 10pm and often much later. Keep yourself going with a tapas and a caña (half pint in a long, thin glass) in the early evening.

The obvious places to visit are cosmopolitan Madrid or hip Barcelona. Madrid is the buzzing, energetic capital, Barcelona the stylish ex-Olympic city that attracts young people from all over the world. For that morning after, take a recuperating walk around Madrid's oldest quarter, the Madrid de los Austrias, or laze around on Barcelona's beaches. For a different atmosphere entirely head to the south, which has a magnificent Moorish heritage. Córdoba boasts a magnificent mosque (Mezquita), free if you visit on Sundays between 9am and 10.45am. The Alhambra in Granada is another breathtaking example of Islamic art and architecture. For the more stereotypical attractions, namely bulls and beaches, head to Pamplona for the *Sanfermines*, the famous Running of the Bulls festival in early July; Mallorca for great beaches; and Cabo de Gata near Cadiz for an uncluttered and more remote beach experience (accessible only by foot).

Galicia is the province on the undiscovered Atlantic coast of Spain. Because its climate is so much rainier than elsewhere in Spain, it is green and lush, and has some excellent walking tracks and wonderful seafood. The lovely city of St James (Sant Iago) is the end point for the famous pilgrimage from the Pyrenees to Santiago de Compostela which thousands of Christians, mystics and keen walkers still follow every year. But beach bums won't be disappointed: a beach expert from the *Guardian* has declared that Las Islas Cies in Galicia is the best beach in continental Europe.

The strongest difference between Spain and Portugal lies in the people: the Portuguese are more reserved and discreet than Spaniards and the food is more varied, with fish and seafood understandably popular. Porto is the place to start if you like Port (which isn't just a drink for your granddad). Visit the cellars and learn more, or just wander around the riverfront Ribeira district. Lisbon has a great nightlife, although dress can be glam so haul out your best glad rags. Or move off the beaten track and sample the delights of Coimbra, a student city where tradition and parties walk hand in hand. Relaxation and/or surfing are best found on the beaches of the Alentejo – the Algarve can get a tad busy, attracting millions of tourists every year.

# ALPINE

## Switzerland, Austria, Slovenia

### CURRENCY

Austria and Slovenia use the euro (£1 = €1.08)

| | |
|---|---|
| £1 = 1.65 Swiss francs | US$1 = 1.03 Swiss francs |

### BUDGET

€35–€65 per day excluding transport for Switzerland and Austria, €25–€45 per day excluding transport for Slovenia.

### HIGHLIGHTS

Gargantuan snow-capped mountains, shimmering melt-water lakes and air so pure that breathing feels like a special treat – if this all sounds appealing then the Alpine countries of Switzerland, Austria and Slovenia are for you. If it all sounds a bit poetic, then how about hurtling down precipitous slopes, chucking yourself out of a plane or crawling around canyons like Spiderman? Although Alpine countries, specifically Switzerland and Austria, tend to have a reputation for being a little stuffy, all formal manners and crisp bank notes, the scenery itself is anything but – a massive playground, perfect for all kinds of winter and summer activities.

Mountains make up 70% of Switzerland's landmass, with the Matterhorn being its most famous peak. Dozens of ski resorts beckon, but for high-adrenaline sports try the Interlaken area: although backpacker-friendly, the lure of bungee-jumping, paragliding, etc. may soon part you from a large wad of cash. If you're in Slovenia head to Bovec in the Julian Alps, where paragliding and canyoning are enthusiastically catered for. In terms of affordability, Austria is middle of the road, and offers some of the world's best snow-boarding and skiing. Tirol is a picture-perfect example of Alpine scenery – base yourself in mediaeval Innsbruck and be sure to see the famous Golden Roof.

In summer, hiking is the vertiginous activity of choice. In Switzerland there are 50,000km of designated hiking paths and it is hard to get lost – this being Switzerland the signs are plentiful. Austria is also well organised and the Austrian Alpine Club maintains a network of alpine huts for overnight stays. Hiking is extremely popular in Slovenia, with around 7,000 km of waymarked trails, certain 'themed trails' and 165 mountain huts. Outdoor enthusiasts might also like to try watersports in Salzkammergut, Austria's answer to the Lake District, and cooling off in one of Switzerland's great lakes – even suited and booted Zurich has an enviable number of open-air bathing spots.

When the great outdoors palls, there are the urban delights of Vienna, Salzburg, Geneva and Ljubljana to appreciate. Wealthy Vienna is stuffed to the gills with history, and you can take a stroll through the inner city and into the past. If the low brow beckons, just nip into a café, or ride the **Riesenrad**, the ferris wheel which stars in *The Third Man*. Salzburg is famous as the birthplace of Mozart and the location for the ever-popular kitsch that is *The Sound of Music,* while Geneva is the *pied à terre* for major European organisations such as the International Red Cross and the UN. Tiny Ljubljana boasts, with some justification, that it is a 'mini Prague'.

# BALKANS

## Greece, Turkey, Albania, Bosnia and Herzegovina, Bulgaria, Croatia, Macedonia, Montenegro and Serbia

### CURRENCY
Greece and Montenegro use the euro (£1 = €1.08)

| | |
|---|---|
| £1 = 2.33 Yeni Turkish lira | US$1 = 1.46 Yeni Turkish lira |
| £1 = 148 Albanian leke | US$1 = 93 Albanian leke |
| £1 = 2.11 Bosnia and Herzegovina marka | US$1 = 1.33 marka |
| £1 = 2.11 Bulgarian lev | US$1 = 1.32 Bulgarian lev |
| £1 = 7.83 Croatian kuna | US$1 = 4.91 Croatian kuna |
| £1 = 66.6 Macedonian denar | US$1 = 41.8 Macedonian denar |
| £1 = 100 Serbian dinar | US$1 = 63 Serbian dinar |

### BUDGET
€25–€50 per day excluding transport, although Greece is at the higher end and can easily cost up to €60 a day. Macedonia and Albania are both at the lower end and Turkey can be a real bargain if you don't go anywhere that is swamped with tourists.

## HIGHLIGHTS
Light reflects off cubist white buildings, sand crinkles between your toes, archaeological sites trace the story of ancient civilisations and you have to pinch yourself to check that

you're not dreaming. Yes, Greece can be this good. A favoured backpacker destination for decades, it offers, to put it crudely, those useful ingredients for a good time: sun, sand, sea and sex. Some islands such as Kos are well known for the latter, others such as Patmos still avoid the party image. Many do both, inviting package holiday tourists into certain 'tourist ghettoes', leaving the rest of the island free for the more determined traveller to explore at leisure. Santorini, with its stunning Caldera, is a good example – if you get out of the main town of Fira and avoid the south-east beaches then the island is refreshingly uncluttered. An excellent way to get around is to hire a moped (you usually need to show a driving licence and pretend knowledge). Island bus drivers are well known for their imitation of Grand Prix drivers, but apart from that 'experience' the pace of life is reassuringly relaxed.

Greater Athens is a law unto itself, home to about a third of the population, and a place of stark contradictions. On the one hand it is up there with Rome as a superb place to explore classical architecture and ancient history. The Acropolis is probably the most important monument of the ancient world. But the city is also ugly, chaotic and sprawling. Love it, hate it, and move on. Mainland Greece, particularly the north, often gets rather brushed under the tourist carpet, but it is here that you can find the 'real' Greece, a place where the Orthodox church shapes people's lives and old men and women gossip endlessly. Northern Greece also has the country's highest mountain, Mt Olympus, ancient home of the Gods, and snow-capped well into spring. The main route to the top takes two days, with a stay overnight in a shelter. The Peloponnesian peninsula in southern Greece is home to Olympia, birthplace of the Olympic Games, the ruined Byzantine city of Mystras and ancient Sparta. Greeks can be conventional, but they temper this with a relaxed approach to the beliefs and behaviour of visitors. What more can you ask?

If Greece were one side of a coin then Turkey would be the other. They are both made up of similar materials – sandy beaches, mesmeric water, civilisation-shaping history – and share a mutual love of family, food and music. But Istanbul (once called Constantinople) was first the capital of the Christian Byzantine Empire and then later the epicentre of the Ottoman Empire. It is the Islamic influence that predominates today. Admire Aya Sofya and the Blue Mosque in 'Old Istanbul', before losing yourself in the Grand Bazaar, also known as the Covered Market, which has 4,500 shops, selling all kinds of trinkets that you never knew you needed.

For the sun 'n' fun aspect, most visitors head to the Mediterranean coast, famed for its incredible scenery and ancient ruins (including the city of Troy). The coast gets less busy east of Antalya. Republican Turkey has mainly adopted a Western lifestyle, at least on the surface, and western Turkey can be very lively. For a hippie vibe, try Olympos, an abandoned port city, which is now famous for its air of dilapidation and ever-expanding treehouse camp. For something rather more crazy than cool, take the long journey east to Cappadocia. The fantastic landscape of strangely eroded rock cones has been inhabited for centuries, first by Byzantine hermits and others escaping persecution, and now by modern Turks who have erected television aerials on their rock towers and converted the caves into backpackers' hostels.

Croatia, Albania, Macedonia, Montenegro, Bulgaria, Serbia and Bosnia Herzegovina: what do they have in common? Well, for a start they were all at one time part of the Yugoslav Federation, which fell apart in recent history. Today they are fairly settled so that tourists – and developers – have been returning in droves. Croatia has always been popular, with 6,000km of coastline and almost 1,100 islands. You could call it 'the new Greece' but that is hardly fair because Croatia has its own Slavic soul. Most travellers head to the stunning Dalmatian coast crowned by Dubrovnik, 'the pearl of the Adriatic' according to no less a personage than the 'mad, bad and dangerous to know' poet, Lord Byron. For something less familiar take the plunge and visit some of the other countries on the Balkan peninsula. They all have their beauties and the people can be very welcoming.

# RUSSIA, BALTIC COUNTRIES AND UKRAINE

## CURRENCY

| | |
|---|---|
| £1 = 47 Russian roubles | US$1 = 29 Russian roubles |
| £1 = 13.1 Ukrainian hryunia | US$1 = 8.2 Ukrainian hryunia |
| £1 = 0.77 Latvian lats | US$1 = 0.48 Latvian lats |
| £1 = 3.72 Lithuanian litas | US$1 = 2.34 Lithuanian litas |
| £1 = 16.9 Estonian kroon | US$1 = 10.6 Estonian kroon |

## BUDGET

€20–€30 in the Baltic Countries, with Estonia the cheapest, and €36–€50 in Russia and the Ukraine.

## HIGHLIGHTS

Russia occupies a special place in the Western imagination: it seems to breed football-club-owning billionaires, to export internet brides and became involved in a James Bond style thriller involving rare poison and the KGB. The gregarious spirit of its people is coupled with a hideous and silted-up bureaucracy. Yet the relics of old-style communism fail to dim the glory of its Imperial heritage. European Russia is familiar, whereas the rest of the country crosses 10 time zones and reaches almost to Alaska. In short, you could spend years trying and failing to understand Russia.

The two great European cities are St Petersburg and Moscow. The former is considered to be Russia's 'Imperial Crown', the second its 'familial heart'. The haunting magnificence of St Petersburg, its calm canals and brooding Winter Palace, cast a spell from which most visitors don't want to wake (although going out to the suburbs is a surefire way of doing this). The Winter Palace was home to the Tsars and the backdrop for the 1905 and 1917 revolutions, but is best known today as the home of the Hermitage Museum, up there with the Louvre when it comes to being awe-inspiringly enormous.

At the last count, the Russians reckoned that about three million artworks were on show. On the Petrograd side of the city visit the Peter and Paul Fortress, which may sound like a nursery rhyme, but was actually mainly used as a political prison. Its most famous residents included Dostoevsky, Gorky and Trotsky. If you can manage a mini-splurge treat yourself to the ballet at Mariinsky Theatre.

Moscow, by contrast, is an enormous city, changing, tense and powerful, mixing a reckless approach to Western capitalism with the relics of the stolid communist life-style. Begin your visit at Red Square, where Lenin's Mausoleum, complete with rever-ential fans, is located opposite a trendy Western-inspired department store called GUM. The other must-see monolith is the Kremlin, almost a city in its own right. If Moscow still feels a bit close to home, then simply take the Trans-Siberian Express and slowly chug your way to China.

Thanks to the Orange Revolution and the election of pro-Western Victor Yushchenko things are changing in the Ukraine. Its capital, Kyiv, has wakened up to flash cars, chic clothes, hot clubs and chilled-out bars, but peel off the flash veneer, and you'll find an old city, whose religious heart is the Caves Monastery. Its underground labyrinths are lined with mummified monks. If that atmosphere (old rather than dead) is more to your taste, take a train to Lviv, whose beautiful architecture showcases most of the architec-tural movements of the last five centuries.

The Baltic countries of Lithuania, Latvia and Estonia have rapidly become a phenom-enon, combining old towns that are World Heritage Sites with a riotous party culture. Stag and hen parties have been quick to descend, but these countries have a lot more to offer than cheap beer. Try bobsledding in Sigulda or canoeing in Gauja National Park, both in Latvia, or admire the world's first Frank Zappa statue in Vilnius.

## GETTING A VISA FOR RUSSIA

*A letter of invitation (LOI) from someone in Russia is a requirement of getting a tourist visa. It is straightforward to use an agent (for a fee of $20–$30) who will file some paperwork in Russia and send you an email with a hotel reference (no obligation to stay there). With this document and a further fee of £75 a week in advance (or a whacking £133 at short notice), the Russian consulate will grant a single entry visa.*

# TRAVEL RESOURCES

## USEFUL WEBSITES

**www.bugeurope.com**, the backpacker's ultimate guide.
**www.flycheapo.com**, links to all the no-frills routes and carriers in Europe
**www.dooyoo.co.uk/transport-international/interrail**, first hand accounts (dated) of InterRailing.

## USEFUL GUIDEBOOKS

*Europe on a Shoestring* (Lonely Planet, October 2009), £15.99.
*Rough Guide to First-time Europe* (Rough Guides, 2007), £10.99.
*Thomas Cook European Rail Timetable*, £15.99.
*Rick Steves' Europe Through the Back Door* (Avalon Travel Publishing, 2010), £12.99.

## TRAVEL READING

### Classic fiction:

Ernest Hemingway, *A Moveable Feast* (Arrow Books). Absorbing memoirs about the author's years in Paris during the 1920s.

Mikhail Bulgakov, *Master and Margarita* (Penguin Classics). An inspiring satire on Russia and the Ukraine written during the 1930s.

Günter Grass, *The Tin Drum* (Vintage Classics, first published in 1959). Written as a memoir and set in the war years in Germany.

Miguel de Cervantes, *Don Quixote*. A literary classic bringing to life the world of ordinary Spanish people in the seventeeth century.

Homer, *The Odyssey*. This is one of two chief ancient Greek epic poems.

*Diary of Anne Frank* (Penguin). A young Jewish girl's diary about living in hiding in Amsterdam during the second world war.

### Lighter/modern travel writers:

Patricia Storace, *Dinner with Persephone* (Granta Books, 1998). A great account of life in Greece as seen through the eyes of an outsider.

Henning Mankell, *The Wallander Mysteries* (Random House). Set of eight crime novels set in Scandinavia.

Tim Parks, *A Season with Verona* or *Italian Neighbours* (Vintage Books, 2003). The author is an English expat living in Italy.

Alan Furst, *The Polish Officer* (Random House, 2001). A gripping tale of espionage revolving around a Polish intelligence officer and set during the time of the second world war.

Graham Greene, *The Third Man*. A novella set in post wartime Austria and turned into a brilliantly atmospheric film starring Orson Welles.

Milan Kundera. *The Joke*. A satirical novel about Communist Europe.

Patrick Leigh Fermor, *A Time of Gifts* (John Murray, first published in 1977) and *Between the Woods and the Water* (John Murray, 2004). The author describes a 1,200 mile walk from Holland to Constantinople undertaken in 1934 when he was 18.

Jan Morris, *Europe*. A personal appreciation of the continent by the doyenne of travel writing.

# AFRICA

Africa is the birthplace of humanity, home to many natural wonders of the world, and full of a pulsing vibrancy that blows away ideas about it being the dark or hopeless continent. Twenty-first century Africa is a remarkable collection of extremes, often right next to each other. The wealth of skyscrapers sits beside slums. The scorching heat of the dry season gives way to torrential downpours. Before going, many people think of Africa in terms of the animals and stunning scenery, but what most visitors remember is the people: hustling and fighting their way through life, often challenging, but generally welcoming and demonstrating insight born of the knowledge that the past and their ancestors are never far away.

## DISCOVERING AFRICA

After Asia, Africa is the world's second largest (30 million km²) and most populous (900 million people) continent. These statistics are a good starting point for talking about Africa because despite its significant size and population it remains marginalised and often forgotten by the wider world. A gap year in Africa provides the chance to discover a diverse place that is often misunderstood and misrepresented. By stepping off the beaten track of safaris (though you must also take the chance to go on a safari) and beach hotels you can look into a place that faces many challenges, but that offers so much more as well. A good example is Ethiopia, tainted for so long by images from the 1980s of starving refugees, images that ignore lush, green landscapes and ancient civilisations that through thousands of years built breathtaking monuments such as obelisks and castles and huge monolithic rock-hewn churches down into the earth.

The outside world tends to view Africa in terms of poverty, corruption and war but Africans are more likely to be positive, and proud to be African. Ideas and roles are always changing but people are still deeply religious, with a spiritual understanding of the world that can be confusing, but hopefully exciting for someone who is used to a more dry, scientific approach. African hospitality warms the hearts of those who encounter it – although some people can find it smothering at times. Family and kin are very important, but so are national pride and African identity. It's all a bit more complex than the 'ancient tribal hatreds' that the Western press talks about.

The majority of Africa's population still lives in rural areas – about 60% across the continent, although much higher in some countries – and getting to know Africa means heading out into the bush. In the countryside you can still find people farming or raising livestock the same way they have for centuries. However, they are also equally likely today to be talking on a mobile phone while they do so. Rural life can demonstrate remarkable knowledge and understanding of the earth and its preservation. It can also be a place to see tremendous problems with land distribution leading to overcrowding, deforestation and erosion.

*Pole pole ndiyo mwendo* (slowly is the way) is a Swahili proverb repeated in different ways across the continent. Time can be understood in a cyclical manner that Westerners can find infuriating. The main point to remember is that things happen for a reason and will happen in good time. On the Mombasa to Nairobi train, for example, look out for the Europeans who demand that they get more soup immediately, only to realise their mistake as the extra soup pours over them as the train goes round a corner. The happiest travellers in Africa are those who take the chance to move at a different pace and take the time to look around and enjoy the journey.

The two most common choices for gappers are probably:

- The full travelling option going overland, for example from Cairo to the Cape or vice versa. This will give you the chance to see the diversity of experiences that the continent has to offer.
- An equally exciting option that gives a more in-depth look at a smaller area is to work in a voluntary programme in one country, explore the area intensively and also take the chance to pass through surrounding countries.

## GETTING THERE

As a gap year student you may like to book your flight through a student travel agent such as STA Travel or the Flight Centre. This is especially useful if your route is complicated. Key Travel (www.keytravel.co.uk) is also knowledgeable and often has some great prices, as well as being the agent of choice for lots of non-profit organisations. For a straightforward return, it's often hard to beat Opodo (www.opodo.co.uk).

As an early introduction to colonial heritage, British Airways flies direct to most places in Anglophone Africa from the UK while for most of Francophone Africa, Air France may be your best option with a transfer in Paris, or even direct. KLM Royal Dutch Airlines, transferring at Schiphol, have many options to the continent, often in cooperation with Kenya Airways. Cheaper options can often be found through Gulf Air and Emirates – but these will require a longer route through the Middle East.

Often cheapest, and cheerful, but leaving at strange times and frequently with lengthy transfers through Addis Ababa, Ethiopian Airlines have one of the most extensive networks of any airline serving Africa. In fact, the Addis transfer sometimes includes a night in a hotel and a chance to see a little bit of a fascinating place. Just don't eat the food on the flight after Addis.

## GETTING AROUND

Getting around the continent by air is very variable. Links are better than they were, but it's still surprisingly common that the cheapest flight to a neighbouring country will require flying via Europe. Internal flights within a given country are often reasonable but you should have a look at a company's reputation with a quick internet search first. Quite a number of African airlines are banned from European airspace but these tend to be the pirate operations found in places that you don't want to be anyway (for example,

# UNMISSABLE HIGHLIGHTS

- See the Serengeti migration, with 1.4 million wildebeest and 200,000 zebra and gazelle making their way across the plains.
- Victoria Falls is where you'll find 'The smoke that thunders', by some measures the largest waterfall on the planet.
- Soweto has the only street in the world where two Nobel Peace Prize winners live, where you can ponder South Africa's painful but inspiring struggle.
- Zanzibar is the spice island with narrow Arab-style streets and laid back golden beaches.
- The holy city in northern Ethiopia, Lalibela, has monolithic churches hewn down into solid rock some 800 years ago.
- Vibrant, colourful Fes is one of the most demanding but rewarding of North Africa's cities.
- Sossusvlei is an ecosystem in Namibia that seems to work without water, shaped into giant red sand dunes.
- An exciting present that defies the brutal history of slavery remembered in Cape Coast, a colonial fort on the coast of Ghana.
- The Great Pyramid of Giza in Egypt is the only surviving wonder of the ancient world.
- Visit the Atlas Mountains for some amazing trekking or the chance to say you went skiing in Africa.

all 50 airlines of the Democratic Republic of Congo are banned). On the more positive side, Kulula (www.kulula-air.com) is fairly priced, reliable and flies within South Africa. Precision Air (www.precisionairtz.com) is a good option for getting around East Africa. You can comparison-shop for flights on www.travelsupermarket.co.za.

Back on the ground, buses of highly diverse quality can get you to most places you want to reach. A very simple rule to be aware of is that generally the more you pay, the more careful the driving and higher the level of comfort. On a strict budget and looking for adventure the cheapest bus will get you to your destination eventually, after contending with burst tyres, sharing a seat with several other people and their animals, and definitely no air conditioning. Even paying a little more should be considered because this increases the chances that the tyres are not bald, that there is a spare tyre and that the brakes function. Sometime the clue is in the name, for example the reassuringly named intercity bus company in Tanzania, Scandinavia Express Services, has a better safety record than cheaper rivals. With long-distance buses it is usually possible to book by going to the ticket office in person, and you should report on time for departure, but don't expect the bus to leave at the time the ticket says. Over shorter distances you can normally just turn up and buses leave once they are full.

Trains can be a fabulous, and staggeringly slow option. Journeys can last for days, rather than hours, so do find out when you expect to arrive. Third class may look appealingly cheap, but looks less attractive in the middle of the night when pickpockets go to work – although at least with no bed it's easier to stay awake. Second or first class may be the option you take the next time.

On top of these standard ways of moving around you may also like to hop into a horse-drawn *gari* in Ethiopia or a whizzy little *tuk-tuk* in many different places. Rules have generally been tightened up in recent years, but you will at some point be able to marvel at the quantity of human cargo that can be crammed into a *bush taxi* (Nigeria), *matatu* (Kenya) or *daladala* (Tanzania). Wear a seat belt when available and avoid the seat next to the driver (sometimes known as the 'death seat' due to its unfortunate position in a head-on collision). Overcrowding and discomfort are reduced in North Africa and travelling by *louage* (shared minibus-taxi) in Tunisia is cheap and efficient.

You are unlikely to find a taxi with a meter, but make sure it's switched on if you do. Otherwise, negotiation will be required. Ensure that you carry this out before setting off. It can be useful to check with local people what they consider reasonable and drivers will often go at least close to this figure. Resign yourself to paying over the odds until you become more skilled or know what the local price is for a given journey (for example 15p for a quarter hour's drive in Ghana). Africa's roads are the most dangerous in the world. A lot of driving, including on small, pothole ridden tracks, is conducted at break-neck speed. Drunk driving is rarely viewed as anything other than necessary. Commercial drivers (passenger and freight) may often drive for days, staying awake only through the use of stimulants such as cola-nut, or *quat*. Paying a bit more, and assessing the sobriety of a driver (including glue sniffing and drugs) will help, but moving by road is always a risk.

## BUDGETING

An idea of how much you will end up spending is given in the country sections below. Prices vary wildly, but generally cities are much more expensive than rural areas. You need to be flexible in your tastes because what might be a cheap snack at home may be imported, and surprisingly pricey. Street food can certainly be an option to keep costs down, but its risks include diarrhoea and even typhoid. Taking organised trips, such as those available in overland trucks, will increase your costs, but may get you to places you wouldn't otherwise reach, and show you things you might not have noticed.

**DANIEL BRACKSTONE'S** route gave him the chance to work in and wonder at Africa, getting to know people and places that he'll never forget.

'When I decided to take a gap year, I wanted something that would challenge me. I wanted to push my limits and make friends at the same time. It was important to really get to know a place, but to keep moving around and seeing new things. I started off taking a Kiswahili language course at the University Institute on Zanzibar ($7 an hour). I wrote to them but you can really just turn up and arrange something. I was also able to set up a homestay with a family. That was expensive but allowed me to really feel I was more than just a tourist.

After enjoying the mysterious nature of Stone Town, and spending delicious time at the beach, I took my new language skills to a volunteer programme at a home for HIV+ children in Kenya (www.nyumbani. org/volunteer.htm). Working with children anywhere is intense, but this was nothing like I'd come across before. Nairobi is also crazy. You have to watch yourself but all the bars and discos can be great fun, and allow you to escape from the emotion of work once in a while. The local staff and the other international volunteers taught me so much, it felt like having 50 mentors who all knew so many things, and looked at the world in so many different ways.

I'd decided to save my safaris for Tanzania, but in Kenya I took the bus up to Fisherman's camp on Lake Naivasha, and then a bus the next day to Hell's Gate National Park. You can just hike through and camp, walking past herds of giraffe on massive plains, and then into the breathtaking gorge. It feels like stepping into some kind of prehistoric landscape, especially with the sound of the geothermal power station at night sounding *like a monster. Tanzania was then all about the Ngorongoro Crater for a beautiful trip, seeing most of the big five game animals. I took the train as well, just to enjoy two days watching the landscape, towns, and hanging out in the bar talking to the other people – not only Tanzanians but also a Congolese guy who was embarrassed that my Swahili was better than his! That got me through to Malawi where I went to the lake. I'd met a man who told me that if he could be promised that heaven was like the shores of Lake Malawi, he'd be good for the rest of his life. I would too.*

*Those are just a few of the things I did. I went wine tasting in South Africa near Cape Town, and in Jo'burg I went to the Hector Pieterson Museum where you learn about how even children were willing to die for a better life. I also went to Ponto D'Ouro in Mozambique, which is really weird because it's full of South Africans playing with their big adventure toys. It was the first time I've seen people who take their own plane on holiday! I focused on eastern and southern Africa, and I loved the bustle of the towns, the quiet of the countryside, the majesty of the animals and the pride of the people. There was so much to be done that I didn't even get to start on the west and the north – but I've been bitten by the Africa bug that everyone told me about. I didn't think it could be true, but it does feel like going home, being where your ancestors came from, and it changed my heart and soul in ways I couldn't have imagined.'*

## EXPECT A CHALLENGE

In Africa you will not just be a stranger but you will be a rich stranger. Any idea of explaining that you are a student and about to incur massive debts or that you don't yet have a job, can be quickly dismissed. If your iPod cost £180 then it is worth more than the amount of money that half of Africa's population survives on in a year. Of course, this doesn't mean that hassle for money and scams are any less irritating. It also doesn't mean that throwing money around will make any dramatic difference to people's lives. It also doesn't mean that everybody in Africa is poor. Some very wealthy people are to be found in some of the most inequitable societies in the world. There is no simple solution to the money issue. Some people find it very hard to make friends either because of their guilt, or because they feel they are being befriended for ulterior motives. It helps if you can relax and just accept that you will be subsidising others if you want to go to certain places.

On the subject of money, it should also be mentioned that Africa can sometimes be surprisingly expensive. Often there can be a lack of mid-range budget accommodation and food. The budgets below are only indicators; be prepared to negotiate prices almost everywhere.

Colonialism and to some extent slavery also need a mention. Power relations between Africa and the West have been distorted for a long time. It can be strange to hear someone talk of things being better under colonial rule or terrifying to hear unfriendly attitudes to white people. It is equally unpleasant to listen to travellers who regard Africans as fools and themselves as wonderfully superior. This is an assumption that is found all too often, and your experience will be better if you identify it and address it. An anecdote may illustrate this well. While sitting on a beach on Zanzibar, a group of travellers saw a fisherman come down to his boat. The tide had gone out and the boat was left dry, out of the water. The travellers were laughing that the silly fisherman had come down too late to go out fishing – misunderstood the tides or overslept clearly. After looking at his boat for a long time, the fisherman brought down his tools and began fixing his craft, having waited for the tide to be out and having carefully considered what needed doing and then expertly fixing it.

A mention of HIV/AIDS is necessary when talking about Africa. As well as a simple warning to be careful and carry condoms (both sexes) be aware of the social effects of the ongoing pandemic, not least AIDS orphans (estimated to number nearly 12 million). It's actually quite difficult to talk about HIV because, unless you are working in a project concerned with 'the scourge', you may barely notice it. HIV is one of Africa's greatest problems, but remains largely invisible. Deaths can still be registered simply as being, for example, from tuberculosis. Knowledge levels are high, but so is stigma and it can appear that HIV and AIDS are things that only happen to 'other people'.

Before going to Africa, you might want to consider following a football team if you don't have one already. The English Premiership is huge in Anglophone Africa and Ligue 1 is big in Francophone Africa. As a way to start conversations, befriend taxi drivers and so on football is hard to beat. Local grounds may be practically deserted, but the FA cup final, crammed into a bar with a television run from a car battery is something not to be missed – particularly if the teams have African players. The team you pick will need to be a big one, so you can choose from the Premier League Man U, Chelsea, Arsenal or Liverpool.

## CORRUPTION

Former Nigerian president Olesegun Obasanjo estimated that corruption costs Africa 25% of its collective national incomes every year. It is certainly prevalent from the looting of national coffers by political leaders, to the payments made by Western countries to secure contracts and bribes to policemen to have charges dropped. It is possible that you will be asked to pay a bribe, although this is less common than it is made out to be, and occurs most often where someone has been arrested, often for possession of drugs. Indeed, a common scam is to sell drugs to an unsuspecting traveller and then tip off the police who will take a cut of the bribe they extort from the traveller. Generally, corruption is likely to be something that occurs around you, for example a driver being required to pay a policeman, and it tends to be done in ways so subtle that you are unlikely to notice.

# EXCITING WAYS TO GET INVOLVED

- Learn to dive in the Red Sea (www.gapyeardiver.com).
- Take a walk with lions in Zimbabwe (www.amanzitravel.co.uk).
- Coach football in a South African township (www.score.org.za).
- Put on HIV-awareness workshops in Zambia (www.spw.org).
- Carry out underwater surveys in Madagascar (www.blueventures.org).
- Build a school in rural Tanzania (www.madventurer.com).
- Assist at a film academy in Accra, Ghana (www.screenartsghana.org).
- Work on a safari camp in the Okavango Delta (www.theleap.co.uk).
- Teach in a primary school in the Kilimanjaro district (www.village-to-village.org.uk).
- Learn Arabic in Fez Morocco (www.cesa.com) or take Swahili lessons while volunteering in Kenya (www.crossculturalsolutions.org).

# EAST AFRICA

## Kenya

| VISA |
| --- |
| £20 (single entry) |

| CURRENCY | |
| --- | --- |
| £1 = 120 Kenya shillings (KShs) | US$1 = 78 KShs |

| BUDGET |
| --- |
| £12–£18 a day in Nairobi, less in rural areas. |

Kenya is the home of the African safari. The name itself is Swahili for journey and European settlers here conducted the first safaris. You can still see an outstanding variety of animals, including the famed Big Five (lion, elephant, buffalo, leopard and black rhino). This can be done in different ways, from luxury motor tours staying in grand lodges, to walking safaris with a Maasai guide, sleeping under the stars. The country straddles the equator and offers remarkable scenery and a variety of cultures. At its centre Mt Kenya presides over grasslands and thorn scrub. To the west the imposing Great Rift Valley is full of lakes teeming with an amazing array of birdlife. The east coast offers white, palm-fringed beaches and coral reefs as well as the remains of ancient Swahili city-states and Arab influenced cultures and festivals. Kenya is also very much the gateway to or hub of East Africa. Connections by road, rail and air are good to Tanzania, Uganda and Ethiopia. This is useful for a traveller or means that someone working in a project can use their holidays to explore the region, including getting down to Zanzibar.

Staying in rural areas can still involve getting used to a lot of attention, especially from local children. More unwelcome attention, such as aggressive taxi drivers or scams – especially fake safaris and investment opportunities – are also to be found, especially in Nairobi. The capital is a great place to party, meet other travellers and visit some decent monuments and museums. However, it is still often referred to as 'Nairobbery' and moving around at night should be done with care, or avoided. A female traveller should take particular care. Regular marriage proposals are a nuisance, but a real risk of violence also exists in some places. In terms of attention from the opposite sex, men will find some amusement in the direct approach adopted by some bar girls, especially at the coast, which has a reputation for sex tourism. A reminder is probably necessary of the economic circumstances that lead bar girls to look for foreign 'boyfriends' and also the very high rates of HIV to be found.

Usual routes for travellers would involve arrival into Nairobi. Accommodation is fairly pricey (Nairobi is also known as 'London 2') but it is accustomed to backpackers, and decent, clean dorm beds can be found starting at £7 per night. Travellers then tend to head out to the Rift Valley for hiking, safaris through the Serengeti and finish up with beach time at the coast. Many of these trips can be arranged through agencies, but for the Rift Valley a great option for those with a tent is to take a *matatu* up to Fisherman's Camp in Nakuru, then after a night there another bus to Hell's Gate and to trek through. A great number of voluntary projects, from environmental care to caring for AIDS orphans, are available for gappers looking for placements.

# Tanzania

**VISA**
£38

**CURRENCY**
£1 = 2114 Tanzanian shillings (TZS)     US$1 = 1336 TZS

**BUDGET**
£15–£20 per day; £75 a day for a safari in the north.

Dar es Salaam, Tanzania's commercial capital (its official capital is Dodoma, chosen for its central location), is taking off economically. Although it is full of construction Dar is a lot more fun than it used to be. However, Tanzania still offers the gap year traveller a real taste of rural Africa and is one of the most popular gap year destinations. The country has been stable and safe since the economically flawed but socially laudable stewardship of *Mwalimu* (teacher) Julius Nyerere ended in 1985. Try to get out of the towns, which tend to be slow and throw yourself into countryside life. Tanzania also has the East African perks of stunning wildlife in game parks that are more expensive than those of Kenya, but the prices have been raised in the name of responsible tourism and they tend to be more remote, and much less busy. Particularly recommended is the Serengeti and Ng'orong'oro Crater.

Time in Tanzania also gives the chance for a visit to Zanzibar. Having bought a ticket at the port (never from touts who offer residents' prices – and then follow it up with extortion on the boat) the ferry to Stone Town from Dar es Salaam only takes a couple of hours. You then find yourself in the most intriguing town, with narrow Arab-style streets and bazaars. In fact, the Swahili culture and language of Zanzibar is a fusion of Arab and African culture, that emerged from its placement on the trade routes using the monsoon winds that meant it was once the headquarters for the Sultan of Oman. Out of town (about an hour in a shared minibus that can be picked up in the morning from Forodhani Gardens near the House of Wonders) you can head to the north coast, but be prepared for the unsettling contrast between the full moon backpacker parties, discos, huge Italian hotel and the desperately poor villages behind. Much more pleasant is the laid back east coast. The sea is not quite as perfect, but the welcome is much more personal.

# Ethiopia

### VISA
£12

### CURRENCY
£1 = 20 birr                    US$1 = 12.8 birr

### BUDGET
£12 per day (more in Addis).

If the only images you have are of starving, dying babies in camps, then prepare yourself for a shock. Droughts have happened in parts, war raged in places, but Ethiopia is lush and intriguing with a huge diversity of intricate cultures with histories to make you gasp. It is the only African country never to have been colonised. A few years of military occupation has left a bit of Italian influence, but if you identify this in the coffee, then remember that coffee culture has been a part of the area for thousands of years – and many a myth and legend refers to it.

Ethiopia is a land of contrasts and extremes – in fact it represents a small empire dominated by the north, once Abyssinia, and incorporates many different peoples. You can explore the ancient Axumite dynasty, whose empire extended into the Middle East, the remnants of the Jewish culture that was dominant before the coming of mystical Orthodox Christianity in 400AD and Islamic practice that has evolved since its arrival 300 years later – still over a thousand years ago.

Ethiopia's highlands have mountains that soar to around 4,300m while the sweltering lowlands plunge to the depths of the Danakil Depression below sea level. It is home to the oldest human remains in the world, well presented in one of the capital's fascinating museums. The 'New Flower' (in Amharic) that is Addis Ababa faces many challenges of urbanisation. However, it remains largely a pleasant and open city and offers a good starting point before heading off to explore the cultures of the south or the history and splendour of the north. On the Northern Historic Route can be seen the mediaeval city of Gondar, with its castles and churches. Also Axum, where the original Ark of the Covenant containing the 10 Commandments is said to be found. These jewels are perhaps even outdone by Lalibela, with its 11th- and 12th-century, monolithic rock-hewn churches, carved down into the ground. These churches are surrounded by mystery and legend, and said to have been built by angels. Remember also to visit the Simien Mountains, and Bahar Dar to explore the myriad of monasteries on Lake Tana's islands.

After a long time as a closed country under a vicious communist regime (the *Dergue* or Council, which ruled until 1987), Ethiopia is now much more open. Its tourist industry is being privatised (although the state-owned Ghion Hotel chain has hotels in places such as Gondar that are sometimes beautiful, e.g. in old colonial palaces, though lacking in plumbing). Due to its history and reputation, Ethiopia is still frequently overlooked. Be sure to consider it as an opportunity to find somewhere truly off the beaten track. Staggering poverty that can surprise even an experienced African traveller is to be found across the country. However, things are improving and Ethiopia is an opportunity that shouldn't be missed.

# SOUTHERN AFRICA

## South Africa

### VISA
Not required.

### CURRENCY
£1 = 12 rand                                          US$1 = 7 rand

### BUDGET
£12–£25 a day.

The billing of South Africa as a 'world in one journey' actually stands up pretty well to experience. Following the end of apartheid it has become a destination of choice for backpackers and more well-heeled travellers alike, who can take in demanding visits to the dusty Transkei, high finance in Johannesburg or stunning scenery and cuisine in the Winelands and Garden Routes of the Cape. It is also the top African destination for gap year volunteers working in projects. It remains an unequal and rather divided society, which is reflected in crime and growing political dissatisfaction – especially in Jo'burg. However, it is also a place of fascinating political awareness with some of the best historical tours and museums in Africa.

To the wealthy, South Africa offers the option of sticking solely to five-star hotels and resorts, wine tastings, expensive cars and professional game drives. However, cheaper travel, animals and scenery are possible for the budget traveller and even more readily for the volunteer (see *Africa* chapter). It is fascinating to see how South Africa engages with its history, and the political struggle against the racist apartheid government (check out Soweto and the Robben Island Museum), colonial warfare (take a visit to the battlefields of the Zulu wars), and the intriguing mentality of Afrikaner nationalism (including the Voortrekker and Afrikaans monuments). Soweto tours can be arranged with most tour companies, which drive you around the main sites, including the Hector

Pieterson Museum and the houses of Nelson Mandela and Desmond Tutu, and arrange a proper (staggeringly heavy) African lunch. Robben Island – departures from Victoria Waterfront in Cape Town – needs to be booked well in advance. Even then, bad weather often leads to cancellations, so unless you have time to keep trying, you may be disappointed. After visiting these sights you will have some insight into the struggle to create Nelson Mandela's vision of a 'rainbow nation'.

Crime is a huge problem in South Africa. Things are improving, including the upgrading of the central business district in Jo'burg, but violent crime – break-ins, muggings, car-jackings – remain prevalent, and many white South Africans live their lives as if under siege. Nonetheless, people are generally friendly and welcoming. As with anywhere, a bit of organisation and awareness will take an informed gapper a long way and make for a better experience. South Africa also has the best infrastructure in Africa, with some no-frills domestic airlines such as Mango (www.flymango.com), high quality roads and decent trains that are often under-rated, but can make for a great trip. Buses can take you most places but a great way to explore is to take a road trip in a car – some backpackers take advantage of cheap second-hand prices to buy something, and hope to get a bit of money back at the end of their trip.

# Botswana

**VISA**
Not required.

**CURRENCY**
£1 = 10.5 pula                    US$1 = 6.7 pula

**BUDGET**
£18–£25 a day with hire car.

Botswana is included here to demonstrate the diversity of experiences that can be found in Africa. It's also added so as to talk about one of the continent's success stories. However, as you will spot in the budget suggestion above, Botswana is not a cheap option for the budget traveller. Seventy per cent of the country is dominated by the Kalahari Desert, meaning that travel needs assistance and is tough going. As part of its development plan and frugal fiscal policies, Botswana has gone for quality not quantity in its tourism and it is expensive. Still, it's an interesting example and worth bearing in mind – but for the average gapper it will have to be regarded as a special treat, rather than taking up a big part of any itinerary.

If you can afford it though, Botswana is something special. It is about the size of France, but with a population of under two million people, the majority of whom live in the east of the country leaving the rest free for some of the most well-preserved and dramatic scenery and wildlife in Africa. The people are friendly and interesting and, if you get the chance, you may want to spend a bit of time in Gabarone playing 'Mma Ramotswe spotting' if you've read Alexander McCall Smith's charming books about the Number One Ladies Detective Agency (and if you haven't, it's recommended that you do).

But, the main reason people go to Botswana is the scenery and the wildlife. The Okavango River drains inland from Angola in Botswana's north-western corner and forms the Okavango Delta, the largest inland delta in the world. The water from this provides for a profusion of wildlife under huge skies, spreading out across grassy plains and stunning lagoons. The Moremi Wildlife Reserve, which covers 700sq miles (1,812sq km) in the north-eastern corner of the Delta, is considered by many to be the ultimate African safari destination.

The story of Botswana as a nation is rather heart warming, with a more recent sting. At independence in 1966 Botswana was one of the 10 poorest nations on earth. A few years later copious diamond deposits were discovered which were managed with well-disciplined fiscal policy that saw the economy grow by an average of 9% per year for many years. Sensible planning continues to draw the benefits from mining and tourism but the economy has been restricted by incredibly high HIV prevalence rates – an estimated one in six citizens has the virus, the second highest rate in the world after Swaziland. This has led to draining levels of health spending.

# Zimbabwe

In the 1980s and 1990s, Zimbabwe was one of the most popular destinations for gap years in Africa, when the country was known as the breadbasket of Africa. A burgeoning middle class saw Harare become one of Africa's most vibrant and cosmopolitan cities. However, inequalities were unresolved and most land and commercial farming remained in the hands of white farmers. Resentment festered especially on the issue of land distribution. This presented a massive threat to President Robert Mugabe's legitimacy so he began acquiescing to demands which led to the violent grabbing of farms. International isolation has seen the Zimbabwean economy collapse. When inflation hit 4,500% in 2007, the Zimbabwe dollar was officially suspended and transactions now take place in US dollars or another hard currency. Food and fuel shortages as well as power cuts have become chronic, and a cholera outbreak at the end of 2008 meant that the country was at breaking point. In 2009, a power-sharing accord between President Mugabe and his rival Morgan Tsvangirai was finally implemented, however political unrest and reports of Zanu-PF violence persist. One hopeful sign is that the ban on BBC and CNN journalists reporting from the country has been lifted.

Some travellers do still pass through to reach Victoria Falls and a handful of voluntary schemes still operates in the beleaguered country, but travel to Zimbabwe is not recommended.

# WEST AFRICA
## Ghana

### VISA
£30

### CURRENCY
£1 = 2.34 cedi                    US$1 = 1.46 cedi

### BUDGET
Less than £12 per day.

There is no bad time to head to Ghana. The weather is always hot, the political climate is stable, and crime is much lower than other places. Since 2007 you no longer need a wheelbarrow for the currency since they lopped four zeros off the value of the cedi. Widely regarded as the friendliest place in West Africa, if not the whole continent, if not the world, Ghana could be the ideal choice to ease you into Africa, or perhaps restore your faith later on. Ghana has an intriguing political history – its first president Kwame Nkrumah was instrumental in establishing the Commonwealth and a prominent exponent of pan-Africanism. Visitors, including gap year workers and travellers, now talk of one of the fastest-growing and most inspiring of African countries that still retains an exotic vitality.

Highlights to visit include Mole National Park famous for its elephants and the rainforests of Kakum National Park with an aerial walkway through the canopy, not to forget beautiful beaches, waterfalls and rolling hills. Buses and *tro-tros* – jampacked minibuses where you might have to share a seat with a bucket of slopping fish – are a good way to get around but, as with most forms of shared taxi across the continent, they only leave when full and this can mean sitting in the heat for some time. Local people often wait in the shade or by the drinks stall until the time they know it will depart. Keep your eyes and ears open and ask discreetly where you can.

Accommodation in Accra is varied, but can cater to the budget traveller in hostels for around £6 per night and hotels for more. The Adabraka area is a good place to head for hotels, such as the Hotel de California and Crown Prince.

Ghana has one of the richest cultural environments in Africa, with masses of festivals, dance, music, colourful outfits and traditional arts and crafts. Culture is dominated by the Ashanti region, but exciting events can be found all over. The Ghanaian government is making a concerted effort to encourage and celebrate its cultural heritage. Its troubled history is reflected in the slave forts and museums along the beautiful Cape Coast. Further west along the coast is Takoradi, where the Bay Inn is a popular destination, good value at £30 for two nights accommodation, all meals, drinks, snacks and use of the private beach where at certain times of year turtles come ashore to lay their eggs. You can also paddle out to a stilt village.

West Africa is also where football fever is at its most intense. Ghana's 'Black Stars' are a respectable outfit and local and international fixtures are well attended.

# Senegal

### VISA
Not required.

### CURRENCY
£1 = 713 West African CFA                    US$1 = 444CFA

### BUDGET
£20–£35 a day.

Coming from the UK it can be easy to forget about Francophone Africa. The Francophone countries such as Cameroon, Togo and Senegal offer different experiences and the chance to make use of your A-Level French, in case you have it. Indeed, if you think you would like to improve your French but listening to tapes asking where the train station is puts you off, then what better opportunity than to learn it in a colourful, musical situation where finding the train station will take you past markets, performers and traditional healers? (And if you are hoping to travel by train, note this recent extract from the rail site www.seat61.com: 'The Dakar-Bamako train is currently running every 8 or 9 days, to no set schedule.')

People are drawn to Senegal by a vision of people wearing white *jallabiyas* (hooded cloaks) and making beautiful music. Small, friendly, and pretty successful, Senegal sits at Africa's most westerly point with the Gambia almost entirely enclosed within it. Though vibrant and modern, Senegalese society remains rooted in the concepts of honour (*Diom*), hospitality (*Teranga*) and respect for older people.

The name Senegal is said to be derived from the Wolof name for dugout canoes that many fishermen (fishing is Senegal's biggest industry) still use today, and are also used in a favourite Senegalese pastime of canoe racing. This takes place along the coast and is quite a sight. Senegal is also renowned for its moving, soulful music. Festivals between November/December and April/May/June are definite highlights. The only downside is you are likely to have to dance at some point, and you may pick up quite a crowd. Football is again huge in Senegal – remember their victory over France in the 2002 World Cup? The national squad has a few Premiership players, but in your language class you might need to brush up your knowledge of French teams as well as your future perfect tense.

**UP AND COMING DESTINATION**

*Mauritania is one of those unexplored gems that travellers have been discovering recently as part of a popular overland route from Morocco to Senegal (and points beyond), now that the western Sahara region is relatively stable and a paved road connects Nouadhibou with the colourful capital Nouakchott. From the coastal road you can see how the red sands of the Sahara change dramatically into the white beach sands of the North Atlantic.*

# NORTH AFRICA

## Morocco

**VISA**

Not required.

**CURRENCY**

£1 = 12.3 dirham                                    US$1 = 7.8 dirham

**BUDGET**

£12–£18 a day.

Just a short hop from Europe is Morocco. Its position at the crossroads of East and West, as well as the Mediterranean and the Atlantic, makes for a unique experience and some fascinating history and culture. Parts of Morocco have become a little overloaded with backpackers and tourists over the past few years. However, if you take the time to find your way to lesser known places then Morocco's mysteries are still there to be enjoyed. Chefchaon in north-west Morocco is a great place to hang out when you first arrive, get acclimatised, adjust yourself to street sellers and meet other backpackers. Small villages and eccentric markets will provide quality crafts and interesting conversation (often in French). Even in the cities, especially Fez (or Fes) and Marrakech, wandering though the souks takes the visitor to a different world of spice merchants and snake charmers. The smell of tanning mingles with mint tea while the call to prayer from the myriad mosques makes its timeless, haunting demand. For the more adventurous adrenaline junkie, the Rif and Atlas Mountains offer stunning trekking and even skiing. The Saharan sands can be explored on camelback, horseback or four-wheel drive. *Nomadic Morocco* (www.nomadicmorocco.com) specialises in guided treks in the mountains.

Finding your way out of the tourist traps and into Morocco's more interesting sides will take some effort. You also need to be aware that where tourists are commonplace, then thieves and conmen do tend to follow. However, if you keep your wits about you and consider what you want and what you'll pay for a given item, you should find yourself some interesting things at reasonable prices. But remember successful haggling requires practice.

# Egypt

### VISA
£15

### CURRENCY
£1 = 8.8 Egyptian pounds             US$1 = 5.5 Egyptian pounds

### BUDGET
Less than £12 a day.

Egypt might seem a bit of a clichéd choice here. In recent years it's come to be known for the Red Sea Riviera, diving and sunbathing, and the pyramids have come to look a little bit hackneyed – expect to be surrounded by coach loads of tourists. Taking a gap year in Africa is all about challenging perceptions though, and having the time to look beyond common ideas. Amid the tatty souvenirs and the camel rides, remember the importance of Egyptian civilisation in developing so much – for instance architecture, medicine and religion. While a little run down, the pyramids remain truly remarkable and the only remaining wonder of the ancient world. With the rise of political Islam and its role in the Middle East, Egypt also remains important in current world politics. This, of course, also leaves it vulnerable to extremism and Egypt has recently seen bombings and other violence.

It is a good idea to get out of Cairo to Egypt's six oases, for picturesque towns and all the dates you can eat. You could even venture into the harsh Sinai region and find the burning bush that spoke to Moses in St Catherine's monastery. Cairo is definitely an intense experience with quite a lot of hassle from those with some kind of sale to make. In the summer, from June to July a heady soup of dust, heat, pollution, noise and rather too many people around makes walking feel more like a test than a pleasure. But there is lots to see, do, buy and experience. One of the world's largest bazaars (Khan el Khalili) allows you to keep your bargaining skills up to scratch. To see experts at work, though probably not make your own purchase, you can also head out to the Camel Market at Birqash, around 35km from Cairo. Most of the hundreds of camels that are sold daily come from Sudan. In fact, just people-watching with some sweet tea and a hookah pipe can take you out of the hustle and bustle and allow you to experience Egypt's more laid back, social side. By making your leisurely way down the Nile, you can really bathe in the history and majesty of Egypt. If you're still feeling adventurous you can even rent a felucca (wooden sailing boat) to cruise down yourself.

# TRAVEL RESOURCES

## USEFUL WEBSITES
**www.atta.co.uk**, African Travel and Tourism Association.
**http://news.bbc.co.uk/1/hi/world/africa/default.stm**, BBC News Africa.
**www.travelblog.org/Africa**, Africa travel blogs.
**www.africaguide.com**, guide to Africa.
**www.avert.org**, HIV/AIDS information and work.

## USEFUL BOOKS
*Africa* (Lonely Planet, 11th edition, 2007), £21.99. Lonely Planet also provides useful regional guides, if you are just visiting one part of Africa.

Charlie Shackell and Illya Bracht, *Africa by Road* (Bradt, 2001). Out of print but available second hand from www.amazon.co.uk, etc.; getting out of date, but great for adventurers making their own way by car, truck or even bicycle. Bradt publish guides to a large number of individual African countries (www.bradt-travelguides.com).

Chris Scott, *Sahara Overland* (Trailblazer, 2004), £19.99.

Don Pinnock, *African Journeys* (Double Storey Books, 2004), £15.99. A collection of travel essays by a South African travel writer. It would be irresponsible to suggest reading some stories and winging it; but showing some imagination is a good thing for African travel.

Paul Theroux, *Dark Star Safari: Overland from Cairo to Cape Town* (Penguin, 2003), £9.99. Theroux's Africa novels (such as *Jungle Lovers*) are also recommended.

## WIDER READING
J M Coetzee, *Disgrace* (Secker & Warburg, 1999), £7.99. This and other novels by this Nobel Prize winning novelist shed light on South Africa both during and after apartheid.

Meja Mwangi, *Striving for the Wind* (Heinemann, 1992), £9.99. A hilarious farce set in post-colonial Kenya.

Thomas Pakenham, *The Scramble for Africa* (Abacus, 1992), £14.99. How to divide up a continent in one easy conference, and all manner of confused marching about.

Martin Meredith, *The State of Africa: A History of Fifty Years of Independence* (Free Press, 2006), £10.99. Does what it says on the tin.

Adam Hochschild, *King Leopold's Ghost: A Story of Greed Terror and Heroism* (Pan, 2006), £8.99. Very readable, but horrific, history of the Belgian Congo.

Nigel Barley, *The Innocent Anthropologist* (1983, re-issued by Waveland Pr Inc, 2000). A laugh-out-loud account by an academic anthropologist of his research with the Dowayo people of Northern Cameroon.

William Boyd, *A Good Man in Africa* and *Brazzaville Beach* (Penguin, both 1999), both £8.99. Boyd grew up in Africa.

Chimamanda Ngozi Adichie, *Half of a Yellow Sun* (Harper, 2006), £7.99. Powerful novel about the chaos that engulfed ordinary people in the Biafran War.

Chimamanda Ngozi Adichie, *The Thing Around Your Neck* (Fourth Estate, 2009), £7.99. A collection of a dozen stories set in Nigeria.

# ASIA

Asia is the largest and most diverse continent in the world stretching from the Pacific Ocean to the Mediterranean Sea (assuming you consider the Middle East as part of Asia). It bundles together Tibetan refugee settlements in the Himalayas and Japanese temple gardens, elegant suburbs in Colombo, the jungles of Borneo and the slums of Kolkata. The 'East' covers such a vast range of geography and culture that it is difficult to know where to begin when planning a route.

## THE LURE OF THE EAST

Asia offers an astonishing range of attitudes and ways of life, which can seem very alien to anything you are used to. A great many gappers feel a little overwhelmed by the unfamiliarity of it all, the noise, colour and craziness, the touts and transport. Many prefer to stick to the beaten track where Western tastes and expectations are catered for. After acclimatising a little, however, it is worth considering stepping off the well-trodden path, at least for a while. The most popular backpacker haunts, such as the famous Khao San Road in Bangkok and Pattaya, do not in any way reflect the local culture. Most young travellers will not want to miss out on the imagined pleasures of full moon parties and banana pancakes, but this kind of commercial tourism often lapses into tackiness.

The hustle and bustle of urban commerce tends to absorb the unique characteristics of small communities. Although this is less true in the cities of Asia, it is true that a more faithful image of any country should be sought in small towns and villages and by using local transport rather than air-conditioned tourist coaches. The best way of course is to settle in one place for an extended period as part of a volunteer project, such as teaching in a village school in Nepal or working at an elephant park in Thailand; for a multitude of suggestions, see the *Asia* chapter in the latter part of this book.

In some places the unhurried pace of life may cause frustration, especially when dealing with officialdom. But this is one of the glories of the continent. After slogging through A-Levels or university exams, it is easy to luxuriate in the nonchalance and to be amused by the absurd amount of paperwork. There is something to be learned from experiencing attitudes and customs so unfamiliar to our ultra-efficient Western ways. No matter how much you read and talk to fellow-travellers, you will be thrilled and surprised, and sometimes shocked and appalled, by the sights and culture that await exploration.

With the explosion of affordable air travel and the opening up of once-closed and mysterious countries such as Laos, not to mention China, young travellers have been swarming to the continent of Asia. Most choose between the Indian subcontinent (India, Nepal and Sri Lanka), South East Asia (Thailand, Malaysia, Indonesia, Vietnam, Cambodia and Laos) and the Far East (China, Japan, Korea and Taiwan). Generalisations are dangerous, but certain issues crop up in various corners of the continent that deserve a little thought beforehand. Obviously Japan and Taiwan have a more Westernised standard of living, but there are profound differences that can cause problems there too.

## UNMISSABLE HIGHLIGHTS

- Visit Angkor Wat, temple complex in Cambodia which is one of the wonders of the world.
- Join the pilgrims climbing Adam's Peak, Sri Lanka's holiest, to see the Buddha's footprint and the sunrise.
- Marvel at the dusk departure of thousands of bats from Niah caves in Sarawak, Borneo.
- Track rhinos on elephant back in Chitwan, Nepal's foremost national park.
- Admire the patience of fishermen at Fort Cochin in South India who use an ancient kind of shore-mounted cantilevered fishing net.
- Contemplate China's recent history while standing in Tiananmen Square in Beijing.
- Find your way to Hunza, a hidden Himalayan valley in Pakistan where people are said to live to a great age because of their diet of apricots.
- Travel by Shinkansen (bullet train) in Japan; a seven-day rail pass costs little more than the Tokyo-Kyoto return.
- Visit Luang Prabang on the Mekong River in Laos, voted top city by readers of Wanderlust magazine.
- Sea kayak under the cliffs at Krabi in Thailand.

## GETTING THERE

Most gap year students will book their flights through a student travel agent such as STA Travel or the Flight Centre, especially if their routes are at all complicated. If you are looking for a straight return, the cheapest flights are not direct and probably available from airlines such as Aeroflot or Biman Bangladesh, which may be considered dodgy by overprotective mothers. Middle Eastern carriers (e.g. Qatar Airways and Emirates) and Asian carriers (e.g. the Taiwanese airline Eva Airways) are often worth investigating for low fares. Flying with them is guaranteed to be more interesting than flying on British Airways or Cathay Pacific. When **Sarah Spiller** fell in love with Sri Lanka after joining a turtle conservation project, she made several subsequent trips on Sri Lankan Airlines and felt that she was already on holiday the minute she stepped aboard.

The famous overland route to Nepal has been problematical for a very long time now, though the relaunched Oz-bus (www.oz-bus.com) travels from London to Sydney via Iran and Pakistan. Assuming you can get a transit visa for Iran, it is not impossible to make the overland trip by public transport which would be very rigorous and very cheap. Most travellers simply take advantage of the competitive discount flight market from London to Asian destinations. For example the cheapest quoted return price London to Mumbai is less than £300 including taxes provided you're prepared to put up with a stopover in Kuwait. The cheapest advertised fare to Bangkok at the time of writing was £380 return. The price of flights to Japan has dropped in the past few years, especially if you are willing to fly on Aeroflot. In London a wide range of travel agents advertise cheap fares to Asia.

**PASCALE HUNTER'S** route started by flying into Bangkok from Sydney. She was excited about rendezvousing with some friends from home and travelling around Thailand and Cambodia:

*F*antastic *white-water rafting near Chiang Mai, sea-kayaking off Krabi in the Gulf of Thailand, sunrise after the Full Moon party on Ko Pha Ngan and a quite different sunrise later with the magnificent temples of Angkor Wat in the foreground, a rescue centre for abandoned pets near Phnom Penh – these were some of the highlights of Pascale's seven-week trip.*

*To avoid hassles, Pascale and her friends mapped out their trip ahead of time through a travel agent in Bangkok to which their first tuk-tuk driver introduced them. The four girls excitedly boarded the sleeper train to Chiang Mai and, since this was their first foray into Asian travel, they were happy to be met at the airport by someone with a placard bearing their names who took them to their pre-booked hostel. They were amused rather than irritated by the many retail opportunities thrust upon them; while taking a tuk-tuk in Chiang Mai, they made unscheduled stops at no fewer than four factories (umbrellas, lacquer, jade and silver).*

*During their five days in the north, they trekked, white-water rafted, joined an elephant trek and did a half-day Thai cookery course. One day the girls decided to hire motorbikes (for about £4 minus petrol), undaunted that they had no licence or driving experience. Pascale lost track of her friends, one of whom it turned out had fallen off in a busy street and got quite a fright, though was unhurt.*

*The next destination in Thailand was the island of Ko Pha Ngan where they arrived in time for one of the famous full moon parties. Their beach lodge arranged a minibus which picked up a number of other passengers whom they gradually realised were all 'lady-boys' going down to work the beach. When later Pascale noticed a backpacker dancing with one of these beauties, she didn't know whether she should alert him or not. Pascale enjoyed celebrating her 19th birthday by visiting a waterfall on Ko Samui and later proceeded to the coast of Krabi, a southern province of Thailand, with striking cliffs rising out of the sea.*

*Pascale's travel agent had fixed up bus transport from Bangkok to Siem Reap, jumping off point for Angkor Wat, plus four-nights in the Hil Ton hostel and Cambodian visa, all for 6,000–7,000 baht (approximately £120). The journey by road from the Thai border to Siem Reap was acutely uncomfortable, which persuaded them to opt for flying back at the end of their Cambodian trip.*

*Having spent a day roaming round the main temples at Angkor Wat, their attention was caught by a notice posted up at their hostel asking for volunteer teachers. They went along to Savong's School (www.savong.com) for two days, to help in the classrooms, first with secondary school-aged children and then with younger ones. Pascale felt that so many Westerners had participated in the scheme that it had become quite commercialised, which had taught the kids to clamour for Western goodies.*

*Because of flight timings they spent a whole week in Phnom Penh which was exceedingly hot. They visited the Killing Fields Museum and chilled* *in the backpacker enclave at Lakeside. They booked on a tour to a wild-life centre where ex-pets were housed. Another 'must-do' tourist activity in the capital is visiting one of the many orphanages that vie for foreign visitors by advertising on the sides of tuk-tuks. A donation of $30 was required, though at this stage Pascale and friends were within days of flying home and were down to almost nothing so they could not afford this and were still taken.*

*This was right at the end of their trip and they had not factored in the Cambodian and Thai departure taxes, which left them completely skint for their last weekend in Bangkok (and they had been looking forward to a final shopping spree). A café was showing their favourite film (The Holiday) and they managed to nurse a single coke for the entire duration. When they got to Bangkok airport with their carefully saved 500 baht each for the departure tax, they were horrified to learn that the tax had just gone up to 700 baht. They had no alternative but to beg the remaining 200 baht from more well-heeled tourists in the check-in queue, a debt which Pascale's parents repaid the minute she got home. Ironically this, her scariest moment, came right at the end of what had been an amazing trip.*

## GETTING AROUND

If you intend to do a lot of flying around the region, it is worth considering the Visit Asia air pass marketed by the Oneworld group of airlines, available only to people who book their intercontinental flight on a member airline, i.e. British Airways, Cathay Pacific, Qantas, JAL and a few others. Flights are available to 50+ cities in China, Hong Kong, India, Indonesia, Japan, Malaysia, Pakistan, the Philippines, Singapore, South Korea, Sri Lanka, Taiwan, Thailand and Vietnam at various sector prices; see the website for details (www.oneworld.com).

Once you're installed in Asia, travel is highly affordable. The railways of the Indian subcontinent are a fascinating social phenomenon and also dirt cheap. Throughout Asia, airfares are not expensive, particularly around the discount triangle of Bangkok, Hong Kong and Singapore. The no-frills discount carrier Air Asia advertises some amazingly low fares for example between Bangkok and Phnom Penh. The notable exception to the generalisation about cheap public transport in Asia is Japan.

In addition to ordinary buses and trains, Asian countries employ an impressive and ingenious range of vehicles to transport people cheaply. The shared taxi takes many forms from the *dolmuş* of Turkey to the Suzuki of northern Pakistan to the *bemo* of Indonesia. On your extended travels in Asia, you might find yourself travelling in a bullock-drawn cart or a horse-drawn *tonga* as well as the more commonplace modes of transport.

If a vehicle has a meter, make sure it is switched on and, if not, always fix the sum you are willing to pay before stepping in. When it comes to buses, you are usually safe if you hop on one that locals are taking. If you get in on your own you may find that you have 'contracted' the vehicle for your private use which will increase the price by an order of magnitude.

Depending on how steady your nerves are, the style of driving may leave you agape. Also some roads are atrocious with massive potholes or unprotected hairpin bends. Keep this in mind if you are signing up for a 12-hour bus journey. Imagine yourself occupying a narrow seat for all those hours with your head hitting the ceiling every time you hit a pothole. The word 'luxury' is sometimes used rather loosely when describing coach travel in Asia.

### TWO-WHEELING ADVICE

*Gappers are often tempted to hire motorcycles in South East Asia, principally because of the very low prices (just a couple of pounds for a day). Companies require no licence and do not automatically provide helmets. According to the Foreign & Commonwealth Office, an average of 38 people die every day in motorcycle accidents in Thailand alone. Many travel insurance policies do not cover the kind of vehicles routinely hired out, so if you are involved in even a minor accident, you may end up having to pay a hefty fee.*

## BUDGETING

An idea of how much you will end up spending is given in the country sections below. On the whole, you will find that travel throughout South Asia is a fantastic bargain and very addictive. However many gappers get caught out by steep visa costs and departure taxes, some of which must be paid in US dollars (as in the $25 tax to leave Cambodia by air) and if you are misinformed, you run the risk of being caught short on your way out of a country if you happen to have run your funds down to zero. In the case of Thailand, the departure tax is now included in the price of the air ticket.

## CULTURE SHOCK

In all Asian countries, particularly India and Cambodia, you will be confronted with poverty such as is not known in the Western world. Beggars are the most obvious outward sign of this poverty, and it is impossible to pass by without feeling pity. They are often disabled, blind or limbless and, as a result, have no other way of making a living. Even if you are not the flashiest dresser, you will look down at your sandals and camera and for the first time realise how privileged you are. Whether you give them money is obviously a personal choice. Your decision will depend on your own financial position, the degree of pity you feel, your conscience, and how worried you are at the possibility of abetting professional begging. Be aware that if you give your spare coins to begging children, it rewards them for skipping school in order to harass foreigners. Many people think that if you are moved to help a community, it is better to fund some pens or books for the local school or give to an orphanage rather than give money to clamouring individuals.

Once you move out of Europe you are entering a world that is based on different religious, social, moral and cultural values. Many young travellers are heedless of these differences and gravitate to beach resorts and party places which do a good job of masking local norms. But if you want to get a little deeper into the culture and visit local temples, be aware that modesty of dress and behaviour is required. The most famous sites such as Wat Pho in Bangkok post signs specifying 'no shorts' and you should remove footwear and headgear before entering any Buddhist temple (and also avoid taking photos of someone standing in front of a statue of the Buddha). Women should not wear clothing that is in any way revealing, particularly in Muslim countries. Outside the Westernised resorts, it is advisable for women to wear loose-fitting tops with sleeves and light trousers; crop tops, singlets and shorts give out a message that you may not intend. Anyone with light skin is bound to be stared at in any case, which can be discomfiting until you get used to it.

One of the most noticeable differences in attitude between the East and West is the attitude to privacy. For example within 60 seconds of sitting down in a Delhi park, you are likely to be surrounded by a peanut salesman, a snake charmer, an ear cleaner and umpteen children clamouring to see the cover of your book. It will sometimes seem as though you have been asked a hundred times a day 'Where are you coming from? How long in my country? What is your good name?' The first few times you are delighted to engage in conversation but will soon grow weary.

## WHAT TO EXPECT

From the minute you arrive, you will be assailed by people touting for your custom. Who can blame them when there is so much competition for the western dollar? If you really do not want to be offered a service, try not to break step, while providing a polite yet dismissive response. If you are getting really fed up, pull your brimmed hat down, don sun glasses and pretend to be a deaf-mute.

All of this is quite harmless compared to the confidence tricksters you may come across. It would be impossible to list all the ploys and ruses that have been successful in the past, but they range from light deception (beggars pretending to be blind) to blatant blackmail (planting drugs on you then threatening to call the police). Between these two extremes there is a lot of scope for ingenuity. Even the most obvious methods (phony tales of relatives' illnesses, promises to repay money, trading in fake gems) are made so convincing that cautious travellers have been caught out by them. Of course there is no need to mistrust everyone you meet. For every thief and swindler, you will meet dozens of friendly concerned locals who will warn you of lurking evil, keep an eye on your luggage in your absence and so on.

# EXCITING WAYS TO
# GET INVOLVED

- Build look-out posts in the jungle of Indonesian Borneo to help protect orangutans (www.orangutan.org.uk).
- Teach at an English-immersion summer camp in Taiwan (www.kidscamp.com.tw).
- Do a work experience placement at a hotel in the Maldives (www.volunteerinternational.com).
- Help on an organic farm in Korea (www.wwoofkorea.com).
- Work for a book publisher in Delhi (www.gapguru.com).
- Take a Thai cookery course in Chiang Mai (www.thaicookeryschool.com).
- Learn to dive in the Philippines in order to help survey a reef (www.coralcay.org).
- Volunteer at an orphanage in Cambodia (www.outreachinternational.co.uk).
- Teach English to Burmese tribal people in the refugee camps of northern Thailand (maesotel@loxinfo.co.th).
- Live in a Himalayan village as part of a community development programme (www.insightnepal.org.np).

## DRUGS

Sooner or later when travelling in Asia, someone will approach you and offer you one substance or another. Drugs in all countries carry heavy penalties. Occasionally, drug sales are also deals between informers and police, either for financial gain or to boost arrest statistics. Carrying any kind of drugs over a border is plain dumb. Anybody tempted should just google 'drug smuggling' and their destination country to come up with tragic cases. The 1999 film *Brokedown Palace* is about two school friends who straight after high school head to Thailand for a cheap holiday where they meet a charming Australian. He persuades them to join him on a trip to Hong Kong and before they know it they are stopped at Bangkok airport carrying heroin and find themselves condemned to serve 33 years in a Thai women's prison. Never consent to carry a bag for someone else through customs; you may be acting as an unwitting courier, and ignorance is impossible to prove in court.

# SOUTH EAST ASIA

## Thailand

**VISA**

Free on arrival, valid 30 days; can be renewed by leaving the country and crossing back on a visa run, but this only extends visa by 15 days.

**CURRENCY**

£1 = 53 Thai baht                    US$1 = 33 Thai baht

**BUDGET**

$30–$50 a day on the tourist trail; cheaper in rural Thailand.

Beaches of powdery sand and swaying coconut palms set against a glistening turquoise sea – this is the picture conjured by most long haul gap year travellers considering a trip to Thailand. Bangkok is pre-eminent as a destination itself or as a stop-over for gappers heading to or from Australia, and has become a favourite jumping-off point for the whole of South East Asia. Enticing images of rainforests and temples, night markets and beach parties draw many in an easterly direction.

The indigenous Thai urban vehicle is the motorised three-wheeler or *tuk-tuk* which Simon Calder of the *Independent* describes as '*a cross between a Reliant Robin and a bus shelter*'. Be sure to settle on a price before you step in, which is easier after you have been there for a while and know what the price range should be. The atrocious traffic of Bangkok can be avoided by taking the elevated Sky Train or the Chao Phraya River ferry. *Tuk-tuk* drivers target tourists and will often offer private tours or try to persuade them to book their travels through an agent. If you succumb to their blandishments, an agent may well simplify your travel arrangements, but you will have to be prepared to pay a premium. Some people will choose to avoid the middle-man altogether.

New arrivals should be prepared to be swept off by the first *tuk-tuk* driver to a travel agent who will purport to be working for the official TAT (Tourism Authority of Thailand) and who will fix up transport, accommodation, tours and visas for an all-in fee. Some gap year students are happy to pay over the odds to avoid the hassle and possible rip-offs along the way, though more experienced travellers can generally make similar arrangements more cheaply.

The usual route for travellers spending a few weeks in Thailand is to head north to Chiang Mai – often on the sleeper train that departs Bangkok at 7.30pm and arrives 14 hours later – to do some trekking or adventure activities. Visits to elephant sanctuaries are very popular, though sometimes newly arrived gappers are not very impressed at the way the animals are treated, so it is better to do your research well.

Travellers then head south to one or more of the party islands, possibly taking in the jungle at Kanchanaburi, where you can ride an elephant along the banks of the River Kwai, or the ancient city of Ayutthaya. The island of Ko Pha Ngan is famous for its full moon parties, attended by between 10,000 and 20,000 people all dancing to the pumping beats of more than a dozen sound systems. Most revellers stay up to watch the sunrise. (The litter left by party-goers is appalling and may eventually prompt the local council to ban parties on this scale.)

Thailand caters to extremes, from the unsavoury Speedo-wearing older European men looking for a Thai girlfriend to those in search of a spiritual break. Although not as cheap as it used to be, the cost of living is still gratifyingly low except in highly developed resorts that have priced backpackers out. You can eat a good meal for only 40 baht and a beer is 60 baht in a bar.

# Cambodia

**VISA**
Buy on arrival by air or in advance in Bangkok (£15/US$20); valid for 30 days.

**CURRENCY**
£1 = 6640 riels (KHR)          US$1 = 4170 riels

**BUDGET**
$20–$30 a day.

From Thailand, backpackers can proceed to Malaysia, Cambodia or Laos and then on to Vietnam, depending on time constraints. The journey by road from Bangkok to Siem Reap is a gruelling one, because the six hours of travel in Cambodia between the Thai border and the jumping off place for Angkor Wat are along unmade-up roads. At least the danger of landmines along this stretch has subsided.

The temple complex at Angkor Wat is one of the wonders of the world. The archaeological park located just outside the city of Siem Reap in northern Cambodia comprises ruined 12th-century temples built by the ancient Khmer regime. The site covers hundreds of kilometres and would take days to see properly; a three-day ticket costs $40, whereas a longer one $60. Few can resist an impulse to see the temples at sunrise or sunset – a ravishing sight as long as you don't mind sharing it with 5,000 other people. Your guide book can recommend some lesser visited places such as the sacred mountain of Phnom Kulen topped with a reclining sandstone Buddha and the River of a Thousand Lingas (Kbal Spean), a riverbed full of carvings of gods and phalluses (some of which will be submerged in the rainy season).

Travel on to the capital Phnom Penh can be by road or by boat, a wonderful six-hour sea trip. Many stay in the backpackers' ghetto Lakeside which inevitably has more than its fair share of hassles, including dodgy moto drivers and scammers. *Tuk-tuk*s are cheaper than in Thailand; you can often hire one for a whole day for less than $10. Many backpacker lodges include free *tuk-tuk* travel as part of the deal.

Highlights include a trip to the Killing Fields Museum at S-21, a notorious Pol Pot prison located in a former school on the outskirts of the city. Many NGOs, wildlife centres and orphanages welcome visiting tourists, such as the JCA Orphanage which puts on weekly dance shows followed by dinner with the children. Various companies offer sunset dinner cruises on the Mekong; the one run by the non-profit Seametry School is more worthwhile than some.

For destinations far removed from the tourist hordes in Phnom Penh and Siem Reap, try the relaxed coastal province of Kampot where you can swim amongst phosphorescence at night, visit NGOs and enjoy the nearby attractions of Kep, a crumbling colonial beach resort with amazing seafood and untouched islands. Elsewhere try not to miss the spooky deserted town in the middle of the jungle up Bokkor mountain, and the wild north-eastern provinces of Mondulkiri and Rattanakiri, where you can go on elephant treks to remote minority hill tribes, swim in spectacular waterfalls, and escape from the sweltering heat of the lowlands.

**TRAVEL TIP**
*Make sure you have $25 for the departure tax if you are leaving Cambodia by air.*

# Laos

**VISA**
Buy on arrival at the airport or Friendship Bridge (US$30); valid for 15 days only.

**CURRENCY**
£1 = 13,500 kip (LAK)          US$1 = 8,500 kip

**BUDGET**
US$15–$20 a day, with no trouble, one of the cheapest destinations in Asia.

In the years after it opened its borders in 1989, Laos was considered the most exotic, the most untravelled country in Asia. It is now a well-established part of the backpackers' trail. Highlights include the former royal city of the north, Luang Prabang, which sits on the Mekong River and is a good starting point for a slowboat trip. The northern hill tribes of Laos are less affected by tourism than those of northern Thailand.

# Vietnam

**VISA**
Buy in advance in London (£38).

**CURRENCY**
£1 = 28,500 dong          US$1 = 17,850 dong

**BUDGET**
$20–$40 a day; ironically hop-on hop-off bus tours can be cheaper than public transport.

Travelling round the region is very affordable, even if you take a flight, because Jetstar is a low cost airline serving Hanoi and Ho Chi Minh City (HCMC). It is possible to get a bus from HCMC to Phnom Penh for less than $10, though you will pay a premium for a more comfortable ride. The *Reunification Express* is a train that runs the full length of the country (more than 30 hours to cover 1,300km) and stops at all the towns you might want to visit between Saigon and Hanoi including Nha Trang (where you can join a trip on a party boat), Da Nang and Hue. There are many natural and human-made things to see in Vietnam such as the spectacular Halong Bay or the Citadel and ancient imperial capital of Hue.

Although Vietnam is still a one-party state, it bears all the trappings (complete with garish advertising hoardings and American pop music) of a capitalist society. There is a two-tier system for utilities and travel in Vietnam, which means foreigners pay substantially more than locals for almost everything. Hanoi in the north is smaller and more beautiful yet bustling and noisy whereas HCMC is a Bangkok in the making with a slightly higher cost of living. This sophisticated, sprawling commercial centre boasts a skyline already dotted with skyscrapers.

The cities are wonderfully packed with good, cheap restaurants serving excellent healthy food and it is quite easy to get by on $5 a day eating at Com Binh Dan or Bia Hoi, the Vietnamese street side restaurants. Some of the very best food can be found at the smallest street stalls at ridiculously cheap prices.

The Vietnamese people are often very friendly. However, what you see is not always what you get. Behind that charming Vietnamese smile is more often than not the intent to extract money. Of particular note are the numerous women in search of a foreign husband, a foreign passport and an airline ticket. Single men should beware. Internet access is widely available and improving although it is still unreliable, slow and censored.

# Indonesia

### VISA
Buy on arrival: $25 for 30 days. No extensions.

### CURRENCY
£1 = 15,000 rupiah U$1 = 9,450 rupiah

### BUDGET
$15–$25 a day.

Three-fifths of the population live on the main island of Java where the hot, dusty, overcrowded, polluted and poverty-stricken capital, Jakarta, is situated. Many young travellers prefer to head for the adjacent island of Sumatra, still largely covered by jungle and wilderness. The tourist industry on Bali suffered terribly after the terrorist bombings, even though the lovely hinterland was largely unaffected. The resort of Kuta, where several of the bombs went off, has long been spoiled by mass tourism and it is impossible to avoid persistent hawkers, tacky souvenir shops and nightclubs. Head instead to the popular tourist centre of Ubud, famous for its puppet theatre and *game-lan* music as well as its monkey temple and tropical ambience. Further inland, you will come to the tranquil inland lake of Bratan near the temple at Bedugal (one of 20,000 on the island) and the flower market at Candikuning. Sarong-clad women throughout the island gracefully make bamboo and flower offerings to the gods with a backdrop of volcanic hills and lush forests. Bali retained Hinduism whereas 87% of the Indonesian population is Muslim.

Indonesia is a fascinating country and most visitors agree that the Indonesian people are fantastic. There are over 17,000 islands, less than half of them inhabited, with many different tribes and cultures, which make it difficult to keep the country unified. In fact there has been quite a lot of unrest in the past few years which is currently ongoing in central Sulawesi, Ambon and Aceh. The Indonesian half of Borneo is called Kalimantan and is off the radar of most gappers and can involve some very challenging travel conditions.

Travel by public transport is cheap but can be time-consuming, though internal flights are within the range of many.

### TRAVEL TIP
*Bahasa Indonesian, almost identical to Malay, was imposed on the people of Indonesia after independence in 1949 and is one of the simplest languages to learn both in structure and pronunciation.*

# Malaysia (including North Borneo)

### VISA
No visa required for stays of less than three months.

### CURRENCY
£1 = 5.5 ringgits                US$1 = 3.4 ringgits

### BUDGET
$30–$40 a day.

The modern state of Malaysia comprises the southern part of the Malay Peninsula between Singapore at the tip and Thailand to the north, plus the two distant provinces of Sabah and Sarawak, which occupy the northern third of the island of Borneo. A mountain range with peaks of up to 3,000m forms a central spine and provides some hill resorts where you can escape the heat. The rainy season on the peninsula falls between November and February, so this is not a good time to plan a beach holiday. Vast stretches of the country are still covered by tropical forest. Compared with Indonesia and Cambodia, Malaysia is a relatively progressive country with a well-developed infrastructure, which (for some) makes it less appealing as a destination. It is also more expensive, so it is wise to budget at least $30 a day. As a result the average age of travellers tends to be older than in Thailand. Cheap backpacker accommodation can be found in most places, though beach resorts tend to be more upmarket and therefore a lot pricier than the equivalent in Thailand.

The great attraction of Malaysia is its varied tropical scenery, from the coral islands and beaches on the east coast of the peninsula to the jungles of Sabah and Sawarak in East Malaysia. Malaysia also has its hill stations, which can make ideal centres for hill and jungle walking, especially Tanah Rata, the travellers' centre in the Cameron Highlands. Only 100km from Kuala Lumpur, Fraser's Hill is less frequented and very pleasant. The town of Malacca (or Melaka) is a picturesque colonial settlement on the coast. The wonderful Taman Negara National Park promotes eco-tourism.

Many beaches are magnificent, especially along the less developed east coast. Although Penang in the north-west is the most famous, the hordes of tourists, hawkers and litter on the beach spoil it.

---

**UP AND COMING DESTINATION**
*Sarawak is a marvellously exotic place with a fascinating history. It was ruled from 1841 to the Japanese invasion exactly 100 years later by a maverick dynasty of 'white rajahs', the British Brooke family. From the gracious colonial town of Kuching, travel into the hinterland along the busy thoroughfare of the Sarawak River is easy on ferries (express boats). It is not unusual to be invited to visit a longhouse. Another of the unmissable sights are the caves at Niah, shared by thousands of bats and swifts.*

---

# Burma

**VISA**
Buy in advance. £14 in London, cheaper and faster in Bangkok.

**CURRENCY**

| | |
|---|---|
| £1 = 10.2 kyat | US$1 = 6.4 kyat |

**BUDGET**
$25–$35 a day (if you take taxis).

Any gapper contemplating a trip to Burma will soon become aware that this destination arouses controversy. It is in the grip of a totalitarian regime that oppresses its citizens and has under house arrest the democratically elected leader Aung San Suu Kyi, who has requested a tourism boycott. Whereas the Rough Guides abide by this, Lonely

Planet argues that discouraging visits from the outside world only cripples the economy further and punishes the ordinary people. One tourist who did the cause no good was the uninvited American who swam across a lake to Aung San Suu Kyi's house in 2009 and thereby prolonged her house arrest by 18 months.

A typical itinerary would include the capital Yangon, Mandalay (now less romantic than its name), Hsipaw, the beautiful Inle Lake, Kalaw, Bagan (an ancient temple complex on the banks of the Irrawaddy River) and back to Yangon.

# INDIAN SUBCONTINENT

## India

### VISA
Buy in advance for £39, valid for up to six months from date of issue.

### CURRENCY
£1 = 74 rupees                                                    US$1 = 46 rupees

### BUDGET
$15–$20 a day.

India's old associations of poverty, famine, squalor and disease are being challenged by the country's booming urban economy partly based on high-tech outsourced business. Lumbering night trains and hip nightclubs, the vast all-encompassing Mother India offers everything in between. All preconceptions give way before the vitality, colour and cheerfulness displayed on the streets. Sights to shock, amaze and amuse are everywhere; you cannot be bored in India. You may think you are prepared for culture shock but not for the sensory overload, for the visceral reaction to the noise and chaos and hassle, the heat and pollution, the astonishing energy. Many feel that a visit to India should be a requirement for all gap year students, to make them aware of how much we all take for granted. But it can be overwhelming for some and a certain level of maturity is needed to process so many contradictory sensations of disgust and exhilaration and every emotion in between. The way to enjoy it is to go with it rather than kick against it.

In contrast to the frenetic activity on the streets, the wheels of bureaucracy can grind exceeding slow. A relatively simple operation such as buying a rail ticket or cashing a traveller's cheque can take the better part of a day. You can almost hear yourself wind down and eventually will learn to be as patient as Buddha.

Young Westerners can often be heard exclaiming with outrage at the discrepancy between the rich and poor in India (as if inequality didn't exist in Europe or North America). Certainly the sight of lepers outside the luxury hotels of Kolkata (formerly Calcutta) or pavement dwellers near the banking complexes of Mumbai is a shocking experience.

A fear of exposure to extreme poverty and suffering discourages some gappers, which is a pity because there is so much more to this vast land than its lepers. Stretching 2,000 miles from the Himalayas to the beaches of the Arabian Sea, this land is capable of allowing any visitor to construct a thrilling itinerary. A civilisation as ancient and as complex as this is in many ways incorruptible, and infinitely rewarding.

India has three main seasons: the hot season, lasting from April to June, followed by the monsoon, which continues until September and winter which lasts from November until March. South of Mumbai, light clothing can be worn year round, but in the more hilly regions warmer clothes will be needed. The best time of year is between October and March, when mid-day temperatures on the plains range from 21°C to 32°C. The south is always so hot that you will feel sweat trickling down your legs when you are sitting still. Keep up your liquid and salt intake to prevent heat exhaustion.

Spend time with your guide book and talking to experienced travellers before deciding where to go. Concentrating on one region will reduce the travel hassles, so that many choose Goa (once a hippie enclave, now a package resort) or the state of Kerala in the south, sacrificing the great sights of the Taj Mahal and the Pink City of Jaipur in the north for the less stressful south. Others concentrate on mountainous regions like the state of Himachal Pradesh (e.g. Dharamsala where the Dalai Lama resides) or Sikkim to the east (for which you will need to obtain a special permit). Visiting a holiday place favoured by Indian tourists or pilgrims is usually delightful and interesting. Try not to think of your first visit as a one-and-only because it is impossible to see more than a fraction of India at a time.

Whereas in most countries you get on a bus or train in order to be transported somewhere, in India you can view these modes of transport primarily as entertainment. Although buses are not necessarily cheaper than trains, they enable access to more remote regions and often they are faster than trains. Windows on ordinary buses often lack glass and so you may be afflicted by swirling dust in the dry season. The railways of India are a wonderful institution. After choosing where on the spectrum of comfort you wish to travel (air-conditioned with sleeping accommodation down to second class unreserved) you must patiently join all the requisite queues to purchase a ticket.

### TRAVEL TIP
*Try to sit as close to the front of a bus as possible since the suspension favoured in Indian buses means that if you are sitting near the back you have to find a fixed object with which to steady yourself.*

Food and accommodation are always easy to locate. India is predominantly vegetarian. Although meat is available, especially in the Mughal-influenced north, it is relatively expensive and more likely than vegetables to lead to digestive problems. Chillies-wise, food is much hotter in the south.

# Sri Lanka

**VISA**
None required for stays of up to 30 days; local extensions available (but are expensive).

**CURRENCY**
£1 = 183 rupees                    US$1 = 115 rupees

**BUDGET**
$20–$30 a day, but easy to spend more on lavish meals, etc.

Once thought of simply as a tropical paradise, this teardrop-shaped island nation off the east coast of southern India has had plenty to cry about in recent years. In addition to the ongoing communal violence between the Hindu Tamils of the north and the Buddhist Singhalese of the south, it suffered terrible devastation in the 2004 tsunami. The Foreign & Commonwealth Office currently advises against all travel to the Jaffna Peninsula and the areas in the north-west of the country. Since the Boxing Day disaster in 2004, a great deal of rebuilding has taken place and people can travel freely among these areas.

As was evident by the number of Britons killed and affected by the tsunami, Sri Lanka has become a very popular package tourist destination, partly because its scale and transport are more manageable than in India. Tourist hotspots such as Sigiriya, site of a ruined palace on top of a striking flat rock, Kandy the city in the interior where the Temple of the Tooth can be visited, and Hikkaduwa, home of many exiled surfers, all of these can become impossibly crowded in the high season (especially Christmas). But there are hundreds of less trammelled beaches and plenty of lush scenery, wildlife and smiling people to discover for yourself.

> **TRAVEL TIP**
> *In many ways Sri Lanka is an easy country in which to travel and a good introduction to Asia for the apprehensive traveller. You should be able to get round comfortably on $20 a day.*

One highlight that should not be missed is climbing the holy mountain Sri Pada, known as Adam's Peak. Thousands of pilgrims gather in the village of Dalhousie where the ascent to see Buddha's footprint at the summit begins. Most foreigners choose to set off at 2am to avoid the daytime heat and to enjoy the surpassing beauty of the sunrise, together with the otherworldly shadow which the peak casts on the cloud to the west just after sunrise. The climb takes about three hours, and many find the descent down all those 5,200 steps tougher on the muscles.

Meals are almost always vegetarian and rice is the staple. Coconut plays a large part in the diet and is mixed with chillies to make a delicious *sambal* or side dish. Sri Lankans think that a meal (including breakfast) without chillies is like a day without sunshine – vendors even sprinkle chilli powder on slices of fresh pineapple.

# Nepal

### VISA
Can be bought on arrival: £35 for 30 days, £75 for up to 90 days.

### CURRENCY
£1 = 118 rupees                          US$1 = 74 rupees

### BUDGET
$5–$10 a day if trekking, $15 otherwise.

Nepal is like another world after the heat, hustle and bustle of the Indian plains. For one thing, a quarter of the land surface is under ice and snow, and steeply terraced fields and villages can be found up to an altitude of nearly 4,500m. Trekking is one of the chief attractions. The scenery is as spectacular as everyone says and though the walking can be hard, the rewards are worth it. Many gap travellers spend an extended period on a volunteer programme in Nepal, many of which include an element of cultural immersion and adventure activities (see section on Nepal in the last part of this book, page 504).

About half the people are of Mongolian (Tibetan) descent. On the whole the people are friendly though more reserved than on the lowlands. There are only seven towns with a population exceeding 100,000 and three of those are in the Kathmandu Valley.

After a decade long campaign against the constitutional monarchy, the Maoist rebels have secured its abolition and formed the government. In June 2008, King Gyanendra and his family quietly moved out of his palace which was turned into a museum in 2009. Nepal's political problems have not completely disappeared but once again Nepal is a promising destination for a gap year. The FCO continues to urge trekkers to join group tours operated by reputable companies, although many of the standard treks (e.g. Pokhara to Jomson) can be done independently. The most popular trekking season is October/November. Trekking during the summer monsoon is possible though you may encounter flooded river paths, leeches and obscured views. Winter is fine for trekking provided you are carrying a good-quality sleeping bag for the very cold nights, and provided you don't plan to cross any high passes.

If you don't have the time or stamina for trekking, the huge Royal Chitwan National Park, south-west of Kathmandu presents a remarkable contrast with the mountainous north. It is the home of many jungle animals, including the rarely seen Bengal tiger and a decent population of rhinos, which can be seen more easily from the back of an elephant. Unfortunately ongoing poaching is a problem. Lodges inside the park are pricey, but you can stay in budget places in the village of Sauraha on the Rapti River.

# Pakistan

**VISA**
Buy in advance: £53 single entry, £76 double entry.

**CURRENCY**
£1 = 133 rupees                    US$1 = 83 rupees

**BUDGET**
$10 a day (even cheaper than India).

Pakistan is a destination favoured only by the more experienced traveller although its fascinating ethnic diversity and wonderful mountain scenery in the Karakorams are accessible to gap travellers too. Unfortunately, a number of terrorist bombs have gone off and the Foreign & Commonwealth Office is advising against all travel to Peshawar, the Swat Valley and Baluchistan. Large tracts of the country remain under-developed for tourists, which makes it attractive to those who are fed up with the backpacking crowds. One place that remains peaceable as it has always been is the gem of northern Pakistan, the Hunza Valley along the Karakoram Highway, which links the capital Islamabad with Kashgar in China. In this part of the world, you can get away with spending $10 a day without too much trouble.

# Bangladesh

**VISA**
Buy in advance: £40 in London, cheaper in Kolkata.

**CURRENCY**
£1 = 110 taka                      US$1 = 69 taka

**BUDGET**
$10–$15 (or even less) a day.

Relatively few travellers venture into Bangladesh, partly because of its uninviting reputation and also because of its inconvenient location. Bangladesh is something of a cul-de-sac because the border with Burma is firmly closed and so there is no route on into South East Asia. With an annual rainfall of over 200cm in many places, Bangladesh is one of the wettest countries in the world and is notoriously prone to flooding because the land is so low-lying. It is wise to avoid travel in the hot season (March to May) when the average daily temperature in Dhaka is about 32°C.

Like Pakistan, Bangladesh is a liberal Muslim state and local customs should be respected, especially during the holy month of Ramadan. English is less widely spoken than in India. The country is sited on two enormous river deltas, the Ganges and the Brahmaputra, and transport by boat is often preferable to travel by land. Many of the passenger services run by the Bangladesh Inland Water Transport Corporation use authentic old paddle steamers, though these are being replaced. Fares are remarkably cheap on the 350km trip from Dhaka to Khulna Ghat, and even first class is quite affordable.

# FAR EAST
## China

**VISA**

Buy in advance: £64.50 in London; quicker and cheaper in Hong Kong.

**CURRENCY**

£1 = 10.8 yuan                                    US$1 = 6.8 yuan

**BUDGET**

From $30 a day, more in big cities, especially Hong Kong and Shanghai.

Generalisations made about China in one year are bound to be obsolete in the next, since the pace of change in that country is astonishing. To take just one example, city roads that were clogged with bicycles just a few years ago are now jammed with cars, evidence of the sudden new affluence of so many Chinese people. Prices are rising fast, especially in Shanghai and Beijing.

You are unlikely to feel as warmly welcomed as you feel in either the Indian Subcontinent or South East Asia. Whereas in India you can always find someone who knows some English, this is not the case in China, and it can be a frustrating challenge trying to communicate to a taxi driver that you want to be taken to the bus station. Outside Beijing, Shanghai and the popular tourist spots such as Xi'an, home of the Terracotta Warriors (be prepared for feeling exploited and disappointed here), and popular stretches of the Great Wall, you may not come across many Western backpackers.

Travel within the People's Republic of China can initially be exasperating as you struggle with the inscrutable bureaucracy and the utterly incomprehensible nature of stations and airports (where little allowance is made for those who do not understand Chinese characters). Trains and buses go everywhere though it can sometimes be tricky reserving a seat or a sleeper (hard or soft class) especially at holiday times when locals book up everything in advance. (It is estimated that in the Golden Week around Chinese New Year, May Day and in October, up to 350,000,000 people are on the move.) Some long-distance buses offer sleeping couchettes.

It isn't always easy to spot a good restaurant in China, though you can usually find a dim sum restaurant where trolleys of steamed dumplings and hard-to-identify dishes are wheeled round to the tables and you can take what you like the look of. The squeamish should probably avoid markets such as the one in Guangzhou in southern China, where you will see civets and domestic cats in cages, and market traders skinning frogs and selling live scorpions. You might prefer to stick to the staple foods of glutinous rice, soy beans and cabbage. The kind of food you may have learned to like in your local Chinese restaurant is not at all easy to track down.

Hong Kong is the exception, and many travellers to Asia find themselves having a stopover in this great city at some point. The fabulous skyscrapers illuminated at night, the view from Victoria Peak (achieved by taking the very steep tram up the mountain) and ferry rides to other islands in Hong Kong harbour can all be enjoyed between shopping trips. Hong Kong is a good place to buy your Chinese visa (for instance from the China Travel Service) and board a train into Guangdong Province.

# Japan

### VISA
None for stays of up to six months.

### CURRENCY
£1 = 142 yen                                    US$1 = 90 yen

### BUDGET
$80–$100 a day – Japan is notoriously expensive.

Knowing a foreigner *(gaijin)* is a considerable status symbol for many Japanese, so you may find yourself befriended and spending time speaking very, very slowly in order to be understood. A glut of Westerners in Tokyo means that your welcome may be less than enthusiastic in that huge city where there is such a shortage of personal space. In fact non-Japanese are refused entrance to some Tokyo bars and restaurants. Many people head straight out of Tokyo for the ancient traditional cities of Kyoto and Nara with their temples and historic sites, which will seem like villages after Tokyo and where you can actually see trees.

The cost of living, especially in Japanese cities, is notoriously high. Any entertainment which smacks of the West such as going out to a fashionable coffee house or a night club will be absurdly expensive. However, if you are content with more modest indigenous food and pastimes, you can get by on $70 a day. A filling bowl of noodles and broth costs less than $10, though you may never take to the standard breakfast of boiled rice and a raw egg.

Accommodation will also be a significant expense. Private rooms can be rented at *ryokan*, which means Japanese-style guest house or in the countryside you can stay in *minshukus* (bed and breakfasts). *Gaijin* houses offer dormitory accommodation to foreigners for about half the price of a private room and there is a network of youth hostels too.

Finding your way around is nothing if not a challenge in a country where almost all road and public transport signs are incomprehensible. What use is an A–Z if you can't read the alphabet? Fortunately some signs are transliterated into *romaji* in the familiar Latin alphabet. Japanese people will sometimes go to embarrassing lengths to help foreigners. This desire to help wedded to a reluctance to lose face means that passers-by may offer advice and instructions based on very little information, so keep checking. Young people in jeans are the best bets. Outside the big cities the people are even more cordial. Wherever you go, you don't have to worry about crime.

Travel can be ruinously expensive. For example the high-tech bullet train from Tokyo to Sendai, a couple of hundred miles north, costs about $180 return. Tour operators do sometimes have special deals on train fares. For example, JR East (www.jreast.co.jp/e which operates in Kanto in Northern Japan) sells rail passes, for example a three-day pass for 10,000 yen which includes bullet trains. Even better value is the Japan Rail Pass available only to foreign tourists, which can be used on buses and ferries as well as trains. Prices start at less than £200 for seven days.

Shopping around for package tours is another good way to get to see Japan at the lowest possible price. Another option is hitchhiking, though it has to be admitted that there is virtually no tradition of hitchhiking in Japan. The risk is not of being left by the roadside or of being mugged but of being taken unbidden to the nearest railway station (which might be a major detour for the hapless driver who feels obliged to do this out of courtesy). Others will buy meals and refreshments and are genuinely interested in foreigners.

---

**TRAVEL TIP**
*The alienness of Japanese culture is one of the main fascinations of the place. It is foolish to become bogged down worrying about transgressing against mysterious customs, e.g. never blow your nose in public. In fact, Japanese people are more tolerant of foreigners than many give them credit for. Outside the metropolises, however, being pointed at, stared at and laughed at is commonplace.*

---

# South Korea

**VISA**

None for up to 90 days.

**CURRENCY**
£1 = 1,850 won                      US$1 = 1,165 won

**BUDGET**
$40–$50 a day.

Korean backpackers show up all over the world but there isn't much return traffic. The foreigners in Korea tend to be in the country for an extended period as English teachers. Visitors are often surprised to discover the richness and complexity of Korean history and culture, which is much less well known in the West than Japanese. Despite being a bustling metropolis of more than 10 million, Seoul has preserved some of its cultural treasures. The country's area is small, the public transport good, though traffic congestion at weekends can be a problem. Expect to spend as much as $50 a day if you are travelling around and staying in *yogwans* (traditional inns) or *minbaks* (homestay).

The people are friendly, though relationships between Western men and Korean women are sometimes disapproved of. Anyone missing home will gravitate to the area of Seoul called Itaewon, where fast food restaurants and discos are concentrated, not to mention pickpockets and souvenir rip-offs.

Most people do not associate Korea with mountain ranges but hill-walking is one of the main attractions, often in conjunction with visiting a Buddhist temple. You can climb Hallasan, a former volcano and highest mountain in the country, on Jeju Island in the south, and many scenic peaks in Sorak National Park. Gyeongju is one of the oldest cities in Asia and is best visited in the spring when the cherry trees are in blossom.

For the curious, it is possible to visit the Demilitarized Zone (DMZ) between South and North Korea, however it is not possible to enter the reclusive Democratic Republic from the south.

Not many people (including taxi drivers) speak much English, so if you are trying to reach an obscure destination, ask someone in your hotel to write the name in Korean.

# Taiwan

**VISA**
Not needed for stays of up to 90 days.

**CURRENCY**
£1 = 51 Taiwanese new $          US$1 = NT$32

**BUDGET**
$35+ a day.

Taipei has a rapid transit system which is far more enjoyable (not to mention safer and cheaper) than running a motorbike. Many hostels are located near the central station. In the old days, not a single visitor to Taipei, which is one of the most densely populated cities in the world, failed to complain of the pollution. But since the opening up of China, much of the industry has moved to the mainland and so the air quality has improved, though the million motorised vehicles haven't moved to China.

The typhoon season lasts from July to October bringing stormy hot humid weather and mouldy clothes. It is advisable therefore to head elsewhere, such as to the historic city of Tainan with many old temples. Kaohsiung on the south-west coast is a large industrial city but has the advantage of being near the popular resort of Kenting Beach and within reach of mountain campsites such as Maolin. The geographical advantage of Taichung further north is proximity to the mountains as well as a good climate and cultural activities. The tranquil East Coast National Scenic Area extends for nearly 200km along the Pacific coast. Volcanic mountains rise inland creating a wide range of eroded landscapes. If you have time catch a ferry to the tiny tropical island of Lanyu where the indigenous people are Yami rather than Chinese and where you can visit interesting caves.

Wherever you go, one of the highlights is the hospitality of the locals. Many Taiwanese will not accept a refusal of any food or drink offered, and even paying for meals or drinks can be a struggle. Shopping is a national pastime. Street markets are lively and colourful and can be found along alleys off main roads in the capital.

Taiwan is virtually crime-free. For the truly homesick there are some English-style pubs with pool tables and darts boards. Eating out is just as much a pastime in Taiwan as it is in Hong Kong. There are countless little family-run restaurants which offer delicious and inexpensive food. Taiwan is also a fruit-lover's paradise.

# TRAVEL RESOURCES

## USEFUL WEBSITES

**http://travelindependent.info**, useful snapshots of individual countries and a superb links page.

**www.thailandguru.com**, intended for expats living and working in Thailand but plenty of useful tips.

**www.travelfish.org**, '100% original Asia travel intelligence authored by dedicated travellers who know what they're talking about'. Covers Cambodia, Laos, Malaysia, Singapore, Vietnam and Thailand.

**www.pmgeiser.ch**, Pongu's travel guide to many countries in Asia including China and Japan.

**www.into-asia.com**, Thailand and Indonesia.

**www.theindiatree.com**, info and active forums.

**www.myanmar-travelnet.com**, maintained by a Berlin-based individual who loves Burma.

## USEFUL BOOKS

Lucy Ridout, *First Time Asia* (Rough Guides, 2006), £9.99.

David Stott and Annie Dare, *India Handbook* (Footprint Guides, 2009), £16.99. Good alternative to the usual Lonely Planet and Rough Guide offerings.

## TRAVEL READING

William Sutcliffe, *Are You Experienced?* (Penguin, 1998), £8.99. Satirical account of the wrong way to go about being a gap year traveller. The anti-hero Dave's travels in India are based on the author's own gap year.

Emily Barr, *Backpack* (Headline, 2001), £7.99. Novel about an obnoxious young Londoner who gradually comes to appreciate the joys of extended travel in Asia (while narrowly escaping murder by a serial killer).

Haing Ngor, *Survival in the Killing Fields* (Avalon, 2003), £9.99. Moving memoir of life under the Khmer Rouge. The author won an Oscar for his role as Dith Pran in the 1984 film *The Killing Fields*.

Denise Chong, *The Girl in the Picture* (Penguin, 2001), £8.99. The biography of Kim Phuc, the girl burned by napalm in the famous photo from the Vietnam War.

Daniel Mason, *The Piano Tuner* (Picador, 2004), £7.99. Beautifully evokes the atmosphere of Burma. Written by a young American medical student who spent a year on the Thai–Burmese border region researching malaria.

Peter Hessler, *River Town: Two Years on the Yangtze* (John Murray, 2002), £9.99. Author was a young American EFL teacher in a remote town in China called Fuling.

# AUSTRALIA AND NEW ZEALAND

The catchy, unmistakeably Australian, slogan, *So Where the Bloody Hell Are You?* adopted by Tourism Australia in one of its advertising campaigns, seems to be working. Australia and New Zealand have been hugely popular destinations for gap year travellers for many years, and yet don't seem to have become stale. Iconic images of the Sydney Opera House and Ayers Rock at sunset retain their power to attract.

## Australia

### CURRENCY
£1 = A$1.78                                      US$1 = A$1.08

### BUDGET
Minimum US$50 a day excluding travel

### THE LURE OF DOWNUNDER
Australia is like nowhere else on earth. If the beach–beer axis were just a tourism authority myth, people would soon desert the country. But it isn't a myth. Australia really can seem like one perpetual party held by sun-bronzed surfers in an endless summer. The frisson of the bizarre and dangerous wildlife just adds to the thrill (though, fortunately, stories are far more common than actual encounters).

In response to its phenomenal popularity as a destination for so many young Europeans, Australia has developed a massive industry to cater specifically for backpackers. Hostels, both official and private, are full of gap year travellers and working holidaymakers who will advise newcomers on the best travel deals and adventures, and the places to go to find jobs (see *Australia* chapter later in this book for information about working and the working holiday visa, page 518). Specialist travel offices specifically target the backpacking community, which in Australia includes everybody from people fresh from school to professionals in their 30s who choose to stay in 'backpackers' (the Australian word for hostels). Alluring possibilities present themselves at every turn – learn-to-surf tips, cave tours with Aboriginal guides, sailing adventures, winery visits, reef snorkelling and so on.

### TRAVEL TIP
*Some gappers are seduced into pre-booking too many of these before leaving home but when they arrive they see how many other choices there are.*

## VISAS

Buying a tourist visa in advance is compulsory. The paperless visa, the ETA (Electronic Travel Authority), must be obtained via a private agency such as Visas Australia (www. visas-australia.com) or from the Australian Immigration Department's website (www. eta.immi.gov.au), which will incur a fee of A$20. The dispensing of visitor visas has

# UNMISSABLE HIGHLIGHTS

- Snorkel at Magnetic Island on the Great Barrier Reef.
- Sample some McLaren Vale Shiraz wines at the cellar door.
- Wander round the ancient domes and gorges of the eerie Olga Rocks (Kata Tjuta) in the Red Centre.
- Join the Neighbours tour of Ramsay Street in Melbourne.
- Cycle round the car-free Rottnest Island near Perth, spotting quokkas (marsupials peculiar to the island).
- Hike the Cradle Mountain track in Tasmania.
- Catch a film at the open-air Moonlight Cinema in Perth.
- Buy provisions at the Vic Market in Melbourne for a picnic at Hanging Rock an hour north of the city.
- Feed the wild dolphins at remote Monkey Mia on the coast of Western Australia.
- Join the glamorous Sydney set, who descend on Bronte Beach for Sunday brunch.

in essence been privatised and specialist visa providers charge various fees. Among the cheaper providers are www.fastozvisa.com (0800 096 4749), which charges US$12/£7.50, and www.australiavisas.com, which charges US$18.

## GETTING THERE

Australia is within reach of many gap year travellers simply because of the falling price of international airfares. Per mile, the flight to the Antipodes is cheaper than most destinations, though recent tax hikes have increased the outlay required. Malaysia Airlines, Emirates, Royal Brunei and JAL often turn out to be the cheapest, although Qantas has been competing strongly with promotional fares of less than £700 return available through specialists like Austravel (0800 988 4676; www.austravel.com). The cheapest time of year to depart for Australia or New Zealand is between March and June, while mid-season prices are charged between July and November and again in February. Normally the cheapest fares go early, so as soon as you decide, start to shop around. Whatever you do, avoid flying in the weeks before and after Christmas.

Australia is almost always included in RTW tickets, which might add only £100–£200 to the cost of a straight return. So even if your main destination is only Australia it is worth thinking about a possible stopover in Asia en route. Spending time in South East Asia will guarantee that your travel fund will last longer, since the cost of living is much less in Phnom Penh than in Perth (see *Asia* chapter).

## GETTING AROUND

Distances in Australia are unimaginably greater than Britons are accustomed to and so you will have to give a lot of thought to how you can pare down your itinerary. Richard Branson's Virgin Blue (www.virginblue.com.au) has some good deals and his Pacific Blue flies across the Tasman to New Zealand. Sample Blue fares in 2009 were A$140 Sydney to Cairns and A$199 Melbourne to Christchurch (via Brisbane). Compare also the no-frills domestic airline Jetstar (www.jetstar.com.au), a subsidiary of Qantas.

If you plan a major tour of Australia you might consider purchasing a Greyhound coach pass although they are expensive. The all-Australia pass valid for 12 months costs an astronomical A$2,700. If you just want to get from one coast to another as quickly as possible, point-to-point tickets, e.g. Sydney–Adelaide (22 hours for A$150) are the best idea. Students and backpackers are eligible for the Rail Explorer Pass which gives six months of unlimited travel on the *Ghan*, the *Indian Pacific* and the *Overland* for A$590 plus fuel surcharges (+61 8 8213 4592; www.gsr.com.au/backpackers).

A multiplicity of private operators has sprung up to serve the backpacking market such as Oz Experience (which has a reputation as a party bus) and Wayward Bus. Firefly Express operates daily services between Melbourne, Sydney and Adelaide; a sample one-way Sydney–Melbourne fare is A$60.

Having your own transport is a possibility for groups of friends travelling together. Some places have second-hand cars and camper vans for sale which they will buy back at the end of your stay, for example Boomerang Cars in Adelaide (261 Currie Street; +61 414 882 559; www.boomerangcars.com.au) or Travellers Auto Barn in Sydney, Melbourne, Brisbane, Cairns, Perth and Darwin (www.travellers-autobarn.com). Expect to pay A$2,000+ for an old car (such as a gas-guzzling Ford Falcon) and more for a camper van; the more you spend the better your chance of its lasting the distance and being saleable at the end of your stay.

Car hire is expensive, but occasionally 'relocations' are available, i.e. hire cars that need to be returned to their depots. Just pick up the *Yellow Pages* and phone through the rental companies asking about for relocation deals, which is exactly what **Roger Blake** did when he wanted to travel from Adelaide to Melbourne:

> *The Great Ocean Road is renowned as one of the most scenic drives in the world and I was determined not to see it from a tour bus window. I phoned a hundred and one rental companies looking for a relocation (taking a vehicle back to its state depot due to one-way rental demands). I got lucky because they desperately needed one to leave the next day. Only a A$1 per day rental and they were so desperate that they even gave me a A$100 for fuel. So I spent the following three days on my own in a flash 4/5 berth Mercedes-Benz motorhome on the spectacular Great Ocean Road along the coast of Victoria. The whole drive is dangerously scenic. And the cost to me? A whopping A$63!*

Apollo Motorhomes lists the dollar-a-day campervan relocations it sometimes has available on its website (www.apollocamper.com.au/reloc.aspx). The best places to start are Cairns, Darwin, Adelaide and Broome, where drivers are sometimes even given several hundred dollars for fuel.

If you can't afford the luxury of organised transport or buying your own vehicle, you might be drawn to the idea of hitching a lift, though this has become an endangered pastime in Australia (as almost everywhere else). The Queensland coastal road has a notorious reputation. Violence is rare, but if you are unlucky you might be evicted from the truck unless you comply with the driver's wishes. Backpackers' hostels are a good bet for finding drivers going your way, provided you are able to wait for a suitable ride. Try also the lift-sharing forum on www.backpackingaround.com.au or www.shareyourride.net.

## BUDGETING

Although the cost of living is not high compared to Europe, especially for eating out, there are so many temptations for a gap year traveller that money seems to soak away like water poured on the Nullarbor desert. Living a relatively spartan existence will still cost A$50 a day. Because the tourism infrastructure for backpackers is so extensive, you have to pay out significant sums to access the Barrier Reef, take some surfing lessons, and so on. The effectively marketed Sydney Bridge Climb – 'for the climb of your life' – illustrates this perfectly. A dawn climb in peak season costs a whopping A$300 for 3 hours. If you are on a budget you will have to resist all these packaged adventures; for example you can walk or cycle across the bridge for nothing or pay A$9.50 to climb the 200 steps up the pylon at the southern end of the bridge which gives a superb view.

> **TRAVEL TIP**
> *Significant discounts on travel, accommodation, etc. are offered to people with a card that identifies them as backpackers including an international student card, YHA membership card or other backpackers' hostel group card such as VIP or Nomad (see next section).*

## ACCOMMODATION

Australia is incredibly well provided for with congenial hostel accommodation. The average cost of a dorm bed in a backpackers is A$22–$28. Often a double room costs only a little more per head, but these are often booked up ahead. Backpackers' accommodation provides more than just a place to sleep; they become the centre of your social life, and the bar or garden often fizzes with conversation about the next unmissable destination or activity. Many hostels hire out bicycles, put on local tours to places difficult to access otherwise, organise barbecues, picnics and adventure sports.

A free booklet listing all 140 YHA hostels is widely available (www.yha.com.au). One of the most successful groups of non-YHA backpackers' hostels is VIP Backpackers Resorts of Australia which is especially strong in New South Wales and Queensland (www.vipbackpackers.com). A booklet listing its Australian hostels is distributed far and wide or can be obtained from overseas by purchasing the VIP card for A$43, which gives discounts and benefits. Many VIP hostels have notice boards advertising jobs, flats, car shares, etc.

The Nomads Backpacker chain has about 25 hostels in Australia, many of them renovated pubs. Nomads (www.nomadsworld.com) sell a discount card called the MAD Card for A$35.

## WHAT TO EXPECT

The seasons in the Southern Hemisphere are opposite to those north of the equator and it can be difficult getting used to university terms downunder, finishing for the summer holidays in December and the ski season beginning in June. With luck you will bask in sunshine and swim in balmy seas. But Australia's vastness means that there are tremendous variations from zone to zone, encompassing alpine zones such as Tasmania and sub-equatorial monsoonal regions such as Darwin. July in Melbourne can be chilly and wet, and the annual rainfall in sunny Perth is higher than in London.

All Australians have been endlessly drilled to 'slip, slop, slap' – slip on a shirt, slop on some high factor sun protection and slap on a hat – and fair-skinned new arrivals should do likewise to avoid sun damage. Darwin and Cairns are true tropical cities and are therefore subject to rainy and dry seasons, invariably referred to in Australia as the Wet and the Dry. These areas are probably best avoided in the wet season, which lasts from about December to April. If you are there long enough to follow the seasons, you would ideally spend June–September in Queensland and the Red Centre, and then enjoy the long balmy evenings and sunny days of summer in the south-east.

Australia is an overwhelmingly urban culture that treasures its bush lore. While the people cling to the edges of their vast island continent (80% live within 20 miles of the sea) they glorify their untamed interior. Another endearing characteristic is their preference for leisure over work. At weekends everyone is at the beach, a barbecue or a sporting event. At their best, Australians can be gifted and colourful raconteurs. Be prepared to take some good-natured joshing, especially on the subject of cricket. Their quirky and ironic sense of humour, aversion to pomposity and prevailing geniality make for some lively conversations.

Eight million Britons have relations living in Australia. If you do set off with a list of addresses to look up and feel inhibited about making contact with strangers, give it a chance. Always make it clear you are a traveller on the move, rather than a freeloader (known locally as a 'bludger').

If the local people are friendly and benign, the wildlife is less cuddly. One of the more staggering facts about Australia is the number of aquatic nasties that will not hesitate to deliver a fatal sting, bite or snap. The chief menaces are sharks (though popular beaches are usually protected by sea nets), crocodiles and an unpleasant little creature known as a marine stinger. These potentially lethal creatures are known as sea wasps and box jellyfish, and are common on the coast of Queensland and the Northern Territory from December to March. The only sensible way to escape the threat is to follow the advice of signs posted on beaches and stay out of the water during the season.

Just as many dangers await on land, though of course very few backpackers actually come across any redback or trapdoor spiders, or deadly Western Taipan or Brown Snakes. They are far more likely to encounter maddening midges and sandflies; take plenty of strong mosquito repellent or use local concoctions such as tea tree oil, or mixing a third of Dettol with two-thirds baby oil (repulsive but effective).

# Sydney and New South Wales

Partying in Sydney is the sole ambition of many first-time world travellers. With one of the most magnificent settings of any city in the world (apart perhaps from Rio), a vibrant youth culture and a taste for hedonism, it is hard to imagine anyone not liking Sydney. Wherever you look there are hip little cafés, fantastic ethnic restaurants (many allow you to bring your own wine), great bookshops and plenty of ambience. Sydneysiders share with New Yorkers the easy confidence that their city is the Big Smoke. But unlike New York, a great deal of Sydney's life is lived outdoors whether swimming at Bondi Beach, listening to free entertainment in Martin Place downtown or supping a beer at a pavement café.

# EXCITING WAYS TO GET INVOLVED

- Take a jackaroo or jillaroo course before getting a paid job on a Queensland country property (www.leconfieldjackaroo.com).
- Stand up on your surfboard on the first day of a course at Byron Bay, New South Wales (www.mojosurf.com.au).
- Earn money by picking apples in the Huon Valley of Tasmania (www.huonvalleybackpackers.com).
- Get a few days well-paid casual work before and after major horse race fixtures in Melbourne (www.melbourneracingclub.net.au).
- Work a season in a ski resort in the Australian Alps (www.thredbo.com.au/about-thredbo/snow-jobs).
- Intern with an Australian PR firm (www.internships.com.au).
- Volunteer in the rainforest at a tropical research centre in far north Queensland (www.austrop.org.au).
- Teach at an indigenous school (www.lattitude.org.uk).

Most gap year travellers gravitate to one of the backpacker ghettoes and make it their base. Once-sleazy King's Cross has been somewhat rehabilitated, though many prefer one of the beach suburbs like Coogee or Manly (try the iconic Shark Bar in the New Brighton Hotel on the Corso), or leafy arty Glebe not far from Sydney University. Newtown has some hostels though is best known for its amazing range of eateries.

Many of the city's pre-eminent pleasures are free or very cheap – a ferry from Circular Quay to Manly Beach ('Seven Miles from Sydney and a Thousand Miles from Care'), a stroll through the Royal Botanic Gardens downtown (looking up to admire the resident colony of flying fox bats), poking around the colourful Saturday markets such as Paddington Market and Glebe Market or the amazing Fish Market (which sells all kinds of food) or nurse a drink at a Sunday afternoon session in a pub that features free jazz.

The sooner you leave Sydney, the better chance you have of not blowing all your money in a few weeks. Most head north along 'The Route' to the favourite backpackers' resort of Byron Bay and on to Queensland. Those who are heading south of Sydney have the chance to explore the wonderful South Coast, often overlooked by foreign travellers. Heading south, the so-called Sapphire Coast between Eden and Bateman's Bay is a favourite vacation destination for Australians.

The state boasts 58 national parks, which come in all shapes and sizes. The Blue Mountains, accessible on an hourly rail service from Sydney to Katoomba, are crisscrossed with walking tracks of varying degrees of difficulty. Even nearer the city, Ku-ring-gai Chase National Park features the Basin Track which leads you to some atmospheric Aboriginal rock carvings of hunters and kangaroos.

All manner of adventure tours can be booked in New South Wales. Among the most popular are a surf tour to Byron Bay and Crescent Head (for example with *Mojo Surf*; www.mojosurf.com.au).

# Queensland

Great expanses of the Queensland coast meet most people's expectation of paradise. Variations on the theme include the many offshore islands turned holiday playgrounds, the sleepy sugar plantation towns, the travellers' haven of Cairns and the outback wilderness beyond. What makes the coastline exceptional is the immense and fascinating Great Barrier Reef lying off most of the eastern shoreline, usually at least a 45-minute (expensive) boat ride away. Less paradisical – except in name – but still extremely popular, are the unabashedly commercialised resorts around Surfers Paradise on the Gold Coast.

As visitors from the southern states began to discover the hedonistic delights of the Gold Coast and the Sunshine Coast, Brisbane – the sleepy state capital that lies between these two touristic gems – began to shed its redneck image. Brisbane is now a curious mix of the crumblingly tropical, the handsomely colonial and the gleamingly modern, embroidered by pleasant parks and the slow, murky Brisbane River. But the condition of the capital is of little concern to the wide spectrum of visitors to Queensland. Most gappers head straight past and up the coast.

One essential reason for the popularity of Queensland is the glorious climate. Places such as Townsville plaster over all their promotional literature '300 days of sunshine a year'. Queensland's weather is sub-tropical in the south of the state and becomes more tropical the further north you go with a summer wet season (October or November to March).

A huge number of travellers trek through Airlie Beach en route to the Whitsunday Islands, often for a pre-booked inter-island sailing trip with a company such as Awegasmic Tours. Expect to pay A$100+ a day for a longish tour or A$200 a day for a shorter one which includes food, etc. Another highly recommended island destination is Fraser Island which is a gigantic sand island with lots of wildlife.

Most gappers end up signing up for a diving course, yacht cruise or four-wheel-drive expedition which they end up enjoying so much that they do not begrudge the drain on their travel coffer. Depending on your tastes, the sheer number of foreign backpackers on The Route can become oppressive. In Cairns, for instance, visitors entirely swamp locals, and competition for the tourist dollar is unceasing and sometimes bitter. But do not be deterred. Queensland is a vast state where it is the simplest thing to camp in a gregarious unspoiled little town or hike in a national park. Try for example Hinchinbrook Island, accessible by launch from Cardwell, with wild mountain scenery and plenty of wildlife. If you don't want to stay at the low key eco-resort where the boat lands, walk about 45 minutes to a simple campsite on the coast where the pleasure of eating oysters prised from the coastal rocks goes some way to compensating for the belligerent sandflies.

# Northern Territory and the Outback

To foreigners and Australians alike, the Northern Territory has traditionally been equated with Ayers Rock, or Uluru – the red rock rising from the red centre of Australia, symbolising the uniqueness of this country. Uluru is the world's largest monolith and its appearance rising suddenly from the stark desert is magical. Only when you get close to it does its massive scale become overwhelming. The most spectacular aspect is the change of colour that sometimes takes place at sunset and sunrise. When this happens, it lasts for only a few minutes but is captured by a thousand cameras. The scenes on the 'sunset strip' west of the rock can be almost comical, with visitors clamouring for the best photographic vantage point, as if waiting for the arrival of a celebrity. You can either climb the rock very early in the morning before the heat of the day makes it impossible or walk round the base (9.5km) pausing to look at paintings by the Anangu Aboriginal people for whom it is sacred.

Close to Uluru are the Olgas, a range emerging from the stark desert that many find even more intriguing. Nearby – always a relative term in the Territory – is the town of Alice Springs. Australia's Red Centre is semi-desert, with hot, dry summers and cold winters. At its heart is Alice Springs, which once epitomised the pioneering spirit of a nation, where visitors plan their assault on the Rock 450km away. One of the best tours is a three-day camping-under-the-stars trip with Mulga's Tours (www.mulgas.com.au); it includes Ayers Rock, the Olgas and Kings Canyon for A$250 plus A$25 entrance fee for Uluru National Park.

'The Track' or Stuart Highway is the central spine that covers the 1,500km distance between Alice and Darwin. Darwin, capital of the territory is surrounded by swamps, gorges and more than a few crocodiles. The north is tropical – hot throughout the year with a pronounced wet season, always referred to as 'the Wet', from November to April. You could easily blow A$1,000 visiting the places of interest around Darwin. Pre-eminent among them is Kakadu National Park, which is the state's other must-see destination. The supply of accommodation inside Kakadu is decidedly finite and should be booked ahead, especially during the high season. One of the most interesting places to stay is Kakadu Culture Camp (www.kakaduculturecamp.com), which is owned and run by an Aboriginal family, whose members are also qualified park rangers; the price is A$160 per person for dinner, breakfast and bed in a safari tent. Night billabong boat tours cost A$70. You can also pitch a tent next door for A$10 per person.

Local tour companies typically offer two, three or five day four-wheel drive trips to Kakadu featuring visits to waterholes to see wildlife, information about Aboriginal culture, bush barbecues and adventure activities such as canoeing and climbing. Although Kakadu is the most popular destination, you might consider the less visited Litchfield Park (Wangi), which is nearer Darwin; it has the scenic Tabletop Range as a backdrop, huge termite mounds, hot springs and waterfalls to compensate for a shortage of crocodiles. This is a feasible destination for people without a four-wheel drive.

> **TRAVEL TIP**
> *Remember that programmes run by local tour companies can be quite different depending on whether it is the Wet or the Dry.*

# Victoria and Tasmania

Although the smallest state in Australia (apart from Tasmania), Victoria contains as great a variety of terrain as any other state, encapsulating almost the entire range of Australian landscapes and climates in microcosm: from the Little Desert to the Snowy Mountains, rich pastures to rainforest, and tumbling vineyards to dramatic coastline. Victoria has a wealth of little-known natural attractions.

From the urban point of view, Victoria comprises both big-city style and small-town country life, laced with a fascinating colonial history. The sprawling city of Melbourne is the only rival to Sydney in terms of sophistication. Sydney has so successfully grabbed the limelight that Melbourne has been relatively neglected by travellers. In recent years the cityscape has shot skywards, old buildings have been renovated and the Yarra River foreshores cleaned up. The glitzy Federation Square piazza provides a focus for Melbourne culture with galleries, art cinemas and restaurants. As well as being a cultural mecca, Melbourne boasts the best sporting venues and arguably the finest food in the country.

Picturesque cosmopolitan neighbourhoods are dotted around the heart of Melbourne: St Kilda, once a seaside resort for the wealthy, now a trendified bohemian beachside suburb; Port Melbourne, a refurbished waterfront area; Carlton, Fitzroy and Richmond, paradises for cut-price gourmets. 'Ramsay Street' in a distant suburb can be visited on the official *Neighbours* tour for A$50 or you can make your own way to Pinoak Grove (train to Glen Waverly, bus 888 to Nunawading).

Outside Melbourne, the highest concentration of backpacker facilities is along the scenic Great Ocean Road (mentioned above). The 200km stretch of road hugs the coastline through picturesque seaside resorts then cuts inland through the lush forested hills of Otway National Park.

Tasmania is distinctly dissimilar to the rest of Australia, softer and damper than the dry environment of the mainland and with spectacular wilderness scenery which has turned it into an eco-destination, especially worth seeing if you are not going to make it to the South Island of New Zealand. Its reputation for wet weather, backwardness and the expense of getting to the island deter many would-be backpackers, thus indirectly preserving the unspoiled character of the island. The discount airline Jetstar advertises one-way fares Melbourne to Hobart for A$69, so the expense is not prohibitive.

The south-east has the historic capital of Hobart and some fascinating remnants of the island's past as a colony of penal servitude. Hobart's setting – overlooking the broad Derwent River estuary and surrounded by rugged hills – is more beautiful than that of any other state capital except Sydney. Salamanca Place with an excellent food market and free weekend concerts contains some splendid sandstone warehouses converted to a pleasant mixture of antique shops, galleries and restaurants, all within easy walking distance.

If your time in Tasmania is limited, get a flavour of the island by sailing or flying to Devonport and heading north-west. The top left-hand corner of Tasmania has the same ingredients of dramatic coastline, rugged mountains, towering forests and undulating pasture that the island possesses in such abundance.

The major hiking trail is the 80km Overland Track which takes five to eight days and passes Tasmania's highest peak, the 1,617m high Mt Ossa. It is so popular that it is necessary to book between November and April (www.parks.tas.gov.au) at a cost of A$160.

# Western Australia

Western Australia (WA as it is invariably known) is a vast and vibrant state with immense variety: the clean and cosmopolitan city of Perth and its pretty port of Fremantle, the fertile south-west and the wild northern regions with their rugged mountains and deserts. More than any other state, WA brings home the immense scale of the Australian continent. Because of the vast distance (and expense) involved in getting there, many gappers neglect it, missing out on a fantastic climate, a young and lively population dedicated to enjoying themselves and encounters with wildlife.

Perth's clubbing scene is centred on Northbridge. For a casual night out, watch for the special backpacker nights advertised widely which may involve three-hour happy hours and free or heavily discounted bar food. Two of the favourites are the Hip-e-Club in Leederville which hosts backpacker party nights on Tuesdays and Black Betty's in Northbridge where Wednesday evenings are 'Starving Student' evenings with discounted food and drink.

Obviously in a limited time it is not possible to see much of this vast state. From Perth you can travel down the lovely south-west coast to great surf beaches or far to the north to Monkey Mia, where dolphins happily frolic with swimmers, and laid-back tropical Broome, a backpackers' mecca. You can choose to get around by bus, by backpacker tour or something in between, the jump-on jump-off bus run by Easy Rider (www.easyridertours.com.au). Many other tour companies compete to take you to the famous Pinnacles, 230km north of Perth, weird calcified humps and pillars of eroded limestone, and to the gorges at Kalbarri.

# South Australia

Adelaide has a grace and charm lacking in bigger brasher cities. A beautifully planned and sited city, with suburbs on the seashore and the Adelaide Hills rising up to the east, it is a pleasant place to spend time on your trans-Australian travels. South Australia has a rich blend of varied coastline, fertile farmland (producing three-fifths of Australia's wine), rugged mountain ranges and seemingly endless stark desert.

In keeping with the relaxed lifestyle which they enjoy, natives of Adelaide and its environs are casual and friendly. Try the pubs and clubs around Hindley Street or clean-cut King William Street, or mix with the student fraternity at the University of Adelaide.

Adelaide is favoured with a continuous stretch of accessible sandy beaches, safe from sharks and overeager developers. From anywhere in the city you need only head west to find somewhere to lay your towel on the 32km of wide gently sloping beach. Don't expect the massive breakers of the Indian and Pacific oceans; the placid waters of Gulf St Vincent are protected from the high seas by the Yorke Peninsula and Kangaroo Island.

Nearly 10 hours driving time from Adelaide, Coober Pedy in the South Australian outback is a bizarre place which is mostly below ground. The name is Aboriginal for 'White Man's Burrow', which accurately describes the dwellings of the opal hunters who live here. The inhabitants escape from the unremitting summer heat by residing underground in homes hewn out of the rock. Several backpackers hostels are underground including the Opal Cave Bedrock Underground Bunkhouse on Hutchison Street (beds for A$23).

# New Zealand

**VISA**

Tourists from the UK need no visa to stay for up to six months. Information about the working holiday visa is given in the chapter on New Zealand near the end of this book.

**CURRENCY**

£1 = NZ$2.25                                          US$1 = NZ$1.36

**BUDGET**

US$40+ a day

## THE LURE OF NEW ZEALAND

New Zealanders sometimes refer to their country as 'Godzone' (God's Own) and assume that foreigners will agree with them that New Zealand combines most of the attributes of an ideal country (other nationalities are guilty of this too but with less justification). Travelling gappers will find themselves the object of much friendly interest and curiosity, which makes New Zealand uniquely attractive. Even people involved in the tourist industry often seem to take a more personal than commercial interest in visitors' welfare. It is hard to imagine a country where travellers will feel as safe and pampered as New Zealand.

New Zealand's spectacular topography is its real trump card. The natural wonders – volcanoes, glaciers, fiords – do not disappoint. This tiny country encompasses alpine ranges and mangrove swamps, glaciers and rainforests. The climate may come as a shock if you have been travelling in the hot, dry areas of Australia. Rainfall is terrifically high on the west coast of the South Island, where some of the country's foremost attractions are located. An entry in the visitor's book of a mountain hut on the Routeburn Track reads, '*In New Zealand you don't tan – you rust*'. But often it's balmy and beautiful.

Almost everybody seems passionate about sport. Not only do they avidly follow the fortunes of their national teams, they pursue outdoor activities themselves like tramping (i.e. hiking), sailing, skiing and diving. They are also amazingly innovative when it comes to exploring their remarkable country and have invented a host of sports and vehicles. The most famous is bungee-jumping, but there is also zorbing, surf-rafting, dune-surfing, rap-jumping (abseiling head first) and river sledging.

## GETTING THERE AND AROUND

Air New Zealand has been offering some very competitive return fares and also round-the-world fares lately. In 2009, a RTW fare to Auckland via Los Angeles and Hong Kong was costing £535 plus tax from Travelmood (www.travelmood.com). A stopover in Sydney could be added for as little as £50.

## UNMISSABLE HIGHLIGHTS

- Go tramping (i.e. hiking) in Tongariro National Park, familiar as the Land of Mordor in Lord of the Rings.
- Visit the albatross colony on the Otago Peninsula near Dunedin.
- Bodyboard down the sand dunes at Ninety Mile Beach in the far north.
- Go on the high-tech High Ride in New Zealand's National Museum Te Papa.
- Jump off a 102m platform above the Shotover River with an elastic band around your ankles.
- Eat sophisticated seafood at one of the trendy eateries on Auckland's Ponsonby Road.
- Go punting on the River Avon in Christchurch.
- Admire the stunning alpine views from the windows of the TranzAlpine train that crosses the South Island coast to coast.
- Explore the huge Polynesian flea market at Otara, a suburb of Auckland.
- Escape the crowds at thermal Rotorua by pedalling a hire bike around the lake.

If you are combining Australia with New Zealand without a RTW ticket, you should investigate the trans-Tasman airfares available from Pacific Blue as mentioned above. If flying within New Zealand, note that Jetstar mentioned above now flies domestic routes. Hope that your visit will coincide with a price war between Qantas and Air New Zealand on domestic flights. Recently Jetstar was advertising a one-way Auckland to Wellington fare of NZ$59 (carry on bags only).

Once in New Zealand, distances are so much more manageable and the scenery more varied than in Oz, that road travel is a delight. Backpackers often decide to buy a vehicle (from about NZ$1,500) or rent a car, though this is available only to those over 21. Car auctions are held on Sundays in the Auckland suburb of Manukau City or try the Ellerslie Car Fair in South Auckland or adverts in www.autotrader.co.nz. In the South Island, backpackers buy and sell cars via http://backpackerscarmarket.co.nz. Look for a vehicle with a couple of months of WOF remaining (equivalent to MOT in the UK).

The integrated coach network is operated by scheduled coach companies Intercity and Newmans. Investigate the coach passes including the innovative Flexipass (http://flexipass.intercity.co.nz) in which you buy a certain number of hours of travel, starting at 15 hours for NZ$169. The New Zealand Travelpass (www.travelpass.co.nz) permits unlimited coach travel plus one rail journey and the trans-Tasman ferry for a limited number of days of travel within one year; seven days of travel costs NZ$579 while 14 days costs NZ$1,283. You can also get cheaper passes limited to one island. But before booking any of these, investigate Naked Bus (www.nakedbus.com), which operates like Megabus in the UK and USA. If you book well in advance you can get some NZ$1 fares. They have also introduced bus passes to undercut their rivals.

In addition, there are private shuttle services between fixed points. Try, for example, Atomic Travel (www.atomictravel.co.nz) between Christchurch and Queenstown, Wanaka and Dunedin, or the West Coast Shuttle operating between Christchurch and Greymouth (mainly for skiers). The main backpacker companies with hop-on hop-off services in New Zealand are Stray Travel (www.straytravel.com), the Magic Travellers Network (+64 9 358 5600; www.magicbus.co.nz), which picks up from hostels around New Zealand, and Kiwi Experience (www.kiwiexperience.com), which has the reputation for being one giant pub crawl for 18–21 year olds.

New Zealand is famously welcoming to hitchhikers. A combination of friendly trusting locals and like-minded travellers with transport means that you don't usually have to wait long. To minimise anxiety try arranging a lift ahead via www.jayride.co.nz.

## BUDGETING

If you stick to all the free activities at your disposal like swimming and tramping and admiring the scenery, the daily cost might be NZ$50. But once you decide to try bungee-jumping or glacier-walking or go out to eat at foodie restaurants, the daily spend will be three times as much.

## ACCOMMODATION

New Zealand has a marvellous network of cheap and cheerful hostels and mountain huts for 'trampers'. Many hostels (also called backpackers as in Australia) belong to the YHA, the VIP network and Budget Backpackers Hostels group (www.bbh.co.nz) which has 320 member hostels and links to travel info. If you buy a membership card in any of these groups, you get a discount every time you stay in one of their hostels.

Camping on beaches, fields and in woodlands is generally permitted if you ask permission of the landlord. Some Department of Conservation sites with no facilities are free of charge, or you might be allowed to camp in the grounds of a hostel and use their facilities for a modest charge.

**CHARLOTTE SNELL** was lucky enough to be given a RTW ticket for her 21st birthday so that she could take the gap year she'd missed before university, before proceeding to do a law conversion course:

'My trip round New Zealand started in Auckland, where we hired a car and decided where we wanted to go in the next five weeks. Auckland itself I found largely uninspiring but the surrounding area was lovely, with Karekare Beach (where they filmed The Piano) being well worth a visit. Our first stop after Auckland was Russell (in the Bay of Islands) where sadly we encountered the worst rain in 50 years, meaning we quickly pushed on to Hahei on the Coromandel Peninsula. There the rain finally cleared and we saw some of the stunning coastline we'd been hoping for. From Hahei we went down to Rotorua – smelliest city in the world – and then on to Taupo. From Taupo we did the Tongariro Crossing, which seemed fully deserving of its reputation as New Zealand's finest day hike. Our next destination was Napier for some Art Deco architecture and more importantly some excellent wine tasting, and then finally down to Wellington, my favourite of the NZ cities we visited.

From Wellington we took the ferry across to Picton where we based ourselves while we explored the Marlborough Sounds by postal boat and the wine regions around Blenheim. Next stop was Nelson and a day trip kayaking in the Abel Tasman National Park (all white beaches and turquoise seas), after which we headed down the West Coast to a superb eco-friendly hostel near Westport. After Westport we made our way to the Franz Josef glacier where we did one of the full day glacier hikes. This was a real highlight and worth every penny, even if walking was a little painful the next day!

We took a leisurely drive to Queenstown, which is spectacular, but we weren't really tempted by any of the activities since I have a chronic fear of heights and my brother thought it was all wildly overpriced. We made *our way to Te Anau and used it as a base to visit Milford Sound and to equip ourselves for our four-day hike on the Kepler Track. This was an excellent, if challenging, four days with some stunning scenery, first class facilities and fun fellow walkers. I would definitely recommend doing one of the Great Walks, even to people whose usual definition of a walk is, like mine, around the shops. After the hike we headed down to Papatowai in the Catlins and then on to Dunedin. Dunedin was followed by a quick trip to Lake Tekapo through some gorgeous Canterbury landscapes, before we ended our trip in Christchurch. Overall I was working to a budget of about £1,000 and ended up going £200 over. We mainly stayed in BBH hostels which were good and averaged NZ$20 a night, but activities like kayaking were the biggest expenses.*

*The main highlights of New Zealand for me were definitely the endlessly spectacular and varied landscapes, some of the best of which you see from the car driving around, and the many outdoor activities you can do in them. My only regret would be that I went all the way to the home of the All Blacks and did not see a single rugby game!'*

# North Island

The North Island is far more densely populated than the South and Auckland is the biggest city, though Wellington is the capital. Whereas the most sensational geographical phenomena of the South Island are due to glaciation, the remarkable feature of the North is its volcanic history.

Auckland's harbourside location, complete with overcrowded bridge and rising number of excellent informal eateries, justifies a comparison with Sydney. But most backpackers head out of the city fairly promptly, often north to the Bay of Islands resort area. Paihia and Russell are jumping off points for experiencing the glorious ocean scenery of the Bay of Islands and also have many places of historical interest such as New Zealand's oldest church and the hotel with the oldest licence. A half-day walk from Opua to Paihia takes you through mangrove forest, populated by strange clicking crabs and snapping shrimp. From Auckland, others set out in a southerly direction, perhaps to the rugged and mountainous Coromandel Peninsula with its lovely unspoiled wilderness and empty beaches even in summer, or to sulphurous (and touristy) Rotorua.

Tongariro National Park, roughly half way between Auckland and Wellington, incorporates the highest peaks of the North Island, all active volcanoes so that the ground is hot to the touch. Many gappers choose to walk the Tongariro Crossing, a long one-day traverse between Mt Tongariro and Mt Ngauruhoe, which Peter Jackson (New Zealand director of *Lord of the Rings*) chose to stand in for Mt Doom.

Wellington is another Antipodean city with a magnificent setting, with steep hills descending to the spacious harbour. For such a small city Wellington is surprisingly cosmopolitan, with a fantastic range of restaurants representing every imaginable cuisine. Don't miss visiting Te Papa and Courtenay Place, a centre for eating out. The splendid National Museum of New Zealand, Te Papa (www.tepapa.govt.nz) features excellent exhibits on Maori and Polynesian culture and an interactive display called Awesome Forces in which an earthquake and volcanic eruption are simulated (free admission).

From Wellington, you can catch the scenic Interislander ferry to Picton on the South Island. The one-way fare for a foot passenger starts at NZ$58 with a student discount.

# South Island

Some say that the further south you travel from Auckland, the further you travel into the past, ending at a fisherman's house on Stewart Island with no electricity, motor car or telephone. Travelling south along the east coast you will pass through laid-back Kaikoura famous for whale-watching and on to the third city of New Zealand. Christchurch continues to promote itself as the most English city outside England: punting takes place on the River Avon, uniformed school boys can be seen cycling home and a red double-decker bus takes tourists on city tours. There are many lovely beaches within easy reach of Christchurch, such as the charmingly named Taylor's Mistake and Scarborough Beach at Sumner for surfing. A little further away is the Banks Peninsula which has a feeling of remoteness. Try the superb fish and chips in the main resort on the peninsula, Akaroa.

Over on the west coast, the spectacularly pristine Franz Josef and Fox Glaciers are worth examining up close. Fox Glacier Guiding (www.foxguides.co.nz) is one of several companies offering hiking tours and ice adventures to suit all fitness levels. An alternative independent walk is to Robert's Point, which is situated beside Franz Josef Glacier, affording good views of the blue and deeply crevassed surface of the glacier. The three-hour walk through dripping temperate rainforest is not overly strenuous, though the slippery stream crossings can become a little tricky and, as throughout New Zealand, people who suffer from vertigo might not enjoy the swing bridges and rockface ladders.

If you have seen just one glossy New Zealand calendar, chances are that the photos of mountains, lakes and fiords were taken in the south-west corner of the South Island, an area of sublime landscapes. Even more attractive to many gap travellers is the social scene and possibilities for adventure in Queenstown, capital of Fiordland. Not many backpackers can withstand the pressure to participate in at least one of Queenstown's attractions; in fact there's not much point in coming unless you do. You will be subjected to a barrage of enticing offers not to miss happy hour, to dabble in a dangerous sport or plan an excursion further afield to Milford or Wanaka. Despite the huge number of beds in Queenstown, it is a good idea to book ahead in the summer and also during the ski season if you want a central location. The busiest time of all is the Winter Festival at the end of June.

## EXCITING WAYS TO GET INVOLVED

- Become a volunteer hut warden for the NZ Department of Conservation (www.doc.govt.nz).
- Earn money by picking kiwifruit in the Bay of Plenty, New Zealand (www.seasonalwork.co.nz).
- Exchange your help for free room and board at a horse trekking centre in New Zealand (www.wwoof.co.nz).
- Work a season in a ski resort in the New Zealand Alps (www3.nzski.com/employment/welcome.jsp).
- Teach at an indigenous school (www.lattitude.org.uk).

You are bound to meet backpackers freshly back from tramping one of the great long-distance routes of the South Island, such as the Abel Tasman, the Routeburn or the Kepler. This is the quintessential New Zealand experience and not to be missed.

## TRAVEL RESOURCES

### USEFUL WEBSITES
**www.australia.com**, official site of the Australian Tourist Commission.
**www.citysearch.com.au**.
**www.australianexplorer.com**.
**www.backpackerboard.co.nz**, lots of useful job info and tips on budget travel for backpackers in New Zealand.

### USEFUL BOOKS
*Bug Australia: The Backpacker's Ultimate Guide* and *Bug New Zealand* (both Explore Australia, 2008), £12.99. A change from the usual guidebook series.

## TRAVEL READING

Peter Carey, *True History of the Kelly Gang* (Faber and Faber, 2004), £8.99. A journal-style book that brings to life the harsh realities of life in 19th-century Australia.

Thomas Keneally, *The Commonwealth of Thieves: Story of the Founding of Australia* (Vintage, 2006), £9.99. A lively depiction of the Sydney experiment, of founding a penal colony.

Clive James, *Unreliable Memoirs* (Picador, 2008), £7.99. Television presenter and author's engaging memoirs.

Nevil Shute, *A Town Like Alice* (House of Stratus, 2000), £7.99. Alice Springs is the setting for this endearing tale about an English woman who is a prisoner of war in Malaya, but then finds love and settles in the Australian outback.

Patrick White, *Voss* (Vintage, 1994), £8.99. Novel with detailed descriptions of colonial life in Australia.

Murray Bail, *Eucalyptus* (The Harvill Press, 2000), £7.99. A romantic tale set in the countryside of New South Wales.

Keri Hulme, *The Bone People* (Picador, 1986), £8.99. Booker prize winner about a reclusive artist, a Maori factory worker and his mute young son, with poetic evocations of South Island landscapes.

Janet Frame, *An Angel at my Table* (Virago Press, 2008), £12.99. Autobiographical account of the author's mental breakdown and years spent in a NZ mental hospital.

### FILMS ABOUT DOWNUNDER

*Many excellent films have come from Australia such as* **10 Canoes** *filmed in remote Arnhem Land and with characters speaking in an indigenous Aboriginal language and* **Jindabyne** *(by the same director as the excellent* **Lantana***) which confronts tensions between white and Aboriginal communities. Also recommended is* **Rabbit Proof Fence**. *Classic films such as* **Picnic at Hanging Rock, Breaker Morant, Gallipoli** *and* **My Brilliant Career** *are good not just as movies, but as comments on aspects of the Australian character and situation.* **Priscilla Queen of the Desert, Muriel's Wedding** *and* **Strictly Ballroom** *are all wonderfully quirky Australian films. You probably won't want to see* **Wolf Creek** *before setting off on a trip to the outback. Baz Luhrmann's over-the-top* **Australia** *(2008) is thoroughly enjoyable.*

# LATIN AMERICA

The Latin American continent is inconceivably vast, stretching from the Caribbean tropics, round the equator, and down to the icy Antarctic glaciers of Patagonia. It is a land of superlatives, home to the world's tallest waterfall, driest desert, largest rainforest, longest river, southernmost city, biggest carnival and most remote tribes. With many places well geared up for tourism, and its wealth of cultures and landscapes, it is an exciting place to explore, whatever your interests. Its mixture of opposites is fascinating, with the Virgin Mary and *Pachamama* (mother earth) worshipped at the same altar, and ancient ruins, colonial architecture and modern cities all vying for attention. Most journeys will take in the monumental (like the Inca fortress Machu Picchu in Peru and the Mayan temple city Chichén Itzá in Mexico), the natural wonders like Iguazu Falls or the Costa Rican cloud forests. Yet even the everyday sights and experiences in markets and bus stations rarely fail to charm visitors.

The gringo trail may be a well-trodden route, but there are still plenty of things left to discover, and those willing to explore further afield, on local 'chicken buses' and to the smaller indigenous towns and villages are likely to be taken aback by the warmth of the people they meet. The Latin passion for life can be infectious, which isn't hard to understand given that fiestas, impassioned football matches and delicious food are all features of daily life. This exoticism leaves many young travellers captivated, but of course it isn't all parties and *playas* (beaches). Some of the world's poorest citizens live in the *favelas* (slums) of Brazil or the *barrios jóvenes* (squatters' settlements, literally young districts) of Lima and Mexico City. The rise of urban poverty is alarming, and is partly why so many Latin Americans are so highly politicised. The region is experiencing a shift leftwards and you are likely to bump into *manifestaciones* (protests) or *huelgas* (strikes) at least once. Less romantic than the ubiquitous face of Che Guevara would have you believe, these can often affect bus routes and travel plans, although thankfully this is probably the most serious it'll get – the days of guerrilla forces and civil war are long gone in all but a very few regions on this map. Should this stir your social conscience, opportunities for volunteering in the Americas abound, as detailed later on in this book. This, as well as allowing you to stay put for a while to learn the language, is by far the best way of experiencing the continent, offering an intimacy with people and places that seems distant along the standard gringo trail.

## CLASSIC ROUTES

Latin America provides thousands of diversions, and it is relatively simple to put together a route that combines a variety of natural settings, from mountain ranges to jungles and rainforests laden with wildlife, and the mysterious ruins of ancient empires, to chill out beaches, sleepy colonial towns and modern metropolises with their lively nightlife.

# UNMISSABLE HIGHLIGHTS

- Hike to the awe-inspiring lost Inca citadel of Machu Picchu.
- Soak up Carnaval in Rio: music and dance are Latin America's lifeblood, and this party tops them all.
- Dive in the Bay Islands, Honduras (world class scuba-diving at rock bottom prices) where, if you time it right, you can swim alongside the world's most majestic fish, the whale shark.
- Lose yourself in the Amazon by taking a slow boat trip from Peru to Brazil.
- If your budget doesn't stretch to the Galápagos, head to Tortuguero, Costa Rica to watch giant sea turtles lay their eggs on the sand by night.
- Live it up like an Argentine in Buenos Aires: sample the you've-got-to-taste-it-to-believe-it steaks, washed down with fine yet affordable vino, then catch a match at the La Boca football stadium or party at a milonga (tango club) till dawn.
- Take a salar trip in Bolivia: surreal multicoloured lakes and geysers next to the endless white of the world's largest salt flats.
- Time travel in Cuba: an island with a revolutionary past and a rebellious present — it looks like it's stuck in the 1950s, yet feels on the brink of massive change.
- Marvel at indigenous medical knowledge and take a leaf, literally, out of the locals' book: chew coca or drink coca tea for altitude sickness in the Andes.
- Go down Potosí's cooperative mines in Bolivia and get to grips with the extreme conditions the miners put up with in the hope of striking gold.

You will have to rein in your ambitions to see too much since if you just rush around ticking off sights, you will come away exhausted and with very superficial impressions.

## CENTRAL AMERICA

Making a zig zag up or down the long thin region of Central America will allow you to visit sights on the Caribbean and Pacific coasts as well as cooler inland hill towns and volcanoes. With one-way fares from London to Mexico City coming in at £250 (on Iberia, October 2009) and £359 return, this is a sensible place to start. Head south to the Yucatán peninsula via Palenque, where you can take in the Mayan ruins at Chichén Itzá. Continue down to the temples at Tikal over the border in Guatemala, rising up from the jungle canopy – breathtaking at dawn. Have a break from ruins at the picturesque Lake Atitlán, surrounded by Mayan villages, perhaps followed by a Spanish course in Antigua or an aside to the famous market town of Chichicastenango. Head east to Copán in Honduras, and then onwards to the Caribbean island of Utila – one of the cheapest places in the world to pick up a PADI dive qualification. If time and budget still allow, travel through Nicaragua's colonial cities of León and Granada down to Costa Rica. Here you have endless eco-tourism opportunities, from the turtle nesting beaches of Tortuguero to the zip wiring in the Monteverde cloud forest. The Arenal volcano spouts fire by night, and you can get off the beaten track in the southern Corcovado National Park. Fewer gap travellers venture further south to Panama, but the ones who do are rewarded with a spot of island hopping in the idyllic Bocas del Toro region. Flying home from San José, capital of Costa Rica, will set you back at least £400, and flights entering Mexico City and leaving San José can be found for less than £600.

## PATAGONIA AND THE SOUTHERN CONE

If you're into the outdoors, Patagonia offers some of the most impressive hiking and scenery in the world. Fly into the Big Apple (Buenos Aires), and head for the Península Valdés for whale watching. Bus or fly to the world's southernmost city, Ushuaia, and spend time checking out the remote Tierra del Fuego (land of fire) National Park. Not far north are the glaciers at Calafate and the beautiful lakes and volcanoes of the Torres del Paine on the Chilean side of the border. Continue to the Lake District and perhaps stop in Bariloche for the skiing between June and September. Rediscover urban pursuits in the many good eateries and drinkeries of the Chilean capital Santiago or Mendoza before heading north into Bolivia on the train, to pick up the next route.

## THE WEST

Start with a trip to the surreal Salar de Uyuni, a desert of salt in south-western Bolivia with geysers and multicoloured lakes (easily accessible from Chile or Argentina). Proceed by bus to Potosí and descend into the silver mines before appreciating the colonial charm of Sucre or the hectic Cochabamba market en route to La Paz. Explore the nearby mountains and valleys, bike down the world's most dangerous road and perhaps divert to Rurrenabaque for a jungle or pampas trip. The stunning Lake Titicaca and the Isla del Sol are worth a few days, and are far less commercialised than the floating islands on the Peruvian side. From here head to Cusco and hike the Inca trail to Machu Picchu (though be aware you have to book this in advance and be accompanied by a guide). Explore the Sacred Valley before setting out on a rainforest trip in the Manu National Park. Continue up the coast, try sand boarding and surfing, with a possible detour to the mysterious Nasca lines, before crossing into Ecuador. From here an aside to the Galápagos and its unique wildlife would be pricey but unforgettable. Quito and Cuenca are perfect for Spanish courses (especially if you are doing this trip in reverse) and you could wind up relaxing on any one of Ecuador's Pacific beaches. You will have to give serious thought to whether or not you want to include Colombia in your travels since it is one of those countries that everyone warns you about, mentioning kidnappings of foreigners. On the other hand many who have braved it have told tales of safe, easy, enjoyable travel in this beautiful, little-visited country, especially in the lovely old town of Cartagena, and you may decide the risks are minimal as long as you avoid dodgy areas.

## THE EAST: BRAZIL AND THE AMAZON

Fly into Rio and enjoy the beaches and nightlife before nipping across to the spectacular Iguaçu Falls (just as accessible from Argentina). From here head for the Pantanal for outstanding wildlife viewing and back to the coast, taking in the musical Salvador before arriving in Belém, gateway to the Amazon. Take a boat to Manaus, the jumping off point for trips into the wild interior. From Manaus go northwards to Guyana for the impressive Kaieteur falls, and a unique mix of Caribbean, African and European cultures, and continue on to Venezuela (more waterfalls here... including the record breaking Angel Falls).

**TIM TAYLOR** designed an ideal route from Cancún, Mexico, down, around and across to Rio de Janeiro, Brazil, but then had an even better time when he missed his first flight:

'With a backpack full of clothes, a bloodstream full of inoculations, and a passport full of potential, I was all set. When I was delayed by US Immigration in New York and forced to miss my flight, I took the first flight to Central America which was to San José and all of a sudden I was just going to have to wing it, which would prove to be the more fulfilling way to travel.

*As a tourist destination, Costa Rica is more commercially advanced than its near neighbours. Thus it was a perfect place to comfortably spend the first days of a year travelling alone. The fact that Costa Rica has become a popular travel destination, especially for the US tourist, means the dollar has flooded the market and pushed up the prices. However, I found with great surprise that the other countries that make up the vertebrae of Central American offer the same experiences only at lower costs. I whiled away many days at the rainforests of Panama, the volcanic lakes of Nicaragua, the diving resorts of Honduras, the surf zones of El Salvador, the remarkable Mayan ruins of Guatemala, and the crystal waters of Belize, most notably diving the Blue Hole beside the Barrier Reef. From Belize I ventured up Mexico's Yucatán Peninsula, skipping among Mayan ruins, until I reached the urban metropolis of Cancún for a bargain priced flight to Cuba.*

*Cuba is a country unlike any other I have visited. It requires far more than the two weeks I had to do it justice. It takes almost that long just to comprehend the dual-currency system. At the moment, Cuba is not set up for wandering backpackers, especially not a lone one. There are no hostels as such. As a budget traveller I stayed in* casas particulares *– government-controlled homestays. Havana is a lively, cultured, buzzing city, and the Museum of the Revolution gives a fascinating (if not altogether balanced) account of Fidel Castro's rise and reign. I had enough time to ride the tourist-only buses around the western half of the island, dropping in on the colonial city of Trinidad, the Che Guevara Memorial at Santa Clara, and numerous beautiful beaches. But before I blew my budget, it was time to move on to the South American mainland.*

*I travelled along the north coast from Colombia – highly under-rated and exceptionally friendly and safe for tourists – and into Venezuela, crossing over into Guyana and gradually working my way along the Amazon River and into Peru. The slow passenger boat from Manaus is one of those experiences I appreciate far more now it's over (secondary enjoyment). Five days of cramped and smelly conditions, continuously watching your belongings, eating cold rice and beans, while tip-toeing along mile after mile of vast river. Yet, it was the most awe-inspiring journey of my entire trip.*

*In contrast to my Amazonian adventure, I stuck with the highlights programme for Peru, Ecuador and Bolivia. The ancient and mysterious Nasca*

*Lines, the strange reed islands upon Lake Titicaca, and amazing Andean hikes in Peru, the pièce de résistance being the spectacular Inca Trail to Machu Picchu.*

*In Ecuador, straddling the eponymous equator, a quick jaunt to evolution's gift of the Galápagos Islands, and more amazing Andean hikes. In Bolivia, a tour of the unimaginably inhumane working conditions of the Potosi mines, the blinding white splendour of the salt deserts at Salar de Uyuni.*

*My next campaign was supposed to be a journey to Patagonia, zigzagging southwards between Chile and Argentina. However, the southern hemispherical seasons, and more accurately my inept knowledge of them, conspired against me. So in mid-June I cut the journey short, and began working my way slowly towards Rio de Janeiro instead.*

*With the final days of an incredible year rapidly disappearing, I am acutely aware that I have but scratched the surface of a remarkable and varied continent. For every 'thing to do' I tick off one list, another two are added to the 'what I mustn't miss next time' list.'*

Luckily British nationals can travel to all the countries of South and Central America without a visa, though they will need one for Cuba and one or two other Caribbean nations. North Americans should check beforehand since they do require visas for Brazil (for a whacking $150) and a few other countries.

## GETTING THERE

For students the cheapest deals can often be found with STA Travel, although their discounts will really come into their own when booking open-ended and multi-destination flights. The biggest hubs and therefore cheapest destinations from Europe are Buenos Aires, Rio de Janeiro, Mexico City and San José. It is also worth keeping an eye on special promotional fares offered by British Airways and Iberia. Best prices for return fares from London at the time of writing were: £425 to San José, £420 to Rio, £550 to Quito, and £500 to Buenos Aires. If wanting to split your trip between two cities, it can make sense to buy an open-jaw ticket, flying into one and out from another. Expect to pay £680–£750+ for instance to fly into Mexico City and out of Buenos Aires, or into Buenos Aires or Rio and out from Lima. Flight prices go up around *Carnaval* in Rio (40 days before Easter) and Inti Raymi (the all-important Inca festival of the sun around the winter solstice in June) in Cusco, so you must weigh up the desire to experience such events against your budget.

Two fully-bonded London-based agencies that specialise in travel to and around this area of the world are Journey Latin America (www.journeylatinamerica.co.uk) and South American Experience (www.southamericanexperience.co.uk), which along with STA consistently offer the lowest fares and the most expertise.

## GETTING AROUND

Travel around the region can involve many twists and turns, and these are not just on the roads themselves. Following in the tracks of the young Che Guevara as seen in the film *The Motorcycle Diaries* is, unfortunately, the exception rather than the rule, and most travellers will find bus travel the most affordable and convenient. Every country has an extensive bus network, with varying levels of comfort on offer. In Argentina, paying a few extra pesos will get you fully reclining seats, waitress service and complimentary champagne, while at the other end of the scale, in most of central America the fabled 'chicken buses' ply the long route between cities, stopping at every single village on the way, to pick up seemingly impossible numbers of people and sacks of produce, including those chickens.

Slicker, direct tourist buses of course exist alongside these (at about 10 times the speed, and price), although there is certainly much to be gained from travelling alongside local people. You'll come away with far more authentic impressions of a place, and getting to know your fellow passengers – especially the two or three with whom you are sharing a seat – will make the time race by (even if the vehicle doesn't). Night time bus travel is also a good way forwards: you save on accommodation and can knock off some of the hours sleeping (bring a blanket along Andean routes, temperatures plummet after sundown). Think carefully however about arrival times, and whether you want to turn up in a bus station in the small hours of the morning, bearing in mind that sleepy, disorientated gringos with bulging backpacks are prime targets for thieves. Many hostels offer pick-ups from bus stations; it's worth booking ahead and securing this if the bus terminal area has a dodgy reputation, as is not infrequently the case. Booking in advance for popular routes and at festival times is a good idea, although tickets bought on the day tend to cost less than those booked beforehand; and getting to the bus terminal at the specified hour – 90% of the time the bus will leave late, but naturally the one time you count on this and turn up late, it will doubtlessly have left you behind.

> **TRAVEL TIP**
> *Keep your wits about you at all times on buses; it's not uncommon for people to wake up and find their wallet missing from their hand luggage, even if they fell asleep with it in their lap.*

The other option for inter-regional travel is by air, the only answer if you are short of time, or can't face another 24-hour rollercoaster bus journey along winding unpaved roads. Short internal flights with national carriers, such as Bolivia's *Amaszonas*, or Honduras' *Sosa Airlines* can cost as little as $25, and bargains are usually available at the last minute as well as in advance. Like buses, flights are subject to inexplicable delays or changes in schedule – *Taca* being a notorious culprit – so try to remain as flexible as possible, and embrace the exasperation!

Certain airlines such as LAN or Brazil's TAM offer flight passes in the region, which represent good value only if you want to cover a lot of ground. The prices of the individual flight sectors depend on the distance and how mainstream the routes are. For example the LAN Visit South America Airpass mainly covers flights within Chile, Argentina and Peru. Sample prices (excluding taxes) are Quito to Lima for $135–$160; Lima to Bogotá $416; Santiago to Easter Island $427–$549 each way. TAM's pass costs $639 and covers up to four flights within Brazil allowing a maximum stay of 30 days. In both cases, the cost of airpass sectors is reduced significantly if you have arrived on an international flight with the relevant airline.

Rail and river travel are also feasible in some areas, yet these are usually the attraction in themselves rather than a means of getting somewhere. Notable exceptions are in the Amazon basin, where roads are scarce, and at Machu Picchu, which can only be accessed by trek or by (extortionately priced) train. It is also worth noting that in many developing countries, heavy rains can render certain routes impassable, so plan your itinerary carefully in the rainy season (mainly January–March), and ask around before setting out.

As far as local travel goes, taxis and minibuses are the most widespread. Taxis can be licensed or unlicensed, and while the former is clearly safer, it is almost impossible to avoid the latter, since many car owners keep a taxi sign in the window, simply to earn a little pocket money. As a rule these aren't dangerous, however be more vigilant when sharing a taxi with others (known as a *colectivo*), and a young woman travelling alone might feel uncomfortable getting into a *colectivo* with only male passengers. The cheapest way of getting around urban areas and their immediate environs (rarely more than a dollar) is by minibus. Known as *combis*, *flotas*, *micros* and myriad other names, these abound in most cities and towns, and are manned by a sort of conductor figure – this is usually a 10-year-old boy, hanging out the door and shouting the destinations at top volume. Just listen for your stop and hop on.

For information on travel in Latin America, it might be worth joining *South America Explorers*, which maintains clubhouses in Lima, Cusco, Quito and Buenos Aires (www. saexplorers.org); membership costs $60 or $90 for a couple.

## WHAT TO EXPECT

The real reason travel in Latin America is rewarding is the attitudes and customs of the people you meet. Latinos are incredibly open and talkative by nature, and visitors who learn some Spanish or Portuguese before or during their trip will find casual conversations with local people one of the most enriching aspects of their trip. No visitor can fail to notice the vast inequalities between today's Latin Americans, with cities such

# EXCITING WAYS TO GET INVOLVED

- Learn to speak Spanish at an eco-hotel in rural Nicaragua (www.spanishschoolnica.com).
- Fix up a work experience placement in accounting, marketing or journalism in Ecuador (www.elep.org).
- Join an expedition in the jungles of Belize (www.trekforce.org.uk).
- Help street children in Rio (www.taskbrasil.org.uk) or Quito (www.cenitecuador.org).
- Join a diving course on the Caribbean coast of Venezuela (www.gapyeardiver.com) or train as a ski instructor in Patagonia (www.peakleaders.co.uk).
- Subsidise a stay on the Galápagos Islands by becoming a student volunteer at the Charles Darwin Research Station (www.darwinfoundation.org).
- Teach English in remote Peruvian villages (www.ecotrekperu.com) or in coastal Ecuador (www.childrenecuador.com).
- Protect turtles in Mexico (www.experiencemexico.co.uk) or maintain forest trails in Costa Rican national parks (www.asvocr.org).
- Arrange a working holiday in Chile's tourist industry (www.chileinside.cl).
- Intern at a dive shop in Honduras while acquiring a PADI scuba diving certificate (www.subwaywatersports.com).

as Rio showcasing the flashy lifestyles of the wealthy, just around the corner from the unimaginable poverty of the slums. Begging is not as widespread as in, say, Asia, but in large cities you will certainly come across entire families living on the streets. It is impossible to ignore the fact that these are almost always indigenous people, whose rights and identities have been trampled on since the first European conquistadors set foot on the continent. Always use the word *indígena* as opposed to *indio* (feminine *india*) when referring to indigenous people, to show respect.

Another aspect Westerners may find frustrating is the *mañana* attitude prevalent, well, everywhere. '9am sharp' means sometime before noon; bureaucracy moves at a snail's pace, and buses will leave when they feel like it. Female travellers may resent the Latin *machista* attitude: catcalls will follow most fair-skinned females (particularly blondes), and while these are generally of a harmless appreciative nature, it can be trying at times.

Latin America is a safe enough place to travel in, providing you are sensible and take the necessary precautions. Pickpockets and bag snatching are the most common forms of crime, and in some places are almost an art form, especially at festivals, in stations and on buses. Keep a good grip on your possessions, or better still, carry only what you need, and girls – keep your money in your bra. Another thing to watch out for are dodgy tour operators who take a deposit one day and are gone the next. As mentioned, protests and strikes are commonplace. Occasionally these turn nasty, and tear gas is sprayed as if it were water: observe such gatherings, if you must, from a distance.

As a rule, travel here is fantastically affordable, with places such as Bolivia and Guatemala requiring little more than $15 a day. Watch out for unexpected departure taxes (Peru's ever increasing one is currently at $30, Ecuador's $45), 'airport use' and 'bus terminal use' fees. Consider paying more to support eco-friendly tour organisations, and always tip porters and guides. You can often opt to pay for tours in dollars, as well as the local currency – sometimes this is cheaper, other times it is not, so always check exchange rates.

# SOUTH AMERICA
## Argentina

**CURRENCY**

£1 = 6.1 pesos                             US$1 = 3.8 pesos

**BUDGET**

$30 per day.

Since the devaluation of the *peso*, tourism in Argentina has boomed, and this should be taken advantage of while it lasts! Buenos Aires is a European city with Latin flavour, a prime party place, bristling with history and culture. It is best explored district by district, each one distinctive in character and appearance. There's the artsy San Telmo with its antiques markets and legendary steak houses; chichi Palermo for boutiques and night-life, and colourful La Boca – a pilgrimage for those who call themselves football fans. Whichever *barrio* (district) you're in, take a look at the omnipresent graffiti – not gorm-less UK-style tags, but witty political quips and pictures. On Thursdays walk around the Plaza de Mayo (pronounced 'masho', in a thick Argentine accent) with the mothers still protesting over the 'disappearance' of their sons during the 1976–1983 dictatorship.

**GAPPER'S TIP**
*If you go out to party at midnight and feel let down by the lack of choice, that's because you're too early. After a hefty steak dinner the norm is to sleep it off until about 1am and then go dancing until daybreak.*

The mighty Iguazu Falls (*Iguaçu* is the Portuguese spelling used in Brazil) are an easy detour from the capital, before getting lost in the vast outdoor playground that is Patagonia. Whale watching at the Península Valdés is awe inspiring, June to Decem-ber being the best season, although sea lions and seals are permanent residents and penguins come to chill out between October and March. Giant glaciers at El Calafate; unparalleled and highly accessible hikes past blue waters in the southern hemisphere's own Lake District, and skiing in Bariloche are all highlights. Bariloche is meant to be the Switzerland of Argentina, but it definitely has its own (superior?) charm, and offers rid-ing, paragliding, mountain biking, etc. A quirkier attraction is the Chubut valley with its Welsh speaking villages, settled back in the 1860s, where those missing home cooking can order scones and afternoon tea. To the north, Mendoza is a deservedly popular region, famed for its highly affordable and good quality wines, offering even the grubbi-est of backpackers the chance to feel slightly civilised again. Cycle tours between vine-yards, stopping to sample the produce are highly recommended. Trips to Aconcagua, the highest peak in the Andes, can be arranged from Mendoza. Barren Northern Argentina is 'off the beaten track', although punctuated by the buzzing university city of Córdoba, pretty colonial Salta, and several natural hot springs.

# Bolivia

**CURRENCY**

£1 = 11.2 bolivianos                    US$1 = 7 bolivianos

**BUDGET**

$15 per day.

Bolivia deserves its billing as the most 'authentic' country in South America. The poorest Latin American country, Bolivia is currently led by Evo Morales, the first indigenous president of the country, whose popularity is partly due to his legalisation of coca growing. 'Different' things to visit in La Paz include the *Museo de la Coca* and the San Pedro prison, effectively a walled city within a city, where the more, ahem, successful inmates have luxury pads on site.

Only outside hectic La Paz ('the Peace') are you likely to find any *paz*, on one of the many scaleable mountains or scenic Inca treks in the immediate environs. A thrilling day out is mountain biking the 'world's most dangerous road' which involves an exhilarating drop from snowcapped peaks to subtropical climes in a few hours.

Most of Bolivia's population is clustered up on the *altiplano*, through which the gringo trail weaves its route. Sucre has beautiful colonial plazas and a pleasingly high concentration of chocolate shops. If you brave the sweltering tunnels with bad smells and low oxygen down in Potosí's silver mines, you will meet the miners (and their young sons) who do this daily, chewing coca to cope with the hunger and solitude, for very little financial reward.

The salt flats of *Salar de Uyuni* are a perspective-free white desert in the dry season, and a glassy mirror during the rains. Tours also take in the geysers, at the dizzying heights (literally) of 5,000m above sea level, and the flamingo-festooned red and green lagoons – your photos just won't do it justice. Cochabamba's sprawling market is interesting, particularly the 100% genuine witchcraft section, where locals really do buy dried llama foetuses for good fortune, unlike in La Paz's touristy version. Another unmissable altiplano destination is sacred Lake Titicaca on the Peruvian border. Locals say that Bolivia has the 'titi', and Peru only got the 'caca', perhaps a little unfair since the sparkling blue waters and intriguing ruins put in an appearance on both sides. The Bolivian side is less touristy than the floating reed islands off Puno, Peru. The more adventurous may head off to the northern pampas for a wildlife boat trip – expect to get close and personal with pink dolphins, parrots, piranhas, monkeys and cayman. The hyper-adventurous can make for the remote and wild Noel Kempff Mercado National Park, one of the most pristine areas of the Amazon jungle, with stunning waterfalls.

# Peru

**CURRENCY**

£1 = 4.56 soles                    US$1 = 2.86 soles

**BUDGET**

$15–$25 per day.

Machu Picchu is the primary destination for many people who travel to the continent. Although some visitors have exceedingly high expectations of the Lost Citadel, it rarely disappoints. However, one word of caution: even at dawn, it's still crawling with tourists. Yet its grandeur and beauty remain intact. Walking up the super steep Huayna Picchu in the early morning is a novel way of seeing the site, although those who have hiked the Inca trail may pale at the sight of so many steps.

The four-day Inca trail proper must be booked at least six months in advance in the high season (mid-April to September), though there are beautiful alternatives in the same area. If taking the train, consider starting from Ollantaytambo in the Sacred Valley, as this is the cheapest option (from $31 one way). Ollanta is a lovely town in itself; stop off at the Hearts Café on the *plaza* and think of something you could donate to a women's shelter like your windproof jacket or other obsolete Inca trail gear.

Cusco is bristling with Inca ruins, great cafés and bars, and souvenir shops, set amongst well kept colonial buildings. Undiscovered it is not, especially during the festival in late June when *Inti* the sun god is honoured. To escape the SAGA busloads, head for one of the many pristine jungle lodges in the south-west, or make for the coast (via the bright white city of Arequipa), where you too can worship the sun, sandboard on the dunes at Huacachina, surf or sail to 'the poor man's Galápagos' – the fauna filled Ballestas Islands – to watch frolicking penguins, sea lions and flamingos. Not to be outdone, the Colca Canyon is home to the giant Andean condor which might just want to share the walking tracks. More superb walking and climbing is to be had around Huaraz in the *Cordillera Blanca* (white mountains), but true off-the-beaten-track adventures are found in Peru's lightly inhabited Amazonian north. Iquitos is its main settlement: purchase a *hamaca* (hammock), and barter passage on a slow boat down the Amazon to Brazil.

# Brazil

### CURRENCY
£1 = 2.8 reais                              US$1 = 1.74 reais

### BUDGET
$35 per day.

Brazil is a country of epic proportions, beauty and style. It has its fair share of icons such as Sugarloaf Mountain and Copacabana Beach in Rio, but it's the locals that leave the strongest impressions: passionate about dancing, football, beaches and food, life is unavoidably fun here. However, crime, drugs and poverty are prevalent: never wander alone after dark, don't stray into *favelas* (slums) and watch the film *City of God* before your trip.

Rio de Janeiro's legendary beaches are made for people-watching, and by night the city swings to the beat of a thousand samba drums, especially during February *Carnaval* which involves manic revelry in all its forms. The serious could even join a samba school beforehand and take part in the processions.

Culturally rich Salvador da Bahia on the north-east coast is distinctive because of the many descendants of African slaves whose culture survives in interesting ways. The *Carnaval* here in the heart of African Brazil beats to the distinctive *axé* and *pagoda* rhythms and is just as flamboyant and marginally less of a crush. In the north you may be fortunate enough to attend a *Candomblé* ritual – a potent blend of African magic, spiritualism and fortune telling (by reading shells). In Salvador you are bound to come across a *capoeira* performance in the street, a mesmerizing martial art-cum-dance. Brazilian cuisine is as sensual as its people, that is to say, *muito* (very). *Feijoada*, the national dish – a sort of meaty beany stew – is addictive.

The obvious top natural attraction is the mighty Amazon: Manaus offers jungle trips and treks of every variety, and anyone headed to the region is bound to travel by boat at some point – evocative at best, and tedious at worst. In the southern part of the interior, the Pantanal is a vast area, offering some of South America's best wildlife watching, especially in the rainy season when the animals are confined on higher patches of land (capybara, armadillos, alligators, anteaters, and for the lucky, jaguars). The culture of Portuguese-speaking Brazil is as diverse as its landscape, with quirks not found elsewhere in Hispanic Latin America.

# Chile

### CURRENCY
£1 = 883 pesos                     US$1 = 554 pesos

### BUDGET
$30 per day.

Long, skinny Chile is a travellers' playground, where the buzzword is *outdoors*. Head south to discover the real meaning of chilly – exploring the Torres del Paine National Park, where it is possible to climb inside ice caves on spectacular glaciers in the lee of gigantic peaks. Another thrill in Chilean Patagonia is the world-renowned Futaleufú river, where the waters are as white as the rafters' knuckles. Also aim for the many hikeable volcanoes, such as Pucón. The more temperate Lake District is another perfect setting for rafting and climbing, or perhaps just chilling out on the black sand lakeside beaches (it's not dirty, it's volcanic). If that sounds too taxing, you can hot foot it to some of the region's many hot springs.

In the warmer north there are many South Pacific beaches, notably at La Serena, or for some added surfing action, head to Arica or Iquique. Although pricey, paragliding at Iquique and skiing June to October shouldn't be left off the outdoors enthusiast's itinerary. Moving north past (or via) the wineries, altiplano Chile offers geysers and more lakes (with flamingos), as well as the world's driest desert, the Atacama. Here duneboarding ticks the thrill seeking boxes, and the small *salares* (salt lakes) give a taster of the mighty *salar de Uyuni* a short train ride over the border in Bolivia.

Urban Chile also has its attractions: the skyscraper-filled, Andes-backed capital, Santiago de Chile, is an entertaining place to hang up your hiking boots for a while, and indulge yourself at some of South America's finest eateries and drinkeries. Most museums are free on Sundays, and one well worth a visit is La Cascona, to learn about one of Latin America's most famous writers, the poet and Communist Pablo Neruda.

# Ecuador

### CURRENCY
£1 = 3,980 sucre                     US$1 = 2,500 sucre

### BUDGET
$20 per day.

Ecuador is another South American country combining the best of the Andes, Amazon and Pacific, but with the unique addition of the Galápagos Islands. The emphasis on eco-tourism and local indigenous traditions distinguishes Ecuador from its neighbours. The capital, Quito, is recognised as one of the best places to study *español* – or *castellano*, as Latin Americans prefer to call it, anxious to shed colonial ties. There are very many highly rated schools, which can also offer homestays, salsa lessons, volunteer placements and so on.

Quito itself is schizophrenically split into the Old Town and New Town, both full of bustling street markets and buses, but only the Old Town has a backdrop of pretty colonial buildings, while the New Town is a silver urban jungle. Street performers and pretty plazas abound in the invitingly wanderable old town. More strenuous pursuits lie just outside the city, such as climbing the Volcán Pichincha or energetically hopping from one hemisphere to the other at the *Mitad del Mundo* (meaning 'half of the world'), a popular Sunday hangout 20km north of the city for *quiteños* (people from Quito), with live music groups adding to the atmosphere.

Guayaquil is Ecuador's largest city and, due to recent gentrification, is no longer a seedy port. All the same few travellers warm to it, as life is hot, sticky and stressful. Up in the highlands, the town of Otavalo is worth a detour, especially on market days, when animals, crafts, foods and other unidentifiable objects are traded at a frenetic pace (and volume) by local indigenous groups in traditional dress. There are also accessible lagoons in the area, and weekly cockfights (not to everyone's taste). The high peaks of Volcán Chimborazo and Cotopaxi provide opportunities to hike, bike and climb, as well as purchase a panama hat (they originated here).

Cuenca is a picture postcard charming colonial town on a river, with a healthy student nightlife scene. The Amazon *Oriente* (east) is perfect for kayaking and paddling, from Coca to Iquitos, Peru, or simply for watching wildlife. Mating whales can often be seen from Machalilla National Park between June and October. But it is the Galápagos that really steal the show. At about $900+ a week they don't come cheap, but live-aboard vessels show you the highlights and can bring you face to face with sea lions, white-tipped reef sharks, spotted rays, penguins, land and marine iguanas, giant tortoises, frigate birds, blue-footed boobies and all the creatures, mostly unafraid of humans, that thrive on this ecological marvel. Another possibility is to stay on land, for example at a hotel in the main town of Puerto Ayora from which you can join all-day excursions to different islands.

# Colombia

| CURRENCY | |
| --- | --- |
| £1 = 2,950 pesos | US$1 = 1,857 pesos |

| BUDGET |
| --- |
| $20 per day. |

Colombia is one of the most rewarding and interesting travel destinations in South America, far less visited than its neighbours, mainly due to its dangerous reputation. Paramilitary and guerrilla groups are still active and kidnappings of foreigners do take place, but only in rebel areas, which can be avoided. Keep abreast of the political and safety situation via the local news and through reports from fellow travellers. The Colombians, not yet jaded by mass tourism, are exceedingly friendly and welcoming to travellers, though petty theft is rampant.

Cartagena, a strikingly attractive colonial port city, dripping with history is deservedly top of many Colombian itineraries; few are left uncharmed by its walled old town, beautiful old buildings and nearby fishing villages, beaches, snorkelling and scuba diving. Take a fun day trip from here to the el Totumo mud volcano, where you can wallow in warm 'therapeutic' mud.

The other imperative dip to take in this country is into a García Márquez book. The Colombian Nobel prize winning author has created an incredible world of fiction in his short stories and novels, which intoxicate and delight as much as Colombia itself. His 'magical realist' style blends historical fact and indigenous beliefs, seen through hazy tropical eyes, and simultaneously helps comprehend the Latin American way of life, while further mystifying it.

Scuba and snorkelling are to be indulged in all along the Caribbean coast, especially off the Islas de Rosario, a national park with unspoilt coral reefs; the San Andres and Providencia archipelago and at Tanganga. Near Santa Marta, also on the coast, you can make an ambitious side trip to see the famous overgrown *Ciudad Perdida* (lost city), one of the largest pre-Colombian settlements found in the Americas. Built between the 11th and 14th centuries, and 'found' again by tomb raiders less than 40 years ago, it can now be reached on a six-day return trek through the rainforest (cost $200).

Cali and Medellín are both vibrant and cultured, while Bogotá is a heaving city where anything is possible for those with the cash. Head to the *salsatecas* (like a *discoteca*, but for salsa) for some dancing, a national obsession. Near Bogotá is a unique cathedral carved from rock salt inside the salt mines at Zipaquirá, as well as the sacred Guatavita Lake.

# Venezuela

### CURRENCY
| £1 = 3.48 bolivares | US$1 = 2.15 bolivares |
| --- | --- |

### BUDGET
$30 per day.

Venezuela is a country synonymous with oil, economic crises, and the burly face of anti-US rhetoric from president Hugo Chavez. Yet the actual meaning of the country's name is Little Venice, after the houses on stilts the Spanish first set eyes on here, centuries back. The capital, Caracas, has little to recommend it – get straight out. Mérida is much more pleasant and offers paragliding, rafting, climbing and so on. It is also home of the world record holding *Heladería Coromoto*, with over 800 ice cream flavours.

The great outdoors really does do amazing things at the *Salto Ángel*, Angel Falls, in the south – the world's tallest waterfall, cascading down from one of Venezuela's many *tepuis*, distinctive table mountains home to loads of unique plants and animals. Roraima is the biggest of these, and a five-day trek up, over and past its waterfalls is reasonably easy to coordinate. Many travellers to Little Venice don't leave without a few days on (or just off) the coast, to follow watery pursuits: the scuba and snorkelling in the Los Roques archipelago are *excelente*.

# Guyana, Suriname and French Guiana

### CURRENCY
French Guiana uses the euro (£1 = €1.08)

| £1 = 324 Guyana dollars | US$1 = 203 Guyana dollars |
| --- | --- |
| £1 = 4.37 Suriname dollars | US$1 = 2.75 Suriname dollars |

### BUDGET
Guyana $35 per day, Suriname $25 per day, French Guiana $60 per day.

A region frequently overlooked by the majority of *mochileros* (backpackers) – mostly because of the higher prices and weaker infrastructure – this trio of countries still has its share of attractions and offers a culturescape very different from the rest of the continent. Guyana in the east is a former British colony, Suriname was Dutch, and French Guiana is still part of France, a *département d'outre-mer* or overseas territory. The Europeans never properly got their teeth into the Amazon interiors of these countries, where indigenous tribes carry on as they have done for centuries. Geographically, the three countries follow a similar pattern: attractive port towns and beaches along the vaguely industrialised northern coast, and dense pristine rainforest inland. French Guiana's highlights include the Îles du Salut (former penal colony islands) and the rocket launches at the Space Centre; Suriname offers a host of canoeing and trekking opportunities, especially up Mt Kasikasima, while Guyana's top trip is to the towering Kaieteur Falls. Ethnically this region is nothing short of surprising, with European influences, Amerindian natives and Asian immigrants – those on RTW tickets pining for Asia can even visit a Hmong refugee crafts market in Cacao, French Guiana.

# Paraguay and Uruguay

| CURRENCY | |
| --- | --- |
| £1 = 7,800 guaraní (Paraguay) | US$1 = 4,900 guaraní |
| £1 = 33 pesos (Uruguay) | US$1 = 20.7 pesos |

| BUDGET |
| --- |
| $25 per day. |

Less superlative than its neighbours, chilled out Paraguay still has enough to entertain its visitors. Wildlife is plentiful and the Chaco and north-eastern wetlands all afford prime animal spotting. Ruins of Jesuit missions and colonial architecture fill in the gaps, with the German-speaking Mennonite colonies offering a cultural contrast to the rest of the country. Uruguay's petite dimensions and relative prosperity make it a manageable destination. Party hard with vacationing *porteños* (from Buenos Aires) in Punta del Este; wander the diminutive cobbled Colonia and ponder its many quirky museums. Not to be outdone in the steak stakes, Uruguayan cuisine is very good – enjoy a slap-up *churrasco* (grilled steak) in a Montevideo restaurant.

# CENTRAL AMERICA
## Costa Rica

**CURRENCY**

£1 = 935 colones                    US$1 = 587 colones

**BUDGET**

$35 per day.

Having missed out on the dictatorships and civil wars suffered by many of its neighbours, Costa Rica is an anomaly in the region. This peaceful, democratic state with no army has famously supported conservation, so that there are now more than 70 national parks. Animals to be ogled include monkeys, manatees, sloths, snakes, iguanas, armadillos, dolphins, whales, four species of giant turtle and countless butterflies, birds and bats. The heart of Costa Rica lies in the natural world, evident in the national buzzword, *pura vida*, which you will hear about 5,000 times a day. This is an all-encompassing phrase, meaning hey, what's up, peace, and cool, among other things, and it translates as 'pure life'.

Costa Rica's Caribbean and Pacific coasts both boast great beaches, yet have a different atmosphere from one another. The northern coast is home to a Caribbean rasta culture, and is more relaxed and easy going than the south, where the Pacific breakers are ideal for surfing. The Cahuita National Park on the Caribbean side has some good snorkelling on the coral reefs, as well as hiking in the park itself. The Tortuguero National Park in the north, whose name refers to the sea turtles which nest on its beaches, is among the most popular. The best seasons to observe the turtles with a guide at night are April/May and July to October. It is nothing short of miraculous to see these enormous creatures slowly heave themselves onto the beach, dig a hole, and proceed to lay hundreds of tiny eggs in the sand, before disappearing as silently as they came. Poaching, once a problem here, is now being brought under control – note that the park is run on tourist revenue. Canoeing trips are popular here, and you stand a good chance of seeing crocodiles or the elusive manatee.

Another worthy contender for best park is in the Monteverde cloud forest in the central highlands, with its rare unspoilt ecosystem. Zip wiring is a fun way to enjoy the forest; this involves 'flying' through the canopy, suspended from a cable in a harness, theoretically observing the animals, but realistically whooping and squealing with adrenaline, scaring them all away. A short bus ride from here is the Arenal volcano – one of many in the country, but the most likely to delight pyromaniacs with its fire-breathing, lava-spitting night-time antics. Worth a trip are the geothermal hot springs nearby.

Many sections of the Pacific coast are built up. The unashamedly Americanised Tamarindo and Montezuma on the Nicoya peninsula are surf havens, and diving and turtles can be found here too. Untouched wilderness is to be found on hikes in the southern Corcovado National Park.

In the centre of the country, San José is a cosmopolitan city, with many *museos*, bars and a stimulating arts scene to recommend it.

# Guatemala

### CURRENCY
£1 = 13.3 quetzales                    US$1 = 8.3 quetzales

### BUDGET
$15 per day.

Guatemala is one of the richest destinations in Central America, culturally speaking. Mayan traditions are alive and kicking, many Catholic saints correspond to Mayan deities, and sacrifices still take place at religious ceremonies. Guatemalans are among the poorest Central American citizens, yet are unbelievably generous with those they meet. Show an interest in learning the Mayan language (most still speak Spanish as a second tongue), and people will certainly be willing to help. Despite a few pleasant parks and plazas, and a lively music scene, Guatemala City is smelly, congested and crime ridden. Most travellers prefer to spend their time in Antigua or Xela (the local name for the city of Quetzaltenango). Guatemala's token postcard colonial town, Antigua is now a veritable gringoville, with all the requisite bars and clubs. There are many language schools here, where the emphasis is less on picking up Spanish than on partying.

If you still have the energy, try climbing the many volcanoes near Antigua, particularly still-active Pacaya (and don't forget to buy marshmallows to roast on the lava). Xela, Guatemala's second largest city, also has a dazzling array of language schools, where students actually seem interested in learning Spanish. Xela also has volcanoes within reach: *Quetzaltrekkers* is a non-profit company held in high local regard which funnels trekkers' fees into a free school and shelter for local street children (see entry in 'Directory of Volunteering Abroad'). You can find similar ventures elsewhere in Guatemala, for example if you go hiking in Nebaj, go with the Trekking Ixil project.

Around Xela, the natural hot springs ('spa') at Fuentes Georgina are definitely worth an afternoon. A centre in Momostenango runs courses in Mayan ceremonies, beliefs and horoscopes for the inquisitive traveller, while Chichicastenango is a famous and colourful market town, best visited on Thursdays and Sundays. Some of the most enjoyable Mayan villages are the scenic settlements on the shores of Lake Atitlán. Skip Panajachel ('gringotenango') unless you want to hire a bike, then visit the lakeside towns of bohemian San Pedro, San Marcos, popular for its retreats, and Santa Cruz, known for its lake diving. Boats connect these towns (see Anna Ling's account on page 557 for more details).

The jungle at Petén is home to Tikal, an eerily beautiful complex of Mayan temples, whose tall stone pyramids peek out over the canopy. At dawn this sight is breathtaking, and accompanied by the tune of thousands of monkeys and birds. Other Mayan ruins lie deeper in the jungle, but are difficult to reach. On the Pacific coast black sand beaches, mangrove swamps and turtle nesting sites of Monterrico (and a turtle hatchery or two looking for volunteers), and deep sea fishing at Iztapa can all be enjoyed. The Caribbean coast is characterised by its *Garífuna* (descendants of black slaves) culture.

Guatemala is a wonderfully cheap place to travel or stay in – language courses with homestays and food rarely cost more than $100 a week. Language institute staff can often put you in touch with volunteer organisations if you want to get more involved in the country.

# El Salvador

### CURRENCY
£1 = 13.9 colones

US$1 = 8.7 colones

### BUDGET
$15 per day.

Long the domain of bullets and guerrillas, El Salvador is better known for its bloody civil war than for its tourist industry. Now however, peace prevails, and those jaded by the *ruta gringa* (gringo trail) find this a refreshing haven – locals are curious towards foreigners, and the landscapes are as dramatic as elsewhere on the continent. A typical itinerary might blend trekking in the mountainous interior, for instance at El Imposible National Park or along the Ruta de las Flores, taking in the volcanoes and crater lakes of the Sierra Apaneca Ilamatepec, followed by some down time on the Pacific *playas*.

# Belize

### CURRENCY
£1 = 3 Belize dollars

US$1 = 1.9 Belize dollars

### BUDGET
$35 per day.

English speaking Belize is very easy to travel in... provided you have the money. Island hopping and water sports reign supreme, and these are more pricey. The legendary Blue Hole (an underwater sinkhole teeming with fish and friendly sharks) and the surrounding reefs offer some of the region's best diving and snorkelling, and Caye Caulker is the ultimate backpacker hideaway. If you find the Latino *mañana* pace a little slow then brace yourself for Belize's Caribbean outlook – you'll be hard pushed to find a more chilled out lifestyle. The buses, however, are as efficient as clockwork, and the energetic will find plenty of hiking and whitewater rafting.

# Honduras

**CURRENCY**

£1 = 30 lempiras                              US$1 = 19 lempiras

**BUDGET**

$15 per day, more expensive on the Bay Islands.

Long a backpacker favourite, Honduras' long lazy Caribbean coast, cool interior and Mayan ruins are the main draws, although those with more time to spare should make for one of the last remaining wilderness areas in the region, the Mosquitia jungle. Not to be missed are the Bay Islands, off the northern coast, with Roatan and Utila being best suited to budgets with backpacks. These English-speaking islands, once a refuge for pirates, have a colourful history. Diving on Utila is spectacular, with pristine coral reefs, vast shoals of tropical fish and, if you go between May and September, the elusive whale shark. Totally harmless, these huge fish play in the shallows so even snorkellers have a chance of meeting one. A PADI Open Water course costs about $220, and most dive shops offer free or discounted accommodation for divers.

The Mayan ruins at Copán (also accessible from Guatemala) are impressive, and can be visited in a day. National parks and cloud forests – Pico Bonito and La Tigre have been receiving rave reviews – grace the interior, but the adventurous should head to the Mosquito coast where travel is by dugout canoe and tourists are rarer than jaguars, so accommodation and food is sparse. Bring insect repellent (even though the name comes from the Miskito natives rather than the pesky insects).

# Nicaragua

**CURRENCY**

£1 = 32.8 cordoba oro                         US$1 = 20.6 cordoba oro

**BUDGET**

$20 per day.

Nicaragua is safe, affordable, and back on the backpackers' list of desirable destinations. Roads are still in their infancy, and travel can be tough, but attractions abound, and the people are talkative and opinionated – all good practice for your Spanish. Granada and León are Nicaragua's rival colonial cities, which more than make up for the big bad Managua. León, the former capital twinned with Oxford, has a pretty cathedral, cobbled streets and shady parks, and is steeped in colonial and revolutionary history. It is near the south coast and has a couple of large climbable volcanoes nearby. Granada is on the shores of the fascinating Lago de Nicaragua, and is just as aesthetically pleasing, with some excellent cafés and restaurants. Nearby Masaya, flattened in 2000 by an earthquake, is now the *artesanía* (handicrafts) epicentre of Nicaragua, with many tempting markets. Explore the Lago's fishing villages, ruins, beaches and wildlife on the Isla de Ometepe, as well as the artistic communities of the Solentiname archipelago in the south. The turtle nesting beaches of the Pacific coast also feature on many itineraries, although many travellers fresh from Costa Rica will be distressed by the different attitudes to conservation.

# Panama

**CURRENCY**

£1 = 1.59 balboa                    US$1 = 1 balboa

**BUDGET**

$20 per day.

There is more to Panama than hats and a canal, but many travellers don't make it this far. It's the *cul de sac* of central America, because travel further south is impossible due to the dense, bandit-ridden jungle of the Darién Gap. Panama City is a delight as far as capitals go, with clubs and bars nestling behind colonial façades, and the obligatory trip to the canal, first proposed by the Spanish as long ago as the 16th century. Whereas the area east of the canal is wild Darién jungle, the Bocas del Toro archipelago to the west is another isn't-life-tough Caribbean watersports paradise, where you take water taxis between bar, beach and turtle sanctuary.

# Mexico

**CURRENCY**

£1 = 21 pesos                    US$1 = 13 pesos

**BUDGET**

$35 per day.

The largest of the Central America countries, Mexico is not a cheap destination, but its beaches, festivals and ruins are an inevitable draw. Stick to the south rather than the industrialised north, where it tends to be more Tex than Mex. Mexico City is a sprawling metropolis, known for its chronic pollution and crime, and most travellers fly in and straight out. The south's most interesting regions are the Yucatán peninsula, and the state of Chiapas. Mayan temples and pyramids are dotted around these areas and Mayan traditions are still upheld. The most impressive Mayan sites are at Chichén Itzá, Palenque (both World Heritage sites), and the ruins of the walled city at Tulum, overlooking the Caribbean. Chichén Itzá has been called the Disneyland of the Mayan world, so expect to jostle for space with the fanny-pack toting crowds. The nightly light show is spectacular or cheesy depending on your sensibilities. These sites are still amazing – get there as early in the day as you can.

The Caribbean coast offers some unparalleled snorkelling and diving, particularly on the Isla Mujeres (check out the turtle farm) and off the island of Cozumel. Swimming is the best way to escape the year-round heat, and visiting the *cenotes* of the Yucatán is a refreshingly novel experience. These are sinkholes of fresh water, some underground, surrounded by stalactites and crazy rock formations.

Cancún, the largest city of the 'Mayan Riviera' is very Costa del Sol, favoured by US frat groups on Spring Break. The smaller Playa del Carmen has a more stayable feel to it, but many recommend staying at Tulum, where you can sleep in rustic cabins on the beach. Mérida is also a pleasant Yucatán destination, one of the cleanest and prettiest cities in Mexico, with a thriving theatre scene and many galleries.

The state of Chiapas, the country's poorest, is home to the Zapatista movement – a left-wing group supporting indigenous rights. Mexico's second city, Guadalajara is the arts capital, with innumerable music, film and book festivals all year round. Moving west, Puerto Vallarta on the Pacific coast is less touristy than its Caribbean cousins, and offers the possibility of humpback whale watching between November and March. If possible time your visit to Mexico to coincide with the *Día de los Muertos* (Day of the Dead) on 1 November, which roughly corresponds to the Anglophone world's Halloween. Families make technicolour shrines to deceased relatives and sit up all night drinking and feasting in graveyards, keeping the dead company.

# Cuba

### VISA
Required: £15 in London.

### CURRENCY
£1 = 1.59 pesos                    US$1 = 1 peso

### BUDGET
$50 per day.

Bridging the link between the Caribbean and Latin worlds, Cuba is a fascinating island brimming with things to be seen, learnt and confused by. New arrivals will have their own romantic images of the country, from Che Guevara and old pastel painted American cars to dressed up old ladies smoking fat cigars, and palm fringed beaches. Unfortunately the state-regulated tourist industry makes travel costs pretty steep, in a country where the average monthly wage is $17. Under Fidel Castro, tourist activities and movements were limited: foreigners had to stay in state-run hotels (think Soviet architecture) or in tourist enclaves from which Cubans were excluded, or in *casas particulares* – family run homestays. It was almost a case of apartheid with foreigners kept at a distance from locals as much as possible and required to pay far higher prices for services. However, the policy of restricting certain hotels and services to tourists was ended by President Raul Castro in 2008 and it is possible that very soon the long-time embargo on US citizens visiting Cuba will be lifted. A Freedom to Travel to Cuba bill is under consideration by a Congressional committee at the time of writing. Until the bill is passed, most travellers will continue to arrive in Havana on cheap flights from Canada or Cancún.

Mosquitoes are not the only things buzzing in *La Habana*, which is cultured, hip and edgy – art and music thrive, and this is the cultural and political focus of the island. The old town is a beautiful colonial zone, with plenty of bars and museums to visit. before heading out to the outlying beaches. Avoid the all-inclusive resorts of Varadero, and try to get to Trinidad – another pretty colonial city, with excursions to waterfalls and beaches, and nearby hiking opportunities, as well as some very vibrant nightlife; the eternal flame and Che Guevara memorial in Santa Clara, and explore the beautiful countryside of the Pinar del Río province in the west by bike or by horse.

## TRAVEL RESOURCES

### USEFUL WEBSITES
**www.bootsnall.com/South-America**, updated monthly, listings, travellers' forums and tips about travel, also covers other regions of the world.
**http://baexpats.org**, the lowdown on Buenos Aires life.
**www.brazilmax.com**, well laid out information about this continent within a continent.

### USEFUL BOOKS
*Footprint South American Handbook* (Footprint, 2009), £22.50. Updated yearly, the most consistently recommended guide for accuracy and background information. Footprint Guides also publishes *Central America and Mexico*.
*South America on a Shoestring* (Lonely Planet, 2007), £20.99.
*The Rough Guide to South America on a Budget* (Rough Guides, 2009), £19.99.

### TRAVEL READING
Gabriel García Márquez, *100 Years of Solitude* (Penguin, 2007), £9.99. Or read one of his quirky short stories, such as *I Only Came to Use the Phone*.

Laura Esquivel, *Like Water for Chocolate* (Black Swan, 1993), £7.99. Amusing tale of love and food in revolutionary Mexico.

Rigoberta Menchú, *I, Rigoberta Menchú: An Indian Woman in Guatemala* (Verso, 1984). The author is a Nobel Peace Prize winner.

Stephen Benz, *Green Dreams: Travels in Central America* (Lonely Planet, 1998). A witty account of fellow travellers and locals, with an emphasis on eco-tourism.

Larry Rice, *Baja to Patagonia: Latin American Adventures* (Fulcrum Publishing, 1994). An informative account of travel in wilderness areas across the continent.

Peter Robb, *A Death in Brazil* (Bloomsbury, 2005), £9.99. Acutely observed account of both the violence and beauty of Brazil.

Louis de Bernières, *The War of Don Emmanuel's Netherparts* (Vintage, 1991), £7.99. About mysticism and traditions. Other hilarious accounts of Latin life by the same author include *The Troublesome Offspring of Cardinal Guzman* (fiery women and passions) and *Señor Uno and the Cocalord* (about drugs wars blighting the continent).

### SOUTH AMERICA ON FILM
City of God *(2002) is a fast-paced, hard-hitting yet uplifting film about life in Rio's most dangerous slum. Also check out films by Walter Salles such as* Central Station *and of course* The Motorcycle Diaries.

# NORTH AMERICA

| CURRENCY | |
| --- | --- |
| £1 = US$1.65 | £1 = C$1.74 |

| BUDGET | |
| --- | --- |
| US$50+ per day in USA | US$40–$60 per day in Canada |

## THE LURE OF NORTH AMERICA

This vast and wealthy continent is crammed with all sorts of wonders, natural and man-made, and is peopled by a fascinating ethnic mix. With the dawn of the Age of Obama, the USA is a more attractive proposition than it was in its previous incarnation. But even if you do have reservations about the stance of the 'moral majority' of Americans, the friendly culture-loving folk of Minneapolis or the liberal-minded students of California should not be tarred with the same brush.

Politics aside, many travellers will derive immense pleasure from visiting some of the great American icons – Walt Disney World, the Statue of Liberty, the Grand Canyon, the Golden Gate Bridge. But on the doorstep of all these fabled landmarks are many less well-known wonders. The Grand Canyon is undoubtedly stupendous, but nearby Monument Valley is also breathtaking and much less crowded. While Manhattan offers the archetypal urban experience, the sleepy artists' colonies and beach resorts on Long Island make a fascinating destination. The bars along Bourbon Street are once again thriving after the disaster of Hurricane Katrina. But also in the French Quarter (which was barely touched by the hurricane), you can visit a voodoo temple.

America is not the known quantity many gappers expect it to be, based on a steady diet of US sitcoms and rock lyrics. At times it can be the futuristic, wild and dangerous place depicted in the media, and at other times as homespun as apple pie. Places such as Las Vegas, Orlando and Hollywood are in many ways as over-the-top and vulgar as anyone could wish, while others like Seattle, or Georgetown in Washington DC are more sophisticated and thoroughly congenial.

The world's second largest country (after Russia), Canada is a thinly populated geo-political eccentricity. It also has a staggering diversity of landscape and people, and is often a welcome antidote to the excesses of the USA. Most gappers confine themselves to the cities of the southern belt; Vancouver, Toronto and Montréal are all within a few degrees of latitude almost straddling the US border. They are all clean, safe, full of character and within reach of natural wonders. But to see the best of Canada, the visitor should try to reach the fringes, such as the national parks, the Maritime provinces on the Atlantic coast, or remote parts of British Columbia in the west.

Travel round North America can be by turns wonderfully rewarding and deeply confusing, practically as well as culturally. Can such a high degree of gregariousness be

## UNMISSABLE HIGHLIGHTS

- Hike the Appalachian Trail (but ignore Bill Bryson on the danger of bear attacks).
- Shop in famous department stores like Macy's on Broadway or Neiman-Marcus in Dallas.
- Watch a baseball game in Boston, Detroit, Toronto or anywhere where the fans are passionate.
- Rent a wreck for US$30 a day and drive the beautiful coastal Highway 1 from LA to SanFran.
- Lose some money at the roulette tables of Las Vegas.
- Sample maple syrup at a sugar bush in Quebec or boiled lobster in the Canadian Maritimes.
- Ride the Empire Builder train from Chicago to Seattle through magisterial mountain scenery.
- Swill bourbon in Kentucky's Blue Grass Country (but only if you're over 21).
- Hire a canoe to explore 7725sq km Algonquin Park in Ontario.
- Be spooked at the sight of the Bates Motel from Hitchcock's Psycho at Universal Studios Hollywood.

genuine or might this friendly American be trying to con or convert you? In all cases, exploring this mighty powerhouse will be a huge and memorable adventure.

## GETTING THERE

The price of flying across the Atlantic has barely risen in real terms for decades, though with increased taxes and fuel surcharges, it is difficult to find a flight for for under than £250 return. To take a random example provided by the top budget travel website www.cheapoair.com, the base price of a Virgin Airlines low-season return London–New York is US$236, but the taxes amount to an additional US$325+. The low-cost Canadian charter operator Canadian Affair (www.canadianaffair.com) and Scotland's flyglobespan.com sell the cheapest flights to Canada from regional airports, though Air Canada has some good low season deals from Heathrow from about £350.

For the USA, competition is fiercest and therefore prices lowest on the main routes between London and New York and Los Angeles/San Francisco, though reasonable deals on mainstream carriers to cities such as Denver and Detroit are readily available outside peak season. In many cases, summer fares will be twice as high as winter ones. One-way fares are also available to eastern seaboard cities such as Washington and Boston; however passengers arriving on the Visa Waiver Program (see below) must show a return or onward ticket as proof that they do not intend to stay in the US. Outside summer and the Christmas period you should have no problems getting a seat across the Atlantic; at peak times, a reliable alternative is to buy a discounted ticket on one of the less fashionable carriers which fly to New York, such as Air India or El Al.

## GETTING AROUND

The USA and Canada share the longest common frontier in the world, which gives some idea of the potential problems and expense of getting around. Bus, train and air travel generally work out to be cheaper per mile than in Europe. In the USA, consult any branch of STA (+1 800 781 4040) and in Canada look for an office of Travel Cuts, the youth and student travel specialist (www.travelcuts.com).

In both the USA and Canada, the car is king. A driving licence is regarded almost as a birthright and many young men spend a lot of time talking about their wheels. Eighteen year olds are permitted to rent by some companies like Rentawreck (www.rentawreck.com) but may be expected to leave a credit card number as a deposit. In states where young drivers are permitted to rent, there may be a surcharge, for example the minimum renting age in Michigan is 18, but Alamo imposes an extra daily fee of US$28 to drivers 20 and under, US$14 for 21–24 year olds. Clubbing together to buy an old banger can be affordable, though insurance costs for young drivers will bump up the cost (though it will still be much less than the UK equivalent).

The term 'drive-away' applies to the widespread practice of delivering private cars within North America. Prosperous Americans and Canadians and also companies are prepared to pay several hundred dollars to delivery firms who agree to arrange delivery of private vehicles to a different city, usually because the car-owner wants his or her car available at their holiday destination but doesn't want to drive it personally. The companies find drivers, arrange insurance and arbitrate in the event of mishaps. You get free use of a car (subject to mileage and time restrictions) and pay for all gas after the first tankful and tolls on the interstates. Usually a time deadline and mileage limit are fixed, though these are often flexible and checks lax. A good time to be travelling east to west or north to south (e.g. Chicago to Phoenix) is September/October when a lot of older people head to a warmer climate. On the other hand, when there is a shortage of vehicles (e.g. leaving New York in the summer), you will be lucky to get a car on any terms.

Unfortunately most companies are looking for drivers over the age of 23 or even 25, so students aren't eligible. If you or an older friend are interested in pursuing this idea, check *the Yellow Pages* under 'Auto Transporters' for a local provider, though the company with national coverage is Auto Driveaway (+1 800 346 2277; www.autodriveaway.com) which has dozens of franchised operators across the US, from Salt Lake City to Syracuse, Saint Louis to Seattle. Go to www.autodriveawaydc.com/carlist.html for a current list of available cars. From Toronto, an established company is Toronto Drive-Away Service (+1 800 561 2658; www.torontodriveaway.com) whose website contains driver recruitment information; the minimum age is 25. An alternative is to ask at a travel information centre for car rental agencies which arrange delivery of rental cars to the places where there is a seasonal demand, for example to Florida or to ski resorts in the winter.

The deregulation of US domestic airlines some years ago resulted in some amazing discounted fares. Southwest Airlines based in Dallas (www.southwest.com) is one of the better known discount airlines offering cheap fares and no-frills service. Southwest was advertising a one-way fare of less than US$150 including taxes between Philadelphia and Los Angeles (2009). Small airlines keep springing up, serving lesser known cities; check out for example Allegiant Air (www.allegiantair.com).

Normally, the cheapest advance purchase coast-to-coast fares are about US$149 plus a few extras. Other low cost airlines include Spirit Airlines (whose hub is Fort Lauderdale and with many connecting flights to the Caribbean and Central America), JetBlue (whose home is New York) and US Airways (with hubs in Philadelphia, Charlotte and Phoenix). The best advice within the USA is to ask locals and study local newspapers, as fare wars are usually fought using full-page advertisements. In Canada, check out the routes and fares available on low cost Air Canada Jazz and WestJet.

Attempts to revive long-distance train travel in the US have not been terribly successful and several grand old routes come under threat from time to time. Amtrak (+1 800 USA RAIL/872 7245; www.amtrak.com) offers limited rail passes such as '7 days in 21' around California for US$159 or the whole network starting at US$389 for eight journeys within 15 days. The basic three-and-a-half day train trip from Toronto to Vancouver costs about C$525 in the summer, C$450 off-season; student discounts are available on some routes but not this one. With fares at those levels, it is worth considering the Canrail pass; the youth fare of C$518 permits 12 days of unlimited travel in economy class throughout the VIA Rail network during a 30-day period. The Via Rail infoline in Canada is +1 888 842 7245 (www.viarail.ca).

South of the Canadian border, bus passes are a travel bargain for people who want to cover a lot of ground. Greyhound still markets bus passes lasting 7, 15, 30 or 60 days, and fares have been dropping, currently US$199, $299, $399 and $499, respectively (www.discoverypass.com). Promotional advance purchase fares of US$99 for any trip within the USA are good value. Megabus (www.megabus.com) is expanding its network in North America and recently started operating between New York and Toronto as well as Chicago–Detroit and connecting routes. The earlier you book online, the better the bargain, e.g. US$1 for New York to Washington or Toronto.

Other forms of transport in the USA are probably more expensive but may have their own attractions, such as the trips run by Green Tortoise (494 Broadway, San Francisco, California 94133; +1 800 867 8647; www.greentortoise.com) which use vehicles converted to sleep about 35 people and which make interesting detours and stopovers. One of the most popular youth tour companies is Trekamerica (www.trekamerica.co.uk). Their biggie is the 64-day Trailblazer tour which costs £3,299 plus a food kitty of US$10 a day.

---

**TRAVEL TIP**

*Hitchhikers are a rare breed throughout the continent, except in mountain resorts or wilderness areas where people need lifts into remote areas, though ride-sharing possibilities exist; try www.erideshare.com. The system of Allo-Stop is well developed in the province of Quebec but has been ruled illegal in Ontario after complaints were received from coach operators; join www.allostop.com for C$6 to access available rides.*

---

## BUDGETING AND ACCOMMODATION

Between the high cost of covering the vast distances whether by air or land and the relatively expensive accommodation costs, the USA and Canada are not countries where your average gapper spends months on the road. Of course many cover their costs by working at a summer camp or at a seasonal job (see *USA* and *Canada* chapters near the end of this book) and then spend the final few weeks of their J-I visa's validity seeing some of the country. Most people estimate a daily spend of US$50–$100.

Travellers should calculate on spending at least US$20 on a dorm bed in American youth hostels and more than twice that for a private room, less if camping with one or more friends. Of interest to travellers with their own transport, budget motels line the approach roads to every town. They can be affordable if you are travelling with a few friends and are prepared to squash up. Cheap national chains include Motel 6 and the more upmarket Super 8. Motel 6 prices are usually in the range of US$40–$70 for a room with two double beds.

Official YHA hostels are listed at www.hiusa.org while the promising sounding www.usahostels.com lists international travellers' hostels only in San Francisco, Los Angeles, San Diego and Las Vegas. Round-the-world backpackers are sometimes shocked by the contrast between your average city hostel in the USA and in Australia/New Zealand or Europe, as gap year student **David Hardie** reported in 2008:

> *In LA the hostel was a dive. This seems to be the case with most hostels in the US. One of the people staying at our LA hostel was a black dwarf named Jacky whose job it was to impersonate Chucky, the evil doll from those films. Another hostel resident wanted us to join him to go and trash his ex-girlfriend's car. There isn't really a backpacking scene in USA. Unlike Australia everyone in US hostels are older and in between jobs, usually low lives.*

Therefore it might be wise to choose your accommodation with more care than elsewhere. For hostel accommodation in Canada, see the hostel links at www.backpackers.ca.

# EXCITING WAYS TO GET INVOLVED

- Study the behaviour of whales and dolphins in Hawaii as a research intern (www.oceanmammalinst.com).
- Look after the children of a Texan executive (www.aupairamerica.co.uk).
- Construct trails in the Grand Canyon or other national parks (www.usaconservation.org).
- Improve your French in the chic yet friendly city of Montréal (www.visavis.org).
- Qualify for an H2-B seasonal work visa and work in a Rocky Mountain ski resort (www.ccusa.com).
- Volunteer to work with First Nations children in the Canadian Arctic (www.frontiersfoundation.ca).
- Work in the British pavilion at Disney World's Epcot World Showcase in Florida (www.yummyjobs.com).
- Learn to snowboard or pick up a winter job at the buzzing resort of Whistler two hours north of Vancouver (www.whistlerblackcomb.com).
- Take up a one-year internship for graduates in an East Coast company (www.istplus.com).
- Coach soccer at a summer camp in New England (www.mlscamps.com) or sports at Canadian camps (www.go-nyquest.com).

To keep costs down, a brave gapper might wish to join one of the free hospitality networks such as www.couchsurfing.com with a large number of North American adherents willing to give travellers a free bed for a night or two, mentioned in the section about accommodation in 'Before You Go' page 51.

## VISAS

Under the Visa-Waiver Program, citizens of the UK and 34 other countries who have a machine-readable passport do not need to apply for a tourist visa in advance for stays of less than 90 days. However as of 2009, they have to obtain prior authorisation via ESTA, the Electronic System for Travel Authorization, which can be easily done online free of charge. Individuals entering visa-free or with a visitor visa for business or tourism are prohibited from engaging in paid or unpaid employment in the USA. Those planning trips of more than 90 days, including those who wish to work or study, must obtain a visa in advance from the Embassy. This now requires a pre-arranged face-to-face interview and a US$131 visa fee (even if the visa is denied) as well as completing a long and detailed form.

British travellers and tourists arriving in the USA on the Visa-Waiver Programme face increasingly rigorous restrictions. Upon arrival you will have a digital photograph and an inkless fingerprint taken. Check the embassy website (www.usembassy.org.uk) or call the premium line 09042 450100 (£1.20 per minute) for visa information and application forms or request an outline of non-immigrant visas from the Visa Branch of the US Embassy (5 Upper Grosvenor Street, London W1A 2JB).

The non-immigrant visa of most interest to gap year students is the J-1, which is available to participants of government-authorised exchange programmes primarily for registered students. For details see the *USA* chapter at the end of this book (page 534). British and Commonwealth citizens do not require visas for entry to Canada as tourists for up to six months. To work or study in Canada, you must obtain the appropriate visa before you leave your home country.

## WHAT TO EXPECT

Like every nationality, the people of the USA have their egocentricities. They take great pride in living in the richest country in the world with its much vaunted belief in freedom, democracy and justice. This sometimes blinds them to the poverty in which so many of their fellow citizens live, as was so poignantly revealed after Hurricane Katrina devastated New Orleans in 2005. There can be a certain narrow focus to their view of the world, partly because relatively few Americans have travelled abroad, and many have a shaky grasp of the geography of the rest of the world. Don't be unduly surprised if you are asked 'What is the capital of London?'

The multi-ethnic character of America is well known. The number of Hispanics and Chicanos (naturalised Americans from Mexico) represents 14.8% of the total US population of 305 million, and has overtaken the number of African Americans who make up 13.4% of the total. Racial sensitivity frequently surfaces. Even among people who appear to be tolerant, you need to tread warily (e.g. in mentioning problems in the Middle East) to avoid inflaming concealed prejudices.

Glamour and squalor vie for supremacy in the great cities of the USA. You should keep your wits about you since a busy shopping street that seems perfectly safe in the day can turn empty and spooky at night. Be careful wandering at random after dark since it is very easy to turn off a safe street into a deprived area which you might find threatening. Muggings are far more common in Washington and Chicago than they are in London, so never count your travel funds in public or display expensive items. If you find yourself being mugged, do not resist. Ideally, you will be carrying US$50–$100 in cash that you can quickly hand over.

Canadians are less volatile and are almost universally friendly and just plain 'nice'. The fastest way to antagonise a Canadian is to mistake him or her for an American, and then to say 'Well there isn't much difference anyway'. Yet Canada is so heavily dependent on the USA both culturally and economically that it isn't always easy to spot the difference, and certainly the accents can easily be mistaken. Attune your ear to the sound 'ou' as in the word 'about' which Canadians pronounce in a short clipped way, almost like 'abote'.

Newly turned 18 year olds who have relished the chance to go to pubs and clubs legally will be disappointed in most of North America. The minimum legal age for the purchase of alcohol is 21 across the USA and 19 in most Canadian provinces except Alberta, Manitoba and Quebec where it is 18 (and not so strictly enforced in the latter, because of the French influence). Elsewhere, do not expect to get away with showing some home-forged ID, since age limits are strictly enforced.

## WHICH TRAIL TO FOLLOW?

The greatest hits of North America are well known to just about everyone, and it will simply be a matter of choosing from among the wealth of options – the great cities of New York, Chicago, San Francisco and Vancouver might form the series of dots to be joined up by an On the Road style trip via Niagara Falls, the Grand Canyon and the Rocky Mountains. Or your lodestar cities might be Atlanta, Nashville, Albuquerque, Los Angeles and Seattle, via the wide open spaces of Texas, Death Valley and the glaciers of Oregon. Most gappers, however, will concentrate on one particular region. Typically travellers go north from New York to Boston or south to Washington, possibly taking in the hip city of Philadelphia or Salem Massachusetts, home of 17th-century witchcraft in America. Manhattan is of course unmissable though you should venture into New York's other boroughs, perhaps to visit the Bronx Zoo or to take the ferry to Staten Island. Ellis Island, a short ferry ride from Lower Manhattan, commemorates a staggering 12 million immigrants who were processed here on arrival in the new world, many with tragic histories. One top pick for New York is Central Park – take a good walk round and spend the rest of your life recognising it in films.

Other favoured trails include the Old South beaches and plantations of the Carolinas and Georgia; the Gulf Coast between Florida and New Orleans; and southern California with side trips to Yosemite National Park and Las Vegas. Arizona is home to the be-all and end-all of natural wonders, the Grand Canyon whose immensity and beauty are sufficient to compensate for the crowds and commercialism. It is also next to the fascinating state of New Mexico whose capital, Santa Fe, is a town for lotus eaters. For the really ambitious (and well-heeled), Alaska and Hawaii are possibilities.

In Canada you will probably have to choose between exploring the centre (the Toronto–Montreal corridor) and the west between the Rocky Mountain resort of Banff and the great coastal city of Vancouver.

## TRAVEL RESOURCES

### USEFUL BOOKS

*Rough Guide to the USA* (Rough Guides, 2009), £16.99.

*Rough Guide to Canada* (Rough Guides, 2007), £15.99.

*USA Travel Guide* (Lonely Planet, 2008), £16.99.

Both Lonely Planet and Rough Guides publish regional and city guides.

*Time Out City Guides.* Available for New York, Boston, Chicago, Las Vegas, San Francisco, Los Angeles and Washington in the USA, plus Vancouver and Toronto in Canada.

# Part III
# GAP YEAR PLACEMENTS

SPECIALIST GAP YEAR PROGRAMMES
EXPEDITIONS
WORK EXPERIENCE
VOLUNTEERING
A YEAR OFF FOR NORTH AMERICANS
PAID SEASONAL JOBS
AU PAIRING
COURSES

# GapGuru

Emily Rosselli

Emily Rosselli did the Journalism Internship in Bangalore, India with GapGuru:

What encouraged Emily to choose the journalism internship in India was her module at university about the anthropology of India; this triggered her interest in the country. Journalism also fitted with her professional objective: 'I aspired to a career in journalism or PR, which are notoriously competitive industries, so I jumped at the chance to gain experience that would help me stand out from the crowd'.

Emily covered various stories for a leading daily newspaper in Bangalore, from a Halloween Banquet at a 5 star hotel, to gun dealers in the City Market, as well as India's forgotten World War II veterans. 'Seeing my name in print was an amazing feeling. I used to scan the newspaper religiously every morning to see if any of my pieces had made it in!'

Discovering India was a fantastic and rewarding experience for Emily: 'there's no "greyness" or anything mundane in India; everywhere you look there are vibrant colours, tastes, smells, sounds... it's an assault on your senses, and overwhelming in the best possible way... I miss the noise and the energy of daily life in India.

Having seen the hardship faced by so many people in India, I quickly realised that I wanted a career where I could help people in less fortunate situations. I now work at a hospice doing PR and Communications. I wouldn't have been lucky enough to get my current job without the experience of this internship; not only did I come home with a really strong portfolio of published articles and the knowledge of a press environment, I also became more confident and resilient.'

Would Emily recommend her GapGuru programme to others? 'Yes! both my internship and my travel journeys were incredible experiences. In particular, Hema (the GapGuru representative in Bangalore) and her husband Kittu were two of the loveliest people I have ever met and were like family! My three months in India were unforgettable and I wouldn't change them for the world. I just wish I'd stayed longer!'

# SPECIALIST GAP YEAR PROGRAMMES

Specialist gap year placement organisations and companies can arrange the logistics and save you (and your parents) a great deal of anxiety. They find voluntary and occasionally paid placements, provide orientation and sometimes group travel and, crucially, provide back-up, usually in the form of an in-country representative who can sort out problems. Mediating agencies come in all shapes and sizes. Some are charities with stable programmes in a range of countries and links forged over many years with certain schools and NGOs. Others are more entrepreneurial and are always seeking new projects in developing countries to which they can send paying volunteers. Gappers on the cusp of choosing should be aware that not all providers are the same, and that they should not just choose the first one that pops up on Google or the one to put on a slick presentation to their sixth form.

A plethora of companies and fewer charities offer a wide range of packaged possibilities, from work experience placements in French businesses to teaching in Himalayan schools. This section provides a general description of the programmes run by companies that specifically market to gap year students. Younger school leavers should be aware that 18 is often quoted as a minimum age. Further details of programmes mentioned here are included in the country-by-country chapters, with stories of people who have done placements.

Mediating agencies charge high fees and all participants must pay or fundraise substantial sums. In recent years the expectation that parents will finance the year off has declined and most companies provide much detailed advice on how to obtain sponsorship and raise money. Fees and services differ enormously, so research is essential, preferably well in advance. Generally speaking, the high-profile organisations that invest a lot in publicity are considerably more expensive than the more obscure small charities active in just one country. Before committing yourself and your backers to a large financial outlay, you must be sure that your choice of organisation is sound and that its programme matches your requirements. Researching all the possibilities is time-consuming and sometimes confusing since it can be difficult to compare programmes simply on the basis of their publicity.

The word 'voluntourism' has been coined for the more superficial kind of volunteer experiences, and in some cases is what is on offer by the profit-driven companies that commercialise and commodify the experience of helping in developing countries. Not long ago the director of VSO (Voluntary Service Overseas) expressed her concern at the rise of this phenomenon, and that many year-out programmes represented a new form of colonialism. This in turn prompted some of the gap year companies committed to their development work to respond in the editorial pages of newspapers with the following:

> *Your prominent coverage of the views of Judith Brodie, director of VSO UK, puts into relief a critical need for greater transparency and accountability amongst organisations*

*operating within the UK's largely unregulated gap year and volunteer travel industry. The proliferation of poorly planned, spurious and increasingly profit-oriented gap year schemes poses a growing threat to the legitimacy of reputable UK-based volunteer organisations, large and small, working throughout the sustainable development sector.*

The non-profit trade association, the Year Out Group, aims to promote and advise on structured years out. Its website (www.yearoutgroup.org) has links to its 37 member organisations and contains guidelines and questions to ask when comparing year out providers, most of which are common sense, e.g. find out whether it is a charity or a profit-making company, look at safety procedures and in-placement support, ask for a breakdown of costs, and so on. The Year Out Group is primarily a trade association, and Tourism Concern has expressed concern that it is not as selective in its membership is it might be, since it has no external auditing procedure and no funds to investigate claims made by members. Note that the Year Out group cannot intervene in any dispute between member companies and disgruntled clients.

## GOOD PRACTICE STANDARDS

*A new national standard of good practice and risk management among gap year and adventure travel providers was introduced by the British Standards Institution in 2007 and is endorsed by the Royal Geographical Society (RGS). The BS 8848 kitemark is granted to companies and organisations that maintain high standards of safety and procedures.* **Shane Winser** *at the RGS feels strongly that gappers and their parents should be encouraged to ask companies if they are BS 8848 compliant and if not why not. In 2009 she wrote to this book:*

*I am getting increasingly concerned about the number of British-based companies who are acting as re-sellers of gap year experiences and yet taking little or no responsibility for carrying out checks on those who are providing the experiences. Worse still some will not even divulge details of the project provider until the deposit is paid.*

A good organisation should be able to tell an applicant exactly what work they will be doing and precise contact details for the overseas project. Assuming you care about such things (and even if you don't beforehand, you probably will after spending some time in a developing country), ask the company what financial contribution they make to the voluntary project and about their ethical tourism policy. Some gap year companies wait until a paying customer has signed up before finding a placement abroad and these are often less satisfactory. Sustainable development means 'development which meets the needs of the present without compromising the ability of future generations to meet their own needs'.

Everybody will tell you that you have to set the wheels in motion about a year before you are ready to go. But in fact lots of people start their gap year with nothing fixed up. It turns out that all those organisations whose literature contains dire warnings of the consequences of procrastination often have last-minute vacancies, so it is worth ringing around whenever you decide you want to go for it. With the recent explosion in gap year provision, there is often an over-supply of places, and in many cases they need you more than you need them.

This chapter sets out the programmes of more than 100 leading organisations which are equipped to organise all or part of your gap year for you. The majority is based in the UK though some American organisations welcome all nationalities onto their programmes. The organisations listed below specifically target gap year students. Many other organisations listed in the other directories in the *Volunteering*, *Work Experience*, *Au Pairing* and *Courses* chapters and also in the country chapters welcome gap year students with open arms but do not specialise in catering for them.

Another consideration is the financial soundness of the company. Not all gap year companies have financial protection for the consumer in the form of an ATOL licence and personalised insurance certificates. The 1992 Package Travel Regulations state that any company that arranges a package (and this is simply two or more elements of travel such as flights, accommodation and transport) should have coverage in place, whether it be a bond, ATOL licence or insurance policy.

## SOURCES OF INFORMATION

The internet is awash with sites that claim to be definitive sources of information for people planning a gap year and yet link to just a handful of advertisers, usually the most commercial companies operating in the field.

The main sites and services are:

***gapyear.com***, (www.gapyear.com). Largest gap year community in the UK dedicated to helping people plan and prepare for a gap year. The massive website www.gapyear.com claims to have more than 100,000 pages of information about 100 countries and a section to help plan an RTW trip (www.gapyear.com/rtw) in association with STA. Users can find travelmates, access a database with thousands of opportunities, pose questions on the message boards and buy kit.

***gapadvice.org***, (www.gapadvice.org). Independent advisory service that provides unbiased up-to-date information, research and advice on gap years for individuals (of all ages) and organisations. The director is Phil Murray. Fees for individual advice are: £50 for basic service; £125 or £200 for more personalised consultation.

***WorldWide Volunteering (WWV)***, (www.wwv.org.uk). Non-profit organisation designed to help people of all ages get involved with volunteering and find a placement that suits them. WWV's online database of 1,700 organisations on its website offers a potential total of 1.5 million placements and is free for all to use. The director is Peter Sharp. The site also carries volunteers' stories.

***Gap Enterprise Consultants***, (Oxfordshire OX27 8DG; 01869 278346; johnvessey@ gapenterprise.co.uk; www.gapenterprise.co.uk). Gap year consultancy that offers private consultations to help plan a structured year out. Consultation fee of £400 covers detailed confidential questionnaire, three-hour interview, comprehensive 50-page written report (including client-specific contacts list) and follow-up. The director is John Vessey.

**Gapwork.com**, (www.gapwork.com). Publisher and provider of gap year and working holiday information. The website provides a range of information on taking a gap year including listings of accommodation providers, employment opportunities and gap year organisations.

**iGapYear.com**, (www.igapyear.com). Has a far from comprehensive database of gap year options. Includes some first-hand content and a blog/travel diary section.

**Careerscope Gap Year Magazine**, (www.careerscope.co.uk). Can be read online (regular price £4). Updated annually (www.careerscope.co.uk/gap/index.html).

Of course Facebook and other networking sites have become the first port of call for students looking for feedback on particular programmes. Last year the mainstream agency Frontier attracted some negative publicity after an article was published in the *Guardian* (www.guardian.co.uk/travel/2008/sep/06/gapyeartravel.workingholidays) describing the experiences of some disappointed participants. One of them, **Hannah Lemkov** aged 19, volunteered through Frontier to work with Peace Child as an English teacher in Bangalore, and afterwards set up a Facebook group called 'Frontier: Charity? No'. Everyone has to weigh up complaints and rebuttals and decide whether or not the evidence justifies eliminating them from your list of possibilities.

Wherever you look, services and niche websites target gap year students, from Gap Year NZ (www.gapyear-newzealand.co.uk) to Traveltree.co.uk, a website directory that enlightens visitors with opportunities for gap year ideas as well as adventure and educational travel, internships and volunteering opportunities. Many of these are referred to in the appropriate context throughout this book.

The *Jobs Abroad Bulletin* is a useful one-man and one-woman site (www.jobs abroadbulletin.co.uk) which dispenses with pretty graphics to deliver actual job vacancy details each month. E-mail subscriptions to what is billed as an 'online magazine for working abroad and taking a gap year' are free. Also look at www.payaway.co.uk/gap. shtml from the same people.

Gap year fairs are held around the country through the spring and early summer and are generally free and open to anyone. One series is organised by Futurewise (www. myfuturewise.org.uk) whose website will direct you to the dozen or so fairs held at various schools between June and October. Visiting one of these fairs gives you a chance to meet in person representatives of various companies as well as real live ex-gappers. Many sixth form careers departments organise gap year information evenings though these are often partisan events at which a few gap year company representatives are pushing their schemes. Remember that there are always more options out there than are in front of you at one of these events. **Ed Fry** went along to one of these at his school but wanted more independent advice:

*I was given some advice at school as to how I might wish to structure my gap year in terms of travel, work and so on but many of the people that came to speak at school had a commercial slant to their talks which made me slightly dubious of their advice. Teachers were very helpful in terms of advising on countries to visit and things to do. A short course was also offered on how to stay safe in your gap year, but it was an extra cost and basically all common sense.*

# DIRECTORY OF SPECIALIST GAP YEAR PROGRAMMES

## ADVENTURE ALTERNATIVE

PO Box 14, Portstewart, Northern
Ireland BT55 7WS
02870 831258
office@adventurealternative.com
www.adventurealternative.com

**PROGRAMME DESCRIPTION:** Combined teaching/
community work, group activities (e.g. climbing,
trekking, rafting, safaris) and independent travel. In
Kenya participants teach and work in rural and slum
schools supported by AA's charity Moving Mountains
(movingmountains.org.uk) and/or in orphanages and
rescue centres. In Nepal, participants help in rural
development projects that can be combined with trek to
Everest Base Camp or to Model Green Village. Medical
electives are also available for medical students and
doctors in both countries.

**DESTINATIONS:** Rural and inner city Kenya and
Himalayan Nepal.

**NUMBER OF PLACEMENTS PER YEAR:** 42 for Kenya,
60 for Nepal.

**PREREQUISITES:** Minimum age 17; average age 22.
Hard-working committed enthusiastic gap year students
who are not fazed by the hardships of living in a
developing country. All nationalities.

**DURATION AND TIME OF PLACEMENTS:** 1–3
months. All trips are tailor-made; longer trips are
available.

**COSTS:** 3-month placement costs £1,850 (excluding
flights).

**CONTACT:** Gavin Bate, Director; Chris Little or Andy
MacDonald, expedition coordinators.

## AFRICA, ASIA & AMERICAS VENTURE

10 Market Place, Devizes, Wiltshire SN10 1HT
01380 729009
av@aventure.co.uk
www.aventure.co.uk

Founding member of the Year Out Group. Africa, Asia
& Americas Venture is an organisation which enables
students to gain teaching, sports coaching, community
and conservation work experience (unpaid). Participants
work in small groups/pairs, but are part of a larger
group of up to 30 18–24-year-old volunteers.

**PROGRAMME DESCRIPTION:** Students are placed
in selected rural secondary and primary schools for
approximately 3 months, teaching a variety of subjects
and helping with extracurricular activities, especially
sports. This is followed by 2–3 weeks of backpacking
before going on safari to areas of interest and outstanding beauty in the chosen country.

**DESTINATIONS:** Uganda, Kenya, Tanzania, Malawi,
South Africa, India, Nepal, Sri Lanka, Thailand, China,
Costa Rica, Ecuador and Mexico.

**NUMBER OF PLACEMENTS PER YEAR:** 380–420.

**PREREQUISITES:** Students going on to further education or undergraduates considering taking time out can
apply. Participants are generally aged 18–24 when
they join the scheme, although any age may apply.
Volunteers should enjoy working with young people.

**DURATION AND TIME OF PLACEMENTS:** 3 weeks to
4/5 months, with departures all year round.

**SELECTION PROCEDURES AND ORIENTATION:**
On application, a company representative will ring to
answer questions and to get to know the potential participant. A face-to-face interview will then take place in

UK (telephone call if applying from outside UK) so that a satisfactory placement and partner can be found.

**COST:** The basic cost (2009/10) is £1,750 for 3 weeks, £2,050 for 5 weeks, £3,125 for 4/5 months, which covers orientation course, living/food allowance, accommodation, a 6–8 day group safari, and in-country back-up. Prices do not include airfares, entry visas and insurance.

### AFRICAN CONSERVATION EXPERIENCE

Unit 1, Manor Farm, Churchend Lane, Charfield, Wotton-Under-Edge, Gloucester GL12 8LJ

℡ 0845 5200 888

✍ info@ConservationAfrica.net

🖥 www.ConservationAfrica.net

Member of the Year Out Group.

**PROGRAMME DESCRIPTION:** Conservation work placements for young people on game reserves in Southern Africa. Tasks may include darting rhino for relocation or elephant for fitting tracking collars. Game capture, tagging, assisting with veterinary work, game counts and monitoring may be part of the work programme. Alien plant control and the re-introduction of indigenous plants is often involved. There are also two marine research assistant projects.

**DESTINATIONS:** Southern Africa including South Africa, Botswana and Mauritius.

**PREREQUISITES:** Must have reasonable physical fitness. Enthusiasm for conservation is most important qualification. Programme may be of special interest to students of environmental, zoological and marine sciences, veterinary science and animal care.

**DURATION AND TIME OF PLACEMENTS:** 2–12 weeks throughout the year.

**SELECTION PROCEDURES AND ORIENTATION:** Candidates are matched to a suitable project on the information provided on their application form but do have final say on their placement. Optional open days are held at various locations in the UK.

**COST:** Varies depending on reserve and time of year. Students can expect an average total cost of about £3,320 for 4 weeks up to £5,220 for 12 weeks, which includes international flights (from London), transfers, accommodation and all meals. Support and advice given on fundraising.

**CONTACT:** Alexia Massey, UK Operations Manager.

### AFRICATRUST NETWORKS

Africatrust Chambers, PO Box 551, Portsmouth, Hampshire PO5 1ZN

℡ 02392 730987

✍ info@africatrust.org.uk

🖥 www.africatrust.org.uk

**PROGRAMME DESCRIPTION:** UK NGO that makes residential placements for pre-university and mainly post-university students, to teach young children, help with disabled, homeless, blind and orphaned children, etc.

**DESTINATIONS:** Ghana (Cape Coast and Kumasi), Cameroon and Morocco working with the Moroccan Children's Trust (www.moroccanchildrenstrust.org).

**PREREQUISITES:** Volunteers must be at least 18 (most are 21+), in good health and preferably non-smokers. A-Level French is needed for Morocco.

**DURATION AND TIME OF PLACEMENTS:** 3 and 6 months.

**SELECTION PROCEDURES AND ORIENTATION:** Application form available on website. References will be taken up and interviews scheduled in London. Briefing information on health, fundraising and projects are sent. There is a compulsory pre-departure briefing in London for volunteers and their families plus induction course.

**COST:** Cameroon project is subsidised: £850 for 3 months, £1,700 for 6 months. Other prices on application.

### AIL MADRID SPANISH LANGUAGE IMMERSION SCHOOL IN SPAIN

C/ Nuñez de Balboa 17, 2° D, 28001 Madrid, Spain

℡ +34 91 72 56 350

✍ info@ailmadrid.com

🖥 www.ailmadrid.com/gap year/home

**PROGRAMME DESCRIPTION:** 12-week Spanish language course in Madrid and other cities in Spain with work placement options.

**PREREQUISITES:** Minimum age 17, average age 22.

**DURATION AND TIME OF PLACEMENTS:** 12–48 weeks with flexible start dates.

**COST:** 12-week programme from €3,500.

**CONTACT:** Maya Bychova.

---

### AMANZI TRAVEL
4 College Road, Westbury on Trym, Bristol
BS9 3EJ
℃ 0117 904 1924
🖱 info@amanzitravel.co.uk
🖥 www.amanzitravel.co.uk

**PROGRAMME DESCRIPTION:** Worthwhile volunteer placements throughout Africa providing opportunities to help conserve endangered wildlife; work on teaching and community development projects and help at medical clinics and hospitals. Projects include working with big cats at the leading Lion Breeding/Release Project at Victoria Falls; helping at the Bushman Medical Clinic in Namibia; looking after AIDS orphans in Cape Town; teaching disadvantaged children in schools in Zambia or Tanzania; coaching the local children's football team in Mwanza, Tanzania; and helping at wildlife sanctuaries throughout Africa. A range of adventure activities and safari trips (3–56 days) is also offered, plus courses in photography and in how to become a Field Guide or Game Ranger.

**DESTINATIONS:** Botswana, Kenya, Mozambique, Namibia, South Africa, Tanzania, Uganda, Zambia and Zimbabwe.

**NUMBER OF PLACEMENTS PER YEAR:** 500.

**DURATION AND TIME OF PLACEMENTS:** 2 weeks to 1 year, with flexible start dates.

**PREREQUISITES:** All ages including gap year students and mature volunteers.

**SELECTION PROCEDURES AND ORIENTATION:**
Comprehensive pre-departure pack and full orientation on arrival.

**OTHER SERVICES:** Tailor-made trip itineraries including flight arrangements and advice on insurance.

**COST:** From £300 for short placements. Sample cost £1,295 for 4 weeks in Namibia.

**CONTACT:** Gemma Whitehouse, Managing Director.

---

### ART HISTORY ABROAD
The Red House, 1 Lambseth Street,
Eye, Suffolk IP23 7AG
℃ 01379 871800
🖱 info@arthistoryabroad.com
🖥 www.arthistoryabroad.com

Year Out Group founding member.

**PROGRAMME DESCRIPTION:** Programme based around the great art, architecture and sculpture of Italy, this course is about European civilisation in the broadest sense. Participants spend 6 weeks travelling throughout Italy including Venice, Verona, Florence, Siena, Naples and Rome. No classroom work is involved and all tuition is on-site and in groups of no more than 10; 2-week summer holiday courses in Italy also available. A new course in Contemporary Art and Architecture based in London has just been introduced.

**NUMBER OF PLACEMENTS PER YEAR:** 27 per course, 4 times per year.

**DURATION AND TIME OF PLACEMENT:** 6-week course offered 4 times a year (autumn, spring, early summer and late summer) and 2-week courses offered in July/August.

**COST:** £6,990 (2010) for the autumn, spring and early summer courses including travel to, from and within Italy, hotel accommodation and breakfast throughout, all museum entry, expert tuition in small groups as well as drawing and Italian conversation classes and a private visit to San Marco in Venice. Fees do not include lunch or supper. Price for 2-week summer courses in Italy is £2,750. London-based courses from £1,090.

**ACCOMMODATION:** Shared rooms in hotels in the centre of each city visited.

## AU PAIR IN AMERICA

37 Queen's Gate, London SW7 5HR

℡ 020 7581 7322

✉ info@aupairamerica.co.uk

🖥 www.aupairamerica.co.uk

Parent organisation (American Institute for Foreign Study) founded in 1967 and the au pair programme authorised in 1986.

**PROGRAMME DESCRIPTION:** Au Pair in America operates the largest and longest established legal childcare programme to the United States. Au pairs are placed with a screened American family for a minimum of 12 months and maximum of 24. Other programmes that run alongside are the EduCare in America (for students who work shorter hours to allow more time for studies and receive less pocket money) and Au Pair Extraordinaire (for qualified and experienced child-carers).

**NUMBER OF PLACEMENTS PER YEAR:** 4,000+.

**DURATION AND TIME OF PLACEMENTS:** 12–24 months. Au pairs provide 45 hours of childcare per week.

**PREREQUISITES:** All nationalities are eligible provided there is an established interviewer network in their country. Ages 18–26. Must have at least 200 hours recent non-family practical childcare experience gained within the past 3 years. Must hold a full driving licence and be available for 12 months.

**SELECTION PROCEDURES AND ORIENTATION:** Applicants must submit a complete application and attend a personal interview with an appointed Au Pair in America interviewer. Au Pair in America has representatives in 45 countries and agent/interviewers throughout the UK.

**COST:** $500 programme fee. Au pairs who successfully complete their 12-month minimum stay will receive a $200 completion payment.

**BENEFITS:** Free return airfare London to New York, 4-day orientation programme held near New York, legal J-1 visa, weekly payment of $195.75, up to $500 study tuition allowance, medical insurance, 2 weeks paid holidays, optional 13th month travel, year-long support from US community counsellor and placement in an established au pair 'cluster group'.

### BASE CAMP GROUP
Unit 30, Baseline Business Studios, Whitchurch Road, London W11 4AT
*℄* 020 7243 6222
*✎* contact@basecampgroup.com
*▤* www.basecampgroup.com

**PROGRAMME DESCRIPTION:** Adventure training company founded in 2002 offering Ski and Snowboard Instructor Courses in the French and Swiss Alps, Canadian Rockies and Argentina. See entry in 'Directory of Sport and Activity Courses'.

### BRITISH COUNCIL ASSISTANTS PROGRAMME
10 Spring Gardens, London SW1A 2BN
*℄* 020 7389 4596
*✎* assistants@britishcouncil.org
*▤* www.britishcouncil.org/languageassistants

**PROGRAMME DESCRIPTION:** English Language Assistants Programme for modern language students and recent graduates. Applicants should be aged 20–30 with at least 2 years of university-level education. For most countries A/AS Level in the language of the destination country is the minimum foreign language requirement. There is no language requirement for China.

**DESTINATIONS:** Country-by-country details are available on the website. Most posts are in Austria, France, Germany, Spain, China and Latin America. Posts also exist in Italy, Belgium, Switzerland, Canada and Senegal.

**DURATION AND TIME OF PLACEMENTS:** One academic year, i.e. September or October to May or June, depending on country.

**SELECTION PROCEDURES AND ORIENTATION:** Application forms are downloadable from the website from October for a deadline of 1 December.

**COST:** Travel costs, visas and vaccinations where necessary. Monthly stipend paid to assistants varies from country to country, e.g. €940 gross in France.

### THE BRITISH INSTITUTE OF FLORENCE
Piazza Strozzi 2, 50123 Florence, Italy
*℄* +39 055 2677 8200
*✎* info@britishinstitute.it
*▤* www.britishinstitute.it

Housed in two historic buildings on the River Arno close to the city's museums, galleries and churches, the British Institute offers students a chance to experience the life and culture of Florence within a structured programme of study.

**PROGRAMME DESCRIPTION:** The British Institute offers year-round courses in Italian language, history of art and life drawing. A summer school takes place in Massa Marittima near the Tuscan coast during the first fortnight in August. The institute also hosts a regular programme of events, many of them free, including lectures, concerts and films in the institute's Harold Acton Library.

**DURATION AND TIME OF PLACEMENTS:** Courses last 1–12 weeks.

**COST:** Tuition fees vary. For example a 1-week Italian language course costs from €205, and a 1-week history of art course costs from €195. Accommodation can be arranged in local homes, *pensione* and hotels plus €25 arrangement fee.

### BSES EXPEDITIONS
Royal Geographical Society, 1 Kensington Gore, London SW7 2AR
*℄* 020 7591 3141
*✎* info@bses.org.uk
*▤* www.bses.org.uk

BSES Expeditions organises overseas expeditions worldwide for 16–23 year olds. See entry in 'Directory of Expeditions'.

## BUNAC

16 Bowling Green Lane, London EC1R 0QH

✆ 020 7251 3472

🖂 enquiries@bunac.org.uk

🖳 www.bunac.org

Founding member of the Year Out Group. BUNAC is a non-profit national student club offering work and travel programmes worldwide. It acts as an aide before and after arrival in the country of travel and acts as a 'security blanket' if situations go wrong while the student is abroad.

**PROGRAMME DESCRIPTION:** Various work programmes in North America and elsewhere. A large number of students and non-students are placed on summer camps (see *USA* chapter). BUNAC makes it possible for candidates to obtain the necessary visas and publishes its own job directories which help members to fix up short-term jobs before or after arrival.

**DESTINATIONS:** Work programmes in USA, Canada, New Zealand, Australia and South Africa; volunteer programmes in South Africa, Ghana, Costa Rica, Peru, Cambodia, India and China.

**PREREQUISITES:** Work America students must have documentary evidence that they are enrolled in a higher education degree course (gap year students not eligible). For Work Canada, evidence of a guaranteed place in higher education is sufficient. Limited places for non-students in Canada and the USA. Work Australia and Work New Zealand are open to all 18–30 year olds (see country chapters).

**DURATION AND TIME OF PLACEMENTS:** 9 weeks on summer camps in the USA. Participants on the Work America programme must return to a full-time course in the UK in September/October. Other programmes in other countries can last up to 2 years.

**SELECTION PROCEDURES AND ORIENTATION:** BUNAC holds information evenings at venues around the country.

**COST:** Applicants need to pay a registration fee (includes £5 BUNAC membership fee) and budget for flights, insurance and spending money.

## CALEDONIA LANGUAGES ABROAD

The Clockhouse, 72 Newhaven Road, Edinburgh EH6 5QG

✆ 0131 621 7721/2

🖂 courses@caledonialanguages.co.uk

🖳 www.caledonialanguages.co.uk

Established in 1994.

**PROGRAMME DESCRIPTION:** Short and long-term language courses throughout Europe and Latin America all year round, ideal as a gap year option. Courses available to suit all levels from beginner to advanced, and all ages from 17. Volunteer work programmes in Latin America for students with at least lower intermediate level Spanish or Portuguese, in ecological, community, conservation and social welfare projects, working and living with local people.

**DESTINATIONS:** Caledonia's partner language schools are in France, Italy, Germany, Spain, Russia, Portugal, Peru, Mexico, Ecuador, Cuba, Bolivia, Chile, Costa Rica, Brazil and Argentina (see entry in 'Directory of Language Courses').

**DURATION OF COURSES:** Language courses from 4 weeks upwards; volunteer work programme from 4 weeks upwards.

**SELECTION PROCEDURES AND ORIENTATION:** Briefing meetings for volunteers are held during the pre-placement language course in-country. Depending on the location, site visits can be organised before the placement. In-country back-up support is given throughout.

**COST:** £250 plus VAT administration fee plus fees for the pre-placement language course in the overseas country plus accommodation and travel. 4-week language course and half-board homestay costs £900 in Bolivia, Ecuador and Peru, £945 in Costa Rica and £1,365 in Argentina. The weekly cost of self-catering accommodation during volunteer project is £65–£70 in most countries except Argentina where it is £125.

## CAMP COUNSELORS USA (CCUSA)

*London office*: Devon House, 171/177 Great Portland Street, London W1W 5PQ

- 📞 020 7637 0779
- ✉ info@ccusa.co.uk
- 🖥 www.ccusa.com

*Scottish office*: 39 Sherwood Terrace, Bonnyrigg, EH19 3NB

- 📞 0131 454 1687
- ✉ Scotland@ccusa.co.uk

*US headquarters*: 2330 Marinship Way, Suite 250, Sausalito, CA 94965

- 📞 +1 415 339 2728

**PROGRAMME DESCRIPTION:** Camp Counsellor placement in the US plus Work Experience in the USA, Australia, New Zealand and Brazil. Placements on summer camps in Russia, Croatia and Canada. Teaching in China. Volunteering in South Africa and many South American countries.

**DESTINATIONS:** USA, Canada, Australia, New Zealand, South Africa, China, Brazil, Russia and Croatia.

**PREREQUISITES:** Ages 18–30 for most programmes.

**DURATION AND TIME OF PLACEMENTS:** 9 weeks for camp counsellors, 3–4 months working in the USA (between late May and October), 4–12 weeks in South Africa, 12–18 month business training programme in America, 6 months in Canada (ski resort jobs November-April), and up to 12 months in Australia and New Zealand.

**COST:** Camp Counselors USA fee from £299, Work Experience USA Placement £580, Independent £354; Practical Training USA £540 (12 months) or £810 (18 months), Work Adventures Downunder £425. First year counsellors aged 18 earn US$675 in pocket money. Prices based on 2008/2009 season and may change.

## CAMPS INTERNATIONAL LIMITED

Unit 1, Kingfisher Park, Headlands Business Park, Salisbury Road, Blashford, Ringwood, Hampshire BH24 3NX

- 📞 01425 485390
- ✉ info@campsinternational.com
- 🖥 www.campsinternational.com

**PROGRAMME DESCRIPTION:** Gap year placements and expeditions in Kenya, Tanzania, Zanzibar and Borneo for 18–24 year olds and community volunteering for adults 25 years upwards and families. Co-located with rural communities, participants undertake a range of community and wildlife projects and also have the opportunity to trek Mt Kenya, Kilimanjaro or Mt Kinabalu, or to do a PADI scuba diving course or a jungle trek.

**DESTINATIONS:** Kenya, Tanzania, Zanzibar and Borneo.

**DURATION AND TIME OF PLACEMENTS:** 1 week to 3 months.

**SELECTION PROCEDURES AND ORIENTATION:** Must be motivated and enthusiastic.

**COST:** £695–£2,860 depending on placement and duration.

**CONTACT:** Lucy Gould or Sammy Baker.

## CESA LANGUAGES ABROAD

CESA House, Pennance Road, Lanner, Cornwall TR16 5TQ

- 📞 01209 211800
- ✉ info@cesalanguages.com
- 🖥 www.cesalanguages.com

Founding member of the Year Out Group (yearoutgroup. org).

**PROGRAMME DESCRIPTION:** Major provider of language courses in France, Guadeloupe, Spain, Ecuador, Argentina, Chile, Costa Rica, Mexico, Germany, Austria, Italy, Portugal, Greece, Russia, Morocco and China. See entry in 'Directory of Courses'.

## CHANGING WORLDS

11 Doctors Lane, Chaldon, Surrey CR3 5AE

℡ 01883 340960

✉ ask@changingworlds.co.uk

🖥 www.changingworlds.co.uk

ATOL licensed and member of the Year Out Group. Aims to provide full cultural immersion through challenging and worthwhile work placements with a safety net if required.

**PROGRAMME DESCRIPTION:** Gap year options ranging from voluntary teaching placements in developing countries to paid placements in prestigious hotels.

**DESTINATIONS:** Argentina, Australia, Brazil, China, Ghana, Honduras, India, Kenya, Latvia, Madagascar, New Zealand, Romania, Serbia, South Africa, Thailand and Uganda.

**NUMBER OF PLACEMENTS PER YEAR:** 120.

**PREREQUISITES:** A Level or equivalent plus initiative, determination, adaptability and social skills.

**DURATION AND TIME OF PLACEMENTS:** 1– 6 months. Placements begin throughout the year.

**SELECTION PROCEDURES AND ORIENTATION:** Interview days held in Surrey every 6–8 weeks. All participants attend a pre-departure briefing; for those going to a developing country, this is a 2-day residential course. Participants are met on arrival in the country and attend orientation with the local representative before proceeding to placement. Local representatives act as support during placement. Changing Worlds is a member of Interhealth which can provide health screening to all participants and act as travel health advisers.

**COST:** From £1,775 for Latvia. Prices include return flights but exclude insurance (approximately £200 for 6 months).

**CONTACT:** David Gill, Director.

## CORAL CAY CONSERVATION

Elizabeth House, 39 York Road, London SE1 7NJ

℡ 020 7620 1411. Fax: 020 7921 0469

✉ info@coralcay.org

🖥 www.coralcay.org

Founding member of the Year Out Group and the FCO's Know Before You Go Campaign. Since 1986, CCC has been an international leader in recognising the importance of managing coral reefs for everyone's prosperity.

**PROGRAMME DESCRIPTION:** Volunteers gather key information about the state and condition of tropical forests and coral reefs around the world, for the benefit of the local communities that depend on these ecosystems for their livelihood. On expedition volunteers learn to survey, identify, record and differentiate between a plethora of plants and animals that thrive in these beautiful yet fragile environments. Furthermore, volunteers are given the opportunity to involve themselves in community conservation, which involves visiting local communities, planning and running environmental workshops, beach clean ups, theatrical education plays, giving snorkelling lessons to young locals and more.

**DESTINATIONS:** Philippines, Tobago and Cambodia.

**NUMBER OF PLACEMENTS PER YEAR:** 300–500. Sites vary in size and therefore in the number of volunteers they can accommodate.

**PREREQUISITES:** No previous experience is required as full training in marine and terrestrial ecology is provided on-site. On all marine expeditions, volunteers are given PADI scuba training if needed, at no additional cost.

**DURATION AND TIME OF PLACEMENTS:** Expeditions depart monthly throughout the year. Minimum stay is 2 weeks.

**SELECTION PROCEDURES AND ORIENTATION:** A free information pack is available on request, and free presentations are held on the second Wednesday and final Saturday of every month; places should be pre-booked.

**COST:** Expeditions start from £650 for 2 weeks. Prices exclude flights and insurance.

**CONTACT:** Peter Mandara, PR & Communications Coordinator.

## CROSS-CULTURAL SOLUTIONS

UK Office: Tower Point 44, North Road, Brighton BN1 1YR

℡ 0845 458 2781/2

✉ infouk@crossculturalsolutions.org

🖥 www.crossculturalsolutions.org

See entry in 'Directory of Volunteering Abroad'.

## CSV

Community Service Volunteers, 5th Floor,
Scala House, 36 Holloway Circus, Queensway,
Birmingham B1 1EQ

℡ 0800 374991

℡ 0121 643 7690

🖱 volunteer@csv.org.uk

📖 www.csv.org.uk/fulltimevolunteering

CSV is the largest voluntary placement organisation
in the UK. It provides voluntary placements to UK/EEA
nationals who are residents in the UK and aged 16–35
who are committed to volunteering full-time and
away from home for up to 12 months in a huge range
of social care projects. See entry in 'Directory of
Volunteering in the UK'. Other international volunteers
can participate provided they apply through one of
CSV's international partnerships (details from
www.csv.org.uk/ftvol).

## DEUTSCH-INSTITUT TIROL

Am Sandhügel 2, 6370 Kitzbühel, Austria

℡ +53 56 712 74

🖱 office@deutschinstitut.com

📖 www.gap-year.at

**PROGRAMME DESCRIPTION:** Gap Year Winter Sports
(Sept to Dec) in conjunction with German language
course, specially designed for gap year students.
Language instruction combined with ski and snowboard
instruction with possibility of training for ski/snowboard
instructor's exams.

**DESTINATIONS:** Gap Year Winter Sports skiing/
snowboarding in October and November takes place
Thursday to Sunday at Kaprun at the foot of a glacier
(45-minute drive from Kitzbühel). German lessons
Monday to Wednesday take place in Kitzbühel.
Programme includes 1-week trip to Salzburg,
Vienna, Budapest, Prague and Budweis.

**PREREQUISITES:** Any level of German or none can
be catered for. Similarly beginners or more advanced
skiers/snowboarders welcome.

**DURATION AND TIME OF PLACEMENT:** 12-week
winter programme (mid-Sept to mid-Dec).

**COST:** €8,200.

**CONTACT:** Louise Ebenhöh.

## DEVELOPMENT IN ACTION

78 York Street, London W1H 1DP

℡ 07813 395957

🖱 info@developmentinaction.org

📖 www.developmentinaction.org

**PROGRAMME DESCRIPTION:** Arrange voluntary
attachments to various locally based development NGOs
in India for 2 months in summer or 5 months from September. See entry in 'Directory of Volunteering Abroad'.

## ECOLOGIA YOUTH TRUST

The Park, Forres, Moray, Scotland IV36 3TD

℡ 01309 690995

🖱 info@ecologia.org.uk

📖 www.ecologia.org.uk

**PROGRAMME DESCRIPTION:** Volunteer programme
open to gap year students at the Kitezh Children's Community for orphans in western Russia. Russian language
is not essential although students of Russian will quickly
become fluent. (See entry in 'Directory of Volunteering
Abroad' and further details in chapter on Russia.)

## EIL UK

Elphick House, 287 Worcester Road, Malvern,
Worcestershire WR14 1AB

℡ 0800 018 4015

℡ 01684 562577

🖱 info@eiluk.org

📖 www.eiluk.org

EIL (Experiment in International Living) is a registered
charity that specialises in increasing understanding
between cultures. Educational and cultural programmes
for young people in their gap year or long vacations. Partner offices in 30 countries. See also www.
volunteering18-30.org.uk and www.overseas
volunteering.org.uk, maintained by EIL UK.

**PROGRAMME DESCRIPTION:** Various programmes include European Voluntary Service (EVS) described below, volunteer programmes, homestays worldwide, language tuition, teaching English, environmental projects, and helping with specialist projects, all in line with the UN Millennium development goals (e.g. halting the spread of HIV/AIDS).

**DESTINATIONS:** Africa, Asia, Australasia, Europe, South America and USA.

**DURATION AND TIME OF PLACEMENTS:** 4 weeks to 1 year.

**COST:** Costs vary depending upon the type of stay chosen.

---

### EL CASAL BARCELONA

Balmes 163, 3–1, 08008 Barcelona, Spain

✆ +34 93 217 9038

✉ info@elcasalbarcelona.com

🖥 www.elcasalbarcelona.com

---

**PROGRAMME DESCRIPTION:** El Casal is a gap year programme for well-motivated high school graduates who want to experience Spanish culture and who are looking for a rewarding and stimulating experience before they begin college.

**NUMBER OF PLACEMENTS:** 16.

**PREREQUISITES:** Minimum age 17, average age 18. All nationalities (though majority are North American). Participants should have at least 2 years of Spanish and a good academic record.

**DURATION AND TIME OF PLACEMENTS:** 100 days.

**SELECTION PROCEDURES AND ORIENTATION:** Normally, participants have been accepted to a selective 4-year college in the USA and have chosen to postpone their enrolment. Week-long orientation programme encompasses 'survival' and practical skills in Barcelona, host family adjustment workshops and intensive Spanish workshops.

**COST:** €8,400 inclusive covers academic programme (spring or fall), room and board with a host family, excursions, day trips, all local transport, all expenses on the 6-day Camino de Santiago hiking portion of the programme, etc. Not included: transportation to and from Barcelona at the beginning/end of the programme, lunches, miscellaneous and personal expenses.

**CONTACT:** John Rosen, Director.

---

### EUROPEAN VOLUNTARY SERVICE (EVS)

Youth in Action, British Council, 10 Spring Gardens, London SW1A 2BN

✆ 020 7389 4030

✉ action2.enquiries@britishcouncil.org

✉ connectyouth.enquiries@britishcouncil.org

🖥 www.britishcouncil.org/connectyouth-programmes-evs.htm

---

**PROGRAMME DESCRIPTION:** Fully funded initiative of the European Commission to promote mobility among Europeans and to encourage young people (aged 18–30) to volunteer in European countries, engaging in cultural, educational and training opportunities. Huge range of projects including social care, youth work, outdoor recreation and rural development.

**DESTINATIONS:** Europe.

**NUMBER OF PLACEMENTS:** EVS provides several thousand volunteers with free travel, food, accommodation and an allowance.

**PREREQUISITES:** Applicants must be aged 18–30 and be a legal resident in one of the EU member states (including Turkey, Norway, Iceland and Liechtenstein). No specific qualifications are needed and language training may be provided.

**DURATION AND TIME OF PLACEMENTS:** Standard voluntary service is for 6–12 months. Shorter-term placements are on offer (2 weeks to 2 months) to young people with fewer opportunities.

**SELECTION PROCEDURES AND ORIENTATION:** Applicants need to apply through an approved sending organisation (details for volunteers and organisations can be obtained through Connect Youth). For further information on potential placements, see http://ec.europa.eu/youth/evs/aod/hei_en.cfm. Sending organisations with entries in this book include ICYE and EIL.

**COST:** No cost to volunteers, as the programme is funded through the European Youth in Action programme. Pocket money is provided weekly or monthly.

## FLYING FISH

25 Union Road, Cowes, Isle of Wight PO31 7TW

℗ 0871 250 2500

✉ mail@flyingfishonline.com

💻 www.flyingfishonline.com

Member of the Year Out Group. Flying Fish trains water and snowsports staff and arranges employment for sailors, divers, surfers and windsurfers, skiers and snowboarders. Founded in 1993 it can help young people to fix up a year of travel, training and adventure, or to start a career in the action sports industry.

**PROGRAMME DESCRIPTION:** A gap year with Flying Fish starts with a course leading to qualification as a surf, sail or windsurf instructor, yacht skipper, divemaster or dive instructor, ski or snowboard instructor (see entry in 'Directory of Sport and Activity Courses'). After qualifying you can choose a period of work experience or go into a paid job in many locations worldwide, with advice from a Flying Fish careers adviser.

**DESTINATIONS:** Training courses are run at Cowes in the UK, at Sydney and the Whitsunday Islands in Australia, the Bay of Islands in New Zealand, Vassiliki in Greece and Whistler Mountain in Canada. Jobs are worldwide with main employers located in Australia, the South Pacific, the Caribbean and the Mediterranean.

**NUMBER OF PLACEMENTS PER YEAR:** 600.

**DURATION AND TIME OF PLACEMENTS:** 1 week to 12 months with start dates year round.

**SELECTION PROCEDURES AND ORIENTATION:** Applicants submit an application before training and will be asked to attend job interviews.

**COST:** Fees range from £800 to £11,000 but most gap year students choose a programme costing about £3,500. Accommodation and airfares are provided, with normal wages during employment.

## FRONTIER

50–52 Rivington Street, London EC2A 3QP

℗ 020 7613 2422

✉ info@frontier.ac.uk

💻 www.frontier.ac.uk

Frontier is a conservation research and development NGO, working in tropical countries since 1989, that is dedicated to saving endangered species, helping build sustainable livelihoods in rural areas and protecting tropical forests and reefs. Frontier works in partnership with international organisations, local governments and community organisations to address conservation and development priorities. Frontier is a founding member of the Year Out Group.

**PROGRAMME DESCRIPTION:** Frontier offers the opportunity to work in coral reefs, savannas, forests and mangrove areas as part of long-term conservation programmes in far-off destinations. Programmes are established in response to problems; surveys of damaged areas are carried out so that possible solutions can be identified. For example, dynamite fishing in Tanzania was damaging the web of delicate marine life. Frontier volunteers carried out more than 6,000 dives, resulting in the establishment of a Marine Park where the marine life is protected.

**DESTINATIONS:** Over 50 countries in Africa, Asia, Pacific Islands, Central and South America.

**NUMBER OF PLACEMENTS PER YEAR:** 900+.

**PREREQUISITES:** Minimum age 17. No specific qualifications required as training is provided in the field leading to a BTEC Advanced Diploma or Certificate in Tropical Habitat Conservation, a TEFL qualification, or PADI Advanced Open Water.

**DURATION AND TIME OF PLACEMENTS:** 2 weeks and longer departing year round.

**SELECTION PROCEDURES AND ORIENTATION:** Informal information sessions are held on Saturdays and Wednesdays (check website for dates) where interested parties can find out more from past volunteers. After an application has been submitted, a consultant will make contact the same day to discuss possible choices.

**COST:** From £350 for 9 days. Many projects include free dive training to PADI Advanced Open Water, free TEFL course and BTEC qualifications.

## GAPFORCE (GREENFORCE/TREKFORCE)

530 Fulham Road, London SW6 5NR

📞 020 7384 3343

📧 info@gapforce.org

🖥 www.gapforce.org

**PROGRAMME DESCRIPTION:** Gap year programmes include conservation and community development activities. Conservation volunteers work as fieldwork assistants, carrying out tasks such as tracking animal movements and studying coral reef species. Choice of land-based or diving projects. In some locations possibility of learning local languages (e.g. Nepali or Maasai). Humanitarian aid volunteers assist partner organisations in helping people in various poverty-stricken circumstances.

**DESTINATIONS:** Projects based around the world, including Fiji, Belize, Bahamas, Tanzania, Ecuador, Nepal, India, Thailand, Borneo, China and South Africa.

**PREREQUISITES:** No previous experience necessary; no qualifications required. Minimum age 17.

**DURATION AND TIME OF PLACEMENTS:** Flexible durations from a week to a year, but most last 2–10 weeks.

**SELECTION PROCEDURES AND ORIENTATION:** Applicants may attend an informal training day. A briefing pack is provided, giving information about fundraising and relevant medical advice, etc. Pre-departure training and a BBQ held in London plus reunion parties held after return to UK.

**COST:** From £590 for short expeditions; approximately £2,500 for 10-week projects and £4,100 for 5-month expeditions.

**CONTACT:** Sam Bliss, Trekker Co-ordinator.

## GAP GURU

Town Hall, Market Place, Newbury, Berkshire RG14 5AA

📞 0800 032 3350

📞 +44 1635 45556

📧 info@gapguru.com

🖥 www.GapGuru.com

Leading ethical gap year provider now allied to Mondo-Challenge (see entry below).

**PROGRAMME DESCRIPTION:** Specialist in India with recently added opportunities in other countries. Large range of volunteer placements and internships in teaching, medical, conservation, sport, business, etc. Add-on travel possibilities include trekking in the mountains, and exploring beaches, cities, deserts and temples.

**DESTINATIONS:** Throughout India. Also Tanzania, Chile, Sri Lanka, Nepal, Romania and Ecuador.

**PREREQUISITES:** Minimum age 18 (at time of travel). No qualifications needed for many projects. Training programmes (e.g. Hotel Management) and openings in some fields such as business and medicine are open to those studying or qualified in the relevant field.

**DURATION AND TIME OF PLACEMENTS:** 4 weeks to 12 months.

**SELECTION PROCEDURES AND ORIENTATION:** Applicants discuss possible projects before choosing. Pre-departure briefings are held and workplace orientations take place in India.

**COST:** Programmes start at £795 for 4 weeks, with a typical programme of 3 months costing around £1,850 including accommodation and most meals but excluding flights and insurance.

**ACCOMMODATION:** A shared twin-bedded room with a local family or other suitable accommodation. All accommodation is checked and vetted.

## GAP YEAR CANADA INCORPORATED

Box 4955, Banff, Alberta, Canada T1L 1G2

📞 020 7096 1632 (UK)

📞 +1 403 762 3625 (Canada)

📧 info@GapYearCanada.com

🖥 www.GapYearCanada.com

**PROGRAMME DESCRIPTION:** Specialist gap year agency for people aged 18–30 who want to work for a season in Banff, Canada. Chalet accommodation and jobs are pre-arranged for the season, and assistance is given with visas, flights and transfers. Sample jobs include guest services, ski rental and repair shop, retail stores, gondola operations, lift services, various food and beverage positions, Trail crew, ski and snowboard instructors, valet parking, and hotel staff. Also offer 3-month summer programme.

**DESTINATIONS:** Banff, Canada.

**NUMBER OF PLACEMENTS:** 65 (restricted by the number of chalets available for the season).

**PREREQUISITES:** Minimum age 18. Any nationality that is eligible for a Canadian student work visa (see *Canada* chapter). Must be adventurous, outgoing, enthusiastic and should be interested in learning to ski or snowboard, or improving skills.

**DURATION AND TIME OF PLACEMENTS:** Winter season (October till the end of May) at the resorts around Banff. Most winter employers prefer 6-month contracts. Minimum 3-month summer programme lasts from May/June to September/October.

**SELECTION PROCEDURES AND ORIENTATION:** Applications accepted on an ongoing basis though early application is recommended for the October start date. Agency helps with CV preparation, job placement, social insurance number processing, orientation to town upon arrival, as well as setting up bank accounts for the season. Gap Year Canada organise activities and events throughout the season.

**COST:** £3,000 for full 8-month winter season, which includes accommodation in furnished chalets and all services. Chalets have two-or three-bedded rooms. £300 per month in summer.

**CONTACT:** Nancy Myles, Programme Director.

---

### GAP YEAR DIVER
Tyte Court, Farbury End, Great Rollright, Oxfordshire OX7 5RS
© 0845 257 3292
📧 info@gapyeardiver.com
🌐 www.gapyeardiver.com

**PROGRAMME DESCRIPTION:** Scuba diving courses for all types of gappers in Egypt, Venezuela, Costa Rica, Thailand, Ecuador, Bahamas, Fiji and Belize. See entry in 'Directory of Sport and Activity Courses' and further details in chapter on Latin America.

---

### GAP YEAR SOUTH AFRICA
PO Box 592, Cambridge CB1 OES
© 020 8144 2423
📧 info@gapyearsouthafrica.com
🌐 www.GapYearSouthAfrica.com

**PROGRAMME DESCRIPTION:** Range of gap year projects arranged by on-the-ground organisation in South Africa including sports coaching, teaching and HIV/AIDS and health awareness, environmental awareness and medical projects.

**DESTINATIONS:** In and around Port Elizabeth, South Africa.

**PREREQUISITES:** Minimum age 17, average age 20. All nationalities accepted. No specific qualifications or skills needed, but rather general knowledge and an enthusiasm to teach or coach under-privileged children.

**DURATION AND TIME OF PLACEMENTS:** 3 months or 5 weeks, with weekly extensions if desired.

**SELECTION PROCEDURES AND ORIENTATION:** Applications accepted on ongoing basis until places are filled. Volunteers receive an induction on arrival in South Africa.

**COST:** For a 3-month trip the project fee is £1,995, for 5 weeks £1,195 and extensions are £125 per week. The project fee includes all accommodation in volunteer house, food, transport including airport transfers, a selection of excursions as well as a donation in the form of resources to partner community schools.

**CONTACT:** Jonathan Rademeyer, Marketing.

---

### GAP YEAR THAILAND
1 Vernon Avenue, Rugby, CV22 5HL
© 01788 552617
© 07899 887276 (mobile)
📧 david@gapyearthailand.org.uk
🌐 www.gapyearthailand.org.uk

Professional education organisation whose key team members have a background in teacher education in universities in UK or in the Rajabhat Universities (teacher training universities) in Thailand. The programme is approved and endorsed by the South East Asian Ministers of Education.

**PROGRAMME DESCRIPTION:** Gap Year Thailand specialises only in Thailand, providing placements for volunteers as assistant teachers, teaching English (particularly conversational English) in schools or universities.

**NUMBER OF PLACEMENTS PER YEAR:** 10+.

**DESTINATIONS:** Thailand.

**PREREQUISITES:** Minimum age 18, average age early 20s. Must speak English as a first language. Teaching qualification not needed.

**DURATION AND TIME OF PLACEMENTS:** Minimum 2 months up to 6+ months.

**SELECTION PROCEDURES AND ORIENTATION:** Applications accepted throughout the year. Telephone interviews. Pre-departure briefing weekend with some TEFL training, and further training in the orientation programme on arrival.

**COST:** £980 including accommodation, which can be homestay with family or in a teacher's house.

**CONTACT:** Dr David Lancaster, Chief Executive.

---

## GLOBAL CHOICES

420 Omega Works, 4 Roach Road, London E3 2LX
℡ 020 8533 2777
℡ +1 646 929 4656 (USA)
🖱 info@globalchoices.co.uk
🖥 www.globalchoices.co.uk

**PROGRAMME DESCRIPTION:** Work and travel programmes worldwide, mainly paid work in hotels, amusement parks, casinos, resorts and restaurants. Voluntary work, internships, practical training and work experience worldwide.

**DESTINATIONS:** Argentina, Australia, Brazil, India, China, Singapore, Canada, Spain, Greece, UK and USA.

**PREREQUISITES:** Majority of programmes open to all over 18.

**DURATION AND TIME OF PLACEMENTS:** 2 weeks to 18 months.

**COST:** Varies by programme.

**CONTACT:** Giedrius Mazurka.

---

## GLOBAL VISION INTERNATIONAL (GVI)

*UK Office*: 3 High Street, St Albans, Hertford shire AL3 4ED
℡ 01727 250250
🖱 info@gviworld.com
🖥 www.gvi.co.uk
*North American office*: 252 Newbury Street, Number 4, Boston, MA 02116
℡ +1 888 653 6028
🖥 www.gviusa.com
*Australian office*: Suite 206, 530 Little Collins Street, Melbourne, VIC 3000
℡ +61 1300 795013
🖥 www.gviaustralia.com

See website for GVI's choice of top 10 gap year programmes.

**PROGRAMME DESCRIPTION:** Volunteer abroad expeditions and projects to assist in environmental research, conservation, education and community development.

**DESTINATIONS:** 30+ countries in Europe, Latin America, Africa and Asia.

**NUMBER OF PLACEMENTS PER YEAR:** 1,000.

**PREREQUISITES:** Minimum age 18. All nationalities welcome. No special training or qualifications are required as all training will be provided in the field.

**DURATION AND TIME OF PLACEMENTS:** 1 week to 1 year.

**SELECTION PROCEDURES AND ORIENTATION:** Online application form plus application assessment over the phone.

**COST:** From £325 (short-term English teaching workshops in Guatemala) to £4,630 (teach and travel in Central and South America).

## GLOBAL VOLUNTEER PROJECTS

7–15 Pink Lane, Newcastle upon Tyne NE1 5DW

0191 222 0404

info@globalvolunteerprojects.org

www.globalvolunteerprojects.org

**PROGRAMME DESCRIPTION:** Specialise in work experience projects for people hoping to go into medicine or the subjects allied to medicine, such as physiotherapy, dentistry and nursing and people looking for work experience in journalism. Opportunities also available to help with teaching, conservation and orphanage work for those keen to get involved in helping local communities. Most programmes include basic language courses as well as 'culture' courses such as drumming in Ghana, yoga in India or learning Swahili in Tanzania.

**DESTINATIONS:** Ghana, Tanzania, China, India, Cambodia, Mexico and Romania.

**NUMBER OF PLACEMENTS:** 100–200.

**PREREQUISITES:** Minimum age 17 (with parental consent) but most are 18/19.

**DURATION AND TIME OF PLACEMENTS:** 2 weeks to 1 year. Most join for 1 month (summer) or 3 months. Projects available throughout the year.

**SELECTION PROCEDURES AND ORIENTATION:**
Applications must be submitted at least 4 weeks prior to departure. References must be provided and CRB checks are compulsory for projects involving work with children. Journalism projects include time on a media course (unless you have a background in media or a media related degree) and some of the medical projects include time in lectures at a medical college. Participants require visas for nearly all programmes; visa support given.

**COST:** £995–£1,795 for 1-month projects.

**CONTACT:** Kevin Dynan, Founder and Director.

## GO GAP SPORT

Swell Surf Camp, Cabarete, Dominican Republic

+ 1 809 571 0562

info@gogapsport.com

http://gogapsport.com

**PROGRAMME DESCRIPTION:** Primarily a Spanish language course but combined with watersports.

**NUMBER OF PLACEMENTS PER YEAR:** 20–50.

**DESTINATIONS:** Dominican Republic.

**PREREQUISITES:** Minimum age 17, average age 17–20. No experience needed.

**DURATION AND TIME OF PLACEMENTS:** 3–6 months.

**SELECTION PROCEDURES AND ORIENTATION:**
Applications accepted year round.

**COST:** Varies with sport chosen, e.g. surfing/Spanish is $599 per week, with discounts for longer term stay. Accommodation is in purpose-built camp offering single, double or dorm beds in secure environment. Camp has pool, air-conditioning on request and pool table. All meals are included.

**CONTACT:** Clare Barnaby-Smith, Co-owner.

## ICYE-UK: INTER-CULTURAL YOUTH EXCHANGE UK

Latin American House, Kingsgate Place, London NW6 4TA

020 7681 0983

info@icye.org.uk

www.icye.org.uk

Non profit-making charity offering both long-term (6 or 12 months) and short-term (1–12 weeks) volunteering opportunities in many countries (see 'Directory of Volunteering Abroad').

## INTERNATIONAL ACADEMY

Sophia House, 28 Cathedral Road, Cardiff CF11 9LJ

029 2066 0200

info@international-academy.com

www.international-academy.com

Member of the Year Out Group. Instructor training in skiing and snowboarding to help people on a gap year, career break or others become qualified as instructors. See 'Directory of Sport and Activity Courses'.

## INTERN OPTIONS

159–161 Temple Chambers, 3–7 Temple
Avenue, London EC4Y 0DA
© 020 7353 7699
info@internoptions.com
www.internoptions.com

**PROGRAMME DESCRIPTION:** Unpaid internships in many industries especially hospitality, horticulture and travel. Entry-level admin jobs available to school leavers.

**NUMBER OF PLACEMENTS PER YEAR:** 30–60+.

**DESTINATIONS:** Sydney and Melbourne mainly. Placements also available in Australia and New Zealand.

**PREREQUISITES:** Students and graduates aged 18–30 (in order to qualify for a working holiday visa). Candidates should be looking for a work experience placement in their field of study or experience.

**DURATION AND TIME OF PLACEMENTS:** 6 weeks to 1 year, though most last 10–26 weeks. Summer internships (June to Sept) are available.

**COST:** £800.

**CONTACT:** Jonathan Carroll, Director.

## IST PLUS

Rosedale House, Rosedale Road, Richmond,
Surrey TW9 2SZ
© 020 8939 9057
info@istplus.com
www.istplus.com

Partner agency in UK delivering programmes on behalf of CIEE (Council on International Educational Exchange) and USA summer camps on behalf of Interexchange.

**PROGRAMME DESCRIPTION:** Work and teaching abroad programmes for UK students, graduates and young professionals. Programmes include Work & Travel USA, Internship USA, Summer Camps USA, Work & Travel Australia, Work & Travel New Zealand, Teach in China and Teach in Thailand.

## i TO i

Woodside House, 261 Low Lane, Horsforth,
Leeds LS18 5NY
© 0870 333 2332
info@i-to-i.com
www.i-to-i.com

Founding member of the Year Out Group and member of WYSE. i-to-i is a teacher training and volunteer travel tour operator.

**PROGRAMME DESCRIPTION:** 500+ volunteer projects in 24 countries including teaching, conservation, community work, building, sports and media placements. Online and classroom TEFL training and paid jobs abroad as well.

**DESTINATIONS:** Projects are available in Argentina, Australia, Brazil, Cambodia, Canada, China, Costa Rica, Ecuador, Honduras, India, Indonesia, Kenya, Malaysia, Nepal, Peru, Philippines, South Africa, Sri Lanka, Swaziland, Tanzania, Thailand, Uganda, Vietnam and Zambia. Paid English teaching placements are available in China, Czech Republic, Ecuador, Indonesia, Japan, South Korea, Slovakia, Spain and Thailand after completing one of i-to-i's intensive TEFL training courses.

**NUMBER OF PLACEMENTS PER YEAR:** 6,000.

**PREREQUISITES:** Native or near-native English speakers are required for teaching placements.

**DURATION AND TIME OF PLACEMENTS:** Volunteer placements are from 1 week to 6 months, starting all year round. Jobs abroad can range from 2 months to 1 year. TEFL courses or voluntary programmes can also be booked through STA Travel.

**SELECTION PROCEDURES AND ORIENTATION:** Volunteer applicants are screened for suitability and prohibitive pre-existing medical conditions. Applicants for Teaching & Community Work placements are required to undergo a criminal record check. All volunteer placements include comprehensive briefing notes, safety information, 24/7 emergency support, in-country staff and an orientation on arrival. All volunteer teaching placements include an accredited i-to-i online TEFL course.

**COST:** Volunteer placements start from £435 (excluding airfares). TEFL courses start from £199. Free 'TEFL Course Taster' online at www.onlinetefl.com.

## JAPAN EXCHANGE & TEACHING (JET) PROGRAMME

JET Desk, c/o Embassy of Japan, 101–104 Piccadilly, London W1J 7JT

℅ 020 7465 6668

info@jet-uk.org

www.jet-uk.org

**PROGRAMME DESCRIPTION:** The Japan Exchange & Teaching (JET) Programme is a Japanese government run scheme to promote international understanding and improve foreign language tuition. UK graduates have the opportunity of working in Japan for a minimum of 1 year.

**DESTINATIONS:** Throughout Japan.

**NUMBER OF PLACEMENTS PER YEAR:** Approximately 200 places are offered to UK candidates, however, the number varies each year.

**PREREQUISITES:** Must have a Bachelor's degree in any subject and be under 39 years of age by the time of departure. Neither teaching qualifications nor Japanese language ability is needed for the assistant language teacher (ALT) positions; however the co-ordinator for international relations (CIR) role does require Japanese language ability sufficient for everyday working situations.

**DURATION AND TIME OF PLACEMENTS:** 1-year contracts begin in late July.

**SELECTION PROCEDURES AND ORIENTATION:** The application deadline is usually the last Friday in November. Orientations are given at the start of July in London and Edinburgh and in Tokyo upon arrival in Japan.

**COST:** None. There is no application fee and return airfares are provided to those who complete their contract. Salary 3,600,000 yen.

## JOHN HALL VENICE COURSE

9 Smeaton Road, London SW18 5JJ

info@johnhallvenice.com

www.johnhallvenice.co.uk

Annual pre-university course on European civilisation specially designed for gap year students, held in London and Venice between January and March. Emphasis is on the visual arts and music. Cost for 1 week in London plus 5 weeks in Venice is £6,990 with optional extra periods in Florence and Rome. See 'Directory of Courses'.

## THE KAREN HILLTRIBES TRUST

Midgley House, Heslington, York YO10 5DX

℅ 01904 411891

penelope@karenhilltribes.org.uk

www.karenhilltribes.org.uk

**PROGRAMME DESCRIPTION:** Volunteer placements for teaching at primary and secondary level (all year round). Also installing water systems (in summer) in northern Thailand. Volunteers live with host families, often the village headman.

**DESTINATIONS:** Upland and hill communities of northwest Thailand.

**NUMBER OF PLACEMENTS PER YEAR:** About 20 but only a few at any one time. Volunteers are usually placed in pairs in different villages.

**PREREQUISITES:** Candidates should be team players, with maturity and a genuine interest in helping the Karen hill tribe people. No TEFL qualification required. Village life can be primitive, with most families living in wooden houses on stilts. Volunteers are encouraged to get involved at all levels.

**DURATION AND TIME OF PLACEMENTS:** for teaching, 3 or 6 months or longer, starting October or January. Water system programme requires volunteers for 1 month in July or August.

**SELECTION PROCEDURES AND ORIENTATION:** Interviews held in York or London or by phone if necessary. Pre-departure briefings, meetings with past volunteers, training weekend and continuing support given. Paid manager in Thailand.

**COST:** £1,000 (3 months), £1,750 (6 months) for teaching, £500 for water systems. Part of these costs is set against the cost of the project. Advice given on fundraising and sponsorship (also on website).

**CONTACT:** Penelope Worsley, Director.

### KWA MADWALA PRIVATE GAME RESERVE – CONSERVATION EXPERIENCE

PO Box 192, Hectorspruit 1330, South Africa

+27 (0)82 779 2153/255 4105

www.kwamadwala.net

www.kwamadwalagapyear.co.za

*UK representative:* Paul Shields

01590 688014

info@kwamadwala.co.uk

Private game reserve located on the south side of the Kruger National Park in South Africa between Swaziland and Mozambique which offers a range of gap year conservation experiences.

**PROGRAMME DESCRIPTION:** Diverse activities available to those who wish to experience life on a private game reserve with the inclusion of a variety of outbound excursions. Programmes include microlight game counting, anti-poaching patrols, camping trips into Kruger National Park, bush survival course, basic ranger training, visits to animal orphanages and breeding projects, interaction with domestic elephants, work at local AIDS orphanage and school, and visits to Mozambique, Swaziland and an extreme sport destination. Accommodation is in Gazebo Lodge with swimming pool overlooking a dam.

**PREREQUISITIES:** Minimum age 18.

**DURATION AND TIME OF PLACEMENTS:** 10-week Culture, Conservation and Adventure Experience, 8-week Culture and Conservation Extra Experience (both with intakes early January, April and September); 6-week Culture and Conservation Experience (starting early January, April, July and September) and a variety of 4-week programmes throughout the year.

**COST:** 10-week programme from £3,399; 8 weeks from £2,799; 6 weeks £2,299 and 4 weeks from £1,499. Fees include all land arrangements, meals, accommodation on and off property, equipment, transport, entrance fees, visiting experts and tuition. Flights, visas and insurance are not included.

### LANGUAGE COURSES ABROAD

67–71 Ashby Road, Loughborough, Leicestershire LE11 3AA

01509 211612

info@languagesabroad.co.uk

www.languagesabroad.co.uk

Parent company, Spanish Study Holidays, is a member of FIYTO (Federation of International Youth Travel Organisations), ALTO (Association of Language Travel Organisations) and WYSE Work Abroad (World Youth Student & Educational).

**PROGRAMME DESCRIPTION:** In-country language courses in Spanish, French, German, Italian, Portuguese, Russian, Chinese and Arabic (see entry in 'Directory of Language Courses') often in conjunction with work experience placements, available in Spain, Latin America, France, Germany and Italy (see entry in 'Directory of Work Experience Abroad').

**CONTACT:** Mike Cummins, Director.

### LATTITUDE GLOBAL VOLUNTEERING

42 Queen's Road, Reading, RG1 4BB. Offices also in Canada, New Zealand and Australia

0118 959 4914

Volunteer@lattitude.org.uk

www.lattitude.org.uk

Registered charity specialising in international volunteering, with more than 35 years' experience. Previously named GAP Activity Projects, it was a founding member of the Year Out Group

**PROGRAMME DESCRIPTION:** Voluntary work placements in teaching, caring, environmental, outdoor activity, medical and community projects. All placements are designed to make a difference in the world and to stretch the capabilities of volunteers.

**DESTINATIONS:** 17 countries worldwide.

**NUMBER OF PLACEMENTS PER YEAR:** 2,000+.

**PREREQUISITES:** Age between 17 and 25.

**DURATION AND TIME OF PLACEMENTS:** 4–12 months (average 6 months).

**SELECTION PROCEDURES AND ORIENTATION:** Volunteers can apply at any time online. After an application is received, an interview will be held, after which the applicant will hear if he or she has been offered a place. There is a group briefing which all volunteers are encouraged to attend and a full orientation programme in-country on arrival. Any necessary courses such as teaching skills or language training must be attended before beginning the placement, either before departure or in-country.

**COST:** Volunteers pay a fee ranging from £1,600 to £2,250 depending on the programme. The fee includes pre-departure administrative support, briefing, orientation in-country, and 24-hour emergency helpline.

### LEARN OVERSEAS

47 Greenheys Centre, Pencroft Way, Manchester Science Park, Manchester M15 6JJ

✆ 0161 226 5300

✆ 0790 3040567 (mobile)

✉ office@learnoverseas.co.uk

🖥 www.learnoverseas.co.uk

**PROGRAMME DESCRIPTION:** Gap year and career break work experience placements in India. Specialists in placements for students applying for medicine and related fields or wanting to complete research projects. Mixture of hands-on, observation and work-shadowing experience in Delhi.

**DESTINATIONS:** Delhi, India.

**PREREQUISITES:** Age 16+.

**DURATION AND TIME OF PLACEMENTS:** From 2 weeks to 6 months throughout the year.

**COST:** From £900 including transport within the country, full board and lodging and weekend breaks, but excluding airfares and insurance.

### MADVENTURER

The Old Smithy, Corbridge, Northumberland NE45 5QD

✆ 0845 121 1996

✉ tribe@madventurer.com

🖥 www.madventurer.com

Member of the Year Out Group.

**PROGRAMME DESCRIPTION:** With projects and adventures in a dozen destinations lasting between 2 weeks and 6 months, all itineraries can be catered for. While on a project, participants live in a rural village with a group of madventurers while volunteering as a teacher, builder, medic and/or sports coach. A typical 2-month expedition includes 6 weeks of volunteering for a grassroots community project, followed by a 3-week group adventure (trekking, rafting, touring). Projects can be booked in blocks of 6 weeks for a prolonged experience (i.e. 3 projects for a total of 18 weeks).

**DESTINATIONS:** Ghana, Togo, Tanzania, Uganda, Kenya, Peru, India, Vietnam, Thailand and Fiji.

**PREREQUISITES:** Minimum age 17. No experience is necessary to make a difference.

**DURATION AND TIME OF PLACEMENTS:** Projects run in blocks of 6 weeks, split into 3 phases of 2 week-activities, and it is possible to just join one of the 2-week phases. Adventures range from 1 to 12 weeks. Departure dates available all year round.

**SELECTION PROCEDURES AND ORIENTATION:** Volunteers are assigned at least one crew member to lend support and guidance throughout placement. Comprehensive pre-departure information given in UK.

**COST:** From £695 (Africa), £795 (Latin America and South Pacific) and £595 (Asia) for short phases, excluding flights.

**CONTACT:** The Tribe at Mad HQ.

### MONDOCHALLENGE

Town Hall, Market Place, Newbury RG14 2QD

✆ 01635 45556

✉ info@mondochallenge.co.uk

🖥 www.mondochallenge.co.uk

UK-based organisation sending volunteers to work on community-based teaching and orphanage projects, as well as business development and medical projects in Africa, Asia and South America.

**PROGRAMME DESCRIPTION:** Volunteers of all ages including some in their gap year (pre- and post-university) are sent to villages in a number of countries, mainly to teach.

**DESTINATIONS:** Nepal, India (many destinations), Sri Lanka, Tanzania, Senegal, Gambia, Ecuador, Chile and Romania.

**NUMBER OF PLACEMENTS PER YEAR:** 200 including 60 to Tanzania.

**PREREQUISITES:** All nationalities accepted. Minimum qualification is A-Level or equivalent in subjects to be taught. Must be able to cope with remote posting and to relate to people of other cultures.

**DURATION AND TIME OF PLACEMENTS:** 6 weeks to 6 months with start dates throughout the year; average 3 months.

**COST:** From £600 for one month, including board and lodging in local family homes.

**CONTACT:** Simon Palferman, Head of Operations.

---

## NONSTOP ADVENTURE

Unit 3B, The Plough Brewery, 516 Wandswoth Road, London SW8 3JX

0845 365 1525

info@nonstopadventure.com

www.nonstopadventure.com

Member of the Year Out Group.

**PROGRAMME DESCRIPTION:** Ski and Snowboard Improvement and Instructor Courses in the Canadian Rockies and New Zealand. Sail training courses from Dartmouth Devon and trans-Atlantic and Caribbean sailing expeditions (see entries in 'Directory of Expeditions' and 'Directory of Sport and Activity Courses').

**CONTACT:** Georgie Bushe, Sales Manager.

---

## OPERATION WALLACEA

Wallace House, Old Bolingbroke, Near Spilsby, Lincolnshire PE23 4EX

01790 763194

info@opwall.com

www.opwall.com

**PROGRAMME DESCRIPTION:** Operation Wallacea is a series of biological and conservation management research programmes that operate in remote locations across the world. These expeditions are designed with specific wildlife conservation aims in mind, from identifying areas needing protection, through to implementing and assessing conservation management programmes. Opportunities for university, school and gap year students.

**DESTINATIONS:** Honduras, Indonesia, Egypt, Cuba, South Africa, Peru, Mozambique and, new for 2010, Madagascar.

**PREREQUISITES:** Minimum age 16. Enthusiasm needed.

**DURATION AND TIME OF PLACEMENTS:** 2, 4, 6, 8 or 10 weeks anytime between June and September.

**SELECTION PROCEDURES AND ORIENTATION:** Telephone interview. No deadlines. All relevant training can be given on-site including in some cases dive training.

---

## ORANGUTAN FOUNDATION

7 Kent Terrace, London NW1 4RP

020 7724 2912

elly@orangutan.org.uk

www.orangutan.org.uk

**PROGRAMME DESCRIPTION:** Volunteers are based in remote locations in Kalimantan, Indonesian Borneo. Most volunteers will be based at a new release site for rehabilitated orangutans. Previous projects have included: general infrastructure repairs, trail cutting, constructing guard-posts, water purification systems and orangutan release sites. Volunteers should note that there is no direct work with orangutans although wild and/or rehabilitated orangutans will be in the vicinity where volunteers work. The work is of a manual labour/ construction nature.

**DESTINATIONS:** Most likely destinations are the Lamandau Reserve near Tanjung Puting National Park in Kalimantan or the Belantikan Arut region in the north west of Central Kalimantan.

**NUMBER OF PLACEMENTS PER YEAR:** 36.

**DURATION AND TIME OF PLACEMENTS:** 6 weeks, 3 or 4 teams of no more than 12, departing April, May June, August and possibly October. Dates are confirmed in September of the previous year.

**PREREQUISITES:** Participants must be at least 18 and be members of the Orangutan Foundation. They must work well in a team, be fit and healthy and adaptable to difficult and demanding conditions.

**SELECTION PROCEDURES AND ORIENTATION:**

Applicants need to submit an application form (available on the website) with accompanying CV and cover letter. All potential UK volunteers are expected to attend an interview at the Foundation office in London. Phone interviews can be conducted for non-UK applicants. Successful UK applicants are expected to attend a pre-departure briefing day in March.

**COST:** Approximately £730 (to be confirmed), includes accommodation, food, equipment, materials and transport for the duration of the programme but does not include international and internal travel to the project site.

**CONTACT:** Elly Sanderson, Volunteer Co-ordinator.

---

**OUTREACH INTERNATIONAL**
Bartletts Farm, Hayes Road, Compton Dundon,
Somerset TA11 6PF
℡ 01458 274957
✉ gap@outreachinternational.co.uk
🖥 www.outreachinternational.co.uk

Member of the Year Out Group. Outreach International is a specialist organisation with carefully selected projects. There is enough variety to ensure that the interests and skills of individual volunteers can be put to good use.

**PROGRAMME DESCRIPTION:** Committed volunteers work on many varied projects including with street children, in orphanages, teaching English, art or sport, doing medical work, conservation, marine biology or participating in humanitarian aid. The needs of these hand-picked projects are constantly assessed so volunteers are placed only where genuinely needed and where skills can be utilised. Placements are ideal for anyone wanting a gap experience and many are suitable for those considering a career in medicine, humanitarian, social or environmental work.

**DESTINATIONS:** Mexico, Costa Rica, Ecuador, Galápagos, Cambodia, Sri Lanka.

**NUMBER OF PLACEMENTS PER YEAR:** 100 per year. Outreach International knows each volunteer and places them in the most appropriate project.

**PREREQUISITES:** Most of the projects are ideal for gap year volunteers aged 18–21 and some are ideal for people with some work experience. Ideal for confident young people with a desire to travel, learn a language and offer their help to a worthwhile cause. The projects focus on the most needy sections of the community.

**DURATION AND TIME OF PLACEMENTS:** 3–6 months. Departure times are January, April, June and September.

**SELECTION PROCEDURES AND ORIENTATION:**

Applicants will be invited to a meeting within 3 weeks of applying, in which projects can be discussed and an informed choice made about whether to proceed. The director visits each project at regular intervals and is familiar with their specific requirements. Volunteers are given a comprehensive briefing and language training, and are offered a good teacher training course and support with fundraising. In all countries Outreach International employs a full-time coordinator, who attends to the welfare of individuals. While the level of support is high, volunteers are encouraged to be autonomous and make their own decisions on their placements.

**COST:** £2,800 for 3 months includes unlimited insurance, visas, local transport, language course, in-country support, airport pick-up, food, accommodation and all project costs. Additional months are approximately £500 each. Outreach International rents spacious houses close to the projects and offers volunteers the opportunity of living with a local family. Volunteers can also live together in an Outreach International house but work in pairs on their project.

**CONTACT:** James Chapman, UK Director.

---

**DURATION AND TIME OF PLACEMENTS:** 1 month minimum. Most participants stay at least 3 months, up to 6 months. Group departures are usually in September, January and May. Others are possible.

**SELECTION PROCEDURES AND ORIENTATION:** Interview and pre-departure training included as well as language training and orientation on arrival. Full support throughout. French language classes provided in Mont Tremblant, Canada.

**COST:** Varies from £1,770 for 1 month in Romania to £3,725 for 4-month Chile placement. Sample prices for Canadian programme: £2,200. All prices include airfares.

**CONTACT:** Roger Salwey, Director.

Gap year ski and snowboard instructor courses in Canada, Switzerland, Argentina, Japan and India (see 'Directory of Ski Training Courses').

Member of the Year Out Group. A number of Oyster's projects are now entering their 10th year of receiving participants.

**PROGRAMME DESCRIPTION:** Volunteering with children and teaching English, helping in orphanages and coaching sports in a range of developing countries or at bear sanctuary in Romania. Paid work is available on a farm in the Australian Outback, or hospitality work in Sydney, and hotels in the Canadian Rockies and Quebec. In each location Oyster has a representative to provide back-up throughout.

**DESTINATIONS:** Australia, Brazil, Canada, Chile, India, Nepal, Kenya, Romania, Tanzania and Zambia.

PoD is a non-profit organisation that aims to provide personal service, quality and benefit for local communities.

**PROGRAMME DESCRIPTION:** Flexible gap year programmes in Africa, Asia and South America. Choice of projects working with people, community, animals and conservation. Examples include caring for elephants and wild animals, joining an Amazon jungle conservation project, scuba diving and marine conservation, community building projects, volunteering at orphanages and care homes, teaching English and running summer English camps.

**DESTINATIONS:** Belize, Cambodia, India, Nepal, Peru, Tanzania, Thailand and Vietnam.

**DURATION AND TIME OF PLACEMENTS:** 1 week to 3 months, with flexible start dates throughout the year. Summer mini-gaps are also available for school leavers going straight to university.

**SELECTION PROCEDURES AND ORIENTATION:** Online application. Reference and phone interview may be required. A comprehensive information booklet is provided before departure with support available by telephone and email from the PoD UK office. Training and introductions are provided on arrival in the country.

**COST:** From £349, depending on project and duration.

**CONTACT:** Alex Tarrant or Mike Beecham.

---

**PLATFORM2**
35 Lower Marsh, London SE1 7RL
℀ 020 7523 2258
✉ platform2@myplatform2.com
🖥 www.myplatform2.com

---

Platform2 is run by Christian Aid, Islamic Relief and BUNAC, and is funded by the Department for International Development (DFID).

**PROGRAMME DESCRIPTION:** Government-funded volunteering programme aimed at young people who would not otherwise get the chance to volunteer in a developing country.

**NUMBER OF PLACEMENTS PER YEAR:** up to 2,500.

**DESTINATIONS:** Ghana, Kenya, South Africa, India, Nepal and Peru.

**PREREQUISITES:** Age 18–25 (at the time of travel) and eligible for a UK passport. Special encouragement is given to young Muslim volunteers.

**DURATION AND TIME OF PLACEMENTS:** 10 weeks.

**SELECTION PROCEDURES AND ORIENTATION:** Applications should be received 3–6 months in advance (e.g. between June and September for a December departure). The programme is intended to create global citizens who will return to their communities and continue the volunteering habit.

**COST:** Nil, except for transport to and from interview, to and from Heathrow Airport and any passport costs.

---

**THE PROJECT TRUST**
Hebridean Centre, Ballyhough, Isle of Coll, Argyll PA78 6TE
℀ 01879 230444
✉ info@projecttrust.org.uk
🖥 www.projecttrust.org.uk

---

Established in 1967. Founding member of the Year Out Group.

**PROGRAMME DESCRIPTION:** Voluntary placements specifically for gap year students throughout the developing world. Volunteers can choose to take part in care work, community development and wildlife projects, educational projects or outdoor activity projects, or they can act as English language assistants at schools.

**DESTINATIONS:** Africa (Uganda, Botswana, South Africa, Namibia, Senegal and Swaziland), South and Central America (Honduras, Chile, Bolivia, Peru, Guyana and the Dominican Republic), Asia (Thailand, China, India, Japan, Malaysia, Hong Kong and Cambodia).

**NUMBER OF PLACEMENTS PER YEAR:** Around 200.

**PREREQUISITES:** Applicants should be aged between 17 and 19 and be aiming for university.

**DURATION AND TIME OF PLACEMENTS:** 12 months from August. Limited number of 8-month placements departing in January, for those needing to attend a university interview in the autumn.

**SELECTION PROCEDURES AND ORIENTATION:** In the period between August and March, candidates attend a 4-day course on the Hebridean Isle of Coll where their skills and interests are assessed. About 80% of those who take the selection course are offered a place within a week of leaving Coll. Training courses are held, also on the Isle of Coll, during July to teach skills relevant to the volunteers' work placements as well as country-specific briefings and how to live safely and healthily overseas. Once in the destination country there is always at least one local representative on hand to help volunteers settle in and a full-time desk officer for each country based on the Isle of Coll.

**COST:** Volunteers are required to raise £4,660 (2010 cost) for the 12-month programme which includes the costs of selection, training, supervision, debriefing, airfares, medical insurance, board and lodging and a living allowance.

## PROJECTS ABROAD
Aldsworth Parade, Goring, West Sussex
BN12 4TX
℅ 01903 708300
🖱 info@projects-abroad.co.uk
🖳 www.projects-abroad.co.uk

Founding member of the Year Out Group. Company arranges volunteering placements overseas in a range of countries. Also arranges work experience placements in medicine, media and other fields in selected destinations (see 'Directory of Work Experience Abroad').

**DESTINATIONS:** Argentina, Bolivia, Cambodia, China, Costa Rica, Ethiopia, Ghana, India, Jamaica, Mexico, Moldova, Mongolia, Morocco, Nepal, Peru, Romania, Russia, Senegal, South Africa, Sri Lanka, Tanzania and Thailand.

**NUMBER OF PLACEMENTS PER YEAR:** 4,000.

**PREREQUISITES:** Minimum age 16. Optional UK briefing and TEFL weekend courses before departure.

**DURATION AND TIME OF PLACEMENTS:** Very flexible, with departures year round. Placements last 2 weeks to 12 months.

**SELECTION PROCEDURES AND ORIENTATION:** Paid staff in all destinations arrange and vet placements, accommodation and work supervisors. They meet volunteers on arrival and provide a final briefing before the placements.

**COST:** Placements are self-funded and the fee charged includes insurance, food, accommodation and overseas support. 3-month placements cost between £1,395 and £2,595, depending on placement, excluding travel costs.

## QUEST OVERSEAS
15A Cambridge Grove, Hove, East Sussex
BN3 3ED
℅ 01273 777206
🖱 info@questoverseas.com
🖳 www.questoverseas.com

A founding member of the Year Out Group, Quest Overseas specialise in combining worthwhile voluntary work projects and challenging expeditions to Africa and South America for volunteers aged 17–24. Since 1996 Quest Overseas participants have raised £1.2 million for their charity and NGO partners.

**PROGRAMME DESCRIPTION:** The South America programme is split into 3 phases: Phase I – 3-week intensive Spanish or Portuguese language course in Ecuador, Bolivia or Brazil; Phase II – 4-week voluntary work projects; either conservation work in the rainforests of Peru, looking after children in shanty towns in Peru or Brazil, or working in Ambue Ari animal rehabilitation project in Bolivia. Phase III – 6-week expedition covering over 1000km of Peru, Chile and Bolivia including Amazon jungle and Machu Picchu, or throughout Brazil, including surfing, diving and hang gliding over Rio. The Africa programme is split into 2 phases: Phase I – 6-week voluntary work project; either conservation work in Swaziland or a community development project in Tanzania, Kenya or Malawi. Phase II – 6-week expedition through Swaziland, Mozambique, South Africa, Botswana and Zambia. Summer trips lasting 4–6 weeks in Bolivia, Peru, Tanzania, Kenya, Malawi or 6-week expeditions to either Southern Africa or the Andean mountains.

**DESTINATIONS:** Ecuador, Peru, Chile, Bolivia and Brazil; or Kenya, Uganda, Swaziland, Lesotho, Tanzania, Mozambique, South Africa, Botswana and Zambia.

**NUMBER OF PLACEMENTS PER YEAR:** 10–16 students in each team and 12 expeditions per year.

**PREREQUISITES:** Volunteers are typically aged 17–24 and are on gap years or breaks from university.

**DURATION AND TIME OF PLACEMENTS:** 13-week programmes depart throughout January to April, with summer projects and expeditions departing June to

August. Flights can be open returns so stays can be extended.

**SELECTION PROCEDURES AND ORIENTATION:** Selection is by phone/in-person interview. Preparation and expedition skills weekends are organised prior to departure.

**COST:** £1,000–£4,000 which includes all internal transfers, accommodation and food. Price excludes return flights, individual insurance (about £140) and personal pocket money for souvenirs and luxuries. Volunteers are also asked to make a minimum project donation.

## RALEIGH
207 Waterloo Road, London SE1 8XD
© 020 7183 1270
info@raleigh.org.uk
www.raleighinternational.org

Founding member of the Year Out Group and leading youth and education charity which inspires people of all ages, backgrounds and nationalities to take part in challenging environmental, community and adventure projects around the world.

**PROGRAMME DESCRIPTION:** Participants aged 17–24 have the option of a 10-week or 5-week expedition. The longer expedition consists of 3 distinct project phases: community, environment and adventure. With the 5-week expedition, participants choose either a community or environmental project plus a team-based adventure challenge. Sample projects include the building of a primary school in remote areas, putting in a suspension bridge in national parks or trekking through mountainous terrain. Volunteers over 25 can join Raleigh as volunteer managers.

**DESTINATIONS:** Costa Rica, Nicaragua, Malaysia (Borneo), India.

**PREREQUISITES:** Applicants must be aged between 17 and 24 to join an expedition as a venturer, or 25–75 to join as a volunteer manager.

**DURATION AND TIME OF PLACEMENTS:** 5- or 10-week programmes run throughout the year with normal start dates in spring, summer and autumn.

**SELECTION PROCEDURES AND ORIENTATION:** Participants from all backgrounds and nationalities are welcome. Participants receive training in the UK and on expedition.

**COST:** Expeditions for participants cost £2,995 for a 10-week programme and £1,750 for a 5-week programme. Prices include food, accommodation, medical insurance, training and in-country travel but exclude flights.

## REAL GAP EXPERIENCE
1 Meadow Road, Tunbridge Wells, Kent TN1 2YG
© 01892 516164
info@realgap.co.uk
www.realgap.co.uk

Leading gap year specialists, offering the most comprehensive range of exciting projects in over 40 countries. ATOL bonded with financial backing. Provider of career breaks (see www.gapyearfor grownups.co.uk) and sports programmes (see www.realsportexperience.co.uk).

**PROGRAMME DESCRIPTION:** Wide range of volunteer and travel options in over 40 countries, including paid work placements, volunteering with wildlife, conservation, teaching, language courses, sports, expeditions, volunteering with children, communities, career breaks, learning new skills and tailor-made gap years.

**DESTINATIONS:** 6 continents: Africa – Senegal, Ghana, Kenya, Uganda, Namibia, Tanzania, South Africa, Zambia, Zimbabwe, Malawi, Ethiopia, Mozambique, Swaziland; Australasia – Australia, New Zealand, Fiji; South East Asia – Thailand, Vietnam, Cambodia, Malaysia, Indonesia, India, Sri Lanka, Nepal, Israel; Central Asia – China, Mongolia, Trans-Siberia; South America – Galápagos Islands, Ecuador, Peru, Bolivia, Chile, Brazil, Argentina, Venezuela; Central America – Guatemala, Costa Rica, Honduras, Belize; North America – USA and Canada; Eastern Europe – Ukraine, Moldova, Romania.

**PREREQUISITES:** None, except as limited by visas. Some programmes require basic level of fitness.

**DURATION AND TIME OF PLACEMENTS:** 2 weeks to 2 years. Programmes available all year round and tailor-made gap year itineraries can be arranged.

**COST:** Varies with programme, from £389 to £10,000+.

## ROTARY INTERNATIONAL IN GREAT BRITAIN AND IRELAND (RIBI)

Kinwarton Road, Alcester, Warwickshire B49 6PB

01789 765411

www.youthribi.org

**PROGRAMME DESCRIPTION:** 1-year international exchanges to promote international understanding and peace through exposure to different cultures. Exchange students stay with families in host country and attend a place of academic or vocational learning.

**NUMBER OF PLACEMENTS PER YEAR:** Over 9,000 worldwide.

**DESTINATIONS:** See website – many countries.

**PREREQUISITES:** Ages 15–19; average age 18. All nationalities. Students are expected to get involved in the activities of their host Rotary Club.

**DURATION AND TIME OF PLACEMENTS:** 10–12 months. Also short-term exchanges in summer of 3–4 weeks.

**COST:** Students pay for costs of travel and insurance plus approximately £200 for orientation and sundries. Pocket money of £60 per month is given.

**SELECTION PROCEDURES AND ORIENTATION:** Schools normally recommend candidates. Deadline for applications is the end of February. Interviews held in candidate's home with parents. Students should be from the top 10% of their school year in overall achievement. Weekend residential orientation in March and local orientation of half a day prior to leaving. Students receive orientation within 1 month of arriving in their host country. Exchangees have regular contact with, and access at all times to, an independent counsellor to ensure their safety and a successful experience.

**CONTACT:** Denis Spiller.

## SHUMBA EXPERIENCE

95 Ditchling Road, Brighton, Sussex BN1 4ST

0845 257 3205

info@shumbaexperience.co.uk

www.shumbaexperience.co.uk

**PROGRAMME DESCRIPTION:** Gap year students have the chance to work as volunteers on game reserves, veterinary projects, marine placements, wildlife sanctuaries and wildlife research projects, working with conservation professionals in South Africa, Botswana or Namibia. The types of experience available include assisting with game capture, working on a 'Big 5' game reserve, veterinary experience, bush survival, and wild dog and rhino conservation.

**DESTINATIONS:** Mainly South Africa, also Botswana and Namibia.

**NUMBER OF PLACEMENTS:** 200+.

**PREREQUISITES:** Minimum age is 17 and the average is 28, except in July/August, when the average age is 20. All nationalities but most are from the UK. No previous experience is required as all training is given on placement.

**DURATION AND TIME OF PLACEMENTS:** 4 or 8 weeks. Mini Adventures last 1–2 weeks.

**SELECTION PROCEDURES AND ORIENTATION:** Informal interviews by phone with open days arranged throughout the year at various UK locations. Volunteers receive pre-departure placement booklets and attend an induction and orientation session on-site.

**COST:** £495–£995 for Mini Adventures. £1,395–£1,795 for 4-week experiences and from £1,995 for 8 weeks. Price includes all accommodation, food, training, pre-departure information and support, guidebook, airport pick up and supervision. Accommodation varies from comfortable lodgings, houses and cabins to camping in the bush and sleep outs under the night sky.

**CONTACT:** Mark Rowley, Director.

## SKI LE GAP

220 Wheeler Street, Mont Tremblant, Quebec
J8E 1V3, Canada
℗ 0800 328 0345 (UK)
℗ +1 819 429 6599
info@skilegap.com
www.skilegap.com

**PROGRAMME DESCRIPTION:** Ski and snowboard instructor's programme in Quebec, Canada, designed for gap year students from Britain. See entry in 'Directory of Sport and Activity Courses' and further details in chapter on Canada.

## SPW – STUDENTS PARTNERSHIP WORLDWIDE

7 Tufton Street, London SW1P 3QB
℗ 020 7808 1783/4
info@spw.org
www.spw.org

An international development charity that recruits young people aged 18–28 from the UK and Europe, USA and Australia to volunteer and work in partnership with counterparts from Africa and Asia. In pairs or groups volunteers live and work in rural communities for 3–12 months. Their input builds knowledge, skills and self-confidence in young people and begins to change attitudes and behaviour to important health, social and environmental issues amongst young people and communities. All volunteers take part in 4 weeks' intensive training which covers health, hygiene, sanitation, nutrition and the environment, with a particular emphasis on HIV transmission as well as cross-cultural awareness, basic development theory and local languages.

**PROGRAMME DESCRIPTION:** SPW runs health education and community resource programmes. These programmes tackle youth problems from different perspectives. All placements are in rural villages.

**DESTINATIONS:** India, Nepal, South Africa, Tanzania, Uganda and Zambia.

**NUMBER OF PLACEMENTS PER YEAR:** 250 places for European volunteers.

**PREREQUISITES:** A Level or equivalent qualifications. Volunteers need to be physically and mentally healthy, hard working, open-minded, enthusiastic and have good communication skills.

**DURATION AND TIME OF PLACEMENTS:** 3–12 months with starting dates throughout the year.

**SELECTION PROCEDURES AND ORIENTATION:** Applicants should download an application form from the website. Every applicant is required to attend an information and selection day in London. This also gives them the opportunity to meet staff and ex-volunteers. Following selection, volunteers are accepted on a first come first served basis, so early application is recommended.

**COST:** £2,900 (India) to £3,600 all-inclusive of open return flight, accommodation, basic living allowance, insurance, in-country visa, extensive overseas training and support, UK briefings and general administrative support. SPW is a non-profit making charity, so volunteer fees cover costs only.

## STARFISH VENTURE

℗ 0845 004 8010
enquiries@starfishventures.co.uk
www.starfishvolunteers.co.uk

Not-for-profit gap year organisation in which volunteers work closely with Thai partner organisations to provide range of volunteer service.

**PROGRAMME DESCRIPTION:** Volunteer programmes in teaching, community development, conservation and medical.

**DESTINATIONS:** Throughout Thailand, in Surin, Maehongson, Rayong and Phuket.

**PREREQUISITES:** Minimum age 18. All nationalities accepted. CRB check certificate essential for UK applicants; non-UK residents must provide evidence of no criminal record.

**DURATION AND TIME OF PLACEMENTS:** 2–12 weeks, longer placements can be arranged.

**COST:** £1,200 for 3 months. Includes preparatory TEFL training weekend, insurance, in-country co-ordinator

and 24-hour support, travel within Thailand, plus accommodation in private room in privately rented house.
**CONTACT:** Dan Moore, Director.

## SUDAN VOLUNTEER PROGRAMME (SVP)
34 Estelle Road, London NW3 2JY
© 020 7485 8619
david@svp-uk.com
www.svp-uk.com

**PROGRAMME DESCRIPTION:** Volunteer teaching programme in Sudan (mainly Khartoum and area) for people aged 20+. See entry in 'Directory of Volunteering Abroad'.

## THE LEAP OVERSEAS
121 High Street, Marlborough, Wiltshire SN8 1LZ
© 01672 519922
info@theleap.co.uk
www.theleap.co.uk

Member of the Year Out Group.
**PROGRAMME DESCRIPTION:** Volunteering programmes that combine projects in safari/eco-tourism, community and conservation, located off the tourist trail.
**DESTINATIONS:** Africa (Kenya, Tanzania, Malawi, Botswana, South Africa, Zambia, Mozambique), South America (Argentina, Guyana, Ecuador, Costa Rica, Venezuela) and Asia (Cambodia, India, Borneo).
**PREREQUISITES:** Minimum age 18. Must be committed, enthusiastic and motivated to work in a team and get stuck in. No previous experience needed.
**DURATION AND TIME OF PLACEMENTS:** 10, 6 or 2 weeks. Flexible departures.
**SELECTION PROCEDURES AND ORIENTATION:** Volunteers attend briefing/ training course in the UK and receive an induction course on arrival in the country.
**OTHER SERVICES:** Flights can be arranged through ATOL partner agency STA Travel. Time given for adventure travel, e.g. whitewater rafting, kite surfing and scuba diving.
**COST:** £1,600–£2,900 (depending on duration and location), includes briefing, food and accommodation,

transport, project donation and 24-hour support. Price does not include airfares or visas.
**CONTACT:** Guy Whitehead, Founder Director.

## TICKET TO RIDE – GAP YEAR SURFING ADVENTURES
263 Putney Bridge Road, London SW15 2PU
© 020 8788 8668
info@ttride.co.uk
www.ttride.co.uk

**PROGRAMME DESCRIPTION:** Ticket to Ride is a small organisation that focuses on surf coaching and getting involved in community projects while travelling to 8 locations around South Africa, and other locations. Surf course includes over 60 hours of professional instruction from South Africa's surfing elite. Riders are on hand to teach or work with children in schools, local townships and on the beach.
**DESTINATIONS:** South Africa, Mozambique, Costa Rica, Morocco, Portugal.
**PREREQUISITES:** Should have reasonable swimming ability. Some trips are for confident surfers.
**DURATION AND TIME OF PLACEMENTS:** 3 weeks to 3 months.
**SELECTION PROCEDURES AND ORIENTATION:** Applications should be received at least a month in advance of departure. Riders are given a light fitness regime prior to the trip. Riders can qualify as SSA Level 1 Surf Instructors and SPA Surf Lifesavers (both qualifications are UK and internationally recognised).

## TRAVELLERS WORLDWIDE
2A Caravelle House, 17/19 Goring Road, Worthing, West Sussex BN12 4AP
© 01903 502595
info@travellersworldwide.com
www.travellersworldwide.com

Travellers is a Founder Member of the Year Out Group.
**PROGRAMME DESCRIPTION:** A wide range of gap year programmes including teaching (Maths, Arts & Crafts, Drama and IT), sports coaching, hands-on

conservation (pandas, lions, orangutans, elephants), language courses (Spanish, Swahili, Portuguese, Mandarin, Tamil), professional work experience internships (Law, Journalism, Medicine, TV, Tourism, Web Design, Architecture) and cultural courses in a wide range of subjects (Tango, Salsa, Photography, Capoeira, Bush Survival, Flying, etc).

**DESTINATIONS:** Argentina, Australia, Brazil, Brunei, Cambodia, China, Ghana, Guatemala, India, Kenya, Malaysia, New Zealand, Peru, South Africa, Sri Lanka, Thailand, Zambia and Zimbabwe.

**NUMBER OF PLACEMENTS PER YEAR:** 1,000+.

**PREREQUISITES:** No formal qualifications required, just a good dose of enthusiasm!

**DURATION AND TIME OF PLACEMENTS:** From 1 week to 1 year, subject to visa requirements, with flexible start and finish dates all year round that you choose.

**COST:** Prices start from £595 and include food, accommodation, airport pick-up, induction, orientation, 24/7 support on the ground and at home but don't include international travel, visas or insurance.

**CONTACT:** Jennifer Perkes, Managing Director.

---

### TRAVEL TO TEACH

Cll 5 De Mayo 505, Jalatlaco Esq. Noche Triste, Oaxaca De Juarez, Oaxaca, Mexico C.P. 68080

☏ +52 951 5132365

☏ +52 122 81259242 (mobile)

✍ info@travel-to-teach.org

🖥 www.travel-to-teach.org

**PROGRAMME DESCRIPTION:** Travel to Teach is an international volunteer organisation, which provides affordable opportunities to volunteer in areas such as English and IT teaching, conservation, eco-tourism and community development. Some placements offer the chance to participate in Buddhist observances.

**DESTINATIONS:** Thailand, Cambodia, Bali, China, Laos, Nepal, Vietnam, India, Costa Rica, Ecuador, El Salvador and Mexico.

**PREREQUISITES:** No qualifications required. Must be adaptable, i.e. willing to live without modern plumbing, hot water and electricity.

**DURATION AND TIME OF PLACEMENTS:** 2 weeks to 6 months, though fees quoted in blocks of 4, 8, 12 or 24 weeks.

**SELECTION PROCEDURES AND ORIENTATION:** Teacher training courses can be arranged in Thailand (with ECC Thailand).

**COST:** €550–€945 for 4 weeks (varies according to destination), €750–€1,245 for 8 weeks, €950–€1,545 for 12 weeks. All fees include an application fee of €200. Thailand and Cambodia are the cheapest countries; India is the most expensive. Fees are used to run the programmes and support different causes in host countries.

**CONTACT:** Renee Holste (International Programme Manager), Charlotte or Kerstin.

---

### TUTORS WORLDWIDE

*UK office:* Tutors Worldwide, Gaufron Villa, Gaufron, Near Rhayader, Powys LD6 5PB

Fax: 01597 810 861; mobile 07768 191 437

✍ r.finney@xtra.co.nz

🖥 www.tutorsworldwide.org

*New Zealand office:* Tutors Worldwide, 2/9 Majesty Plc, Half Moon Bay, Auckland 1706

☏ +64 9 534 9999; mobile +64 21–995 553

**PROGRAMME DESCRIPTION:** School leavers are given the opportunity to work in an overseas school environment as a tutor at either a prep or secondary (high) school in the UK, New Zealand, Australia and occasionally South Africa

**DESTINATIONS:** New Zealand mostly with some in Australia and South Africa (and UK for New Zealanders, Australians and South Africans).

**PREREQUISITES:** Must be students from the list above. Initiative, enthusiasm, adaptability, flexibility, communication, commitment, motivation, reliability and responsibility needed. Many posts involve a lot of sporting activities with children, including coaching and supervision.

**DURATION AND TIME OF PLACEMENTS:** One full academic year.

**SELECTION PROCEDURES AND ORIENTATION:**
Application and referee support forms need to be completed and forwarded. Application deadline is early January. Extensive interview with each applicant to try to get the best match between school overseas and student assistant.

**COST:** £75 registration fee. Placement fee of £450 is charged only to candidates who are offered and accept a place overseas. All posts are residential and board and lodging are provided.

**CONTACT:** Robin Finney.

---

## TWIN WORK AND VOLUNTEER ABROAD

67–71 Lewisham High Street, Lewisham, London SE13 5JX

© 0800 804 8380

workandvolunteer@twinuk.com

www.workandvolunteer.com

**PROGRAMME DESCRIPTION:** Range of work and volunteer programmes in developing countries. Project types include community development, conservation, medical and teaching. Also Work Experience programmes, both paid and unpaid, mostly in Europe (including government-funded vocational training programmes).

**DESTINATIONS:** Volunteer programmes in Asia, Africa, Australasia, Europe, North and South America. Work experience in Europe.

**NUMBER OF PLACEMENTS PER YEAR:** 700–800.

**PREREQUISITES:** Minimum age 18. Average age 25. All nationalities accepted, subject to visa requirements. Generally there are no specific skills required, just enthusiasm, an open mind and a willingness to get involved.

**DURATION AND TIME OF PLACEMENTS:** From 2 weeks to 1 year.

**SELECTION PROCEDURES AND ORIENTATION:** Some programmes require 3 months' notice, others need much less processing time. Interviews are sometimes required, some programmes include a UK-based induction programme. All programmes have some form of orientation/induction/training in the host country.

**COST:** Varying programme costs. Some programmes offer comfortable fully furnished rooms with en-suite

facilities; in other cases, participants will be camping in the wilderness for short periods with limited facilities.

**CONTACT:** Barry Johnson and Peter Talbolt.

---

## UKSA THE MARITIME ACADEMY

West Cowes, Isle of Wight PO31 7PQ

© 01983 294941

info@uksa.org

www.uksa.org

**PROGRAMME DESCRIPTION:** Gap year programmes last up to 1 year, covering range of watersports and work experience in UK and overseas.

**COST:** Fees ranges from £3,250 to £14,400 (see entry in 'Directory of Sport and Activity Courses').

---

## VAE TEACHERS KENYA

*UK office:* Bell Lane Cottage, Pudleston, Near Leominster, Herefordshire HR6 0RE

© 01568 750329

vaekenya@googlemail.com

www.vaekenya.co.uk

*Kenya address:* PO Box 246, Gilgil, 20116 Kenya

© + 254 (0)50 50080

VAE runs two associated charities: Harambee Schools Kenya providing educational infrastructure and materials (www.hsk.org.uk) and Langalanga Scholarship Fund providing secondary education to bright children who would not otherwise be able to afford it (www.llsf.org.uk).

**PROGRAMME DESCRIPTION:** British school leavers and graduates teach in extremely poor rural schools based around the town of Gilgil in Kenya. Volunteers are placed only in schools with a shortage of teachers and resources, and must assume major responsibility as they become integrated and live as part of an African community. VAE is also involved with the local town street children.

**DURATION AND TIME OF PLACEMENTS:** Preferred departure time January for 6 months. Places can sometimes be filled as much as two years in advance.

**COST:** About £3,350 including flight, insurance, salary, accommodation, etc.

**CONTACT:** Simon C D Harris, Director.

## VENTURE CO WORLDWIDE

The Ironyard, 64–66 The Market Place,
Warwick CV34 4SD

☎ 01926 411122

✉ mail@ventureco-worldwide.com

🖥 www.ventureco-worldwide.com

🖥 www.ventureco.org

ATOL licence. Member of the Year Out Group.

**PROGRAMME DESCRIPTION:** Specialists in Gap Years and volunteer projects with programmes that combine language schools, local aid projects and expeditions.

**DESTINATIONS:** Inca Venture: Ecuador, Peru, Chile and Bolivia. Patagonia Venture: Peru, Bolivia, Chile, Argentina and Tierra del Fuego. Aztec Maya Venture: Mexico, Guatemala, Belize, Honduras, Nicaragua, Costa Rica and Cuba. Himalaya Venture: India and Nepal. Kilimanjaro Venture: Uganda, Kenya and Tanzania. Indochina Venture: Cambodia, Vietnam, Laos and China. Detailed itineraries are available on website.

**NUMBER OF PLACEMENTS PER YEAR:** 200–300.

**PREREQUISITES:** Must have motivation, enthusiasm and desire to be part of a Venture team.

**DURATION AND TIME OF PLACEMENTS:** 3–4 months long with departures all year round. Shorter summer Ventures are available (1–3 months) in Peru, India, the Galápagos and East Africa departing July; these trips can be fitted into the long summer vacation. Volunteer projects from 2 weeks.

**SELECTION PROCEDURES AND ORIENTATION:** Online application form. Preparation weekends held in UK, and expedition skills training in-country.

**COST:** Range from £500 to £5,000; all prices are available on the website.

**CONTACTS:** Mark Davison and David Gordon.

## VILLAGE-TO-VILLAGE

Callmate House, 1 Wilton Street, Bradford
BD5 0AX

☎ 01274 397830

✉ enquiries@village-to-village.org.uk

🖥 www.village-to-village.org.uk

Village-to-Village is a charity which has been working to reduce poverty in Tanzania for over 10 years. Member of the Year Out Group.

**PROGRAMME DESCRIPTION:** Volunteers are sent to the Kilimanjaro region to assist on various projects including teaching English in primary schools and orphanages, teacher training as well as construction and sustainable agriculture projects.

**NUMBER OF PLACEMENTS PER YEAR:** 40.

**DESTINATIONS:** Tanzania.

**PREREQUISITES:** Minimum age 16 (with parental consent). Most are gap year and university students. All nationalities welcome, provided volunteers can speak English or Swahili.

**DURATION AND TIME OF PLACEMENTS:** Minimum 2 months for teaching placements starting year round; otherwise timing is flexible.

**SELECTION PROCEDURES AND ORIENTATION:** Volunteers are required to attend an induction day before their placement which will offer some Swahili language training. Orientation will be held on arrival in Tanzania. Volunteers are required to obtain a B3 Class Visa prior to travel.

**COST:** Typical 8-week placement requires a minimum donation of £1,450 (excluding international flights). The third and fourth months are charged at £300 each, and the following two months at £150 each. Accommodation is provided in volunteer centre or homestay.

**CONTACT:** Libby James, UK Programme Director (libby@village-to-village.org.uk).

## VOLUNTEER ADVENTURES

915 S. Colorado Boulevard, Denver, CO 80246, USA

☎ +1 866 574 8606 (toll-free in the USA and Canada)

☎ 0808 120 7613 (toll-free in the UK)

✉ volunteer@volunteeradventures.com

🖥 www.volunteeradventures.com

Affiliated to Bridge Linguatec (see entry in 'Directories of Courses').

**PROGRAMMES OFFERED:** Volunteers can choose to work in the areas of Community Development, Conservation, Public Health, Sports Coaching, Construction, Youth Outreach or English Teaching in many countries in Africa, Asia and Latin America. Teacher training, language courses, and host families are also available on many projects.

**DESTINATIONS:** Africa (Zambia), Asia (India), and South America (Argentina, Brazil, Chile and Peru).

**DURATION OF PROGRAMMES:** Variable. From 1 week to 1 year. Average project length is 2 weeks, though there are some that last 4 weeks and longer.

**ACCOMMODATION:** Local host families, hostel or volunteer housing.

**OTHER SERVICES:** TEFL Online training for volunteer teaching projects, language immersion courses, activities and excursions to get to know the local culture.

**COST:** Sample costs would be £1,130 for a fortnight in youth outreach work in Argentina, £1,650 for 4 weeks teaching in Zambia.

### WORLDWIDE EXPERIENCE
The Oak Suite, Guardian House, Borough Road, Godalming, Surrey GU7 2AE
℅ 01483 860560
info@WorldwideExperience.com
www.WorldwideExperience.com

**PROGRAMME DESCRIPTION:** Specialist conservation placements in Southern Africa that give participants the chance to get actively involved in conservation on various game reserves, animal rehabilitation centres and ocean research projects. Other projects include community placements, game ranger courses, a wildlife film academy and a sculpting course.

**DESTINATIONS:** Projects are located in South Africa, Kenya, Malawi, India and Sri Lanka.

**NUMBER OF PLACEMENTS PER YEAR:** 400+.

**PREREQUISITES:** No particular skills needed. All nationalities accepted.

**DURATION AND TIME OF PLACEMENTS:** 2–12 weeks. Placements are available all year round (gap year, summer break and sabbatical).

**SELECTION PROCEDURES AND ORIENTATION:** Applications accepted year round. Interviews are informal and can be done by telephone. Open days are arranged throughout the year when Worldwide Experience crew meet potential volunteers. Full medical and personal checklist is supplied during preparation.

**COST:** From £599 for 2 weeks, inclusive of transfers, meals, accommodation (furnished and comfortable, shared between two) and placement activities.

### YEAR IN INDUSTRY
The University of Southampton, Southampton SO17 1BJ
℅ 023 8059 7061
info@yini.org.uk
www.yini.org.uk

Founding member of the Year Out Group. Major provider of gap year industrial placements throughout the UK. See entry in 'Directory of Work Experience in the UK'.

### YEAR OUT DRAMA COMPANY
Stratford-upon-Avon College, Alcester Road, Stratford-upon-Avon, Warwickshire CV37 9QR
℅ 01789 266245
yearoutdrama@stratford.ac.uk

Founding member of the Year Out Group. One-year course covers acting, directing, performance, voice work, movement and design. See entry in 'Directories of Courses'.

### YOMPS
10 Woodland Way, Brighton, East Sussex, BN1 8BA
℅ 0845 006 1435. Fax: 020 7149 9933
info@yomps.co.uk
www.yomps.co.uk

**PROGRAMME DESCRIPTION:** Volunteering, adventure, training courses, exploration and cultural experiences.

**DESTINATIONS:** South Africa, Namibia, Malawi, Kenya, Botswana, Zambia, Zimbabwe, Mozambique, Mexico,

Ecuador, Venezuela, Guatemala, Honduras, Chile, Peru, Argentina, Thailand, Fiji, USA and Switzerland.

**NUMBER OF PLACEMENTS PER YEAR:** 200+.

**DURATION AND TIME OF PLACEMENTS:** 2 weeks to 2 years; average trip lasts 8–12 weeks.

**PREREQUISITES:** Open to people of all nationalities. Most participants are aged 18–25 but other age groups are also welcome.

**SELECTION PROCEDURES AND ORIENTATION:** Online applications accepted throughout the year. Field Manual provided pre-departure and project orientation on arrival.

**COST:** From £649 for short trips. Sample cost of 4 weeks of Wildlife Research Volunteering in South Africa is £995. Prices include accommodation which varies, for example chalet in Switzerland, tented camp in South Africa, beach marine base in Mexico, coastal volunteer base in Lake Malawi, overlanding vehicle in Southern Africa, host family in Guatemala, under the stars in Namibia, Amazonian rainforest research base in Ecuador and camping out in the Patagonian wilderness of Argentina.

**CONTACT:** Tom Smith, Volunteer Coordinator.

---

**ZANZIGAP**

18 Melrose Road, Sheffield S3 9DN

℡ 0114 249 1661

✉ enquiries@zanzigap.com

🖥 www.zanzigap.com

---

Zanzigap was set up in 2007 and is run by a group of teachers and ex-teachers in Sheffield, who are familiar with this part of Tanzania and with experience of organising long-term visits.

**PROGRAMME DESCRIPTION:** Teaching English (or any preferred specialist subject) to GCSE level in secondary schools in Zanzibar.

**NUMBER OF PLACEMENTS PER YEAR:** Up to 60.

**PREREQUISITES:** Minimum age 16, average 19. Mainly but not exclusively British. GCSEs and/or A-Levels preferred.

**DURATION AND TIME OF PLACEMENTS:** 3–9 months, though full academic year (end of January to beginning of November) preferred.

**SELECTION PROCEDURES AND ORIENTATION:** Applications should be made a year in advance. No interview needed. Pre-departure bonding weekend is part of programme. Full orientation given, including CD-ROM, risk assessment, packing list and medical information. Support given in situ, lesson observation, training and teaching practice. 24-hour hotline to UK.

**COST:** £2,500 for 9 months, all-inclusive of insurance, airfares, visa, accommodation and living expenses. Local accommodation only which may not have water/electricity. Mobile phone signal available in all locations.

**CONTACT:** John Errington, MBE (Director).

*Also see directories at the end of the chapters on Volunteering, Work Experience, Au Pairing and Courses for other organisations that welcome gap year students (among others).*

# EXPEDITIONS

Adolescence is a good time to discover tales of adventure from the literature of exploration whether it is the casual descriptions of suffering by mountaineers or sailors, classics by Robert Byron or Freya Stark, or more recent classics by Bruce Chatwin, Redmond O'Hanlon and Dervla Murphy.

Visiting a wild and woolly part of the world might seem an impossible dream for a 17-year-old with no money and no travel experience beyond a youth hostelling weekend in the Peak District. But a number of organisations cater specifically for gap year students looking for challenging adventures in remote places. These are open to anyone who is mentally and physically fit and who is prepared to raise funds for the fees (typically starting at £3,000 plus equipment, etc.).

If you feel the need for a testing adventure or would like to show your friends and family what stern stuff you are made of, then a gap year is the perfect time to think about going on an expedition. In a recent Radio 4 interview, the director of the Wilderness Foundation tried to explain the value of spending time in wild places and why it fosters tolerance: 'Wilderness creates a sense of vulnerability... and vulnerability is the greatest way of finding a common sense of humanity between people'.

## EXPEDITIONS AND THE DUKE OF EDINBURGH AWARD
School-leavers who have attended schools with a tradition of sending students on expeditions will be at an advantage in tracking down suitable opportunities in their gap year. An expedition forms part of the requirements to gain a Duke of Edinburgh Award. Most people become involved through their local school or youth club though it is possible to enlist through an Open Award Centre. Most take place in the UK (usually the Lake District or Wales) but some go abroad, e.g. on canoeing expeditions to Canada. The Duke of Edinburgh's Award Scheme (www.dofe.org) supports personal and social development of young people aged 14–25 and has links with the main youth expedition organisers.

## HELPFUL ORGANISATIONS
The *Royal Geographical Society* (RGS; 1 Kensington Gore, London SW7 2AR; www.rgs.org) encourages and assists many British expeditions. The RGS is now allied with the Institute of British Geographers (IBG) and keeps files of expedition reports and maps in the Foyle Reading Room that might be of assistance to expedition planners. The old Expedition Advisory Centre is now known as Geography Outdoors. The RGS hosts an annual weekend seminar called 'Explore' in November on expedition and fieldwork planning (www.rgs.org/explore) which covers fundraising and budgeting for expeditions as well as issues of safety and logistics (attendance fee £65 for students). The RGS has put online the list of grant-giving organisations from its publication *The Expedition Handbook* (2004, £16.99). Although many grants are ring-fenced (e.g. must live within

eight miles of Exmouth Town Hall) it is certainly worth checking and applying as widely as possible.

The RGS's new Leading and Learning programme (020 7591 3180) has recently begun offering gap year scholarships (www.rgs.org/LandL) aimed at A-Level students from challenging backgrounds who would benefit from a bursary to enable them to do fieldwork, go on a meaningful gap year, or attend fieldwork summer schools.

The Young Explorers' Trust (YET; www.theyet.org) affiliated to the RGS is a registered charity that promotes safe and responsible expeditions. It offers advice and support to groups of students who wish to organise their own expedition during their gap year. YET does not offer pre-arranged expeditions but offers an expert panel of advisers and assessors for expedition plans. It also organises occasional weekend Expedition Leaders' Planning Courses in Sheffield every October, open to everyone for a residential fee of £80. Some grant aid may be made available to YET-approved expeditions.

*Raleigh* (www.raleighinternational.org) is a well-established youth and education charity that since 1984 has sent on expeditions worldwide more than 30,000 people from all walks of life, nationalities and ages. Participants develop new skills, friendships and make a difference to communities and environments across the world. It offers 5 or 10 week expeditions consisting of community, environmental and adventure projects. 17–24 year olds can sign up as participants and 25+ can volunteer as managers. When **Felicia Royaards** decided to take time out before starting university, she signed up to the Costa Rica expedition after hearing about Raleigh from a friend. She fundraised with support from friends and family and got creative by selling her own jewellery designs at a local fair. Her enthusiasm for choosing a Raleigh expedition is boundless:

> *Raleigh puts you in such a different situation; in a new environment, new people, and a new country with another spoken language. It gives you a great opportunity to do three totally different things in one expedition. Not only do you learn a lot about yourself through adventure, you get to appreciate the community and environment. Changing groups every phase made me more confident and more independent. Furthermore you get to know a lot of people from different kinds of backgrounds. My highlight has been finishing the Kamuk trek. It was a personal challenge: you push yourself to the limit and find out how strong you are. Raleigh changed me in positive ways and I reckon it will help me in the future when I'm looking for a job after my university degree.*

The British Schools Exploring Society (see entry for *BSES Expeditions* page 242) organises an impressive range of expeditions which combine scientific research projects and adventurous activities. This youth development charity has been running wilderness expeditions for over 75 years. Visiting some of the world's most remote and challenging environments, from the Arctic to the Amazon, BSES offers the opportunity to explore and learn about environmental issues facing the world today. Expedition members take part in a UK-based training weekend so that they can meet the rest of the team and find out more about the science and adventure objectives. It is a chance to become familiar with kit and equipment and gain some of the essential skills required for living in an extreme environment.

**SARAH PHILLIPS** thinks that although the fund-raising target is high, so are the rewards. She joined an Extreme Arctic Expedition to Svalbard through BSES in 2009. Being at such a high latitude (78° north) means that the sun never sets during the spring and summer. The cold is unbelievable. At night breath vapour condenses against the ceiling of tents where it instantly freezes and then falls on you as soon as a gust of wind hits the tent:

'The total cost of the expedition came to around £8,000, which I felt was quite expensive for a gap year, but I would rather spend it on something like that where I am doing something completely different and unforgettable, than go around New Zealand, Thailand and Fiji which is commonplace with gap year students. Furthermore, the kit was very costly. But you have to get the right kit, because it is not something you can take a shortcut with, and I didn't mind paying out for something that will keep me alive!

We had some absolutely unforgettable days. Our leader Richard had managed to cast his mind back and relocate an untouched ice cave up a steep valley. He was concerned about the huge cornice overhanging the valley, especially since the snow was heavily piling up and the weather was vicious. So we ventured up the side of the valley in the relentless wind that tries to knock you over as you wobble and sway up the incline.

We were lowered into the little slot of the cave, which opened up into a huge church-like cavern. It was stunning. The ceiling glistened and sparkled, secretly twinkling out of the corner of your eye. I really had the sense of the Snow Queen's forgotten lair. We excitedly ventured further in, coming across untouched beauty such as cascading water paused delicately as it splashed to the floor and fragile glass-like icicles ranging in all sizes balanced from the starry ceiling.

> *We settled to do our scientific discoveries of the cave, planning to map it out by taking detailed measurements at frequent intervals along the 240m tunnel. We eventually hope to turn our results into a 3D model of the cave and create a task for future expeditioners to investigate. When we reached the back of the cave, we turned off our head torches and simply appreciated the still darkness and utter silence. It was truly a special moment of meditating and appreciating these simple things. Richard reckoned there had been fewer people in the cave than on Everest. After five hours of hardcore science and spectacular adventure, we rugged up and braved the angry weather outside the cave. After a short while we reached our beloved camp and escaped the harrowing wind. All in all a magical day that can't really be described.'*

These highlights compensated for the downsides that Sarah encountered, such as not being in contact with anyone at home for three months and feeling uncomfortably isolated.

## SAILING ADVENTURES

Several youth-oriented organisations and charities take young people on Sail Training expeditions. Fees vary but most tend to be £60–£80 a day. The Association of Sail Training Organisations (ASTO) is the umbrella group for sail training organisations in the UK, and its website (www.sailtraining.co.uk) is a useful link to about 30 member organisations with more than 50 boats including RTW racing yachts, gaff-rigged classics and large square-rigged ships. UK Sail Training organisations predominantly operate around European waters, with many taking part in the Tall Ships Races. A few vessels operate in the Caribbean or Canaries. Sea Sail Training (www.atseasailtraining.com) coordinates crew placement for vessels taking part in an annual series of Tall Ships Races. More than half the trainees are obliged to be aged 18–25 and of mixed nationalities; some use the trip as the residential element of the Duke of Edinburgh Gold Award. No experience is needed to join the crew. The full daily cost of a berth is £60–£90. For example the youth cost of joining the seven-week transatlantic crossing from Charleston in the USA to Belfast is €4,320.

## FUNDRAISING

Expeditions tend to be among the most expensive among gap year placements, and some of the targets fixed by the major organisations are truly daunting. See the section on Fundraising in the chapter 'Before You Go' for ideas on how to earn, save and persuade others to give you the necessary funds.

Those with a specialised project might discover that targeted funds are available from trusts and charities. However many, like the Mt Everest Foundation (www.mef.org.

uk/mefguide.htm), are earmarked for high level expeditions undertaking first ascents, new routes and scientific research on mountains, so that, according to the MEF's Honorary Secretary 'Gap Year projects are extremely unlikely to be eligible for support'.

Relevant companies are sometimes willing to give equipment in lieu of a cheque, though most manufacturers of hiking and camping equipment are inundated with requests. Successful supplicants often present imaginative ways in which they plan to publicise their benefactors' products.

## SPONSORED EXPEDITIONS FOR CHARITY

A large and growing number of charities in the UK now offer adventurous group travel to individuals who are prepared to undertake some serious fundraising on their behalf. Household names such as Oxfam, the Youth Hostels Association and the Children's Society organise sponsored trips, as do many more obscure good causes. Specialist agent Charity Challenge (www.charitychallenge.com) allows you to select your trip (most of which last no more than a fortnight) and which charity you would like to support. Participants are asked to raise £2,300 (say) for the charity and in return receive a 'free' trip. You are in a far stronger position to ask people for donations if you can say you are supporting the Children's Society/British Heart Foundation/Whale Conservation Society or whatever, than if you say you are trying to raise money for a holiday to Morocco/Patagonia/Borneo. These trips are usually more attractive to older people looking for an interesting way to take a gap than to school-leavers.

# DIRECTORY OF EXPEDITIONS

## BORDERS EXPLORATION GROUP

enquiries@borders-exploration-group.org.uk

www.borders-exploration-group.org.uk

Borders Exploration Group is a non-profit making voluntary organisation that organises international and European expeditions for young people living in the Scottish border area.

**DESTINATIONS:** 4-week expedition to Chile (summer 2010).

**NUMBER OF PLACEMENTS PER EXPEDITION:** About 35 on a major expedition, 15 on a European trip.

**PREREQUISITES:** Must live in Scottish Border catchment area. Ages 16–25.

**CONTACT:** Jono Ellis, Vice Chair.

## BRATHAY EXPLORATION GROUP TRUST

Brathay Hall, Ambleside, Cumbria LA22 0HP

01539 433942

admin@brathayexploration.org.uk

www.brathayexploration.org.uk

Established 1947.

**PROGRAMME DESCRIPTION:** Mounts expeditions and expeditionary courses for young adults. Wide-ranging activities including adventure and environmental awareness.

**DESTINATIONS:** Worldwide, varying from year to year. 2010 expeditions to Morocco, Norway and Foula (a remote Shetland Island).

**NUMBER OF PLACEMENTS PER YEAR:** 200.

**PREREQUISITES:** Ages 15–25, with most aged 16–21. No qualifications needed. People with disabilities welcome to apply.

**DURATION AND TIME OF PLACEMENTS:** 1–5 weeks summer holiday period.

**SELECTION PROCEDURES AND ORIENTATION:** Briefing and pre-departure training sessions on outdoor skills and first aid.

**COST:** Up to £2,000 for a month-long overseas expedition (excluding airfares); less for trips in UK.

## BSES EXPEDITIONS

Royal Geographical Society, 1 Kensington Gore, London SW7 2AR

020 7591 3141

info@bses.org.uk

www.bses.org.uk

The British Schools Exploring Society is a youth development charity which was founded in 1932 by an original member of Captain Scott's ill-fated Antarctic Expedition of 1910–1913. It provides opportunities for young people to take part in challenging scientific expeditions to remote wild environments.

**PROGRAMME DESCRIPTION:** The expeditions aim to combine living in extreme and challenging conditions with valuable scientific and environmental research. Past expeditions have included climbing a 6,000m peak in India, protecting 30,000 turtle eggs from poachers by building artificial nesting sites in the Amazon, glaciology field-work through the arctic winter in Eastern Greenland, sea kayaking in Alaska and other expeditions in the Arctic. In 2010 there will be a 3-month spring expedition to Arctic Svalbard, and month-long summer expeditions to Ladakh in the Himalayas, the Amazon Rainforest and again to Svalbard. All expeditions can count towards the Duke of Edinburgh's Gold Award Residential and Expedition sections.

**DESTINATIONS:** Arctic, jungle, desert and mountain environments worldwide, for example the Amazon rainforest, Libya, Sinai, the Himalayas, Svalbard, Madagascar and Greenland. Destinations change from year to year.

**NUMBER OF PLACEMENTS PER YEAR:** 180–220.

**PREREQUISITES:** Must be aged between 16 and 23, be well motivated and have a good level of fitness. However, no previous experience is necessary.

**DURATION AND TIME OF PLACEMENT:** Expedition lengths vary from 1 month in the summer holidays to 3 months for Gap Year expeditions.

**SELECTION PROCEDURES AND ORIENTATION:** Applicants will be interviewed regionally. Places are allocated on a first come first served basis on completion of a successful interview. On accepting the offer of a place, Young Explorers take part in a briefing weekend held prior to their expedition. Following the expedition the BSES Annual Gathering Presentations take place in the Royal Geographical Society.

**COST:** £3,500–£5,500. BSES Expeditions offers lots of help and guidance on fundraising, including a bursary and mentoring scheme. No one showing appropriate commitment and effort in raising the contribution will be denied a place.

---

### CORAL CAY CONSERVATION (CCC)
Elizabeth House, 39 York Road, London SE1 7NJ
020 7620 1411
info@coralcay.org
www.coralcay.org

CCC runs tropical forest and coral reef expeditions in the Philippines, Tobago and Cambodia. Volunteers are trained to survey scientifically some of the world's most beautiful yet endangered tropical environments. For details, see 'Directory of Specialist Gap Year Programmes'.

---

### DORSET EXPEDITIONARY SOCIETY/ LEADING EDGE EXPEDITIONS
Lupins Business Centre, 1–3 Greenhill, Weymouth, Dorset DT4 7SP
01305 816222
dorsetexp@googlemail.com
www.dorsetexp.co.uk
www.leadingedge.org.uk

The Dorset Expeditionary Society promotes adventurous opportunities for young people from throughout the UK.

---

All expedition leaders are volunteers. Expeditions can qualify for part of the Duke of Edinburgh Gold Award.

**PROGRAMME DESCRIPTION:** Expeditions include trekking, mountain climbing, kayaking, white water rafting, mountain biking and safaris, and experience of other world cultures.

**DESTINATIONS:** Europe, North and South America, Africa, India and Asia, always to wilderness areas off the tourist track.

**PREREQUISITES:** Participants must be fit and healthy. Minimum age 15 for some expeditions, 16/18 for others.

**DURATION AND TIME OF PLACEMENTS:** 3–5 weeks, usually in the summer holidays.

**SELECTION PROCEDURES AND ORIENTATION:** Selection weekend to choose suitable candidates. Training courses for aspiring leaders are organised to gain nationally recognised qualifications such as Emergency Rescue First Aid Certificate, Single Pitch Assessment, Cave Leadership and Mountain Leadership Awards.

**COST:** £50 for the selection weekend plus expedition costs (roughly £500–£2,500). Guidance on fundraising is given.

**CONTACT:** Lucy Demontis, Secretary.

---

### GAPFORCE
530 Fulham Road, London SW6 5NR
020 7384 3343
info@gapforce.org
www.gapforce.org

Trekforce, part of Gapforce, offers extreme expeditions and jungle trekking that include conservation work.

**DESTINATIONS:** Belize, Borneo, Nepal and Thailand.

**DURATION AND TIME OF PLACEMENTS:** Expeditions all-year round with flexible durations.

---

### GLOBAL VISION INTERNATIONAL (GVI)
*UK office:* 3 High Street, St Albans, Hertfordshire AL3 4ED
01727 250250
info@gviworld.com
www.gvi.co.uk

*North American office*: 252 Newbury Street, Number 4, Boston, MA 02116

☎ +1 888 653 6028

🖥 www.gviusa.com

*Australian office*: Suite 206, 530 Little Collins Street, Melbourne, Victoria 3000

☎ +61 1300 795013

🖥 www.gviaustralia.com

**PROGRAMME DESCRIPTION:** Since 1998, GVI has been running overseas expeditions and projects in Africa, Latin America and Asia.

**DESTINATIONS:** South Africa, Kenya, Seychelles, Ecuador, Mexico, Costa Rica and Patagonia.

**NUMBER OF PLACEMENTS PER YEAR:** 1,000.

**PREREQUISITES:** None. Minimum age 18. All nationalities welcome. No special training or qualifications are required as all training will be provided in the field.

**DURATION AND TIME OF PLACEMENTS:** 5, 20 or 15 weeks.

**SELECTION PROCEDURES AND ORIENTATION:** Online application form plus application assessment over the phone.

**COST:** From £1,345 for 5-week rainforest expedition in Ecuador.

---

**JUBILEE SAILING TRUST YOUTH LEADERSHIP @ SEA SCHEME**

JST, Hazel Road, Woolston, Southampton SO19 7GB

☎ 023 8044 9108

🖥 sales@jst.org.uk

🖥 www.jst.org.uk

**COURSES OFFERED:** Leadership course on a sea voyage to develop communication, leadership and team skills, while building an understanding of disability.

**PREREQUISITES:** Ages 16–25. Must be prepared to act as a full part of a tall ship voyage crew for the duration of the voyage.

**SELECTION PROCEDURES AND ORIENTATION:** By written application; mark form with 'Youth Leadership @ Sea' and enclose short personal statement of 200–400 words, detailing why you think you should be chosen. Places are limited.

**COST:** Prices start from £399 for a 5-day voyage. This includes all accommodation, meals and training. Subsidies of up to £300 are offered towards the cost of the Jubilee Sailing Trust Youth Leadership @ Sea Scheme.

---

**NONSTOP SAIL**

Unit 3B, The Plough Brewery, 516 Wandsworth Road, London SW8 3JX

☎ 0845 365 1525

🖥 info@nonstopsail.com

🖥 www.nonstopsail.com

Member of the Year Out Group.

**PROGRAMME DESCRIPTION:** Transatlantic crossings and Caribbean adventure sail trips.

**DESTINATIONS:** Choice of transatlantic crossing; island hopping in the Caribbean starting and finishing in Antigua, cruising from island to island, swimming, snorkelling and exploring the islands; and sailing around Britain and Ireland while gaining RYA qualifications. Opportunity to participate in the Fastnet ocean race among others.

**PREREQUISITES:** Minimum age 18 (about half of participants are gappers).

**NUMBER OF PLACEMENTS:** 5–10 per boat.

**Duration:** 2, 4 or 6 weeks.

**COST:** £1,550 for 2 weeks, £2,990 for four weeks and £4,395 for six weeks.

**CONTACT:** Georgie Bushe, Sales Manager.

---

**OASIS OVERLAND**

The Marsh, Henstridge, Somerset BA8 0TF

☎ 01963 363400

🖥 info@oasisoverland.co.uk

🖥 www.oasisoverland.co.uk

Overland expedition company founded in 1997.

**DESTINATIONS:** South America, Africa, Middle East and Egypt, and the Silk Road.

**NUMBER OF PLACEMENTS PER EXPEDITION:** Purpose-built trucks carry up to 24.

**DURATION:** Large choice (see website) between 10 days and 40 weeks.

**COST:** From £92 a week plus £37 kitty on longest trips, rising to £140 plus £70 kitty in South America. Sample expedition 15 weeks Quito to Rio costs £2,075 plus $1,690 kitty paid locally.

**CONTACT:** Chris Wrede, Director.

---

## RALEIGH
207 Waterloo Road, London SE1 8XD
📞 020 7371 8585
📧 info@raleigh.org.uk
🖥 www.raleighinternational.org

Expeditions for young people aged 17–24 comprise a diverse mix of people including gap year students, graduates and people from the expedition country. The aim is to make a positive contribution to the host countries – Costa Rica, Nicaragua, Malaysia (Borneo) and India. Participants take part in adventure, community and environmental projects. See listing in the 'Directory of Specialist Gap Year Programmes'.

---

## REAL GAP EXPERIENCE
1 Meadow Road, Tunbridge Wells, Kent TN1 2YG
📞 01892 516164
📧 info@realgap.co.uk
🖥 www.realgap.co.uk

Leading gap year specialists, ATOL bonded with financial backing.

**PROGRAMME DESCRIPTION:** Gap year adventure expeditions combining travel, adventure and volunteer work to a range of destinations.

**DESTINATIONS:** Everest base camp, Ecuador, Peru, Venezuela, India, Indonesian Islands, Kenya and Tanzania.

**PREREQUISITES:** None, except as limited by visas. Some programmes require basic level of fitness.

**DURATION AND TIME OF PLACEMENTS:** Everest trip is 35 days, most others last 4, 6 or 8 weeks.

**COST:** Everest expedition costs £2,199, others vary from £1,450 to £2,300+.

---

## THE RONA TRUST
Universal Marina, Crableck Lane, Sarisbury Green, Southampton SO31 7ZN
📞 01489 885098
📧 office@ronatrust.com
🖥 www.ronatrust.com

**PROGRAMME DESCRIPTION:** Sail training voyages for young people on three large sail training yachts. Older trainees sail in the two larger vessels and cross the Channel to France or the Channel Islands.

**DESTINATIONS:** South coast, France or Channel Islands.

**PREREQUISITES:** for ages 14–25.

**DURATION AND TIME OF PLACEMENTS:** mostly 1 week.

**SELECTION PROCEDURES AND ORIENTATION:** charity aims for broad social mix on each sailing. Most applicants come via recognised organisations such as scouts, sea cadets, youth clubs, schools and colleges, but individuals may also book directly.

**COST:** £100 a week (because charitable project is subsidised).

**CONTACT:** Ann Bowers, Project Secretary.

---

## SEA | MESTER PROGRAMS
PO Box 5477, Sarasota, FL 34277, USA
📞 941 924 6789
📧 info@seamester.com
🖥 www.seamester.com

Parent company (ActionQuest) has been operating experiential education programmes for youth for over 30 years and 'Sea | mester' programmes since 1998.

**PROGRAMME DESCRIPTION:** Educational adventures on an 88 or 112ft schooner. Primary academic foci are oceanography, nautical science, communication and leadership skills development. Students undertake research and service projects with local government and private organisations while working toward certification in sailing and scuba diving. Voyages are available in the Caribbean and worldwide destinations with ocean crossings.

**NUMBER OF PLACEMENTS PER YEAR:** About 200.

**DESTINATIONS:** Worldwide destinations include Mediterranean, Caribbean, South East Asia, Pacific, Australia and ocean crossings.

**PREREQUISITES:** No experience necessary. Minimum age 17 (many students are pre-matriculates). All nationalities.

**DURATION AND TIME OF PLACEMENTS:** 80- and 90-day voyages during the autumn and spring. Also 40- and 20-day voyages during the summer.

**COST:** US$14,600 for 80 days, US$15,800 for 90 days, US$7,100 for 40 days, US$3,970 for 20 days.

**CONTACT:** Jo Meighan, PR and Marketing Manager, ActionQuest, Lifeworks and 'Sea|mester' Programs (jo@actionquest.com).

---

## TALL SHIPS YOUTH TRUST

2A The Hard, Portsmouth, Hampshire PO1 3PT

023 9283 2055

info@tallships.org

www.tallships.org

Youth charity dedicated to the personal development of young people through crewing on its two 60sq m rigged ships *Prince William* and *Stavros S Niarchos*.

**PROGRAMME DESCRIPTION:** Tall ships adventures and adventure sail training voyages mostly lasting 7–10 days though longest voyage is 25 days. These take place year round in the waters around the UK and Northern Europe in the summer and around the Canaries, Azores and Caribbean in the winter/spring.

**PREREQUISITES:** Minimum age 16 with an upper age limit of 25 on youth voyages, 18–75 for adult voyages.

**SELECTION PROCEDURES AND ORIENTATION:** No previous sailing experience needed. Enthusiasm and an ability to work well with others is all that is required.

**COST:** About £80–£90 per day (plus flights for voyages abroad). Bursaries may be available.

## VENTURE CO WORLDWIDE

The Ironyard, 64–66 The Market Place, Warwick CV34 4SD

01926 411122

mail@ventureco-worldwide.com

www.ventureco-worldwide.com

**PROGRAMME DESCRIPTION:** Gap year and career gap specialist organising 4-month programmes in Latin America, India/Nepal, East Africa and Indochina incorporating an 8–9-week expedition through the Andes, Himalayas, Rift Valley and China highlands (including the Everest Base Camp Trek). Route planning and day-to-day organisation is done by team members, and leadership roles are shared out (see entry in 'Directory of Specialist Gap Year Programmes'.

---

## YORKSHIRE SCHOOLS EXPLORING SOCIETY

579 Denby Dale Road, Calder Grove, Wakefield, Yorkshire WF4 3DA

01484 663 678

01924 267 144 (answering machine)

info@yses.org.uk

www.yses.org.uk

**PROGRAMME DESCRIPTION:** Expeditions are organised to wilderness areas, most recently to Tibet and the Yukon. Young leaders are needed to assist with the expeditions.

**DESTINATIONS:** Mongolia, Alaska, Ireland in 2008; Kenya 2009; Grand Canyon 2010.

**NUMBER OF PLACEMENTS PER YEAR:** Around 70/80.

**PREREQUISITES:** Students on the expeditions must be in full-time education in Yorkshire (aged 14–18, excluding Gap Year students). Leaders can come from anywhere and need not be in full-time education.

**DURATION AND TIME OF PLACEMENTS:** 4–5 weeks in summer.

# WORK EXPERIENCE

Focused school leavers who have a clear idea of what career path they intend to follow can try to build into their gap year a component of working in a related field, which will also feed into their university course. This works better with Engineering than English Literature, but in all cases will look impressive on future CVs. Work experience considered in its broadest terms applies to any experience of the world of work, which can also be in a developing country, and is very often unpaid.

In the current disastrous economic climate with rising unemployment, an already competitive workplace has just become more so. Work experience placements may be all that a new graduate can aspire to. The new buzzword in this context is 'intern' as a means of kickstarting careers, and the British government launched a campaign to increase the number of internships to absorb some of the 400,000 graduates leaving UK universities in 2009 (see Graduate Talent Pool information below).

Experience in a working environment, preferably in your chosen career field, is a valuable asset for any serious job search. And if this can be combined with cultural immersion and the chance to cope with a foreign working environment, your profile will be enhanced even more. The troubled economy is predicted to send more students and graduates to untraditional places from China to California searching for an opportunity to extend their CVs and provide potential for future job references. Even if an overseas work placement is irrelevant to your future career plans, it will at least provide a useful introduction to how companies or organisations function in a different culture. This applies to people taking a pre- or post-university gap year.

Although UK schools are obliged to organise five or 10-day work experience placements for students in Year 10 or 11, a longer period spent working in a particular area gives a much clearer idea of what a job is about and whether it is of interest for your potential future. Work placements are looked on favourably by university admissions officers; experience of the 'real world' often helps students to develop a more mature outlook on life which enables them to do relatively better at university than their peers who come straight from school or a Thai island. Similarly, employers view students with work experience as more desirable. There is less risk for an employer in choosing someone who has already had some exposure to a particular career, and also less expense in training.

Employers, especially in companies with an international profile, look for employees who have demonstrated that they are open-minded and can adapt to different cultures. One way to impress these employers is with a CV that shows that you have successfully completed a period of work experience abroad. This is particularly impressive if the student uses or learns a foreign language as part of this experience. However, experience in the USA or Australia will also boost your CV.

Nowadays, the demand for many careers often outweighs supply, and exam qualifications no longer seem to be enough to get a job. Work experience can be used as a means of getting a foot in the door with particular companies and occupations. If you are interested in gaining work experience in a competitive field such as the media, publishing, broadcasting, museology, medicine, veterinary science, wildlife conservation, etc. you may find it very difficult to obtain paid work.

If you are serious about enhancing your CV or simply getting a taste of what it will be really like, you should be prepared initially to work on a voluntary basis, which is now standard practice in many professions such as conservation. Some UK companies specialise in arranging work experience abroad in fields allied to medicine, journalism and others; see entries below for *Global Volunteer Projects* and *Learn Overseas* and also see website of Work the World (www.worktheworld.co.uk), which organises placements for student medics, nurses, dentists and physiotherapists to gain experience working in Ghana, Tanzania, India and Argentina. Gap Medics (www.gapmedics.co.uk) has placements in Namibia, Tanzania and Nepal.

If you foresee yourself working in business, engineering, banking, accountancy or industry after graduation, you may be able to arrange a relevant paid work experience placement in your year between school and university. Not only are you likely to be able to earn and save money but with luck they will like you enough to offer you future vacation jobs or even a permanent career. **Nicky Stead** from West Yorkshire found herself in the unwelcome position of being forced to take a gap year when her A-Level results were worse than expected. Undaunted, she decided to work locally before embarking on some world travels (see *Australia* chapter):

> *I had to get a job and decided that to make the best of things I should get a job that was relevant to my preferred career and would look good on my CV as well as raise money for travelling. I got a job inputting mortgage applications for Skipton Building Society for six months, which I really enjoyed. I made so many friends and I loved the business environment. I felt grown up, and it was great. My appraisal was good and they encouraged me to stay.*

# FINDING A PLACEMENT

Several companies that take students for work placements for a substantial period are listed at the end of this chapter. It is worth visiting the local Connexions office for the names of local companies that might take on students. Students can also write directly to companies enclosing a CV to ask if they offer work placements, though the ratio of replies is likely to be discouraging (let alone favourable ones). The direct approach is more personal and likely to please potential employers, especially if there is a particular aspect of the company which students can say has attracted them.

Much can be achieved by confidently and persistently asking for the chance to help out in your chosen workplace unpaid. **Laura Hitchcock** (from the USA) managed to fix up two three-month positions in the field of her career interest by agreeing to pay her own expenses if they would take her on and help her find accommodation in local homes. Her jobs were in the publicity departments of the Ironbridge Museums and then in a theatre-arts centre in East Anglia. Laura discovered that if you are willing to help yourself people can be helpful and encouraging.

Specific gap year programmes offered by big companies are generally fiercely competitive. If applying for one of these competitive schemes, such as the ones offered by Deloitte or KPMG, be prepared to undergo psychometric tests and other rigorous selection procedures. At interview you will be expected to talk about market issues in the financial world affecting the service line for which you are applying, i.e. tax or assurance/audit. Also you should have an example prepared that demonstrates how you solve problems in a team. And of course they will want to know your reasons for taking a gap year. Whatever the question, use it to demonstrate a strength of yours, not a weakness.

The fortunate few who are successful are usually paid a reasonable salary and many other benefits. The companies offer these schemes in order to attract the best possible candidates to join their companies after university. They tend to make their programmes interesting and varied to impress students. For example, the *Accenture Horizons Gap Year Scheme* is a programme that lasts eight months from September and combines training with paid work experience. Accenture pays £18,500 (pro rata, so equivalent to about £12,400 for the eight months) plus a London housing allowance travel bursary or university sponsorship worth £1,500 on completion of a satisfactory period of work, which leaves plenty of time and money for travelling before university in the autumn.

Other gap year schemes, such as the one run by *IBM*, are hanging in there, although *PricewaterhouseCoopers* cancelled its programme for gap year students in 2009, blaming the economic downturn. Many students seeking work experience will entertain more modest ambitions than these gold-plated companies. Agency temping experience in different kinds of office can be a useful stepping stone not only to well-paid holiday work in the future but also to acquiring a broad acquaintance with the working world.

Try also WEXO (Work Experience Online; www.wexo.co.uk), a networking community for those requiring or offering work experience, internships and jobs. In the current climate, there are far more internship-seekers registered than there are offers from companies. But WEXO hosts occasional job fairs that claim to deal with gap year ideas as well, so could be worth attending.

The majority of work experience placements are designed for university students, typically in their third year, and many university careers services have excellent databases of prospective hiring companies. Individual universities cater mainly to a local population but their careers webpages can be worth searching. Try Imperial College, for example, which is affiliated to City & Guilds College internship listings at www.cgcu.net/internships and which focuses on placements in technical and financial companies. The Windsor Fellowship (www.windsor-fellowship.org) offers sponsorship to high-achieving undergraduates (first or second year) from African, African Caribbean and Asian communities in the UK. The fully funded two-year leadership programme includes paid work experience placements and community involvement. Similarly Sponsors for Educational Opportunity (SEO), a non-profit organisation based in London, assists exceptional undergraduates from under-represented ethnic minority backgrounds to find summer internships with banks, corporate law firms and other UK businesses.

> **GRADUATES' TIP**
> The Graduate Talent Pool (http://graduatetalentpool.direct.gov.uk) is a new government initiative that helps recent graduates get internships with companies; registration is free.

## YEAR IN INDUSTRY

The *Year in Industry* (YINI) is a leading provider of gap year work placements throughout the UK and is run by the education charity, the Engineering Development Trust (EDT). Last year nearly 600 students took part in the scheme, gaining skills and experience to enhance their degree course while earning a real salary. There are opportunities in all branches of engineering, science, technology, IT, business and other fields. It's a great chance for students to confirm their degree choice and get a feel for the working world before starting university. Students develop skills, which will enhance their university education and maximise their graduate job prospects. Many companies view The Year in Industry as a part of their graduate recruitment programme and go on to sponsor placement students through university or offer vacation work. Around one in four students go on to receive financial support from their company throughout university and many students are subsequently offered jobs on graduation.

Placements generally last for 10–12 months from August/September to June/July and are paid, so students get valuable work experience while saving for university or travels. YINI has launched YINI Combo to provide a structured gap year experience that offers students a YINI work placement followed by an overseas travel experience during July/August/September. The opportunities available include YINI plus one of the following: conservation, summer camp, expedition or voluntary work. When **Helen Dawson** took a gap year with The Year in Industry, she was placed with Goodrich Engine Control Systems. After going on to graduate from Imperial College, London with a 1st in Mechanical Engineering, Helen took her first graduate job with the same company.

> *I chose to take a gap year, not only for experience and money but I also needed a bit of a break from academia and the constant pressure of homework and exams. The Year in Industry gave me the opportunity to experience the working world, which has made me a lot more focused as a student. It sounds a bit clichéd but in short The Year in Industry scheme was the best thing I could have done for my year out and I don't regret any part of it.*

## WORK EXPERIENCE ABROAD

Anyone with sufficient determination and patience has a good chance of persuading a company or organisation overseas that they could use an unpaid assistant keen to gain exposure to that particular profession. **Kate Day** wanted to travel after university while advancing her ambition of becoming a journalist:

> *I spent a year getting a range of work experience after graduating from university. I had decided I wanted to be a journalist rather late and was ill during my undergraduate degree so had no journalism experience when I graduated. I worked on a couple of local papers in this country and then went out to California for three months last March where I was a reporter for a tiny paper called the* **Los Altos Town Crier** *in Silicon Valley. I then went to India last summer with Projects Abroad and stayed on in India after my placement finished to travel a little bit and spent a week at* **The Hindu** *office in Chennai at the end. I am now doing a newspaper journalism diploma at City University in London and spent the Christmas holidays working for* **Times Online.**

In order to fix up the internship near San Francisco, Kate says she did endless googling (Journalism Jobs/Internships) and concentrated her efforts on small local papers. She didn't hear back from most of them but did succeed with one. Getting paid was out of the question for visa reasons. After signing up with a gap year agency to arrange a placement in south India, she says now that she was naïve in expecting everything to be laid on, because it wasn't. Undaunted she made a private arrangement to do some work shadowing at the main Indian daily *The Hindu*, experience that must have counted in her favour when she was applying for work experience in London later.

Work experience is also one of the fastest growing sectors in the youth travel industry. *Projects Abroad* is just one of many fee-charging placement agencies. The international association of work experience providers called WYSE Work Abroad (www.wyseworkabroad.org) has more than 150 member organisations around the world, many of which are affiliated to language schools that provide a preparatory language course before assignment to a work place. WYSE Work's stated aim is to '*facilitate and increase international youth travel and exchange through the promotion of culturally-oriented work exchange and work experience activities*'. Its website includes links to its members and is a good starting place for anyone interested in fixing up work experience abroad, almost all of which is unpaid. Most mediating organisations charge a substantial fee for their services, usually between €750 and €1,500, which may not include living expenses.

Although a study abroad placement was incorporated into her course at the University of Oregon, **Melissa Hunt** was determined to gain some work experience rather than just study. She spent 10 weeks in Madagascar with *Azafady* (see entry in 'Directory of Volunteering Abroad'):

> *I chose the programme because I had always known that I wanted to go to Africa first of all and I knew that I didn't really want to study abroad because I feel as though an internship is a much less selfish experience in a way. Studying abroad is something one does more for their own benefit and I think doing an internship, especially a service-based one, is working for someone else. I really liked the challenging nature of the in-*

*ternship and the fact that I pretty much had no idea what I was getting into, I basically wanted to make myself as uncomfortable as possible, as strange as that sounds, I felt that I was at a place in my life where I could really test my limits.*

Students and recent graduates in business, management, marketing, accounting, finance, computing, education or economics may be interested in an organisation run by a global student network based in 90 countries. *AIESEC*, an acronym for the International Association for Students of Economics and Management, (www.aiesec.co.uk) can organise placements in any of its member countries, aimed at giving participants an insight into living and working in another culture. *IAESTE* stands for the International Association for the Exchange of Students for Technical Experience. It provides international course-related vacation training for thousands of university-level students in 80 member countries. Placements are available in engineering, science, agriculture, architecture and related fields. British undergraduates should apply directly to IAESTE UK at the British Council (www.iaeste.org.uk). The US affiliate is the Association for International Practical Training or AIPT (+410 997 3069; www.aipt.org), which can arrange long and short-term placements for graduates and young professionals as well as college students in related fields.

*Raleigh*, through its overseas expeditions combining community, environmental and adventure projects, enables people of all ages to gain work experience skills such as team working, problem-solving, leadership and cultural awareness.

# WORKING IN EUROPE

Legislation has existed for many years guaranteeing the rights of all nationals of the European Union to travel, reside, study and work in any member country. The accession of two new countries to the European Union in 2007 (Bulgaria and Romania) in addition to the 10 new countries that joined in May 2004 means that the EU now consists of the original 15 member states (Austria, Belgium, Denmark, Finland, France, Germany, Greece, Ireland, Italy, Luxembourg, the Netherlands, Portugal, Spain, Sweden and the UK) plus Hungary, Poland, the Czech Republic, Slovakia, Slovenia, Estonia, Latvia, Lithuania, Malta, Cyprus, Romania and Bulgaria. However some transitional barriers to the full mobility of labour linger on.

The computerised, pan-European job information network EURES (EURopean Employment Service) is accessible through JobcentrePlus offices around the UK and all national employment services in Europe. Throughout Europe hundreds of specially trained EuroAdvisers can advise on vacancies within Europe. It is also possible to access the EURES database online via the EURES portal http://ec.europa.eu/eures to see the kinds of vacancies available from Iceland to Greece. Registered vacancies are usually for six months or longer, and are often in hotels and catering, personal services or for skilled, semi-skilled and (increasingly) managerial jobs. Naturally, language skills are very often a requirement.

A number of special exchanges and youth programmes help young Europeans move easily across borders for short and longer periods. Some of these projects cannot be applied for directly by the student, but must be supported by their school, university or local youth agency. The aim of the EU's *Leonardo da Vinci* scheme is to improve the quality of vocational and language training in Europe. It grants students and recent graduates mobility and in some cases full funding to undertake overseas work placements of between 3 and 12 months (for students) or between 2 and 12 months (recent graduates).

Applications for Leonardo funding must be submitted by organisations, not individuals. Details are available from university placement offices or International Relations Offices, or directly from ECOTEC, acting as the Leonardo UK National Agency in Birmingham (0845 199 2929; leonardo@ecotec.com; www.leonardo.org.uk). One provider of the scheme, *Twin Work and Volunteer Abroad*, based in London, (www.workandvolunteer.com), can assist with 9-week placements in an EU country (in 2009 the choices were Spain and Portugal) in which training and orientation, job placement, flights, allowance and expenses are all free. The terms of the programme are quite prescriptive (e.g. they cover 'linguistic preparation' but not 'language courses') so candidates must be prepared to conform to the specifications.

The well-established Erasmus student exchange incorporates an Internship in Europe component which is integrated throughout the EU. Students from all the participating countries can do an Erasmus internship somewhere in the European Union, plus Norway, Iceland, Liechtenstein and Turkey. The Erasmus internship should last at least three months, but no more than 12 and it should be relevant to the trainee's degree studies (www.eu-student.eu).

**GAPPERS' TIP**

*High flyers who would like to work for the European Commission as administrators, translators, secretaries, etc. must compete in open competitions (http://ec.europa.eu/stages). (See* Belgium *chapter for further information, page 402).*

# DIRECTORY OF WORK EXPERIENCE IN THE UK

## ACCENTURE HORIZONS SCHOOL SPONSORSHIP SCHEME

60 Queen Victoria Street, London EC4N 4TW

📞 0500 100189 (recruiting helpline)

✉ ukgraduates@accenture.com; UKI_
peopleline_HR@accenture.com

🖥 https://microsite.accenture.com/UK_
graduate_joiners/Where_will_I_fit_in/
Internships_and_placements/Pages/
Horizons.aspx

**PROGRAMME DESCRIPTION:** Provides students looking to take a gap year with a combination of training, work experience and the opportunity to travel before going to university. The job involves working alongside high-profile clients to deliver management and IT consultancy solutions. Upon successful completion of the placement, an opportunity is given to do further paid summer vacation work while at university and potentially an offer of a permanent position on graduation.

**DESTINATIONS:** London base, however the work will require travel to client sites across the UK.

**PREREQUISITES:** Must be an A-Level student currently in the upper sixth year with a strong interest in business and technology. A strong record of academic achievement is important with good grades in Maths and English at GCSE level and a minimum of 340 UCAS points or 5 Bs at Scottish Highers predicted. Candidates should be confident, enthusiastic and mature with excellent communication and team working skills.

**DURATION AND TIME OF PLACEMENTS:** 8-month internships from early September to April.

**SELECTION PROCEDURES AND ORIENTATION:** All applications should be made online between 1 September and 25 January. Interviews will be held from the September of the candidate's final year at school.

**REMUNERATION:** Candidates are paid the pro rata equivalent of £18,500 per year, with a possible choice of travel bursary of £1,500 awarded at the end of the scheme or the same amount for university. Depending on performance, financial sponsorship through university and the chance to come back and work during summer holidays is extended.

## BBC WORK EXPERIENCE PLACEMENTS
🖥 www.bbc.co.uk/workexperience

**PROGRAMME DESCRIPTION:** A chance for people to see what the working life of the BBC is like for a few days or up to 4 weeks.

**NUMBER OF PLACEMENTS:** 150+ placement areas from which to choose, based at various UK locations.

**PREREQUISITES:** See searchable database of opportunities online for specific criteria.

**REMUNERATION:** None.

**SELECTION PROCEDURES AND ORIENTATION:** Deadlines vary according to business area (e.g. production, business management and support, journalism). Up to 3 months needed to process applications.

## CIVIL SERVICE CAREERS
🖥 www.civilservice.gov.uk/jobs/Under
graduates-Graduates/Work-Experience.aspx

More than 170 departments and executive agencies, employing nearly half a million people, make the Civil Service one of the largest employers in the UK. Very few government departments and agencies offer vacation opportunities for students. Most opportunities that exist are open to graduates and possibly undergraduates in relevant fields and not to school leavers. For example the Government Legal Service (www.gls.gov.uk) has a 2–3-week vacation scheme open to 70 students who have completed or are in the penultimate year of a law degree or the final year of a non-law degree. Students are advised to apply early as most opportunities have deadlines for applications early in the year and by the end of March at the latest. The Civil Service Fast Stream runs a Summer Diversity Internship Programme for ethnic minority and disabled students.

## CORAL CAY CONSERVATION (CCC)
Elizabeth House, 39 York Road, London
SE1 7NJ
✆ 020 7620 1411
✉ info@coralcay.org
🖥 www.coralcay.org

Founding member of the Year Out Group. CCC sends hundreds of volunteers to assist in conserving endangered tropical marine and terrestrial environments in the Philippines, Tobago and Cambodia (see 'Directory of Specialist Gap Year Programmes'.

**PROGRAMME DESCRIPTION:** Opportunities for PR and Marketing interns to work at London head office. Positions are part-time and unwaged but travel and other expenses are paid. Marketing interns may be asked to attend careers fairs, exhibitions and networking events.

**CONTACT:** Pete Mandara, PR & Communications Coordinator (pm@coralcay.org).

## CORUS PLACEMENT SCHEME
Ashorne Hill Conference Centre, Leamington
Spa, Warwickshire CV33 9PY
✆ 01926 488025
✉ recruitment@corusgroup.com
🖥 www.corusgroup.com/en/careers/
     graduates_and_placements/placements

Due to the recession, Corus is not offering at present its usual 1-year funded placements in engineering, metallurgy and process technology, manufacturing management, research and development and finance or related degree fields. A small number of vacancies for summer placements to start work in July 2010 are available.

**DURATION AND TIME OF PLACEMENTS:**
3 months.
**PREREQUISITES:** Must be undergraduates.
**SELECTION PROCEDURES AND ORIENTATION:**
Application should be made online via www.corusgroup. com.
**REMUNERATION:** £14,500 per year (pro-rated for shorter placements). If successful, possibility of receiving sponsorship for following academic year.

## DELOITTE
Stonecutter Court, 1 Stonecutter Street,
London EC4A 4TR
✆ 020 7303 7019
✉ vconisbee@deloitte.co.uk
🖥 www.deloitte.co.uk/scholars

**PROGRAMME DESCRIPTION:** Scholars scheme offers financial sponsorship and work experience in the financial industry to high-calibre students from the start of a gap year through to when they graduate from university.

**NUMBER OF PLACEMENTS PER YEAR:** 40.

**DESTINATIONS:** Placements offered in a number of regional offices (including St Albans, Reading, Bristol, Cambridge, Birmingham, Nottingham, Manchester, Leeds, Edinburgh and Glasgow) as well as London office (on the Strand) and others.

**PREREQUISITES:** Good A-Levels (any subject) with intention to go on to study at a top UK university after their gap year. Must have achieved at least B in GCSE Maths and C in English language, be predicted 320 UCAS tariff points in first 3 A-Levels excluding General Studies. Should have interest in business/finance.

**DURATION AND TIME OF PLACEMENTS:** Gap year placements last 30 weeks from the end of August. Successful candidates remain involved in the scheme throughout their university education.

**SELECTION PROCEDURES AND ORIENTATION:**
Applications open on 1 July (13 months before scheme begins); no closing date since the scheme remains

open until places are filled with suitable candidates on a first come first served basis. Applications are made on line from website above.

**REMUNERATION:** Scholars receive a competitive salary and receive £1,500 travel bursary to spend in the remainder of their gap year. Once at university, they receive £1,500 academic bursary each year and return to Deloitte for at least 4 weeks a year in their holidays for further paid work.

**CONTACT:** Victoria Conisbee, Early Identification Administrator.

---

### EARTHWATCH INSTITUTE (EUROPE)
Mayfield House, 265 Banbury Road,
Oxford OX2 7DE
✆ 01865 318838
📧 info@earthwatch.org.uk
🖥 www.earthwatch.org/europe

Earthwatch is an international environmental charity which engages people worldwide in scientific field research and education to promote the understanding and action necessary for a sustainable environment.

**PROGRAMME DESCRIPTION:** Various unpaid internship positions are available in the Oxford office, offering useful experience to those wishing to enter the charity/environmental sector.

**DURATION AND TIME OF PLACEMENTS:** 4–6 months.

**SELECTION PROCEDURES AND ORIENTATION:** Internship candidates must submit a CV and are selected subject to interview.

---

### GLOBE EDUCATION
International Shakespeare Globe Centre, Globe Education, 21 New Globe Walk, London SE1 9DT
✆ 020 7902 1433
🖥 www.shakespeares-globe.org/
    information/jobvacancies/internships

**PROGRAMME DESCRIPTION:** Paid gap year student internships to run the 'Lively Action Schools Programme' (the theatre's workshop and lecture pro-

gramme caters for 45,000 students annually). Shorter unpaid administrative work experience placements in various departments: exhibition, appeals/fundraising and communications. Students will be able to work on special projects and events and act as stewards during the summer.

**NUMBER OF PLACEMENTS:** 2 paid internships for school leavers who want to develop a career in arts or education administration. Possibility of 30 short internships.

**DURATION AND TIME OF PLACEMENTS:** 12 months from 1 September for internship. 1–2 weeks work experience (or longer if gap year placement) or minimum 3 months unpaid internship.

**REMUNERATION:** Stipend paid with 25 days holiday, free access to the majority of Globe Education events and some free theatre tickets. No wage paid for short work experience placements and travel expenses are not covered.

**SELECTION PROCEDURES AND ORIENTATION:** Deadline 25 May.

**CONTACT:** Rob Norman, Personnel Manager (robert. n@shakespearesglobe.com).

---

### IBM UK
PO Box 41, North Harbour, Portsmouth PO6 3AU
✆ 023 92 564104 (Student Recruitment
    Hotline)
📧 ibmstudent@uk.ibm.com
🖥 www-05.ibm.com/employment/uk/futures

**PROGRAMME DESCRIPTION:** IBM Futures Programme is a gap year scheme for academically outstanding students. Pre-university employment (e.g. in technology, marketing, consulting and human resources) lasts 9 months followed by 3 months working with Raleigh (see entry in 'Directory of Specialist Gap Year Programmes') among other options. The Raleigh expedition complements the competencies that IBM recruits against and IBM will be flexible (business permitting) to support any student wishing to pursue this unique opportunity.

**PREREQUISITES:** Selection against a number of competencies based on tangible evidence. Must have a deferred place or be planning a deferred place at university.

**DURATION AND TIME OF PLACEMENTS:** 9–12 months starting in August/September. Deadline for applications is May.

**OTHER SERVICES:** Residential induction course at beginning of year. Salary of £13,500 pro-rated and up to £1,500 performance-related bonus awarded at end of the initial 9-month contract depending on performance against key objectives.

## INDEPENDENT TELEVISION

**PROGRAMME DESCRIPTION:** A limited number of work experience placements is sometimes available with the regional ITV companies. Vacancies are rarely known in advance and demand constantly outstrips supply.

**PREREQUISITES:** Applicants must be students on a recognised course of study at a college or university; their course must lead to the possibility of employment within the television industry (ideally, work experience would be a compulsory part of the course); and the student must be resident in the transmission area of the company offering the attachment, or in some cases, attending a course in that region. However, opportunities occasionally exist for students following computing, librarianship, finance, legal, administrative or management courses.

**DURATION AND TIME OF PLACEMENTS:** Placements vary in length from half a day to several weeks or months, depending upon the work available and the candidate's requirements.

**REMUNERATION:** Students do not normally receive payment, although possibility that expenses will be paid. Students from sandwich courses who are on long-term attachments may be regarded as short-term employees and paid accordingly.

**SELECTION PROCEDURES AND ORIENTATION:** General information on working in media can be obtained from the Sectors Skills Council for the Audio Visual Industries (broadcast, film, video, interactive media and photo imaging) on www.skillset.org. Their careers service, Skillset Careers, offers media careers information, advice and guidance to anyone wanting to enter or progress in the media industry. Visit www.skillset.org/careers/work_experience or call one of the free helplines – 08080 300 900 in England, 0808 100 8094 in Scotland or 0800 0121815 in Wales.

### KPMG
ukfmgraduate@kpmg.co.uk
www.kpmgcareers.co.uk (search for A-Level Trainees and then the Gap Programme)

**PROGRAMME DESCRIPTION:** Gap Year Programme in Audit department, which provides hands-on commercial experience and an understanding of the professional services industry. May involve travel to clients' premises.

**DESTINATIONS:** Offices throughout the UK.

**PREREQUISITES:** Prediction of good A-Levels (e.g. 300 UCAS points). Must be pro-active individual who can demonstrate commitment to their chosen team.

**DURATION AND TIME OF PLACEMENTS:** 6 months from October to April.

**SELECTION PROCEDURES AND ORIENTATION:** Online application in first instance. Acceptance is very competitive at the next stages of online numeracy and verbal reasoning tests followed by a competency-based interview. Chosen candidates are then given a 1-week induction, and then assigned to a mentor for informal support and guidance, a manager who oversees the day-to-day work and a senior manager who will review performance.

### METASWITCH NETWORKS
100 Church Street, Enfield EN2 6BQ
020 8366 1177
recruit@metaswitch.com
www.metaswitch.com/careers/internships/pre-university

Metaswitch Networks is a leading technology company.

**PROGRAMME DESCRIPTION:** Vacation work and year-long placements are offered to exceptional pre-university and university students with an interest in the development of complex software. The company provides challenging programming assignments, while offering help and support.

**PREREQUISITES:** Successful applicants usually have all A grades at A-Level or equivalent. Computing experience not required, but must have a real interest in technology.

**DURATION AND TIME OF PLACEMENTS:** Minimum of 8 weeks over the summer or for a gap year.

**SELECTION PROCEDURES:** Recruitment takes place year round. One-stage interview process with results known within 3 days.

**REMUNERATION:** A salary of £1,100+ per month for pre-university students. Also subsidised accommodation in the company house, a few minutes walk from the office.

**CONTACT:** The Recruitment Team.

---

## THE NATIONAL CENTRE FOR YOUNG PEOPLE WITH EPILEPSY (NCYPE)

St Piers Lane, Lingfield, Surrey RH7 6PW

01342 831234

recruitment@ncype.org.uk

www.ncype.org.uk

**PROGRAMME DESCRIPTION:** Student support worker residential positions to support student development by contribution to student's education and social and developmental curriculum, as part of a coordinated team.

**NUMBER OF PLACEMENTS:** Up to 5.

**PREREQUISITES:** Minimum age 19; suitable for pre-university. Must be legally entitled to work in the UK, obtain enhanced police disclosure and have desire to work with young students.

**DURATION AND TIME OF PLACEMENTS:** 1 year minimum (Sept to July).

**REMUNERATION:** From £15,101.

**OTHER SERVICES:** Single hostel accommodation arranged.

---

## OXFAM

Volunteering Team, Oxfam House, John Smith Drive, Cowley, Oxford OX4 2JY

01865 472028

internship@oxfam.org.uk

www.oxfam.org.uk/ get_involved/ volunteer/interns.html

**PROGRAMME DESCRIPTION:** Voluntary internship scheme in NGO sector. Successful candidates can make a contribution to Oxfam's goal of reducing poverty and suffering by working in one of several divisions, such as campaigns, humanitarian or trading. Opportunities for specific training if relevant to assigned project, e.g. project management, time management, negotiation skills.

**DESTINATIONS:** UK only; most positions are in the Oxford headquarters.

**PREREQUISITES:** Most candidates are post-university. Required skills and experience vary depending on the specific role. Should have basic office and IT skills.

**DURATION AND TIME OF PLACEMENTS:** Up to 3 days per week for 3–6 or 12 months depending on position. Recruitment is ongoing throughout the year.

**REMUNERATION:** Positions are unpaid. Lunch and reasonable travel expenses are reimbursed.

---

## PRICEWATERHOUSECOOPERS

Plumtree Court, London EC4A 4HT

0808 100 1500 (Student Information Line)

schoolsteam@uk.pwc.com

www.pwc.com/uk/careers

The member firms of the PricewaterhouseCoopers network (www.pwc.com/uk) provide assurance, tax and advisory services to clients and their stakeholders in 149 countries.

**PROGRAMME DESCRIPTION:** PricewaterhouseCoopers' gap year programme was cancelled in 2009. Now it offers internships to penultimate year undergraduates and graduates only.

---

## ROYAL OPERA HOUSE

Covent Garden, London WC2E 9DD

www.roh.org.uk/workhere/
workexperience/index.aspx

**PLACEMENTS OFFERED:** Work placements/
internships offered across the organisation but
predominantly in technical and production areas (for
example model room, costume production or stage
management).

**PREREQUISITES:** Selection criteria and minimum age
limits vary, depending on the placement type. Applications accepted from UK residents only. Minimum age
18. Students should have an interest in ballet, opera or
music with a view to working in the arts.

**DURATION OF COURSES:** Depends on placement type,
from 2 days to several months.

**CONTACT:** Lowri Jones, Work Experience Administrator.

## SIR ROBERT MCALPINE

Eaton Court, Maylands Avenue, Hemel
Hempstead, Hertfordshire HP2 7TR

01442 412909

www.sir-robert-mcalpine.com

A long-established building and civil engineering
contractor which has suspended its gap year scheme
but will review the decision in autumn 2010.

## STEP (SHELL TECHNOLOGY ENTERPRISE PROGRAMME)

14 Bridgford Road, West Bridgford,
Nottingham NG2 6AB

0870 036 5450

enquiries@shellstep.org.uk

www.shellstep.org.uk

Initiative sponsored primarily by Shell UK to match
undergraduates and new graduates with small and
medium-sized businesses and community organisations
for work projects.

**PROGRAMME DESCRIPTION:** Work experience
projects, mostly in the summer, for second and higher
year university students and new graduates.

**NUMBER OF PROJECTS:** Approximately 600.

**PREREQUISITES:** Must be studying full-time at a UK
university in either second or penultimate year or (as of
2009) recent graduates. No age restrictions.

**DURATION AND TIME OF PLACEMENTS:** 8–12 weeks.

**SELECTION PROCEDURES AND ORIENTATION:**
Application can be made online. Deadline for summer
placements falls in the second week of June.

**REMUNERATION:** Summer students receive about
£200 per week. Travelling expenses are paid at the
employer's discretion.

## YEAR IN INDUSTRY

University of Southampton, Southampton
SO17 1BJ

023 8059 7061

info@yini.org.uk

www.yini.org.uk

Founding member of the Year Out Group. The Year in
Industry is a major provider of gap year industrial placements throughout the UK.

**PROGRAMME DESCRIPTION:** The Year in Industry programme provides paid, structured and fully supported
work experience from which students gain career and
personal development, confirm their career choice and
prepare for their degree. Participants are encouraged to
enter an end-of-year competition with cash prizes.

**NUMBER OF PLACEMENTS PER YEAR:** 500–600.

**PREREQUISITES:** Students should be interested in
gaining experience in industry and must be intending to
go to university. Most participants are intending to study
engineering, science, technology or business, although
opportunities are available for other disciplines.

**DURATION AND TIME OF PLACEMENTS:** Placements
generally last for 10–12 months, from August/Septem-
ber to mid-July.

**SELECTION PROCEDURES AND ORIENTATION:** All
applicants will be interviewed by the Year in Industry.
Participants are also offered Management Training Level
3 Certificate via the Chartered Management Institute.

**REMUNERATION:** Students earn competitive salaries
during their placements.

# DIRECTORY OF WORK EXPERIENCE ABROAD

## AGRIVENTURE

International Agricultural Exchange Association
(IAEA), Speedwell Farm Bungalow, Nettle Bank,
Wisbech, Cambridgeshire PE14 0SA

✆ 01945 450999
🖰 uk@agriventure.com
💻 www.agriventure.net

**PROGRAMME DESCRIPTION:** International agricultural and horticultural work placements for British and EU participants.

**DESTINATIONS:** Placements for UK and European participants in the USA, Canada, Australia, New Zealand and Japan.

**PREREQUISITES:** Aged 18–30 with an aptitude or interest in working in agriculture or horticulture.

**DURATION AND TIME OF PLACEMENTS:** Placements in the USA and Canada begin in February and April and last for 7 or 9 months. Placements for Australia and New Zealand run throughout the year and last 4–12 months. Placements in Japan begin in April and last 4–12 months. The Workabout programme in Canada, Australia and New Zealand offers short-term placements as the participants travel around a country. There are also several round-the-world itineraries which depart in the autumn to the southern hemisphere for 6–7 months followed by another 6–7 months in the northern hemisphere.

**SELECTION PROCEDURES AND ORIENTATION:** Selection by interview. Pre-departure information meeting and orientation seminar on arrival.

**COST:** Participants pay between £2,030 and £4,500, which includes airline tickets, visas, insurance, orientation seminar, back-up and board and lodging throughout with an approved hosting enterprise. Trainees are paid a realistic wage.

## AIL MADRID SPANISH LANGUAGE IMMERSION SCHOOL IN SPAIN

C/ Nuñez de Balboa 17, 2˚D, 28001 Madrid,
Spain

✆ +34 91 72 56 350
🖰 info@ailmadrid.com
💻 www.ailmadrid.com/gap year/home

**PROGRAMME DESCRIPTION:** 12-week Spanish language course in Madrid and other cities in Spain with work placement options.

**PREREQUISITES:** Minimum age 17, average age 22.

**DURATION AND TIME OF PLACEMENTS:** 12–48 weeks with flexible start dates.

**COST:** 12-week programme from €3,500.

**CONTACT:** Maya Bychova.

## AUSTRALIAN INTERNSHIPS

Suite 1, Savoir Faire, 20 Park Road, Milton,
Brisbane, Queensland 4064, Australia

✆ +61 7 3305 8408
🖰 info@internships.com.au
💻 www.internships.com.au

**PROGRAMME DESCRIPTION:** Two programme options for candidates interested in seeking international hands-on experience: Professional Internship Programme and Hospitality Internship Programme. Professional Internship Programme offers hands-on experience in most fields (apart from medicine) especially administration, education, engineering, finance, government, graphic design, journalism, marketing and trade. Professional Hospitality Internship Programme offers paid positions for hospitality students willing to work in hands-on fields such as cookery, food and beverage, and housekeeping. Candidates should be flexible with their destinations as positions vary from capital cities to islands and resorts in remote locations.

**DESTINATIONS:** Throughout Australia.

**NUMBER OF PLACEMENTS:** 600–1,000.

**PREREQUISITES:** Ages 18–30. Pre-university students are eligible but will be placed in entry-level roles.

**DURATION AND TIME OF PLACEMENTS:** 6–52 weeks, but usual maximum is 6 months.

**SELECTION PROCEDURES AND ORIENTATION:** All details for the internship are confirmed with each candidate in a formal training agreement, which defines the terms and conditions for their training in Australia. All interns must be interviewed by telephone.

**REMUNERATION:** Hospitality interns are paid according to the Australian standard: the minimum hourly rate is A$12.

**COST:** Sample fees for professional internship placements are A$1,950 for 7–12 weeks, A$2,700 for 21–26 weeks; and for hospitality interns A$3,340 for 26 weeks, A$3,750 for 38 weeks and A$4,150 for 52 weeks. Agency can arrange homestay and other accommodation at extra cost.

**CONTACT:** Rebekah Gilchrist, Marketing Executive.

---

### C.E.I./CLUB DES 4 VENTS1 RUE GOZLIN, 75006 PARIS, FRANCE
📞 + 33 1 43 29 13 39
✉ wif@cei4vents.com
🖥 www.cei4vents.com

**PROGRAMME DESCRIPTION:** Paid job and internship placement service.

**PREREQUISITES:** Ages 18–30.

**DURATION AND TIME OF PLACEMENTS:** 3 months (mostly) year round.

**COST:** €575 job placement for EU nationals, €980 for nationalities that require a visa for France. Internships for students of all nationalities arranged for a fee of €825.

**OTHER SERVICES:** C.E.I. offers homestay and residential summer French courses for young people aged 12–18 in a number of places including Paris. Runs residential language courses in Paris at the French school Paris Langues (www.parislangues.com).

**CONTACT:** José Luis Ponti, Incoming Programmes Manager.

---

### CHILE INSIDE
Román Díaz 205 Of. 405, Providencia, Santiago, Chile
📞 +56 2 235 7170
📞 +56 2 235 7184
✉ info@chileinside.cl
🖥 www.chileinside.cl

**PROGRAMME DESCRIPTION:** Internships, working holidays, volunteer work, farm stays, Spanish language courses (see separate entry page 364) and accommodation throughout Chile.

**NUMBER OF PLACEMENTS PER YEAR:** 200–300.

**DESTINATIONS:** Chile.

**PREREQUISITES:** Minimum age 18 (average 21–25). All nationalities accepted. Programmes tailored to individual backgrounds and education.

**DURATION AND TIME OF PLACEMENTS:** Programmes last between 6 weeks and 6+ months.

**SELECTION PROCEDURES AND ORIENTATION:** No special selection criteria. Candidates need to send CV and fill in registration form. Applications should be sent 3–10 weeks. Orientation talk will be held upon arrival in Chile. Personal assistance and regular participants' meetings and activities arranged throughout stay. 24-hour support available.

**COST:** $50 registration fee and programme fees range from $180 to $800.

**ACCOMMODATION:** Host family, shared apartment, student residences, furnished rooms.

**CONTACT:** Marion Ruhland, Founder and Executive Director.

---

### CRCC ASIA
106 Weston Street, London, SE1 3QB
📞 020 7378 6220
✉ internships@crccasia.com
🖥 www.crccasia.com

Consulting company that runs internship programmes in Beijing.

**PROGRAMME DESCRIPTION:** 1–2 month internships in a variety of company sectors in Beijing, including legal, financial, general business, environment, energy and consulting. Programme includes arrangement of visas, accommodation, Chinese business culture training, language induction, English speaking mentor within company and full support.

**DESTINATIONS:** Beijing, China.

**NUMBER OF PLACEMENTS PER YEAR:** 300.

**PREREQUISITES:** All fluent English speakers. Must have interest in China, and be diligent and enthusiastic.

**DURATION AND TIME OF PLACEMENTS:** 1 departure per month, year round.

**SELECTION PROCEDURES AND ORIENTATION:** Applications accepted year round. Telephone interview arranged within a week of application.

**COST:** £1,295 (1 month), £1,795 (2 months) includes accommodation and visa cost.

---

### EARTHCORPS

6310 NE 74th Street, Suite 201E, Seattle, WA 98115

☏ +1 206 322 9296 (ext 224)

✉ mark@earthcorps.org

🖥 www.earthcorps.org

**PROGRAMME DESCRIPTION:** 6-month skill-based environmental restoration experience in Seattle. Trail construction, environmental education and invasive plant removal.

**NUMBER OF PLACEMENTS PER YEAR:** 20–25 (2 per country).

**PREREQUISITES:** All nationalities, so cross-cultural communication skills needed. Ages 20–25. People preferred who have experience of working in the field of environmental restoration.

**DURATION AND TIME OF PLACEMENTS:** June to December or March to August.

**SELECTION PROCEDURES AND ORIENTATION:** Competitive selection. Applications due by middle of

December (for June start) or September (for February start).

**REMUNERATION:** All basic needs covered including room and board plus a small stipend. Airfare reimbursement scholarship available that pays 30% of transport costs up to $500.

**CONTACT:** Mark Howard, Senior International Programme Manager.

---

### ELEP (EXPERIENTIAL LEARNING ECUADORIAN PROGRAMS)

Mosquera Narvaez Oe3–163 y Av. America, Quito, Ecuador

☏ +593 9 940 0851

☏ +593 9 996 3605

✉ info@elep.org

✉ programs@elep.org

🖥 www.elep.org

**PROGRAMME DESCRIPTION:** Customised internships in many fields, e.g. audit/finance, accounting, human resources, foreign trade, marketing/PR, IT, graphic design, engineering, architecture, medicine, environment, journalism, law and social work. Also arranges placements in humanitarian and ecological volunteer sector: childcare, HIV/AIDS, human rights, teaching English, healthcare/nursing, micro-enterprise, infrastructure and construction work, agriculture, organic farming and agroforestry, animal care and veterinary medicine, etc. Spanish language training is available for beginners, intermediate and advanced individuals and groups.

**DESTINATIONS:** Throughout Ecuador including Highlands, coastal areas, Amazonia and the Galápagos Islands.

**PREREQUISITES:** Good knowledge of Spanish is required for the internships and basic knowledge for the volunteer work. Must have an open mind and be able to adapt to different culture.

**DURATION OF PLACEMENTS:** 2 weeks to 6 months for volunteer programme. From 4 weeks to 6 months for internships (depending on field). Available any time of year. No special visa needed for stays of less than 6 months.

**COST:** Application fee $100, placement fee $200 includes transfer from airport to host family. Private language lessons cost $6 an hour (20 hours a week). Special offers include 20 hours of Spanish plus 4 weeks volunteering or interning plus accommodation for $700, 40 hours of language lessons plus 8 weeks of internship or volunteering for $1,100, and 4 weeks of Spanish lessons plus 8 weeks internship or volunteering for $1,620.

**ACCOMMODATION:** Accommodation with host families in private room costs $105 a week on the mainland, $155 on the Galápagos; 3 meals a day and laundry service included.

**CONTACT:** Patricia Parrales (Programme Consultant), Kleber Parrales (Programme Officer), Patricio Fernández (Managing Director).

---

## EUROGROUP

472 rue de la Leysse, BP 429, 73004 Chambéry Cedex, France

*C* +33 479 65 08 06 801

info candidatures@eurogroup-vacances.com

www.madamevacances.com

**PROGRAMME DESCRIPTION:** Work placement programme that places students in 86 hotels and residences in France managed by Eurogroup. Provides professional experience and chance to improve spoken French. Resort placements are available on reception, in the restaurant and in other roles, including customer services and management support.

**NUMBER OF PLACEMENTS PER YEAR:** 20+.

**DESTINATIONS:** France including ski resorts, the southern and western coasts, the Dordogne and Vendée regions, and cities such as Montpellier. Also some placements in head office in Chambéry in the following departments: marketing, human resources, legal, reservations, planning, purchasing, quality, e-commerce, accounts and finance.

**PREREQUISITES:** Students must be enrolled in a school or university of the EU at the time of applying. Open to gap year as well as year abroad students.

**DURATION AND TIME OF PLACEMENTS:** Minimum 2 months in resorts, 4 months in head office. Resort placements are seasonal, normally up to 4 months. Head office positions available for up to 9 months.

**SELECTION PROCEDURES AND ORIENTATION:** A good command of French and possibly previous experience in a work environment. Applications accepted year round. All candidates must undergo an interview by telephone, during which their level of French is assessed.

**REMUNERATION:** €398 per month if food and accommodation are found independently or €198 per month live-in, usually a shared room in a staff apartment. Ski passes are often provided for those working in ski resorts. Eurogroup has also negotiated favourable rates with various ski shops in resorts for their employees.

**CONTACT:** Mlle Hyacinthe Eisenmann, Work Placement Co-ordinator.

---

## EUROINTERNS

Solano 11, 3°-C, Pozuelo de Alarcon, 28223 Madrid, Spain

*C* +34 66 783 8136

*C* +34 91 518 9985

info info@eurointerns.com

www.eurointerns.com

**PROGRAMME DESCRIPTION:** Internships in Spanish and Belgian firms for practical language enhancement and work experience.

**DESTINATIONS:** Spain and Brussels.

**NUMBER OF PLACEMENTS:** 100.

**PREREQUISITES:** Ideal candidates will have professional or academic experience in the area chosen for the internship as well as intermediate language skills in either Spanish or French although these are not always necessary.

**DURATION AND TIME OF PLACEMENTS:** 2–6 months.

**SELECTION PROCEDURES AND ORIENTATION:** 2–4 weeks intensive language training in Spanish or French is recommended.

**Fee:** €1,100.

**CONTACT:** Susana Thomas, Internship Co-ordinator.

---

## EUROPEAN COMMISSION

Bureau des Stages, 200 Rue de la Loi, 1049
Brussels, Belgium

📞 02 299 33 20

📧 eac-stages@ec.europa.eu

🖥 http://ec.europa.eu/stages/index_en.htm

The scheme is open to university graduates from all
over the world and is administered by the Training Office at the European Commission's Directorate General
for Education and Culture.

**PROGRAMME DESCRIPTION:** Twice a year the Commission organises in-service training periods to give
trainees a general idea of the objectives and problems
of European integration and provide them with practical knowledge of the workings of the Commission's
departments.

**DESTINATIONS:** Most are in Brussels, some in
Luxembourg and Representation Offices in the Member
States.

**NUMBER OF PLACEMENTS PER YEAR:** Approximately 600 per period (out of 7,000 applications), i.e.
1,200 per year.

**PREREQUISITES:** Applicants must have a thorough
knowledge of one other EU official language in addition
to their mother tongue. Applicants must also have
completed their degree.

**DURATION AND TIME OF PLACEMENTS:** 3 or 5
months. Training periods begin in first week of March or
October every year.

**SELECTION PROCEDURES AND ORIENTATION:** Application forms must be submitted online. Deadlines are
1 September and 15 February.

**REMUNERATION:** All official trainees are paid a grant
of €1,047 per month and their travel expenses.

---

## GLOBAL VISION INTERNATIONAL (GVI)

*UK office:* 3 High Street, St Albans, Hertfordshire
AL3 4ED

📞 01727 250250

📧 info@gviworld.com

🖥 www.gvi.co.uk/internships-abroad

*North American office:* 252 Newbury Street,
Number 4, Boston, MA 02116

📞 +1 888 653 6028

🖥 www.gviusa.com

GVI Traineeships offer those seeking a career change
and or practical experience in a specific field a unique
opportunity to develop new skills, practical experience
and opportunities. Main fields are marine biology and
conservation, environmental research and conservation
with coral reefs, monkeys, lions, turtles and other
species; teaching in developing communities, childcare,
English language teaching and organic farming.

**DURATION AND TIME OF PLACEMENTS:** Short- and
long-term from 2 weeks to 1 year.

---

## GLOBAL VOLUNTEER PROJECTS

7–15 Pink Lane, Newcastle upon Tyne NE1 5DW

📞 0191 222 0404

📧 info@globalvolunteerprojects.org

🖥 www.globalvolunteerprojects.org

**PROGRAMME DESCRIPTION:** Specialise in work experience projects for people hoping to go into medicine
or the subjects allied to medicine, such as physiotherapy, dentistry and nursing and people looking for
work experience in journalism. Placements are available
in Ghana, Tanzania, India, China, Cambodia, Mexico and
Romania. See entry in 'Directory of Specialist Gap Year
Programmes'.

---

## GLS SPRACHENZENTRUM BERLIN

Kastanienallee 82, 10435 Berlin, Germany

📞 30 78 00 89 15

📧 germancourses@gls-berlin.de

🖥 www.german-berlin.de

**PROGRAMME DESCRIPTION:** Minimum 4-week
language course followed by an internship lasting 6,
8 or 12+ weeks in a company in or near Berlin.

Traineeships available in range of fields such as marketing, government and banking.

**PREREQUISITES:** Students should have at least level B1 (intermediate), i.e. able to express themselves in German and understand everyday conversations. Must also show initiative. Minimum age 18/19.

**COST:** Placement fee is €450.

**OTHER SERVICES:** GLS is a leading centre in Berlin for teaching German as a foreign language and is a key member of WYSE Work Abroad.

**CONTACT:** Anna Bartnikowska (anna.bartnikowska@gls-berlin.de).

---

## IST PLUS

Rosedale House, Rosedale Road, Richmond, Surrey TW9 2SZ

✆ 020 8939 9057

✉ info@istplus.com

🖥 www.istplus.com

---

Partner agency in UK delivering programmes on behalf of the Council on International Educational Exchange and USA summer camps on behalf of Interexchange.

**PROGRAMME DESCRIPTION:** Work and teaching abroad programmes including Work & Travel USA, Camp USA, Internship USA, Work & Travel Australia, Work & Travel New Zealand, Teach in China and Teach in Thailand.

**DESTINATIONS:** USA, Australia, New Zealand, China and Thailand.

**PREREQUISITES:** Different eligibility requirements for each programme. To work in the USA, the participant must either be a student, graduate or young professional. To work in Australasia, they must be over 18. To teach in Asia they must be a degree-holder.

**DURATION AND TIME OF PLACEMENTS:** Anything from a few weeks up to 18 months. The Work & Travel USA summer programme is open between June and October. Internship USA can last up to 18 months and runs all year round. Students bound for Australia and New Zealand can go out for 12 months at any time of year. 5- or 10-month contracts for Teaching in China

start in August or February and for Thailand they begin in May or October.

**SELECTION PROCEDURES AND ORIENTATION:** The application deadlines are the end of June for Work and Travel USA; mid-November or early May for Teach in China; and mid-February and mid-July for Thailand. Participants receive 7 days of orientation in Shanghai or Bangkok, covering the essentials of TEFL and an introduction to Asia, its culture and language. Students participating in Work and Travel USA receive a pre-departure orientation.

**COST:** Teach in China and Thailand programme fee from £775 plus flights. Participants receive a local wage which allows for a comfortable lifestyle and on completion of 10-month contract have their return flight reimbursed. Work and Travel USA fee starts from £455 which includes insurance, US government SEVIS fee and all support services. Other programme fees are listed in application materials, available on request or from the website.

---

## JUNIOR EXPAT

PT JuniorExpat Indonesia, Jl. Tengger Barat III No. 38, Semarang, Java, Indonesia

✆ +6 22 49 124 4068

✉ azzan@juniorexpat.com

🖥 www.juniorexpat.com

---

Registered in the Netherlands (JuniorExpat Netherlands), Indonesia (PT JuniorExpat Indonesia), Hong Kong (JuniorExpat HongKong) and the USA (Junior Expat LLC).

**PROGRAMME DESCRIPTION:** The majority of internship/work experience opportunities are in the areas of marketing, logistics, law, hospitality, finance and information technology. Internship possibilities also available for junior teachers, aviation students, product development and design students, and event management students.

**DESTINATIONS:** Semarang and Jakarta in Indonesia, also Hong Kong.

**NUMBER OF PLACEMENTS PER YEAR:** 250.

**PREREQUISITES:** Minimum age 18. Students must be about to start or part way through higher education. Candidates with Bachelor's and Master's degrees accepted too. Open to all nationalities but must be English speaking; most participants are from UK, France, Netherlands, Belgium, Germany, USA, Canada, Australia, and New Zealand.

**DURATION AND TIME OF PLACEMENTS:** Normally 3–6 months starting throughout the year.

**SELECTION PROCEDURES AND ORIENTATION:** Pre-arrival intake interview and assistance given with visa sponsorship, contracts, finding accommodation, etc. JuniorExpat has Western-style accommodation available for applicants from abroad in Semarang and Jakarta in Indonesia, but not in Hong Kong.

**REMUNERATION:** The majority of internships are unpaid, however, companies provide lunch and local transport for foreign interns.

**COST:** Standard placement fee €495 (2010).

**CONTACT:** Azzan Goeting, International Relations Manager.

---

### LANGUAGE COURSES ABROAD

67–71 Ashby Road, Loughborough, Leicestershire LE11 3AA

℡ 01509 211612

✉ info@languagesabroad.co.uk

🖳 www.languagesabroad.co.uk

Spanish Study Holidays, the parent company, is a member of WYSE Work Abroad (World Youth Student & Educational).

**PROGRAMME DESCRIPTION:** Work experience placements in range of countries. Any type of work experience can be provided as long as the student has relevant qualifications. A few work placements available in company's own schools.

**DESTINATIONS:** Spain, Latin America, France, Germany and Italy.

**NUMBER OF PLACEMENTS PER YEAR:** 100–200.

**PREREQUISITES:** Work placements require at least an intermediate level of the language. Most work placements are preceded by a 4-week in-country

language course (see entry in 'Directory of Language Courses'.

**DURATION AND TIME OF PLACEMENTS:** 4 weeks minimum, normally 8–16 weeks.

**SELECTION PROCEDURES AND ORIENTATION:** Applications should be sent at least 8 and preferably 12 weeks in advance. Personal monitor is appointed to oversee work placement.

**COST:** Work placements not normally paid, except those in the hotel and catering industry for which students normally receive free board and lodging and sometimes also payment at national minimum wage levels. Fees included on company website.

**CONTACT:** Mike Cummins, Director.

---

### LEARN OVERSEAS

47 Greenheys Centre, Pencroft Way, Manchester Science Park, Manchester M15 6JJ

℡ 0161 226 5300

℡ 0790 3040567 (mobile)

✉ office@learnoverseas.co.uk

🖳 www.learnoverseas.co.uk

**PROGRAMME DESCRIPTION:** Work experience available along with other gap year placements in India. Specialists in placements for students applying for medicine and related fields or wanting to complete research projects. Mixture of hands-on, observation and work-shadowing experience in Delhi.

**DESTINATIONS:** Delhi, India

**PREREQUISITES:** Ages 16+.

**DURATION AND TIME OF PLACEMENTS:** From 2 weeks to 6 months throughout the year.

**COST:** From £900 including transport within the country, full board and lodging and weekend breaks, but excluding airfares and insurance.

**CONTACT:** Poonam Puri.

---

### M.B. LANGUAGE ASBL

41 rue Henri Bergé, 1030 Brussels, Belgium

℡ +32 2 242 27 66

✉ macbaron@telenet.be

🖳 www.mblanguage.be

Promotes linguistic and cultural exchanges within Europe.

**PROGRAMME DESCRIPTION:** Organises work experience abroad for European students aged 16–18/20.

**DESTINATIONS:** Mainly in Brussels; also Lübeck for students of German.

**NUMBER OF PLACEMENTS PER YEAR:** 100–200.

**PREREQUISITES:** Language skills (French or German), organisation, enthusiasm and self-motivation are needed. Students ought to have studied French or German at school.

**DURATION AND TIME OF PLACEMENTS:** 1 or 2 weeks, occasionally longer if requested throughout the year.

**SELECTION PROCEDURES AND ORIENTATION:** A CV is required, but interviews are not essential.

**COST:** Work experience fees are €300 for 1 week between October and May and €375 in July and August. Fortnight-long placements cost €450 in winter, €475 in summer.

**CONTACT:** Xavier Mouffe, Manager.

---

## NEXT STEP CONNECTIONS

Suite 1004, Hui Jin Tower 515 Hankou Road, Huang Pu District 2000001 Shanghai, China (PRC)

℡ +86 21 6351 5182

✉ contact@nextstepconnections.com

🖥 www.nextstepconnections.com

**PROGRAMME DESCRIPTION:** Professional internship programme offering work placements in Shanghai (year round) and Beijing and Hong Kong (summer only). Placements may be found in many fields such as architecture, art, design, finance, IT, engineering, journalism, law, medicine, pharmaceuticals, advertising, marketing and public relations. Links with big companies such as McCann Group, Publicis, CIBA, China Daily, Shanghai Business Review, Wieden & Kennedy and more.

**NUMBER OF PLACEMENTS PER YEAR:** 100.

**DESTINATIONS:** China and Hong Kong.

**PREREQUISITES:** Ages 18–35. Must be fluent in English, have motivation, good-quality CV and interest in professional career-geared programme.

**DURATION AND TIME OF PLACEMENTS:** 1–6 months. Participants choose their start date, length of stay and field of placement.

**SELECTION PROCEDURES AND ORIENTATION:** Online application at least 2 months (preferably 3) before proposed arrival. 3 hours per week of Chinese lessons are part of programme. Monthly career and professional meeting with an executive recruiter at Next Step Connections office to carry out programme monitoring and overview. Each meeting tackles a different topic, and provides a better insight into the Chinese job market and how to improve a CV.

**REMUNERATION:** Monthly stipend between RMB1,500 and 2,000.

**COST:** £2,000 for 1 month, £6,430 for 6 months including internship placement, housing, insurance, airport transfers and back-up.

**CONTACT:** Jerome Le Carrou. Director.

---

## NYQUEST TRAINING AND PLACEMENT

571 Roselawn Avenue, Toronto, Ontario, M5N 1K6, Canada

℡ +416 932 1370

✉ info@go-nyquest.com

🖥 www.go-nyquest.com

**PROGRAMME DESCRIPTION:** The Canadian Camp Experience programme trains and places leaders for work experience at day and residential summer camps in Canada, working and living with children aged 7–16. Camp counsellors work directly with children, leading activities and supervising campers. Support staff work behind the scenes setting up the camp, maintaining camp facilities and helping out in the dining hall and kitchen.

**DESTINATIONS:** All over Canada.

**NUMBER OF PARTICIPANTS:** 190 in 2009, estimated 300+ in 2010.

**PREREQUISITES:** Ages 19–26 (average 20–23). Should have leadership qualities and an interest in travel and outdoor education. Gap year students must submit very strong applications and have some experience teaching and supervising children.

**DURATION AND TIME OF PLACEMENTS:** Minimum work period 8 weeks between mid-June and the end of August or from the end of August to the beginning of November. Many participants work for 6 months at camps from May to October and then travel or start working at a winter resort in Canada.

**SELECTION PROCEDURES AND ORIENTATION:** British applicants must apply through CCUSA (see entry page 210). Provides training, work placement assistance and on-going support. NYQUEST will arrange work permits and provide health insurance, free Canadian bank account, Canadian Social Insurance Number (SIN), 2 nights accommodation and 1-day orientation in Canadian host city, internet access and free phone card, transport from airport to accommodation in host city and on to camp placement.

**COST:** C$300–C$500 excluding flights; CCUSA fee for Britons is £299 for early applicants; £399 for later ones.

**CONTACT:** Jonathan Nyquist, Founder & Operations Director.

## PRACTIGO GMBH
Neidenburger Str. 8, D-28207 Bremen, 28207 Germany
℃ +49 421 437 7280
🖂 info@practigo.com
🖥 www.practigo.com

**PROGRAMME DESCRIPTION:** Personalised internships and Spanish language courses arranged in Spain and South America.

**NUMBER OF PLACEMENTS PER YEAR:** 1,000–1,500.

**DESTINATIONS:** Argentina, Chile, Ecuador, Spain.

**PREREQUISITES:** Interns must have European citizenship and must be able to speak Spanish.

**DURATION AND TIME OF PLACEMENTS:** Participants decide where and for how long they want to go abroad.

**SELECTION PROCEDURES AND ORIENTATION:** Applications should be submitted at least 8 weeks in advance. Language interview given by phone to test language skills and decide whether participation in a language course is necessary before starting an internship. Sometimes companies interview prospective interns on arrival; in other cases participants are assigned to companies before leaving home. PractiGo can arrange language course, internship, insurance, accommodation and flight, contact person in the foreign country and 24-hour emergency hotline.

**COST:** Internship fee from €250; language course fee from €90. Accommodation can be fixed up for €46 a week (single room in a shared flat); other options include host families, student residences, apartments and hotels.

## PROJECTS ABROAD
Aldsworth Parade, Goring, West Sussex BN12 4TX
℃ 01903 708300
🖂 info@projects-abroad.co.uk
🖥 www.projects-abroad.co.uk

Projects Abroad arranges unpaid work experience in many countries as well as placing fee-paying volunteers in a variety of placements.

**PROGRAMME DESCRIPTION:** Voluntary work experience opportunities in selected destinations for business, conservation and other fields including archaeology, care, medical, media/journalism and supervised dissertations for degree courses.

**DESTINATIONS:** Argentina, Bolivia, Cambodia, China, Costa Rica, Ethiopia, Ghana, India, Jamaica, Mexico, Moldova, Mongolia, Morocco, Nepal, Peru, Romania, Russia, Senegal, South Africa, Sri Lanka, Tanzania and Thailand. Destinations and programmes can be combined.

**NUMBER OF PLACEMENTS:** 4,000 in total of which 75% are project placements and 25% teaching.

**PREREQUISITES:** Minimum age 16.

**DURATION AND TIME OF PLACEMENTS:** Very flexible, with departures year round and varying lengths of placement.

**COST:** Placements are self-funded and the fee charged includes insurance, food, accommodation and overseas support. 3-month placements cost between £1,395 and £2,595, excluding travel costs.

## SPANNOCCHIA FOUNDATION FARM INTERNSHIP PROGRAMME
Tenuta di Spannocchia, 53012 Chiusdino, Siena (SI), Italy
+39 57 775 211
internships@spannocchia.org
www.spannocchia.org

**PROGRAMME DESCRIPTION:** Hands-on internships on a 1,200-acre community organic farm and education centre in the hills of Tuscany, about 30 minutes from Siena; 7 farm interns spend three-quarters of time working alongside Italian farm staff in the vegetable garden, vineyards, olive groves, forestry operations, etc. The Spannocchia Guest Services Internship Programme accepts 1 intern per session, who works in the guest services operation, setting up breakfast, bottling and labelling products, assisting with grounds maintenance, help in kitchen when needed, etc. The rest of the interns' time is devoted to structured courses, particularly in Italian language and culture.

**NUMBER OF PLACEMENTS:** 8 per session, 24 per year.

**PREREQUISITES:** All nationalities welcome to apply, although programme and *agriturismo* attract a mostly American clientele. A very strong interest in manual labour and community living and a positive attitude are essential.

**DURATION AND TIME OF PLACEMENTS:** 3-month internships each year in spring, summer and autumn.

**COST:** One-time $250 education fee plus student membership of Spannocchia Foundation ($25). Interns are responsible for their airfare to Italy plus international health insurance coverage and spending money.

**OTHER SERVICES:** Accommodation and meals are provided in exchange for the 30 hours per week of farm work.

**CONTACT:** Bronwen Hanna-Korpi, Education Director.

## SPW UK – STUDENTS PARTNERSHIP WORLDWIDE
7 Tufton Street, London SW1P 3QB
020 7808 1783/4
info@spw.org
www.spw.org

An international development charity that recruits young people to volunteer and work in rural communities, with a particular emphasis on HIV transmission.

**PROGRAMME DESCRIPTION:** New for 2010, SPW is offering internships and opportunities for technical assistants in their country offices. These are short-term placements focusing on capacity building in specific technical areas.

**DESTINATIONS:** India, Nepal, South Africa, Tanzania, Uganda and Zambia.

**CONTACT:** Rachael Glover, International Youth-led Development Programme Officer.

## SUBWAY WATERSPORTS
Brick Bay, Roatan, Bay Islands, Honduras, Central America
internship@subwaywatersports.com
www.subwaywatersports.com/Courses/internship.htm

**PROGRAMME DESCRIPTION:** Internship working in a dive shop while training towards a professional PADI Divemaster (see entry in 'Directory of Sport and Activity Courses'.

## THAILAND GAP INTERNSHIPS
GPO Mae Haad, Koh Tao, Suratthani 84360, Thailand
+66 86 271 2212
+66 86 059 1590
darius@gapinternshipsthailand.com;
info@gapinternshipsthailand.com
www.gapinternshipsthailand.com

Thailand Gap Internships was set up at the beginning of 2009 by divers who have been living and training divers on Koh Tao island for many years.

**PROGRAMME DESCRIPTION:** Internship programmes on this beautiful island in the Gulf of Thailand include professional-level scuba training (divemaster or instructor), underwater videographer, freediver (master freediver/apnoea), Muay Thai training and marine conservation.

**NUMBER OF PLACEMENTS PER YEAR:** 10–15 per month.

**PREREQUISITES:** Most interns are 18–25 years.

**DURATION AND TIME OF PLACEMENTS:** Variable, but 3–7 months is ideal.

**SELECTION PROCEDURES AND ORIENTATION:**

**COST:** 7-month package that includes everything except food will cost about 45,000 Thai baht (£835) per month. 3-month Muay Thai internship can be done for less than 25,000 Thai baht per month (£465). Clean comfortable accommodation with a fan and private hot water bathroom is included in the price.

**CONTACT:** Darius Moazzami and Gary Bain, co-owners.

---

### TRAVELLERS WORLDWIDE
2A Caravelle House, 17/19 Goring Road, Worthing, West Sussex BN12 4AP
℡ 01903 502595
✉ info@travellersworldwide.com
🖥 www.travellersworldwide.com

---

Travellers is a Founder Member of the Year Out Group.

**PROGRAMME DESCRIPTION:** A wide range of professional work experience internship placements across the world, available in Law, Journalism, Medicine, TV, Tourism, Web Design, Architecture, Physiotherapy, Radio, Veterinary and many more. Placements are tailored to preferences and experience and are open to everyone, from students to professionals or career-breakers.

**DESTINATIONS:** Argentina, Australia, Brazil, Cambodia, China, Ghana, Guatemala, India, Kenya, Malaysia, New Zealand, Peru, South Africa, Sri Lanka and Zambia.

**NUMBER OF PLACEMENTS PER YEAR:** 1,000+.

**PREREQUISITES:** Qualifications required depend on the placement. Staff can advise on the most beneficial placements for individuals. All placements do require you to have initiative, adaptability and patience (and a good sense of humour helps!)

**DURATION AND TIME OF PLACEMENTS:** From 1 week to 1 year, subject to visa requirements, with flexible start and finish dates all year round.

**COST:** Prices start from £595 and include food, accommodation, airport pick-up, induction, orientation, 24/7 support on the ground and at home but don't include international travel, visas or insurance.

**CONTACT:** Jennifer Perkes, Managing Director.

---

### TWIN WORK AND VOLUNTEER ABROAD
67–71 Lewisham High Street, Lewisham, London SE13 5JX
℡ 020 8297 3251
✉ workandvolunteer@twinuk.com
🖥 www.workandvolunteer.com

---

**PROGRAMME DESCRIPTION:** Internships, language assistants, Leonardo Da Vinci programme, unpaid work and working holidays in various locations worldwide.

**DESTINATIONS:** Primarily Australia, Canada, Germany and Ghana but with unpaid work opportunities in other countries such as France, Italy, Norway, Portugal, Spain, Bolivia, and China.

**PREREQUISITES:** Must meet the age requirements of the relevant visa. Other requirements vary. Language course may be compulsory before work experience/job placement.

**DURATION AND TIME OF PLACEMENTS:** Vary with maximum usually 12 months (according to visa).

**SELECTION PROCEDURES AND ORIENTATION:** Enrolment online. Processing time 1–3 months.

**COST:** Placement fees usually about £300–£600 excluding courses and accommodation.

**CONTACT:** Barry Johnson, Peter Talbolt and Patrycja Maslanka (for Leonardo programmes).

**YOU VOLUNTEER**
1 Riverside Close, Oundle, Peterborough
PE8 4DN
☎ 01832 275038
✉ nick@youvolunteer.org
🖳 www.youvolunteer.org

Part of the Great Aves non-profit organisation.

**PROGRAMME DESCRIPTION:** Arajuno Road Project offers volunteers the opportunity to work and teach in schools in Ecuador.

**DESTINATIONS:** Amazon jungle of Ecuador.

**COST:** $100 a week.

**CONTACT:** Nick Greatrex.

# VOLUNTEERING

Throughout its time in power, the Labour Party has strongly supported the ethos of volunteering and the Labour government poured large sums of money into schemes to encourage volunteering at all levels, especially among the young. For example in 2008, it implemented a programme called *Platform2* in which up to 2,500 British young people aged 18–25 from backgrounds not normally associated with gap years have been awarded full funding to volunteer abroad for 10 weeks (see section below and entry in directory page 226). The veteran Labour MP, Frank Field, has gone much further by proposing the introduction of a mandatory national citizenship service programme. He has been campaigning for every British young person, aged 16–25, to be paid the minimum wage to spend at least six months, and preferably a full year, working on projects supporting Britain's children, the sick and elderly, the environment, and international development. However, this ambitious scheme is considered to be too expensive, so it is unlikely that it will come to fruition.

Another idea that has been mooted is to reward with lower tuition fees young people from non-affluent backgrounds who have volunteered in their gap year. For example in Scotland, the government-backed Project Scotland scheme (www.projectscotland. co.uk) encourages full-time volunteering (30 hours a week) for 3–6 months among young people aged 16–25 including students taking a gap year. They even receive pocket money of £55 a week.

Voluntary work can be not only fulfilling and satisfying in itself but can provide a unique stepping stone to interesting possibilities later on. By participating in a project such as digging wells in a Turkish village, playing football with Ghanaian kids or just helping out at a youth hostel, gap year students have the unique opportunity to live and work in a remote community, and the chance to meet up with young people from many countries. You may be able to improve or acquire a language skill and to learn something of the customs of the society in which you are volunteering. You will also gain practical experience, for instance in the fields of construction, archaeology, museums or social welfare, which will later stand you in good stead when applying for paid work. Less tangible but equally marketable benefits include the acquisition of new skills like problem solving, leadership, relationship building, communication skills and self-development generally. Research based on findings of the recruitment group Reed Executive showed that three-quarters of employers in business prefer applicants with experience of volunteering.

Although this book is devoted largely to canvassing options abroad, do not discount the possibility of spending some of your gap year in the UK doing something worthwhile away from home. A number of such organisations are listed in the UK Directory just below. Unlike placements abroad, you are unlikely to be out of pocket at the end of an attachment to British organisations which sometimes pay your travel and living expenses and may even pay an allowance. Also your carbon footprint will be much lighter. Note that volunteer organisations taking on people to work with children or vulnerable adults have a statutory obligation to run a police check on new volunteers. It is the responsibility of the organisation rather than the individual to apply to the Criminal Records Bureau (www.crb.gov.uk).

The Rank Foundation runs a Gap Award Scheme open to volunteers aged 17–24 who are recommended by their school/college or already active in a member charity in the Rank Charities network. Up to 40 volunteers are selected to work full-time in the UK for 6–9 months and receive board and lodging, training, travel and a personal allowance of £40–£45 a week, a bonus on completing the scheme of £600–£1,200 plus a Certificate that carries some weight in youth work (details from Youth Projects, Rank Foundation, 28 Bridgegate, Hebden Bridge, West Yorkshire HX7 8EX; www.rankyouthwork.org/gap/index.htm).

## COMMUNITY SERVICE VOLUNTEERS

*Community Service Volunteers* (*CSV*) provides voluntary opportunities in the UK to those aged 16 to 35 who commit themselves to volunteer full-time away from home for between four and 12 months. As many as 1,000 volunteers throughout the UK receive £34 a week pocket money in addition to accommodation and meals. Details can be obtained from CSV (contact details below). CSV produces oodles of persuasive literature demonstrating how worthwhile a stint as a CSV volunteer can be. Projects are usually with people who need help, such as children with special needs, adults with learning difficulties, teenagers at risk of offending and homeless people. Interestingly, two-thirds of volunteers are women and one-third are men. CSV is always looking to expand the scheme and would like to see an NHS Corps, Education Corps and Care Corps created to increase opportunities to volunteer in public services.

**Elizabeth Moore-Bick** volunteered with CSV just after graduating from Cambridge. Studying for a degree in Classics had meant that she had led a fairly rarefied existence and she decided it was time to develop her 'people skills'. Despite initial doubts, she decided to take the plunge and did a placement supporting a woman who had been left paralysed by a car accident 20 years before.

CSV has links with disability services at most British universities and a stint supporting a student might provide a useful initiation as it did for 19-year-old **Jo Scluz** who supported three students at Loughborough University for her year between school and university:

> *After finishing A Levels, I wanted to have a break from study and give something back. Being on placement at a university means that everyone is my own age. I've made so many friends. The other students think it is really great that I get to have all the perks of student life without having to do all the study, but of course I've got that to look forward to next September when I start my geology course. Being a CSV volunteer has been a crash course in university life.*

## PLATFORM2

By investing in the Platform2 scheme to fund 2,500 young people to volunteer over-seas, the government has proved its commitment to the culture of youth volunteering. Britons aged 18–25 who would not otherwise be in a position to take a gap year are urged to participate on the fully funded scheme. The long-term goal is that returning participants will be persuaded of the benefits of volunteering and will continue at home and gain skills that will impress potential employers.

Platform2 has secured funding at least until the end of 2010.

**SHO KONNO** was among the early beneficiaries of the Platform2 scheme and travelled to South Africa for the 10-week programme in October to December 2008. When he finished a History university course at Warwick, he noticed a newspaper article about the brand new Platform2 scheme and, after completing the online application process, was called to an informal interview:

The interviewer was not interested in Sho's skills or working experience but rather in gauging his level of interest in volunteering and brief-ing him on the possible challenges he might face. They were making an effort to lower expectations, in contrast to the commercial gap year pro-grammes, which raise them.

Despite the newness of the programme, Sho found that it was well re-sourced and structured, since the highly experienced agencies Christian Aid, BUNAC and Islamic Relief administer it on behalf of the Department for International Development (DFID). His placement was at a wetlands ecology centre 40km south of Cape Town. Before allocating this place to him, the organisers made sure he liked animals – though at the time he did not anticipate that one of the most challenging chores would be rounding up an injured ostrich which had got loose. He and the other 12 volunteers in his group noticed that the line between work and leisure time became blurred, and he soon learned to show initiative in undertak-ing useful tasks in what was technically his free time.

The programme places a strong emphasis on group cooperation and on ongoing volunteering on return to the UK especially campaigning on development issues. All returning volunteers from the participating *countries (Ghana, Kenya, South Africa, India, Nepal and Peru) attend a three-day residential camp to consolidate what they have learned and to talk about campaigning strategies. At times Sho could not believe that he was benefiting from this completely free programme. The only outlay was transport from his home to Heathrow plus buying a few gifts for friends and family. Participants even received a travel allowance which covered most of their weekend trips. En route to their project, the Platform2 group met other international volunteers who were paying a great deal for a similar programme.*

*Because Sho appreciated how much the government had invested in him, he (like the majority of the others) is happy to carry on volunteering, for Christian Aid, volunteer teaching and helping put on workshops for prospective Platform2 volunteers.*

## EUROPEAN VOLUNTARY SERVICE

Thousands of young people aged 18–30 are eligible to take up fully funded placements lasting six but preferably 12 months in Europe or beyond through the EU-funded *European Voluntary Service (EVS)* programme. Full details are available from Youth in Action at the *British Council* (see entry for European Voluntary Service in the *Directory of Specialist Gap Year Programmes* and also http://ec.europa.eu/youth/evs/aod/hei_en.cfm). Also check out www.evsguide.eu and www. action2.eu.

The programme is generally regarded as excellent though the usual way in is slightly complicated. After making contact with a national agency, you have to find a sending organisation from the list of youth exchange and other participating voluntary organisations supplied by the EVS department. Alternatively, you can ask a group that you already work or volunteer for (e.g. a youth centre, women's refuge, etc.) to become your sending sponsor. When you have found a sending organisation, they will give you a password to the database of host projects across Europe. These are extremely varied, from conference centres to film workshops, orphanages to environmental projects, though all are socially based with the aim of making contacts across Europe and of benefiting the community.

The programme is open to European nationals of all social and educational backgrounds. In fact young people from disadvantaged situations are especially encouraged. Participants pay nothing to take part. Both the sending and the host organisations receive funding from the European Youth in Action programme (with a budget allocated until 2013) and the volunteers get their travel costs, insurance, board and lodging, language classes, pocket money, orientation and mid-term programme all provided free. There is also a tutor in each project who is available to help with any difficulties and guide the volunteer.

## VOLUNTEERING ABROAD

Time spent in an Ecuadorian orphanage, an orangutan rehabilitation centre or working with street children in India can be a wonderfully liberating release from the exam struggle, whether at school or university, a welcome break before entering the next fray, the search for a job. The spirit to help others may be willing but the cash supplies may be weak. While charities in the UK might be able to cover their volunteers' basic costs, this is almost never the case abroad. We have already seen how expensive specialist gap programmes can be. The organisations listed in this chapter do not specialise in gap year students and the initial outlay of joining one of these organisations will usually be less than for the high-profile specialist agencies. As a consequence they may not be so geared up for integrating volunteers as young as 18, which is not usually a problem if the volunteer does not carry unreasonable expectations.

Most voluntary jobs undertaken abroad will leave the volunteer seriously out-of-pocket, which can be disillusioning for those who think that a desire to help the world should be enough. After participating in several prearranged voluntary projects in the USA, **Catherine Brewin** did not resent the fee she had paid to *Involvement Volunteers*:

> *The whole business of paying to do voluntary work is a bit hard to swallow. But having looked into the matter quite a bit, it does seem to be the norm. While it may be a bit unfair (who knows how much profit or loss these voluntary organisations make or how worthy their projects?), most people I've met did seem to feel good about the experience. The group I was with did raise the odd comment about it all, but did not seem unduly concerned. However I should mention that most were around 18 years old and their parents were paying some if not all the costs.*

## SOURCES OF INFORMATION

The website of *Volunteering England* (www.volunteering.org.uk) has a listing of UK agencies that send volunteers abroad, as well as disseminating a great deal of other information about volunteering generally. The revolution in information technology has made it easier for the individual to become acquainted with the amazing range of possibilities. There are some superb websites with a multitude of links to organisations big and small that can make use of volunteers. *WorldWide Volunteering* (*WWV*) is a non-profit organisation that maintains an extensive database of opportunities (www.wwv.org.uk).

Another website directory www.traveltree.co.uk covers gap year ideas and volunteering opportunities worldwide as well as internships, educational travel and related matters. University careers websites often carry a page of gap year volunteering listings, for example, www.bath.ac.uk/careers/earlybird/cvgy.pdf.

Hosted by *Action Without Borders*, www.idealist.org is an easily searchable site that will take you to the great monolithic charities such as the Peace Corps as well as to small grassroots organisations in Armenia, Tenerife or anywhere else. It lists 20,000 organisations in 105 countries. When planning her gap year, **Katie White** says she spent hours browsing the amazing opportunities on www.idealist.org and www.goabroad. com and felt '*like a kid in a candy shop*'.

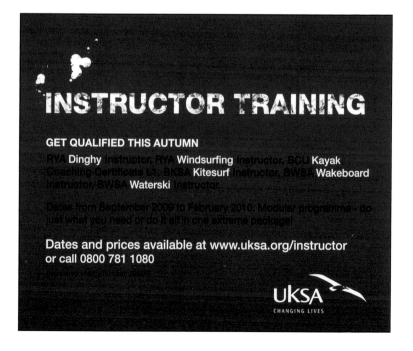

I want to see the world.
I want to save the world.
I want to be thrilled, to be fulfilled.
I want to learn, I want to teach.
I want to dance, I want independence.
I want to share, I want to care.
I want to try, I want to find out why.
I want to know, I want to grow.
I want in, because I want time out.
I want to soar, I want to explore.
I want to rock I want to roll.
I want stories to tell.
I want to L.O.L.
I want the best year of my life.
(well, the best year yet)
creating memories I'll never forget.
I want to give, I want to take.
I need a break
for goodness sake...
what do you want out of your year?
Visit our website or call 01879 230444 to discover more about our 8 & 12 month volunteer placements in Africa, Asia and the Americas.
project TRUST
Changing lives, year in, year out...
Registered as a Charity in Scotland No. SCO25668
projectrust.org.uk

# pacsafe....?

Fully encases and secur
your belongings with
eXomesh Ultimate

Slashproof eXomesh c

Locks closed

Locks to secure fixtu

Enables user to Lock,
Leave and Relax

eXomesh
**ultim⌂te**
the complete lock & leave syste

---

## *pacsafe*™ (55/85/120/140) with eXomesh®

### anti-theft backpack & bag protector

Keeping an eye on your pack and its contents at all times when travelling is near impossible. Crowded trains, buses or hostel dorm rooms can all be prime locations for pickpockets and thieves - potentially bringing your trip to an early end.

With a Pacsafe backpack protector, you can encase your gear in eXomesh - a high tensile steel mesh. Slashproof and tamperproof, you can lock it off to a secure object and ensure prying hands stay out, leaving you free to take in the adventure.

As we like to say, "When your gear's secure, you can do more."

**packs small**

☑ **slashproof**

☑ **snatchproc**

☑ **tamperproc**

## pacsafe®
*travel security*

Available from all good outdoor retailers or call 0116 234 4644 for your nearest stockist

Students with a church affiliation and Christian faith have a broader choice of opportunities since a number of mission societies and charities are looking for young Christians (see the separate listing in this chapter of Religious Organisations). Whereas some religious organisations focus on practical work, such as working with street children, orphans, in schools, building libraries, etc., others are predominantly proselytising, which will appeal only to the very committed. *Christian Vocations* (St James House, Trinity Road, Dudley, West Midlands DY1 1JB; 0121 288 0854; www.christian vocations.org) publishes a searchable online directory of short-term opportunities with Christian agencies.

---

**SEARCH TIP**
*The search engine at www.do-it.org is very useful for finding suitable projects in the UK and specifically near your post code.*

---

## AVOIDING PROBLEMS

It is impossible to predict the circumstances in which you will find yourself. Whereas some gappers have a ready-made social life because of their location, others will find themselves fairly isolated. The picture on the brochure of the smiling volunteer teacher at the blackboard addressing some bright-eyed eager students might not be your day-to-day experience. **Abi Cooke** found herself the only European in a Thai village and had to get used to everyone shouting and pointing, stopping and staring.

> *The teaching itself had its ups and downs. Some days when the kids were keen and the weather not too sticky were great, and the enthusiasm you receive makes the effort worth the while. It is difficult though when you are faced with a class of 50 and half the kids are unable to read and write in their own language, never mind read and write in English. The time I spent with the English Club I started was my favourite, when I met kids who really wanted to learn and weren't afraid to voice the few words they knew. In class it was very difficult to have individual conversations with separate kids.*

Bear in mind that voluntary work, especially in the developing world, can be not only tough and character-building but also disillusioning. Misunderstandings can arise, and promises can be broken just as easily in the context of unpaid work as paid work. If you are in any doubt about an organisation you are considering working for, ask for the names of one or two past volunteers whom you can contact for an informal reference. Any worthy organisation should be happy to oblige.

## WORKCAMPS/VOLUNTEER PROJECTS

Voluntary work in developed countries often takes the form of workcamps which accept unskilled short-term labour. The term 'workcamp' is falling out of favour and is often replaced by 'volunteer project'. These short-term projects are an excellent introduction to travelling for 18–21 year olds who have never before been away from a family-type social structure. Certain projects in the UK are open to 16 and 17 year olds. As part of an established international network of voluntary organisations they are not subject to the irregularities of some privately run projects. As well as providing gap year and other volunteers with the means to live cheaply for two to four weeks in a foreign country, workcamps enable volunteers to become involved in what is usually useful work for the community, to meet people from many different backgrounds and to increase their awareness of other lifestyles, social problems and their responsibility to society.

Within Europe, and to a lesser extent further afield, there is a massive effort to coordinate workcamp programmes. This usually means that the prospective volunteer should apply in the first instance to the appropriate organisation in his or her own country, or to a centralised international headquarters. The vast majority of camps take place in the summer months, and camp details are usually published online in March/April with a flurry of placements made in the month or two following. It is necessary to pay a registration fee which has become standard across the different agencies recruiting volunteers, usually £150 for a project in Europe, £180 for one in a developing country to help finance future projects or to pay for specialised training. The fee covers board and lodging but not of course travel.

The largest workcamp organisation is *Service Civil International* with branches in 41 countries. The UK branch is *International Voluntary Service* (*IVS-GB*) in Edinburgh (0131 243 2745; info@ivsgb.org). The cost of registration on IVS workcamps outside the UK is £190, which includes £35 IVS membership fees. IVS has linked with the four other main agencies listed below to form *VINE-UK* (vine-uk.org), all of whom organise international volunteer exchange programmes. The other organisations in the network are:

**Concordia International Volunteers**, Brighton BN41 1DH (01273 422218; www. concordiavolunteers.org.uk). Programme of workcamps in 30 countries worldwide. Registration fee £180. (For projects in Latin America, Asia, Middle East and Africa volunteers pay an extra fee of about £150 to cover food and accommodation, etc.)

**UNA Exchange**, Cardiff (029 2022 3088; www.unaexchange.org). Membership costs £12 plus £150 for overseas projects, £200+ for longer term ones.

**Voluntary Action for Peace/VAP**, London SE22 0PH (0844 209 0927; www.vap. org.uk). Workcamps held in many countries in Western and Eastern Europe, plus Mexico, the Middle East and Bangladesh. Administrative fee £120–£160.

**Xchange Scotland**, Glasgow G1 1LH (xchange.scotland@yahoo.com; www.xchange scotland.org).

## ARCHAEOLOGY

Taking part in archaeological excavations is another popular form of voluntary work especially among gap year students planning to study a related subject at university. Volunteers are almost always expected to make a contribution towards their board and lodging. Also, you may be asked to bring your own trowel, work clothes, tent, etc. (see entry for *Archaeology Abroad* page 287). *Archaeology Abroad* subscribers are eligible to apply for Fieldwork Awards of up to £500 to help with their dig expenses. Excavations applied for must be listed in the annual bulletin of *Archaeology Abroad* or in one of their email updates.

For those who are not students of archaeology, the chances of finding a place on an overseas dig will be greatly enhanced by having some digging experience nearer home. Anyone who wants to participate on an archaeological dig should read information available from the Council for British Archaeology (CBA) in York; some of its fieldwork listings are freely available on its website (www.britarch.ac.uk/briefing/field.asp). Otherwise you can subscribe to CBA's briefings, which lists the archaeological digs to which volunteers can apply.

**Anthony Blake** joined a dig sponsored by the University of Reims in France and warns that '*archaeology is hard work, and applicants must be aware of what working for eight hours in the baking heat means!*' Nevertheless Anthony found the company excellent and the opportunity to improve his French welcome.

Israel is probably the country with the most active archaeology digs. Information on volunteering at archaeological digs in Israel is available on the website of the Israeli Ministry of Foreign Affairs (though it's a little difficult to locate; try googling 'mfa digs 2010'). After choosing an excavation of interest, you make contact directly with the person in charge of the research, some of them in the Department of Classical Studies at Tel Aviv University and others at universities elsewhere in Israel or abroad.

Volunteers are needed to do the mundane work of digging and sifting on a range of archaeological digs. In the majority of cases, volunteers must pay a daily fee of $35–$50+ to cover food and accommodation and sometimes considerably more, plus a registration fee (typically $50–$75). Most camps take place during university holidays between May and September when temperatures soar. Volunteers must be in good physical condition and able to work long hours in hot weather. Valid health insurance is required.

## CONSERVATION

People interested in protecting the environment can often slot into conservation organisations abroad. To fix up a short conservation holiday, contact *BTCV* (*British Trust for Conservation Volunteers*) which runs a programme of UK and international projects in a dozen countries including Iceland, France, Bulgaria, USA, Cameroon and Japan. Accommodation, meals and insurance are provided; sample prices are £460 for a week of nest-building on the Black Sea to £510 for two weeks planting trees in a Cameroonian village, excluding flights.

The international system of working-for-keep on organic farms is another good way of visiting unexplored corners of the world cheaply (see entry for *World Wide Opportunities on Organic Farms/WWOOF* page 309). Of the several thousand WWOOF members in the UK about half are aged 18–25.

# Project Trust

Susan Molloy

**Project Trust** is an educational charity, specialising in sending 17-19 year old school-leavers overseas for long-term placements. Currently operating in over twenty countries across Africa, Asia and The Americas, projects include teaching, social care and medical work and outward bound instructing. All of the projects are vetted to ensure that volunteers add to the community in a positive way, rather than taking roles that could be filled by locals.

Thembelihle Home in South Africa is for children who need protection from previous family members or care givers. Most children have been sexually abused, and the volunteers are essential when it comes to re-building their lives. **Susan Molloy** volunteered at Thembelihle last year. She explains more about the place she made home for a year.

'Because Thembelihle Home is a place of safety, the children cannot go to local schools. The home has a small classroom in the back yard where schooling takes place five days a week. My Project partner and I were the only teachers (for up to 30 children of ages between 5-18) and wrote and set up the lesson plans, curriculum and exams. Without Project Trust volunteers, the home school would not run, therefore the children would be without education. Thembelihle could not afford to employ full time teachers, let alone teachers who would agree to live on-site 24/7 and be social care workers, friends and listeners!

Not only do the volunteers run the school and support the children when they need it, but they are also a huge support for the other staff members. Resources are scarce, but the available materials are cherished and loved, just like all those, including children and staff, who are involved in the success and triumph of such a small home.'

Susan describes what an impression her volunteering in South Africa has had on her.

'I have definitely matured in leaps and bounds since returning from South Africa. I feel like I have a better understanding of how difficult life is for people and how I have been handed everything I have ever wanted on a silver plate. I am now more grateful for everything I have. Nothing should be taken for granted. My year has opened my eyes to what really matters and what I really want from my life now. I learnt to have patience and an understanding of how other people live.

I think life in South Africa is a pace slower than the UK but that's not a bad thing. I learnt to take things one at a time. Try to enjoy things more. Before I left for South Africa my life was a rat race of deadlines and things to be done and places to be. Now, I have learned to relax, to slow down, to enjoy things and realise what really matters and what things don't. Never again, will I ever be ungrateful for anything I receive.'

Several organisations assist scientific expeditions by supplying fee-paying volunteers, in addition to *Earthwatch* (entry below). For details of scientific expedition organisations which use self-financing volunteers, investigate *Biosphere Expeditions* (0870 446 0801; www.biosphere-expeditions.org) and *Coral Cay Conservation*, *Gapforce* and *Frontier* in the 'Directory of Specialist Gap Year Programmes'.

## DEVELOPING COUNTRIES

Commitment, no matter how fervent, is not enough to work for an aid organisation in the developing world. You must be able to offer some kind of useful training or skill. However if you are travelling in underdeveloped countries and take the time to investigate local possibilities, you may discover wildlife projects, children's homes, special schools, etc. in which it will be possible to work voluntarily for a short or longer time. You may simply want to join your new Vietnamese, Sri Lankan or Ecuadorian friends wherever they are working. You may get the chance to trade your assistance for a straw mat and simple meals but more likely the only rewards will be the experience and the camaraderie.

# DIRECTORY OF VOLUNTEERING IN THE UK

## L'ARCHE

10 Briggate, Silsden, Keighley, West Yorkshire
BD20 9JT
℡ 01535 656186
✉ info@larche.org.uk
🖥 www.larche.org.uk

**PROGRAMME DESCRIPTION:** L'Arche is a worldwide network of communities where assistants help people with learning disabilities to live in a congenial atmosphere. The aim is to provide a real home, with spiritual and emotional support.
**DESTINATIONS:** Kent, Liverpool, Inverness, Lambeth, Bognor Regis, Ipswich, Brecon, Edinburgh and Preston.
**NUMBER OF PLACEMENTS PER YEAR:** 190–200.
**PREREQUISITES:** Assistants need an ability and willingness to live communally and to share life with people with learning disabilities.
**DURATION AND TIME OF PLACEMENTS:** Generally 12 months, although shorter and longer stays are sometimes acceptable.
**SELECTION PROCEDURES AND ORIENTATION:** Enquirers are sent an information pack along with a detailed application form. They are invited to visit the community, meet the members and have an informal interview with house leaders/assistants/coordinators. All assistants work for a probationary period and receive a one-to-one induction with the community leader.
**COST:** Assistants must pay their own travel costs and personal insurance. Free board and lodging are provided and a modest allowance is paid.

## CSV – COMMUNITY SERVICE VOLUNTEERS

5th Floor, Scala House, 36 Holloway Circus,
Birmingham B1 1EQ
℡ 0800 374991
℡ 0121 643 7690
✉ volunteer@csv.org.uk
🖥 www.csv.org.uk/fulltimevolunteering

CSV is the largest voluntary placement organisation in the UK. It provides a voluntary placement for those aged 16+ for 4–12 months.
**PROGRAMME DESCRIPTION:** CSV volunteers help people throughout the UK in a huge range of social care projects, e.g. working with the homeless, mentoring young offenders, supporting children in special schools or helping the disabled to live independently in their homes, and at the same time learn new skills. CSV volunteers are full-time and live away from home anywhere within the UK.
**NUMBER OF PLACEMENTS PER YEAR:** 1,000.
**PREREQUISITES:** No specific qualifications or experience are needed. Open to UK citizens or EEA citizens who are residents in the UK. Other international volunteers can participate provided they apply through one of CSV's international partnerships (details from www.csv.org/ftvol).
**SELECTION PROCEDURES AND ORIENTATION:** Volunteers receive regular supervision and back-up support from their local CSV office.
**COST:** CSV volunteers receive £34 per week living allowance; plus food (or food allowance of £40 per week), accommodation and travel expenses are also provided.

## HESSE STUDENT SCHEME

Aldeburgh Festival, Aldeburgh Music, Snape
Maltings Concert Hall, Snape, Saxmundham,
Suffolk IP17 1SP

✆ 01728 687127

✉ jalexander@aldeburgh.co.uk

🖥 www.aldeburgh.co.uk

**PROGRAMME DESCRIPTION:** Volunteers assist in the day-to-day running of the Aldeburgh Festival of Music and the Arts in June and prepare for the weekly Hesse Students Concert. Duties include selling programmes, conducting shuttle buses, page turning and assisting Aldeburgh staff with a variety of light tasks. Students are also expected to devise and perform a concert as part of the festival events.

**NUMBER OF PLACEMENTS PER YEAR:** 2 sets of 10 students are chosen for each half of the festival.

**PREREQUISITES:** Ages 18–25. Must be a music lover, willing to help with the general running of the festival and have a cheerful disposition and a professional approach.

**DURATION AND TIME OF PLACEMENTS:** 1 week during the festival, which runs over the middle 2 weeks in June.

**COST:** Volunteers receive bed and breakfast accommodation and tickets to festival events.

**CONTACT:** Jane Alexander (jalexander@aldeburgh.co.uk).

## LOSANG DRAGPA CENTRE

Buddhist College and Meditation Centre,
Dobroyd Castle, Pexwood Road, Todmorden,
West Yorkshire OL14 7JJ

✆ 01706 812247 (ext 201)

✉ info@losangdragpa.com or workingvisits
@losangdragpa.com

🖥 www.losangdragpa.com

An opportunity to enjoy a break and experience living in a Buddhist spiritual community in the Pennines. During the week volunteers (who contribute £40 per week) work alongside residents maintaining Victorian Dobroyd Castle. In the evenings and at weekends they can participate in meditation classes and explore the surrounding countryside and villages. Other Buddhist centres that welcome volunteers who may have to pay a small contribution are Madhyamaka Buddhist Centre, Pocklington, York (www.madhyamaka.org) and Manjushri Kadampa Meditation Centre in Ulverston, in the Lake District (workingvisits@manjushri.org).

## OPTIONS TRUST

4 Plantation Way, Whitehill, Bordon, Hampshire
GU35 9HD

✆ 01420 474261

✉ optionstrust@pvm.ndo.co.uk

🖥 www.optionstrust.co.uk

**PROGRAMME DESCRIPTION:** Placements arranged for live-in carers, providing assistance to disabled clients who require help with washing, dressing, moving around, household tasks and driving about.

**NUMBER OF PLACEMENTS PER YEAR:** 12.

**DESTINATIONS:** Clients all live in their own homes, mostly in the south of England.

**PREREQUISITES:** Minimum age 18. Many workers are on a gap year or are from abroad and want to improve their English; must be EU nationals.

**DURATION AND TIME OF PLACEMENTS:** 6–12 months.

**COST:** None. Workers live in with disabled employer and receive free accommodation, normally in own room. Sometimes employers pay a small wage.

**CONTACT:** Virginia Mason, Co-ordinator.

## OXFAM

Oxfam House, John Smith Drive, Cowley,
Oxford OX4 2JY

✆ 0870 010 8553

✉ stewards@oxfam.org.uk

🖥 www.oxfam.org.uk/what_you_can_do/
events/stewards/index.htm

**PROGRAMME DESCRIPTION:** Volunteer stewards recruited for various summer musical festivals including Glastonbury and WOMAD.

**NUMBER OF PLACEMENTS PER YEAR:** 1,400.

## SHAD – SUPPORT AND HOUSING ASSISTANCE FOR PEOPLE WITH DISABILITIES

SHAD Wandsworth, 5 Bedford Hill, London
SW12 9ET

📞 020 8675 6095

✉ volunteering@shad.org.uk

🖥 www.shad.org.uk

SHAD enables tenants with physical disabilities to live in their own homes. Volunteers are needed to act as the tenants' arms and legs, following their instructions.

**DURATION AND TIME OF PLACEMENTS:** Minimum 3–4 months, maximum 12 months. Work is on a rota basis: volunteers can expect a minimum of 4 days off a fortnight. A shift system is worked by volunteers allowing plenty of free time to explore London.

**PREREQUISITES:** No experience is necessary and support is guaranteed. Opportunity to gain good work experience in a friendly and supportive environment, and to live and work with people from all over the world. Volunteers from overseas welcome.

**SELECTION PROCEDURES AND ORIENTATION:** Through application form, interview and suitable references. Induction and safe manual handling training is provided.

**REMUNERATION:** Volunteers receive an allowance of £60+ a week, free accommodation (shared with other volunteers) and expenses. Certificates and references provided on successful completion of a placement.

## V-INSPIRED

5th Floor, Dean Bradley House, 52 Horseferry
Road, London SW1P 2AF

📞 0800 089 9000

📞 020 7960 7000

✉ info@vinspired.com

🖥 www.vinspired.com

**v** took over the Millennium Volunteers programme in 2007. It is a publicly funded body with a budget of £50 million and remit to create a million volunteers by 2012.

**PROGRAMME DESCRIPTION:** UK-wide initiative provides volunteering opportunities for young volunteers aged 16–25 in the UK.

**DESTINATIONS:** Throughout the UK regions.

**NUMBER OF PLACEMENTS PER YEAR:** Unlimited.

**COST:** Out-of-pocket expenses covered.

## VITALISE (FORMERLY WINGED FELLOWSHIP TRUST)

*London office*: 12 City Forum, 250 City Road,
London, EC1V 8AF

📞 0845 345 1972

✉ admin@vitalise.org.uk

🖥 www.vitalise.org.uk

*Kendal volunteer office*:

📞 0845 330 0148

✉ volunteer@vitalise.org.uk

Charity that provides essential breaks for disabled people and carers and inspirational opportunities for volunteers.

**PROGRAMME DESCRIPTION:** Volunteers are recruited to support people with disabilities and carers on holiday.

**DESTINATIONS:** Centres in Cornwall, Southampton, Chigwell, Nottingham and Southport.

**PREREQUISITES:** Minimum age 16. No experience necessary.

**DURATION AND TIME OF PLACEMENTS:** All year round availability (especially spring and autumn). Anything from 1 week (most common) to 1 year.

**SELECTION PROCEDURES AND ORIENTATION:** Booking form, references, CRB check. Trained care staff are always around and induction training and ongoing support are given.

**COST:** Completely free. All board, lodging and travel to centres is paid.

## WORLDWRITE

WORLDwrite Centre, Millfields Lodge, 201
Millfields Road, Hackney, London E5 0AL

📞 020 8985 5435

✉ world.write@btconnect.com

🖥 www.worldwrite.org.uk

**PROGRAMME DESCRIPTION:** WORLDwrite is an education charity that uses documentary film-making as a medium for campaigning on domestic and global issues and uses lots of London-based volunteers for varying periods. Their new news channel WORLDbytes (www.worldbytes.org), run by volunteers, covers a lot of domestic as well as international issues.

**CONTACT:** Patrick Hayes (Volunteer Coordinator), Ceri Dingle (Director) and Viv Regan (Assistant Director).

---

**WWOOF UK**
World Wide Opportunities on Organic Farms;
PO Box 2154, Winslow, Buckingham MK18 3WS
📖 www.wwoof.org.uk

Helps people interested in organic farming to exchange their manual labour for a chance to stay on farms throughout the UK and Ireland. Membership costs £20 for one, £30 for two for one year. Access to about 300 UK properties that accept working volunteers. See also entry in 'Directory of Volunteering Abroad'.

---

# DIRECTORY OF VOLUNTEERING ABROAD

## AFRICAN IMPACT/PATHFINDERS

6 Carlton Close, Noordhoek, Cape Town 7985,
South Africa

☎ +27 21 7854319

☎ 0800 5200926 (UK toll-free)

☎ 0877 2532899 (USA toll-free)

✉ sarah@africanencounter.org

🖥 www.africanimpact.com or
www.pathfindersafrica.com

African Impact facilitates conservation and community
development volunteer programmes, internships and
small group adventures in Southern and East Africa.

**PROGRAMME DESCRIPTION:** Volunteer opportunities in lion rehabilitation and release programme in
Zimbabwe, whale shark research in Mozambique and
mobile clinics in rural Kenya, among others.

**DESTINATIONS:** Southern and East Africa.

**NUMBER OF PLACEMENTS:** 1,000.

**PREREQUISITES:** Minimum age 18.

**DURATION AND TIME OF PLACEMENTS:** typically
2–4 weeks.

**SELECTION PROCEDURES AND ORIENTATION:**
Telephone interviews are conducted for more complex
and sensitive placements; otherwise a CV is sufficient.

**COST:** Average cost is £1,195 per month.

**CONTACT:** Sarah and Rob Graham, Directors.

## AMERICAN CONSERVATION EXPERIENCE (ACE)

418 Leroux Street, Flagstaff, AZ 86001, USA

☎ +1 928 226 6960

✉ cbaker@usaconservation.org

🖥 www.usaconservation.org

**PROGRAMME DESCRIPTION:** Environmental conservation projects in America's National Parks and public
lands. Typical projects include walking track construction, revegetation, weed eradication, fencing, habitat
surveys, erosion control and watershed restoration.

**DESTINATIONS:** Grand Canyon, Zion, Bryce, Can-
yonlands, Arches, Yosemite, Sequoia and many other
National Parks throughout America's West.

**NUMBER OF PLACEMENTS:** 250.

**PREREQUISITES:** All nationalities. Minimum age 18
(average 23).

**DURATION AND TIME OF PLACEMENTS:** 8, 10 or
12 weeks.

**SELECTION PROCEDURES AND ORIENTATION:**
Applications must be sent to partner agent, e.g. BUNAC
in the UK.

**COST:** BUNAC fee is £250 for 10 or 12 weeks, £475
for 8 weeks. Volunteers must fund their airfares to
Phoenix or San Francisco, plus pay for food on their
days off. Dorm accommodation and meals while on
project are provided.

**CONTACT:** Chris Baker, Director.

## AMERISPAN

PO Box 58129, Philadelphia, PA 19103, USA

☎ +1 800 879 6640

☎ 020 8123 6086 (UK)

✉ info@amerispan.com

🖥 www.amerispan.com/volunteer_intern

Specialist Spanish-language travel organisation with
expertise in arranging language courses, voluntary
placements and internships throughout South and Central
America as well as other language courses worldwide.

**PROGRAMME DESCRIPTION:** Many choices of volunteer placements and internships, all listed on website. Some come with free accommodation. Many set a minimum age for volunteers of 20. A typical programme would be a 2-week language programme followed by a 4-month volunteer placement in healthcare, education, tourism/marketing, national parks or social work.

**COST:** Fees start at $1,560 for a 4-week placement in Argentina that includes homestay, language lessons and volunteer placement.

## AMIGOS DE IRACAMBI – SAVING FORESTS, CHANGING LIVES

Caixa Postal No 1, Rosário da Limeira, 36878–000, Minas Gerais, Brazil
✆ +55 32 3231 2756
🖰 volunteers@iracambi.com
🖳 www.iracambi.com

Organisation working at the cutting edge of conservation and sustainability to make the conservation of the rainforests more attractive than their destruction, in one of the world's top five biodiversity hotspots, the Atlantic Forest in south-east Brazil.

**PROGRAMME DESCRIPTION:** Volunteers (and professionals) needed in three programme areas: natural resource management, forest restoration and alternative income generation. Support activities include working in the forest nursery, forest monitoring, trail maintenance, GIS (geographic information system), marketing, fundraising and administrative support.

**NUMBER OF PLACEMENTS PER YEAR:** 110.

**PREREQUISITES:** Volunteers must be enthusiastic, flexible, self-motivated people who want to make a valid contribution.

**DURATION AND TIME OF PLACEMENTS:** Minimum stay 1 month.

**SELECTION PROCEDURES AND ORIENTATION:** Rolling acceptance year round. After receiving application and CV, volunteer's skills are matched with programme needs. Support and advice available throughout stay.

**COST:** R$1,200 for first month, R$1,150 for second month, R$1,100 for third and subsequent months. Cost includes full board accommodation in shared housing.

**CONTACT:** Jemma, Volunteer Co-ordinator.

## APES (ANIMAL PROTECTION AND ENVIRONMENTAL SANCTUARY)

Greytown, 3250 KwaZulu-Natal, South Africa
✆ +27 03 3413 2219
🖰 apes1@gom.co.za or apes1@vodamail. co.za
🖳 www.apes.org.za

APES is a non-profit organisation specialising in primate rehabilitation and rescue.

**PROGRAMME DESCRIPTION:** Committed volunteers accepted year round to work with the animals, especially infant vervet monkeys. Tasks may include snare/trap clearing; game counts and environmental management. APES also promotes community development and environmental education in local Zulu schools.

**DESTINATIONS:** Umpalazi Reserve, KwaZulu-Natal.

**DURATION AND TIME OF PLACEMENTS:** Discretionary.

**COST:** £610 per month.

**CONTACT:** Dawn Magowan and Rodney Pendleton.

## ARCHAEOLOGY ABROAD

31–34 Gordon Square, London WC1H 0PY
✆ 020 8537 0849
🖰 arch.abroad@ucl.ac.uk
🖳 www.britarch.ac.uk/archabroad

Established in 1972 and based at University College London.

**PROGRAMME DESCRIPTION:** Provides information about archaeological fieldwork opportunities outside the UK through its annual publication *Archaeology Abroad* (published on CD-ROM) and via occasional email updates throughout the year. Also publishes free fact sheets including one called *Digging Abroad in a Gap Year*, available in exchange for a large, stamped self-addressed envelope.

**DESTINATIONS:** Worldwide.

**NUMBER OF PLACEMENTS PER YEAR:** 700–1,000.

**PREREQUISITES:** Archaeological fieldwork involves physical labour. Volunteers need to be fit and healthy and enjoy working as part of a team. Previous experience useful, though not essential.

**DURATION AND TIME OF PLACEMENTS:** From 1 week.

**SELECTION PROCEDURES AND ORIENTATION:** Applications from people with a definite interest in the subject are generally though not always preferred. Basic training is usually offered to those with no excavation experience.

**COST:** Annual subscription to *Archaeology Abroad* costs £22 (£24 in Europe, £26 elsewhere). Fieldwork Awards available to subscribers towards cost of joining excavation projects listed in *Archaeology Abroad*.

**CONTACT:** Wendy Rix Morton, Honorary Editor and Secretary.

---

### AZAFADY

Studio 7, 1A Beethoven Street, London W10 4LG

℡ 020 8960 6629

✉ mark@azafady.org

🖥 www.madagascar.co.uk

Registered UK charity and Malagasy NGO.

**PROGRAMME DESCRIPTION:** The Pioneer programme, Conservation programme and short-term programmes in community construction or English teaching allow volunteers to work with a grassroots organisation tackling conservation issues and extreme poverty in Madagascar. Volunteers gain experience in sustainable development, health infrastructure and education, and environmental conservation with sample projects including tree planting, school building and teaching English. Pioneers work with a group of international volunteers and permanent Malagasy staff on projects across Azafady's three interrelated departments: sustainable livelihoods, conservation and development. New for 2010, the Conservation programme offers the opportunity to get involved in all aspects of Azafady's community conservation work which integrates flora and fauna research, especially of lemurs, with community initiatives.

**DESTINATIONS:** South-east Madagascar.

**NUMBER OF PLACEMENTS PER YEAR:** 14–20 per group, 8 groups per year.

**PREREQUISITES:** Enthusiasm, cultural sensitivity and an interest in a future career with non-profit organisations would be beneficial. Training given. Volunteers learn basic Malagasy and gather skills relevant to working in the fields of development and conservation. Minimum age 18, no maximum.

**DURATION AND TIME OF PLACEMENTS:** 10-week Pioneer programme starting in January, April, July and October (5–10 weeks also available). Conservation programme lasts 2–10 weeks with programmes starting throughout the year. English teaching and community construction 2–3 weeks. Applications preferred in advance to give ample time to prepare.

**COST:** Successful applicants pay for pre-project costs such as flight, insurance and visa and are required to raise a minimum direct charitable donation of £2,000 for Pioneer, £600 for 2-week Conservation and other short-term programmes (discounts for additional weeks). These funds help to run the NGO in Madagascar and many of the projects. Applicants are provided with extensive fundraising resources and advice.

**CONTACT:** Mark Jacobs, Managing Director.

---

### THE BACKPACK & AFRICA TRAVEL CENTRE

74 New Church Street, Tamboerskloof, Cape Town, South Africa

℡ +27 21 423 5555

✉ toni@backpackers.co.za

🖥 www.backpackers.co.za

**PROGRAMME DESCRIPTION:** Volunteers teach maths, science and English in a local community in Cape Town 10am–2pm daily with option of assisting sport coaches with football or with the life skills programme until 6pm.

**NUMBER OF PLACEMENTS PER YEAR:** 20.

**DESTINATIONS:** Cape Town.

**PREREQUISITES:** Minimum age 18.

**DURATION AND TIME OF PLACEMENTS:** Monday to Thursday for 6 weeks with weekends free to travel.

**SELECTION PROCEDURES AND ORIENTATION:** Backpackers' introduction to Cape Town given.

**COST:** R9,200 for 6 weeks.

**CONTACT:** Toni Shina, Co-owner.

### BIMINI BIOLOGICAL FIELD STATION
9300 SW 99 Street, Miami, FL 33176 2050, USA
- +1 305 274 0628
- +1 305 799 9048 (mobile)
- sgruber@rsmas.miami.edu;
  bbfssharklab@gmail.com
- www.miami.edu/sharklab

Privately owned shark research station in the Bahamas.

**PROGRAMME DESCRIPTION:** Active research on lemon sharks and other captive animals. Studies consist of genetics, behaviour, telemetry-tracking, etc. Volunteers perform all tasks including research, plus routine maintenance and cooking.

**DURATION AND TIME OF PLACEMENTS:** Minimum 1 month from the 15th of the month.

**NUMBER OF PLACEMENTS:** About 20 per year (5–7 volunteers at any one time).

**PREREQUISITES:** Must speak English, have a biological background and an interest in sharks.

**SELECTION PROCEDURES AND ORIENTATION:** Applications via email accepted year round. Two academic references must be submitted.

**COST:** $695 per month to cover meals and housing.

**CONTACT:** Professor Samuel H Gruber, Director.

### BLUE VENTURES
Unit 2D, 22–24 Highbury Grove, Islington, London N5 2EA
- 020 3176 0548
- enquiries@blueventures.org
- www.blueventures.org

**PROGRAMME DESCRIPTION:** Field research is carried out in Madagascar, Fiji and Malaysia by overseas volunteers, who work closely with field research scientists and camp staff. Volunteers learn to dive and develop practical research and conservation skills in some of the world's most biodiverse coral habitats. Working with local communities, schools, NGOs and marine institutes, volunteers experience the full spectrum of conservation in remote coastal communities.

**NUMBER OF PLACEMENTS PER YEAR:** Up to 18 at one time, with 8 expeditions in Madagascar, and 7 in Fiji and Malaysia throughout the year.

**DESTINATIONS:** Andavadoaka, southwest Madagascar. Newer destinations are Leleuvia in Fiji and Tioman island off Peninsular Malaysia.

**PREREQUISITES:** Volunteers wishing to dive must be 18 or over, although there is no age limit on non-diving volunteers. Volunteers must be competent swimmers, fit enough to pass a diving medical examination, and enthusiastic about working as part of a team in a remote and often challenging environment. No previous diving or science experience is needed as all dive training and research training is provided on site.

**DURATION AND TIME OF PLACEMENTS:** Departures every 6 weeks. Minimum stay 3 weeks, typical stay is 6 weeks, but volunteers are welcome to stay for as long as they wish.

**SELECTION PROCEDURES AND ORIENTATION:** Volunteers can apply year round via blueventures.org. All volunteers are contacted by phone for interview and briefing on registering for an expedition.

**COST:** From £2,100 for non-qualified diver and £1,900 for a qualified diver for expeditions to Madagascar. Prices for Fiji and Malaysia are available online. All expedition costs include full training and equipment hire along with accommodation and board but exclude flights, visas and diving apparel.

**CONTACT:** Kathleen Edie, Volunteer Coordinator.

### BOTTLENOSE DOLPHINS RESEARCH INSTITUTE (BDRI)
Via A. Diaz 4, Golfo Aranci, Olbia-Tempio, Sardinia 07020, Italy
- +39 0789 183 1197

*C* +39 338 469 5878

*C* +39 346 081 5414 (mobile)

✆ info@thebdri.com

▣ www.thebdri.com

**PROGRAMME DESCRIPTION:** Boat-based field work, marine conservation and dolphin research project for paying volunteers.

**NUMBER OF PLACEMENTS PER YEAR:** 75.

**DESTINATIONS:** Emerald Coast of northern Sardinia.

**PREREQUISITES:** All welcome.

**DURATION AND TIME OF PLACEMENTS:** Minimum 6 days; standard stay 13 days. No maximum.

**COST:** €75–€100 per day.

**CONTACT:** Bruno Diaz Lopez, Chief Biologist and Director.

## BUENOS AIRES VOLUNTEER (BAV)

Av. Rivadavia 2431, 3rd Entrance, 4° floor, office 9, (C1034ACD) Ciudad Autónoma de Buenos Aires, Argentina

*C* +54 11 4952 4779

✆ info@bavolunteer.org.ar

▣ www.bavolunteer.org.ar

BAV is one of Amartya's programmes, a social enterprise based in Argentina with a branch in Scandinavia.

**PROGRAMME DESCRIPTION:** Organises and coordinates volunteer work projects for people from all over the world with the objective of contributing to the strengthening of social organisations in Argentina, focused on child services development, arts and development, social inclusion, poverty relief and micro-enterprises.

**NUMBER OF PLACEMENTS PER YEAR:** 40.

**DESTINATIONS:** BAV works with over 50 grassroots and other organisations of different types in and around Buenos Aires, as well as in different provinces of Argentina.

**PREREQUISITES:** Minimum age 18. Average age 24. Volunteers should know basic Spanish. Should be flexible and pro-active.

**DURATION AND TIME OF PLACEMENTS:** Minimum 3 months.

**SELECTION PROCEDURES AND ORIENTATION:** Applications accepted year round.

**COST:** Programme fee $600 includes assistance with finding homestay or private accommodation, intensive Spanish course, information about cultural events, bi-weekly meetings and seminars, etc.

**CONTACT:** Cecilia Levy, Institutional Coordinator.

## CENIT (CENTRE FOR THE WORKING GIRL)

Calle Huacho 150 y Jos Peralta, Barrio El Camal, Quito, Ecuador

*C* +593 2 265 4260

✆ contact@cenitecuador.org or volunteer-office@cenitecuador.org

▣ www.cenitecuador.org

**PROGRAMME DESCRIPTION:** CENIT relies heavily on volunteers from all over the world to help them achieve their aim to allow families to send their children to school rather than have them working on the streets. Volunteers work in projects such as street outreach, English classes, the medical clinic, dental programme, literacy classes, art and jewellery-making workshops and drop-in tutoring centres, mainly in south Quito.

**NUMBER OF PLACEMENTS:** 40–60, usually for short periods, although longer-term volunteers are preferred as they can take on more responsibilities at the project.

**DURATION AND TIME OF PLACEMENTS:** Minimum 2 months. Placement depends on the amount of time committed and level of Spanish.

**PREREQUISITES:** All ages. Basic knowledge of Spanish required. Volunteers should be outgoing and self-motivating and (for some projects) willing to work with children who have suffered severe neglect or abuse.

**COST:** One time administrative fee $75. Volunteers are responsible for finding (and funding) their own accommodation, though advice on homestays and hostels is available from CENIT; the latter will cost $80–$150 a month.

**CONTACT:** Marianne Pownall or Gladys Pérez, Volunteer Coordinators.

## CHALLENGES WORLDWIDE

54 Manor Place, Edinburgh, EH3 7EH

📞 0845 2000 342

📧 info@challengesworldwide.com

🖥 www.challengesworldwide.com

An award-winning international development charity that recruits volunteers with professional training and experience only.

## CHILE INSIDE LTDA/SOUTH AMERICA INSIDE

Román Díaz 205 Of. 405, Providencia, Santiago, Chile

📞 +56 2 235 7170

📞 +56 2 235 7184

📧 info@southamerica-inside.com

🖥 www.southamerica-inside.com

**PROGRAMME DESCRIPTION:** Volunteering placements, working holidays and language courses throughout Latin America.

**NUMBER OF PLACEMENTS PER YEAR:** 200–300.

**DESTINATIONS:** Throughout Latin America.

**PREREQUISITES:** Minimum age 18. All nationalities accepted.

**DURATION AND TIME OF PLACEMENTS:** Programmes last between 2 weeks and 6+ months.

**SELECTION PROCEDURES AND ORIENTATION:** No special selection criteria. Candidates need to send CV and registration form 3–10 weeks in advance.

**COST:** Programme cost depends on each programme and the length of stay, from about $200 for 2 weeks volunteer work or language course.

**ACCOMMODATION:** Host family, volunteer house.

**CONTACT:** Marion Ruhland, Founder and Executive Director.

## CONCORDIA

19 North Street, Portslade, Brighton, Sussex BN41 1DH

📞 01273 422218

📧 info@concordiavolunteers.org.uk

🖥 www.concordiavolunteers.org.uk

Concordia is a small not-for-profit education charity (no. 305991) committed to international youth exchange since 1943, whose aims are to bring people together from different countries to move towards the common goal of breaking down cultural stereotypes and promoting greater international understanding and peace.

**PROGRAMME DESCRIPTION:** Programme of short-term international volunteer projects in more than 60 countries. Projects range from nature conservation, renovation, construction and archaeology to social work including working with adults and children with learning or physical disabilities, children's playschemes, youth work and teaching.

**DESTINATIONS:** Western, Central and Eastern Europe, Russia, Japan, South Korea, Africa, the Middle East, South East Asia, India and North, Central and South America.

**PREREQUISITES:** Aged 18+ and resident in the UK. A selection of projects is available for teenagers aged 16 and 17. No experience or specific skills needed though motivation is essential. For projects in Asia, Latin America and Africa volunteers must attend a preparation weekend in Brighton; dates are set in February, June, July and October, and the participation fee is from £30.

**DURATION AND TIME OF PLACEMENTS:** 2–4 weeks, mainly between June and September with a smaller winter/spring programme. Some longer term placements for 3–12 months available.

**COST:** Volunteers pay a registration fee of £180 and fund their own travel and insurance. Board and accommodation are free of charge for projects in Europe, North America, Japan and South Korea. For projects in Latin America, Asia, Middle East and Africa, volunteers pay a fee on arrival of approx. £150 that covers food and accommodation, as well as funding the programme in the country.

**CONTACT:** Francesco Bonini, International Volunteer Co-ordinator.

## CROSS-CULTURAL SOLUTIONS

UK Office: Tower Point 44, North Road, Brighton
BN1 1YR

📞 0845 458 2781/2

✉ infouk@crossculturalsolutions.org

💻 www.crossculturalsolutions.org

See website for US address

A not-for-profit international volunteer organisation founded in 1995 and a registered charity in the UK (Number 1106741).

**PROGRAMME DESCRIPTION:** Opportunity for participants to work side-by-side with local people, on community-led initiatives. Volunteer programmes are designed to combine hands-on service and cultural exchange with the aim of fostering cultural understanding.

**DESTINATIONS:** Latin America, Africa, Asia and Eastern Europe.

**NUMBER OF PLACEMENTS PER YEAR:** 4,000+.

**PREREQUISITES:** No language or specialist skills are necessary. All nationalities welcome. No upper age limit.

**DURATION AND TIME OF PLACEMENTS:** 1–12 weeks. Start dates are offered all year round.

**COST:** Programme fees start at £960 for 1 week. Fees cover the cost of lodging, meals, bottled water and ground transport, plus individual attention and guidance from an experienced programme manager, coordination of the placement, cultural and learning activities, a 24-hour emergency hotline, travel, medical insurance and more. Airfares not included.

## DEVELOPMENT IN ACTION

78 York Street, London W1H 1DP

📞 07813 395957

✉ info@developmentinaction.org

💻 www.developmentinaction.org

Formerly Student Action India.

**PROGRAMME DESCRIPTION:** Arrange voluntary attachments to various locally based development NGOs in India. Partner organisations require volunteers to work in a wide variety of areas: from non-formal education, working with vulnerable children, or deaf and blind children, to fieldwork and research, working on solar energy projects, and administrative and office work.

**DESTINATIONS:** India, with projects in the Mumbai area (rural placements), Pune, Indore, Bhopal and Pondicherry.

**PREREQUISITES:** Energy and enthusiasm, a commitment to volunteering and an interest in grassroots development. All ages welcome.

**DURATION AND TIME OF PLACEMENTS:** 2-month summer placements (July-August) or year-out 5-month placements (September-February).

**SELECTION PROCEDURES AND ORIENTATION:** University recruitment talks/careers fairs take place October to March (see website). Application deadlines around the end of January and March; interviews held in February and April. Pre-departure training over one weekend plus orientation on arrival. Sessions led by recently returned volunteers, and include some basic Hindi language training.

**COST:** £690 for summer; £1,290 for 5 months (covers placement, training, support and accommodation). Flights, insurance, visa and subsistence costs are extra.

**CONTACT:** Kate Jeffery, UK Co-ordinator.

## THE DODWELL TRUST

16 Lanark Mansions, Pennard Road, London
W12 8DT

📞 020 8740 6302

✉ dodwell@madagascar.freeserve.co.uk

💻 www.dodwell-trust.org

**PROGRAMME DESCRIPTION:** Hands-on experience in English teaching, working with children, French-language conversation tuition, conservation, research or zoology (depending on time of year).

**DESTINATIONS:** Madagascar.

**NUMBER OF PLACEMENTS PER YEAR:** 60–70.

**DURATION AND TIME OF PLACEMENTS:** 3 weeks to 8 months. Flexible timing.

**PREREQUISITES:** No skills required. All nationalities welcome provided English is spoken and programme open to gap year students and career breakers. Placements matched with volunteers' skills and interests where possible for example local radio and TV, French practice, IT computer literacy, tennis, choir, conservation and animal studies at zoo.

**SELECTION PROCEDURES AND ORIENTATION:** Interviews not essential, though frequent optional meetings and briefings are held in London. Two-day training and orientation course on arrival in Madagascar at placement. Volunteers normally placed in pairs.

**COST:** In-country placement costs from £670 for 3 weeks, £1,340 for 12 weeks. Self-contained accommodation with cooking facilities provided, in quaint small towns in highlands, rainforest, or seaside. Volunteers usually placed in pairs. Volunteers are responsible for obtaining their own visas and health insurance.

**CONTACT:** Christina Dodwell, Head of Projects.

## DRAGONFLY

1719 Soi 13, Mookamontri, A. Muang, Nakhon Ratchasima 30000, Thailand

+66 4428 1073

martin@thai-dragonfly.com

www.thai-dragonfly.com

**PROGRAMME DESCRIPTION:** Volunteer work with wildlife, English teaching, football coaching, building, and orphanage care work projects.

**DESTINATIONS:** Thailand.

**NUMBER OF PLACEMENTS PER YEAR:** 150.

**PREREQUISITES:** Applicants should be fluent in English. Coaching project requires coaching certification. For all other projects, no experience is necessary as training is provided.

**DURATION AND TIME OF PLACEMENTS:** 2–52 weeks in length. Hours vary with placement type. Volunteers usually work 5–6 days and 20–40 hours each week.

**SELECTION PROCEDURES AND ORIENTATION:** Online applications accepted.

**OTHER SERVICES:** Visa assistance, airport pick-ups, online Thai lessons, language and culture training, and project orientation are provided for all placements. Different TEFL training courses are available for those without prior teaching experience, from 3-day intensive, to 4-week or online for varying prices.

**COST:** Fees vary with project type from £350 (teaching) to £765 (wildlife) for a 4-week placement. Volunteers pay an extra £35 a week for longer placements. Homestay or on-site accommodation is provided for all placements, and meals are also provided for all but the gibbon rehabilitation project. Long TEFL training course plus placement fee is £1,150.

**CONTACT:** Martin Walsh, Project Director.

## EARTHWATCH INSTITUTE (EUROPE)

Mayfield House, 265 Banbury Road, Oxford OX2 7HT

01865 318831

info@earthwatch.org.uk

www.earthwatch.org/europe

Earthwatch is an international environmental charity that engages people worldwide in scientific field research and education to promote the understanding and action necessary for a sustainable environment.

**PROGRAMME DESCRIPTION:** Earthwatch currently supports more than 50 research projects in the UK, Europe and beyond, addressing important environmental issues from climate change to oceans. UK projects include whale and dolphin surveys in Scotland and an archaeological project in the north of England. International projects range from turtle conservation in Costa Rica to climate change studies at the Arctic's edge. (Earthwatch also offers internships in its Oxford office, see *Work Experience* chapter.)

**DESTINATIONS:** Volunteer field assistants needed throughout the UK and worldwide.

**DURATION AND TIME OF PLACEMENTS:** Projects last around 2 weeks and run throughout the year. In 2010 some shorter duration teams will be available on selected projects.

**SELECTION PROCEDURES:** No previous experience necessary. The standard minimum age is 18 years, unless participating in a family team and teen-only team. Family teams have a minimum age of 10 and teen teams are exclusively for 16–17 year olds. There is no maximum age limit.

**COST:** The cost of joining an expedition ranges from £475 to £2,075 (excluding travel to the location).

## ECOLOGIA YOUTH TRUST

The Park, Forres, Moray, Scotland IV36 3TD
📞 01309 690995
📧 info@ecologia.org.uk
🖥 www.ecologia.org.uk

The trust promotes creative change in Russia through youth, ecology and education.

**PROGRAMME DESCRIPTION:** Volunteer programme ideal for gap year students at the Kitezh Children's Community for orphans in western Russia. (See chapter on Russia for first-hand account.)

**DESTINATIONS:** Kaluga, Russia.

**NUMBER OF PLACEMENTS PER YEAR:** 16.

**PREREQUISITES:** Minimum age 18; most are 18–35. No specific skills needed though any of the following would be useful: some knowledge of Russian, TEFL, experience working with children (sports, arts and crafts, music, drama), building, cooking and gardening. An interest in children and a willingness to participate fully in the life of the community are essential.

**DURATION AND TIME OF PLACEMENTS:** 2–3 months.

**SELECTION PROCEDURES AND ORIENTATION:** Introductory questionnaire required to apply. Police check in country of residence required. Extensive preparatory materials are sent including feedback from previous volunteers. Informal orientation given on arrival and ongoing support including email contact with Ecologia Trust and weekly meeting for volunteers.

**COST:** 2 months costs £1,320, 3 months £1,450 plus consular visa fee, travel insurance and airfare (from £280 depending on time of year).

**CONTACT:** Liza Hollingshead, Director.

## ECOTEER

23 Bearsdown Close, Plymouth PL6 5TX
📞 01752 426285
📧 contact@ecoteer.com
🖥 www.ecoteer.com

Ecoteer is a non-profit organisation.

**PROGRAMME DESCRIPTION:** Ecoteer is a collection of around 150 projects worldwide that need volunteers and are willing to provide food and accommodation at no, or at little, cost. Ecoteer provides contact information to members so they can organise their placement directly with the projects. Teaching English projects are among the most common.

**DESTINATIONS:** Worldwide.

**NUMBER OF PLACEMENTS:** 100.

**PREREQUISITES:** Varies among projects. Most of the projects are remote so require volunteers to be tolerant with a willingness to participate.

**DURATION AND TIME OF PLACEMENTS:** Minimum 1 month; no maximum.

**COST:** Membership is £20 per year.

**CONTACT:** Daniel Quilter, Owner.

## EUROPEAN VOLUNTARY SERVICE (EVS)

Youth in Action, British Council, 10 Spring Gardens, London SW1A 2BN
📞 020 7389 4030
📧 action2.enquiries@britishcouncil.org
🖥 www.britishcouncil.org/connectyouth-programmes-evs.htm

**PROGRAMME DESCRIPTION:** EVS gives young people aged 18–30 the opportunity to spend time in a European country (including Eastern Europe) as full-time volunteers on a social project, e.g. working with children with special needs. Volunteers do not have to pay for their placement. Further details in the 'Directory of Specialist Gap Year Programmes'.

## EXPERIENCE MEXICO

12 Salisbury Terrace, Armley, Leeds LS12 7AY
📞 07825 339422
📧 info@experiencemexico.co.uk
🖥 www.experiencemexico.co.uk

Non-profit organisation arranging volunteer placements in Mexico.

**PROGRAMME DESCRIPTION:** Volunteer placements and/or Spanish course in Mexico. Choice of project might include turtle protection, teaching, deer reserve, Huichol village (Huichol are an indigenous ethnic group), an aviary or nature reserve islands.

**DESTINATIONS:** On or near the Pacific coast of Mexico, north of Puerto Vallarta.

**NUMBER OF PLACEMENTS:** 16 at any one time.

**PREREQUISITES:** Preferred minimum age 18; most volunteers are aged 18–25, but all ages welcome.

**DURATION AND TIME OF PLACEMENTS:** 3-month commitment preferred, but all applications considered. 1–2 week options available.

**SELECTION PROCEDURES AND ORIENTATION:** All participants meet with a member of the volunteer team prior to final acceptance onto the projects.

**COST:** All-inclusive fee includes flight, travel insurance, food and accommodation (with host family or shared flat) and full project support. Tailored quotes provided via website.

**CONTACT:** Rachel Vokes, UK Director.

---

### FUNDACION JATUN SACHA

Eugenio de Santillán N34 248 y Maurián, Casilla 17 12 867, Quito, Ecuador

℃ +593 2 432240

℃ +593 2 432246

🖱 volunteer@jatunsacha.org

🖾 www.jatunsacha.org

Jatun Sacha Biological Station is a 2,000 hectare tropical rainforest reserve. All reserves protect endangered ecosystems critical to Ecuador, located in all four regions of the country.

**PROGRAMME DESCRIPTION:** Volunteers and interns participate in research, education, community service, station maintenance, plant conservation and agroforestry.

**DESTINATIONS:** Amazonian Ecuador and the Galagapos.

**NUMBER OF PLACEMENTS PER YEAR:** 800 on different projects.

**PREREQUISITES:** Minimum age 16 (with parental authorisation); average 23.

**DURATION AND TIME OF PLACEMENTS:** Minimum 15 days at any reserve, though the majority stay for 1 month, and some stay 3, 6 or 12 months.

**COST:** $47 or $67 application fee plus reserve fees (including lodging and meals) of $475 for the first month $380 afterwards; some reserves are more expensive; special offers included on website.

**CONTACT:** Santiago Paz y Miño, Volunteer Programme Coordinator.

---

### GLOBALTEER

Globalteer House, TheaChamrat Road, Wat Bo Village, Salakamroeuk Commune, Siem Reap, Cambodia

℃ +855 63761802

🖱 volunteer.camkids@globalteer.org

🖾 www.globalteer.org

**PROGRAMME DESCRIPTION:** Globalteer provides financial support and volunteers to teach and assist in the daily running of their partner in-country projects, including 3 in Siem Reap to assist 800 underprivileged Khmer children, a project in Mondulkiri, Cambodia that assist the Bunong, the indigenous tribal people. Also projects with orphaned and street children in Peru and Colombia, and maltreated elephants in Thailand and Cambodia.

**PREREQUISITES:** Minimum age 18. Should speak English as a first language.

**DURATION AND TIME OF PLACEMENTS:** 1 week to 3 months.

**SELECTION PROCEDURES AND ORIENTATION:** Applications should be sent at least 2 months in advance. Each project has a native-speaking manager who works alongside local staff and the volunteer coordinator.

**COST:** Each project asks for a donation for the duration that the volunteer attends, which helps to fund the project. Donations (see website) cover accommodation and in some cases meals, airport pick up, in-country support and administration costs.

**CONTACT:** Trixie O'Sullivan, Office Administrator.

---

## GLOBAL VOLUNTEER NETWORK

PO Box 30–968, Lower Hutt 5040, Wellington,
New Zealand

ⓒ +64 4 920 1451

✉ info@volunteer.org.nz

🖥 www.volunteer.org.nz

**PROGRAMME DESCRIPTION:** Volunteers recruited for a variety of educational, environmental and community aid programmes in many countries. Projects include teaching (English and other subjects), working with orphans, environmental/conservation work, animal welfare, health/medical, maintenance/construction and cultural homestays. Fundraising treks to Everest, Kilimanjaro, and Machu Picchu also arranged.

**DESTINATIONS:** Cambodia, China, Costa Rica, Ecuador, Ethiopia, Ghana, Honduras, India, Kenya, Nepal, New Zealand, Panama, Peru, Philippines, Romania, Rwanda, South Africa, Thailand, Uganda, USA, and Vietnam.

**DURATION AND TIME OF PLACEMENTS:** 1 week to 6+ months depending on the placement. Applications accepted year round.

**PREREQUISITES:** Minimum age 18 (average 19–23). No special skills or qualifications needed in most cases. All nationalities placed, although projects in China accept only Australians, Canadians, Europeans, Irish, British, American and New Zealanders.

**COST:** US$350 application fee covers personal staff support, programme guide, fundraising guide and software, online journal, online video 'Preparing for your trip', and opportunities for discounts on airfares. Programme fees vary according to in-country costs and range from US$597 to US$1,297 per month which covers accommodation, meals, orientation, transport, supervision, and an administrative charge (with some variation between programmes).

**CONTACT:** Erin Cassidy, CEO.

## GLOBALXCHANGE PROGRAMME

c/o VSO, 317 Putney Bridge Road, London
SW15 2PN

ⓒ 020 8780 7500

✉ Enquiry@globalxchange.org.uk

🖥 www.vso.org.uk/globalxchange

**PROGRAMME DESCRIPTION:** Reciprocal youth exchange programme whereby volunteers from the UK (or EEA nationals who live in the UK) spend 3 months working abroad and 3 months in UK hosting partner volunteers.

**DESTINATIONS:** Indonesia, Nigeria, India and Kazakhstan, with more recent addition of Pakistan, Malawi, Kenya, Philippines, Mongolia and South Africa.

**DURATION AND TIME OF PLACEMENTS:** 6 months total.

**PREREQUISITES:** Ages 18–25.

**COST:** £600. All other expenses covered by programme.

## GO DIFFERENTLY

Flat 1, The White House, 24 Third Avenue,
Hove BN3 2PD

ⓒ 01273 451372

✉ info@godifferently.com

🖥 www.godifferently.com

**PROGRAMME DESCRIPTION:** Several volunteering programmes throughout Thailand including working with elephants, *langurs* (monkeys), teaching English and providing assistance with various local village projects (e.g. tsunami recovery, supporting local craft workshops etc). Participants at the elephant project learn to ride and care for elephants and about the traditional life of the mahouts. Teaching projects involve teaching English to village children while living with a family and helping with household and farm duties. Also 'voluntourism' tours lasting 2 weeks which offer a combination of short-term volunteering together with some adventure and exploration.

**NUMBER OF PLACEMENTS PER YEAR:** 200–300.

**DESTINATIONS:** Elephant Project is in Pattaya (southern Thailand), while teaching takes place among Karen tribal people in Um-Phang (in mountainous Tak province) or in Andaman villages in southern Thailand.

**PREREQUISITES:** Volunteers should be willing to respect Thai culture (guidance will be given), be open-minded and have a sociable attitude towards the local people. All ages are welcome.

**DURATION AND TIME OF PLACEMENTS:** 1–4 weeks (elephants/langurs), 1 week to 6+ months (teaching), 2 weeks voluntourism tours.

**SELECTION PROCEDURES AND ORIENTATION:** Visits can normally be arranged at short notice.

**COST:** Average cost for 2 weeks including accommodation and meals but excluding flights is £700 per person which includes homestay accommodation. Part of fees supports sustainable tourism in the villages.

**CONTACT:** Nikki Bond, Director.

## GREENPEACE

Canonbury Villas, London N1 2PN

© 020 7865 8100

✆ info@uk.greenpeace.org

🖳 www.greenpeace.org.uk

🖳 www.greenpeace.org/international/about/
  worldwide

Greenpeace has offices around the world and volunteer participation is sometimes welcomed locally. Greenpeace UK regrets that it is unable to offer internships or work experience, nor does it offer sponsorship. Voluntary input is occasionally needed at London office and Greenpeace has groups of volunteers around the UK.

## HANDS FOR HELP NEPAL

Baluwatar Kusum Galli, Kathmandu, Nepal

© +977 98510 517 36

© +977 1444 0652

✆ hforh@wlink.com.np

🖳 www.handsforhelp.org.np

**PROGRAMME DESCRIPTION:** Teaching in schools, orphanage assistant, environmental and conservation, health and first aid, community building and various internship programmes.

**NUMBER OF PLACEMENTS PER YEAR:** 300.

**PREREQUISITES:** All nationalities welcome. Most volunteers are aged 19–28. Applicants must have at least high school education and ability to communicate in English.

**DURATION AND TIME OF PLACEMENTS:** 1 week to 5 months, though average is 2 months. Applications

should be sent at least a month in advance for start dates throughout the year.

**SELECTION PROCEDURES AND ORIENTATION:** Orientation provided plus training lasting from 1 to 7 days covering cultural adjustment, personal safety, health, Nepali language, project description and travel information.

**COST:** €400 for first month; €180 for subsequent months, including host family accommodation.

**CONTACT:** Badri Raj, Programme Director.

## ICEYOM/CAMEROON VISION TRUST/ SWEET AFRICA FOUNDATION

International Centre for Education Youth Orientation and Mobilisation, c/o Cameroon Vision Trust, PO Box 1075, Limbe, South West Province, Republic of Cameroon

© +237 74190403

© +237 99580292

✆ sweetafrica09@gmail.com

✆ iceyom@yahoo.co.uk

🖳 www.womenearthalliance.org

Several charities under single leadership, including one in Liberia: Society for Women Empowerment Education and Training (SWEET), c/o Action Against Climate Change (AACC), 23 MacDonald Street, Monrovia, Liberia (+231 6242236).

**PROGRAMME DESCRIPTION:** Placements for all kinds of voluntary service including hospitality, conservation, climate change, sports, community service and fundraising.

**NUMBER OF VOLUNTEERS PER YEAR:** 100.

**DESTINATIONS:** Liberia, Cameroon, Ghana, Nigeria, Malawi, Tanzania, Kenya, Uganda, Republic of Congo, Equatorial Guinea, Rwanda, and more.

**PREREQUISITES:** Minimum GCSEs or high school graduation. Gap year students welcome.

**DURATION AND TIME OF PLACEMENTS:** Minimum 6 months, maximum 2 years with option to extend.

**SELECTION PROCEDURES AND ORIENTATION:** Applications accepted year round.

**COST:** £350/$500/€400. Projects usually provide accommodation, holiday schemes, in-country transport and some allowance depending on placement.

**CONTACT:** Rosemary Olive Mbone Enie, Executive Director (Cameroon Vision Trust) & ICEYOM Co-ordinator/WICO Africa President and SWEET Africa Foundation President.

## ICYE-UK: INTER-CULTURAL YOUTH EXCHANGE UK

Latin American House, Kingsgate Place, London NW6 4TA

℡ 020 7681 0983

✉ info@icye.org.uk

🖥 www.icye.org.uk

ICYE-UK is a non profit-making charity that offers international exchange and volunteering opportunities in many countries around the world.

**PROGRAMME DESCRIPTION:** ICYE-UK works with three main volunteering programmes: long-term (6–12 months) or short-term (3–12 weeks) in Africa, Latin America and Asia, and the European Voluntary Service (EVS) scheme (see main entry in 'Directory of Specialist Gap Year Programmes'). On the long-term programme, volunteers spend 6 or 12 months abroad and undertake voluntary work placements with grassroots organisations, for example working with street children, assisting projects supporting people with HIV/AIDS or working on an ecological project. The emphasis of the programme is on both volunteering and cultural interaction. The short-term programme is similar but not reciprocal and lasts 3–12 weeks.

**DESTINATIONS:** Africa (Ghana, Kenya, Morocco, Mozambique, Nigeria, Uganda); Asia (India, Japan, Nepal, South Korea, Taiwan, Thailand); Latin America (Bolivia, Brazil, Colombia, Costa Rica, Ecuador, Honduras, Mexico) and throughout Europe.

**NUMBER OF PLACEMENTS PER YEAR:** Approximately 100.

**PREREQUISITES:** For the long-term programme, applicants must be aged 18–30 (upper limit may be flexible). For the European programme 18–30. The short-term programme is open to all ages.

**DURATION AND TIME OF PLACEMENTS:** 12- and 6-month placements start in August or January. Short-term opportunities are available all year round.

**SELECTION PROCEDURES AND ORIENTATION:** Information and recruitment days are held every month to allow prospective volunteers the chance to learn about the volunteering opportunities and the organisation. Selection is based on an interview which focuses on matching the needs of the volunteer with the opportunities on offer. The long-term programme offers pre-departure training (3 days) and orientation-on-arrival training in country (8–10 days), which includes a 30-hour language course. For the short-term programme a training day is held prior to departure and induction is held on arrival (depending on the project).

**COST:** Long-term placements cost approximately £4,495 for 12 months (covering flights, visas, insurance, board and lodging for the year, work placement and pocket money) and approximately £3,795 for 6 months. Discounts are available if volunteers gift aid the costs. The EVS programme is fully funded by the EU for European citizens and costs for the short-term programme vary according to duration and country (see website for up-to-date information).

**CONTACT:** Catherine Udal, Office Administrator.

## INSPIRE VOLUNTEERING

28 Chatsworth Drive, Market Harborough, Leicestershire LE16 8BS

℡ 07773 874545

✉ sales@inspirekenya.com

🖥 www.inspirevolunteering.com

**PROGRAMME DESCRIPTION:** Volunteer programmes in Kenya (children's homes, teaching in schools, medical projects and internships in journalism, radio and law); and in Sri Lanka (children's homes, teaching monks, hospital work, and conservation projects with turtles and elephants).

**NUMBER OF PLACEMENTS PER YEAR:** 60+.

**DESTINATIONS:** Kenya, Sri Lanka.

**PREREQUISITES:** Minimum age 17. Volunteers are from all walks of life; should be keen, flexible people who like to help others.

**DURATION AND TIME OF PLACEMENTS:** 2 weeks to 3+ months.

**SELECTION PROCEDURES AND ORIENTATION:** Application deadline 3 weeks before departure.

**COST:** From £699. Accommodation with host family or in hotel.

**CONTACT:** Mathew Muckle, Manager.

## INTERNATIONAL SOCIETY FOR ECOLOGY AND CULTURE

*UK office:* ISEC, Foxhole, Dartington, Devon TQ9 6EB

infoUK@isec.org.uk

01803 868651

*US HQ:* PO Box 9475, Berkeley, CA 94709, USA

+1 510 548 4915

www.isec.org.uk

**PROGRAMME DESCRIPTION:** 'Learning from Ladakh' allows volunteers to understand the pressures on rural communities worldwide and ways to strengthen threatened cultures and economies. Participants live with a Ladakhi farming family, help with farm and household work and participate in educational workshops.

**DESTINATIONS:** Ladakh (200 miles and 2 days drive from Kargil in the politically unstable state of Jammu and Kashmir, India).

**PREREQUISITES:** Should be in good health to withstand the risks of living and working at high altitude. All nationalities accepted.

**DURATION AND TIME OF PLACEMENTS:** 1 month: July or August.

**SELECTION PROCEDURES AND ORIENTATION:** Programme is oversubscribed so early application recommended.

**COST:** £350/$600 for one month.

**CONTACT:** Lin Etherden, UK Programme Administrator; Victoria Clarke, US Programme Administrator.

## INVOLVEMENT VOLUNTEERS ASSOCIATION INC (IVI)

PO Box 218, Port Melbourne, Victoria 3207, Australia

+61 3 9646 9392

ivworldwide@volunteering.org.au

www.volunteering.org.au

Involvement Volunteers was established in 1988 with the original aim of making volunteering available to young people wanting to assist and learn from volunteer experiences.

**PROGRAMME DESCRIPTION:** IVI arranges individual volunteer placements worldwide lasting at least 2 weeks (up to 52). Projects are concerned with conservation, the environment, animal welfare, social and community service, medicine, education and childcare.

**DESTINATIONS:** Dozens of countries worldwide.

**PREREQUISITES:** Minimum age 18; minimum age 21 for some projects

**DURATION AND TIME OF PLACEMENTS:** 2–6 weeks with chance to arrange series of back-to-back placements. A series of one or more projects can be arranged lasting up to 1 year for a multicultural round-the-world experience.

**COST:** The One-Placement Package cost is A$1,200; two-placement package is A$2,070 and so on.

## IONIAN SEA RESEARCH CENTRE

Fiskardo's Nautical and Environmental Club, 28084 Fiskardo, Kephalonia, Greece

+30 26740 41182

info@fnec.gr

www.fnec.gr

FNEC is a non-profit-making environmental NGO which runs the Northern Kephalonia Cetacean Observation Project.

**PROGRAMME DESCRIPTION:** Volunteers monitor cetacean populations by observing from the coast and from boats, by collecting opportunistic sightings from visitors, promoting awareness of cetaceans among visitors and locals, and carrying out underwater research on seahorses in collaboration with the National Aquarium of Plymouth.

**NUMBER OF PLACEMENTS PER YEAR:** 50.

**DESTINATIONS:** Kephalonia, Ionian Islands, Greece.

**PREREQUISITES:** All ages. No training needed. Horse patrols organised for people with extensive riding experience. Participants can undertake PADI scuba diving instruction.

**DURATION AND TIME OF PLACEMENTS:** 3-week placements; more than one period can be applied for (see website www.fnec.gr/dolphin/availab.htm).

**SELECTION PROCEDURES AND ORIENTATION:** Applications can be made online; CVs can be sent by email to dolphins@fnec.gr.

**COST:** €570 for each 3-week period, excluding flights and insurance. Cost can include PADI Scuba Diving instruction.

**CONTACT:** Andreas Petalas, Volunteer Co-ordinator.

---

### KIBBUTZ PROGRAM CENTER

Volunteer Department, 6 Frishman Street, Corner of Hayarkon Street, Tel Aviv 61030, Israel

📞 +972 3 524 6154/6

📧 kpc@volunteer.co.il

🖥 www.kibbutz.org.il/volunteers

The office is open Sunday to Thursday 8am–2pm. The buses needed to reach the office are: number 475 from the airport, 10 from the railway station and 4 from the Central Bus Station.

**PROGRAMME DESCRIPTION:** Placements on 250 kibbutzim throughout Israel.

**DESTINATIONS:** Throughout Israel. Most kibbutzim are situated in the fertile lands of northern and southern Israel. The north can be cold and rainy in winter, whereas the Jordan Rift Valley can be one of the hottest and driest places in the world.

**PREREQUISITES:** As of October 2009, age range accepted is 20–35. Must be free to stay for a minimum of 10 weeks.

**DURATION AND TIME OF PLACEMENTS:** $2\frac{1}{2}$–6 months.

**SELECTION PROCEDURES AND ORIENTATION:** Volunteers can be assigned to a kibbutz after arrival in Israel. They must take their passport, medical certificate, airline ticket out of Israel, proof of funds ($250),

two passport photos and registration fee to the KPC. The KPC sells specialised health insurance for about $90 which provides cover for up to 12 months.

**COST:** $90 registration fee covers volunteers for 12 months, plus returnable deposit of $50–$100.

---

### KIYA SURVIVORS

Suite 42, 41–43 Portland Road, Hove, East Sussex BN3 2DG

📞 01273 721092

📧 info@kiyasurvivors.org

🖥 www.kiyasurvivors.org

**PROGRAMME DESCRIPTION:** Volunteers work as assistant teachers/therapists with special needs children in Peru. They help to organise art, drama, sports, music and dance workshops, alongside professionals.

**NUMBER OF PLACEMENTS PER YEAR:** 40.

**DESTINATIONS:** 2 projects in Peru: Mama Cocha children's home and Early Bird Centre in Los Organos, Piura or The Rainbow Centre in Urubamba, Cusco.

**PREREQUISITES:** No experience needed although Spanish helps as does any experience of working with children or adults with learning disabilities. Should be enthusiastic, caring individuals who are able to work alone or as a team using their own initiative.

**DURATION AND TIME OF PLACEMENTS:** 2, 3, 4 or 6 month placements.

**SELECTION PROCEDURES AND ORIENTATION:** UK volunteers participate in obligatory training in UK and all programmes include a short training programme. Spanish courses also available.

**COST:** £800–£3,150.

**CONTACT:** Andrew Murphy, Volunteer Programme Co-ordinator (andrew@kiyasurvivors.org).

---

### LANGUAGECORPS

53 Whispering Way, Stow, MA 011775, USA

📞 +1 978 562 2100

📧 info@languagecorps.com;
jan.patton@languagecorps.com

🖥 www.languagecorps.com;
www.languagecorps.org

**PROGRAMME DESCRIPTION:** English teaching programmes in various countries, all of which include an intensive 4-week TESOL training and certification course, pre-departure support, and assistance finding a paid teaching position.

**NUMBER OF PLACEMENTS PER YEAR:** 300–400.

**DESTINATIONS:** Latin America, Asia, and Europe.

**PREREQUISITES:** Minimum age 19. Average age 25. Some countries require a college degree in addition to the TESOL certification. If someone between school and university demonstrates a solid level of maturity and independence, they may qualify. Applicants must be native English speakers, or have native level English speaking skills.

**DURATION AND TIME OF PLACEMENTS:** 6–12 months in most cases. Short-term volunteer programme available in Thailand, Vietnam, and Cambodia.

**SELECTION PROCEDURES AND ORIENTATION:** Applications welcomed 2–6 months in advance. A phone interview is required for some programmes. Some programmes include local language and cultural training, medical insurance, accommodation, excursions and other support services.

**COST:** $1,500–$3,995.

**CONTACT:** Jan Patton, Admissions Director.

---

## OTRA COSA NETWORK

Las Camelias 431, Huanchaco Trujillo, Peru
*C* +51 44 461302
otracosavoluntario@gmail.com
www.otracosa.org

**PROGRAMME DESCRIPTION:** Examples of volunteer projects include teaching English to children in a shanty town school or environmental guides, working with children at a day centre, helping at an organic coffee and sugar farm, and many others.

**DESTINATIONS:** Most projects are in and around Huanchaco and Trujillo, but also some opportunities in northern Peru and as far south as Nazca.

**PREREQUISITES:** Knowledge of Spanish not essential; cheap lessons can be arranged.

**COST:** €75 for administration and housing arrangement fee.

**CONTACT:** Peter and Juany Murphy-Gerente.

---

## PEACE CHILD INDIA

No. 952, 18th A Main Road, B Cross, Ideal Homes Phase 1, Rajarajeshwari Nagar, Bangalore 560 098, India
*C* +91 80 28600463
*C* +91 98 86515711
india@peacechild.org
www.peacechildindia.org

Established in 2001, this is the Indian Field Office of the UK-based organisation Peace Child International.

**PROGRAMME DESCRIPTION:** Implements youth action programme 'Be the Change' in local schools in marginalised communities. Volunteers usually teach English and organise extracurricular projects. Also works with Government Home for street and working children, in collaboration with local NGO Arivu.

**NUMBER OF PLACEMENTS PER YEAR:** 100.

**DESTINATIONS:** In and around Bangalore, India.

**PREREQUISITES:** Minimum age 18. Must have initiative since interns are put in charge of a project, and expected to use their own skills and initiative.

**DURATION AND TIME OF PLACEMENTS:** Normally 1 month, but longer stays are welcomed.

**SELECTION PROCEDURES AND ORIENTATION:** Orientation held on arrival. Volunteers visit various projects before choosing one.

**COST:** £350/$560 per month and £300/$480 per month for stays of more than 3 months. Fee includes shared accommodation with resident housemother who cooks and takes care of maintenance. Internet access available.

**CONTACT:** Amaidhi Devaraj, Director.

---

## QUETZALTREKKERS

Casa Argentina, 12 Diagonal, 8–37, Zona 1, Quetzaltenango, Guatemala
*C* +502 7765 5895
info@quetzaltrekkers.com
www.quetzaltrekkers.com

Non-profit trekking company that relies on volunteer guides and uses trekkers' fees to assist free school and programme for local street children.

**PROGRAMME DESCRIPTION:** Volunteer guides recruit customers for treks, prepare food and equipment, maintain and clean equipment and guide treks. Volunteers also needed for street school and dormitory in Las Rosas.

**DESTINATIONS:** Quetzaltenango and environs in Guatemala plus programme in Nicaragua.

**NUMBER OF PLACEMENTS:** 60.

**PREREQUISITES:** Must know intermediate Spanish. Training given in any skills that are lacking.

**DURATION AND TIME OF PLACEMENTS:** Volunteer guides work at least 3 months. Volunteers working with children stay at least 3 months.

**COST:** Guides receive all expenses and food on treks, and discount on room in Casa Argentina. Rent charged to volunteers is 600 quetzals per month and food will cost a further 400 quetzals.

## REAL GAP EXPERIENCE

1 Meadow Road, Tunbridge Wells, Kent TN1 2YG

📞 01892 516164

📧 info@realgap.co.uk

🖥 www.realgap.co.uk

Leading Gap Year specialists, offering a comprehensive range of volunteering projects in dozens of countries. ATOL bonded with financial backing.

**PROGRAMME DESCRIPTION:** Wide range of volunteer and travel options in over 40 countries, including volunteering with wildlife, conservation, teaching, sports, expeditions, volunteering with children, communities and tailor-made gap years.

**DESTINATIONS:** see entry in 'Directory of Specialist Gap Year Programmes'.

**PREREQUISITES:** None, except as limited by visas. Some programmes require basic level of fitness.

**DURATION AND TIME OF PLACEMENTS:** 2 weeks to 2 years. Programmes available all year round and tailor-made gap year itineraries can be arranged.

**COST:** Varies with programme, prices start from £389 to £10,000+.

## SCORE INTERNATIONAL

3rd Floor, Burleigh House, 25 Barrack Street, Cape Town, South Africa

📞 +27 21 461 0466

📧 info@score.org.za

📧 info.nl@score.org.za

🖥 www.score.org.za

🖥 www.scorefoundation.nl (Dutch website)

In operation since 1991 implementing sports and community development programmes.

**PROGRAMME DESCRIPTION:** SCORE is a South African NGO that uses volunteers to teach physical education, and coach and train children, youth and adults in deprived communities in a variety of sports. Volunteers either live in a programme house or with a local family.

**DESTINATIONS:** Rural and urban locations throughout South Africa: Western Cape, Eastern Cape, Northern Cape, Mpumalanga Province, Limpopo Province and North-West. Some volunteers work in Namibia and Zambia as well.

**PREREQUISITES:** Minimum age 20 unless volunteer has specialist background. Volunteers should have skill, experience, enthusiasm, creativity and an ability to adjust to other cultures. Variety of nationalities accepted including British and North American.

**DURATION AND TIME OF PLACEMENTS:** Students: 6 or 12 months; graduates: 12 months. Starting in July or January.

**SELECTION PROCEDURES AND ORIENTATION:** Applications for January intake should be submitted by 15 September, and for July intake by 15 March.

**COST:** Fee of €2,500 for 6 months, €3,500 for 12 months, covers health insurance, room, board, transport within South Africa, orientation and back-up but not international airfares. Airfares are covered for EU citizens. Volunteers receive nominal monthly stipend.

**CONTACT:** Suzanne van Esser, Manager (SCORE NL) (stichting.score@planet.nl).

## SKIP (SUPPORTING KIDS IN PERU)

volunteering@skipperu.org

www.skipperu.org

**PROGRAMME DESCRIPTION:** Non-profit organisation running projects to help economically disadvantaged children in El Porvenir to realise their right to an education. Projects include English teaching, extracurricular tutoring and group activities for parents.

**DESTINATIONS:** El Porvenir, Trujillo, Peru

**PREREQUISITES:** Minimum age 18. SKIP can provide training suitable for volunteers who want to learn about working in an NGO. Volunteers must be comfortable working with and around children.

**DURATION AND TIME OF PLACEMENTS:** Minimum 1 month.

**SELECTION PROCEDURES AND ORIENTATION:** Rolling applications accepted year round. Specific vacancies are advertised on idealist.org. Telephone interviews held in some cases.

**COST:** $350 per month for the first two months, $250 for 3–5 months, $180 for 6–8 months and $125 for 9–12 months. Accommodation in the volunteer house (for up to 12 volunteers) is included but not food and travel. Volunteers may also stay with a local host family.

**CONTACT:** Liz Wilson, Volunteer Coordinator.

## SOFT POWER EDUCATION

PO Box 1493, Jinja, Uganda, East Africa.
*UK address* 55 Guildhall Street, Bury
St Edmunds, Suffolk IP33 1QF

+256 774 162541

volunteering@softpowereducation.com

www.softpowereducation.com

British registered non-religious charity to enhance the education facilities for hundreds of Ugandan children.

**PROGRAMME DESCRIPTION:** Primary school refurbishment programme, education programmes through the Amagezi Education Centre, conservation projects, pre-schools for orphans and special needs projects. Work involves assisting with building projects, painting classrooms, painting teaching aids in classrooms, assistant teaching at pre-schools, hosting art and sports workshops, etc.

**NUMBER OF PLACEMENTS PER YEAR:** About 100 independent volunteers and 150+ in student groups.

**PREREQUISITES:** Minimum age 18, no maximum. No qualifications needed. All nationalities accepted. All that is needed is a sense of humour, independence, creativity, initiative and a willingness to fundraise. Any experience or skill in building is a bonus.

**DURATION AND TIME OF PLACEMENTS:** 1 day to 12 months.

**SELECTION PROCEDURES AND ORIENTATION:** Arrival should be arranged at least a month in advance.

**COST:** Volunteers must cover their own living and travel expenses as well as a donation to the charity. Recommended amount is £75 a week.

**ACCOMMODATION:** Camping, dorms or living within the local community. Guest houses in Jinja are also an option, but they are located some distance from the network of schools which means longer travelling times to site.

**CONTACT:** Sharon Webb, Volunteer Manager.

## SUDAN VOLUNTEER PROGRAMME

34 Estelle Road, London NW3 2JY

020 7485 8619

david@svp-uk.com

www.svp-uk.com

**PROGRAMME DESCRIPTION:** SVP works with undergraduates and graduates who are native English speakers and who wish to teach English in Sudan. Teaching tends to be informal in style, with only 4–5 hours of contact a day. Volunteers can plan their own teaching schemes, such as arranging games, dramas, competitions and tests for assessing skills learned by the students.

**DESTINATIONS:** Sudan around Khartoum and also smaller towns in northern Sudan.

**PREREQUISITES:** Minimum age 20. TEFL certificate and knowledge of Arabic are helpful but not obligatory.

Volunteers must be in good health and be native English speakers. It is preferred that volunteers have already had experience of travelling in developing countries.

**DURATION AND TIME OF PLACEMENTS:** Minimum 7 months with start dates in September or early January.

**SELECTION PROCEDURES AND ORIENTATION:** Application forms must be completed and sent by email. Two referees are also required. Prior to departure, interviews, orientation and briefings take place. Volunteers are required to write a report of their experiences and to advise new volunteers.

**COST:** Volunteers must raise the cost of the airfare to Sudan (currently £425 for ticket valid for 12 months) plus travel costs to selection interviews and briefings plus £60 (towards the first 3 months insurance). Host institutions cover living expenses, accommodation and SVP covers insurance beyond the initial 3 months.

**CONTACT:** David Wolton.

---

### TEACHERS FOR VIETNAM
159 Piermont Avenue, Piermont NY 10968, USA
845 680 6560
info@teachersforvietnam.org
www.teachersforvietnam.org

**PROGRAMME DESCRIPTION:** Recruit teachers of ESL for university posts in Vietnam to further Vietnam's educational development by increasing fluency of spoken English and to build bridges between people in Vietnam and the West, particularly the USA.

**NUMBER OF PLACEMENTS PER YEAR:** 5.

**PREREQUISITES:** Must be university graduate so most volunteers are over 21. Some experience and/or training in TESL needed, plus eagerness to live and work in Vietnam.

**DURATION AND TIME OF PLACEMENTS:** Academic year September to June.

**SELECTION PROCEDURES AND ORIENTATION:** Deadline for applications is 1 April. Face-to-face interviews preferred but can be done by phone. In-country

orientation session provided, which covers cultural issues as well as practical matters for foreigners newly arrived in Vietnam.

**COST:** Application fee $40. Programme pays for airfare, health insurance and travel during Tet holiday. Host universities pay a cost-of-living salary and in most cases provide free housing, usually a room or suite in a campus guesthouse.

**CONTACT:** John Dippel, Executive Director.

---

### THAI-EXPERIENCE.ORG
1133/4 Kaewworrawut Road, Moo 1, Meaung District, Nongkhai 43000, Thailand
+66 8444 92022 (mobile)
www.Thai-Experience.org

**PROGRAMME DESCRIPTION:** Teaching English, computer skills or vocational skills to disadvantaged children and/or adults in Thailand. Maintaining computers.

**NUMBER OF PLACEMENTS PER YEAR:** 80.

**DESTINATIONS:** Mainly north-eastern Thailand (Isan province).

**PREREQUISITES:** Minimum age 18. Good command of English language. Computer trainers need computer skills, open mind and patience to deal with the different environment. No TEFL certificate needed as volunteers do not replace teachers but assist them, encouraging students to use their English language skills to speak, practise and motivate them to learn more.

**DURATION AND TIME OF PLACEMENTS:** 1 week to 1 year; typically 2–3 months.

**SELECTION PROCEDURES AND ORIENTATION:** Application can be made online. Volunteers can be placed at short notice but 2–3 months advance warning preferred.

**COST:** €350 for 1–2 weeks, €450 for 3 weeks, €500 for 1 month, €1,380 for 24 weeks. Fees include orientation, pre-arranged accommodation, travels within the project, cultural outings and support before and during the stay.

**CONTACT:** Sabine Lindemann, Project Manager.

## TWIN WORK AND VOLUNTEER ABROAD

67–71 Lewisham High Street, Lewisham,
London SE13 5JX

ⓒ 0800 804 8380

✉ workandvolunteer@twinuk.com

🖥 www.workandvolunteer.com

**PROGRAMME DESCRIPTION:** Volunteer programmes around the world providing assistance to orphans, disadvantaged children, elderly people and so on and working in healthcare, language assistance, animal conservation, community development projects, etc.

**DESTINATIONS:** China, India, Indonesia, Nepal, Thailand, Ghana, Namibia, South Africa, Uganda, Romania, Australia, New Zealand, Argentina, Bolivia, Costa Rica, Ecuador, Guatemala and Peru.

**PREREQUISITES:** Previous experience needed for some of the projects, e.g. basic knowledge of Spanish. Must be enthusiastic and eager to help people.

**DURATION AND TIME OF PLACEMENTS:** 2 weeks to 12 months.

**SELECTION PROCEDURES AND ORIENTATION:** Enrolment online. Processing time 1–3 months.

**COST:** Sample costs are £690/£890 for Volunteer Peru (for 2/3 months); £420 for Volunteer Costa Rica (for 2–12 months); £950 for Volunteer South Africa (8 weeks plus £100 per extra week), from £380 for Volunteer Ghana. Accommodation usually included.

**CONTACT:** Barry Johnson and Peter Talbolt.

Organisation for sharing Spanish language and Guatemalan culture run by a group of experienced Guatemalan Spanish teachers.

**PROGRAMME DESCRIPTION:** Voluntary placements in a day-care centre (for the children of single impoverished mothers), in a hospital, in a home for elderly people, rebuilding homes and (for longer stays) as assistants in schools.

**NUMBER OF PARTICIPANTS:** 100.

**DURATION OF COURSES:** Flexible from 1–2 weeks to many months.

**COST:** $25 weekly when not taking lessons, or none when volunteers take Spanish lessons, though volunteers pay for their accommodation and other expenses.

**ACCOMMODATION:** Homestays with full board (3 meals a day Monday to Saturday and 7 nights lodging) cost $70 a week when taking lessons and/or doing volunteer job or $95 when just visiting.

**CONTACT:** Juan Carlos Martinez, General Director.

Formerly Volunteers for English in Sri Lanka, VESL is a charity registered in the UK that sends volunteers to work on projects to Sri Lanka, India and across Asia.

**PROGRAMME DESCRIPTION:** Volunteers (and qualified teachers) are sent to run English language summer schools and for longer periods in remote communities.

**DESTINATIONS:** Sri Lanka mainly, also India and Thailand, with possibility of expanding to Surin province, Cambodia. Southern, Central and Uva provinces of Sri Lanka only, because it is too dangerous to work in VESL's projects in Jaffna, Trincomalee and Battacaloa. Also Andhra Pradesh in India and Chiang Rai Province, Thailand.

**NUMBER OF PLACEMENTS PER YEAR:** Up to 40.

**PREREQUISITES:** Minimum age 18, though most volunteers are older. Volunteers should be enthusiastic, motivated and up for a challenge. TEFL experience and some experience overseas are helpful but not a requirement.

**DURATION AND TIME OF PLACEMENTS:** 3+ months and also 4–6 week summer programmes in July and August.

**SELECTION PROCEDURES AND ORIENTATION:** Applications accepted throughout the year. All candidates are invited to information and selection days that take place throughout the UK.

**COST:** £900 for summer programme, £1,350 for 3 months, includes induction and training day, in-country travel, insurance, visas, food, accommodation and comprehensive back-up and support.

**CONTACT:** Tom Harrison, Programme Director.

## VET (VOLUNTEER ENGLISH TEACHERS) PROGRAM

No.78 Lane 1 Longyue Road, Yangshuo, Guilin, Guangxi, P.R. China 541900

📞 +86 773 8811420

✉️ vetchina.yangshuo@gmail.com

🖥️ www.vet-china.org

Licensed charity set up in 2004 by retired Canadian professor living in Yangshuo.

**PROGRAMME DESCRIPTION:** Volunteers help students in village schools improve their verbal English skills and give them an opportunity to meet foreigners, to improve their chances of getting out of poverty and finding employment in the tourist and service industry around Yangshuo.

**NUMBER OF PLACEMENTS:** VET works in 4–5 rural primary schools and one orphanage.

**PREREQUISITES:** Minimum age 18, no maximum. Anyone with a strong proficiency in English and an easily understood accent is acceptable. Previous work with children aged 9–12 is desirable. Volunteers should be imaginative and creative, energetic, motivated, patient, with the ability to work independently and as a member of a team.

**DURATION AND TIME OF PLACEMENTS:** 3 + months; shorter stays by arrangement.

**SELECTION PROCEDURES AND ORIENTATION:** Volunteers accepted throughout regular school year but not during exam or holiday periods; terms run September to mid-January and March to mid-June. Interviews are not required. All volunteers have a 2-day

orientation with a qualified teacher trainer and on-going support from the VET team.

**COST:** Volunteers must cover return airfare from the country of origin; a 3-month tourist visa (if a volunteer stays longer VET will assist with a visa extension), spending money.

**CONTACT:** Laurie Mackenzie (Founder/Director) or Jennifer Jiang (Assistant Director).

## VILLAGE AFRICA

126 Hambledon Road, Waterlooville, Hants. PO7 6XA

📞 01242 250 901

✉️ info@villageafrica.org.uk

🖥️ www.villageafrica.org.uk

The aim of the project is 'to alleviate poverty through health and education'.

**PROGRAMME DESCRIPTION:** Current initiatives are to provide volunteers to teach English, help with local building projects and to establish a fully equipped and staffed health post. In the primary school teaching programme volunteers work in local schools, improving speaking and listening skills and building the children's confidence to communicate.

**NUMBER OF PLACEMENTS PER YEAR:** 30.

**DESTINATIONS:** Yamba and Milingano, villages in the West Usambara Mountains of Tanzania.

**PREREQUISITES:** The charity is open to people bringing their own skills from administration to knitting.

**DURATION AND TIME OF PLACEMENTS:** 3 months for teaching (can be extended), from 2 weeks for other roles.

**SELECTION PROCEDURES AND ORIENTATION:** 1 month's notice is preferred but placements can be arranged at very short notice. Volunteers receive a telephone interview and references are required. Teachers must also have a CRB check. On arrival, volunteers receive orientation and training appropriate to their role including TEFL training for teachers.

**COST:** Volunteers fund themselves and pay a fee to cover their training, support and costs in-country, in addition to paying for flights, insurance and other costs.

Volunteers are encouraged to fundraise towards these costs and fundraising support is provided. Volunteers live together in simple houses in the village, with a short walk to work. A house girl is employed to fetch water, shop, cook and clean and a watchman is employed to oversee the houses at night.

**CONTACT:** Caroline Johnston (Director, Tanzania), Andrea Ward (UK Administrator).

## VILLAGE EDUCATION PROJECT (KILIMANJARO)

Mint Cottage, Prospect Road, Sevenoaks, Kent TN13 3UA

- 01732 743000
- 01732 459799
- project@kiliproject.org
- www.kiliproject.org

This organisation was set up in 1994 with an overall aim to improve the education of primary school children. The Tanzanian Central Ministry of Education is in full support of the work of the charity.

**PROGRAMME DESCRIPTION:** Volunteers live in the beauty of Marangu and teach basic English as a foreign language in primary schools in the area. Class sizes range between 17 and 40 and good textbooks and teaching aids are available. Extra periods are assigned where volunteers can play football or other sport with the children or undertake art/music/drama extra-curricular activities. School outings are arranged to a national park and to the coast.

**DESTINATIONS:** Marangu, Tanzania.

**NUMBER OF PLACEMENTS PER YEAR:** 6–8 UK students.

**PREREQUISITES:** Good spoken English and an outgoing personality are required. Art/sport/music skills are an advantage.

**DURATION AND TIME OF PLACEMENTS:** 6–9 months, starting in January.

**SELECTION PROCEDURES AND ORIENTATION:** On receipt of an application, an interview is arranged. Pre-departure training is given, including preparing for work,

using the textbooks and basic Swahili. A project leader in Tanzania meets the students and helps them settle in. Local staff are always on hand to support volunteers.

**COST:** £3,250 to be paid to the charity. Additional costs include living expenses, medical insurance and initial entry visas (currently £38).

**CONTACT:** Katy Allen, Trustee and Director.

## VOLUNTEER LATIN AMERICA

BM Volunteer Latin America, London WC1N 3XX

- 020 7193 9163
- info@volunteerlatinamerica.com
- www.volunteerlatinamerica.com

**PROGRAMME DESCRIPTION:** Volunteer Latin America is an advisory service enabling clients to set up their own volunteer placement in environmental or humanitarian projects in Central and South America, and also to find Spanish language schools in the region. Volunteers are directed towards a range of environmental projects in Latin America ranging from building nature trails in the Amazon to monitoring big cats such as puma, as well as working with a diverse range of species and habitats. Other projects provide humanitarian assistance to disadvantaged communities by means of child welfare, community development, education and health programmes.

**NUMBER OF PLACEMENTS PER YEAR:** 1,000.

**DURATION AND TIME OF PLACEMENTS:** 1 week to 1 year.

**COST:** Some projects are free; others require a participation fee. Volunteer Latin America charges clients for its advisory service: £22.50 for a standard guide, £28.50 includes information on Spanish language courses.

**CONTACT:** Stephen Knight, Manager.

## VOLUNTEER NEPAL NATIONAL GROUP

Jhaukhel 4, Bhaktapur, Nepal

- +977 1 661 3724
- info@volnepal.np.org; volunteer_nepal 2002@yahoo.com
- www.volnepal.np.org

Community-based non-profit organisation that coordinates local and international work camps to empower community self-help initiatives.

**PROGRAMME DESCRIPTION:** Placements for volunteers in schools, colleges and universities. Volunteers help with sports, music, extracurricular activities, English teaching and other administrative and social welfare work. Also arrange internships in fields of medicine, media, conservation, etc.

**NUMBER OF PLACEMENTS PER YEAR:** 100.

**DESTINATIONS:** Kathmandu Valley near the historic city of Bhaktapur.

**PREREQUISITES:** Minimum age 18.

**DURATION AND TIME OF PLACEMENTS:** 2 weeks to 5 months, starting January, April, August and November.

**SELECTION PROCEDURES AND ORIENTATION:** Application form, CV and references needed.

**COST:** Volnepal programme fee is $250 for up to 8 weeks, $750 for 18 weeks, includes pre-service training, language instruction, homestay and meals, trekking, rafting, jungle safari and volunteering. Sample costs are $550 for first month for medical interns (includes donation to hospital), $450 for school and orphanage volunteers. Second and third months cost $150–$200.

**CONTACT:** Anish Neupane, Director.

---

**VOLUNTEER TEACHER THAILAND**
Khao Lak, Phang Nga 82190, Thailand
© +66 828 022 811
🖑 volunteer.teachers@yahoo.com
🖥 www.volunteerteacherthailand.org

**PROGRAMME DESCRIPTION:** Volunteer Teacher Thailand continues the work of the Tsunami Volunteer Centre's English Teaching Project which was set up to alleviate the loss of 4 out of 5 English-speaking Thai people in the area. English teaching is offered free to schools and people in the communities, where it is requested by the Thai people, mainly to enhance their job prospects in the tourism industry.

**NUMBER OF PLACEMENTS PER YEAR:** 800.

**PREREQUISITES:** Minimum age 18. Must be fluent in English Volunteers need to be open-minded and focus on what they can give rather than get.

**DURATION AND TIME OF PLACEMENTS:** 2 weeks – 1 year (though visas are a problem for stays of more than 3 months).

**SELECTION PROCEDURES AND ORIENTATION:** References or police check required for those working with children. Orientation, training and ongoing support in the classroom are given.

**COST:** 3000 baht (£55) to cover teaching materials and transport to the schools. Volunteers pay their own expenses while in Thailand, e.g. in cheap guest house (which are plentiful).

**CONTACT:** Ken Hyde, Director.

---

**VOLUNTEER UGANDA**
🖑 gapyear@volunteeruganda.org
🖥 www.volunteeruganda.org/gapyear.html

New charity, sending its first volunteers in February 2010.

**PROGRAMME DESCRIPTION:** Volunteer teaching in local primary schools in a very poor area of south-west Uganda. Volunteers also work on outreach programmes teaching teenagers and young people about family planning and HIV avoidance. Programmes also include white water rating, chimpanzee tracking, Pygmy community visits and a 3-day safari.

**NUMBER OF PLACEMENTS PER YEAR:** 20–60.

**DESTINATIONS:** South-west Uganda.

**PREREQUISITES:** Ages 18–25. All nationalities but should be fluent in English. Should be enthusiastic and outgoing. Volunteers are encouraged to obtain a TEFL qualification before departure but this is not essential.

**DURATION AND TIME OF PLACEMENTS:** 3 months starting February and July.

**SELECTION PROCEDURES AND ORIENTATION:** Informal telephone interviews conducted to ensure programme is suitable. The first week in Kinkizi is an induction week, consisting of structured discussions on teaching methods, practice peer teaching, talks on Uganda's education, health, wildlife, religion and local culture. Volunteers will also be given basic local language lessons.

**COST:** £2,400 for 3 months, including accommodation in a mountain lodge overlooking Bwindi Impenetrable Forest. Volunteers share a log cabin in groups of 2–4. Adventure and wildlife activities included.

**CONTACT:** Simon Graffy, Group Leader & Founding Director (simongraffy@hotmail.com).

## VOLUNTHAI: VOLUNTEERS FOR THAILAND
86/24 Soi Kanprapa, Prachacheun Road,
Bahng Sue, Bangkok 10800, Thailand
✆ +1 202 403 1540 (US number)
✉ info@volunthai.com
🖥 www.volunthai.com

**PROGRAMME DESCRIPTION:** Volunteer teaching in 20 target schools with homestay. Volunteers teach conversational English in the classroom for 3–4 hours a day.

**DESTINATIONS:** Rural areas in remote provinces of Thailand.

**NUMBER OF PLACEMENTS PER YEAR:** 100.

**DURATION AND TIME OF PLACEMENTS:** 1 month minimum.

**PREREQUISITES:** Ages 21–60. College degree required. Must be speaker of English native or non-native. Must be willing to live with and learn from the locals.

**SELECTION PROCEDURES AND ORIENTATION:**
Rolling admissions. Online interviews. Volunteers are met in Bangkok for an introduction, and then go to the headquarters in rural Chaiyaphum for a 2-day training in Thai culture and language. A Thai teacher is available at the homestay to help with teaching and to answer any questions.

**COST:** Modest monthly fee ($375 for two months) to cover comfortable homestay and three fine Thai meals a day. Volunteers pay for their own travel costs.

**CONTACT:** Michael Anderson, Founder and Leader.

## WILD AT HEART
Suite 8, Corporate Park, 11 Sinembe Crescent,
La Lucia Ridge, Umhlanga Rocks, 4320
Kwa-Zulu Natal, South Africa
✆ +27 31 566 5264
✉ info@wah.co.za
🖥 www.wah.co.za

Working with wildlife at rehabilitation centres, wildlife areas, parks and reserves in Kenya, South Africa and Namibia.

**PROGRAMME DESCRIPTION:** Gap Year programme consists of 24 weeks in 3 countries (Kenya, Namibia and South Africa).

**DESTINATIONS:** South Africa (Kruger National Park and Hartbeespoort Dam), Kenya and Namibia.

**PREREQUISITES:** Ages 18–45; maximum age for Namibia is 40.

**DURATION AND TIME OF PLACEMENTS:** Minimum 2 weeks, maximum 3 months. Gap year programme is 24 weeks. Start dates year-round.

**SELECTION PROCEDURES AND ORIENTATION:** All welcome. Orientation is offered at each project on arrival.

**CONTACT:** Tanya Venter, Volunteer Coordinator.

## WWOOF – WORLD WIDE OPPORTUNITIES ON ORGANIC FARMS
🖥 www.wwoof.org;
www.wwoofinternational.org

The International WWOOF Association (IWA) website has links to both the national organisations in the countries that have a WWOOF coordinator and to those that do not, known as WWOOF Independents. National WWOOF coordinators compile a list of member farmers willing to provide bed and board in a non-monetary exchange with volunteers who help out and who are genuinely interested in furthering the aims of the organic movement.

**PROGRAMME DESCRIPTION:** Visitors are expected to work around 6 hours per day in return for free accommodation and food. Visitors have the opportunity to learn about the organic growing of crops and food.

**DESTINATIONS OFFERED:** Worldwide.

**PREREQUISITES:** Minimum age 18. Should be prepared to work hard and have an interest in organic growing and environmental issues.

**DURATION AND TIME OF PLACEMENTS:** Anything from a few days upwards.

**SELECTION PROCEDURES AND ORIENTATION:** Most WWOOF organisations have an online application process.

**COST:** Varies according to which country WWOOF you wish to join. WWOOF UK membership costs £20. Countries which have national WWOOF organisations have to be joined separately (e.g. Denmark, Sweden, Germany, Switzerland, Austria, Italy, Australia, New Zealand, Canada, Ghana, Japan, Korea and many more – some are mentioned in country chapters).

---

**YOUTH FOR DEVELOPMENT PROGRAMME**
317 Putney Bridge Road, London SW15 2PN
℡ 020 8780 7500
✉ yfd@vso.org.uk
🖥 www.vso.org.uk/youth

VSO's Youth for Development (YfD) programme gives young volunteers the opportunity to gain work experience and develop skills in an international setting.

**PROGRAMME DESCRIPTION:** VSO's development projects are in the fields of education, HIV and AIDS, disability, health and social well-being, secure livelihoods, participation and governance.

**PREREQUISITES:** Participants must be aged 18–25 and living in the UK or Ireland. They must be committed to volunteering, and demonstrate that they have at least 12 months' volunteering or community work experience. They should be interested in longer-term involvement in development work, either in the UK or overseas.

**DURATION AND TIME OF PLACEMENTS:** 12 months beginning at any time.

**SELECTION PROCEDURES AND ORIENTATION:** Closing deadline for applications is early January for departure between August and October. Applicants take part in a competitive assessment process. Selected volunteers are matched to placements developed by VSO programme offices in more than 34 countries. Volunteers also complete a global education project which makes a practical contribution to raising awareness of development issues in the UK and overseas. All volunteers complete pre-departure training to help them explore their motivation to volunteer, increase their understanding of cross-cultural issues, and to help volunteers develop their existing skills for working in a development context.

**COST:** Volunteers must raise £900 towards their placement.

**CONTACT:** YfD Team.

---

# DIRECTORY OF RELIGIOUS ORGANISATIONS

## BMS WORLD MISSION

PO Box 49, Baptist House, Didcot,
Oxfordshire OX11 8XA

℡ 01235 517653

✉ shortterm@bmsworldmission.org

🖥 www.bmsworldmission.org/actionteams

**PROGRAMME DESCRIPTION:** Action Teams enable young people to spend 6 months living and working alongside BMS missionaries or a partner organisation involved in church work, community development work, basic TEFL teaching, youth and children's work, drama and music outreach.

**DESTINATIONS:** Asia, Europe, Africa, Central and South America.

**NUMBER OF PLACEMENTS PER YEAR:** 50 or more.

**PREREQUISITES:** Aged between 18 and 23. Must be a committed Christian with support from their local UK church. Health clearance required.

**DURATION AND TIME OF PLACEMENTS:**
10 months including 1 month's training, 6 months overseas and a 2-month tour of UK churches upon return to share experiences and inspire others for mission.

**SELECTION PROCEDURES AND ORIENTATION:** Interviews are held over a weekend at BMS International Training Centre in Birmingham. A 1-month period of training and preparation follows. Debriefing is given on return.

**COST:** Contribution of approximately £3,590 to include flights, accommodation and living expenses overseas, insurance, visas and training.

**CONTACT:** Sarah Lewney, Mission Teams Assistant.

## BOSCO VOLUNTEERING ACTION (BOVA)

Savio House, Ingersley Road, Bollington,
Cheshire SK10 5RW

℡ 01625 560724

✉ bova@salesianyouthministry.com

🖥 http://boscovolunteeraction.co.uk

BOVA is the overseas volunteering group of the Salesians of Don Bosco in the UK, a Catholic Religious order focussed on serving the young and the poor.

**PROGRAMME DESCRIPTION:** Volunteer programmes in Salesian communities around the world, assisting in their work with the young and the poor while experiencing life in other countries. Previous volunteers have assisted in schools, vocational training centres, youth centres and residential centres, done office work and administration, coached sport, led music, taught maths, ICT (computers) and English.

**NUMBER OF PLACEMENTS PER YEAR:** 25.

**DESTINATIONS:** Don Bosco works in 130 countries. So far, BOVA volunteers have lived and worked with host communities in Bolivia, Ghana, India, the Philippines, Sierra Leone, Tanzania, Kenya, Azerbaijan, the Solomon Islands, Swaziland, El Salvador and Nigeria. BOVA aims to match volunteers to communities' needs, so cannot guarantee a placement in a particular country.

**PREREQUISITES:** Minimum age 18. BOVA accepts non-Catholics and people of no faith who are willing to work in a Catholic context.

**DURATION AND TIME OF PLACEMENTS:** 1 month to 2 years.

**SELECTION PROCEDURES AND ORIENTATION:**
Reference check and CRB check. Two pre-departure training weekends organised (at volunteers' expense).

**COST:** £25 administration charge, £100 for 2 training weekends, £50 training fee. Volunteers cover airfares, insurance, visas and spending money; host community provides lodging and food.

**CONTACT:** James Trewby.

---

### CAREFORCE

35 Elm Road, New Malden, Surrey KT3 3HB

📞 020 8942 3331

📧 enquiry@careforce.co.uk

🖥 www.careforce.co.uk

---

Established in 1980, Careforce enables Christians to serve in areas of need in the UK.

**PROGRAMME DESCRIPTION:** A year designed for committed Christians in their gap year is spent in the UK working as volunteers with churches and Christian projects amongst vulnerable and needy people.

**NUMBER OF PLACEMENTS PER YEAR:** 125.

**PREREQUISITES:** Ages 17–30. No specific qualifications are required except commitment to Christianity.

**DURATION AND TIME OF PLACEMENTS:** Usually 11/12 months from September or January each year.

**SELECTION PROCEDURES AND ORIENTATION:** Interviews are essential, first locally and then at the site of the potential placement. Orientation takes place in the first fortnight of the placement. An induction course for all volunteers is also held within the first month.

**COST:** None. All volunteers receive a weekly allowance of £35 per week plus full board and lodging. However, on acceptance, volunteers are asked to raise some financial support to help cover Careforce central costs.

---

### CHRISTIAN AID GAP YEAR

2 Deans Court Lane, Wimborne, Dorset BH21 1EE

📞 01202 840764

📧 gapyear@christian-aid.org

🖥 www.christianaid.org.uk/getinvolved/
volunteer/gapyear/gap_year.aspx

---

Christian Aid is a non-governmental development charity. It is not evangelistic, but has as its mission to help eradicate poverty and to challenge the root causes of poverty.

**PROGRAMME DESCRIPTION:** Gap year scheme involves working in an area office in the UK and getting local teenagers, university students and youth leaders interested and engaged in Christian Aid's global campaigns and activities. Overseas trip will be included. Role includes fundraising and visiting up to four summer festivals to promote the work of Christian Aid.

**NUMBER OF PLACEMENTS:** 20.

**PREREQUISITES:** Minimum age 18, average 22. Christian Aid works with people of all faiths and none, although much of the gap year youth work is undertaken with church-connected young people. A passion for global justice is essential.

**DURATION AND TIME OF PLACEMENTS:** 10 months.

**SELECTION PROCEDURES AND ORIENTATION:** Application deadline is 31 March. Briefing and interview days are held in the spring and placements are agreed by the end of June. Extensive on-the-job training given.

**COST:** Subsistence money provided by Christian Aid will have to be supplemented with own funds. Christian Aid gap year volunteers are usually placed with a family or in a shared house close to the area office where they work.

**CONTACT:** Olivia Flint, Youth Marketing Project Manager.

---

### CMS – CHURCH MISSION SOCIETY

Watlington Road, Cowley, Oxford OX4 6BZ

📞 01865 787400

📧 vro@cms-uk.org

🖥 www.cms-uk.org

---

**PROGRAMME DESCRIPTION:** CMS Encounters are short-term placements that provide an experience of mission service alongside Christians in other cultures, whether overseas or the UK. Examples including youth worker in Brazil, nursing assistant in Nepal, English teaching in Uganda, working with visually- or hearing-impaired children in Lebanon, church planting in France.

**DESTINATIONS:** Various countries in Africa, Asia, Europe, the Middle East and South America. Also the UK.

**PREREQUISITES:** Christians living in Britain, who are involved with their local church, interested in learning about and sharing in cross-cultural mission. Ages: 18–30 for Summer Encounters.

**DURATION AND TIME OF PLACEMENTS:** 4 months to 2 years. Short placements of 2–4 weeks also available.

**SELECTION PROCEDURES AND ORIENTATION:** Application form, interview process, CRB and medical check. 12-day preparatory training and debrief.

**COST:** Volunteers must be self-financing, though CMS can advise on fundraising.

**CONTACT:** Rebecca Thomlinson, Vocational Recruitment Officer (for Individuals); Debbie James, Discipleship Team Leader (for Groups).

---

### LATIN LINK STEP & STRIDE PROGRAMMES
87 London Street, Reading, Berkshire RG1 4QA
- 0118 957 7100
- step.uk@latinlink.org or stride.uk@latinlink.org
- www.latinlink.org

---

**PROGRAMME DESCRIPTION:** STEP: Self-funded team-based programme working on small-scale building projects and church work in Latin America for committed Christians only. STRIDE: Individual placements in Latin America using participants' specific skills and gifts according to the needs of the Latin American church. Opportunities include school and TEFL teaching, children's work, church work, agricultural and engineering work, project development and prison ministry. STRIDE also provides opportunities for short-term medical elective and bible college placements, from a minimum of 8 weeks.

**DESTINATIONS:** Argentina, Bolivia, Brazil, Cuba, Costa Rica, Ecuador, Guatemala, Honduras, Mexico, Peru and Spain.

**NUMBER OF PLACEMENTS PER YEAR:** STEP: 150; STRIDE: 25–30.

**PREREQUISITES:** Minimum age 17 years for 3-week to 6-month STEP Programme; minimum age 18 for 6-month to 2-year STRIDE programme. Volunteers must have an active Christian faith. Applicants need to be flexible, have initiative and be open to learn. Knowledge of Spanish or Portuguese is not essential but it is a great help. It is suggested that volunteers attend evening classes to prepare for the project.

**DURATION AND TIME OF PLACEMENTS:** STEP: Spring projects run from March to July and summer ones during July and August (7 weeks). STRIDE: Orientation and departures in September and January.

**COST:** STEP: From £1,500–£2,000 in total; details on application. The cost of the STRIDE programme varies from country to country, but is around £1,950 for initial costs followed by £450 per month. As with STEP, the cost includes flights, insurance, training, debriefing, food and accommodation but not language lessons and visa costs.

---

### OASIS UK
75 Westminster Bridge Road, London SE1 7HS
- 020 7921 4200
- enquiries@oasisuk.org; globalprojects@oasisuk.org
- www.oasisuk.org

---

In operation since 1985.

**PROGRAMME DESCRIPTION:** Global Action Teams and Short-term Summer Teams. Practical projects run alongside local Christian groups and churches to help transform communities in some of the poorest areas of the world. Activities vary from children's holiday clubs to teaching English, community health work with those affected by HIV/AIDS to youth discipleship, etc. Activities include youth and children's work, drama, music and projects with slum-dwellers and AIDS orphans.

**DESTINATIONS:** Uganda, Zambia, Mozambique, Zimbabwe, South Africa, India, Bangladesh, Thailand, USA and Brazil.

**NUMBER OF PLACEMENTS PER YEAR:** 250.

**PREREQUISITES:** Minimum age 18. Applicants should be committed Christians and in sympathy with the aims of the Oasis Trust.

**DURATION AND TIME OF PLACEMENTS:** Gap Year (Global Action) Teams depart twice a year for 3–6 months. Summer teams last 2–6 weeks.

**COST:** From £3,000 for 3 month Global Action Team; £4,250 for 4.5 months. From £2,000 for 2–6 week Short-Term Summer Teams.

## SALESIAN VOLUNTEERS
Ingersley Road, Bollington, Macclesfield
SK10 5RW
℗ 01625 575405
✉ jessica@saviohouse.org.uk
🖥 www.saviohouse.org.uk

**PROGRAMME DESCRIPTION:** Gap year scheme for living and working in a Catholic residential community with other volunteers doing hands-on youth work on various projects including retreat programmes, outreach and roadshows.

**PREREQUISITES:** Committed Christians aged 18–30.

**DURATION AND TIME OF PLACEMENTS:** September to July.

**SELECTION PROCEDURES AND ORIENTATION:** Interview, including week's residential experience. All new volunteers are given in-house and external training and preparation and on-going developmental personal and professional support.

**COST:** None. Weekly allowance is paid.

**CONTACT:** Jessica Wilkinson, Retreat Team Leader.

## TEARFUND
100 Church Road, Teddington, Middlesex
TW11 8QE
℗ 020 8943 7777
✉ transform@tearfund.org
🖥 www.tearfund.org/Transform/
Youth+and+student

A Christian charity working with local church partners to bring justice and transform lives by overcoming global poverty.

**PROGRAMME DESCRIPTION:** 'Transform Teams' work practically supporting Tearfund partners overseas with their projects, mainly with children and the vulnerable, holiday clubs, AIDS education, etc.

**DESTINATIONS:** Kenya, Malawi, Rwanda, Zambia, Tanzania, Madagascar, Burkina Faso, Cameroon, Uganda, Bangladesh, Thailand, India, Russia, South Africa, Peru, Argentina, Brazil, Mexico and Bolivia.

**DURATION AND TIME OF PLACEMENTS:** 4-month trips leave in March/April, 6-month trips leave in January, or 6 month gap year trips; 4–6 week teams leave July and August.

**COST:** 4-month teams £2,900, 6-month teams £3,600 excluding flights and visas.

## TIME FOR GOD (TFG)
North Bank, 28 Pages Lane, Muswell Hill,
London N10 1PP
℗ 020 8883 1504
✉ office@timeforgod.org
🖥 www.timeforgod.org

One of the most longstanding organisations in the UK working in the field of voluntary service, gap years and career breaks.

**PROGRAMME DESCRIPTION:** Gap year and career break organisation with an interdenominational and international focus. UK placements include but are not limited to inner city projects with the homeless and disadvantaged, caring for children with special needs, assisting the ministry team in a Church, children's and youth work, youth retreat centres/outdoor activity centres, drug and alcohol rehabilitation centres and more.

**NUMBER OF PLACEMENTS PER YEAR:** 150.

**DESTINATIONS:** UK, Europe, USA, Canada, Hong Kong and South Korea.

**PREREQUISITES:** Minimum age 18. Must be open to explore the Christian faith.

**DURATION AND TIME OF PLACEMENTS:** 3–12 months from September or January.

**COST:** Fees vary according to programme selected, and range from a free gap year in Europe for UK young adults (subject to approval through EVS – see Volunteering entry page 294), to £1,500 for a year in

Hong Kong, America or South Korea, excluding travel expenses, insurance, visa and immunisation fees. Includes orientation and re-entry training, ongoing training and support while in placement, accommodation, food expenses and pocket money.

**CONTACT:** Susann Haehnel, Field Team Leader.

---

### YEAR FOR GOD

Youth With a Mission, Holmsted Manor, Staplefield Road, Cuckfield, West Sussex RH17 5JF

📞 01444 440229
📞 07805 154486 (mobile)
✉ yfg@holmsted.org.uk
🖥 www.yearforgod.co.uk

**PROGRAMME DESCRIPTION:** Year For God is a 12-month opportunity for Christian missions training and experience in a different culture.

**DESTINATIONS:** Bolivia, Singapore/Asia, Uganda and others.

Gap Year Programme of Youth with a Mission for Christians to devote 12 months to 'radical discipleship' and missions in one of several countries. Locations include Bolivia, Tanzania, India, Malaysia/Indonesia and Europe. Cost is £3,000–£4,000.

**NUMBER OF PLACEMENTS PER YEAR:** 30–40.

**DURATION AND TIME OF PLACEMENTS:** 12 months starting either in August or February (2 intakes per year).

**SELECTION PROCEDURES AND ORIENTATION:** Application form with references. Informal interview at Holmsted. Orientation week at start of the year.

**COST:** The year will cost £4,000–£7,500 depending on location. This includes airfare, food and accommodation, medical insurance, immunisations, visas and DTS (Discipleship Training School) fees. Extra needed for personal spending money.

**CONTACT:** Caroline Morgan, YFG Co-ordinator (YWAM England).

---

# A YEAR OFF FOR NORTH AMERICANS

Once completely unknown in North America, the concept and even the term gap year is catching on. Gradually colleges are getting to grips with the concept of deferred entry, though it is still an alien notion to some. Be aware that some (such as Connecticut College) will grant a deferral but require the student to sign a pledge that they will not apply elsewhere.

The trend may have started with an article published by the Admissions Office of Harvard University which continues to have wide circulation, entitled 'Time Out or Burn Out for the Next Generation' which argued strenuously for having a break from the intense pressures affecting students trying to get into the top universities. More recently Princeton University has created a programme by which up to 10% of its intake participate in a year of social service abroad before they arrive. The university's president is quoted as citing the advantages as giving students a more international perspective, adding to their maturity and giving them a break from academic pressures.

**ELISABETH WEISKITTEL** is one young American who decided that she did not want to go straight to college:

*I* was the only person in my graduating high school class to take a gap year or probably even to consider doing it. My friends, after blinking and looking shocked for a minute, thought it was a great idea but, like the adults, shook their heads and said, 'Oh, you'll never be able to go back to finish college.' My family was used to the idea because I had first brought it up in my sophomore year of high school, and they approved wholeheartedly. I knew that I was going to need a break from school, and I've always loved to travel. The only reason not to go was that I would be a year behind my high school classmates, and a year older than my new classmates at college. But I decided that that wasn't so terrible an idea.

I had already applied to college during my senior year of high school, which is the normal time, and had been accepted at several. When I chose one, I included a letter saying that I was planning to take a year off. The college wrote back saying I had permission, and that they would hold

> *my space in the upcoming class the following year. Deciding where to go turned out to be more difficult than deciding to go.'*
>
> *Elisabeth ended up doing courses in Oxford and Florence plus an internship in Hawaii and had a very full and productive year out. Although she admits the year was expensive, it wasn't as expensive as a year at college would have been.*

Post-college gap years are more common in North America, though even here there is pressure on many new graduates to get immediately onto the career ladder. Yet those who have never travelled outside their home continent may leave college with a nagging feeling that their horizons need broadening.

Canada has definitely seen an upsurge of interest in taking a year off before university. The national student travel agency Travel CUTS and its work abroad programmes called SWAP have launched a new website www.gapyearabroad.ca. **Graham Milner** from Victoria BC took advantage of a gap year scheme and spent a happy year at a residential school between London and Cambridge. He soon realised his school was not far from Stansted Airport and became an aficionado of cheap European flights with no-frills airlines from Stansted, which he could afford even on his modest salary. In order to find a travelling companion, he simply sent a round-robin email to the other participants from Canada and offered to search out the cheapest flights and accommodation, and as a result he and a young woman gapper spent a long weekend in Milan not long after they both arrived in England.

**Halael Craig** from Vancouver wanted to spend the second half of her gap year in England, because she had enjoyed a year in Cambridge previously when her family was on sabbatical. Partly because she had family contacts, she wanted to fix her gap year up independently. However, when she gradually realised that she was not going to be able to pin down either a job or accommodation in advance, she began to lose heart. But she had managed to save C$5,000 by working at a chain clothes store and decided to go for it anyway, arriving in cold and rainy February:

> *Moving to England by myself without any parental assistance really showed me what I was capable of doing (although I do fully recognise all those who were very helpful during my initial period there). However, the fact that I was able to find a room to rent and a job all by myself without going broke was very satisfying and gave me confidence in my capabilities. I really enjoyed my job at Laura Ashley where there were some really nice girls who worked part-time and with whom I would go out for drinks or dinner. The low points of my year out were the drudgery of working for five months in Canada. I was only able to get part-time work which meant that I was quite bored and my parents would nag at me to do something helpful etc.... blah blah.*

*Having a year out from school was one of the best decisions I've ever made. My experiences gave me more confidence and maturity as I arrived at university. I had travelled and been in situations where I had to meet complete strangers and these experiences helped me overcome shyness and gave me confidence when faced with this new rather daunting social experience. Throughout the six months I was in Britain/Europe, I managed to save money so that after all travel, rent and food payments had been made, I had still saved money that would go to university expenses. It was an excellent year out and I look back on it fondly.*

One changing trend is for British gap year organisations to accept more clients from North America. It seems that the increase in competition among the companies has prompted many of the British agencies to stop worrying about the reputed litigiousness of Americans and to start not just welcoming but actively recruiting Americans onto their programmes. Several such as *Global Visions International* and *Projects Abroad* have offices in the USA.

Of course many Americans taking a gap year do not leave the shores of their country. Some who may be undecided about the next step may join AmeriCorps, the national service programme instituted by President Clinton in 1993, which has been described as a domestic Peace Corps. In exchange for 1,700 hours of community service over a 10-month period, AmeriCorps volunteers aged 18–24 receive a US$5,000 education voucher and a living allowance of US$100 or more a week. President Barack Obama would like to extend this so that students willing to volunteer 100 hours a year would become eligible for a US$4,000 tax credit. President Obama's proposal also includes the funding of an online clearinghouse of volunteer vacancies.

The Federal Work Study programme is another scheme that encourages a volunteering culture with monetary rewards: financial assistance is given to students in financial need who work in community service positions during term-time or while on holiday, e.g. working with deprived children to raise literacy rates. The Labour government in the UK is attracted to such incentives and has been considering a similar scheme for Britain.

**LAURA WERNER** turned to mediating agencies after graduating from Harvard as access to Europe is not as easy for American students as for EU nationals. After carrying out quite a lot of detailed research, she opted for a gap year internship arranged by Adelante (listed below) and wrote from Spain several months into the experience:

*I spent the entirety of my senior spring stressing over what to do after college. I was worried because I couldn't find anything that I wanted to pursue whole-heartedly. Instead, I ended up in my hometown working for a marketing and distribution company. I knew I was meant to do more and see more of the world. I found my mind turning back to one idea, that I wanted to travel. I had studied Spanish in college and wanted to expand on my language set. Since there are so many programmes, it's hard to know which ones are reliable unless you've met somebody who's already been through it. Adelante offers to help you find an internship in several cities in Spain, lasting one to six months plus housing and assistance with visas. It seemed right on target with what I wanted: to live abroad, to work on my Spanish, and to try a new job without the pressures of a contract. The only drawback, aside from my family and best friends being so far away, was financial. As a recent graduate, I had not managed to save much. So, I decided to take out a loan calculated to cover my six months in Barcelona. I didn't really think about what would happen when I came home or if I ran out of money. I just wanted to go!*

*I was very excited on arrival in Barcelona and was lucky to be placed in an apartment with an outgoing and helpful woman from the city studying for her Masters. My other roommate was also on the Adelante programme and we were at the same point in our lives, recent grads, unsure of our futures. The first two weeks, we went to the Kingsbrook Language School which was a great way to reintroduce yourself to the language and start to understand the colloquial speech of Barcelona, however, the lack of structure made it tough to improve by leaps and bounds as you might wish.*

*From the stories I had heard, I thought I could find ways of earning money, even though I wasn't legally permitted to work in Spain. Unfortunately, this was only partially the case. I found work babysitting, but the income was hardly enough to cover my needs, as I had not anticipated so many extra expenses such as public transport, internet, cell phone and WATER (which isn't free like in the States). I didn't live like a rock star, but I certainly learned how much money you need if you want to live abroad. If you haven't saved up a lot, you probably shouldn't be doing an unpaid internship (as I did).*

*After the course, I started my five-month internship with a small publishing company called ACV Global. The company is absolutely wonderful! The atmosphere is bright and welcoming and the employees are very friendly. The friends that I made through my internship, as well as my roommates, helped pull me out of occasional spells of homesickness. The small company gave me the opportunity to participate in a variety of projects, and I am thrilled with my work in the design and communication sector. Since my experience has been so positive, I feel that I have strengths that have been revealed by this trip and I certainly plan on emphasising them in the job search. I've already started making contacts in NYC and sent some CVs to a few companies. I hope that my transition into the working world will be a lot smoother than it might have been otherwise!'*

## ADVISORY SERVICES

Companies that maintain databases of gap year semester programmes and a wealth of opportunities (mostly unpaid) and offer personalised consultations to fee-paying clients (often young people aged 16–25) attempt to match them with a suitable work, volunteer or study placement abroad:

*Taking Off*, Boston (+1 617 424 1606; www.takingoff.net). Taking Off provides ongoing personal assistance to those looking for international experiences that include volunteer work, internships and custom-designed situations (not paying jobs). Consultation fee US$1,200; ongoing consulting service US$2,000.

*Center for Interim Programs LLC*, Princeton (+1 609 683 4300; www.interimprograms.com). Consulting service with offices near Princeton and Harvard aimed primarily at pre-university and university students looking to arrange an internship or volunteer work. Consulting fee from US$2,100.

*LEAPNow*, Calistoga, California (+1 888 424 5327; www.leapnow.org). Various internships and experiential programmes in 126 countries, e.g. wildlife hospital in Greece, school in Honduras and orphanage in India. Agency fee of US$750 in addition to the programme costs.

*Horizon Cosmopolite*, Montreal, Canada (+1 514 935 8436; www.horizon cosmopolite.com). Database of volunteer work, internships and Spanish immersion in 30+ countries around the world. Tries to match clients with suitable placements. Registration fee C$555 plus varying programme fees.

## KEY NORTH AMERICAN ORGANISATIONS

Of the thousands of organisations large and small throughout North America which are involved with student exchanges and assisting young people to undertake worthwhile projects or internships abroad, paid or voluntary, here is a small selection.

*Adelante LLC*, Seal Beach, California (+1 562 799 9133; adelanteabroad.com). Internships, volunteer placements, teaching abroad and semester/summer study opportunities from 1–12 months in Spain (several cities), Costa Rica (San José), Mexico (Oaxaca), Chile (Vina del Mar/Valparaiso) and Uruguay (Montevideo). Prices start from US$1,995 for 1 month in Chile, Uruguay and Mexico to include language classes, various housing options and work assignment placement.

*AFS International Youth Development*, (+1 800 AFS INFO (237 4636); www.usa. afs.org). Gap year icon on website. Full intercultural programme lasting 4/6–12 months in 28 countries, including many in Europe, for volunteers aged 18–29. Most programmes include language training prior to volunteer placement, home-stay accommodation and participation in local voluntary projects.

*Agriventure (International Agricultural Exchange Association)*, Alberta, Canada (+1 403 255 7799; www.agriventure.com). Details of the international farm exchange may be found in the chapter 'Work Experience'.

*AIDE (Association of International Development and Exchange)*, (+1 512 457 8062; +1 866 6-ABROAD (227623); reinventyourself@aideabroad.org; www. aideabroad.org). Variety of overseas placements in volunteer, internship, work, and teach abroad programmes lasting 2 weeks to 12 months in Argentina, Australia, Chile, China, Costa Rica, Ecuador, England, Guatemala, India, Ireland, Peru, South Africa, Spain and the USA. Participants pay a programme fee to cover placement, airport pick-up, accommodation, meals, local support, medical insurance and optional language courses. Programmes can also include cultural and adventure tours.

*AIPT (Association for International Practical Training)* (www.aipt.org or www. iaesteunitedstates.org). Short- and long-term placements in more than 80 countries through the International Association for the Exchange of Students for Technical Experience (IAESTE) available to students in science, engineering, math, agriculture or architecture. Other work exchange schemes with selected countries.

*Amerispan Unlimited*, Philadelphia (+1 800 879 6640; info@amerispan.com). Specialist Spanish-language travel organisation with expertise in arranging language courses, voluntary placements and internships throughout South and Central America.

**Amigos de las Americas**, Houston (+1 800 231 7796; amigoslink.org). Summer training programme for 700+ high school and college student volunteers mostly in community health projects throughout Central and South America. Participation fee is US$4,040 including travel from the USA. All volunteers must have studied Spanish at school or university and undergone training.

**ArchaeoSpain**, Connecticut (+1 866 932 0003; www.archaeospain.com). Summer archaeological programmes for anyone over 18 in Spain and Italy. Sample cost US$2,450 for a month working on a Roman excavation in Spain.

**British American Education Foundation** (+1 914 834 2064; www.baef.org). Offers students from North America the opportunity to spend a term or a year in a British boarding school following the normal Sixth Form curriculum. Cost approximately US$36,000.

**Brown Ledge Gap Year** (+1 888 74-FOCUS (36287); www.brownledgegapyear. org). 4-month programme August to Christmas; first phase is 4 weeks documentary film training at camp in Vermont, then road trip to Salt Lake City for a 6-week internship or community service; on to New Orleans for the last phase. Participants identify subjects for documentaries along the way. Costs US$14,500.

**BUNAC USA** (+1 203 264 0901; www.bunac.org). Administers a number of programmes for US students and young people including Intern in Britain, Work in Ireland, Work Australia, Work New Zealand, Work Canada, Volunteer South Africa, Volunteer Peru and Volunteer Cambodia. Note that the old Work in Britain Program has been cancelled due to UK visa changes.

**CCI – Center for Cultural Interchange**, Chicago (+1 888-ABROAD1; www.cci-exchange.com). Language courses, homestays, internships lasting 1–3 months and volunteering programmes in many countries worldwide.

**CCUSA (Camp Counselors USA)** (www.ccusa.com). Work Experience programmes in Australia/New Zealand, internships in Brazil and summer camp counsellors in Russia and Croatia.

**CDS International** (+1 212 497 3500; info@cdsintl.org). Practical training internships for American students or recent graduates mainly in Germany but also in Spain, Argentina and Switzerland.

**CIEE-Portland** (toll-free +1 800 40 STUDY; www.ciee.org/hsabroad/gap/index.html). Gap years or gap semesters for pre-university students arranged in China, Japan, Chile, the Dominican Republic, France and Spain. Programme includes housing and meals with local families, language classes, and English teaching internship or community service. Prices from about US$12,000 for one semester. Also organise teach abroad programmes in Chile, China, Korea, Spain and Thailand (www.ciee.org/teach).

*City Year* (www.cityyear.org). Community service and leadership development for young people of all backgrounds, ages 17–24, for a demanding year of community service in 19 US communities and Johannesburg, South Africa.

*Cross-Cultural Solutions*, New Rochelle, New York (+1 800 380 4777; www.crossculturalsolutions.org). Volunteers work side-by-side with local people on community-led initiatives in the areas of caregiving, teaching, healthcare and community development in Africa, Asia, Eastern Europe and Latin America.

*Cultural Embrace*, Austin, Texas (+1 888 214 8570; www.culturalembrace.com). Internships, volunteer teaching and work programmes in lots of countries.

*Dynamy*, Worcester, Massachusetts (508 755 2571; www.dynamy.org). Residential internship year for 30–40 people aged 17–22; Outward Bound expedition, community service and optional college credit. Tuition for 9-month programme is US$17,900 plus housing US$7,000; for one semester fees are half as much. Scholarships are available.

*Earthwatch Institute* (+1 800 776 0188; www.earthwatch.org). An international environmental charity that engages people worldwide in scientific field research and education to promote the understanding and action necessary for a sustainable environment. Earthwatch recruits 3,000 volunteers a year to assist scientific field research projects around the world. Prices range from US$759 to US$5,750, excluding travel to the location.

*Educators Abroad* (www.eltap.org). Placement programme open to gap year students among others. Participants are sent to 25 countries on all continents for 4–10 weeks throughout the year. Fees total US$2,300–$4,200 excluding travel. Accommodation and board are provided by host schools.

*EIL (Experiment in International Living)*, Vermont (+1 800 345 2929; www.experimentinternational.org). Programmes lasting 3–5 weeks include some language training.

*Experiential Learning International*, Denver, Colorado (+1 303 321 8278; www.eliabroad.com). Immersion, intern and volunteering programmes in South and Central America, Africa, Asia and Europe.

*Explorations in Travel*, Guildford, Vermont (+1 802 257 0152; www.volunteertravel.com). International volunteers for rainforest conservation, wildlife, community and many other projects worldwide.

*Foundation for Sustainable Development*, San Francisco, California (+1 415 288 4873; www.fsdinternational.org). Short summer and longer term internships for anyone over 18 in the field of development in certain Latin American and African countries plus India. Volunteers in Latin America will be usually expected to converse in Spanish. Prices from US$3,000 for 9 weeks.

*GeoVisions*, Connecticut (+1 203 453 5838/+1 877 949 9998/toll-free; from UK: 0800 043 4822; www.geovisions.org). Volunteer or teach abroad in range of countries from Russia to Jordan.

**Global Citizens Network**, Minneapolis (+1 800 644 9292; www.globalcitizens.org). Volunteer vacations in Kenya, Nepal, Mexico, Guatemala, Peru, Tanzania, and others.

**Global Crossroad**, Irving, Texas (+1 866 387 7816; www.globalcrossroad.com). Volunteer teaching and internships in 23 countries. Paid teaching in China (1–12 months). Placement fees from US$799 for China, but more typically US$1,399 for Peru.

**Global Experiences** (+1 877-GE-ABROAD (43 227623); www.globalexperiences. com). Range of customised international internships for university-level students and recent graduates in Ireland, Italy, France Spain, UK and Australia. Internships are available in nearly all career fields and include accommodation, for-credit components, on-site support, and more.

**Global Intern** (+1 973 537 6800; www.theglobalintern.com). Professional internships arranged in UK, Israel, Italy and China. Placement fees from US$1,500–$5,000 excluding accommodation.

**Global Learning Across Borders** (+1 800 984 4522; www.global-lab.org). International cultural immersion, experiential education, and community service programmes for young adults aged 16–22 and others. Semester Programs in Morocco, India, China/Tibet, and Greece.

**Global Routes**, Northampton, Massachusetts (+1 413 585 8895; globalroutes.org). Offers 12-week voluntary internships to students over 17 for teaching English and other subjects in village schools in Tanzania, Costa Rica, Peru, Ghana, India and Thailand. Participation fee US$6,250–$6,750.

**Global Service Corps**, San Francisco (415 551 0000; globalservicecorps.org). Co-operates with grass-roots organisations in Thailand, Cambodia and Tanzania and sends volunteers and interns for two or three weeks or longer.

**Global Visions International**, Boston, Massachusetts (+1 888 653 6028; www. gviusa.com). Large range of expeditions and volunteer projects worldwide (see entry in 'Directory of Specialist Gap Year Programmes').

**Global Volunteers**, St Paul, Minnesota (+1 800 487 1074; globalvolunteers. org). 'Granddaddy of the volunteer vacation movement'.

**ICADS**, San José, Costa Rica (+1 506 2225 0508; www.icads.org). Institute for Central American Development Studies combines study of the Spanish language and development issues with structured internships in Costa Rica and Nicaragua lasting a semester (US$9,850) or a summer (US$4,200).

**ICYE: Inter-Cultural Youth Exchange**, United Planet, Boston, Massachusetts (+1 800 292 2316; www.unitedplanet.org). International exchange organisation that sends volunteers to spend a year abroad with a host family and undertake voluntary work placements, after a one-month orientation including intensive language study. Placements worldwide but programme particularly strong in South and Central America.

**Institute for Cultural Ecology**, Hilo, Hawaii (+1 808 854 9806; www.cultural-ecology.com). Academic internships in Fiji, Thailand, Hawaii and others, working on marine biology projects, environmental advocacy or custom-designed projects in student's major. 4, 6, 8 or 12 weeks. Sample fees: US$1,895 for 4 weeks, US$3,850 for 12 weeks, e.g. reef mapping on the Fiji coast.

**InterExchange**, New York (+1 212 924 0446/+1 800 597 3675; www.inter exchange.org). Homestay tutors in Spain; au pair placements in France, Germany, Netherlands, Spain; short-term work in Australia, internships in France, the UK and Costa Rica. Volunteer opportunities in South Africa, India, Peru, Costa Rica, Australia, Namibia, Kenya. Fees from US$600 for au pair placements.

**International Co-operative Education**, Menlo Park, California (+1 415 323 4944; www.icemenlo.com). Arranges paid and unpaid summer internships in England, Germany, Switzerland, Belgium, Singapore, Japan, China, Australia, Ghana, Mongolia and Argentina. Jobs include retail sales, banking, computer technology, hotels and restaurants, offices, etc.; most require knowledge of relevant language. Placement fee is US$900 plus application fee of US$250.

**International Cultural Adventures** (+1 888 339 0460; www.ICAdventures.com). Cultural, educational and volunteer service experiences in Peru and Sikkim (India). Fees for 6-week summer programmes from US$3,150 and from US$4,150 for 12-week extended programmes beginning in February/March and September.

**Kibbutz Program Center**, New York (+1 212 462 2764; www.kibbutzprogramcenter. org). Volunteer placement service for candidates aged 20–35 on Israeli kibbutzim, US$350 fee.

**Knowledge Exchange**, New York (+1 800 831 5095/212 931 9953; www. keiabroad.org). Study and intern abroad programme for students including pre-college. Subject-specific internship placement and professional opportunities available in many countries.

**Living Routes**, Amherst (+1 888 515 7333; www.LivingRoutes.org). Semester, summer and year-abroad programmes based in eco-villages around the world that help people of all ages gain the knowledge, skills and inspiration to build a sustainable lifestyle. Current programmes in India, Scotland, Senegal, USA, Mexico, Brazil and Peru.

**Map the Gap International**, Connecticut (+1 203 672 5950/866 356 7120 (toll-free); www.mapthegapinternational.com). Programmes in Italy (US$10,000+), Ecuador, etc.

**Mountbatten Internship Programme**, New York (+1 212 557 5380; www. mountbatten.org). Reciprocal programme places American graduates in London so that they can acquire practical training in business for 12 months. Participation fee is US$4,000.

**Pacific Challenge**, Eugene, Oregon (+1 800 655 3513; www.pacificchallenge. org). 2-month and shorter experiential travel programmes through New Zealand/ Australia and South East Asia (Thailand and Vietnam) plus summer programme in South Africa, Nepal, etc.

**Nikitas Language Abroad Schools**, New York (+1 646 502 8677; www.nik-las. com). Internship and language study programmes in Italy, Spain, Portugal and France.

**Peace Corps**, Washington, DC (+1 800 424 8580; www.peacecorps.gov). Sends volunteers on 2-year assignments to 70 countries.

**Projects Abroad**, New York (toll-free +1 888 839 3535; info@projects-abroad.org). US office of British counterpart (see 'Directory of Specialist Gap Year Programmes').

**ProWorld Service Corps** (+1 877 429 6753; www.myproworld.org/internships.htm). Offers a range of internships in fields from business to journalism, lasting 2–26 weeks with aid agencies in Peru, Belize, Mexico and Brazil. Fees start at US$1,895 which includes project work with local NGOs, language training, room and board, and cultural activities. ProWorld has a UK office in Sheffield (0870 750 7202).

**SCI-IVS (Service Civil International-International Voluntary Service)** (206 350 6585; www.sci-ivs.org). International workcamps.

**SWAP (Student Work Abroad Program)** (+1 416 996 2887; swapinfo@swap.ca, www.swap.ca). Administered by the Canadian Federation of Students. Coordinates a working holiday programme for Canadian students and non-students in the UK, Ireland, France, Germany, Austria, New Zealand, Australia, Japan, and South Africa. Has a dedicated website – www.gapyearabroad.ca.

**Thinking Beyond Borders** (www.thinkingbeyondborders.org). Programme designed for gap year students to explore international development through global service learning and academic study. US$39,000 for 35-week programme.

**Visions Service Adventures** (+1 800 813 9283; www.visionsserviceadventures. com). Summer volunteering programmes in the Dominican Republic, Guadeloupe, the British Virgin Islands and many others, which cost from US$4,750 for one month.

**Volunteers for Peace** (+1 802 259 2759; www.vfp.org). Annual membership US$30. VFP publishes an online 'International Workcamp Directory' with more than 2,500 listings in nearly 100 countries, available from early April. Registration for most programmes is US$300 (US$500+ if under 18).

**Where There Be Dragons**, Boulder, Colorado (+1 800 982 9203; www.wherethere bedragons.com). 12-week semester in Asia, Africa and Latin America (aimed at 17–22 years olds). Also 6-week summer programmes for ages 15–19 in a range of developing countries.

**Wildlands Studies** (+1 831 477 9955; www.wildlandsstudies.com). Conservation projects lasting 6 weeks in the USA (including Alaska and Hawaii), Belize, Thailand, Nepal, etc.

**World Endeavors**, Minneapolis, Minnesota (+1 612 729 3400; www.world endeavors.com). Volunteer, internship and study programmes lasting 2 weeks to 2 months in many countries.

**WISE, Worldwide International Student Exchange** (731 287 9948; www.wise-foundation.com). Academic year abroad (ages 15–18) in Germany, Austria, Denmark, Japan and Brazil for 5 or 10 months.

**WorldTeach**, Harvard University (+1 617 495 5527/+1 800 4-TEACH (83224)-0; www.worldteach.org.) Private, non-profit organisation which places several hundred volunteers as teachers of EFL or ESL in countries which request assistance. WorldTeach provides college graduates with one-year contracts in American Samoa, Bangladesh, Costa Rica, Ecuador, Namibia, Kenya, the Marshall Islands, China, Venezuela, Chile, Pohnpei, Mongolia, Rwanda, South Africa and Guyana. 8-week summer programmes in Bulgaria, China, Costa Rica, Ecuador, Poland, Namibia and South Africa. Many participants pay a volunteer contribution ranging from US$500 to US$7,990, but several new programmes are fully funded by the host country.

**Your World to Discover**, Richmond Hill, Ontario (www.yourworldtodiscover.ca). Partnered with volunteer agencies such as Cosmic Volunteers and offers large range of gap year and volunteering programmes.

**Youth Challenge International**, Toronto, Canada (+1 416 504 3370; www.yci.org). Teams of volunteers carry out community development projects lasting from 5 to 10 weeks in Costa Rica, Nicaragua, Guyana and a number of others. Sample fundraising required costs C$3,000 for 5 weeks, C$3,900 for 10 weeks.

**Youth International (Experience the World)**, 232 Wright Avenue, Toronto, Ontario M6R 1L3, Canada (+1 416 538 0152; www.youthinternational.org). One semester programmes to Asia, Africa and Latin America for people 18–25; US$8,900.

The first organisation that American volunteers think of is the *Peace Corps* (www.peacecorps.gov) which sends both skilled and unskilled volunteers on two-year assignments to scores of countries. **Kristie McComb** was posted to Burkina Faso and gradually concluded that the Peace Corps programme places less emphasis on development than on cultural exchange, i.e. sharing American culture with the host country nationals and then sharing the culture of your host country with Americans on your return:

> The cool thing for Americans is that you don't have to be qualified in anything to be accepted by the Peace Corps. There are many generalist programmes where you can learn what you need to know once you get there through the three-month pre-service training. I would encourage interested parties to be honest about what they can and cannot tolerate since not all volunteers are sent to live in mud huts. In a world changed by terrorism it is comforting to know how much of an active interest the US government takes in the safety and well being of its citizens abroad. However some people might find this stifling and not adventurous enough. How well PC keeps tabs on volunteers in any given country depends on the local PC leadership but, regardless, you are still in a high profile group of well locatable people. Risk reduction is the buzz word in Washington these days.
>
> Overall I am happy with my experience though I am often frustrated by the inertia, the corruption and bureaucracy that makes me question whether anything will ever change. But you do gain a lot by (if nothing else) witnessing poverty on a regular basis. You quickly learn to recognise the difference between a problem and an inconvenience and to see how lucky we are as Americans to have some of the 'problems' we have.

# LANGUAGE COURSES FOR NORTH AMERICANS

At a time when Americans seem to be reaching out under Barack Obama, going abroad to learn or improve a foreign language may have special appeal. Classroom learning has its place. But it is axiomatic that the fastest progress will be made when you are forced to use a language in every-day situations both at home and work. Programmes that combine structured study of a language or culture with volunteering are arguably a paradigm of the kind of foreign travel experience that can more than justify taking a year out before proceeding to college. Many organisations both international and local can arrange such placements, often in conjunction with a homestay to maximise exposure to the language.

Using a mediating agency simplifies the process of choosing a language school since they tend to deal with well-established schools and programmes on the ground. These agencies also provide a useful back-up service if something goes wrong. An effective US-based search engine for locating courses is provided by the Institute of International Education on www.iiepassport.org. Alternatives are www.abroadlanguages.com and www.worldwide.edu.

Here is a list of language course providers and agents of possible interest to North Americans planning a gap year.

**AmeriSpan** (+1 800 879 6640; www.amerispan.com). Language training organisation that started as a Latin America specialist but now offers programmes worldwide learning 10 languages.

**Bridge-Linguatec**, see entry in 'Directory of Language Courses'.

**Center for Cultural Interchange**, Chicago (+1 888-ABROAD(227623)1; www.cci-exchange.com). Language courses, volunteering and internship programmes in many countries. High school semester or year abroad in Australia, and a number of European countries.

**Eduvacations**, Washington, DC (+1 202 857 8384; www.eduvacations.com). Travel company specialising in customised language courses combined with sports, art instruction, etc. throughout Europe, Latin America, the Caribbean, Russia, the USA, etc.

**Language Liaison** (+1 800 284 4448; www.languageliaison.com). Total immersion language/culture study programmes and leisure learning courses.

**Language Link** (+1 800 552 2051; www.langlink.com). Long-established agency which represents dozens of Spanish language schools in Spain and Latin America.

**The Learning Traveller**, Guelph, Ontario, Canada (+1 888 364 1411; www.learning traveller.com). Agent for many language schools worldwide.

**Lexia International**, Hanover, New Hampshire (+1 800 775 3942; info@lexiaintl.org; www.lexiaintl.org). Overseas academic programmes, which include intensive language study, civilisation course, research methodology course, academic research project, elective course, internships and community service projects in Argentina,

China, Cuba, Czech Republic, England, France, Germany, Spain, Hungary, Italy, Poland, Turkey, South Africa and Thailand.

**Lingua Service Worldwide**, Connecticut (800 394 5327; www.linguaserviceworld wide.com). Represents range of private language schools at all levels.

**National Registration Center for Study Abroad**, Milwaukee (414 278 0631; study@nrcsa.com/ ww.nrcsa.com). Full language and culture immersion and other courses offered at 125 language schools and universities in 43 countries. Varying lengths of stay. Gap year students studying at a university may be able to apply the credit to their subsequent university.

**University Studies Abroad Consortium**, Virginia Street Gym 5, University of Nevada, USAC/323, Reno, Nevada 89557 (+1 775 784 6569; usac@unr.edu; http://usac. unr.edu). University-accredited courses in Spanish, Basque, Chinese, Danish and many other languages, plus art history, business, communications, etc.

# PAID SEASONAL JOBS

The fastest way to save money is of course to live at home and find a job which pays more than the national minimum wage and has scope for working lots of overtime. Vast numbers of students register with a local temp agency and request as many hours as possible or simply find the highest paying job locally that will involve the least expenditure. In addition to allowing you to save for your gap year project, doing a dull unskilled job might have other benefits, as **Alice Mundy** discovered when she spent months at a motorway services (because it was a short walk from her home and so required no outlay in petrol) working in the restaurant area, to save for a snowboard instructor's course in Canada:

> *Probably the lowest point of my gap year was working in certain jobs where there were a lot of people who didn't enjoy their jobs and so didn't put much effort in, but at the same time lacked either the resources or the ambition to do anything about changing it. However, on the positive side of that, my gap year has certainly highlighted to me just how lucky I am to have the opportunity of higher education, a privilege that a lot of people in the world don't have. This has definitely encouraged me to make the most of the next three years at university.*

The majority of gappers work locally in the autumn to fund travels or foreign projects after Christmas. With dedication and self-denial, it is amazing how fast you can hit your target, as **Melissa Evans** testifies: '*Financing my Gap Year was fairly difficult, and it required long hours and very minimal spending. I had two jobs that I worked full time, one in a call centre 9–5 Monday to Friday, and any overtime, then a job in a pub as a barmaid on Sat and Sun in addition to 3–4 other shifts during the week. I worked approximately 13 hours a day 5 days a week, and also weekends. This allowed me to raise the money I needed quickly. I started the jobs in the September and by December, I had paid for my flights and travel for 7 months away.*'

If you can manage to do it the other way round, you will probably find it much easier to land a job. For example **Ed Fry** scraped and borrowed to fund a sailing course in Australia between September and January and then returned to London where he found that so many gap year students had taken off, finding a job was very easy.

If the time comes when you can't stand the sight of the same old high street or the same old workmates, and want a complete break while still earning, you might want to consider some of the suggestions canvassed in this chapter. Although it is more difficult to save if working away from home, hotel work sometimes comes with meals and accommodation, and can be a more interesting way to save than the usual range of local jobs in stores, restaurants and offices. **Mark Smith** ended up really enjoying the saving part of his gap year:

> *I worked at the Gleneagles Hotel in Perthshire. I wanted somewhere that I could both work and stay so I thought big hotels were a good idea. It was fantastic. I found that*

*this was a great way to make money without having to spend a lot. They always need staff and you can stay in staff accommodation for really cheap and just earn loads of money while having a great experience too. I hunted around a few other hotels and it can be a bit tedious applying but there are loads of them about and a lot of the staff are temporary, only staying for six months or so at a time. This was all part of the gap year experience for me. I always thought this would be the boring bit that I had to endure in order to go on my travels but it turned out to be just as fun and rewarding as the trip itself. Living and working away from home was an absolute blast and I made good friends and gained valuable experience.*

Depending on the time of year, you may be able to arrange a short sharp change of routine by, say, working at a Scottish country house hotel over Christmas or going to pick grapes in France or Switzerland in September. The possibilities are so numerous that this chapter can only skim the surface. For much more comprehensive listings of seasonal jobs, look at *Work Your Way Around the World 2009* (£12.99).

While opening up an enormous range of possibilities, the internet can be a bewildering place to job-hunt. One of the best specialist recruitment websites is www.seasonworkers.com, a website that has been designed to help people find a summer job, outdoor sports job, gap year project or ski resort job quickly and easily. Another website that can prove invaluable for job-seeking travellers is the non-commercial, free Jobs Abroad Bulletin website (www.jobsabroadbulletin.co.uk), which will send a free monthly jobs listing by email to subscribers. A sample issue from summer 2009 included advertisements for chalet staff for the Bulgarian ski resort of Bansko, and poolside snack bar attendants at a beach apartment complex on the Algarve, as well as a range of teaching, au pairing and other vacancies worldwide.

Otherwise try www.gapwork.com, www.anyworkanywhere.com, www.jobmonkey.com (especially for North America), www.hotrecruit.com and so on. Everywhere you look on the internet potentially useful links can be found. A surprising number of company home pages feature an icon you can click to find out about jobs/recruitment/careers.

Registration on sites such as www.justjobs4students.co.uk is usually free of charge, and will soon see your inbox cluttered up with quite a high proportion of unsuitable jobs. Among the kinds of firm that recruit quite aggressively (possibly because there is such a high turnover) are 'charity fundraising' firms. These are commercial companies hired by mainstream and other charities to raise money on the streets of British cities.

Companies such as Flow Caritas (www.flowcaritas.co.uk), Dialogue Direct (www.dialoguedirect.co.uk), Inspired People (www.inspiredpeople.org), Tim Lilley Fundraising (www.tlfc.org/fundraising-jobs) and Wesser (www.wesser.co.uk) use worthy sounding lines such as 'championing the search for a better world' in their bid to hire an army of young people to accost passers-by and try to persuade them to sign direct debit donation forms. This activity has been dubbed 'charity mugging' and hence the employees are sometimes referred to as 'chuggers'. Unless you are a gifted salesperson, it is very difficult to get into the high-earning area, and in fact it is possible to make a loss. If you don't meet your target of 20 sign-ups a week, then you don't get your basic salary and you have to pay the accommodation charge. If considering this job, check out feedback sites online such as Facebook or www.thestudentroom.co.uk.

Employees are moved from town to town, so it can suit a foreigner on a working holiday. Eighteen-year-old **David Cox** from Ontario was hired soon after arriving in London. He was invited to attend a day's training in Oxford before being dispatched to his first location, and looked forward to a chance to see different places:

> *The last three weeks have been very interesting, but I'm starting to get into the swing of things. So far I've been posted in Brighton, Portsmouth and Newcastle areas and am leaving for Manchester tonight. I love the job but it's literally 7 days a week and can be very stressful so I'm looking forward to time off, I'm going to Norway in 2 weeks.*

Not everybody ends up loving the job by any means. **Anna Ling** was attracted partly by idealism to do this job in Bristol but came to consider it iniquitous since so much of the money raised goes to the 'middle-men'. She was paid £4 an hour plus a commission per donor.

Working for a local employer abroad is arguably one of the best ways of getting inside a culture, though the kind of job you find will determine the stratum of society which you experience. The student who spends a few weeks picking fruit in Canada will get a very different insight into North American culture from the one who looks after the children of a Texan millionaire. Yet both will have the chance to participate temporarily in the life of a culture and get to know one place well.

Most gap year students looking for holiday jobs abroad will have to depend on the two industries that survive on seasonal labour: tourism and agriculture. School leavers and their parents will probably feel happier with a pre-arranged job, possibly with a British tour operator, but that does limit the choice. Like job-hunting in any context, the competition for seasonal work will be hard to beat unless you are available for interview. If looking for farm work or a berth on a transatlantic yacht, a visit to a village pub frequented by farmers or yachties is worth dozens of speculative applications from home.

The other major fields of paid overseas employment for students are au pairing (see separate chapter) and English teaching (discussed below and also in the relevant country chapters). The more unusual and interesting the job the more competition it will attract. For example it is to be assumed that only a small percentage of applicants for advertised jobs actually gets the chance to work as underwater photographic models in the Caribbean, history coordinators for a European tour company or assistants at a museum bookshop in Paris.

# TOURISM

Hotels, restaurants, pubs and campsites from Cannes to Canada depend on transient workers. Anyone with some home-town restaurant experience and perhaps some knowledge of a second language should be able to fix up a summer job in a European resort. If you secure a hotel job without speaking the language of the country and lacking relevant experience, you will probably be placed at the bottom of the pecking order, e.g. in the laundry or washing dishes.

Even if the job is fairly grim, you will probably collect some good anecdotes as **S C Firn** did in an upmarket restaurant in Oberstdorf in the Bavarian Alps:

> *I had to peel vegetables, wash dishes, prepare food, clean the kitchen and sometimes serve food. Everything was done at a very fast pace, and was expected to be very professional. One German cook, aged 16, who didn't come up to standard, was punched in the face three times by the owner. On another occasion the assistant chef had a container of hot carrots tipped over his head for having food sent back. During my three months there, all the other British workers left, apart from the chef, but were always replaced by more.*

So if you can't stand the heat… read on.

## AGENCIES AND WEBSITES

The earlier you decide to apply for seasonal hotel work the better are your chances. Hotels in a country such as Switzerland recruit months before the summer season, and it is advisable to contact as many hotel addresses as possible by March, preferably in their own language. A knowledge of more than one language is an immense asset for work in Europe. Those who have a GCSE or A-Level in German are at a particular advantage since many tourist resorts in Spain, Italy and Greece cater mainly to a German clientele, so they like their staff to be able to communicate. Do not put too much faith in sending out a shower of speculative emails since these are routinely ignored by employers.

Specialist recruitment websites can be invaluable such as those mentioned above, e.g. www.seasonworkers.com. Dozens of other sites may prove useful such as www.seasonal-jobs.com (formerly www.voovs.com) and www.resortjobs.co.uk (part of www.natives.co.uk).

Wherever there is a demand for jobs, there will be an agency charging clients to make the necessary arrangements. Air-Pro Working Holidays in Wembley (020 8123 7693; www.air-pro.co.uk) arranges for sun-worshipping party types to find work in Tenerife, Magaluf, Ibiza and the other usual suspects. Punters pay £68 to register and from £370 for an 'option fee' to have a job and accommodation found for them.

On the other hand you might not be able to plan so far ahead, or you may have no luck with advance applications, so it will be necessary to look for hotel work once you've arrived in a foreign country. All but the most desperate hoteliers are far more willing to consider a candidate who is standing there in the flesh than one who sends in a CV out of the blue. One job-seeker recommends showing up bright and early (about 8am) to impress prospective employers. Perseverance is necessary when you're asking door to door at hotels since plenty of rejections are inevitable.

Hotels represent just one aspect of the tourist trade, and many more interesting venues exist for cooking and serving, including luxury yachts, prawn trawlers, holiday ranches, safari camps and ski chalets. People with some training in catering will find it much easier to find a lucrative job abroad than most. When applying for jobs which are not seasonal, you should stress that you intend to work for an indefinite period, make a career of fast food catering, etc. In fact staff turnover is usually very high. This will also aid your case when you are obliged to badger them to give you extra hours.

A good way of gaining initial experience is to work for a large organisation with huge staff requirements, such as PGL Adventure (www.pgl.co.uk/recruitment) in Britain and Europe, and Village Camps (www.villagecamps.ch) in Europe. Since they have so many vacancies (most of which pay only pocket money), the chances of being hired for a first season are reasonably good.

Mark Warner (08717 033955; visit www.markwarner-recruitment.co.uk) is a leading tour operator with resort hotels located around the Mediterranean and Aegean, and chalet hotels in top ski resorts in the Alps. The company recruits staff to work in Greece, Turkey, Corsica, Sardinia and Italy for the summer season and in Austria, France and Italy for the ski season. Positions are open for chefs, restaurant and bar staff, nursery nurses and children's activity leaders, watersport, tennis and aerobic instructors, pool attendants, customer service and shop staff, ski hosts and many others. Employees are provided with a competitive package including full board, medical insurance, travel expenses, use of watersport and activity facilities (summer) and ski pass, skis and boots (winter).

## CAMPSITE COURIERS

British camping holiday firms hire large numbers of people to remain on one campsite throughout Europe for several months. Holidaybreak (www.holidaybreakjobs.com) alone recruits up to 2,000 campsite couriers and children's couriers for the self-drive camping brands Eurocamp and Keycamp. The courier's job is to clean the tents and caravans between visitors, greet clients and deal with difficulties (particularly illness or car breakdowns) and introduce clients to the attractions of the area or even arrange and host social functions and amuse the children. All of this will be rewarded with on average £100–£125 a week in addition to free tent accommodation. Many companies offer half-season contracts April to mid-July and mid-July to the end of September.

The massive camping holiday industry generates winter work as well. Brad Europe has depots in Nantes and Beaucaire near Avignon that clean and repair tents and bedding on behalf of many of the major companies. Staff (who need not speak French though it is an advantage) are needed for the laundry and distribution for four to six months in winter and summer. *Gite* accommodation is provided free of charge in addition to the UK minimum wage. A driving licence is essential for the delivery drivers but not for the laundry operatives. Brad Europe's UK office is in Wigan (01942 829747; info@bradeurope.com; www.bradeurope.com/vacancies.html).

Some camping holiday and tour operators based in Britain are as follows (with the European countries in which they are active):

*Canvas Holidays*, Dunfermline, Scotland (01383 629012; www.canvasholidays recruitment.com). Mainly France but also Germany, Austria, Switzerland, Italy, Luxembourg, Netherlands and Spain.

*Club Cantabrica Holidays*, St Albans, Hertfordshire (01727 866177; www.cantabrica. co.uk). France, Austria and Spain (including Majorca). Summer and winter positions.

*Eurocamp*, Overseas Recruitment Department (Ref WW/09) (01606 787525; www. holidaybreakjobs.com). Up to 1,500 staff for 200 campsites in most Euro-pean countries. Applications accepted from October. Interviews held in Hartford, Cheshire over the winter. Average wage £131 a week (2009).

*Siblu Holidays*, Recruitment Team, Hemel Hempstead (01442 293230; recruitment@ siblu.com). Park reps and children's courier staff for France, Spain and Italy.

*Keycamp Holidays*, Overseas Recruitment Department, Northwich, Cheshire (01606 787525; www.holidaybreakjobs.com). Operate in most European countries.

*Vacansoleil*, Eindhoven, Netherlands (+31 040 8447748; camping-jobs@ vacansoleil.com). Application form for seasonal work is available online at www. vacansoleil.com. Supply summer staff to campsites around France, Spain, Italy, Denmark, Belgium and Holland.

**Caroline Nicholls'** problems at a campsite in Brittany included frequent power fail-ures, blocked loos and leaking tents, though most of the sites belonging to the estab-lished companies are well managed with clean and functioning facilities:

> *Every time there was a steady downpour, one of the tents developed an indoor lake, due to the unfortunate angle at which we had pitched it. I would appear, mop in hand, with cries of 'I don't understand. This has never happened before.' Working as a courier would be a good grounding for an acting career.*

Caroline goes on to say that despite enjoying the company of the client families, she was glad to have the use of a company bicycle to escape the insular life on the camp-site every so often. Some companies guarantee one day off-site which is considered essential for maintaining sanity. The companies do vary in the conditions of work and some offer much better support than others. For example a company for which **Hannah Start** worked ignored her pleas for advice and assistance when one of her clients had appendicitis.

The big companies interview hundreds of candidates and have filled most posts by the end of January. But there is a very high dropout rate (over 50%) and vacancies are filled from a reserve list, so it is worth ringing around the companies as late as April for cancellations. Despite competition, anyone who has studied a European language and has an outgoing personality stands a good chance if he or she applies early and widely enough.

# UKSA

Rory Munro

**RORY MUNRO talks about his gap year at UKSA:**

Rory took part in a UKSA Watersports Extreme programme as part of a gap year between 6th form and college. With multiple start dates all year around, Rory chose to start his programme in February 2009.

UKSA's Watersports Extreme is a combined programme of training modules designed to take anyone from complete beginner up to an instructor level in popular watersports. The programme is designed for people wanting to embark on a career in water sports, which offers fantastic opportunities for travel and work worldwide. With large portions of time training overseas in some amazing venues, it is a popular option for Gappers looking for a fun, rewarding, and stimulating experience.

On his programme Rory learned to teach Kayaking, Dinghy sailing, Windsurfing and Kitesurfing. The programme included 10 weeks training at UKSA's bases in Egypt where Rory perfected his Windsurfing and Kitesurfing skills.

While living and training in Egypt there are a whole host of opportunities to soak up the local sights and culture, and the wind and beach conditions are perfect for mastering watersports. Rory commented,'this was a fantastic experience to find out what you want to do and have a new enthusiasm for other sports.'

Rory has returned to college this year to complete his Engineering studies and inspired by his time at UKSA, is hoping to study Maritime Studies at university. Although now wanting to focus on his academic studies, since completing his training Rory has been offered work with Mark Warner for the 2010 peak season in Greece, which should make for some interesting holiday work.

# Flying Fish

Andrew Merriman

Andrew Merriman decided to do a Dinghy Instructor Course with Flying Fish on the Greek island of Levkas in his gap year:

'I was keen to do a Dinghy Instructor course but I didn't really want to do it in Scotland, where I live! I was looking for a gap year where I could gain new skills but really enjoy myself. A course with Flying Fish seemed like the perfect solution. My brother had done a similar kind of course and had spent time during summers teaching water sports. I could think of no better way of spending my summers.

Just being in such a stunning location and being able to go sailing every day was amazing. Going out and being able to handle the high winds was always really exhilarating. It was always great to be on the water in whatever the weather (even though it was really sunny most of the time) and it was so rewarding to pass the instructor course.

The mountain biking was great too. Vass is a stunning location and the morning rides were really beautiful. It got even more fun after I lost my exceptional fear of going down hill. I cannot mention my weeks in Vass without mentioning the brilliant night life and, specifically, the Zeus bar shelf. Whether it was the barbecues or just chilling and watching a film, it was always easy to have a good time. Everybody in Vass is so cool there that it would be a monumental difficulty to not enjoy yourself.

The most valuable thing that I gained from the course? Blond hair. Only joking! I gained a massive enthusiasm for sailing and for teaching people how to do it. When I taught my first beginner it was such a brilliant experience that I couldn't wait to do it again. And now I can't wait until I can get more instructing done.

The course is also a pretty good preparation for student life. I learned how to cook in Vass which was definitely advantageous. I'd be scuppered if I couldn't cook now. Also, good training for late nights and early mornings. You'll come back to the UK and be surprised by how early everything closes.

Since getting back from the Fish course I have been able to get on the water teaching sailing to the Dundee Sea Cadets and beginners at the University. This has been a great way to meet new people who were interested in sailing. I'm currently at uni, studying medicine. But the plan for next summer is to get a job in the Med and to teach some sailing.'

## ACTIVITY HOLIDAYS

Many specialist tour companies employ leaders for their clients, whether children or adults, on walking, cycling, watersports holidays, etc. Any competent sailor, canoeist, diver, climber, rider, etc. should have no difficulty marketing their skills in the UK and abroad. Try for example Acorn Adventure (www.acorn-jobs.co.uk) or In2action based on the Isle of Wight (recruitment@in2action.co.uk), which recruits action teams to lead children in sports and activities, in resorts from Turkey to Mexico. For more ideas, check the website www.adventurejobs.co.uk.

If you would like to do a watersports course with a view to working abroad, see the entries for Flying Fish and UK Sailing Academy in the 'Directory of Sport and Activity Courses'. They offer training as instructors in windsurfing, diving, dinghy sailing and yachting, followed by a job recruitment service.

## SKI RESORTS

The winter season in the European Alps lasts from about Christmas until late April/early May. Between Christmas and New Year is a terrifically busy time as are the middle two weeks of February during half-term. Because jobs in ski resorts are so popular among the travelling community, wages can be low. So many gap year and older students are (or become) such avid skiers that in their view it is recompense enough to have easy access to the slopes during their time off. One of the best ways to improve your chances of being hired is to do a catering course, some of which specialise in ski chalet cooking (see 'Directory of Cookery Courses').

Specialist ski recruitment websites can be extremely helpful. Three excellent re-cruitment websites are www.natives.co.uk, www.seasonworkers.com and www.free radicals.co.uk, all of which describe themselves as one-stop shops for recruitment of winter staff for Europe and worldwide. Also check out www.snowworkers.com which recently carried a number of ski resort jobs in Japan. Qualified/experienced nannies are especially sought after for the Alps and worldwide.

Either you can try to fix up a job with a British-based ski tour company before you leave (which has more security but lower wages and tends to isolate you in an English-speaking ghetto), or you can look for work on the spot. In the spring preceding the winter season in which you want to work, research ski tour companies (some of which are listed below). Their websites will describe the range of positions they wish to fill. These may vary slightly from company to company but will probably include resort representatives (who may need language skills), chalet staff (who must be able to cook to a high standard), odd jobbers and ski guides/instructors. An increasing number of companies are offering nanny and crèche facilities, so this is a further possibility for the suitably qualified.

Here are some of the major ski tour companies in the UK. Some have a limited number of vacancies which they can fill from a list of people who have worked for them during the summer season or have been personally recommended by former employ-ees. So you should not be too disappointed if you are initially unsuccessful.

**Crystal Holidays** (0845 055 0258; www.jobsinwinter.co.uk/crystal). Part of TUI. 1,500 resort reps and chalet/hotel staff for 140 ski resorts in Europe (especially France, Austria and Italy) and North America (visa required).

**Equity Travel** (01273 648273; www.equity.co.uk/employment). Recruits chefs, house-keeping and waiting staff, handymen, night porters, plongeurs and bar staff (EU nationality essential) as well as ski reps and tour reps for its sizeable operation in Austria, France and Italy.

**Esprit Holidays**, Fleet, Hampshire GU51 3BL, (01252 618318; recruitment@esprit-holidays.co.uk; www.workaseason.com). Vacancies for resort managers, hotel managers, chalet controllers, resort reps, chalet chefs and host/cooks, chalet and hotel assistants, nannies and alpine rangers to work in resorts in France, Austria and Italy.

**First Choice/Skibound/Travelbound**, Crawley, West Sussex RH11 0PQ, (0870 750 1204; overseas.recruitment@firstchoice.co.uk; www.firstchoice4jobs.co.uk). 750 winter staff from EU employed in France, Italy, Austria, etc.

**Inghams Travel**, London SW15 (020 8780 4400 or 020 8780 8803; www.inghams. co.uk/general_pages/job.html). 450 chalet, chalet hotel or bar work jobs for winter season in France, Italy, Austria, Switzerland and Bulgaria. Perks include free ski pass, ski and boot hire, meals, accommodation and return travel from the UK.

**NBV Leisure**, Bromley, Kent BN3 6BD (0870 220 2148; www.nbvleisure.com/recruitment.html). Catered chalet summer and winter holidays in France and Austria.

**Neilson Overseas**, Brighton BN2 5HA, (www.neilson.co.uk/jobs.aspx). Part of Thomas Cook Group. Resorts in Andorra, Austria, Bulgaria, Canada, France and Italy among others.

**Powder Byrne**, London SW15 6TG, (020 8246 5342; www.powderbyrne.com). Up-market company operating in Switzerland, France, Italy and Austria. Also recruit staff for summer resorts programme in Greece, Tunisia, etc.

**Scott Dunn**, London SW17 7PH, (www.scottdunn.com). Established in 1986 offers both summer and winter season recruitment.

**Simply Ski**, part of TUI group (www.shgjobs.co.uk). Chalet and other staff needed in Austria, France and Switzerland.

**Skibound** (www. skibound.co.uk). Snow sports holidays for school parties. Owned by TUI.

**Skiworld**, London W6 9NU, (0870 420 5914/3; recruitment@skiworld.ltd.uk; www. skiworld.ltd.uk). Catered chalet and hotel holidays in France, Austria, Switzerland, Canada, USA and others.

**Snowline VIP** (www.snowline.co.uk). Employs 180 winter staff each year; usual minimum age 21.

**Supertravel Ski** (020 7962 1369; skijobs@lotusgroup.co.uk; www.supertravel.co.uk/jobs.asp). Takes on winter staff for France and Austria. All applicants must hold an EU passport and have a National Insurance number.

If you attend the Metro Ski & Snowboard Show held each October at Olympia in London, some ski companies hand out job descriptions and application forms. An added bonus is that you can attend the Natives Jobs Fair free at the same time.

A classic job for the gap year is as a 'chalet girl' (or boy). The number of chalets in the Alps has hugely increased over the past decade or so with the biggest areas of expansion for British holidaymakers being Méribel, Courchevel and Val d'Isère in France, Verbier in Switzerland and St Anton in Austria. Clients in chalets are looked after by a chalet girl or (increasingly) chalet boy. The chalet host does everything (sometimes with an assistant) from cooking first-class meals for the 10 or so guests to clearing the snow from the footpath (or delegating that job). She is responsible for keeping the chalet clean, preparing breakfast, packed lunches, tea and dinner, providing ice and advice, and generally keeping everybody happy.

Although this sounds an impossible regimen, many chalet hosts manage to fit in several hours of skiing in the middle of each day. The standards of cookery skills required vary from company to company depending on the degree of luxury (i.e. the price) of the holidays. In most cases, you will have to cook a trial meal for the tour company before being accepted for the job or at least submit detailed menu plans. Average pay for a chalet host starts at about £75 a week, plus perks including accommodation, food and a ski pass (worth about £1,000 for the season). Recruitment of the 1000+ chalet hosts needed in Europe gets underway in May so early application is essential.

Eighteen-year-old **Dan Hanfling** baked a creditable cake for his interview in the autumn and was pleased to be offered a chalet job. But on arriving in the Alps, he learned that chalet staff in their first season are not always assigned their own chalet, but are expected to service a number of them by carrying supplies, cleaning toilets, etc. This job was a lot less glamorous than he had imagined, and he returned to England after just a few weeks (to the consternation of his parents who had booked a Christmas holiday in the same resort).

If you wait until you arrive to look for a ski resort job in the Alps, be prepared for lots of refusals. The situation is not as tight in resorts in Canada and New Zealand, so if you have a working holiday visa for those countries, you might try resorts like Whistler, Banff and Queenstown (see country chapters).

If you are already a good skier and interested in qualifying as an instructor, contact BASI, the *British Association of Snowsport Instructors*, or one of the gap year instructor courses such as *Ski Le Gap*, *Peakleaders* or the *International Academy* (see 'Directory of Sport and Activity Courses'). The recent explosion in snowboarding has resulted in many young people qualifying as instructors, though with not much demand, since snowboarders tend to be self-taught.

# FARM WORK

Itinerant workers have traditionally travelled hundreds of miles to gather in the fruits of the land, from the tiny blueberry to the mighty watermelon. Living and working in rural areas is often a more authentic way of experiencing another culture than working in the tourist industry. The availability of harvesting work in Europe has been greatly reduced by the large numbers of Slovaks, Romanians, Albanians, etc. who have moved into every corner of Europe trying to earn the money their own struggling economies cannot provide.

To find out which farmers are short of help, check www.pickingjobs.com, which is strongest on the UK and Australia or, if already on the road, ask in the youth hostel, campsite or local café/pub. (According to one experienced traveller, this is great for people who are good at meeting prospective employers in pubs, unlike him who just gets drunk and falls over.) The great advantage of job-hunting in rural areas rather than in cities is that people are more likely to know their neighbours' labour requirements and often are more sympathetic and helpful in their attitudes.

Picking fruit may not be as easy as it sounds. If you are part of a large team you may be expected to work at the same speed as the most experienced picker, which can be both exhausting and discouraging. Having even a little experience can make the whole business more enjoyable, not to mention more financially worthwhile if you are being paid piece work rates. The vast majority of picking jobs is paid piece work (with the notable exception of grape harvests in Europe), though a minimum level of productivity will be expected, particularly if you are being given room and board.

Anyone with a farming background could consider placing an advert in a farmers' journal or small town newspaper in your favoured destination. Something might work, along the lines of: '19-year-old Briton taking a year out before university seeks farm work. Willing to exchange labour for board and lodging and chance to get to know the country.' The usual caution must be exercised when considering any replies. If possible, talk to your prospective employer on the telephone and ask them for a reference. Always try to obtain the terms of employment in writing.

IEPUK (www.iepuk.com), the rural employment specialist, places suitable applicants in all rural industries including agriculture, horticulture, winemaking. For people with relevant equine experience, live-in vacancies in dozens of countries in Europe and worldwide can be tracked down.

Some European countries have programmes whereby young people spend a month or two assisting on a farm, e.g. Norway and Switzerland (see country chapters). A farming background is not necessary for participating in these schemes, though of course it always helps. The work-for-keep exchange on organic farms known collectively as World Wide Opportunities on Organic Farms (WWOOF) is described in the chapter on 'Volunteering'.

# TEACHING ENGLISH

The English language is the language which literally millions of people around the world want to learn. There are areas of the world where the boom in English language learning seems to know no bounds, from Ecuador to China, Lithuania to Vietnam. People who are lucky enough to have been born native speakers of English find their skills universally in demand, though it is far easier to land a teaching job in a language school once you have a university degree.

As is obvious by the programme descriptions of the major gap year placement agencies in an earlier chapter, a high percentage of all gap year volunteer placements revolve around teaching English to young children, in secondary schools and to adult learners. One of the best sources of information about the whole topic of English teaching (if I may be permitted to say so) is the 2009 edition of *Teaching English Abroad* by Susan Griffith (Vacation-Work/Crimson Publishing, £14.99) which covers in great detail training courses, recruitment agencies and lists individual language schools around the world.

Your chances of gaining employment in a gap year are much stronger if you have undergone some training, preferably the four-week certificate course (see *Courses* chapter for further information).

## JOB-HUNTING

Printed advertisements have been largely replaced by the internet, though it is probably still worth checking advertisements in Tuesday's *Guardian* between February and June. Most advertisers are looking for teachers who have some training or experience but in some cases, a carefully crafted CV and enthusiastic personality are as important as EFL training and experience.

For schools, a website advert offers an easy and instantaneous means of publicising a vacancy to an international audience. People looking for employment can use search engines to look for all pages with references to EFL, English language schools and recruitment. CVs can be e-mailed quickly and cheaply to advertising schools, who can then use e-mail themselves to chase up references. The internet has very quickly taken over as the primary means of recruitment.

Arguably it has become a little too easy to advertise and answer job adverts online. At the press of a button, your CV can be clogging up dozens, nay, hundreds of computers. But everywhere you look on the internet, potentially useful links can be found, especially the long established Dave's ESL Café (www.eslcafe.com) which dominates the field, along with www.tefl.com. 'Dave' provides a mind-boggling but well-organised amount of material for the future or current teacher including accounts of people's experiences of teaching abroad (but bear in mind that these are the opinions of individuals). It also provides links to specific institutes and language school chains in each country.

Native speaker teachers are nearly always employed to stimulate conversation rather than to teach grammar. Yet a basic knowledge of English grammar is a great asset when pupils come to ask awkward questions. The book *English Grammar in Use* by Raymond Murphy is recommended for its clear explanations and accompanying student exercises.

Most schools practise the direct method (total immersion in English) so not knowing the language shouldn't prevent you from getting a job. Some employers may provide nothing more than a scratched blackboard and will expect you to dive in using the 'chalk and talk' method. If you are very alarmed at this prospect you could ask a sympathetic colleague if you could sit in on a few classes to give you some ideas. Brochures picked up from tourist offices or airlines can be a useful peg on which to hang a lesson. If you're stranded without any ideas, write the lyrics of a pop song on the board and discuss them.

Whatever the kind of teaching you find, things probably won't go as smoothly as you would wish. After a year of teaching English in Italy, **Andrew Spence** had this sensible advice:

> *Teaching is perhaps the best way there is of experiencing another country but you must be prepared for periods when not all is as it should be. The work is sometimes arduous and frustrating, or it can be very exhilarating. Be prepared to take the very rough with the fairly smooth.*

# AU PAIRING

Gap year students who choose to become au pairs are generally looking for an affordable way to improve their knowledge of a country's language and culture. For several generations, female school leavers have been flocking to the Continent, and more recently to the USA and even Australia, attracted by the safe and stable environment that a family placement can provide. When the au pair arrangement works well, it is ideal for young, under-confident and impecunious students who want to work abroad. Occasionally, young men can find live-in jobs, but the number of families and therefore agencies willing to entertain the possibility of having a male au pair is still painfully small.

The terms au pair, mother's help and nanny are often applied rather loosely, since all are primarily live-in jobs concerned with looking after children. Nannies may have some formal training and take full charge of the children. Mother's helps work full-time and undertake general housework and/or cooking as well as childcare. Au pairs are supposed to work for no more than 30 hours a week and are expected to learn a foreign language while living with a family. Although the term au pair is used in the American context, the hours are much longer and there is no language learning element for British au pairs (see *USA* chapter).

One of the great advantages of these live-in positions generally is that they are relatively easy to get (at least for women over 18). After proving to an agency or a family that you are reasonably sensible, you will in the majority of cases be able to find a placement, though it is much easier and quicker in some countries than others, e.g. easy in France, Switzerland and Italy, but more difficult in Scandinavia and Portugal. Furthermore au pairs can usually benefit from legislation that exempts them from work permit requirements.

The minimum age can be a stumbling-block for some school leavers who are not yet 18. The majority of agencies prefer to accept applications only from candidates over 18, as **Camilla Preeston** discovered:

> *I had decided even before I had finished school that I would take a year off between school and university, and au pairing seemed like the perfect way to do this. Being 17 and a half made things much more difficult in the beginning though I sent off endless letters to agencies in Britain and overseas. Most flatly replied that I was too young, though a couple said that they would try anyway. I eventually had success with a foreign agency. The reason they didn't turn me away may have been because the fee they levy is paid upfront before a family is found. By the time they had found me a family in Calais, four months of my year off had already gone by and I was almost ready to give up. I immediately accepted the offer, perhaps a little hastily. However, had I refused it, I might not have found another family willing to accept me due to my age, and it was the first family offer I had received in the four months I had been trying.*

Camilla's youth did not prevent her from coping with what turned out to be a difficult situation in which she was expected to accept a lot of responsibility for the children (including a newborn baby) and the running of the household, while the mother was away for five days and two nights a week.

The standard length of au pair stay is for one academic year, typically September to June. Summer stays can also be arranged to coincide with the school holidays and there is some inevitable turn-over at Christmas when homesick au pairs go home to their families and then decide not to return. The advantage of a summer placement is that the au pair will accompany the family to their holiday destination at the seaside or in the mountains; the disadvantage is that the children will be your responsibility for more hours than they would be if they were at school, and also most language classes will close for the summer. Make enquiries as early as possible, since there is a shortage of summer-only positions.

## PROS AND CONS

### THE GROUND RULES REGARDING AU PAIRING IN EUROPE

*The Council of Europe guidelines stipulate that au pairs should be aged 18–27 (though these limits are flexible), should be expected to work about five hours a day, five days per week, plus a couple of evenings of babysitting, must be given a private room and full board, health insurance, opportunities to learn the language and pocket money. The standard pocket money paid to au pairs in Europe is €260 a month, though it can be more, for example in Switzerland.*

The relationship of au pair to family is not like the usual employer/employee relationship; in fact the term au pair means 'on equal terms'. The terminology used is of 'host family' rather than 'employer'. Therefore the success of the arrangement depends more than usual on whether individuals hit it off, so there is always an element of risk when living in a family of strangers.

Once you have arrived in the family, it is important to clarify immediately what your hours and duties will be, which day you will be paid, whether you can expect a rise and how much notice either party must give if they wish to terminate the arrangement. This gets everyone off to a business-like start. But no matter how well-defined your duties are, there are bound to be occasions when your extra services will be taken for granted. It may seem that your time is not your own. So the standard working hours can soon turn into an unofficial string of 14 hour days. Whether you can tolerate this depends entirely on your disposition and on the compensating benefits of the job, e.g. free use of car and telephone, nice kids, good food, lots of sunshine, etc.

**Gillian Forsyth's** au pairing experience in Bavaria was a great success:

*I had no official day off or free time but was treated as a member of the family. Wherever they went I went too. I found this much more interesting than being treated as an employee as I really got to know the country and the people. In the evenings I did not have to sit in my room, but chatted with the family. Three years later we still keep in close contact and I have been skiing with them twice since, on an au pair/friend basis.*

If you do not have such a friendly arrangement with your family, you may feel lonely and cut off in a foreign country. Many au pairs make friends at their language classes. Some agencies issue lists of other au pairs in the vicinity.

Most au pairs' duties revolve around the children. For some, taking sole responsibility for a child can be even more alarming than cooking for the first time. You should be prepared to handle a few emergencies (for example sick or lost children) as well as the usual excursions to the park or collecting them from school. The agency questionnaire will ask you in detail what experience you have had with children and whether you are willing to look after infants, etc., so your preferences should be made known early.

## APPLYING

Many au pair agencies now operate only as online matching services. The old-fashioned one-woman agency that used to arrange family placements with the help of a partner agency in France, Germany, Italy, etc. has all but disappeared. This is primarily due to 2004 UK legislation which makes it illegal for any au pair agency to charge au pairs a fee for finding them work, either in the UK or abroad. As a result agencies which at one time sent many British girls abroad are now concentrating exclusively on placing foreign girls with paying client families in the UK.

If you are already abroad, check in the local English language newspaper or visit an au pair agency office in the country where you are (addresses provided in country chapters). Many European agencies charge a substantial fee of €200+ which they claim is necessary to guarantee a minimum quality of service.

Many leading au pair agencies and youth exchange organisations in Europe belong to IAPA, the International Au Pair Association, an international body trying to regulate the industry. The IAPA website (www.iapa.org) has links to its member agencies around the world. Agencies that specialise in one country are mentioned in the country chapters.

Other ways of hearing about openings are to check the notice boards at the local English-speaking churches or ask the head teacher of a junior school if she/he knows of any families wanting an au pair. One tip for finding babysitting jobs in resorts is to introduce yourself to the *portière* or receptionist on the desk of good hotels and ask them to refer guests looking for a babysitter to you, possibly offering them a small commission. With more suspicion around these days, informal arrangements like this are less likely to succeed; some potential clients might be reassured if you have good references.

## THE INTERNET

Cyberspace buzzes with an exchange of information about live-in childcare. Finding agency details is very easy with several clicks of a mouse. Au pair placement was something that was always done by telephone and correspondence rather than requiring a face-to-face interview, so it is an activity that is well suited to an online database. Among the most popular sites are aupair-agency.com, greataupair.com, findaupair. com, au-pair-box.com and aupair-world.net (German-based), aupairconnect.com (US-based), aupair-select.com and aupairs.co.uk. With nearly 20,000 registered au pairs and nannies and nearly 4,000 vacancies, *GreatAuPair* claims to be the largest agency.

Internet agencies enable families and applicants to engage in DIY arrangements. They invite prospective au pairs to register their details, including age, nationality, relevant experience and in many cases a photo, to be uploaded onto a website which then becomes accessible to registered families. The families then make contact with suitable au pairs after paying an introduction fee to the web-based agency. Registration is invariably free for the job-seeker.

One problem identified by the traditional agencies is that this method makes it very difficult to carry out any effective screening of either party. On the other hand, the same could be said for 'situations vacant' advertising in the conventional way (see below). If relying on the internet, it is essential to ascertain exactly the nature of the situation and the expectations of your new employer. Work out in your mind what you will do in the event the arrangement does not work out; if the agency is simply a database-provider, they will be able to offer no back-up. **Jean-Marc Cressini**, director of the French agency *Oliver Twist*, thinks that this book '*should really warn applicants about free websites, as we have just been informed by Interpol that some girls have paid large amounts of money to families who do not exist. A person pretending to be a family has been arrested in England for asking applicants for large bank transfers.*' You should always be suspicious of any individual, family and even company that asks for money upfront.

**Jayde Cahir** turned to the internet, found an agency, was emailed several families' portfolios from which she was able to make direct contact, and eventually chose a family in Germany. In initial discussions with the host family, she was misled on several counts and found that she was expected to be more a paid companion for the neglected wife than an au pair. Even though she did develop a good relationship with the wife and boy, the husband took against her and unceremoniously dismissed her: '*I left the house within two hours of receiving his note asking me to leave or he would "throw me out". So I was left in a foreign country, unable to speak the language with nowhere to live. In most cases, the agencies are there to support you, however, mine never returned my phone calls. This ended up being a very expensive experience as I am still owed unpaid wages.*'

# COURSES

After the rigours and stresses of sitting A Levels, many school leavers aspire to spend the following 15 months reading nothing more challenging than *The Beach* by Alex Garland set on a fantasy Thai island. But after a decent recovery period has elapsed after exams, the idea of studying something either for fun or with a view to your future at university or in a career may come to seem more bearable. Whatever course is embarked on, extra qualifications and skills are viewed favourably by universities and potential employers, and students will gain practical knowledge for use at university and in later life.

Several course providers, principally *Objective Gap Safety*, *Safetrek* and *Ultimate Gap Year*, offer short preparatory courses for gap year students embarking on expeditions and world travel. See entries under 'Gap Year Safety and Preparation' below. One of the course organisers describes a potentially lethal situation for which his course prepared the clients well:

> *About 18 months ago, we trained a group going off to Belize. On arrival they went to pick up the two 4WDs they had arranged (through Avis) and found one of them to be seriously sub-standard. They were told that there was no alternative but that the vehicle would be replaced the next day and so they reluctantly took the vehicle. Before they signed their life away though, they took very thorough photos of all aspects of the vehicle. Halfway through their journey, the rear axle sheared and the vehicle rolled off the road. Thanks to sensible planning, they only had the two team leaders in the 'dodgy' vehicle and all the gear. The two escaped with only bad scrapes thanks to the kit being correctly packed and stopping the vehicle from being squashed too much. On return to the car hire company, they were given short shrift and so went straight to the police with the photographs. On return to the shop, they got a much better response!*

## RANGE OF COURSES

Depending on how you have decided to divide up your gap year, you may find yourself spending a good chunk at the beginning trying to earn money in a less-than-stimulating workplace like a supermarket or rowdy pub. If most of your friends have gone off to university or travelling, you may have the leisure to take a course locally (see section below). This can provide an ideal chance to get your driving licence, obtain a life-saving qualification or sports instructor certificate, etc.

If you go abroad later in the year with no pre-arranged placement, it is a good idea to take documentary evidence of any qualifications you have earned in case you have the chance to work as an office temp in Sydney or spend a week cooking on a private yacht. A multitude of short leisure courses can be searched on the very good search engine supported by GoLearnTo (www.golearnto.com; 0844 502 0445), anything from beginners' Chinese in Beijing to short gladiator courses in Lazio, to Spanish and tango in Argentina.

# LANGUAGE COURSES

The gap year is an ideal opportunity for students to brush up on a barely remembered GCSE language or even start from scratch with a new language. Most employers will view this as a very constructive allocation of time, and anyone with competence in another language has an advantage in many job hunts. Even people who are not planning to study modern languages at university should consider the advantages of getting to grips with one of the main European languages. Evening language classes offered by local authorities usually follow the academic year and are aimed at hobby learners. Intensive courses offered privately are much more expensive. If you are really dedicated, consider using a self-study programme with books and CDs, online or broadcast language course, though discipline is required to make progress. Hold out a carrot to yourself of a trip to a country where your target language is spoken. Even if you don't make much headway with the course at home, take the books and tapes with you since you will have more incentive to learn once you are immersed in a language.

Although many people have been turning to the web to teach them a language, many conventional teach-yourself courses are still on the market, for example the Take Off in… series from Oxford University Press (www.askoxford.com/languages) available as mp3 downloads, the BBC (bbc.co.uk/languages), Linguaphone (0800 136973; linguaphone.co.uk) and Audioforum (audioforum.com). Linguaphone recommends half an hour of study a day for three months to master the basics of a language. A more enjoyable way of learning a language (and usually a more successful one) is by speaking it with the natives. Numerous British companies represent a range of language schools abroad offering in-country language courses. They are very familiar with differences between schools, qualifications, locations, etc. and what is most suitable for clients. *CESA Languages Abroad*, *Caledonia Languages Abroad*, *Cactus Language* and *Language Courses Abroad*, among others, all have wide-ranging programmes in Europe and beyond. These agencies also provide a useful back-up service if the course does not fulfil your requirements in any way (see list at the beginning of the 'Directory of Language Courses' later in this chapter).

Of course it is also possible to book a course directly with a language school abroad which is the route that **Annabel Iglehart** from Edinburgh chose in her post-university gap year:

> *After completing my university degree, I decided to take a year (or two) out to gain new skills and participate in interesting activities around the world. After working in a variety of jobs at home, I went to Salamanca to do a three-month intensive Spanish language course with Mester. I planned and paid for my course and accommodation directly through Mester and this saved me a lot of money; it was by far the most economical way to organise the trip. The course was fantastic. The classes were fast-paced and the teachers excellent. I lived with a Spanish family for a while and then moved to a flat with other students. I met loads of people with whom I am still in touch.*

While learning a language at secondary school, you usually have two or three hours of classes a week which could work out at as little as 80 hours a year. While doing an eight-week intensive course, you might have 240 hours, the equivalent of three years of school instruction plus you will be speaking the language outside the classroom, so progress is usually very quick.

Literally thousands of language schools around the world would like your business, so care needs to be taken in choosing one that suits individual needs. Possible sources of language school addresses on the web are http://language.studyabroad.com, http://languagestudy.goabroad.com/search.cfm and http://language.shawguides.com. After considering the obvious factors such as price and location when choosing a language school, also try to find out the average age and likely nationalities of your fellow learners, whether there will be any one-to-one tuition and whether the course concentrates on oral or written skills, whether there are extracurricular activities and excursions included in the fee, and generally as much as you can. One key factor is whether or not a school prepares its students for exams. If they do and you are there only for the fun of it, you may find that lessons are not suitable (and vice versa).

Whereas some language schools run purely recreational courses, others offer some kind of qualification. Some schools are instantly recognised such as the Alliance Française and the Goethe Institute. At the other end of the spectrum, some schools offer nothing more than a certificate outlining the period of study and perhaps the level of language reached or work covered in the course, which may be of limited value if you ever need to show proof of language attainment.

Serious language schools on the continent usually offer the possibility of preparing for one of the internationally recognised exams. In France, the qualification for aspiring language learners is the DELF *(Diplôm Elémentaire de Langue Français)* while the Spanish counterpart is the DELE *(Diploma de Español como Lengua Extranjera)* both of which are recognised by employers, universities, officialdom, etc. The DELE is split into three levels: *Certificado Inicial de Español, Diploma Básico de Español* and the *Diploma Superior de Español.* Most schools say that even the Basic Diploma requires at least eight or nine months of study in Spain. A prior knowledge of the language, of course, allows the student to enrol at a higher level and attain the award more quickly. No single qualification in Italy is as dominant as the DELE or the DELF. Typical of Italian exams is CILS *(Certificato di Italiano come Lingua Straniera)* which was established by Siena University and is authorised by the Italian Ministry of Foreign Affairs.

Recreational language courses are offered by virtually every school and are preferred by many gap year students. Some programmes are much more structured than others, so students need to look for flexible courses which allow them to progress at their own rate. Many people agree that the fastest way to improve fluency is to have one-to-one lessons, though of course these are more expensive than group classes. Usually a combination of the two works best.

Another factor that can impede progress is if you are in the midst of your compatriots. A class in which many languages are represented is more likely to use the target language rather than slip into English. Even if you get to spend a lot of time in the company of locals, you may be expected to help them improve their English. One wily young woman studying French in Bordeaux during her gap year arrived at a solution to this problem:

> *The only real frustration of my time so far has to be coming across French people who wish to improve their English. They respond to your attempt in French with their own attempt in English. However I have developed a cunning solution. I provide them with a quick explanation that I am in fact Icelandic or Russian and we are soon back on track.*

Increasingly, major language schools are offering work experience placements to their 'graduates'. Many belong to WYSE Work Abroad mentioned in the chapter on 'Work Experience'. Many language courses abroad combine language tuition with cultural and other studies. For instance while learning Spanish, you can also take lessons in dance or cookery or follow the course up with an unpaid internship; while studying Italian in Florence, you can also take drawing classes, and so on. The possibilities are endless. Living with a family is highly recommended especially for beginners since it usually forces you to speak the target language from the beginning.

## TEFL TRAINING

In some cases, a preparatory course in Teaching English as a Foreign Language (known as TEFL, pronounced 'teffle') is required by year out placement agencies or individual language schools, whereas in others a willingness to communicate is sufficient.

If you are entertaining the idea of teaching English in your gap year, the best way to outrival the competition and make the job-hunt (not to mention the job itself) easier is to do a TEFL training course of which there is an enormous choice in the UK. Two standard recognised qualifications will improve your range of job options. The best known is the Cambridge Certificate in English Language Teaching to Adults (CELTA) administered and awarded by *Cambridge Assessment* (01223 553355; www.cambridgeESOL.org/teaching). The other is the Certificate in TESOL (Teaching English to Speakers of Other Languages) offered by *Trinity College London* (020 7820 6100; www.trinitycollege.co.uk).

Both are very intensive and expensive, averaging £850–£950. These courses involve at least 100 hours of rigorous training with a practical emphasis (full-time for four weeks or part-time over several months). Most centres expect applicants to have the equivalent of university entrance qualifications, i.e. three GCSEs and two A-Levels, but some admit only university graduates.

For people confused by the number of TEFL training courses jostling for attention in the marketplace, Cactus TEFL (0845 130 4775; www.cactustefl.com) is the only international admissions and jobs service for TEFL. It delivers up-to-date information on hundreds of TEFL courses throughout the world, which can be used to compare prices. Cactus TEFL offers an impartial and informed advice service for anyone new to TEFL. The company sends over 1,000 trainees on training courses all over the world every year.

A list of centres in the UK and abroad offering the Cambridge Certificate is available from Cambridge Assessment, which oversees the ESOL exams mentioned above; they are all linked from their website as well. CELTA courses are also offered at more than 250 overseas centres from the Middle East to Queensland, including 10 in the USA and 30 in Australia and New Zealand.

Centres that offer short introductory courses in TEFL or their own proprietary certificates vary enormously in quality and price. Although they are mainly intended to act as preparatory programmes for more serious courses, many people who hold just a short certificate go on to teach. Among the best known are:

**EF English First Teacher Training** (0161 256 1400; www.englishfirst.com). 4-week EF Certificate course offered monthly in Manchester and occasionally other locations. Cost £575 (this course is subsidised, with successful trainees guaranteed teaching posts in China, Indonesia or Russia) or £875 for those who do not wish to commit to working for EF.

**i-to-i**, Leeds LS18 5NY, (0871 423 9941; www.onlinetefl.com). Intensive TEFL weekend courses at venues in UK/Eire cities. Price for online course from £199. A free 'TEFL Course Taster' can be checked online at www.onlinetefl.com.

**Saxoncourt Teacher Training**, London W1K 5SN, (020 7499 8533; www.saxoncourt.com). Subsidised 1-week introductory TEFL course throughout the year for positions in China, Japan and Taiwan.

**TEFL Time**, West Sussex BN12 4AP, (020 7558 8721; www.tefltime.com). Weekend courses affiliated with the volunteer placement agency Travellers Worldwide. Course fee £189.

**TEFL Training**, Witney, Oxfordshire (01993 891121; www.tefltraining.co.uk). 20-hour practical and intensive weekend seminars in cities around the UK. £210.

Many advantages can be gained by signing up for a TEFL course in the place where you want to work, from Barcelona to Bangkok. Most TEFL training centres have excellent contacts with language schools and can assist with the job hunt. Among the best known providers of CELTA courses are the *British Council* and *International House*, offering the training in many cities from Madrid to Sydney. But scores of independent providers provide TEFL training courses of varying lengths; this small selection gives a flavour of the range available:

**Boland School**, Brno, Czech Republic, and Suzhou, China (www.boland-czech.com and www.boland-china.com). Intensive 148-hour 4-week graded courses lead to an International TEFL Diploma qualification. The cost is €1,295 in the Czech Republic (plus €350 for accommodation) and €1,250 in China (plus €300 for single-room accommodation).

**BridgeTEFL**, Denver, USA (+1 888 827 4757 toll-free in North America; 0800 028 8051 toll-free in the UK; tefl-celta@bridgelinguatec.com; www.bridgetefl.com).

# CESA

Stefania

**Stefania spent 24 weeks in Florence on an Italian Gap year programme:**

'I have an Italian background but I had little knowledge of the language. I was looking forward to the linguistic challenge, but was very nervous and excited. I definitely felt better prepared for the experience after talking to the CESA staff.

Having lessons solidly in Italian was the real challenge - but it made learning the language easier. I found the lessons fantastic; all the staff were lovely and helped as much as they could when you couldn't understand something. The school was really good and the location was so convenient, right in the centre of Florence.

Florence is a buzzing, small, safe town with an amazing culture and architecture. In free afternoons I loved visiting the galleries and museums. I made some great friends and it was brilliant to be able to travel around Italy and share the experiences with so many great people.

I found CESA Languages very reliable and helpful and recommend them to you! I just hope I get the chance to do it all again!'

**Phoebe spent 12 weeks in Cannes on a French Gap Year Programme:**

'The important thing to come out of my gap year is my French. I have every confidence it has flourished under the instruction of my professor Katia, who was amazing and extremely patient. The teachers are brilliant, and with lessons taught solely in French, it is a steep learning curve. It is always challenging, but I made so much progress every month that you just await the next lesson with impatience as you know you're going to meet something new.

The college atmosphere is unbelievable. Everyone becomes so close; living, eating and learning together. The beach is so close and beautiful and there are so many things to see and to do. I now feel very well travelled, from meeting people from all over the globe.

There is so much to do at the college and of course outside of college. Whether it is riding, scuba diving or an excursion to a museum, the office was always packed with great ideas and helpful advice. The bar organised some great nights - karaoke, crepe soirees, cheese and wine nights, ice-cream soirees - they were always brilliant and the best way to meet new people. All in all it is impossible to be bored, and it was always more of a challenge to find free time as opposed to finding something to do. I think that the best testimonial of my time at the college is in the fact that I'm actually extending my stay for a further six months and cannot wait to see what adventures the future has to hold.

If you're thinking about it - just pick up the phone and call CESA.'

Bridge-TEFL is an accredited language training company which offers TEFL, IDELT (their proprietary qualification) and CELTA teacher certification and job placement programmes in Asia, Europe, the Middle East and Latin America. Also offers online TEFL course (www.TEFLOnline.com). TEFL training (2–4 weeks) available in Argentina, Brazil, Cambodia, Chile, China, Costa Rica, Czech Republic, England, Greece, Hungary, Italy, Mexico, Peru, Russia, Spain, Thailand, Turkey, Vietnam and the USA.

*Íbero School Argentina*, Buenos Aires (+54 5218 0240; www.iberospanish.com). TEFL/TESOL Certification Programme. 4 weeks with 95 hours of input classes and 6 hours of teaching practice with real students. $870.

After finishing A-Levels, **Sam James** and **Sophie Ellison** from Yorkshire decided to spend their gap year in Barcelona if possible. They both signed up to do the Trinity Certificate in TESOL course at Oxford TEFL in their destination city, deciding that this would give them the introduction they needed, and it worked (see *Spain* chapter).

## IT AND BUSINESS SKILLS COURSES

Colleges of Further Education and private colleges offer a wealth of courses that many gap year students might choose to pursue, possibly with a view to earning money quickly for a planned placement or expedition later in the year. IT and Business skills courses can prove very useful for finding well-paid temporary work before and during university. Many vocational courses attract government grants for students and the college should be able to tell you whether funding is available and how to apply.

The British Accreditation Council for Independent Further and Higher Education or BAC (www.the-bac.org) accredits around 230 private colleges in the UK. Many of these offer business and IT courses, while others specialise in subjects such as hospitality management and cookery, which may be useful to those wishing to spend part of their gap year working for a tour company or in a ski resort. Note that many of BAC's accredited colleges specialise in tutoring students from abroad (e.g. for A-Levels) and not all of the colleges run short courses. The BAC website includes links to the colleges' own websites with details of the courses on offer.

## OUTDOOR PURSUITS AND SPORTS COURSES

A recognised qualification in any sport will make it very easy to pick up work later in your gap year and find enjoyable holiday jobs throughout your university career. Skilled sportsmen and women can often find gainful employment in their area of expertise whether instructing tennis locally, joining a scheme to coach soccer in the USA or South Africa (see country chapters) or making money teaching dinghy sailing in Sydney. Numerous multi-activity centres in Britain and Europe recruit staff to lead and instruct and offer their own pre-season training, sometimes free of charge.

A structured way of acquiring skills and qualifications during your sporting gap year is to participate in the Duke of Edinburgh Award scheme (described in the *Expeditions* chapter). This can lead to a qualification in a variety of activity and sporting areas, including expedition skills.

A life-saving qualification allows you to work as a lifeguard, though there are different qualifications for pool and beach lifeguarding. Further afield, diving instructors work at Red Sea resorts, mountain leaders are hired to guide groups in the Himalayas, trainee parachutists find work packing parachutes in the USA and Competent Crew get positions on ocean-going yachts. The best starting place for acquiring the necessary training and certification is the governing body of the sport that interests you which will be able to point you towards instructors' courses in the UK and beyond. For example see entries for the *British Association of Snowsport Instructors*, which offers a 10-week course aimed specifically at gap year students, and the *Royal Yachting Association* below. Others include the *British Canoe Union* (www.bcu.org.uk), the *British Mountaineering Council* (www.thebmc.co.uk) and the *British Horse Society* (www.bhs.org.uk). *Mountain Leader Training England* (www.mlte.org) offers certificates at different levels e.g. Walking Group Leader and the Single Pitch Award, some of which are offered by the *Edale Youth Hostel* (01433 670302; edaleactivities@yha.org.uk).

Many companies and youth training organisations run expedition and related courses at varying levels. The *Plas y Brenin National Mountain Centre* in Snowdonia (www.pyb.co.uk) runs 2- and 5-day residential courses in a range of disciplines. The most ambitious courses are run by companies such as *Jagged Globe* based in Sheffield (www.jagged-globe.com), which runs ice climbing and other courses in Scotland, Wales and the Alps.

Surf-mad 18-year-old **Nick Braithwaite** spent part of his gap year in Australia doing a Surf Instructor/Lifesaving Traineeship with *Flying Fish* before starting his geography degree at Swansea University (see the *Australia* chapter for more information and a case history from another Flying Fish 'graduate').

There are global shortages of qualified instructors in several sports including diving, watersports and snowsports. Ross Fairgrieve chose a diving course for his gap year:

'*O*ver the course of my gap year I went from a dive virgin to a PADI Divemaster on the Thai island of Koh Tao. Although I had wanted to learn to dive for a few years, it seemed destined to remain on the 'fifty things to forget to do before you die' list. But I decided on the Personal Overseas Development programme because I really liked the look of the experience that it offered and I wanted to do something that could be helpful to me in the future (i.e. gaining a professional diving qualification) rather than 'just' travelling. I considered joining the organisations that offer marine conservation opportunities but in the end I decided to concentrate on diving, knowing that I could always do something more

> *conservation-based after university when I'm armed with an oceanogra-phy degree. I knew that I could just book the diving through a dive school and it would be cheaper that way. As this was my first time away from home for this length of time however, and because I had never been to Thailand before, I decided to pay a little bit of extra money for the support and peace of mind that having a bit of guidance and support provided. It was also nice to have diving, accommodation, visas, full travel and dive insurance and transport advice all arranged in one go.'*

Exotic courses are available worldwide from kitesurfing on the Pacific coast of Ecuador with the *Academia de Español Surpacifico* to polo training on an *estancia* in Argentina with *Shoestring Polo*, based in Wiltshire (though it is not a very convincing shoestring since one month costs from $6,000).

## SKI TRAINING

The past five years have seen a remarkable increase in the number of programmes specially tailored to avid or just aspiring skiers and snowboarders taking a year out who want to improve their skiing or to train as instructors. For instance the major focus of **Alice Mundy's** year out was an 11-week course in the Canadian Rockies to become a snowboard instructor with *NONSTOP Ski & Snowboard*:

> *I decided on a course of this kind as I felt it combined one of my passions with a globally recognised qualification which would open up the future possibility of travelling around the world while being able to make a living. The course was expensive – just over £6,000 (covering flights and transfers, accommodation, weekday breakfast and evening meals, full season lift pass, 20 hours a week coaching, CASI Level 1 exam fee and selected week-end trips and activities) plus £200 dangerous sports insurance and £2,000–£3,000 spending money. So, it didn't come cheap for something that could be arranged on an individual basis (sorting out your own flights and accommodation and then entering for your instructor exams off your own bat). But by doing that you would miss out on the high-level 5-days-a-week coaching, which was the overwhelming advantage of this course for me. You receive invaluable preparation for the instructor examinations and the world of work as a snow sports instructor so, if it is your aim to use the qualification at some point in the future, the cost of the course is definitely justified. Also, it provided exactly the right balance that a lot of people my age were looking for – plenty of in-dependence and the experience of living away from home but enough aspects already taken care of and organised for you not to be totally terrified of having to make all the arrangements by yourself on your first big trip away.*

Many companies arrange these courses in a number of locations worldwide, mainly in Canada and more recently in New Zealand, but also in Europe and Patagonia. So far instructor training has not been generally available in the USA to non-Americans. The providers usually claim that they can accommodate beginner skiers, though the majority have been on regular ski holidays for some years. There was no one on Alice's course who had never skied before and in her view it would defy logic for someone who had never even tried a sport to want to become an instructor in it. On the other hand a number of gap year skiers simply want to improve rather than qualify as an instructor. The pass rate for Level 1 in Alice's case was 100%, which indicates that it is an achievable goal even for those with minimal skiing experience.

Those who want to arrange to spend a whole season in a ski resort without joining one of these elite programmes can book accommodation through an operator that specialises in long-stay ski and snowboard holidays, such as *Seasonaires* (0870 068 4545; www.seasonaires.com), which has properties in a large number of resorts from Tignes in the French Alps to Breckenridge in Colorado.

## COOKERY COURSES

The days of the finishing school are over, however, a practical cookery course can prove immensely useful in finding temporary employment both at home and abroad. (It can also put you in a class of your own when you come to share a house with friends at university.) A catering certificate opens up many appealing employment options in ski resorts, private villas or private yachts. A number are aimed specifically at young gappers who want to master enough impressive dishes to land a job in a ski chalet or for a yacht cruise company. In addition to the courses listed in the Directory, try the *Well-Seasoned Chalet Cookery Course* (www.well-seasoned.co.uk) offered in the off-season in Tignes, France.

The private courses are expensive, but some students (and their parents) decide to splash out in order to acquire an instantly recognised qualification such as *Cordon Bleu* or *Tante Marie*. A Food Safety in Catering Certificate can be acquired in half a day or even online (£35 via www.onlinefoodhygiene.com) and is useful for picking up casual work in restaurants to help fund your gap year.

## CREATIVE ARTS COURSES

While the vast majority of school leavers have no fixed idea what they want to pursue, a few may already have developed a leaning towards one of the creative arts or another vocation. Some do an art foundation course in their gap year purely for pleasure rather than as a springboard for applying to art college; further education courses like this are free of charge to those under 19. Some may want to pursue a creative interest in their gap year before heading to university, though more usually this kind of course is taken post-university.

The *London College of Fashion* runs summer courses in London. You might take the opportunity to build up a portfolio of photographs. Budding actors might consider auditioning for the National Youth Theatre in London (www.nyt.org.uk). Workshop auditions (both acting and technical) are held around the country during the spring half-term or at weekends following the end-of-January deadline for applications. *Northern Gap* (www.northern-gap.co.uk) is a small company set up by a director and drama teacher in Cheshire to give gap year students a chance to perform in a professional venue.

The boom in interest in media studies show no signs of abating, and many of those school leavers think of themselves as up-and-coming film makers. The idea of making a film while travelling abroad is very appealing, and many gappers add a clip to YouTube for their friends to enjoy, but even the most naïve 18-year-old will have worked out that it will be next to impossible to make such a venture a commercial success. Although **Hannah Adcock** was post-university when she braved this field and was already involved with a theatre company, her experiences are instructive. She and some friends out of university had set up a semi-professional production company with a strong theatrical background, specialising in Greek tragedy and Shakespeare. They then turned their hands to film making and set up 'Outlook Productions' to make a film in Greece. Plans for making a film adaptation of Shakespeare's *Twelfth Night* had been discussed over a long period but it wasn't until the director and producer visited the Greek island of Patmos that they realised Patmos *was* the Illyria of their dreams (the magical island where the action in *Twelfth Night* takes place). The island was so perfect that even one of *Twelfth Night*'s more inconsequential lines took on a deeper meaning, 'prithee foolish Greek, depart from me'!

The company felt confident that it could sell the film, either to digital TV channels, educational institutions, even to a distributor, because *Twelfth Night* is a well-known play, and school children have to study it. The company couldn't get funding from organisations such as the Arts Council but it did attract private investors: people who had come to theatrical shows liked what they saw and believed in the company. It is a good idea if you are a theatre/production company to keep a mailing list of people who appreciate your work. However, private investment only goes so far when you are making a digital feature film. Paying wages was out of the question so cast and crew were invited to 'profit share'. This way all cast and crew rise or fall on the success or failure of the production, which is a huge risk but a good incentive to work hard! Hannah concludes: '*This is a great way to get into a tough sector – and not just by making the tea. You should get respect for initiative, but this is not a guaranteed money spinner.*'

# DIRECTORIES OF COURSES

## LANGUAGE COURSES

The following entries represent a tiny proportion of language schools worldwide. Of key interest are the first 14 entries which are for companies, the majority in the UK, which represent a selection of language schools. Using an agency simplifies the selection process. Schools and agencies of interest to North Americans are listed in the chapter *A Year Off for North Americans*.

---

### AMERISPAN

PO Box 58129, Philadelphia, PA 19103, USA

☎ +1 800 879 6640

☎ 020 8123 6086 (UK)

💬 Skype: amerispan

✉ info@amerispan.com

🖥 www.amerispan.com/language_schools

Specialist Spanish language travel organisation with expertise in arranging language courses, voluntary placements and internships throughout South and Central America.

**COURSES OFFERED:** Wealth of options throughout South and Central America. Also offers other languages in other countries, e.g. French in Montreal and Quebec, French in Nice and Paris, German in Frankfurt, Italian in Florence plus Chinese, Japanese, Arabic, Russian and Thai.

**ACCOMMODATION:** Mostly homestays.

**OTHER SERVICES:** Unpaid volunteer placements in Costa Rica, Bolivia, Brazil, Chile, Mexico, Guatemala, Ecuador, Argentina and Peru (see entry in 'Directory of Volunteering Abroad').

---

### BRIDGE-LINGUATEC LANGUAGE STUDY ABROAD

915 S. Colorado Boulevard, Denver, CO 80246, USA

☎ +1 866 574 8606 (toll-free in the US and Canada)

☎ 0808 120 7613 (toll-free in the UK)

☎ +1 303 242 8704

✉ traveladviser@bridgeabroad.com

🖥 www.bridgeabroad.com

Bridge-Linguatec is a language training company with language study and culture immersion programmes in Europe and Latin America.

**COURSES OFFERED:** Spanish, French, German, Italian, Portuguese, Russian, Chinese, Japanese and Arabic. Group, private, and combination group/private classes available. Courses include activities and excursions to help students get to know the local culture, as well as comfortable host family accommodation.

**DESTINATIONS:** Argentina, Brazil, Bolivia, Chile, Ecuador, Peru, Uruguay, Venezuela, Costa Rica, Guatemala, Mexico, Puerto Rica, Dominican Republic, France, Germany, Switzerland, Italy, Spain, Russia, Japan, China, Morocco and Egypt.

**DURATION OF COURSES:** Minimum 1 or 2 weeks. Classes start every Monday year-round in most locations, some have specific start dates.

**ACCOMMODATION:** Local host families, shared apartments, hostels, bed and breakfasts and student residences.

**OTHER SERVICES:** Activities and excursions, special language and culture courses such as Business Spanish, French Cuisine, Roman Archaeology and Brazilian Dance.

### CACTUS LANGUAGE TRAINING
4 Clarence House, 30–31 North Street,
Brighton BN1 1EB
℃ 0845 130 4775
✆ info@cactuslanguagetraining.com
🖳 www.cactuslanguagetraining.com

Cactus is a specialist language travel agency. Learning options include language holidays abroad, evening courses in 41 locations and 24 languages across the UK, private and remote tuition, in-company language and cultural training.

**COST:** Varies hugely from course to course (see website). One example: French and surfing in Biarritz; fortnight long courses cost from £1,009 per person, £1,589 with accommodation (excluding flights).

**OTHER SERVICES:** Cactus cooperates with Global Vision International to arrange language courses in conjunction with GVI volunteer placements.

### CALEDONIA LANGUAGES ABROAD
The Clockhouse, 72 Newhaven Road,
Edinburgh EH6 5QG
℃ 0131 621 7721/2
✆ courses@caledonialanguages.co.uk
🖳 www.caledonialanguages.co.uk

Caledonia was established in 1994 and offers language courses in Europe and Latin America suitable for anyone travelling overseas during their gap year. Students can choose either an intensive beginner's course to provide basic language skills to help with travelling, or a course to consolidate existing language skills. Courses are available in Europe or Central/South America, and include staying with a local family and complementary cultural/social activities to help students become integrated into local life.

**COURSES OFFERED:** Language courses for general interest, exam revision, language and culture. These can often be combined with special interest courses such as walking, cooking, dancing, diving and skiing. There are also opportunities to participate in volunteer work programmes in Latin America (see entry in 'Directory of Specialist Gap Year Programmes'). Two or more language programmes can be taken consecutively in different countries to give a long-term gap year trip.

**DURATION OF COURSES:** Classes for all levels for a minimum of 2 weeks, starting throughout the year, and lasting for up to a year.

**COST:** 2-week programme of French plus surfing in Biarritz would cost from £845 including accommodation. 4-week Spanish course plus half-board accommodation and dance/music/percussion classes in Cuba from £1,495. Prices exclude travel.

**ACCOMMODATION:** Students can stay with local host families or in self-catering residential accommodation, depending on the location.

### CESA LANGUAGES ABROAD
CESA House, Pennance Road, Lanner,
Cornwall TR16 5TQ
℃ 01209 211800
✆ info@cesalanguages.com
🖳 www.cesalanguages.com

Founding member of Year Out Group (yearoutgroup. org).

**COURSES OFFERED:** Beginner, intermediate and advanced courses in French (Cannes, Nice, Montpellier, Tours, Bordeaux, Biarritz, Paris or, for a more exotic option, Guadeloupe), Spanish (Seville, Nerja, Salamanca, Malaga, Barcelona, Alicante, Valencia or Madrid in Spain, plus Argentina, Chile, Mexico, Costa Rica, Peru or Ecuador), German (Berlin, Lindau, Munich, Cologne, Kitzbühel or Vienna in Austria), Italian (Florence, Rome, San Giovanni, Sorrento, Siena and Viareggio), Portuguese, Japanese, Chinese, Russian, Greek and Arabic (in Morocco).

**DURATION OF COURSES:** 1–30+ weeks with possibility of studying in more than 1 location during a year-out programme. At least 1 start date per month year round.

**QUALIFICATIONS OFFERED:** DELE preparation offered in Spain; DELF, Alliance Française and CCIP exams in France; TRKI exams in Russia. Full range of exams including the Z Daf exam offered in Germany and Austria.

**COST:** Languages for Life 16-week course in Seville or Madrid costs from £3,700 including shared apartment accommodation and 20 hours tuition per week. A 4-week course with college residence accommodation and 20 lessons a week in Nice costs from £1,360.

**ACCOMMODATION:** Options include student apartments or residences, on-campus accommodation, host families, sole-occupancy apartments and hotels.

---

### DON QUIJOTE
2–4 Stoneleigh Park Road, Epsom,
Surrey KT19 0QT
✆ 020 8786 8081
✉ uk@donquijote.org
🖥 www.donquijote.org

**COURSES OFFERED:** Intensive (20 lessons a week) and super-intensive (30 lessons a week) courses for all levels throughout Spain: Alicante, Barcelona, Granada, Madrid, Malaga, Marbella, Puerto de La Cruz (Tenerife), Salamanca, Seville, Valencia, Cusco (Peru) and Guanajuato (Mexico) plus many other destinations in Mexico and Latin America. Also available is 'Spanish for Life' (12 weeks and longer) and in Cusco and Guanajuato a 'Spanish Study and Volunteer Programme'.

**DURATION OF COURSES:** 1–40 weeks.

**QUALIFICATIONS OFFERED:** Students will receive a Don Quijote certificate of attendance and level attained at the end of the course.

**COST:** From €600 for 2 weeks intensive course and single room lodging in a self-catering student flat. Spanish for Life courses start at £2,300 for 12 weeks including student flat accommodation.

**ACCOMMODATION:** Homestay, residence and flats.

**FOLLOW-UP:** Specialised courses available including a 'Spanish and Paid Jobs in Spain' programme. Private tuition is available at all schools.

---

### EIL UK
Elphick House, 287 Worcester Road, Malvern,
Worcestershire WR14 1AB
✆ 0800 018 4015
✆ 01684 562577
✉ info@eiluk.org
🖥 www.eiluk.org

EIL is a registered charity specialising in increasing understanding between cultures. Language learning programme with homestay offered in a range of countries. For example one-to-one Spanish tuition in Ecuador with homestay starts from £465 for 2 weeks (travel not included).

---

### EN FAMILLE OVERSEAS
58 Abbey Close, Peacehaven, East Sussex
BN10 7SD
✆ 01273 588636
✉ info@enfamilleoverseas.co.uk
🖥 www.enfamilleoverseas.co.uk

Arranges immersion language homestays in France with or without tuition. Also in Spain, Italy and Germany.
**CONTACT:** Clare Cox.

---

### IALC (INTERNATIONAL ASSOCIATION OF LANGUAGE CENTRES)
Lombard House, 12/17 Upper Bridge Street,
Canterbury CT1 2NF
✆ 01227 769007
✉ info@ialc.org
🖥 www.ialc.org

Language school association that accredits private language schools teaching the official language(s) of their country, currently around 100 members in 24 countries.
**COURSES OFFERED:** Wide choice of French, German, Italian, Japanese, Chinese, Portuguese, Russian and

Spanish courses worldwide, from short- to long-term and general to specialised, or in combination with cultural studies, cookery, dance, art, sport, etc. Some IALC schools arrange work experience, au pairing and volunteering.

**ACCOMMODATION:** Normally a choice of family stay, hall of residence, guesthouse or flat-share.

**APPLICATION PROCEDURES:** Canterbury office is not a booking office. Contact details for member schools appear on the IALC website.

**CONTACT:** Jan Capper.

## LANACOS

High Street, Wrotham, Sevenoaks,
Kent TN15 7AH
*C* 01732 456543
languages@lanacos.com
www.lanacos.com

Language agency run by linguists.

**COURSES OFFERED:** Language courses in more than 200 locations: Spanish in many Spanish and Latin American cities; French in Paris, Cote d'Azur, Montpellier, Bordeaux and Aix-en-Provence; German in Berlin, Cologne, Bavaria, Vienna and Salzburg; Italian in Rome, Florence, Milan, Venice and Genoa; Portuguese in Lisbon, Algarve and Brazil; Greek in Athens and Crete; Japanese in Tokyo; Mandarin in Shanghai; and Arabic in Cairo.

**DURATION OF COURSES:** 2+ weeks. Special 12-week gap year courses in France, Spain, Italy, Germany, China and Latin America.

**COST:** £505 for a fortnight in Granada to £1,620 for 12-week course in Berlin/Cologne.

**ACCOMMODATION:** Homestays with full or half board, B&Bs, single or shared apartments.

## LANGUAGE COURSES ABROAD

67–71 Ashby Road, Loughborough,
Leicestershire LE11 3AA
*C* 01509 211612
info@languagesabroad.co.uk
www.languagesabroad.co.uk

Parent company, Spanish Study Holidays, is a member of FIYTO (Federation of International Youth Travel Organisations) and ALTO (Association of Language Travel Organisations).

**PROGRAMME DESCRIPTION:** In-country language courses in Spanish, French, German, Italian, Portuguese, Russian, Chinese and Arabic, sometimes in preparation for work experience placements (see entry in 'Directory of Work Experience Abroad').

**PREREQUISITES:** Minimum age 16 for junior courses, otherwise 18, average age 18–26.

**DURATION AND TIME OF PLACEMENTS:** 1–40 weeks.

**ACCOMMODATION:** Shared self-catering student apartments, private studio apartments, host families, student residences or hotels.

## SIBS

Beech House, Commercial Road, Uffculme,
Devon EX15 3EB
*C* 01884 841330
trish@sibs.co.uk
www.sibs.co.uk

Language consultancy that arranges language courses abroad for clients.

**COURSES OFFERED:** For business and pleasure in France, Italy, Germany, Austria, Portugal, Japan, Spain, Greece, Russia, Argentina, Ecuador and Mexico.

**COST:** From £300 per week including accommodation.

**OTHER SERVICES:** Variety of courses and locations can be combined with cultural subjects, work experience, etc.

**CONTACT:** Patricia Cooper, Director.

## TRAVELLERS WORLDWIDE

Caravelle House, 17/19 Goring Road, Worthing,
West Sussex BN12 4AP
*C* 01903 502595
info@travellersworldwide.com
www.travellersworldwide.com

Travellers is a Founder Member of the Year Out Group.

**PROGRAMME DESCRIPTION:** A wide variety of language courses available for individuals or groups, including Spanish in Argentina (Mendoza or Buenos Aires) or Guatemala, Portuguese in Brazil (Rio de Janeiro or Florianopolis), Mandarin in China, Tamil in India, Swahili in Kenya. Courses suitable for all levels from beginners to the experienced and can be taken as individual placements or combined with a volunteer or work experience placement. (Please see Directory of Specialist Gap Year Programmes for further details.)

**DESTINATIONS:** Argentina, Brazil, China, Guatemala, India, Kenya.

**NUMBER OF PLACEMENTS PER YEAR:** 1,000+.

**PREREQUISITES:** No formal qualifications required, just a good dose of enthusiasm.

**DURATION AND TIME OF PLACEMENTS:** From 1 week to 1 year, subject to visa requirements, with flexible start and finish dates all year round that you choose.

**COST:** Prices start from £395 and include food, accommodation, airport pick-up, induction, orientation, 24/7 support on the ground and at home but do not include international travel, visas or insurance.

**CONTACT:** Jennifer Perkes, Managing Director.

---

### VIS-À-VIS
2–4 Stoneleigh Park Road, Epsom KT19 0QT
© 020 8786 8021
info@visavis.org
www.visavis.org

---

**COURSES OFFERED:** Courses for all levels in French at schools in France (Paris, Annecy, Antibes, Montpellier, Nice, Royan, Montreux and Vichy), Belgium (Brussels) and Canada (Montréal). Many activities and excursions available in all locations.

**DURATION OF COURSES:** Minimum 1 week.

**COST:** Prices start at about £938 (2009) for a 2-week course (20 lessons a week) including single room half-board accommodation with a family in Annecy. Additional enrolment fee of £50 and accommodation booking fee of £90.

**QUALIFICATIONS OFFERED:** Some courses prepare students for official language diplomas, such as the DELF and the more advanced level (DALF). These can be worked towards at the student's own pace.

**ACCOMMODATION:** Student flats and halls of residence are available for those wishing to mingle with other students. Host families also accommodate students which allows the student an insight into French culture.

# LANGUAGE SCHOOLS ABROAD

## SPANISH

---

### ACADEMIA DE ESPANOL SURPACIFICO
Avenida 24 y Calle 15, Edificio Barre, 3er Piso, Manabi, Ecuador
© + 593 5 2610 838
surpacifico@easynet.net.ec
www.surpacifico.k12.ec
www.ecuadorspanishschools.com

---

**COURSES OFFERED:** Intensive Spanish programmes, private or group lessons. Range of special courses and combinations with activities such as Spanish and surfing, Spanish and kitesurfing and medical Spanish. Also offer an ecological volunteer programme on an organic farm, volunteering with children, etc.

**DURATION OF COURSES:** Language courses last 2–24 weeks. Spanish and surfing: 1–8 weeks; Spanish and kitesurfing: 2–8 weeks. All courses can be started on any Monday of the year.

**QUALIFICATIONS OFFERED:** Courses are accredited by the Ecuadorian Ministry of Education and Culture.

**COST:** $160 per week for 20 hours of private lessons; $120 for group lessons. Intensive Manta Activo programme (30–35 hours combining Spanish classes with excursions on which students use the Spanish they have learned) costs $270–$310 per week. Spanish and surfing $400 a week, Spanish and kitesurfing

$912 for 2 weeks. Ecological volunteer programme costs $1,152 for 6 weeks.

**ACCOMMODATION:** Homestay (private bedroom, all meals and laundry service) or shared student apartment (private bedroom in a furnished apartment).

**CONTACT:** Manuel Bucheli, Director.

## ACADEMIA HISPANO AMERICANA

Mesones 4, San Miguel de Allende, 37700, GTO, Mexico

☎ +52 415 152 0349

✉ info@ahaspeakspanish.com

🖥 www.ahaspeakspanish.com

Established in 1959.

**COURSES OFFERED:** Intensive and semi-intensive Spanish; Diploma in Spanish as a Second Language; One on One Spanish; Mexican history, literature and sociology, and language workshops.

**DURATION OF COURSES:** 1–4 weeks. 35 hours of lessons and activities per week.

**QUALIFICATIONS OFFERED:** Diploma in Spanish as a Second Language. Seven semester units of credit are offered per session.

**COST:** One-time enrolment fee $50. First 4-week session $600, second session $480, third session $415. One on one classes $17 per hour.

**ACCOMMODATION:** Homestays: $28 per person per night for a single room and $18 for a shared room with 3 meals a day included; $22 for a shared room with meals. Mexican cooking classes and field trips also available.

**CONTACT:** Paulina Hawkins, Director.

## ALL MADRID SPANISH LANGUAGE IMMERSION SCHOOL IN SPAIN

C/ Nuñez de Balboa 17, 2°D, 28001 Madrid, Spain

☎ +34 91 725 63 50

✉ info@ailmadrid.com

🖥 www.ailmadrid.com/gap year/home

**PROGRAMME DESCRIPTION:** 12-week Spanish language course in Madrid and other cities in Spain with work placement options.

**PREREQUISITES:** Minimum age 17, average age 22.

**DURATION AND TIME OF PLACEMENTS:** 12–48 weeks with flexible start dates.

**COST:** 12-week programme from €3,500.

**CONTACT:** Maya Bychova.

## CHILE INSIDE

Address: Román Díaz 205 Of. 405, Providencia, Santiago, Chile

☎ +56 2 2357170

☎ +56 2 2357184

✉ info@chileinside.cl

🖥 www.chileinside.cl

**PROGRAMME DESCRIPTION:** Spanish language courses and accommodation throughout Chile.

**NUMBER OF PLACEMENTS PER YEAR:** 200–300.

**DESTINATIONS:** Chile.

**PREREQUISITES:** Minimum age 18.

**COST:** Programme fee depends on the Spanish course (group or intensive course, private classes), the location of the school and the length of the programme. 1-week Spanish course with accommodation in Santiago starts from $270.

**CONTACT:** Marion Ruhland, Founder and Executive Director.

## CIS – CENTRO DE INTERCAMBIO SOLIDARIDAD

*El Salvador office*: Mélida Anaya Montes Language School, Ave. Aguilares y Ave. Bolivar #103, Colonia Libertad, San Salvador, El Salvador

☎ +503 2235 1330

☎ +503 2226 5362

✉ cis_elsalvador@yahoo.com

🖥 www.cis-elsalvador.org

*US office*: Los Olivos CIS, PO Box 76, Westmont, IL 60559–0076

**COURSES OFFERED:** Spanish classes and political-cultural programme. English teaching volunteer opportunities also available.

**DURATION OF COURSES:** Classes start every Monday. Any number of weeks can be booked. Volunteers must commit to teaching for a 9-week English cycle.

**QUALIFICATIONS OFFERED:** Recreational courses.

**COST:** US$115 per week for 4 hours of morning classes plus 1-time $25 application fee and $10 for first 4 weeks. $40 per week for afternoon political-cultural programme. Volunteers are eligible to receive a half-price discount on Spanish classes. Volunteers must also pay a 1-time programme fee of $100.

**ACCOMMODATION:** Homestays with breakfast and dinner cost $80 a week. Alternatives in guest houses or shared flats can be arranged.

**CONTACT:** Rachel Burrage.

---

**ÍBERO SPANISH SCHOOL ARGENTINA**
Uruguay 150, Capital Federal (1015), Argentina
+54 5218 0240
info@iberospanish.com
www.iberospanish.com

**COURSES OFFERED:** Spanish language immersion courses in Buenos Aires. 8 levels of Spanish classes from absolute beginner to superior. Course involves weekly activities that allow learners to practise Spanish in an informal environment. Students can choose themed course, e.g. on Che Guevara, Diego Maradona or Jorge Louis Borges. TEFL training also offered.

**DESTINATIONS:** Buenos Aires, Argentina.

**DURATION OF COURSES:** All courses last 3 weeks. Courses run Monday to Friday throughout the year. Students take a placement exam to establish the correct level, and a final exam upon the completion of each 3-week level. Standard course consists of 20 group lessons per week. 40, 20 or 10 hours per week of private lessons can also be arranged.

**QUALIFICATIONS OFFERED:** Courses can lead to CELU qualification (international examination from Argentina) or DELE from Spain.

**COST:** US$100 per week group lessons plus $25 for textbook. Accommodation can be arranged in shared apartments, homestays or private apartments in downtown Buenos Aires.

**CONTACT:** Florencia Bozzano, Director.

---

**MALACA INSTITUTO**
Calle Cortada 6, Cerrado de Calderón, 29018
Málaga, Spain
+34 952 29 3242
espano@malacainstituto.com
www.MalacaInstituto.com

Students at Malaca Instituto from all over the world create a cosmopolitan environment and a culturally enriching experience. The Instituto is inspected by and meets the quality criteria of the Instituto Cervantes, CEELE, EAQUALS and IALC.

**COURSES OFFERED:** A variety of Spanish language and culture classes are offered, from standard beginner to preparation for university entrance. Gap year students usually take courses of between 16 and 36 weeks. Hispanic Studies programme is especially suitable. In addition, a range of courses short and long includes Spanish + Dance, Spanish + Cookery, Spanish + Internships, as well as General Intensive Spanish, Summer Courses and one-to-one tuition.

**DURATION OF COURSES:** Hispanic Studies Term I – 16 weeks; Term II – 20 weeks.

**QUALIFICATIONS OFFERED:** Students can work towards the DELE examinations or Spanish university entrance if their level of language is suitably advanced.

**ACCOMMODATION:** All types with single and twin rooms.

---

**MARIPOSA SPANISH SCHOOL & ECO HOTEL**
San Juan de la Concepcion, Masaya, Nicaragua
+505 4866 99455
paulette.goudge@googlemail.com
www.mariposaspanishschool.com

**COURSES OFFERED:** Intensive Spanish courses for all levels run year round: 20 hours per week in the mornings or 28 hours per week. Emphasis on Spanish as used in Nicaragua. 2 hours per day of grammar, 2 hours of conversation. Opportunities to integrate with the local community by volunteering in gardens, farms, etc. Income from school and hotel (owned by a British expat) supports a range of local projects from solar power to adult literacy. Combination language course offered, with other special interest such as Nicaraguan culture and history, or food.

**COST:** From $300 for 1-week family stay or hotel room plus language course and activities. Full time volunteers pay less for hotel or homestay. Cost of 3 months combination of Spanish course with homestay and community volunteering is $2,000.

**CONTACT:** Paulette Goudge.

## MESTER SPANISH COURSES
Vázquez Coronado 5, 37002 Salamanca, Spain
📞 +34 923 21 38 35
📧 mester@mester.com
🖥 www.mester.com

**COURSES OFFERED:** Spanish at all levels offered in Granada, Salamanca and Seville.

**DURATION OF COURSES:** 1–40 weeks starting every Monday. 40-week academic year course includes language classes (including Business Spanish) and Spanish culture classes. Students do not need to know any Spanish before coming to the school.

**QUALIFICATIONS OFFERED:** Some courses are recreational; others lead to DELE and Certificate of Business Spanish (exam fees extra). All students who successfully complete their course are given a diploma or certificate of study on leaving.

**COST:** From €150 for a week-long course of twice daily lessons of conversation and grammar to €3,680 for an academic year (800 lessons).

**ACCOMMODATION:** Full range including homestays, student flats, university residences and independent apartments.

**CONTACT:** Julia Parnell, Registration Department.

## MONTANITA SPANISH SCHOOL
En Frente de Cana Grill, Montanita,
Provincia de Santa Elena, Ecuador
📞 +593 08 979 1305
📧 info@montanitaspanishschool.com
🖥 www.montanitaspanishschool.com

**COURSES OFFERED:** Spanish language courses alongside lessons in Latin American history and culture. Most popular option is Spanish with surfing. Salsa and other classes also available. Volunteer service can be arranged at local hospital and in primary schools.

**DURATION OF COURSES:** Average stay is 6 weeks, but can be shorter or up to 12 weeks (no visa requirements in Ecuador for stays of less than 3 months).

**COST:** $20 registration fee plus $140 per week for group classes, $195 for private lessons. Surf lessons cost $75 a week, salsa or yoga lessons $65. Volunteering is free.

**ACCOMMODATION:** Accommodation is extra; student dormitory accommodation costs $56 a week, private cabanas $105.

**CONTACT:** Warwick White, Owner.

## SPANISH IN THE MOUNTAINS
Isla Victoria s/n Bariloche, Patagonia, Argentina
📞 +54 2944 467597
📧 info@spanishinthemountains.com
🖥 www.spanishinthemountains.com

**COURSES OFFERED:** Spanish as a second language. Lessons can be combined with outdoor activities in the mountains.

**DURATION OF COURSES:** Tailor-made.

**QUALIFICATIONS OFFERED:** Recreational only.

**COST:** $13 per hour for tuition.

**ACCOMMODATION:** Homestay at a cost of $15 per night.

**CONTACT:** Maria Eugenia Favret, Programme Coordinator.

# ITALIAN

## ACCADEMIA DEL GIGLIO
Via Ghibellina 116, 50122 Florence, Italy
+39 055 230 2467
info@adg.it
www.adg.it or www.italyhometuition.com

**COURSES OFFERED:** Italian courses for foreigners plus Art and Art History courses (see below). Intensive classes or one-to-one tuition.

**DURATION OF COURSES:** From 1 week to 6 months. Choice of 2–5 hours of classes a day.

**QUALIFICATIONS OFFERED:** Certificate attesting to the programme/level and the number of hours that the student has attended.

**COST:** 1-week intensive course costs €165, 8 weeks costs €910. Enrolment fee of €45.

**ACCOMMODATION:** All kinds of accommodation can be arranged from single room in a family for €30 a day half-board to €400 for 4 weeks in a single room in a flat sharing kitchen and other facilities. School located in a peaceful area of the city centre.

**OTHER SERVICES:** Visits and social activities included in the price. Free Wi-Fi area for students. Library and video library.

**CONTACT:** Lorenzo Capanni, Assistant Director.

## THE BRITISH INSTITUTE OF FLORENCE
Piazza Strozzi 2, 50123 Florence, Italy
+39 055 2677 8200
info@britishinstitute.it
www.britishinstitute.it

**COURSES OFFERED:** Italian language courses are designed for beginner, intermediate and advanced level students with classroom activity being directed towards building confidence in the spoken language. Materials used in class have an emphasis on the city of Florence to enable students to learn about the city, its culture and customs through the study of the language. Short A2 and AS overview courses and 2-week Italian language courses in Massa Marittima near the Tuscan coast are also offered. Italian language courses can be combined with History of Art, which is taught in English.

**DURATION OF COURSES:** Standard Italian language courses from 1 to 12 weeks can be joined throughout the year.

**COST:** Tuition fees vary. For example a 1-week Italian language course costs from €205, and a 1-week History of Art course costs from €195.

**ACCOMMODATION:** Can be arranged in local homes, *pensione* and hotels.

## CENTRO CULTURALE GIACOMO PUCCINI
Via Vespucci 173, 55049 Viareggio (LU), Italy
+39 058 443 0253
infopack@centropuccini.it
www.centropuccini.it

**COURSES OFFERED:** Italian language.

**DESTINATION:** Viagreggio is a seaside resort in Tuscany.

**DURATION OF COURSES:** Standard 2-week course includes 4 lessons per day; intensive course includes extra 10 or 20 hours of private tuition over the fortnight. Courses offered year round. 32-week courses suitable for a gap year (mid-Jan to mid-Aug, early May to Dec, or Sept to May).

**QUALIFICATIONS OFFERED:** Firenze Diploma Examination preparatory courses available (leading to DELI, DILI, DILC, DALI, DALC; see www.acad.it).

**COST:** Courses lasting for 32–34 weeks cost €5,720. Standard course costs €280 for 2 weeks plus registration fee of €70. Family accommodation with breakfast from €234 in a shared room in low season per fortnight or single room in an apartment for €598 (high season).

**OTHER ACTIVITIES:** Sailing, riding, culinary courses, music courses, etc.

**CONTACT:** Elisa Campioni.

## KOINE
Via Pandolfini 27, 50122 Florence, Italy
+39 055 213881
info@koinecenter.com
www.koinecenter.com

**COURSES OFFERED:** Italian language for foreigners offered year round in Florence, Lucca and Bologna, Cortona and Elba Island. Sister company Vinarium also offers guided wine tastings and cooking lessons in Florence and Lucca, wine tours to Chianti Classico area, Montalcino and Montepulciano.

**DURATION OF COURSES:** 1 week to 6 months.

**QUALIFICATIONS OFFERED:** Certificate CILS from Siena University.

**COST:** Sample cost in Florence: €1,620 for a month's tuition (20 hours a week) plus €310 for a month's basic accommodation without use of kitchen.

**ACCOMMODATION:** With an Italian family or independent apartment.

---

### PICCOLA UNIVERSITÀ ITALIANA
Largo Antonio Pandullo 6, 89861 Tropea, Italy
- +39 096 360 3284
- info@piccolauniversitaitaliana.com
- www.piccolauniversitaitaliana.com.
- Skype: piccola.universita.italiana

---

**COURSES OFFERED:** Italian language courses recognised by the Italian Ministry of Education, University and Research; special courses for the hotel and tourism industry; individual crash courses in business Italian. Courses can be combined with activities and lessons in windsurfing, catamaran sailing, scuba diving, mountain biking or painting. Courses are given to small groups of a maximum of 3–6 students.

**DURATION OF COURSES:** Any duration from 1 week. Courses begin every Monday year round.

**QUALIFICATIONS OFFERED:** Opportunity to work towards the CILS examination.

**COST:** 8-week conversation course costs €670; 8-week main course costs €1,205; 8-week intensive course costs €2,387. Special rates for long stays. Registration fee of €100 includes transfer from and to the airport/train station at Lamezia Terme or 2 excursions of the weekly cultural programme.

**ACCOMMODATION:** Accommodation is extra at €950 for 8 weeks in a single room (shared flat) or €1,365 in a single room apartment. Generally holiday flats in the centre of Tropea, with a sea or mountain view. Flats usually have 1–3 rooms, kitchen and terrace or balcony.

**OTHER ACTIVITIES:** Piccola Università Italiana (at the same address) offers surfing, sailing, diving, tennis and horse riding. The school offers excursion programmes in Calabria and Sicily. Further courses available in *aquarelle* or oil painting, history of art and cookery; can be combined with language course.

---

# FRENCH

---

### ALLIANCE FRANCAISE
101 Boulevard Raspail, 75270
Paris Cedex 06, France
- +33 1 42 84 90 00
- info@alliancefr.org
- www.alliancefr.org

---

Alliance Française has 1,000 language centres in 129 countries, including in the UK, where students can study French in their own country.

**COURSES OFFERED IN PARIS:** French language courses at 5 levels with a choice of shared or individual classes at the school in Paris. Students have the chance to study general French or specialised French, e.g. French for tourism, hotel work or secretarial.

**DURATION OF COURSES:** 20 or 26 hours a week intensive, or 9 or 15 hours a week extensive (minimum 2 weeks extensive).

**QUALIFICATIONS OFFERED:** Various French diplomas can be awarded including Paris Chamber of Commerce & Industry and the Ministry of National Education. Normally test can be sat after 128 hours.

**COST:** €220 a week for intensive, €85 a week for 9 hours instruction, plus annual enrolment fee of €55.

**ACCOMMODATION:** Provided on demand in student residence or in studios.

## ELFCA – INSTITUT D' ENSEIGNEMENT DE LA LANGUE FRANÇAISE SUR LA COTE D'AZUR

66 avenue de Toulon, 83400 Hyères, Provence, France

(C) +33 04 94 65 03 31

elfca@elfca.com

www.elfca.com

**COURSES OFFERED:** Total immersion French language courses.

**DURATION OF COURSES:** 1–24 weeks.

**QUALIFICATIONS OFFERED:** Long-term courses lead to recognised qualifications; ELFCA is an exam centre for the TEF (Test d'Evaluation de Français).

**COST:** From €180 per week for long-term courses lasting more than 12 weeks. Weekly charge for shorter stays is €280 plus homestay accommodation with half-board costs €190 per week (shared) or €210 (single).

**ACCOMMODATION:** Homestay accommodation, apartment or hotel.

## INTER-SEJOURS

179 rue de Courcelles, 75017 Paris, France

(C) +33 1 47 63 06 81

aideinfo.intersejours@wanadoo.fr

www.inter-sejours.fr

**COURSES OFFERED:** Language courses as part of a homestay in Paris (and French students placed abroad in England, Australia, New Zealand, USA, etc.). Language courses also arranged in Spain, Germany, Italy, Costa Rica and Canada. European students are placed as au pairs in France, Spain, Italy, Germany, Austria (and French students in English-speaking countries including Canada, Australia and New Zealand) or in hotel or restaurant jobs in the UK and Spain, internships in Ireland, etc. Volunteering opportunities in USA, Latin America, Asia and Africa.

**DURATION OF COURSES:** Minimum 1 week up to 34 weeks, with Monday start dates throughout the year. Specified start dates for beginners or for courses leading to exams.

**QUALIFICATIONS OFFERED:** Opportunity to work towards the DELF examination and the *Certificat Pratique de Français*.

**COST:** Examples of price in Paris: 30 lessons in 2 weeks would cost €725. A standard course with 20 lessons over 2 weeks costs €545 (2010).

**ACCOMMODATION:** Accommodation and breakfast with a host family costs €189 per week in Paris or €210 half board in the suburbs.

**CONTACT:** Marie-Helene Pierrot, Director.

# GERMAN

## BWS GERMANLINGUA

Hackenstrasse 7c, D-80331 Munich, Germany

(C) +49 89 59 98 92 00

info@bws-germanlingua.de

www.bws-germanlingua.de

**COURSES OFFERED:** German language courses in Munich or Berlin, standard (20 lessons per week), intensive (25 lessons) or one-to-one.

**DURATION OF COURSES:** 2–48 weeks. Minimum 1 week for a tailor-made course. Can join on any Monday (unless total beginner).

**COST:** €370 for 2 weeks to €5,010 for 48 weeks. Prices higher for intensive courses (from €440) and one-to-one (€410 for 1 week with 10 lessons).

**ACCOMMODATION:** With a German family, in a flat shared with students or in a studio apartment.

**CONTACT:** Florian Meierhofer, Proprietor.

## CAMPUS AUSTRIA

Wiener Internationale Hochschulkurse, Universität Wien, Alserstrasse 4, A-1090 Vienna

(C) +43 01 42 77 24 101

info@campus-austria.at

www.campus-austria.at

Source of information about German language courses at 16 different centres in Austria.

**COURSES OFFERED:** Some courses lead to Goethe Institut qualifications or the Austrian Diploma for German as a Foreign Language (OESD).

**DURATION OF COURSES:** Normally 2 or more weeks, year round with choice of holiday courses and youth programmes.

**COST:** Prices vary, but approximately €500 per fortnight excluding accommodation.

## DEUTSCH-INSTITUT TIROL

Am Sandhügel 2, 6370 Kitzbühel, Austria
*C* +43 53 56 71 274
office@deutschinstitut.com
www.gap-year.at

**COURSES OFFERED:** German language combined with ski and snowboard instruction specially designed for gap year students. (See 'Directory of Specialist Gap Year Programmes').

## DID DEUTSCH-INSTITUT

Hauptstrasse 26, 63811 Stockstadt am Main, Germany
*C* +49 60 27 41 770
office@did.de
www.did.de

**COURSES OFFERED:** Short and long-term intensive German language courses year round for adults (17+) in Berlin, Frankfurt, Hamburg and Munich. Standard, Intensive, Premium courses. Summer programmes for juniors in many more cities throughout Germany. Group tuition in small classes or on individual basis.

**DURATION OF COURSES:** Short-term 1–7 weeks. Long-term courses last 8–48 weeks in Berlin, Munich and Frankfurt.

**QUALIFICATIONS OFFERED:** Diploma examinations for long-term stays, at the end of each course level, B1, B2, C1 and C2 under supervision of GfdS, the German Language Society, Wiesbaden.

**ACCOMMODATION:** Choice of homestays with German families; youth hotels and apartments also available.

**OTHER SERVICES:** Internships are also offered.

## GLS SPRACHENZENTRUM BERLIN

Kastanienallee 82, 10435 Berlin, Germany
*C* +49 30 78 00 89 0
germancourses@gls-berlin.de
www.german-berlin.de

**COURSES OFFERED:** Language courses offered year round at all levels, starting every Monday. Central location near Brandenburg Gate and New Reichstag.

**DURATION OF COURSES:** 20, 30 or 40 lessons per week for any number of weeks. International mix in classes of about 8.

**COST:** Sample price for 2 weeks German language course with 20 weekly lessons, activity programme and self-catering single room in a flat shared with Berliners is €558.

**ACCOMMODATION:** Shared apartments, bed and breakfast, host family or budget hotels available through accommodation service. Single rooms on adult courses; double or multi-bedded for junior summer programmes.

**OTHER SERVICES:** Extended sightseeing programme in and around Berlin. GLS runs an internship programme combining a language course of at least 4 weeks with a work experience placement in a Berlin-based company (see entry in 'Directory of Work Experience').

## GOETHE INSTITUT

Headquarters in Munich, Germany
www.goethe.de
*UK office:* 50 Princes Gate, London SW7 2PH
*C* 020 7596 4000
german@london.goethe.org
www.goethe.de/london

**COURSES OFFERED:** German language courses at all levels in 13 attractive locations in Germany and 144 locations in 80 countries worldwide. All course details and institute addresses are on website. Summer courses offered in several locations including Heidelberg and Lake Constance.

**DURATION OF COURSES:** 2–12 weeks.

**QUALIFICATIONS OFFERED:** The Goethe Institut administers its own language exams at all levels, e.g. Start Deutsch 1 and 2, ZD, ZdaF, KDS and GDS and others.

# OTHER LANGUAGES

## THE ATHENS CENTRE

48 Archimidous Street, 116 36 Athens, Greece

☎ +30 21 0701 2268

✉ info@athenscentre.gr

🖥 www.athenscentre.gr

**COURSES OFFERED:** Modern Greek.

**DURATION OF COURSES:** 3, 4, 5, 7 or 12 weeks throughout the year and summer immersion course (3 weeks on the island of Spetses).

**QUALIFICATIONS OFFERED:** Serious courses with certificate given at end.

**ACCOMMODATION:** Hotels, pensions, apartment sublets and studios but no homestays.

**COST:** From €670 for 2-week course plus accommodation in efficiency apartment.

**CONTACT:** Nina Lorum, Assistant Programme Director.

## CIAL CENTRO DE LINGUAS

*Lisbon office*: Av. da República, 41–8°E, 1050–187, Lisbon, Portugal

☎ +351 21 794 04 48

✉ portuguese@cial.pt

🖥 www.cial.pt

*Algarve office*: Rua Almeida Garrett, 44 r/c, 8000–206 Faro, Portugal

☎ +351 289 807 611

✉ algarve@cial.pt

**COURSES OFFERED:** Full Portuguese language and culture course in six levels, with 60 lessons of language tuition for every level.

**DURATION OF COURSES:** 4 weeks for each course, with new courses every month.

**QUALIFICATIONS OFFERED:** Possibility of qualifying for the Diploma of Portuguese as a Foreign Language.

**COST:** 4-week course will cost €952 (2010) including textbook, audio CD and social programme.

**ACCOMMODATION:** In private homes in individual rooms with breakfast included.

**CONTACT:** Dr Alexandra Borges de Sousa, Director of Studies.

## FOREIGN STUDENT SERVICE

Oranje Nassaulaan 5, 1075 AH, Amsterdam, Netherlands

☎ 020 671 5915

✉ info@foreignstudents.nl

🖥 www.foreignstudents.nl

Organisation provides information about Dutch language courses and assistance to foreign students in the Netherlands.

## LIDEN & DENZ LANGUAGE CENTRES

St Petersburg and Moscow, Central Booking Office, Transportny per. 11, 191119 St Petersburg, Russia

☎ +7 812 334 0788

☎ +7 812 600 7550

Gruzinski per. 3–181, Ground floor, 123056 Moscow, Russian Federation

☎ +7 495 254 4991

✉ bookings@lidenz.ru

🖥 www.lidenz.ru or www.russiancourses. com

**COURSES OFFERED:** Russian language offered at all levels from leisure course to crash course, plus academic year courses and work experience and volunteer programmes.

**DURATION OF COURSES:** Minimum 2 weeks in a group with choice of 20 hours (standard), 25 (intensive) or 25 (combination course: 20 group plus 5 hours one-to-one). One-to-one lessons available with choice of frequency (15, 20, 30 or 40 hours a week; minimum duration 1 week). Fixed duration of academic year courses are 24, 36 or 48 weeks.

**QUALIFICATIONS OFFERED:** All students receive a graded certificate (in Russian) at the end of their stay, indicating course type, course dates, numbers of lessons and level achieved. Liden and Denz in St Petersburg and Moscow are official preparation and testing centres for the state exam TRKI (Russian as a Foreign Language).

**COST:** Standard course costs €225–€270 per week depending on overall duration. Surcharges apply in peak season.

**ACCOMMODATION:** Homestay in single room with half board is the most popular option, at a cost of €190 per week in St Petersburg and €220 in Moscow. Shared flats, etc. also offered.

**CONTACT:** Julia Patasheva (julia.patasheva@lidenz.ru), International Relations.

# ART, DESIGN, DRAMA, FILM AND MUSIC COURSES

## ART AND DESIGN

### ACCADEMIA DEL GIGLIO
Lingue Arte Cultura, Via Ghibellina 116, 50122 Florence, Italy
℡ + 39 055 230 2467
info@adg.it
www.adg.it

**COURSES OFFERED:** Drawing, painting and art history courses in addition to Italian language courses described above. Fresco workshop available over 4 weeks.

**DURATION OF COURSES:** 1 week to 9 months, with 14 hours of tuition per week.

**COST:** 1-week art course costs €180, 2 weeks costs €340, 12 weeks costs €1,710. Enrolment fee of €45.

**ACCOMMODATION:** All kinds of accommodation can be arranged from single room in a family for €30 a day half-board to €400 for 4 weeks in a single room in a flat sharing kitchen and other facilities.

**OTHER SERVICES:** Visits and social activities included in the price. Free Wi-Fi area for students. Library and video library.

**CONTACT:** Lorenzo Capanni, Assistant Director.

### ART HISTORY ABROAD
The Red House
1 Lambseth Street Eye, Suffolk IP23 7AG
℡ 01379 871800
info@arthistoryabroad.com
www.arthistoryabroad.com

Year Out Group founding member.

**PROGRAMME DESCRIPTION:** Art and cultural programme in various cities in Italy lasting 6 weeks. See 'Directory of Specialist Gap Year Programmes' for further information.

### JOHN HALL VENICE COURSE
9 Smeaton Road, London SW18 5JJ
info@johnhallvenice.com
www.johnhallvenice.co.uk

**COURSES OFFERED:** A pre-university course for students of the arts and sciences, covering art, art history, architecture, music, opera, literature, global ecological and political issues, history and world cinema. Introductory week in London including the museum and commercial art world is followed by five weeks in Venice where daily lectures and visits (including a private visit to San Marco) are combined with practical classes in life-drawing and photography, with optional Italian classes and visits to Padova, Ravenna and Palladian villas in the Veneto. The extensions of a week in Florence and 6 days in Rome continue the study of history, art, music and architecture on-site and include private visits to the Uffizi, the Accademia, Settignano, the Keats Shelley Memorial House, the Villa Borghese Gallery and the Vatican and Sistine Chapel.

**DURATION OF COURSES:** 1 week in London, 5 weeks in Venice. Extensions: 1 week in Florence, 6 days in Rome. Offered annually from late January.

**QUALIFICATIONS OFFERED:** Interest and enthusiasm.

**COST:** 1 week London and 5 weeks Venice: £6,990; Florence £1,170, Rome £1,120. Travel to and from Italy, entrances, accommodation including breakfast and dinner in Italy, are included in fees. Accommodation in London not included.

**CONTACT:** Victoria Gillions, Secretary.

---

## LONDON COLLEGE OF FASHION

20 John Princes Street, London W1G 0BJ

© 020 7514 7566

shortcourses@fashion.arts.ac.uk

www.fashion.arts.ac.uk/shortcourses

Member of University of the Arts London.

**COURSES OFFERED:** Intensive evening, weekend and daytime courses in makeup, beauty and all fashion-related subjects, held at one of the University of the Arts' six central London sites. Also some online courses are available.

**DURATION OF COURSES:** 1–15 days intensive short courses or up to 10 weeks as evening classes. Evening classes are held during autumn, spring and summer terms, and intensive courses are offered at Christmas, Easter and during the summer.

**QUALIFICATIONS OFFERED:** Certificate of attendance.

**COST:** Prices range from £150.

**OTHER SERVICES:** Help can be given finding accommodation.

**CONTACT:** Short Course Office or courses can be booked online.

---

## STUDIO ART CENTERS INTERNATIONAL (SACI)

Palazzo dei Cartelloni, Via Sant'Antonino 11, Florence 50123, Italy

© +39 212 248 7225

admissions@saci-florence.org

www.saci-florence.org

**COURSES OFFERED:** Accredited courses for university-level students (minimum age 18). Semester/Year Abroad, Master of Fine Art (MFA), Post-Baccalaureate Certificate in Studio Art, Art History, or Art Conservation, and Summer Studies. Studio art, art history, design, art conservation, and Italian cultural studies. Courses offered in 40 different studio and academic disciplines: drawing, painting, fresco, etching, lithography, serigraphy, sculpture, ceramics, black-and-white photography, colour photography, video, animation, digital multimedia, illustration, graphic design, interior design, contemporary furniture design, eco design studio, design futures: a seminar, batik, book arts, weaving, jewellery design, Italian late medieval and early Renaissance art history, Italian high Renaissance, Mannerist, and early Baroque art history, high Baroque and Rococo European and Italian art history, 19th century European and Italian art history, modern European and Italian art, contemporary European and Italian art, history of photography, art history seminar, museology, art conservation, history of Italian opera, history of Italian cinema, creative writing, literature and visual art, Italian language.

**DURATION OF COURSES:** Fall semester: 13 weeks (Sept to Dec); spring: 13 weeks (Jan to Apr); Late spring: 5 weeks (May/June); summer: 4 weeks (June/July).

**QUALIFICATIONS OFFERED:** Post-Baccalaureate Certificate in Studio Art, Art History, or Art Conservation. Bowling Green State University MFA in Studio Art: First Year at SACI in Florence.

**COST:** Tuition from $4,300 for 4–5 weeks late spring or summer plus $1,500–$1,650 for housing. Semester tuition fees are $11,200–$11,450 plus $4,300 for housing.

**ACCOMMODATION:** Furnished apartments near the school in Florence's historic centre.

---

# DANCE, DRAMA, FILM AND JOURNALISM

## ASAD – ACADEMY OF THE SCIENCE OF ACTING & DIRECTING

9–15 Elthorne Road, Archway, London N19 4AJ

© 020 7272 0027

info@asad.org.uk

www.asad.org.uk

**COURSES OFFERED:** Acting and directing courses. 1-year course is for the students to understand the basic laws of good acting and to become competent professionals. Students study the syllabus through lessons in theory and a series of assessed exercises. In addition students have classes in the study of Voice, Movement, Dance and other subjects including histories of Art, Music, Psychology and Philosophy. Students take part in the Directing students' exercises, exam days and the Edinburgh Festival. This accumulated knowledge and experience leads to the presentation of 2 end-of-course plays. New part-time course in 2010 in the theory of acting (Tuesday and Friday evenings for 3 terms).

**DURATION OF COURSES:** 1 year of 4 11-week terms.

**QUALIFICATIONS OFFERED:** Certificate of Merit issued by the school.

**COST:** From £3,770 first term, £2,450 subsequent terms. Evening courses, directing courses, etc. have varying fees.

**ACCOMMODATION:** Not provided but help given with finding it.

### DORA STRATOU GREEK DANCES THEATRE
8 Scholiou Street, Plaka, 105 58 Athens, Greece
+30 210 324 4395
mail@grdance.org
www.grdance.org

**COURSES OFFERED:** Short courses for foreigners in Greek folk dance and folk culture in conjunction with lectures and evening performances in outdoor theatre near the Acropolis.

**DURATION OF COURSES:** 1 week between May and September. 4 hours of instruction every afternoon.

**COST:** €120. Volunteers must fund their own stay in Athens.

**CONTACT:** Adamantia Angeli.

### NEW YORK FILM ACADEMY
100 E 17th Street, New York, NY 10003, USA
+1 212 674 4300
film@nyfa.com
www.nyfa.com

**COURSES OFFERED:** Film-making (write, shoot, direct and edit) Acting for Film, Screenwriting, Producing, 3D Animation and Editing. Course offered in many cities as well as New York, including London, Florence and Paris.

**DURATION OF COURSES:** 1- and 2-year programmes, 2-year MFA as well as short-term workshops (1, 4, 6 and 8 weeks).

**COST:** $17,000 per semester for the Filmmaking programmes. $3,500 for the short-term 4-week Film-making workshops.

### PRAGUE FILM SCHOOL
Pstrossova 19, Prague 110 00,
Czech Republic
+420 257 534013
info@filmstudies.cz
www.filmstudies.cz

**COURSES OFFERED:** Fast-track studies in practical filmmaking. Full-time programmes include directing, editing, screenwriting and cinematography; acting for film; animation, and documentary production.

**DURATION OF COURSES:** Year programme, semester programme, summer workshop (4 weeks).

**PREREQUISITES:** Minimum age 17.

**QUALIFICATIONS OFFERED:** Qualification accredited by the Czech Ministry of Education under the rubric of professional training.

**COST:** €2,460–€14,800.

**ACCOMMODATION:** Shared or private accommodation in school flats.

### UP TO SPEED JOURNALISM TRAINING
c/o Daily Echo, Richmond Hill, Bournemouth
BH2 6HH
01202 761944
thill@uptospeedjournalism.com
www.uptospeedjournalism.com

**COURSES OFFERED:** 22-week Fast-Track Course in Journalism. The course is based in a newspaper building and accredited by the National Council for the Training of Journalists, the news industry's vocational training organisation. Students take the NCTJ's examinations in Public Affairs, Media Law, News Writing and Shorthand. They also produce assessed coursework in both print and video journalism, learning to shoot and edit video and radio pieces. Feedback on all assignments is given by professional journalists.

**DURATION OF COURSES:** 22 weeks (Sept to Feb or Feb to July).

**QUALIFICATIONS OFFERED:** The 22-week course leads to the NCTJ Certificate in Journalism and gives people a chance of landing jobs in journalism during the remainder of their gap year, during their time at university, and when they graduate.

**COST:** £3,600. Advice given on local accommodation.

**CONTACT:** Tom Hill, Course Director.

## WORLDWRITE

WORLDwrite Centre, Millfields Lodge, 201 Millfields Road, Hackney, London E5 0AL

✆ 020 8985 5435

✉ world.write@btconnect.com

🖥 www.worldwrite.org.uk

**COURSES OFFERED:** WORLDwrite is an education charity that uses documentary film-making as a medium for campaigning on global issues. The charity has broadcast quality equipment and offers a free training programme to volunteers with a passionate commitment to global equality. Courses are taught by TV and film professionals and tutors, and aim to give young people a fresh perspective through a first-hand, investigative filmmaking experience. Volunteers learn all aspects of production from camera to sound to compression and their work features on the charity's news channel WORLDbytes.

**DURATION OF COURSES:** 2–3 days over long intensive weekends.

**PREREQUISITES:** Ages 16–25. Must feel strongly about global inequality and be familiar with the work of WORLDwrite (see website).

**CONTACT:** Ceri Dingle, Director, and Viv Regan, Assistant Director.

## YEAR OUT DRAMA COMPANY

Stratford-upon-Avon College, Alcester Road, Stratford-upon-Avon, Warwickshire CV37 9QR

✆ 01789 266245

✉ yearoutdrama@stratford.ac.uk

Founding member of Year Out Group.

**COURSES OFFERED:** Challenging, intensive, practical drama course specific to gap year students. Led by experts in professionally equipped performance spaces. Students benefit from working with theatre professionals on varying disciplines including Acting Techniques, Voice, Movement, Directing, Text Study and Performance. Students have the option to perform at the Edinburgh Fringe Festival.

**DURATION OF COURSES:** September to July, split into 3 terms.

**COST:** From £5,000 for the year which includes production costs, travel and tickets for frequent theatre trips. Accommodation costs are extra.

**ACCOMMODATION:** Students can live in halls of residence, with landladies or in shared houses.

**FOLLOW-UP:** Students are given help with auditions and UCAS applications. The Company has strong support from the Royal Shakespeare Company and other working professionals.

# MUSIC

## ROYAL COLLEGE OF MUSIC

Prince Consort Road, London SW7 2BS

✆ 020 591 4362

✉ dharpham@rcm.ac.uk

🖥 www.rcm.ac.uk/Studying/Courses/
   Experience + Programmes

**COURSES OFFERED:** Gap Year Experience Programme for talented young musicians who are accepted after audition. Course provides individual lessons on main instrument, opportunities for involvement in orchestras, ensembles, choral groups, etc., participation in core academic classes, concerts, masterclasses and workshops.

**DURATION OF COURSES:** 1 academic year, September to July only.

**QUALIFICATIONS OFFERED:** Most students who enrol on the gap year programme decide to stay on and continue into year 2 of the BMus Programme (subject to passing exams).

**COST:** £6,800.

**ACCOMMODATION:** Possibility of residence in halls, not included in price.

**CONTACT:** David Harpham, Registry Officer.

# BUSINESS SKILLS COURSES

## KUDOS TRAINING LIMITED

Suite 10, The Sanctuary, 23 Oakhill Grove, Surbiton, Surrey KT6 6DU

✆ 020 8288 8766

✉ enquiry@kudostraining.org

🖵 www.kudostraining.org

**COURSES AND QUALIFICATIONS OFFERED:** Qualifications in Administrative Management awarded by the Institute of Administrative Management: Certificate (3rd level), Diploma (4th level) and Advanced Diploma (5th level). Secretarial course offered: Certificate for Secretarial PAs (3rd level), and Diploma in Administration for Executive Assistants (4th level). All courses are offered intensively, part-time or via distance learning with Saturday workshops. Some courses offer progression routes to a degree.

**ACCOMMODATION:** Can be arranged; accommodation always provided during weekend intensive courses and examination periods.

**CONTACT:** Elaine Howard, Principal.

## OXFORD MEDIA & BUSINESS SCHOOL

5 Cambridge Terrace, Oxford OX1 1UP

✆ 01865 240963

✉ courses@oxfordbusiness.co.uk

🖵 www.oxfordbusiness.co.uk

**COURSES OFFERED:** 12-week gap year 'life skills' course covering IT and business skills to help students earn higher wages during their gap year and during university vacations. Intensive tuition in Microsoft IT and communication skills; essential project work to tight deadlines simulates a temping assignment in terms of prioritising, time management, working in teams, and production quality; all of these are part of the course assessment. The school also offers a 9-month executive PA course and 12-week graduate course.

**DURATION OF COURSES:** 12 week gap course starting September, January and April; 9-month course also available.

**QUALIFICATIONS OFFERED:** OMBS College Certificate.

**COST:** 12 weeks is £2,264.

**ACCOMMODATION:** Shared houses within walking or cycling distance or host families in the locality.

**FOLLOW-UP:** Specialist in-house recruitment service, giving ongoing help with CV writing and interview technique as well as help in finding a job.

## QUEST BUSINESS TRAINING

5 Grosvenor Gardens, London SW1W 0BD

✆ 020 7233 5957

✉ info@questcollege.co.uk

🖵 www.questcollege.co.uk

Formed after the long established Queen's College amalgamated with St James's and Lucie Clayton College.

**COURSES OFFERED:** Professional programmes (24 and 36 weeks) and short courses lasting 2–10 weeks on offer. The latter focus on providing training in MS Office Skills as well as other business-related topics. They offer a 10-week gap year course (starting September, January and April) aimed at students who hope to use the rest of their gap year earning money by temping or working in an office. Course ends with an introduction to some of London's top temping agencies, and individual recruitment consultations.

**COST:** £3,154 for gap year course.

# COOKERY COURSES

## THE AVENUE COOKERY SCHOOL

74 Chartfield Avenue, Putney, London SW15 6HQ

020 8788 3025

info@theavenuecookeryschool.com

www.theavenuecookeryschool.com

**COURSES OFFERED:** The 'Really Useful Course' is an intensive 1-week cooking course that includes useful day-to-day skills as well as first aid, car maintenance and travel tips, ideal for gap year students and undergraduates. There is also the 2-week 'Basic to Brilliant Course' and 4-week 'Complete Cooking Course' as well as the 2-week 'Chalet Cooking Course'. Also offered are 6-week courses of evening classes (1 basic and 1 more advanced).

**DURATION OF COURSES:** 1 week, 2 weeks, 4 weeks plus weekly evening classes for 6 weeks.

**QUALIFICATIONS OFFERED:** Certificated First Aid from the Really Useful Course; plus The Avenue Cookery School certificates for all courses.

**COST:** Really Useful Course: £620; Even More Useful/ Advanced Course: £620**;** Basic to Brilliant: £1,200; Chalet Cooking Course: £1,200 (2 weeks); Complete Cooking Course: £2,300; 6 Evening Classes: £330.

**ACCOMMODATION:** Fully residential if required. £120 per week (Mon to Fri), including dinner and breakfast.

**PARTNERS:** Mary Forde and Diana Horsford.

**CONTACT:** Sally Strahan, info@theavenuecookery-school.com.

## BALLYMALOE COOKERY SCHOOL

Shanagarry, Midleton, County Cork, Ireland

+ 353 21 46 46 785

info@cookingisfun.ie

www.cookingisfun.ie

Situated on organic farm by the coast with access to excellent ingredients. Affiliated with www.jobsforcooks.com.

**COURSES OFFERED:** 12-week Certificate in Cookery course. Range of short courses also offered.

**DURATION OF COURSES:** Certificate course starting January, April and September last 12 weeks. Short courses given between April and July, including a 1-week introductory course in July or September.

**QUALIFICATIONS OFFERED:** Students who pass written and practical exams at end of course are awarded the Ballymaloe Cookery School Certificate of Food and Wine.

**COST:** €9,975 for Certificate course excluding accommodation. 1-day courses cost €245, $2^1/_2$-day course €550 and 5-day Intro course €875.

**ACCOMMODATION:** Self-catering student accommodation in converted farm cottages costs €105 per week in twin room and €145 in single (2009 prices). Nightly charges for short courses are €28 shared, €45 single.

**CONTACT:** Rosalie Dunne.

## CHALET ACADEMY

Broomlea, Lingfield Road, East Grinstead, West Sussex RH19 2EJ

020 3287 6839

info@chaletacademy.com

www.chaletacademy.com

**COURSES OFFERED:** Intense chalet preparation cookery course in Chamonix, within view of Mont Blanc.

**DURATION OF COURSES:** 6 days, Wednesday to Wednesday. September, October and May.

**QUALIFICATIONS OFFERED:** CIEH Food Hygiene Level 2 Award.

**COST:** £495.

**OTHER SERVICES:** Employment guaranteed.

**CONTACT:** Simon Sutcliffe.

## LE CORDON BLEU CULINARY INSTITUTE

114 Marylebone Lane, London W1V 2HH

020 7935 3503

london@cordonbleu.edu

www.cordonbleu.net

Institute has branch in Paris and many other cities.

**COURSES OFFERED:** Le Cordon Bleu Essentials Course leaves beginners confident cooks.

**DURATION OF COURSES:** 4 weeks. Many shorter and longer full-time and part-time courses.

**COST:** £2,408 for 4 weeks includes overnight in Paris.

**ACCOMMODATION:** A list of accommodation agencies, hostels and hotels is available from the Admissions office. They are selected according to proximity to the school.

**FOLLOW-UP:** Le Cordon Bleu has strong links with some of the top ski companies, many of whom recruit directly from the school. The course is ideal for those wishing to work on yachts or find employment during their gap year or school and university holidays.

### EDINBURGH SCHOOL OF FOOD & WINE
The Coach House, Newliston, Edinburgh
EH29 9EB

✆ 00 44 (0)131 333 5001
✍ info@esfw.com
🖳 www.esfw.com

**COURSES OFFERED:** Practical hands-on cookery – from 1 day to 6-month diploma course.

**COST:** 4 week intensive course costs £2,450; 6-month (Jan to June) Diploma in Food and Wine course costs £9,500.

**ACCOMMODATION:** Assistance always offered.

**FOLLOW-UP:** The School works closely with ski companies, agencies and restaurants offering opportunities in the UK and abroad.

### FOOD OF COURSE COOKERY SCHOOL
Middle Farm House, Sutton, Shepton Mallet, Somerset BA4 6QF

✆ 01749 860116
✍ info@foodofcourse.co.uk
🖳 www.foodofcourse.co.uk

The Principal, Lou Hutton, was the principal teacher at The Grange and has extensive experience running chalets as well as her own catering business.

**COURSES OFFERED:** 4-week Foundation Cookery Course is suitable for gap year students who want to work in chalets, lodges and galleys, or simply to

broaden their culinary expertise. Also offer a 5- or 10-day Essential Chalet Course in November. The school is based in a family home and offers individual attention while students gain confidence and develop their skills. This intensive hands-on course covers classic and modern methods of cookery, budgeting and menu-planning. Students can take the Basic Food Hygiene Course and examination while on the course. Wine tasting, guest cooks and visits to local markets are organised throughout the course. For the experienced cook the 5-day intensive New Food Course introduces new tastes and timesaving recipes.

**COST:** 4-week Foundation Course £3,350: 5-day Essential Chalet course is £1,490.

**ACCOMMODATION:** In twin guest rooms with en-suite bathrooms and comfortable student sitting room with TV/DVD.

**FOLLOW-UP:** Graduates of the course can be put in touch with ski companies and employment agencies.

**CONTACT:** Lou Hutton, Principal.

## THE GABLES SCHOOL OF COOKERY
Pipers Lodge, Bristol Road, Falfield,
Gloucestershire GL12 8DF
01454 260444
info@thegablesschoolofcookery.co.uk
www.thegablesschoolofcookery.co.uk

Specialists in training chalet hosts and yacht cooks.

**COURSES OFFERED:** 4-week cookery courses ideal for working in chalets or on yachts as well as providing lifelong cookery skills.

**DURATION OF COURSES:** 4 weeks available year round.

**PREREQUISITES:** Minimum age 16; average ages 18–50.

**QUALIFICATIONS OFFERED:** School certificate equivalent to NVQ 2/3.

**COST:** £3,150 inclusive.

**ACCOMMODATION:** 3-star accommodation in twin rooms with en-suite bathrooms.

**FOLLOW-UP:** School aims to find positions for all graduates.

**CONTACT:** Chris Winston, Partner.

## LEITHS SCHOOL OF FOOD AND WINE
16–20 Wendell Road, London W12 9RT
info@leiths.com
www.leiths.com

Leiths School of Food and Wine is based in London and is non-residential.

**COURSES OFFERED:** The Leiths Basic Certificate in Practical Cookery is designed for gap year students and anyone wishing to assist in chalets, villas and lodges. Alternatively the Beginners' Certificate in Food and Wine is a longer course for those looking to work in private catering. On both courses the day is divided between demonstrations and practical cooking sessions. Topics covered include meat, fish and vegetable preparation and cooking, menu planning, costing and time-planning. Each class is divided into suitable age groups and run by experienced, friendly, professional chefs.

**DURATION OF COURSES:** Leiths Basic Certificate lasts 4 weeks full-time, running in Aug/Sept each year. Leiths Beginners' Certificate lasts 10 weeks full-time (Sept to Dec).

**QUALIFICATIONS OFFERED:** Basic Certificate in practical cookery. Beginners' Certificate in Food and Wine.

**COST:** 4-week Basic Certificate £2,650; 10-week Beginners Certificate £6,000. The fees cover teaching, equipment and food (which can be eaten at the school or taken home). Extra items including cookery books, uniforms and chef knives, will need to be bought separately and will cost around £115.

**FOLLOW-UP:** The company also runs Leiths List (www.leithslist.com), an agency for cooks, which helps to place students in suitable positions, once qualified.

## THE MURRAY SCHOOL OF COOKERY
Glenbervie House, Holt Pound, Farnham,
Surrey GU10 4LE
/fax 01420 23049
KMPMMSC@aol.com
www.cookeryschool.net

**COURSES OFFERED:** Cookery certificate courses.
**DURATION OF COURSES:** Certificate course lasts 4 weeks; Chalet Chef course lasts 1 week. Held in January, March, July and September. For dates of future courses refer to website.
**QUALIFICATIONS OFFERED:** The Certificate Course is accredited by major ski chalet operators, yacht catering agencies and by major companies offering retraining schemes. The Chalet Chef course is approved by major ski holiday operators.
**COST:** £1,600 for a 4-week course. Chalet Chef course costs £420.
**ACCOMMODATION:** Local bed and breakfasts are available at £25 per night.
**FOLLOW-UP:** The courses are designed for people wanting to work in ski chalets or on yachts for those interested in catering to a high standard for small groups.
**CONTACT:** Paulette Murray.

## NATIVES.CO.UK
263 Putney Bridge Road, London SW15 2PU
020 8788 4271
vicky@natives.co.uk
www.natives.co.uk/skijobs/cookery/
index.htm

UK's leading recruitment website for finding jobs in ski and summer resorts.
**COURSES OFFERED:** Chalet cookery courses are run annually in England (at girls' schools in Surey and Salisbury) and in Morzine, France.
**DURATION OF COURSES:** 5 days, with starting dates between April and October.
**PREREQUISITES:** Minimum age 18 (unless Duke of Edinburgh candidate, or not intending to work a season).

**QUALIFICATIONS OFFERED:** Natives Cookery course is recognised throughout the industry and candidates are guaranteed a job through Natives.co.uk if they pass with a Grade C or above. Chartered Institute of Environmental Health Level 2 award in food safety in catering.
**COST:** £449 for UK courses, £595 for course in French Alps. £50 deposit is needed to secure a place.
**FOLLOW-UP:** Guaranteed job through natives.co.uk for those who pass.
**OTHER SERVICES:** Natives Jobs Fair is the company's main seasonal recruitment event (www.natives.co.uk/skijobs/jobsfair/index.html). Check the website for upcoming dates. Season2season has a snow season (cookery course included) and a surf season (www.natives.co.uk/season2season/index.htm).

## ORCHARDS COOKERY
The Orchards, Salford Priors, Near Evesham,
Worcestershire WR11 8UU
01789 490 259
Isabel@orchardscookery.co.uk
www.orchardscookery.co.uk

**COURSES OFFERED:** Chalet Cooks and recruitment, Off to University, Designer Dinners for Beginners.
**DURATION OF COURSES:** 5 days and 2 weeks, year round.
**QUALIFICATIONS OFFERED:** Certificate on completion of the course which is well recognised in the chalet industry. Access organisation for the Gold Duke of Edinburgh's Award so participants can be awarded a certificate to certify they have completed their residential project.
**COST:** Chalet Cooks (5 days) £795, (2 weeks) £1,590. Off to University (5 days) £795. Designer Dinners (5 days) £695 including accommodation.
**ACCOMMODATION:** Students live on-site in cottages adjoining the family farm house.
**CONTACT:** Isabel Bomford, Director.

## ROSIE DAVIES COURSES FOR COOKS

Penny's Mill, Nunney, Frome,
Somerset BA11 4NP

© 01373 836210

info@rosiedavies.co.uk

www.rosiedavies.co.uk

**COURSES OFFERED:** A cookery course beginning with essential skills and basic techniques but moving on to more complex aspects. Part of the course will include the specialist skills needed to cook in a chalet or on board a yacht.

**DURATION OF COURSES:** 4 weeks.

**QUALIFICATIONS OFFERED:** Certificate of completion and a Food Safety in Catering Certificate.

**COST:** £3,350 including shared accommodation.

**ACCOMMODATION:** Twin-bedded rooms with toilet/shower room and sitting area with TV/video and broadband internet.

**FOLLOW-UP:** Ideal for aspiring chalet hosts and yacht cooks.

## SNOWCRAZY

La Rosière, France

© UK: 01342 302910;
France: +33 4 79 09 14 86

laura@snowcrazy.co.uk

www.snowcrazy.co.uk;
www.chaletcookerycourse.co.uk

**COURSES OFFERED:** Ultimate Chalet Host Cookery Course in the Alps to teach participants the practicalities of how to run a successful chalet with style and a minimum of fuss. Course teaches tasty recipes that are quick and easy to cook for large numbers, using ingredients which will be available in winter alpine resorts, using methods of cooking specific to altitude. It also covers with how to deal with special dietary requirements including 6 day vegetarian menu and wheat-free/dairy-free/vegan, etc. Tips are given on menu planning (useful if asked to present a weekly plan to your manager), managing a tight shopping budget,

health and safety practices, tricks of the trade and how to maximise your ski time,

**DURATION OF COURSES:** 1 week (6$\frac{1}{2}$ days) in summer and autumn (starting on a selection of Saturdays between mid-August and late November).

**QUALIFICATIONS OFFERED:** Links with tour operators (especially Ski Esprit, Crystal/Thomson and Ski Olympic who come to course to recruit) and independently run chalet operators. Almost all students who want to work a season after the course secure a job in a ski resort.

**COST:** £495 excluding flights, insurance, recreational activities and drinks from honesty bar.

**ACCOMMODATION:** Chalet Chantelauze with outdoor hot-tub (in rooms shared with one other) included in course fee.

**CONTACT:** Laura Clarke, Director.

## TANTE MARIE SCHOOL OF COOKERY

Woodham House, Carlton Road, Woking,
Surrey GU21 4HF

© 01483 726957

info@tantemarie.co.uk

www.tantemarie.co.uk

UK's largest independent cookery school, accredited by the BAC (British Accreditation Council) and member of the Year Out Group.

**COURSES OFFERED:** Variety of practical courses suitable for gap year students. Cordon Bleu Certificate course (11 weeks) offers a formal qualification useful for students who wish to work in ski chalets and on yachts as well as gaining temporary employment during university vacations. The Essential Skills course (4 weeks) is a good foundation though there is no formal qualification. Beginners Course lasts 1 or 2 weeks and is a basic introduction to cookery.

**DURATION OF COURSES:** Essential Skills course offered in July and September; Cordon Bleu Certificate course begins September. Beginners course offered in mid-July.

**QUALIFICATIONS OFFERED:** Internationally recognised qualifications including Cordon Bleu Diploma and Certificate. Certificate of attendance for other courses.

**COST:** £2,825 for Essential Skills, £6,950 for Certificate Course and £650 for 1-week Beginners or £1,100 for 2-week Beginners. Prices are inclusive of chef's whites (where applicable), knives, personalised recipe folder, all ingredients and lunch each day.

**ACCOMMODATION:** With homestay families arranged via the school

**FOLLOW-UP:** Certificate courses are excellent for short-term employment during vacations. Essential Skills course recognised by many ski operators. Tante Marie offers employment advice and has good industry contacts.

**CONTACT:** Debbie Volans.

# SKI TRAINING COURSES

## ALLTRACKS ACADEMY
3 Egbert Road, Winchester, Hampshire SO23 7ED
01962 864203
info@alltracksacademy.com
www.alltracksacademy.com

**COURSES OFFERED:** Ski and snowboard instructor courses and improvement training camps at Whistler, Revelstoke and Red Mountain in Canada.

**DURATION OF COURSES:** 3–11 weeks throughout winter from November to April. 11-week Ski/Snowboard Instructor Course, 11-week Ski/Snowboard Improvement Course, 8-week Off-Piste Backcountry Ski/Snowboard Course, 4-week Ski/Snowboard Instructor Course; 3-week Ski/Snowboard Improvement Course.

**QUALIFICATIONS OFFERED:** Courses lead to instructor qualifications as well as recreational improvement camps.

**COST:** £2,950–£7,450. Fees include expert tuition from professional instructors and mountain guides, exam fees, return flights, central accommodation with hot tubs, Wi-Fi, etc, meals, official Avalanche Skills Training and overnight backcountry adventures.

**ACCOMMODATION:** Comfortable chalets.

**CONTACT:** Paul Beard, Director.

## ALTITUDE FUTURES
Verbier, Switzerland
0+41 (0) 7953 05224
info@altitude-futures.co.uk
www.altitude-futures.co.uk

**COURSES OFFERED:** Ski Instructor and Snowboard Instructor Gap Course.

**PREREQUISITES:** Minimum age 18.

**DURATION OF COURSES:** 10 weeks with 3 possible start dates, November, January or February.

**QUALIFICATIONS OFFERED:** BASI qualifications. Some successful participants stay on working as instructors or return in university holidays.

**COST:** £7,450 including half-board accommodation. Early bird booking discount of £450.

**CONTACT:** Laura Turner (Office Manager) or Jon West (General Manager, Jon.West@altitude-verbier.com).

## BAHARA SKI INSTRUCTOR TRAINING
Highway 73, Springfield, Canterbury, South Island, New Zealand
www.nonstopski.com

**COURSES OFFERED:** 10-week Ski Instructor Training Programme. 10 weeks personal training in the Craigieburn Range (45 minutes from Christchurch). Privately run course for no more than 2 groups of 8 students, which allows the course to be adjusted to the needs of individual trainees. Also 4-week extensions available for level 2 exam.

**DURATION OF COURSES:** 10 or 14 weeks from July to October.

**QUALIFICATIONS OFFERED:** NZSIA (New Zealand Ski Instructors Alliance) Level 1 Exam ( level 2 for 14 week course); exams included in course. Written reference from the ski school director will be useful when applying for jobs.

**COST:** Approximately £6,000 (excluding ski equipment and flights).

**ACCOMMODATION:** Homely local motel style accommodation with meals included at local restaurant.

**PROGRAMME DESCRIPTION:** Ski and Snowboard Instructor courses in the Alps, Rockies and Andes to improve all round ability and gain a recognised European and North American ski or snowboard instructor's qualification. Chance to improve skiing and riding (off-piste, freestyle, racing, etc.). Courses include Avalanche courses, First Aid courses, Ski/Snowboard Tuning Clinics, French lessons, weekend trips and social events. Assistance can be given in finding work after the course. As well as instructor courses they offer 'Improvement Camps' which are courses specially designed to take students' all-round skiing to the next level, and 'Performance Courses' which concentrate on specific disciplines: Freestyle and Freeride.

**DESTINATIONS:** Val d'Isère (France), Méribel (France), Verbier (Switzerland), Whistler (Canada), Banff (Canada) and Bariloche (Argentina).

**DURATION AND TIME OF PLACEMENTS:** 4–11 week courses begin in November and from beginning of January.

**NUMBER OF PLACEMENTS PER YEAR:** Up to 200.

**PREREQUISITES:** Beginners welcome since many clients are spending their first winter in the mountains and are new to the industry. Several Freestyle and Freeskiing camps are run for more experienced skiers.

**COST:** £6,695–£7,925 excluding insurance for 11-week programmes; £3,295–£4,945 for 4–6 week programmes. Includes accommodation throughout.

**ACCOMMODATION:** Whistler accommodation in 7–8 bedded chalets is located a short walk or bus ride from the centre of Whistler village and the lifts. Other accommodation mostly in 4-person flats, but always near the ski centres.

BASI runs training and grading courses throughout the year in five disciplines: Alpine Skiing, Snowboarding, Telemark, Nordic and Adaptive. BASI also publishes the *BASI News* in which job advertisements for ski and snowboard instructors appear.

**GAP COURSES OFFERED:** BASI gap year course offered over 10 weeks leading to Level 2 ski or snowboard instructor's qualification. Courses take place from January to March in Courchevel, Meribel and Val d'Isère.

**PREREQUISITES:** Minimum age 16. Students should be able to ski parallel or ride confidently on red runs coping with a variety of snow conditions.

**COST:** £6,995–£7,995.

**CONTACT:** BASI Administration Department.

**COURSES OFFERED:** Coronet Peak Instructor Training Programme (CPIT).

**PREREQUISITES:** Minimum age 17, average age 20.

**DURATION OF COURSES:** 10 weeks every winter from July to September.

**QUALIFICATIONS OFFERED:** Course prepares candidates for the NZSIA/SBINZ new Level One and Level Two certification. With these qualifications, past graduates have gone on to teach in resorts in both the northern and southern hemispheres.

**COST:** From about NZ$5,610 to NZ$10,475 depending on what is included. Accommodation can be included at a lodge, i.e. shared accommodation in a unit within the lodge complex.

**CONTACT:** Michel Marchand, Snowsports School Director.

---

## DEUTSCH-INSTITUT TIROL
Am Sandhügel 2, 6370 Kitzbühel, Austria
*(C)* +43 53 56 712 74
office@deutschinstitut.com
www.gap year.at

**COURSES OFFERED:** German language combined with ski and snowboard instruction specially designed for gap year students.

**DURATION OF COURSES:** 12 weeks from end of September to just before Christmas. Course includes 8 weeks intensive German tuition at DIT in Kitzbühel interspersed with 8 3-day weekends skiing/snowboarding on the glacier at Kaprun. Also 7-day trip to Eastern Europe.

**QUALIFICATIONS OFFERED:** Preparation for Austrian ski/snowboard instructor exams.

**COST:** €8,200 inclusive of everything except travel to Kitzbühel and insurance.

**ACCOMMODATION:** Half-board accommodation in Kitzbühel; full board in Kaprun.

---

## ECOLE DE SKI & SNOWBOARD C. JORLY
Rue César, 65110 Cauterets, France
*(C)* +33 6 08 68 88 54; fax +33 5 59 54 81 78
contact@ecole-ski-jorly.com
www.gapskifrance.com

Ski and Snowboard school established in 2006 at Cauterets in the Pyrenees near Lourdes. Affiliated to Ecole de Surf de Guéthary on the Basque coast of France (see entry in 'Directory of Sport and Activity Courses').

**PROGRAMME DESCRIPTION:** Instructor course leading to BASI Levels 1 and 2 plus French immersion and language teaching.

**DESTINATIONS:** South-west France.

**PREREQUISITES:** Minimum age 18. Must be able to ski confidently and in control on all kinds of runs,

coping with a variety of conditions including off-piste and have completed at least 10 weeks on snow and be able to make short, medium and long radius turns close to the fall line.

**DURATION AND TIME OF PLACEMENTS:** 10 weeks from early January; 5–6 hours a day, 5 days a week. Course includes 21 hours of French tuition with a qualified French teacher (3 hours a week).

**COST:** £6,040.

**CONTACT:** Christophe Jorly, Co-Director and Instructor.

---

## ICE – INTERNATIONAL CENTRE OF EXCELLENCE
*UK office:* 3–4 Bath Place, Aberdovey, Gwynedd LL35 0LN
*(C)* 08770 760 7360
info@icesi.org
www.icesi.org
*French office:* 17, Le Cret 2, 73150, Val d'Isère

**COURSES OFFERED:** Official BASI gap courses for ski and snowboard instructors. Also BASI Level 1 and Level 2 Instructor courses, performance and preparation courses, and all terrain 4 week courses.

**DURATION OF COURSES:** BASI instructor courses last 10 weeks, 6 weeks or 4 weeks.

**QUALIFICATIONS OFFERED:** Students can be placed in work following successful qualification and can gain workplace experience as part of the course. ICE uses BASI trainers exclusively for all ski instructor training, snowboard instructor training and assessing.

**PREREQUISITES:** Minimum age 16 with parental consent; average age 19.

**COST:** 10-week residential course costs £6,995, 6 weeks for £5,495 and 4 weeks for £3,995. Course only fees are Level 1 (5 days) £390; Level 2 (10 days) £520.

**ACCOMMODATION:** Apartment accommodation, with evening restaurant meals provided throughout residential courses.

**CONTACT:** Rupert Tildesley, Director.

---

**COST:** C$4,550 for 3-week course, C$9,320 for 6-week course and C$12,750 for 11-week course; prices include accommodation, most meals, lift pass and all tuition. Long course also includes weekend trips.

**ACCOMMODATION:** Twin rooms in hotels or houses depending on resort. Recent acquisition of two chalets in Meribel Mottaret run by ex-clients with access to a local guide.

**OTHER SERVICES:** Work experience may be arranged with local ski school and contacts with other ski schools for instructing jobs.

**CONTACT:** Georgie Bushe, Sales Manager.

## PEAK LEADERS UK

Mansfield, Strathmiglo, Fife KY14 7QE, Scotland

📞 01337 860079

🖱 info@peakleaders.com

💻 www.peakleaders.com

**OURSES OFFERED:** Gap year Ski and Snowboard ⌐structor courses in Canada, Switzerland, Austria, ⌐rgentina and Japan. Course includes structured ⌐rogrammes of mountain safety, first aid, avalanche ⌐wareness and leadership. Courses held in Whistler and ⌐anff in the Canadian Rockies, Saas Fee, Zermatt and ⌐rbier in Switzerland, St Anton in Austria, Bariloche in ⌐atagonia and Myoko in Japan.

**⌐RATION OF COURSES:** Instructor courses mainly ⌐st 9–10 weeks with various start times: September ⌐ Saas Fee, November or February in Verbier and ⌐istler, etc. Courses in Argentina and (possibly) New ⌐aland are run in July to September. Shorter improver ⌐rses available in Gulmarg (India), St Anton and Banff.

**⌐ALIFICATIONS OFFERED:** 5 internationally recog- ⌐ed qualifications: instructor, leader, mountain safety ⌐ avalanche awareness. Some courses offer a level ⌐ward in Team Leading, validated by the Institute of ⌐ dership & Management (www.i-l-m.com).

**⌐ST:** £6,500–£8,240 for 9–12 weeks.

**⌐ ER SERVICES:** On winter courses, extras offered ⌐ as skidoo driving, backcountry training, field trips

to Argentine Patagonia and Chile. Work experience and advice on job opportunities worldwide.

## PRO RIDE SNOWBOARD CAMPS

PO Box 1351, Whistler, BC V0N 1B0 Canada

📞 +1 604 935 2115

📞 0800 404 6390 (UK toll-free)

🖱 snowboard@pro-ride.com

💻 www.pro-ride.com

**COURSES OFFERED:** Freeride, freestyle and snowboard instructor training. Opportunity to ride with professionally sponsored pro riders and Olympic level coaches. Courses cater for the intermediate to advanced rider.

**DURATION OF COURSES:** 5 days to 12 weeks. Flexible start dates and length of training according to ability.

**QUALIFICATIONS OFFERED:** Both recreational courses and snowboard instructor training to work towards achieving Canadian Association of Snowboard Instructor certification.

**COST:** From C$3,495 for 2 weeks to C$14,885 for 12 weeks.

**ACCOMMODATION:** Twin share in bright clean houses and condos in Whistler.

**CONTACT:** Karen Crute, Director.

## ROOKIE ACADEMY

PO Box 402, Wanaka, New Zealand

📞 +64 3 443 5100

🖱 info@rookieacademy.com

💻 www.rookieacademy.com

**COURSES OFFERED:** Ski and snowboard instructor courses.

**DESTINATIONS:** New Zealand and USA.

**DURATION OF COURSES:** 12, 8 and 5 weeks for NZ courses; 19, 8 and 5 weeks for US courses.

**QUALIFICATIONS OFFERED:** All courses include an internationally recognised ski or snowboard instructor exam. Only company in New Zealand to offer British and Canadian instructor qualifications in conjunction with the New Zealand qualifications.

## MOUNTAIN LODGE

10 Bankhead Crescent, Arbroath, Angus,
Scotland DD11 2DP

info@mountainlodge.co.uk
www.mountainlodge.co.uk

**COURSES OFFERED:** 10-week ski instructor training
course based in Courchevel, France. Course run by
BASI ski examiners.

**DURATION OF COURSES:** Early January to mid-March
every year.

**QUALIFICATIONS OFFERED:** Successful candidates
will achieve their BASI ski instructor qualification.

**COST:** £6,000. Catered chalet accommodation is
provided as part of the package (through an in-house
chalet company Skivo2).

**CONTACT:** Dave Beattie and Dave Morris, Directors.

## NEW GENERATION SKI AND SNOWBOARD SCHOOL

*French office:* Rue de la Chappelle, Le Praz,
73120 Courchevel, France

+ 33 479 01 03 18
instructorcourses@skinewgen.com
www.skinewgen.com
*UK office:* 0870 068 7519

New Generation runs the official BASI (British Association of Snowsport Instructors) GAP courses. New
Generation is a training centre for students wishing to
pursue a career in ski or snowboard instruction.

**COURSES OFFERED:** Ski GAP courses in Meribel and
Courchevel.

**DURATION OF COURSES:** Once a year, January to
March, for 10 weeks.

**QUALIFICATIONS OFFERED:** All courses include
instructor exams; successful candidates can teach
in most countries including on dry slopes and indoor
slopes in the UK.

**COST:** £6,995 including fully catered chalet accommodation.

**CONTACT:** Euan Wright, New Generation Head Coach.

## NONSTOP SKI & SNOWBOARD

Unit 3B, The Plough Brewery, 516 Wan
Road, London SW8 3JX

0845 365 1525
info@nonstopadventure.com
www.nonstopadventure.com
www.nonstopski.com
www.nonstopsnowboard.com

Member of the Year Out Group.

**COURSES OFFERED:** Ski and Snowboard
and Instructor Courses in Banff, Fernie, K
and Red Mountain in the Canadian Rocki
Craigieburn, New Zealand (see entry for
above). Training in addition to the on-snc
includes mountain safety, avalanche awa
backcountry, winter survival skills, first a
and snowboard maintenance. Weekend
resorts, snowmobiling and heli/cat skiir
classes in French, Spanish, yoga and c
be taken.

**NUMBER OF PARTICIPANTS:** 70–80
course, 30–40 on 3-week course and
6-week course.

**DURATION OF COURSES:** 3-week co
cember to mid-January. 6-week cours
February. 11-week programme runs f
early April. Also 2-week Snow Safaris
ski coaching at different resorts in dif

**PREREQUISITES:** Minimum age 18
participants are gappers).

**QUALIFICATIONS OFFERED:** Inter
recognised CSIA (Canadian Ski Inst
CASI (Canadian Association of Sno
Also CAA (Canadian Avalanche As
tional Avalanche 1 certificate and
Basic first aid certificate. In New Z
Level 1 can be achieved in 10 we
possibility of an extra 4 weeks to
Freestyle and race coach qualific
be obtained.

**COST:** NZ$19,950 for 12 weeks, NZ$12,950 for 8 weeks and NZ$9,000 for 5 weeks. Prices for USA are US$14,950, US$9,450 and US$7,450, respectively.

**ACCOMMODATION:** Shared apartment style, fully furnished includes cleaning and linen service.

**CONTACT:** Garett Shore, Director.

## SKI ACADEMY SWITZERLAND
6 Lane Side, Kirkburton, Huddersfield HD8 0TN
- 0141 416 0146
- 07810 502204 (mobile)
- info@skiacademyswitzerland.com
- www.skiacademyswitzerland.com

**COURSES OFFERED:** Autumn programme: 9–11 weeks of training and qualifications before the winter season. Completion of BASI (British Association of Snowsports Instructors) or PSIA (Professional Ski Instructors of America) instructor course allows participants to work for the remainder of the season as a ski instructor in partnered ski schools across Europe and USA. Winter programmes: 9–11 weeks (shorter courses available) of training and qualifications during the winter season and chance to complete BASI or PSIA instructor course. Spring and Summer Programmes: 4-week training course, and qualifying for PSIA qualifications.

**DESTINATION:** Summer programme at Saas-Fee (for year-round glacier skiing); Autumn and Winter programmes are based in Saas-Fee and Gstaad.

**QUALIFICATIONS OFFERED:** All courses lead to a BASI or PSIA qualification.

**COST:** £2,950 for July/August course, £5,600–£6,600 for other programmes. Prices include 3-star hotel accommodation with half board.

**CONTACT:** James Wilkinson, Director.

## SITCO – SKI & SNOWBOARD INSTRUCTOR TRAINING CO
PO Box 791, Queenstown, New Zealand
- +64 21 341 214/5
- info@skiinstructortraining.co.nz/ info@snowboardinstructortraining.co.nz
- www.sitco.co.nz; www.skiinstructort raining.co.nz; www.snowboardinstructor training.co.nz

**COURSES OFFERED:** Keen skiers and boarders are trained to develop and achieve their Ski & Snowboard Instructor Qualifications in Queenstown, New Zealand. Courses also expose candidates to freestyle, freeride and race influences and includes an Avalanche Awareness course, First Aid course or Off-piste Awareness course, and a Heli-Ski/Board day (included in fee). SITCo. now also offers a 6-week course based out of Snowbird, Utah in the USA (www.sitcosnowbird.com).

**DURATION OF COURSES:** 11, 8, 6 and 5 week courses beginning July and ending September. Each course runs once per season. Training given on 3 days a week.

**PREREQUISITES:** Ski trainees should be able to ski a red/black run in control, with confidence so that there is a realistic chance of achieving the NZSIA Level 2. Snowboarders should be able to ride blue runs on and off trail, linking turns consistently and riding with confidence.

**QUALIFICATIONS OFFERED:** NZSIA Level 1 and NZSIA Level 2.

**COST:** From NZ$14,400 for 11-week course and NZ$12,100 for 8-week course, NZ$10,100 for 6 weeks and NZ$8,200 for 5 weeks. Inclusive of accommodation, whole-season lift pass, transport between Queenstown and the mountain, and exam fees. Early booking prices available.

**ACCOMMODATION:** 5, 6, 8 or 11 weeks of accommodation at Pinewood Lodge in central Queenstown; price based on 2 people sharing a quadruple room.

**CONTACT:** Gavin McAuliffe or Colin Tanner, Founding Partners.

## SKI LE GAP
220 Wheeler Street, Mont Tremblant, Quebec J8E 1V3, Canada
- +1 819 429 6599
- 0800 328 0345 (freephone from UK)
- info@skilegap
- www.skilegap.com

**PROGRAMME DESCRIPTION:** Ski and Snowboard instructor's programme operating since 1994 specifically designed for gap year students from Britain. The course combines ski/snowboard instruction with French conversation lessons plus other activities such as igloo-building, dogsledding, extreme snowshoeing, and trips to Montreal, Quebec City and Ottawa.

**DESTINATIONS:** Quebec, Canada.

**NUMBER OF PLACEMENTS PER YEAR:** 200.

**PREREQUISITES:** All nationalities. Must be passionate about skiing, but all levels of ability accepted from beginners to expert.

**DURATION AND TIME OF PLACEMENTS:** 3 months from January and 1 month intensive training course from late November.

**SELECTION PROCEDURES AND ORIENTATION:** Places are reserved on a first-come, first-served basis so early reservations are advised.

**COST:** £6,970 (plus £500 in tax) for 2010 for 3-month course. Price includes return London–Montreal airfare and full room and board, but not medical insurance or ski equipment. £3,255 for 1-month course excluding flights.

**CONTACT:** Amelia Puddifer, Programme Director.

---

### SNOW TRAINERS

PO Box 846, Queenstown, New Zealand

+64 21 258 6259

+64 21 232 5708

info@snowtrainers.com

www.snowtrainers.com

---

**COURSES OFFERED:** Ski and Snowboard Instructor Courses in Queenstown, New Zealand, Wanaka and Niseko (Hokkaido, Japan). Trainers are NZSIA examiners, trainers and highly qualified coaches.

**DURATION OF COURSES:** NZ: 10-week (July-September) or 5-week (July-August) Instructor courses. Japan: 8-week Instructor course January-February or 2-week Improvement course in February.

**QUALIFICATIONS OFFERED:** Participants train towards the internationally recognised New Zealand Level One

teaching qualification on the short course and towards Levels 1 and 2 on the 8- or 10-week courses.

**COST:** 10-week Instructor course in Queenstown and 8-week Instructor course in Japan cost NZ$14,950. Queenstown 5-week Instructor course costs NZ$8,950; Japan 2-week improvement course costs NZ$4,950. Early booking discounts available.

**ACCOMMODATION:** Centrally located lodge-style accommodation.

**CONTACT:** Matt Phare and Tony Macri, Course Directors.

---

### SNOWORKS

Tignes, France

+33 6 84 44 07 48

+33 6 80165348 (mobile)

08701 225549 (UK booking)

info@snoworks.co.uk

www.snoworks.co.uk

---

**COURSES OFFERED:** 8-week Ski Instructors GAP course leading to BASI qualifications in Tignes, France.

**DURATION OF COURSES:** 8 weeks starting approximately 24 October.

**PREREQUISITES:** Minimum age 18, average age 20.

**QUALIFICATIONS OFFERED:** Successful candidates will be qualified Level 1 and 2 ski instructors by Christmas, allowing them to work a season in the Alps, America and Canada (job advice given).

**COST:** £6,485.

**ACCOMMODATION:** half-board accommodation in Hotel Aguille Percee (Mark Warner hotel) in Tignes.

**CONTACT:** Phil Smith and Emma Carrick-Anderson, Directors.

---

### SNOWSKOOL

37–39 Southgate Street, Winchester, Hampshire, SO23 9EH

0871 223 0060

team@sportskool.co.uk

www.sportskool.co.uk

---

**COURSES OFFERED:** Ski & Snowboard Instructor training courses in the Canadian resorts of Sunshine Village (Banff) and Big White (British Columbia), as well as Cardrona Ski Resort in New Zealand and France's Three Valleys.

**NUMBER OF PLACEMENTS PER YEAR:** 150 for SnowSkool Canada, 40 for SnowSkool New Zealand and 25 for SnowSkool France.

**DURATION OF COURSES:** Northern hemisphere courses run from January to April and southern hemisphere courses from July to September. Courses range in length: 4, 5, 11 and 14 weeks in Canada, 10 weeks in New Zealand and 11 weeks in France.

**QUALIFICATIONS OFFERED:** Internationally recognised CSIA, CASI, BASI, NZSIA and SBINZ qualifications.

**COST:** SnowSkool short courses from £3,550 (including accommodation, meals, tuition and lift pass) and full season long courses from £6,995 (including flights, accommodation, meals, tuition and lift pass).

**CONTACT:** Sales enquiries to team@snowskool.co.uk and for all other enquiries contact Philip Purdie, Director (phil@sportskool.co.uk)

## SUNSHINE WORLD

8 Brompton Place, Knightsbridge,
London SW3 1QE

℅ 020 7581 4736

✉ alan@sunshineworld.co.uk

▦ www.sunshineworld.co.uk
www.sunshineworldpoland.com

**COURSES OFFERED:** All-inclusive and customisable ski and snowboarding instructor training courses in resort of Zakopane in Poland. Ski and snowboard improvement courses also available.

**DURATION OF COURSES:** from 1 week to full 20-week season.

**QUALIFICATIONS OFFERED:** Option available of taking official Canadian qualifications: CSIA for skiing, CASI for snowboarding.

**COST:** 4-week instructor training courses from £800, 8-weeks from £1,600, full season of 20 weeks from

just £3,500. Fees include return flights from the UK, accommodation in Sunshine World's luxury chalet, food, equipment rental, lift passes and instruction.

**ACCOMMODATION:** 20-person chalet with log fireplace, plasma TVs, games consoles and DVD players, Jacuzzi room with heated stone floor, fully equipped kitchen with dishwasher, utility room with washing machine and dryer, ski and boot room and large communal living area. Located just 5 minutes walk from supermarket, bars and clubs, and 10 minutes walk from the main high street.

**CONTACT:** Alan Garcia, Managing Director.

## WARREN SMITH SKI ACADEMY

Snowsport Synergy, Merlewood, Kenyon Lane,
Dinckley, Lancashire BB6 8AN

℅ 01525 374757 (UK)

℅ +41 79 359 6566 (Switzerland)

✉ warrensmith@snowsportsynergy.com

✉ theteam@warrensmith-skiacademy.com

▦ www.warrensmith-skiacademy.com/
gap-program.htm

**COURSES OFFERED:** Gap year ski instructor course in Verbier, Switzerland.

**DURATION OF COURSES:** 9 weeks (9 Jan to 13 Mar).

**PREREQUISITES:** Minimum age 16; average age 30.

**QUALIFICATIONS OFFERED:** BASI qualifications.

**COST:** £6,999 with accommodation, £4,799 without accommodation.

**ACCOMMODATION:** Half board, excellent food, en suite, near lift station. Chalets through Peak Ski.

**CONTACT:** Warren Smith, Director.

# SPORT AND ACTIVITY COURSES

## FLYING FISH

25 Union Road, Cowes, Isle of Wight PO31 7TW

℅ 0871 250 2500

✉ mail@flyingfishonline.com

▦ www.flyingfishonline.com

Flying Fish trains water and snowsports staff and arranges employment for sailors, divers, surfers and windsurfers, skiers and snowboarders (see programme details in 'Directory of Specialist Gap Year Programmes').

**COURSES OFFERED:** Professional Dive Training, International Yacht Training and Sail and Board Sports Instructor training programmes. There is a specially organised modular scheme for gap year students offering training followed by work experience and a period of employment in Australia or Greece. Ski and snowboard instructor courses take place at Whistler in Canada.

**DESTINATIONS:** Training takes place at Cowes on the Isle of Wight (UK), at Sydney and the Whitsunday Islands in Australia, the Bay of Islands in New Zealand, Vassiliki in Greece and Whistler Mountain in Canada. Jobs are worldwide with main employers located in Australia, the South Pacific, the Caribbean and the Mediterranean.

**DURATION OF COURSES:** Courses last from 1 week to 4 months. Courses come with a 'professional' option where trainees take part in a period of work experience as an instructor.

**QUALIFICATIONS OFFERED:** Flying Fish courses lead to qualifications from the Royal Yachting Association (RYA), Professional Association of Dive Instructors (PADI), the Yachting Australia Federation (YA), Surfing Australia (SA), Canadian Ski Instructors Alliance (CSIA), and the Canadian Association of Snowboard Instructors (CASI).

**COST:** Prices range from £460 for a 1-week Learn to Dinghy Sail course in Greece to a 17-week Yachtmaster Professional Traineeship in Sydney for £11,000.

**ACCOMMODATION:** Self-catering apartments. Varies according to course and destination but always provided.

**FOLLOW-UP:** Possibility of employment following qualification. Placements in the Mediterranean, the Caribbean and Australia. Qualifications gained can be used after the year out in holiday periods to gain extra cash.

## GAP YEAR DIVER

Tyte Court, Farbury End, Great Rollright, Oxfordshire OX7 5RS

0845 257 3292

info@gapyeardiver.com

www.gapyeardiver.com

**PROGRAMME DESCRIPTION:** Specialists in the field of recreational, professional, marine conservation and technical scuba diving for all types of gappers, from school and university leavers to career breakers.

**DESTINATIONS:** Egypt, Venezuela, Costa Rica, Thailand, Ecuador, Bahamas, Fiji and Belize.

**DURATION OF COURSES:** Range from intensive 2-week 'learn to dive' trips to extensive 10–15 -week 'Go Pro' and marine conservation programmes.

**QUALIFICATIONS OFFERED:** PADI Open Water Diver to Instructor and marine science training.

**COST:** £660–£6,000 (depends on duration and destination). Includes transfers, accommodation, diving equipment, materials, PADI certification costs, professional scuba tuition and range of specialised diving trips and local land-based activities. In some locations, language courses in Arabic, Spanish or French are included and/ or marine conservation initiatives, videography and photography courses and community work.

**ACCOMMODATION:** Dorm rooms, self-catered houses or camp-style accommodation depending on location.

**CONTACT:** Ben Stillwell, Director.

## INTERNATIONAL ACADEMY

Sophia House, 28 Cathedral Road, Cardiff CF11 9LJ

029 2066 0200

info@international-academy.com

www.international-academy.com

Member of the Year Out Group.

**COURSES OFFERED:** Ski and Snowboard Instructor training courses that lead to internationally recognised qualifications.

**DURATION OF COURSES:** 5–12 weeks.

**DESTINATIONS:** Whistler Blackcomb or Lake Louise in Canada (Jan to Apr) or Cardrona in New Zealand (July to Sept). Also 5-week course at Lake Louise/Banff in November to December. Job opportunities available after course.

**COST:** £3,900–£7,750 depending on course duration and resort.

**CONTACT:** Alan Bates, General Manager.

## ECOLE DE SURF DE GUÉTHARY

Jorly SARL, 168 rue de Souhara,
64210 Bidart, France

*C* +33 6 08 68 88 54

surf.guethary@wanadoo.fr

http://surf.guethary.free.fr

www.gap.surf.france.free.fr

**COURSES OFFERED:** Surf and French language programme; cooking optional.

**DESTINATION:** Basque coast of France.

**DURATION OF COURSES:** 4 weeks in September, best time of year to enjoy the Basque coast.

**QUALIFICATIONS OFFERED:** Mostly recreational but courses do lead to a French qualification.

**COST:** €3,125 including accommodation in 2- to 4-bedded rooms.

**CONTACT:** Christophe Jorly, Co-Director.

## NONSTOP SAIL

Unit 3B, The Plough Brewery, 516 Wandswoth
Road, London SW8 3JX

*C* 0845 365 1525

info@nonstopadventure.com

www.nonstopsail.com

Member of the Year Out Group.

**COURSES OFFERED:** RYA yacht sail training courses and adventure sailing based at sailing school in Dartmouth, Devon, leading to Royal Yachting Association (RYA) qualifications. Adventure sail trips are also run (see 'Directory of Expeditions').

**NUMBER OF PARTICIPANTS:** 5–10 per boat.

**DURATION OF COURSES:** 6, 8 and 14 weeks. All courses run all year.

**PREREQUISITES:** Minimum age 18 (about half of participants are gappers).

**QUALIFICATIONS OFFERED:** RYA Start Yachting, Competent Crew, Day Skipper, Coastal Skipper and Yachtmaster.

**COST:** £150–£7,000.

**ACCOMMODATION:** On board Yachts for most of time.

**OTHER SERVICES:** Careers advice.

**CONTACT:** Georgie Bushe, Sales Manager.

## PERSONAL OVERSEAS DEVELOPMENT (POD)

Linden Cottage, The Burgage, Prestbury,
Cheltenham, Gloucestershire GL52 3DJ

*C* 01242 250901

info@divepod.co.uk

www.divepod.co.uk

**PROGRAMME DESCRIPTION:** PoD Diving offers PADI Learn to Dive and Advanced diver courses; PADI Go Pro Divemaster, Videographer and Instructor professional diving courses leading to a new career; Marine Conservation projects where you can combine diving with learning about and helping to protect the underwater environment.

**DESTINATIONS:** Australia, Belize, Thailand.

**DURATION AND TIME OF PLACEMENTS:** 1 week to 6 months; flexible start dates throughout the year.

**COST:** From £349 for Learn-to-Dive in Thailand. Gap year packages are provided including: pre-departure information and support, transfers, dive courses, manuals, fees and dive kit pack, accommodation, and specialist diving insurance.

**CONTACT:** Alex Tarrant or Mike Beecham.

## PLAS MENAI

The National Watersports Centre, Caernarfon,
Gwynedd LL55 1UE, Wales

*C* 01248 670964

*C* 0845 846 0029

info@plasmenai.co.uk

www.plasmenai.co.uk

**COURSES OFFERED:** Multi-watersports instructor training (26 weeks, including a training module in Dahab (Egypt)); professional yachtmaster training (14 weeks), sailing and windsurfing instructor (12 weeks, includes Dahab training module); fast-track powerboat instructor (3 weeks). Work experience programme.

**DURATION OF COURSES:** 3, 12, 14 and 26 weeks.

**QUALIFICATIONS OFFERED:** All courses lead to national governing body qualifications which allow graduates to become multi-qualified and teach a range of outdoor activities such as dinghy sailing, kayaking, climbing, cruising and windsurfing. Other job opportunities include yacht deliveries, professional race crew and expedition leaders.

**COST:** From £1,500 for 3-week fast-track powerboat instructor; £7,800 for multi-watersports instructor course (including Dahab). All prices include full board and accommodation for the duration of the course.

**FOLLOW-UP:** Graduates go on to teach at centres across the UK, abroad or to join a paid work experience programme.

---

### REAL SPORT EXPERIENCE

1 Meadow Road, Tunbridge Wells, Kent TN1 2YG

📞 01892 516164

✉ info@realsportexperience.co.uk

🖥 www.realsportexperience.co.uk

Part of Real Gap (www.realgap.co.uk), the UK's largest gap year provider.

**PROGRAMME DESCRIPTION:** Gap year sports programmes in 20 countries, including academy training programmes, sports volunteer projects, sports qualification courses and extreme expeditions.

**DESTINATIONS:** 20 countries. Sports Adventure through South Africa, Swaziland and Mozambique: camping safari, volunteer sports coaching and scuba diving course. Australia Beach lifeguard course, South Africa volunteer sports coaching, and many others.

**DURATION AND TIME OF PLACEMENTS:** Mainly 4 weeks.

**COST:** Prices differ, e.g. 4-week Kruger to Coast Sports Adventure costs £1,979; Australia Beach Lifeguard course £2,949; Sports volunteer projects in South Africa from £1,099.

---

### SUBWAY WATERSPORTS

Turquoise Bay Resort and Palmetto Bay Plantation, Roatan, Bay Islands, Honduras, Central America

✉ internship@subwaywatersports.com

🖥 www.subwaywatersports.com/Courses/internship.htm

**PROGRAMME DESCRIPTION:** Internship working in a dive shop while training towards a professional PADI Divemaster. Chance to learn about customer service and how to run a small business focusing on adventure in a resort atmosphere. Good introduction to life in the dive industry.

**NUMBER OF PLACEMENTS PER YEAR:** Average 30 per year (maximum 6 per month).

**DESTINATIONS:** Roatan is a tropical island in the Caribbean.

**PREREQUISITES:** Minimum 20 years. Open Water diving certification recommended. Must be friendly, fun, motivated and a water-lover. Must be in good physical shape.

**DURATION AND TIME OF PLACEMENTS:** 4–8 weeks.

**COST:** $1,350 for 4 weeks; $1,950 for 6 weeks; $2,490 for 8 weeks. Prices include instruction, diving, equipment, accommodation, lunches and airport pick-up. Prices do not include PADI certification cards, PADI books or insurance.

**ACCOMMODATION:** Room in apartments, shared with other interns.

**CONTACT:** Patrick Zingg, Owner (patrick@subwaywatersports.com).

---

### UKSA THE MARITIME ACADEMY

West Cowes, Isle of Wight PO31 7PQ

📞 01983 294941

✉ info@uksa.org

🖥 www.uksa.org

**COURSES OFFERED:** UKSA offer a range of professional watersports and yachting programmes for those wishing to work in the marine industry during their gap year. Gap year programmes can be tailor made from any of UKSA's range of courses.

**DURATION OF COURSES:** 4–23 weeks.

**QUALIFICATIONS OFFERED:** RYA, BKSA (British Kite Surfing Association), and BCU watersports qualifications. MCA (Motor Cruising) and RYA yachting qualifications.

**COST:** From £3,380 to £14,980 for gap year programmes.

**ACCOMMODATION:** Range of options, included in the cost.

**OTHER SERVICES:** On-site gym, bar and dining facilities. All professional courses include industry guidance for support with finding work after training.

### WATER BY NATURE RAFTING JOURNEY
3 Wath Road, Elsecar, South Yorkshire S74 8HJ
01226 740444
rivers@waterbynature.com
www.waterbynature.com

**COURSES OFFERED:** Whitewater raft and kayak guide training in Morocco and Turkey. Trainee raft guides will be taught to kayak on rivers up to Grade 3. Prospective river guides can also join 2-week course in June on the Coruh River in north-eastern Turkey where they can achieve BCU qualifications, leading to a chance to guide in other destinations around the world. (www.waterbynature.com/turkey_rafting/guide_course.html).

**DURATION OF COURSES:** 2 months in each country. 2 weeks for short course in Turkey in June.

**PREREQUISITES:** Very suitable for gap year. Affinity with whitewater useful. Should have driving licence because may be expected to drive vehicles. All nationalities accepted provided they can obtain visas for relevant countries.

**COST:** £1,695 for 2-trip course in either Morocco or Turkey (excluding flights, insurance and spending money). A full season in Morocco or Turkey (maximum 4 trips) would be £2,895 including a kayak or rafting course. Both seasons including all land transport and food en route: £4,295.

**SELECTION PROCEDURES AND ORIENTATION:** Deadline for applications for a handful of places falls in mid-January.

**CONTACT:** Hamish McMaster, Managing Director.

# GAP YEAR SAFETY AND PREPARATION

### OBJECTIVE GAP SAFETY
Bragborough Lodge Farm, Braunston, Daventry, Northants NN11 7HA
01788 899029
office@objectiveteam.com
www.objectivegapyear.com

**COURSES OFFERED:** One-day pre-gap year preparation and safety awareness training. Course covers situation awareness, crime prevention, security advice, kit and equipment, safe food and water, dealing with corrupt officials, travel safety, legal and etiquette concerns, emergency first aid, and handling extreme situations such as kidnapping and environmental dangers.

**DURATION OF COURSES:** Course runs most weeks, usually Tuesdays or Wednesdays in Earl's Court, London. Private courses and bespoke courses for schools are available.

**COST:** £150 including a simple lunch.

**SPECIAL FEATURES:** The company runs safety training courses for travellers ranging from gap year travellers to journalists covering conflict zones. (Objective trained Ewan McGregor and Charlie Boorman prior to their Long Way Round motorbike expedition to Mongolia.) At the end of the day's training, a separate briefing is held for female travellers.

### SAFETREK

East Culme, Cullompton, Devon EX15 1NX

✆ 01884 839704

🖰 info@safetrek.co.uk

🖳 www.safetrek.co.uk

**COURSES OFFERED:** Travel preparation and awareness for gap year and university students. Also skills for life.

**DURATION OF COURSES:** One-day course run at above address on Tuesdays, Bristol on Wednesdays or at different locations by appointment for groups of 5+.

**COST:** £140.

**CONTACT:** John Cummings, Director of Training.

### ULTIMATE GAP YEAR

5 Beaumont Crescent, London W14 9LX

✆ 020 7386 9101

🖰 info@ultimategapyear.co.uk

🖳 www.ultimategapyear.co.uk

**COURSES OFFERED:** Gap year safety training: personalised individual 2-hour training suitable for anyone embarking on a gap year or independent travel. Training held at private homes in London or at address above in West Kensington.

**COST:** £200 per student (free place for second person).

**CONTACT:** Alex Cormack, Managing Director.

# MISCELLANEOUS COURSES

### JUBILEE SAILING TRUST YOUTH LEADERSHIP @ SEA SCHEME

JST, Hazel Road, Woolston, Southampton SO19 7GB

✆ 023 8044 9108

🖰 sales@jst.org.uk

🖳 www.jst.org.uk

**COURSES OFFERED:** Leadership course to develop communication, leadership and team skills, while build-

ing a better understanding of disability. Skills will be built through the medium of tall ship sailing.

**PREREQUISITES:** Ages 16–25. Must be prepared to act as a full part of a tall ship voyage crew for the duration of the voyage.

**SELECTION PROCEDURES AND ORIENTATION:** By written application; mark form with 'Youth Leadership @ Sea' and enclose short personal statement of 200–400 words detailing why you think you should be chosen. Places are limited.

**COST:** Prices start from £399 for a 5-day voyage. This includes all accommodation, meals and training. Subsidies of up to £300 are offered towards the cost of the Jubilee Sailing Trust Youth Leadership @ Sea Scheme.

### VISITOZ

Springbrook Farm, 8921 Burnett Highway, Goomeri, 4601 Queensland, Australia

✆ +61 07 4168 6185

🖰 info@visitoz.org

🖳 www.visitoz.org

*UK contacts in Oxford:* Will and Jules Taunton-Burnet

✆ 07966 528644

🖰 will@visitoz.org

**COURSES OFFERED:** Programme for young people who wish to live and work in outback and rural Australia for up to 1 year. 4 days Meet and Greet, paperwork and Jet Lag Recovery at the beach followed by 5 days on the farm having an introduction to Australian agricultural techniques. Participants go to their first job on the 9th day in Australia. Jobs are guaranteed for the duration of the working holiday visa as the participant travels around Australia, with holiday breaks in between. VisitOz has links with 1,800 potential employers Australia-wide. Jobs are in agriculture, with horses, in hospitality, child care and distance education teaching.

**COST:** A$1,990. Some places are available after arrival in Australia but most people book direct from home.

**CONTACT:** Joanna and Dan Burnet in Australia; Will and Julia Taunton-Burnet in UK.

## WEST ISLAND COLLEGE INTERNATIONAL – CLASS AFLOAT

97 Kaulbach Street, PO Box 10, Lunenburg,
Nova Scotia B0J 2C0, Canada

📞 +1 902 634 1895
📞 +1 1 800 301 SAIL (7245)
✉ ckelley@classafloat.com
🖥 www.classafloat.com

**COURSES OFFERED:** Gap year programme challenges youth academically, physically and personally to become well-rounded, responsible global citizens. Students spend 10 months exploring over 20 ports of call worldwide while completing their first year of university at one of Canada's top undergraduate universities, Acadia University. They can choose courses such as marine biology, anthropology and political science.

**DESTINATION:** Canada, Portugal, Ireland, Spain, France, Malta, Corsica, Turkey, Tunisia, Morocco, Dakar, Brazil, Tristan da Cunha, South Africa, Namibia, St Helena, Trinidad, Bermuda.

**NUMBER OF PLACEMENTS:** 25 gap year and university students.

**DURATION OF COURSES:** Full year programme from September to June, semester courses from September to December/January, and second semester from February to June.

**QUALIFICATIONS OFFERED:** Gap year programme is designed to build leadership skills, foster personal development and offer the opportunity to travel and become global citizens before embarking on a college or university career.

**COST:** Full year costs C$47,000; single semester C$32,000.

**CONTACT:** Craig Kelley, Director of Development.

# Part IV
# Country guide: Europe

BENELUX
FRANCE
GERMANY
GREECE
ITALY
RUSSIA AND EASTERN EUROPE
SCANDINAVIA
SPAIN AND PORTUGAL
SWITZERLAND AND AUSTRIA

# BENELUX

## Netherlands

The Dutch language is studied by so few students at university that the Netherlands does not attract very many gap year students. However for those who want to experience the country's liberal traditions of tolerance, longer term stays are better than just a brief sightseeing trip to Amsterdam.

Most Dutch people speak excellent English so a knowledge of Dutch is generally not essential for voluntary or seasonal work. The market for unskilled non-Dutch-speaking workers is far from saturated since unemployment is the lowest in the EU at 2.7% with youth unemployment less than one-third of the Eurozone average. The Dutch have some of the most progressive laws in the world to minimise exploitation of workers.

### AU PAIRING

Since Dutch is not a language which attracts a large number of students, au pairing in the Netherlands is not well known; however there is an established programme for those interested and able to stay at least six months. Working conditions are favourable in that pocket money of €300–€340 is paid per month in addition to health insurance costs. The main agencies are reputed to offer solid back-up, guidance on contacting fellow au pairs and advice on local courses. The agency with the largest incoming au pair programme is *Travel Active* in Venray (0478 551900; aupair@travelactive.nl) which places au pairs aged 18–25 as well as sending Dutch young people abroad on various work exchanges.

**Jill Weseman** was very pleased with her au pair placement in a village of just 500 people, 30km from Groningen:

> *After graduation I accepted an au pairing position in Holland, mainly because there is no prior language requirement here. I really lucked out and ended up with a family who has been great to me. Though the situation sounds difficult at best – four children aged 1½, 3, 5 and 7, one day off a week and a rather remote location in the very north of Holland – I have benefited a great deal. The social life is surprisingly good for such a rural area.*

Two other agencies are located in the Hague: *Au Pair Agency Mondial* (+31 070 365 1401; www.aupair-agency.nl) and the *House o Orange Au Pairs* (+31 070 324 5903; www.house-o-orange.nl), which also has lots of families in Belgium as well. For others see the website for the Dutch Au Pair Association *NAPO* (Nederlandse Au Pair Organisatie; www.napoweb.nl).

### OPPORTUNITIES FOR PAID WORK

**Neil Datta** decided he wanted to spend part of his gap year in the Netherlands before applying to study medicine. He simply enquired at his local Jobcentre which passed on details of a heavy labouring job registered through EURES, the Europe-wide employment service. Although the work itself was unexciting, he greatly enjoyed being based in small-town Holland especially during the winter carnival in February (comparable to Mardi Gras). Furthermore he was able to save enough money to fund a big trip to South East Asia afterwards.

The state employment service has recently been rechristened *UWV WERKbedrijf* and is a one-stop shop for job-seekers. However, both in cities and the country, many employers turn to private employment agencies (*uitzendbureaux* – pronounced 'outzend') for temporary workers. Therefore they can be a very useful source of temporary work in Holland. They proliferate in large towns, for example there are nearly 350 in Amsterdam alone, though not all will accept non-Dutch-speaking applicants. *Uitzendbureaux* deal only with jobs lasting less than six months. Most of the work on their books will be unskilled work such as stocking warehouse shelves, factory or agricultural work, etc. Among the largest *uitzendbureaux* are *Randstad* with up to 700 branches, *Manpower*, *Creyf's* and *Tempo Team*, all of whose websites are only in Dutch. A good online recruiter is megajobs.nl.

The largest employer of seasonal work is the bulb industry, and Dutch agriculture generally employs thousands of short-term helpers. Hordes of young travellers descend on the bulb-producing area between Leiden and Haarlem without a pre-arranged job; it is easier to find openings in the early spring and through the autumn than in high summer. Traditionally, itinerant workers congregate on big campsites, where the seasonal regulars will advise newcomers. Excellent earnings are possible with employers who offer a lot of overtime (paid at a premium rate). But the work is hard and boring and the area attracts hardened long-term travellers looking to save money for further travels.

In this richly agricultural land, other opportunities present themselves for students looking for outdoor work. The area around Roermond (about 50km southeast of Eindhoven and north of Maastricht in the province of Limburg) is populated by asparagus growers and other farmers who need people to harvest their crops of strawberries, potatoes and vegetables, especially in the spring. Elsewhere, the area of Westland between Rotterdam, the Hook of Holland and Den Haag is well known for tomato production; the whole region is a honeycomb of greenhouses.

Dutch hotels and other tourist establishments occasionally employ foreigners, especially those with a knowledge of more than one European language. A few tour operators such as *Eurocamp/Holidaybreak* employ British young people as staff at their camps for the summer season. In **Adam Skuse's** year off before university, he almost succeeded in finding hotel work but not quite:

> *One very useful resource I found was the website holland.com, where I got a list of hotels and then systematically emailed them all asking for a job. Most had no vacancies, a couple told me to call them when I was in Amsterdam, and one actually arranged an interview with me. But even the knockbacks were pleasant. Quite a few offered to buy me a drink anyway. Alas, I never managed to find the hotel in time, ran out of funds and am now back in Blighty. I had plans for my gap year, but just ended up sitting around on the dole.*

*positions for graduates; even then places are limited and highly sought after. Many stagiaires are unpaid; others gain a meagre allowance or anything up to €1,500 a month. Fortunately, my MEP was generous, giving me a comfortable salary and expenses including Eurostar travel, language lessons and a contribution to my rent. The young woman who disembarked from the train at Waterloo seven months later had grown up a lot from the nervous 18-year-old of last September. She'd worked in a graduate job, paid bills to her French landlady, thrown dinner parties without a microwave. So I would encourage anyone to take a gap year, and to spend that time pursuing their passions. In my case it was politics, for others it's baboons – but don't be intimidated. I always feel it's wishy-washy of people to say they took a gap year to find out who they were, but in Brussels I found out who I wanted to be. I worked alongside them every day, admiring their commitment, passion and drive. That's right: a politician.*

Links to MEPs can be found at www.europarl.europa.eu. If you do pursue this idea, do plenty of research beforehand about which special interests the MEP has and which committees they sit on.

People who live in the south-east of England can make use of the *EURES Channel Network* (www.eureschannel.org), which assists people looking for jobs in West Flanders and Hainaut in western Belgium, Nord-pas-de-Calais in northern France and Kent, with bilingual Euro-Advisers in Mons, Lille and Dover.

## CASUAL JOBS

Odd jobs might be available at the popular hostel St Christophers at the Bauhaus at Langestraat 133–137 in Bruges (www.st-christophers.co.uk/bruges-hostels). *Venture Abroad*, based in Derbyshire (01332 342050; www.ventureabroad.co.uk), employs a few reps, including students with a background in scouting or guiding, for its programme in Belgium. *Ski-Ten International* takes on French-speaking tennis instructors and monitors to work at summer camps (+32 081 21 30 51; martine@ski-ten.be).

For more casual opportunities, the best way to find out about short-term general work is to visit a branch of the Belgian employment service in any town. A special division called T-Interim in Brussels (www.tbrussels.be) specialises in placing people in temporary jobs. Most jobs will require a good knowledge of at least one foreign language. As the capital of the European Union, Belgium has a high demand for au pairs. The government stipulates that au pairs be paid €450 a month for 20 hours of work a week. While many British and North Americans make their arrangements over the internet, *Stufam* in Wemmel (+32 02 460 33 95; aupair.stufam@scarlet.be; www.aupair-stufam.be) and *Au Pair International* in West Flanders (+32 051 460 525; www.aupairinternational.be) make placements throughout Belgium.

## VOLUNTEERING

The Flemish association of young environmentalists called *Natuur 2000* in Antwerp (+32 03 231 26 04; www.natuur2000.be) organises short summer conservation workcamps open to all nationalities. The fee of €60 for five days covers accommodation, food, insurance and local transport. Young people interested in participating in residential archaeological digs in Namur lasting one to three weeks in the summer should contact *Archeolo-j* in Rixensart (+32 81 611073; archeolo-J@skynet.be; www. skene.be). Residential archaeological digs accept paying volunteers, some for teenagers, some for adults. The fee is €299 for 8 days, €549 for 15 days and €670 for 22 days (2009).

## COURSES AND INFORMATION

A few UK-based language course agencies send candidates to Belgium to learn French, including *Vis-à-Vis*. A number of language schools advertise in the English language weekly magazine *The Bulletin*, on sale on Thursdays at newsstands in Brussels.

The *Federation Infor Jeunes Wallonie-Bruxelles* is a non-profit organisation that co-ordinates youth information offices in French-speaking Belgium (www.inforjeunes.be). These can give advice on work as well as leisure, youth rights, accommodation, etc. The website of the Brussels branch has links to useful job info at www.inforjeunes-bxl. be/offresdejob.htm.

# Luxembourg

If Belgium is sometimes neglected, Luxembourg is completely by-passed. Yet it is an independent country with a low rate of unemployment, and a number of useful facilities for foreign students. The national employment service *(Administration de l'Emploi)* or ADEM at 10 rue Bender, L-1229 Luxembourg (+352 2478 53 00) operates a Student Employment Service for students looking for summer jobs in warehouses, restaurants, etc. To find out about possibilities, you must visit this office in person, although EU nationals looking for long-term jobs may receive some assistance from EURES counsellors. The *Centre Information Jeunes* (CIJ) in Luxembourg City (+352 26 29 32 00; www.cij.lu) also runs a holiday job service between January and August for students from the EU. Wages in Luxembourg are very high; for example as of 2009, the minimum for those over 18 is €1,122 per month and the hourly minimum is €10.

Opportunities for gap year work experience may be available for linguists since many multinational companies are based in Luxembourg. Addresses of potential employers can be obtained from the membership list of the British Chamber of Commerce in Luxembourg (www.bcc.lu). *Prolinguis* runs summer language courses for teenagers in remote countryside near Arlon though its offices are in Thiaumont, 6717 Belgium (+32 063 22 04 62; www.prolinguis.be).

# FRANCE

Near destinations have been somewhat eclipsed in recent years by the more exotic far-flung gap year destinations such as Peru and Ghana, but there is still plenty of glamour to be found in good old France. Your ambition may be to get to know Paris, to spend the winter in a French ski resort, to live with a provincial family as an au pair or a paying guest or simply to improve your schoolboy/girl French by conversing with the natives. All are worthy aims for occupying part of your gap year.

## SOURCES OF INFORMATION

The former *Agence National pour l'Emploi* or ANPE is now known as *Pôle emploi* (www.pole-emploi.fr). The national employment service of France has dozens of offices in Paris and hundreds throughout the country. The website lists all the branches by region or postcode (anpe.fr), providing addresses, telephone and fax numbers. For example the ANPE in Narbonne (ANPE, BP 802, 29 rue Mazzini, 11108 Narbonne Cedex) has seasonal hotel vacancies from May to September, and others can provide details of when agricultural work is available. Although EU nationals should have equal access to the employment facilities in other member states, this is not always the case in France unless the job-seeker speaks good French and has a stable local address.

One of the 27 regional offices of the *Centres d'Information Jeunesse* (CIJ) may be of use to the newly arrived gap year traveller. They can advise on cheap accommodation, local jobs, the legal rights of temporary workers, etc. The main Paris branch is CIDJ *(Centre d'Information et de Documentation Jeunesse)* whose foyer notice board is a useful starting place for the job- or accommodation-seeker in Paris. It can also provide booklets and leaflets for varying fees on such subjects as seasonal agricultural work, possibilities for work in the summer or winter, and the regulations that affect foreign students in France. Check the website www.cidj-librairie.com for a complete list which includes *Etrangers en France: Vos Droits* for €22. CIDJ may be visited at 101 Quai Branly, 75740 Paris Cedex 15 (+33 01 44 49 12 00; www.cidj.com). In order to find out about actual vacancies you must visit the CIDJ offices in person, preferably first thing in the morning. CIDJ Paris annually registers about 10,000 summer jobs.

## COURSES AND HOMESTAYS

A good transition between the A-Level classroom and a holiday or job in France is an intensive French language course in Britain (see entry for *Alliance Français* - or try the Institut Français attached to the French Embassy at 14 Cromwell Place, London SW7; www.institut-francais.org.uk/courses). An even better one would be a French course abroad (see listings in the 'Directory of Courses').

The British Council manages several student exchanges with France including the *Charles de Gaulle Bursary Trust*, which bequeaths up to £1,000 on 17–19 year olds who submit an impressive proposal of what project they want to pursue or study for up to a month. For details, contact the Council's Belfast office on 028 9024 8220 ext 258 (charlesdegaulle@britishcouncil.org) and plan to apply by the end of January. Recently bursary holders have completed projects on Scouting in France, *L'influence arabe et égyptienne sur la culture française* and *Les écrivains irlandais en France*. For further information or to download application forms, visit www.britishcouncil.org/nireland.

Hundreds of British students do an exchange term or year in France. For example, more than 1,000 British students participate in the *Erasmus European* student exchange, though this scheme is open to undergraduates not school leavers. Several hundred more attach themselves to the *British Institute* in Paris (part of the University of London), and of course the *Sorbonne* is a magnet for students wanting to take language and civilisation courses.

During her gap year, **Jennifer** from England was as pleased with the extracurricular activities on her eight-week course in Cannes fixed up through *CESA* as she was with the lessons:

> *Cannes was definitely the best part of my overseas gap year last year. The college was perfect for me, and being able to see the festival was just amazing. A Norwegian friend from college and I actually walked the red carpet and saw a film due to some unbelievably good luck in being at the right place at the right time. Just crossing the road on the way home from a bar, a car stopped us and offered us two tickets to see the film Blindness. We initially thought they were fakes, and politely declined. However the driver insisted we take them, and left us with two tickets to the balcony. Lots of photos and laughs later, we were possibly the luckiest people in Cannes! That was just one of the many fun experiences I had in Cannes, and now only wish I could go back.*

A rough estimate of how much a 20-hour course will cost outside Paris per week would be €340 plus a further €220–€250 for half-board with a host family. Obviously prices are higher in Paris. Some language schools double as au pair agencies such as *Inter-Séjours* (bureau.intersejours@wanadoo.fr) and *Institut Euro'Provence* in Marseille; myriam@europrovence.org), which makes a language course much more affordable. A cheap way to have a base in France from which to improve your knowledge of the language is to participate in a work exchange, for example the one offered by the *Centre International d'Antibes*, a French language school on the Côte d'Azur. Volunteers with the right to work in Europe do administrative or domestic work in exchange for free accommodation and/or French tuition (+33 04 92 90 71 70; www.learn-french.fr/work_exchange_program/htm).

As elsewhere, language studies can be combined with other activities. One of the most interesting is a gap year course offered near Biarritz on the Basque cost of France where you can learn to surf while improving your French with the option of also doing classes in French cookery. The four-week course will cost a cool €3,125; see entry for *Ecole De Surf De Guéthary Jorly SARL* in the 'Directory of Courses'.

## WORK EXPERIENCE

Work experience placements are referred to as *stages* in France and are widely available through a number of organisations. The major language school *France Langue*, with centres in Paris and Nice, arranges for its trainees to work in hotels and if desired to obtain the Paris Chamber of Commerce and Industries Hotel and Tourism Industry French certificate; see www.france-langue.fr/en/specialized_programs/hotel_and_tourism_industry_french.php.

*Eurolingua* offers hotel work experience in the south of France lasting three to six months. The work is paid and comes with free staff accommodation and meals in the hotel. The programme is preceded by an appropriate language course at the nearest Eurolingua school, for instance in Montpellier, Nice and Toulon; details at eurolingua.com/Work_Experience(France).htm. The programme fee is €995 for 2–3 months, and €1,290 for 4–6 months (30% extra for non-EU students).

A small company run by a French woman called *Boost your French,* based in Aberystwyth (01970 626884; catherine@boostyourfrench.co.uk), sends Britons on both paid and unpaid work placements in France lasting from one month to a whole year. A gap year student recounts her experience on the website www.boostyourfrench.co.uk:

> *I had just passed my A-Levels and wanted to earn some money during the summer, but I also wanted to have an interesting time and learn more French. So I decided to look for a job in France. I was not successful in my search until I came across Catherine's website. She offered me a job as a shop assistant on the coast near Bordeaux. I had a fantastic time, making lots of friends, I earned money and definitely learned more French. Now, I am in my first year at university and I intend to go back to work in France next summer.*

The long-established *Club des 4 Vents* (www.cei4vents.com) has a variety of workplace openings for young people over 18 who have an intermediate standard of French (see entry for *CEI* in 'Directory of Work Experience Abroad').

After spending a tough but rewarding six months volunteering at a city mission in North Cape Town, **Ollie Perkins** had a treat in store for him in the northern hemisphere in the summer before uni. He met up with some fellow-musicians in France to attend the Marciac Jazz Festival (www.jazzinmarciac.com) for one month: '*Basically all the big European players and some great American players were there. We stayed at a campsite, but didn't know at the time that you can work there and that pays your rent and food, as well as free gigs. I learned so much and really got a huge lift musically.*'

## PAID OPPORTUNITIES FOR YEAR OUT STUDENTS

The best areas to look for work in the tourist industry of France are the Alps for the winter season, December to April, and the Côte d'Azur for the summer season, June to September, though jobs exist throughout the country. The least stressful course of action is to fix up work ahead of time with a UK campsite or holiday company in summer or ski company in winter. For example *First Choice Holidays* (www.firstchoice4jobs.com) hires reps (resort, transfer, children's) over the age of 18 to work in hotels and chalets in the Alps and Normandy. Applicants must have EU nationality but need not have relevant experience.

One important feature of working for a French employer in France is that you should be paid at least the *SMIC (salaire minimum interprofessionel de croissance)* or national minimum wage. There are slightly different rates for seasonal agricultural work and full-time employees; at present the basic SMIC is €8.71 per hour gross with a maximum working week of 35 hours. The rate is adjusted every July to take account of inflation.

With a deferred place to read French and Spanish at university, **Frances Pountain** knew that she wanted to spend part of her gap year in a French-speaking environment. Based on previous trips to France, she and a friend decided to head for Montpellier, not least because they were able to get a dirt-cheap flight with Ryanair in February (but spent nearly 10 times that on an eight-month insurance policy with *Endsleigh*). They arrived cold, with nothing pre-arranged:

> *At first we worked solely on improving our French and having some fun. But after a few months we found jobs with a newspaper and leaflet distributing agency called Adrexo (www.adrexo.fr). We found this job by looking in local publications especially 'Top Hebdo' (www.topannonces.fr). The job of distributing publicity was fairly easy and still allowed time to enjoy being in Montpellier.*
>
> *Going to France was exciting yet had lots of very trying times at the beginning since we hadn't arranged anything before going. With hindsight I would have probably tried to set up either a work placement/job or a language course ahead of time, as sometimes we didn't feel we had much direction there. Yet I feel my gap year has been very rewarding. Going to live in France has helped my French no end.*

*Twin Work And Volunteer Abroad*, South London (0800 804 8380; www.workandvolunteer.com) offers work in France, whereby entry-level jobs that pay the SMIC wage lasting two to three months in tourism, agriculture, sales, etc. are sourced for clients. Intermediate French is a pre-requisite. The £675 fee guarantees placement.

## CAMPSITES AND HOLIDAY CENTRES

British camping tour operators hire an army of language students to staff their network of campsites throughout France. These companies offer holidaymakers a complete package providing pre-assembled tents and a campsite courier to look after any problems that arise. Since this kind of holiday appeals to families, people who can organise children's activities are especially in demand. In addition to Europe-wide companies such as *Eurocamp* and *Canvas* (mentioned in 'Paid Seasonal Jobs'), the following all take on campsite reps/couriers and other seasonal staff for France:

***Carisma Holidays*** (01923 287344; personnel@carisma.co.uk; www.carismaholiday jobs.co.uk). 2009 wage range £125–£175 per week.

***In2Camping***, Blackpool FY2 0AS, (01253 593333; www.in2camping.com).

***Matthews Holidays***, Surrey KT24 6RP, (01483 284044; www.matthewsfrance.co.uk/ MH/jobs.html).

***Venue Holidays***, Kent TN23 1QU, (01233 629950; jobs@venueholidays.co.uk; www. venueholidays.co.uk).

The best time to start looking for summer season jobs from England is between September and February. In most cases candidates are expected to have at least A-Level standard French, though some companies claim that a knowledge of French is merely 'preferred'. It is amazing how far a good dictionary and a knack for making polite noises in French can get you. Many impose a minimum age of 21.

The massive camping holiday industry generates winter work as well. *Brad Europe* has depots in Nantes and Beaucaire near Avignon that clean and repair tents and bedding on behalf of many of the major companies. Staff (who need not speak French though it is an advantage) are needed for the laundry and distribution for four to six months in winter and summer. *Gite* accommodation is provided free of charge in addition to the UK minimum wage. A driving licence is essential for the delivery drivers but not for the laundry operatives. Brad Europe's UK office is in Wigan (01942 829747; info@bradeurope.com; www.bradeurope.com/vacancies.html).

Outdoor activity centres are another major employer of summer staff, both general domestic staff and sports instructors. Try the major tour operators such as *Acorn Adventure* (www.acorn-jobs.co.uk) and *PGL* (www.pgl.co.uk/recruitment). *Manor Adventure*, based in Shropshire (01584 861333; manoradventurejobs.com), hires holiday coordinators and sports instructors for its adventure centre Le Chateau du Broutel along the coast from Boulogne.

For work in an unusual activity holiday, contact either *Bombard Balloon Adventures*, in Beaune (+33 03 80 26 63 30; www.bombardsociety.org/jobs) or *France Montgolfieres* based in Montrichard (+33 02 54 32 20 48; jane@franceballoons.com). Ground crew are hired by these hot-air balloon companies for the summer season May to October. The job requires excellent physical fitness and strength, a cheerful personality, clean-cut appearance and a clean driving licence. Montgolfieres requires its staff to speak French.

## SKI RESORTS

France is the best of all countries in Europe for finding jobs in ski resorts, mainly because it is the number one country for British skiers, 200,000 of whom go there every year. The main problem is the shortage of worker accommodation; unless you find a live-in job you will have to pay nearly holiday prices or find a friend willing to rent out his or her sofa. If trying to fix up a job from Britain, *Jobs in the Alps* (www.jobs-in-the-alps. co.uk) recruits young people of EU nationality and a very good knowledge of French to work in ski resorts.

Another agency is *UK Overseas Handling* (*UKOH*) in Hove (0870 220 2148; ukoh recruitment@fastmail.fm), which provides seasonal and annual staff to the French tour operator Eurogroup. Eurogroup owns hotels, restaurants and chalets in ski and beach resorts in France (and the rest of Europe). Applicants must hold an EU passport and have a UK National Insurance number; the contact person is Jennifer Averill-Richards. Excellent ski recruitment websites include www.natives.co.uk, www.seasonworkers.com and www.freeradicals.co.uk, which match job-seekers with alpine and other vacancies.

If you attempt to find work in a ski resort on your own, success is far from guaranteed and competition for work is increasing. Val d'Isère attracts as many as 500 ski bums every November/December, many of whom hang around bars or the Jobcentre for days in the hope that work will come their way.

Several companies can arrange for you to train as a ski or snowboard instructor in the French Alps; see entries in the 'Directory of Ski Training Courses' for *BASI* and *Base Camp Group*, which run courses in Val d'Isère and Méribel, and *New Generation* and *Mountain Lodge* (in Courchevel).

## YACHTS

A few months on the Riviera would be hard for someone taking a gap year to fund unless some means of earning money could be found. Yachts may provide the answer. It is not impossible to penetrate the world of yacht owners and skippers in glamorous resorts such as Antibes and St Tropez. It is essential to start looking early, preferably the beginning of March, since by late April most of the jobs have been filled. Boats frequently take on people as day workers first and then employ them as crew for the charter season if they like them. Deckhands on charter yachts are paid a weekly wage, usually around £100 which can sometimes be doubled with tips from big-rollers. The charter season ends in late September (convenient if you're returning to university) when many yachts begin organising their crew for the trip to the West Indies.

**Kevin Gorringe** headed for the south of France in June with the intention of finding work on a private yacht. His destination was Antibes, where so many British congregate, and he began frequenting likely meeting places such as La Gaffe English Pub and the Irish bars. The main crewing agencies in Antibes are housed in the same building, viz. La Galerie du Port on Boulevard d'Aguillon and include Blue Water Yacht Crew Agency.

---

### GAPPERS' TIP
*Competition will be fierce, so doggedness together with charm and a good measure of luck will be needed for success. Look tidy and neat, be polite and when you get a job work hard. The first job is the hardest to get, but once you get in with the community of yachties, people will help you move onto other boats.*

## GRAPE-PICKING

Although the French tourist industry offers many seasonal jobs, there are even more in agriculture, especially the grape harvest. Farmers almost always provide some sort of accommodation, but this can vary from a rough and ready dormitory to a comfortable room in their own house. Food is usually provided, but again this can vary from the barely adequate to the sublime: one picker can write that '*the food was better than that in a five-star hotel, so we bought flowers for the cook at the end of the harvest*', while another may complain of instant mashed potatoes or of having to depend on whatever he or she can manage to buy and prepare. When both food and accommodation are provided there is usually a deduction of one or two hours' pay from each day's wage.

The work itself will consist either of picking or portering. Picking involves bending to get the grapes from a vine that may be only 3½ft tall, and filling a pannier which you drag along behind you. The panniers full of grapes are emptied into an *hotte*, a large basket weighing up to 100lb which the porters carry to a trailer.

After visiting the French equivalent of a Jobcentre and also a private agency in Epernay at the beginning of September, 19-year-old **Anna Ling** and her boyfriend were given a list of phone numbers of potential farm employers. Preparing for a marathon of phoning, they bought a local phone card but struck lucky on their very first call. They visited the vineyard in Champagne, were interviewed in the home of the wine-grower and told to come back when the harvest started, which was 20 September.

A Dutch agency called *Appellation Controllée* (+31 50 549 2434; info@apcon.nl; www.apcon.nl) mediates between grape-growers in Beaujolais north of Lyon, Burgundy, Chablis and Champagne and up to 500 Europeans looking for jobs in the *vendange*. Work lasts between one and three weeks in September. In exchange for working eight hours a day, seven days a week you will earn €57 a day plus get full board and lodging. The ApCon agency fee is €99 and they have a good message board. After signing up with ApCon, **Danielle Thomas** from the Netherlands was set up with a grape-picking job in Beaune at the beginning of her gap year. In 11 days, she earned about €650 gross, €550 after deductions were made for tax and food costs. At her farm in Meloisey, accommodation was provided for grape-pickers who had worked with the farming family before, but first-timers were asked to bring their own tents and sleep in the garden. Danielle had no trouble identifying the good and bad aspects of her experience:

> The work was very hard, though very enjoyable because of the team. Back pain was experienced often and at the end I had a lot of cuts in my hand, 22 to be exact. I would not advise sleeping in a tent, since at that time of year, I woke up cold every day and not in the right mental mood for the day's work. Breakfast was limited, though both lunch and dinner were very large and impressive, five course meals, including soup and bread, salad and vegetables, meat or fish, a variety of cheeses and finally a dessert. With each lunch and dinner, local wine or their own wine was also provided. Dinners were very social and fun. This was my first Vendange and I must say, even though the work was

*hard, it was a very pleasant experience. The family was very welcoming and the food was exceptional! I met a lot of really nice people and I hope to go back some time. I'd advise anyone thinking of doing Vendange in the future, that it would certainly be a good idea – as long as you have an open mind and are ready for hard work!*

### DANIELLE'S TIPS FOR GRAPE PICKING

- *Bring waterproof clothing and Wellingtons, as the weather may change at any moment.*
- *Bring rubber washing-up gloves (not cloth gloves), since in the mornings the grapes are wet and your hands get very wet.*
- *Hand cream is also a good idea.*
- *And most importantly do not expect the French to be able to speak English, so bring a phrase book.*

The demand for pickers in all regions is highly unpredictable. Whereas there is usually a glut of pickers looking for work at the beginning of the harvest (early to mid-September), there is sometimes a shortage later on in the month. Harvests differ dramatically from year to year; a late spring frost can wreak havoc. The element of uncertainty makes it very difficult for farmers to make any fixed commitment in advance.

## ENGLISH TEACHING

A more realistic possibility than finding employment with a language school is to offset the high cost of living in Paris or the other cities by doing some tutoring which sometimes shades into au pairing. Language exchanges for room and board are commonplace in Paris and are usually arranged through advertisements (in the places described below in the section on Paris) or by word of mouth. Many long-stayers in Paris have used the notice board at the American Church (65 Quai d'Orsay, *métro* Invalides) to good effect. Sometimes families post notices offering accommodation in exchange for English conversation with their children.

The British Council sends hundreds of undergraduates studying French at British universities and recent graduates aged 20–30 to spend an academic year in primary or secondary schools throughout France as assistants (assistants@britishcouncil.org). *Assistants* give conversation classes for 12 hours a week and are paid €940 (gross) a month. *Twin Work And Volunteer Abroad* (0800 804 8380; www.workandvolunteer.com) arranges a Language Assistant in France programme in the Montpellier region in which participants learn French while teaching English to a host family (fee £950).

Occasionally pre-university students are accepted in this capacity. For example a local education authority in the Vendée offers a 'Gap Year for Francophiles' in French primary schools or acting as an assistant in the local lycée. The only requirements are that you be aged 18–25, have an A Level in French and have some experience of living in France. In exchange for 20 hours of teaching a week between the end of September and the end of May, you receive free board and lodging with a local family and a monthly allowance of €170 (after national insurance contributions); further details at www.gapyear-france.com.

## AU PAIRING

Au pairing has always been a favoured way for young women in their gap year to improve their French and, increasingly, for young men too. The pocket money for au pairs in France is linked to the minimum wage (SMIC) and is currently €67.50 per 30-hour week plus a city transport pass. Most British agencies with an outgoing programme deal with France (see list in introductory chapter on au pairing) but applying directly through a French agency is commonplace. The most established agencies are members of UFAAP, the Union Francaise des Associations Au Pair, an umbrella group set up in 1999. Member agencies have links from their website www.ufaap.org. While some agencies charge nothing, others charge a registration fee, which can be steep (€160+). Here are some agencies to contact:

*Alliance Française*, Marseille (+33 4 96 10 24 60; info@alliancefrmarseille.org).

*Association Familles & Jeunesse*, Nice (+33 4 93 82 28 22; info@afj-aupair.org; www.afj-aupair.org). Places more than 300 au pair girls and boys, mainly in the South of France plus the French Riviera and Corsica.

*Butterfly et Papillon*, Annecy (+33 4 50 67 01 33; aupair.france@wanadoo.fr; www.butterfly-papillon.com). Member of IAPA.

*Europair Services*, Paris (+33 1 43 29 80 01; europairservices@wanadoo.fr; www.europairservices.com). Member of IAPA.

*France Au Pair – Eurojobs*, Saint Palais sur Mer (+33 5 46 23 99 88; contact@eurojob.fr; www.eurojob.fr).

*Inter-Séjours*, Paris (+33 1 47 63 06 81; bureau.intersejours@wanadoo.fr; www.intersejours.fr). Registration fee of €240.

*Oliver Twist Work & Study*, Pessac (+33 5 57 26 93 26; oliver.twist@orange.fr; www.oliver-twist.fr).

Quite a few foreigners are too hasty in arranging what seems at the outset a cushy number and only gradually realise how little they enjoy the company of children and how isolated they are if their family lives in the suburbs (as most do). Unless you genuinely enjoy small children, it might be better to look for a free room in exchange for minimal babysitting (e.g. 12 hours a week). **Matt Tomlinson** went into his au pair job with his eyes open:

> *I'd heard too many horror stories from overworked and underpaid au pair friends to be careless, so chose quite carefully from the people who replied to my notice on the upstairs notice board of the British Church (just off the rue de Faubourg St Honoré).*

*My employers were really laid back, in their mid-20s so more like living with an older brother and sister. The little boy was just over two while the little girl was three months old, and they were both completely adorable. On the whole it was great fun. Baking chocolate brownies, playing football and finger-painting may not be everybody's idea of a good time but there are certainly worse ways to earn a living (and learn French at the same time).*

# VOLUNTEERING

Anyone who is prepared to exchange work for subsidised board and lodging should consider joining one of France's many volunteering associations. The majority of short-term projects last two or three weeks during the summer and cost between €8 and €18 a day. Many gap students join one of these to learn basic French and make French contacts as well as to have fun.

## ARCHAEOLOGY

A great many archaeological digs and building restoration projects are carried out each year. Every May the Ministry of Culture (Direction de l'Architecture et du Patrimoine, Sous-Direction de l'Archéologie) publishes a national list of summer excavations throughout France requiring up to 5,000 volunteers, which can be consulted on its website (www. culture.gouv.fr/fouilles). Without relevant experience you will probably be given only menial jobs but many like to share in the satisfaction of seeing progress made.

Anthony Blake describes the dig he joined which the History Department of the University of Le Mans runs: '*Archaeology is hard work. Applicants must be aware of what working 8.30am-noon and 2–6.30pm in baking heat means! That said, I thoroughly enjoyed the working holiday: excellent company (75% French so fine opportunity to practise French), weekends free after noon on Saturday, good lunches in SNCF canteen, evening meals more haphazard as prepared by fellow diggers. Accommodation simple but adequate.*'

## CONSERVATION

France takes the preservation of its heritage *(patrimoine)* very seriously and there are numerous groups both local and national engaged in restoring churches, windmills, forts and other historic monuments. Many are set up to accept foreign volunteers, though they tend to charge more than archaeological digs:

**APARE/GEC**, Association pour la Participation et l'Action Régionale, L'Isle sur la Sorgue (+33 4 90 85 51 15; mireillepons.apare@yahoo.fr; www.apare-gec.org). An umbrella organisation that runs volunteer workcamps at historic sites in Provence (plus a few in North Africa). Cost of €133 for 2 weeks, €169 for 3 weeks.

**Chantier Histoire et Architecture Médiévale (CHAM)**, Paris 75014 (+33 1 43 35 15 51; cham@cham.asso.fr; www.cham.asso.fr). Volunteer projects to protect historic buildings, not just in mainland France but in farflung places including Réunion Island (a *département* of France in the Indian Ocean near Mauritius) and in Africa.

See the CHAM website (which is in English) for details. Camps cost €10 a day plus €30 registration fee.

**REMPART**, Paris (+33 1 42 71 96 55; www.rempart.com). Similar to the National Trust in Britain, in charge of endangered monuments throughout France. Most projects charge €5–8 per day plus €38 for membership plus insurance.

**UNAREC (Etudes et Chantiers)**, Délégué International, Clermont-Ferrand (+33 4 73 31 98 04; unarec.di@wanadoo.fr; www.unarec.org). Hundreds of international volunteers for short-term conservation projects and longer-term professional training, accepted via partner agencies.

Try to be patient if the project you choose turns out to have its drawbacks, since these organisations depend on voluntary leaders as well as participants. **Judy Greene** volunteered to work with a conservation organisation and felt herself to be '*personally victimised by the lack of organisation and leadership*' or more specifically by one unpleasantly racist individual on her project. Tolerance may be called for, especially if your fellow volunteers lack it.

# Paris

Like all major cities in the developed world, Paris presents thousands of ways to earn your keep, while being difficult to afford from day to day. Unless you are very lucky, you will have to arrive with some money with which to support yourself while you look around.

Expatriate grapevines all over Paris should prove helpful for finding work and accommodation. Many people find their jobs as well as accommodation through one of the city's many notice boards *(panneaux)*. The one in the foyer of the CIDJ near the *métro* stop Bir-Hakeim has already been mentioned as being good for student-type jobs such as extras in movies, but sometimes there are adverts for full-time jobs or *soutien scolaire en Anglais* (English tutor). It is worth arriving early to check for new notices.

The other mecca for job and flat-hunters is the American Church at 65 Quai d'Orsay (*métro* Invalides). Official notices are posted on various notice boards inside and out; the cork board in the basement is a free board where anybody can stick up a notice. Obviously it is necessary to consult the notices in person; they are not available by phoning the church or on the internet.

Arguably the most eccentric bookshop in Europe is Shakespeare and Company at 37 rue de la Bûcherie in the fifth *arrondissement* (on the south side of the Seine). It has a notice board and is also useful as a place to chat to other expats about work and accommodation. The shop operates as a writer's guesthouse. If you are prepared to write a short account of yourself and pitch in with doing chores for a couple of hours a day, you may be allowed to stay free for a limited period, assuming there is space. **Hannah Adcock** describes herself as a 'rather solemn' 18-year-old when she read *Work Your Way Around the World* and found out about this opportunity:

> *Soon after, I found myself living at this hippie Parisien bookstore with a view of Notre Dame, a treat of inedible pancakes to look forward to and orders to clean the floor using*

*newspaper and cold water. Kids staying at Shakespeare's do most of the jobs for free. You'll only get a paid job if (a) the owner really likes you, (b) you went to a university like Cambridge or Harvard and (c) you're really cute. The room overlooking Notre Dame is lovely but when I was there it smelt foul and a highly evolved species of bed bug lurked, as big as rats (ok – exaggeration). Shakespeare's is brilliant, but working there has its 'interesting' aspects!*

Most expat places such as *Shakespeare & Co*, the WH Smith Bookshop on the rue de Rivoli and dozens of others distribute the free bilingual newsletter *France-USA Contacts* or *FUSAC* (www.fusac.org) which comes out the first Tuesday of the month. It comprises mainly classified adverts which are best followed up on the day the paper appears. An advert under the heading 'Work Wanted in France' starts at €36.

## DISNEYLAND PARIS

The enormous complex of Disneyland Paris, 30km east of Paris at Marne-la-Vallée, employs about 12,000 people in high season both on long-term and seasonal contracts. Seasonal positions from March or May to September are open to EU nationals. The minimum period covers the high season from the end of June to the end of August.

'Cast members' (Disneyspeak for employees) must all be over 18, have a conversational level of French and preferably a third European language. The majority of jobs are in food and beverage, housekeeping, merchandising and custodial departments, though one of the best(?) jobs is as a Disney character. Further details are available from Service du Recrutement-Casting, Disneyland Paris, BP 110, 77777 Marne-la-Vallée Cedex 4 (http://disneylandparis-casting.com). Casting tours are conducted around Europe in February for the start of the season in March. For all jobs the well-scrubbed look is required (though they do now tolerate neatly trimmed facial hair), and of course they are looking for the usual friendly, cheerful and outgoing personalities. The monthly gross starting wage is €1,216 from which deductions are made for social security (from €170). Staff accommodation costs €250 per month and a contribution is made to travel expenses on completion of a contract.

**KEITH LEISHMAN** from Dundee was a cast member several summers ago before taking a law degree (with French):

'Getting the job was initially quite frustrating. I first sent a letter to the company around November. After another couple of letters and e-mails without reply, I was just about giving up hope. Finally around March I received notification of an interview in Edinburgh and was offered the job. After that you are pretty much left to your own devices and simply expected to turn up at Disney the day before your contract begins. (This was rather a shock to me after working for Eurocamp the year before who provided transport to France and some preparatory material beforehand.)

I was employed on the ticketing side of operations. I had to wear a Prince Charming costume and supervise the entrance of guests to the Park, stamping their hands for readmission. This meant standing for the whole shift in what were often scorching conditions. This was very beneficial for my French as people would ask a whole range of weird and wonderful questions.

The staff apartments were comfortable enough and equipped with kitchens, though I did not cook much due to the cheapness and accessibility of Disney canteens. I could eat well for a few euros a day. Another of the main advantages of working at Disneyland is the mixture of nationalities. The sheer number of young people from all over the world means there are always lots of parties and barbecues in the residences. On days off I usually went into Paris which is only 40 minutes away on the train. I stayed for two months of the peak summer season and found it quite hard to keep up the Disney smile when I was hot and tired. The job is demanding because you are creating an illusion. All the same I would urge anybody with an interest in people and a desire to improve their French to try the experience.'

# GERMANY

Students who have studied German at school and may intend to pursue those studies in higher education should consider spending at least part of their gap year in Germany, either doing a language course or a work experience placement, as an au pair or a volunteer. Even if you are not planning to specialise in modern languages, German can be combined with many commercial and other subjects to make you ultimately very employable. The economic powerhouse of Europe can absorb a great many foreign students in various capacities. Despite the current high level of unemployment, it is possible to arrange paid work experience independently, though easier with the help of a mediating organisation, teacher or contact.

The stereotype of the obsessively efficient and hard-working German is found by many gap year students to have a basis in truth but is not the whole truth. Germany can be inflexible and rule-bound, but on an individual level, many Germans are helpful and humorous.

## PLACEMENT ORGANISATIONS

The *Zentrale Auslands- und Fachvermittlung* (International Placement Services), ZAV, part of the German Federal Employment Agency, has an international department (Auslandsvermittlung) for dealing with applications from German-speaking students abroad. Details and application forms are available from ZAV (Villemombler Strasse 76, 53123 Bonn; +49 0228 713 1330; ZAV-Bonn.Ferienbeschaeftigung@arbeitsagentur.de). All applications from abroad are handled by this office. Although people of any nationality can apply through the ZAV, only citizens of old EU countries (who have German language skills) are entitled to expect the same treatment as a German. This special department of the ZAV finds summer jobs for students of any nationality (Team 327 – Ferienbeschäftigung). Students must be at least 18 years, be available to work for at least two months and apply by March. ZAV places students in all kinds of jobs, but mainly in hotels and restaurants, in industry, cleaning and agriculture.

The *IJAB* (International Youth Exchange) in Bonn has a EuroDesk which administers European student exchanges (+49 0228 95 06 250; www.eurodesk.de). The website www.prabo.de, available in English, describes itself as '*the free internship database for companies, students and anyone else who is offering or searching for internships*' in Germany.

The Working Holidays in Germany scheme places language and gap year students from the UK and the old EU countries in the field of rural tourism. Participants are given weekly pocket money of €51 and full board and lodging with families on farms or in country hotels. In return they look after children and/or horses and farm animals or take up serving and kitchen duties. The preferred stay is three to six months though a six-week commitment is also allowed; details available from Terre des Langues e.V. in Regensburg (+49 0941 565602; terre-des-langues@t-online.de; workingholidays.de).

A fee of €180 is payable after the placement is agreed, at least 4 weeks before the start date.

Internships for American students and graduates up to the age of 30 who can function in German are available in business, finance, engineering or technical fields through *CDS International* in New York (+1 212 497 3502; www.cdsintl.org). If appropriate, the first month can be spent at an intensive language course, after which participants undertake a paid or unpaid internship which they have secured previously with the help of CDS's partner agency InWEnt (Internationale Weiterbildung und Entwicklung GmbH) in Bonn (www.inwent.org). The average monthly remuneration will cover living expenses. The CDS programme fee is $575.

## WORK EXPERIENCE

Work placements can be organised in a wide range of sectors including tourism, trade, telecommunications, marketing and banking, depending on timing and availability. Most internships are organised in conjunction with an intensive language course. Usually an upper intermediate level of language ability is required for work experience to be successful. Most are unpaid or are rewarded only with a subsistence wage. Board and lodging will generally be provided only in the tourism sector.

*DID-Deutsch Institute* is a major language course provider (see 'Directory of Courses') which can also arrange two to six month internships following on from their four-week language courses in Berlin, Frankfurt and Munich; the processing fee for an unskilled work placement is €350 while a qualified internship placement will cost €450 in addition to the preceding language course (e.g. €740 for 4 weeks). Similarly *GLS (Global Language Services)* combines a minimum 4-week language course with an internship in a Berlin-based company of 6, 8 or 12+ weeks. Host companies want their trainees to speak German to at least an intermediate (B1) level.

*Astur GmbH* (+49 661 92802 0; info@astur-gmbh.de; www.astur-gmbh.de) organises linguistic stays in about 50 cities and towns around Germany with unpaid work experience placements lasting four to 12 weeks. Applicants must be students from the old Europe aged 18–25 with an excellent standard of German to work in a German company, normally in industry, sales, marketing, administration, accountancy, tourism, law, translation or computers. Astur also arrange hotel experience placements for which candidates need an intermediate level of German after a compulsory pre-placement language course. The Astur fee (2009) includes homestay accommodation starting at €1,280 for four weeks, €2,290 for 10 weeks.

*Twin Work and Volunteer Abroad* tries to match a student's area of interest with an internship in companies in Berlin and other major cities. Unless they are fluent in German, participants must do a 4-week German course (from £600). Accommodation and food can also be arranged. The Brussels-based linguistic and cultural exchange agency *M B Language* (+32 2 242 27 66; www.mblanguage.be) arranges short placements in

Lübeck for students aged 16–18 studying German; the placement fee for a two-week summer placement and homestay is €475.

Graduates with a background in economics or business who can speak German have a reasonable chance of finding teaching work in a German city, since most of the demand comes from companies. A TEFL Certificate has less clout than relevant experience when looking for freelance English teaching work. University students and recent graduates who would like to spend a year as an English language assistant in a German secondary school should contact the British Council at assistants@britishcouncil.org or www.languageassistant.co.uk. They send students with at least an AS level in German and recent graduates aged 20–30 to spend an academic year in mainly secondary schools throughout Germany. Altogether they place about 400 assistants who work 12 hours a week and are paid about €800 a month (net).

School leavers with a particular field of interest can try to pursue it in their gap year in Germany. For example **Robin Lloyd** from Hampshire had always been interested in car design. With an A Level in German and a place at Bristol University to do a German and engineering degree, he wrote to a number of motor car manufacturers in Germany only to be told that he was too young and that they accepted only students already embarked on a university-level engineering degree. The one exception was BMW in Munich which runs a scheme for young trainees and who provided Robin with a pleasant flat on his own and enough wages to support himself in Munich for nine months. Although he found the formal protocol of German industry a little hard to swallow, he greatly enjoyed Munich and quickly developed a social life based on the city's Irish pubs. If you intend to look for a placement with a company, take evidence of any qualifications and some good references *(zeugnisse)*, which are essential in Germany.

## AU PAIRING

Among the longest established agencies is the non-profit Roman Catholic agency IN VIA with 40 branches throughout Germany (+49 0761 200206; aupair.invia@caritas.de; www.aupair-invia.de). Its Protestant counterpart is affiliated to the YWCA: Verein für Internationale Jugendarbeit headquartered in Frankfurt (+49 069 469 39 700; au-pair-vij.org). VIJ has 14 offices in Germany and places both male and female au pairs for a preferred minimum stay of one year, though six-month stays are also common. Scores of private agents operate all over Germany, many of them members of the German Aupair-Society (www.au-pair-society.org), which has contact details for its 45 members. Commercial au pair agencies do not charge a placement fee to incoming au pairs.

*Au-Pair Vermittlung AMS*, c/o Anna-Maria Schlegel, Freiburg (+49 0761 70 76 917; info@aupair-ams.de; aupair-ams.de). Information in English on website.

*Abroad Connection*, Landsberg (+49 08191 941378; abroadconnection.de).

*MultiKultur AuPair Service*, Köln (0221 921 30 40; multikultur.info). Places international au pairs throughout Germany.

The minimum monthly pocket money for an au pair in Germany is fixed by the government at €260. Some families offer to pay for a monthly travel pass, a contribution of up to €100 per semester to your language course and even your fare home if you have stayed for the promised period of nine months, typically up to €150. In return they will expect hard work which usually involves more housework than au pairs usually do.

## VOLUNTEERING

Countless opportunities exist throughout the vast nation of Germany for undertaking voluntary work whether in environmental protection or in community service. The green movement in Germany is very strong and many organisations concentrate their efforts on arranging projects to protect the environment or preserve old buildings.

*IJGD*, Bonn (+49 0228 22 80 00; www.ijgd.de). Scores of camps in Germany. British applications accepted by Concordia and UNA Exchange.

*Internationale Begegnung in Gemeinschaftsdiensten (IBG)*, Stuttgart (+49 0711 649 11 28/ www. ibg-workcamps.org ). Projects in both eastern and western Germany. Applications in UK as above plus via VFP (vfp@vfp.org) in the USA.

*Mountain Forest Project (Bergwald Projekt e.V.)*, Würzburg (+49 0931 452 6261; bergwaldprojekt.de). 1-week education and conservation projects in the alpine forests of southern Germany. Basic knowledge of German is essential since the foresters conduct the camps in German only. Hut accommodation, food and insurance are provided free though participants must pay an annual membership fee of SFr60/€40.

*Vereinigung Junger Freiwilliger (VJF)*, Berlin (+49 030 428 506 03; office@vjf. de). Camps take place in the former East Germany. Registration fee €60.

## COURSES AND HOMESTAYS

The *Goethe Institut* is the long-established provider of German language tuition, whether as preparation for university studies or simply to speak it for leisure purposes. A list of addresses in Germany with full course details offered by each one is available from the website (www.goethe.de) or from the Goethe Institut in London. The Goethe Institut administers language exams at all levels, leading to internationally recognised certificates such as the ZdaF, KDS and GDS. **Alastair Holt** decided to spend 12 weeks of his gap year learning German in Berlin arranged through *CESA:*

*I met people from all corners of the world and had the opportunity to explore the un-derschön city that is Berlin. Due to the length of my programme and the full immersion technique, I was very happy with my progress. I felt that staying with a host family was invaluable; meal times in particular offered an opportunity to listen and speak German. I also conducted my social life exclusively in German. My main memories from the course are: strolling around Berlin by night with friends from the language school, going to an excellent jazz bar, watching Hertha Berlin at the Olympia Stadium, drinking German beer in a scenic beer garden, playing ultimate Frisbee in the Tiergarten, and having lots of fun and laughs in class! If you have a gap year it is worth taking an extended course to make significant progress.*

In addition to CESA, all the major language course agencies run extensive programmes in Germany. Among the most popular destinations for year-out language students are Munich, Heidelberg and Freiberg, though less picturesque places will be cheaper. It might be worth noting that the purest German is spoken in the north, but even if you are living in Bavaria where there is a pronounced accent, the teaching will be of standard German.

As mentioned, language courses can sometimes be followed by *stages* (internships) for those who achieve a satisfactory level of German. One of the great educational institutions of Germany is the *Volkshochschulen (VHS)* or folk high schools which can be found in nearly every town of the republic. In addition to offering 'German for Foreigners', it offers a range of evening classes in drama, handicrafts, sport and so on, all at subsidised prices. Most bookshops sell the prospectus of courses available for terms beginning in September and January.

# GREECE

Once the darling of backpackers, Greece has lost some of its lustre over the past two decades. Some consider Greece old hat, and mass tourism has been moving away, as more long haul beach paradises like Thailand have come into vogue. Some gappers are still attracted by the party scenes in Corfu and Rhodes, while others might be put off that it has been spoiled. Although many young people may want to spend time relaxing on a Greek island, few consider longer-term possibilities in Greece during their gap year. Anyone planning to read classics or archaeology at university will be attracted to the great sites of Greek antiquity as well as to the beautiful scenery and climate, friendly and carefree people, memorable wine and food.

## AU PAIRING AND TEACHING

Living with a Greek family is one of the best ways of organising an extended stay. Yet au pairing hours tend to be longer in Greece than elsewhere, partly because there is no expectation that a gap year student will need time off to study the language. The *Nine Muses Agency* accepts applications from young European and American women for au pair positions and can also place candidates after arrival in Athens. Hotel positions are also sometimes available. Contact the Athens agency on +30 210 931 6588; www.ninemuses.gr. The owner Kalliope (Popy) Raekou prides herself on her after-placement service, meeting regularly with au pairs at coffee afternoons. There is no fee to au pairs. Among her satisfied au pairs is **Riitta Koivula** from Finland who, from an unsatisfactory situation on Kos, moved with Popy Raekou's help to a much better one in Athens:

> *I started my work as an au pair on Kos when I was 19. At first I was so excited about my new family and the new place since I had never been to Greece before and I loved the sun and the beach. I lived in a small village called Pili where almost no one spoke English. But soon I got tired of the village because winter came, tourists left and it wasn't so warm to spend time on the beach any more. I also got tired of the family. The three little girls didn't speak English and they were very lively. The working hours were also terrible: 8 to 12 in the morning and then 4 to 10 in the evening every day except Sundays. I was very homesick on Kos and decided I wanted things to change. So I went to Athens in November and was soon given a new family. I fell in love with Athens and its people right away. My new family was the best and we are still very close. I met other au pairs and one Finnish au pair became my best friend. I learned so many things, even to read and write and speak Greek because we took Greek lessons during the spring with Popy. I have many happy memories of Athens and friends who are still dear to me.*

Thousands of private language schools called *frontisteria* are scattered throughout Greece creating a huge demand for native English speaker teachers. Unfortunately for gap year students, all but the dodgiest schools will expect to see a university degree (which is a government requirement for a teacher's licence). The basic hourly wage is currently about €9 gross. Earnings can be increased substantially by compulsory bonuses at Christmas and Easter and holiday pay at the end of the contract.

University graduates who fancy the idea of taking a gap year teaching English in Greece after graduation should be aware that agencies exist to match graduates with 10-month vacant posts. Interviews are carried out in Greece and the UK during the summer for contracts starting in September. These agencies are looking for people with at least a BA and usually a TEFL certificate (depending on the client *frontisterion*'s requirements). The following undertake to match EU nationals with *frontisteria* and do not charge teachers a fee:

**Anglo-Hellenic Teacher Recruitment**, PO Box 263, 201 00 Corinth (+30 27410 53511; jobs@anglo-hellenic.com/ www.anglo-hellenic.com). Scores of posts in wide choice of locations for university graduates from the UK, preferably with a recognised TEFL Certificate including one offered locally every month by TEFL Corinth (www.teflcorinth.com).

**Cambridge Teachers Recruitment**, 17 Metron Street, New Philadelphia, 143 42 Athens (+30 210 258 5155). Interviews conducted in UK in summer by Andrew MacLeod-Smith (macleod_smith_andrew@hotmail.com). One of the largest agencies, placing up to 60 teachers per year in vetted schools. Applicants must have a degree and a TEFL Certificate, a friendly personality and conscientious attitude.

# OTHER GAP YEAR OPPORTUNITIES

## SEASONAL WORK

Seasonal jobs can be arranged from the UK, preferably by contacting relevant tour operators in February or March. *Mark Warner* (0871 703 3955; www.markwarner-recruitment.co.uk) runs several resort hotels in Greece requiring British staff who are paid a weekly wage starting at £50 on top of free travel, accommodation, meals, use of facilities, medical insurance and so on. Other possibilities exist with Olympic Holidays (0870 499 6739 or 6742; www.olympicholidays.co.uk) who are always on the lookout for outgoing EU nationals to work a season as resort reps (candidates must have at least 12 months' customer service experience).

Yachting holiday companies are a possible source of jobs, which can be fixed up either ahead of time or on the spot. Sailing holiday operator *Sunsail* (0844 463 6512; www.sunsail.co.uk/hr) uses an online recruitment process to hire a large number of sailors, watersports instructors and qualified nannies, etc. for their Sunsail Club Vounaki and their flotilla holidays in Greece. Sailing Holidays in London (www.sailingholidays.com) look to hire flotilla skippers and hostesses, boat builders and marine engineers for their upmarket holiday programme in the Greek and Dalmatian islands. The specialist tour operator *Setsail Holidays* in Suffolk (01787 310445; boats@setsail.co.uk) recruits a similar range of staff for the May to September season in the eastern Med, promising pocket money of £120–£160 per week.

*In-Globe Agency* is a recruitment agency based in Thessaloniki and registered with the Ministry of Labour. It aims to find staff from all over Europe to fill positions in holiday resorts in Greece and Cyprus and recruits up to 2,000 Europeans aged 18–55 for tourist hotels on the islands through its 'Work & Travel in Greece' programme and its internship programme for trainees. In most cases jobs last from four to 18 months. Basic monthly salaries start at €400 in addition to free accommodation, meals, social insurance and the possibility of paid flights. For details contact Maria Tsilempi Kaltsidou (+30 2310 588200; maria@inglobe.com.gr). Internships open to students only last four months (June to September) and pay €400 a month; contact the internship coordinator Stella Kampa (info@inglobe.com.gr).

The internet is bound to turn up further possibilities. The monthly electronic jobs listing *Jobs Abroad Bulletin* (www.jobsabroadbulletin.co.uk) carries a sprinkling of vacancies in Greece in the spring. For example, the June 2009 issue carried adverts for bar staff at the Pilot Beach Resort in Crete and for an unnamed 'party island', one for a yachties' bar in Lefkas and another for the Halkidiki peninsula in northern Greece (where their preference was for someone who speaks Hungarian or Slovakian). Be aware that many of these ask that applicants submit a photo, and they are clearly interested in hiring fit and attractive staff. Patient surfing will lead you to the websites of individual bars and restaurants that have a 'Jobs' icon.

### BE INTERNET-WISE

*As always, young people, especially young women, considering a job overseas found over the internet, should go very cautiously and should ask to be put in touch with one or two previous student workers before accepting.*

While hunting on the net for a suitable summer vacancy, **Annelies van der Plas** made use of www.wereldwijzer.nl, the largest online travel community in her native Holland. After spending days of online searching and placing adverts, she finally received a reply from a Dutch man who asked her if she would like to work behind the bar at the Camel Bar on Kos (www.camel.gr/jobs.html). She was asked to send a picture to the Greek boss and was soon offered a job but no contract (which is typical):

*It was a kind of gamble to go alone as a blonde girl of 19, and my parents were a little bit worried, but they did not object to it, especially because many Dutch people worked on Kos. My plan was to work about two months at the Camel bar. The boss had an apartment ready for me, for €200 per month or €100 if I shared. The apartment itself was nothing special but the beautiful view of the harbour from the balcony made it worth the money. When I was working at the Camel bar I saw that it was not hard to find another job on the island. Mostly jobs behind the bar were already taken so the jobs consisted of getting people in. I noticed that the salary was most of the time the same, about €30 a night, paid daily, weekly or monthly. I luckily received my money every week, although I did not get my salary for my last week which means I worked a whole week for nothing. There was nothing I could do; the police were very corrupt. A good feature of the job was the free drinking and the contact with the people. I met a lot of people and every evening seemed like a night out. Sometimes people say that you have to smile or act more happy, which is hard when you are tired, and irritating because tourists don't understand that you work seven nights a week. The boss was happy with me because there were people who only wanted to be served by me. Also the tips were much better on the terrace and I could talk more to the people. Be careful when you are working in Greece. Most bosses don't care about you. A good colleague of mine got very sick for many days. She did not get her money that week. In two months I have seen that most Greek people see the tourists as idiots. Most bosses think only of money, and they don't care if the customer is not happy with their drink because they will never see them again. My last piece of advice: if you are a (blonde) girl, be careful of the Greek men.*

Undoubtedly the motives of some employers in hiring women are less than honourable. If you get bad vibes, move on. Some women find the legendary attention paid by prowling male Greeks intolerable; others have said this unwanted admiration is not unduly difficult to handle. Once you have established your reputation (one way or the other) you will be treated accordingly, at least by the regulars. On her gap year, **Emma Hoare** lasted precisely 20 days in a job as receptionist in a hotel on Mykonos before realising that she was being totally ripped off and her boss was a big, fat, disgusting, immoral bully, whom another disgruntled ex-employee described as 'feral'.

It is also possible to show up and shop around for a job, but don't expect anything to happen quickly. Young women are far more likely to be hired by a bar or restaurant than chaps. Many gap year travellers stop a while in one place and swap some labour for free hostel accommodation. They enjoy the hostel atmosphere and the camaraderie among hostel workers, and regard the job as a useful stop-gap while travel plans are formulated, often based on the advice of fellow travellers. Those who stick at it for any length of time may find themselves 'promoted' to reception; in this business a fortnight might qualify you for the honour of being a long-term employee. The work is easy-come, easy-go, and is seldom secure even when you want it to be.

It is sometimes worth checking the classified advertisements on the website of the English language daily *Athens News* (www.athensnews.gr), which is updated every Thursday. Another interesting possibility for people over 18 is at the holistic holiday centre on the island of Skyros in the northern Aegean. A number of 'work scholars' help with cleaning, bar work and domestic and maintenance duties in exchange for pocket money of £50 a week and the opportunity to join one of the 250 courses on offer, from yoga to windsurfing (www.skyros.com).

## CONSERVATION

*Elix-Conservation Volunteers Greece* in Athens (+30 210 382 5506; www.elix.org.gr) is a non-profit organisation promoting intercultural exchanges and nature and heritage conservation. Projects include work in protected landscapes, conservation of traditional buildings and work on archaeological sites. Applications can be sent directly or through a partner organisation in your country (e.g. UNA Exchange and Concordia in the UK).

*Earth, Sea and Sky* (www.earthseasky.org), a UK-based NGO, recruits volunteers to carry out island-based wildlife research, conservation and tourist awareness work on the Ionian island of Zakynthos. 2010 will see the planned opening of their SOS Sea Turtle rescue station. The rescue station will require volunteers with a range of skills, for short- or long-term placements.

On the same island, a project to protect sea turtles actively uses volunteer helpers. *Archelon* is the sea turtle protection society of Greece (+30 210 523 1342; www.archelon.gr) which carries out research and conservation on the loggerhead turtle on Zakynthos, Crete and the Peloponnese. A free campsite is provided for those who stay at least a month; volunteers will need at least €15 a day for food plus pay a registration fee of €150 or €250 (the lower fee is for those who arrive before mid-June or after August 21).

Another turtle conservation organisation is *MEDASSET* (Mediterranean Association to Save the Sea Turtles; +30 210 361 3572; medasset@medasset.org) which offers volunteers free accommodation at the Head Office in Athens in exchange for working for a minimum of three weeks. Volunteer work is office-based only and includes assisting staff with projects, letter writing, computer orientated and archiving tasks, database updating, internet research, etc. No prior knowledge in sea turtle conservation is required, just a passion and interest in the environment.

Bears are even more threatened than marine turtles. *Arcturos* accepts short-term volunteers at its environmental centre in the Prefecture of Florina in northern Greece, which serves as a bear protection centre (+30 23860 41500; mstyliadou@arcturos.gr; www.arcturos.gr).

## COURSES

Enjoyable as it is to master the Greek alphabet and learn simple greetings with which to befriend the locals, not many gap year students want to make a formal study of Modern Greek. Any that do should enquire about courses in Athens, Thessaloniki and Crete or summer courses on islands as is offered in Evia by *Nine Muses* mentioned above (www.ninemuses.gr/school.htm). *CELT Athens* (www.celt.edu.gr) puts on Modern Greek summer schools in Athens and Paros.

**Emily Reardon** decided she would like to spend the month of February in Greece, since she had been studying Greek in New York. She contacted a couple of language agencies and did her own research on the internet (checking past clients' feedback online) and chose the *Athens Centre*. Emily loved everything about Athens and Greece. She adored the Athens Centre, her coursework, classmates, the staff, the set-up and the accommodation they offered (small, clean, Ikea-furnished studio/efficiency apartments shared between two). The group planned things like eating out and travelling to one of the islands together, yet Emily felt safe and explored on her own as well.

An alternative to the Athens Centre is The Aegean Center for the Fine Arts (+30 22840 23 287; studyart@aegeancenter.org), which has been offering fine arts courses to individuals in small groups for more than 40 years at its centre on the Cycladic island of Paros. Students can create their individual curriculum with the help of artists-in-residence choosing from among the visual arts (photography, printmaking, painting and drawing) and literary arts (creative writing, literature, voice). One student said that she felt as though she had spent a whole semester on a film set rather than real life. The 14-week session from early March costs from €7,500; tuition fees can be reduced on the Work-Study programme.

Anyone interested in Greek folk culture might wish to contact the *Dora Stratou Greek Dances Theatre* in Athens (www.grdance.org) which runs short courses and workshops on traditional dance and theatre over the summer, as well as daily classes during the winter. The organisation presents daily summer performances at the outdoor theatre on Philopappou Hill in Athens and takes on about 10 unpaid foreign student volunteers to help look after the large costume collection and assist at performances.

# ITALY

Italy has always been a favourite destination for young people wanting to expand their cultural horizons. In the 18th century, the Grand Tour of Europe, which was considered to be an essential part of the education of young men of good breeding or fortune, was centred on Italy; and generations of educated people journeyed between the great artistic centres of Venice, Florence and Rome. Although their modern-day equivalents are more likely to be young women, seldom accompanied by a private tutor, many gappers do enrol in courses that will help them to appreciate the art and civilisation of ancient Rome and Renaissance Italy.

Italy is still a remarkably welcoming country and Italians are capable of breathtaking generosity and hospitality, with no expectation of anything in return.

## SPECIALIST GAP YEAR PROGRAMMES

Two exclusive cultural programmes in Italy maintain the tradition of the Grand Tour and are still aimed at young people of fortune since they are expensive. *Art History Abroad* and the *John Hall Venice Course* both provide a superb introduction to European art and culture. Both are aimed at school leavers who may be planning to go on to university to study art history or who may just have an independent interest in Western history and civilisation. For an account of the benefits that **Ella Hickson** reaped from the AHA course, see her case study on page 18.

*John Hall* offers courses in Italy for non-specialists on European civilisation, especially the visual arts and music, including architecture, conservation, opera, design, literature and world cinema. Practical options include Italian language, drawing, painting and photography. The spring course consists of an introductory week in London followed by five weeks in Venice where accommodation, meals, lectures, visits and classes are included in the price of £6,990, with optional extra periods in Florence and Rome.

**LOUISA INGHAM** enrolled in the John Hall course in 2009:

*I chose the John Hall Course in Italy over the rivals because I preferred the more lecture-based course structure, as well as the opportunity to live and really get to know Venice for six weeks, rather than hopping quickly from place to place. Both my brothers had done the John Hall course and came back with unforgettable memories, so I really had no choice but to take the chance to experience it.*

*My six weeks of living in Venice with lectures on art, music, architecture, literature, films and Venice in general included an unforgettable private visit to St Marks Cathedral and many day visits to Ravenna, Vicenza and other neighbouring places of interest. Venice is now the city I know best in the whole of Europe, a city which I will never be able to revisit without totally reliving this gap year experience. The chance to be lectured by such significant people was obviously one of the main rewards of the course. To keep so many teenagers interested and engaged in what they were lecturing on was amazing, and 99% of lectures really were fascinating. Italian lessons were available for an extra £100 or so and many people took the opportunity to learn while living in Venice.*

*During one-week stays in Florence and Rome we had private visits to all the major art galleries and main churches, as well as art classes at the prestigious Charles Cecil studio. From witnessing the highest 'Aqua alta' Venice has had for 30 years, to celebrating St Patrick's day around the Duomo in Florence, the whole trip was full of highlights. The low point was sharing a TINY room with three other girls for six weeks. One wardrobe, one table, and we celebrated when we could see parts of the floor! All part of the experience... and it certainly meant we were firm friends by the end of it! Living in a mixed group of students for such a significant period of time was a perfect way to prepare for university, particularly coming from a single-sex school. Living with no rules and regulations, yet having to follow a timetable of lectures and outings, was also a great introduction to University.'*

*Art History Abroad* offers four six-week programmes in the autumn, spring, early summer and late summer plus two-week courses in July and August. Their six-week programme involves travel throughout Italy, with all tuition on-site and not in classrooms, so that students are introduced to a broad spectrum of Italian life; the inclusive fee is £6,990 from summer 2010.

## COURSES AND HOMESTAYS

Italian is one of the easiest and most satisfying languages to learn, especially if you already have some knowledge of a Latin-based language. Many courses combine Italian language lessons with art history, cuisine, etc. The *British Institute of Florence* runs year round courses in Italian language, history of art and life drawing, with other courses in opera, etc. Summer courses relocate to Massa Marittima near the Tuscan coast, though **Fiona Roberts** was happy to spend her summer in 'the inescapably Italian' city of Florence where she recommends folding up your map and just wandering around the tiny winding streets (avoiding the crocodiles of American tourists plugged into their headphones):

> *When my friend and I first arrived in Florence, our Italian extended no further than 'si', 'grazie', and not-so-useful pizza and pasta names. Although having languages at GCSE and especially A Level was for me an advantage in learning Italian, the course would be perfectly approachable and manageable without it. The classes were often extremely funny, sped by and, to cap the lot, the vending machines sold chocolate croissants. Easily pleased, perhaps? Probably the most atmospheric evening was the first Sunday where, fresh from a week of classes, we watched Italy win the World Cup. The atmosphere was incredible, as everyone seemed to dash back home, grab a vespa, an Italian flag and a small child and race round the city, beeping their horns, until dawn. Sleep may have been difficult but I think we all fell in love with their good-natured enthusiasm.*

**CHARLOTTE SNELL** from Aberdeenshire had been desperate to travel ever since she could remember but had missed out on taking a year out after school because her parents were moving house that year. She couldn't face going straight from finals at Durham to a law conversion course in London so investigated gap year alternatives:

'Deferring the start date of the conversion course was easy and the law firms that I asked all said that they encouraged prospective applicants to take time out and gain some wider experience of the world. So my decision was made. With regards to financing my gap year I was very lucky. My parents were very supportive of my plans and agreed to pay for the course at the British Institute in Italy on the basis that it furthered my education. My three months in Florence were without a doubt the highlight of my gap year (even though the travelling I did afterwards was amazing!) and I would recommend it to anyone without hesitation. I was in the intermediate group for Italian, having done it for GCSE several years previously. The lessons were very conversation-orientated but backed up with a thorough teaching of the grammar. This made a pleasant change from learning languages at school in England and consequently I feel I have a much more useful vocabulary. My teacher was first *class and taught us a lot about Italian culture, the way of life, and modern issues as well as just the language. Also the staff made living abroad as easy as it possibly could be and it was this that made the price of the Institute (which is quite high) worthwhile.*

*I also studied History of Art at the Institute. Having previously had no interest in art history, I decided after a month of wandering around Florence and feeling ignorant that I had better learn. As my budget was quite tight, the Institute kindly allowed me to do a selection of the lectures. The lecturers were excellent – and after three years at university I've seen some bad ones! – dynamic and interesting. There was also a good balance between lectures and tours, the tours being very important as they brought the many wonders of Florence to life. The Institute also runs a number of other courses, such as cookery, which I didn't attend, and organises all sorts of cultural programmes. For example, when I was there they were running a film series, showing the films of Elizabeth Taylor and Richard Burton on a Wednesday night. I went to several and had a lot of fun debating the films afterwards with the random mix of people who turned up to watch. One of the highlights was waking up at 5am and climbing up to the Piazza Michelangelo to watch the sun rise over one of the most beautiful cities in the world.'*

Other institutes to consider include the Accademia Italiana in Florence (www.accademiaitaliana.com) which offers courses in Italian plus design (fashion, furniture, graphic, textile, etc.), while Linguaviva (www.linguaviva.it) offers a range of courses on Italian culture and language plus organises internships in Florence and Milan. The *Accademia del Giglio* in Florence offers Italian courses for foreigners plus drawing, painting and art history courses.

An excellent source of Italian language, art and cookery school listings is the website www.it-schools.com. Serious courses often work towards the Certificazione di Italiano come Lingua Straniera (CILS) exam of the University of Siena and authorised by the Italian Ministry of Foreign Affairs which is divided into four levels. Some language schools are in lovely settings like the *Piccola Università Italiana* in Tropea (see entry page 368). **Isobel Pyrke** spent 11 enjoyable weeks studying Italian in beautiful Sorrento on the Bay of Naples, arranged by CESA:

*As I had never heard or spoken to anyone who had taken a language course in their gap year and I had never studied Italian before, I didn't know what to expect. Linguistically I felt I improved much more than I expected. The teachers were fantastic and I feel I formed some good relationships with them during my time there. The lessons were good, although two hours of solid language learning followed by another two solid hours is quite hard going. I liked the way it left my afternoons free however. The school was in a good position, easily accessible from the main square. Sorrento is a small town so it is easy to meet and socialise with people. By the time I left I couldn't walk down the street without bumping into someone I knew. It is also very safe, much more so than London. I'm going back in the summer so I suppose that speaks for itself.*

An average starting price for one week's intensive study of Italian would be €180–€240 and €550 for four weeks. Accommodation in one of the major cities would cost a further €15–€30 a night or €500+ a month bed and breakfast with a host family. Needless to say, courses in central Florence or Venice will be more costly than ones in more obscure towns.

**Matteo Symonds**, a 19-year-old client of *CESA*, put to the test the maxim that the longer you stay, the more fluent you become:

*The 32-week academic year in Italy was fantastic. I divided my time between Rome, Milan and Florence, three months in each. On the course I met people from all four corners of the planet including Serbia, Holland, China, Brazil and many from Japan. Only 6% of the students were British which is to our advantage because we spoke Italian to each other. It was about 3 months into studying that I could start to put coherent sentences together. The extra curricular activities in Milan were diverse, including trips to San Siro to watch prestigious teams in Serie A like AC Milan and Internazionale; and weekly outings to Casablanca Bar, with its happy hour deal of €6 for a drink and all you could eat. I ended up in Florence where the clubs are fantastic and the city is small enough to be accessible by foot.*

Milan is the fashion capital of the world, and many students go there to study fashion and design. Some centres offer courses taught in English, for example the *Istituto Europeo di Design* (www.ied.edu) which attracts a lot of Americans including **Lauren McHale** from California. Not only did she have a long held interest in fashion design but, while pursuing her passion for snowboarding in the Rockies two years earlier, she had fallen in love with an Italian snowboarder, and was determined to move to Italy: '*I have always wanted to do fashion design, so Max showed me round the schools in Milan while I was visiting in the summer. I found IED, went back home for a month, convinced my parents that it was a good idea, and within a few months, I was going to fashion school in Milan, and living my dream in Italy.*'

The *Spannocchia Foundation* offers an intriguing internship opportunity, mainly to young Americans, to spend time on an *agriturismo* farm in Tuscany while studying the language (see entry in 'Directory of Work Experience Abroad'). **Katie White** from Massachusetts loved her spring-time experience there before college:

*I was one of eight interns at the Tenuta di Spannocchia, a 1,200-acre farm, agriturismo, and educational facility. The internship program included daily farm work, Italian lessons, field trips to surrounding areas of interest, and educational presentations on food issues and Italian culture. The interns worked 30+ hours a week for three months. The conditions were excellent; our intern group lived together in a house on the property which was cleaned regularly, we received meals from the farm, and the work was never too taxing. My gap year included so many exquisite moments that I really don't think I can pick one out. I remember distinctly one moment this spring while I was harvesting leeks on a sunny morning overlooking the Tuscan landscape and thinking that I was the luckiest, happiest, healthiest girl alive (or at least that I knew of).*

# PAID OPPORTUNITIES FOR GAP STUDENTS

## TEACHING

Hundreds of English language schools around Italy employ native English speakers though the majority are not suitable for gap year students unless they have acquired a qualification in Teaching English as a Foreign Language. But some do manage to find openings, despite their lack of a TEFL certificate. Natalia de Cuba could not persuade any of the language schools in the northern town of Rovereto where she was based to hire her without qualifications. So she decided to enrol in the Cambridge Certificate course run by International House in Rome. She found the month-long course strenuous but not terribly difficult, and worth the fee (which now stands at €1,750 plus accommodation; www.ihromamz.it). Good training centres will have links with potential employers throughout Italy.

Several Italian-based chains of language schools account for a large number of teaching jobs, though most operate as independent franchises so must be applied to individually. Chains include the *British Schools Group* (www.britishschool.com) with more than 60 member schools. Other chains include *British Institutes* with 175 associated schools (www.britishinstitutes.it) and *Oxford Schools* based in Venice (www.oxforditalia.it) with 13 schools in north-eastern Italy.

As in other European countries, summer camps for unaccompanied young people usually offer English as well as a range of sports. *ACLE Summer & City Camps* in San Remo, Liguria (+39 0184 506070; www.acle.org) advertises heavily for more than 200 young people with a genuine interest in children who must be 'fun-loving, energetic and have high moral standards' to teach English and organise activities including drama for two, four or more weeks. The promised wage is €220–€260 per week plus board, lodging, insurance and travel between camps within Italy. However, summer staff must enrol in a compulsory four-day introductory TEFL course for which a deduction of €150 will be made from earned wages.

A less well-known organisation also based in San Remo might be worth comparing: *Lingue Senza Frontiere* (+39 0184 508650; www.linguesenzafrontiere.org). They promise to pay their tutors €450 net plus board and lodging every two weeks in their English immersion summer camps. A smaller outfit to try is the *English Camp Company* (info@theenglishcampcompany.com).

## AU PAIRING

Summer-only positions are readily available. Most Italian families that can afford live-in childcare go to holiday homes by the sea or in the mountains during the summer and at other holiday times.

The average weekly pocket money for au pairs is in the range €70–€100+ and for mother's helps €500–€800 a month. Wages are slightly higher in the north of Italy than central and southern parts of the country because the cost of living is higher. The demand for nannies and mothers' helps able to work 40+ hours is especially strong since a high percentage of families in Italy have two working parents. The London-based agency *Totalnannies.com* (020 8542 3067) specialises in Italy and has up to 100 vacancies in Italy at any given moment. Most staff at Italian agencies speak English and welcome applications from British au pairs. Make sure first that you won't be liable to pay a hefty registration fee. Try the following:

**ARCE (Attivita Relazioni Culturali con l'Estero)**, Genoa (+39 010 583020; www. arceaupair.it). Long established agency makes placements throughout the country.

**Celtic Childcare**, Via Sant Antonio Da Padova 14, 10121 Turin (+39 011 533606; www.celticchildcare.com).

**Euroma**, Rome (+39 06 806 92130; www.euroma.info).

**Intermediate SNC**, Via Bramante 13, 00153 Rome (+39 06 57 300683; www. intermediateonline.com). Intermediate has its own language school in the Aventino district of Rome. Registration fee €280.

**Roma Au Pair**, Via Pietro Mascagni 138, 00199 Rome (+39 06 863 21519; www. romaaupair.com). No placement fee for au pairs.

Working in Italy is something of a hit and miss situation and if you can't speak a word of Italian, you will be at a distinct disadvantage. Contacts are even more important in Italy than in other countries. **Louise Rollett**, for example, first went out as a paying guest to a town near Bologna and then extended her stay on a work-for-keep basis as an English tutor. **Dustie Hickey** went for treatment to a doctor in Milan who immediately offered to pay her to tutor his children in English.

You are not expected to speak Italian if you work for a British tour operator; in fact German is probably more sought after than Italian because of the high number of German tourists in Italy. Try any of the major campsite tour companies such as *Canvas*, *Holidaybreak, Eurosites or Keycamp*, which are looking primarily for people over 18 with customer service skills. The smaller *Venue Holidays* (www.venueholidays.co.uk) employs summer season reps at campsites on the Venetian Riviera, Lake Garda and in Tuscany.

## WINTER RESORTS

*Crystal Holidays*, part of the TUI Travel Group (020 8541 2223; www.jobsinwinter.co.uk) hires resort reps and chalet staff for work in the Italian Alps as well as staff for summer holidays. The ski department of *PGL Travel* (www.pgl.co.uk/recruitment) offers some jobs as ski reps, leaders and ski/snowboard instructors (to BASI-qualified skiers), especially for short periods during half-term and Easter holidays. If you haven't fixed up a job with a UK tour operator, job openings can be found (with difficulty) on the spot in the winter resorts of the Alps, Dolomites and Apennines. Many are part-time and not very well paid.

## OTHER JOBS IN TOURISM

As throughout the world, backpackers' haunts such as hostels and campsites often employ travellers for short periods. While planning her escape route from a less-than-satisfactory summer au pairing job in Naples, **Jacqueline Edwards** asked in the Sorrento youth hostel about job possibilities and a few weeks later moved in to take over breakfast duties in exchange for free bed and breakfast.

By making use of www.hostels.com **Stephanie Fuccio** from the USA had little difficulty pre-arranging a hostel job:

> *Never in a million years did I think that watching MTV would be part of my daily life in Rome. The hostel I was working at was Hostel Casanova (Via Ottorino Lazzarini, 12, 00136 Rome; +39 06 397 45228; hostelcasanova@yahoo.com). I was working 7 days a week (I was a bit scared about running out of money since this was the first leg of the trip). The shifts would alternate from evening to morning every day: one day doing the morning shift when the hostel was cleaned and the next day the evening shift. As well as getting to stay there for free, they paid me and my co-worker €20 per day in cash which was really nice. Rome was so cheap (from a San Francisco point of view) and with great weather, it was easy to save. I came to Italy with $700 cash and a plane ticket, I left with about $600 and a plane ticket to England and Ireland, having been there about five weeks total.*

## VOLUNTEERING

Many Italian organisations arrange summer work projects which are as disparate as selling recyclable materials to finance development projects in the developing world to restoring old convents or preventing forest fires. An intercultural exchange organisation with a website in English and a far-reaching long-term incoming programme is *AFSAI* (Viale dei Colli, Portugensi 345 B2, 00151 Rome; 06–537 0332; www.afsai.it).

Here is a selection of voluntary organisations that run working holidays. In some cases, it will be necessary to apply through a partner organisation in your home country:

***Abruzzo, Lazio and Molise National Park***, Centro Operativo Servizio Educazione, Via Roma, 67030 Villetta Barrea (+39 0864 89102; centroservizi.villetta@ parcoabruzzo.it; www.parcoabruzzo.it). Volunteers carry out research and protection of flora and fauna in remote locations, e.g. in Pescasseroli and Villetta Barrea. Volunteers must cover their insurance and registration fees: €80 for 7 days, €140 for 14 days.

**Emmaus Italia**, Boves (+39 0171 387834; www.emmauscuneo.it). Workcamps to collect, sort and sell second hand equipment to raise funds for social and community projects worldwide.

**LIPU (Lega Italiana Protezione Uccelli)**, Trento (+39 0521 273043; www.lipu.it). Long-established environmental and bird conservation association which publishes a catalogue of summer projects at its bird reserves *(gasi)* throughout Italy.

**Pithekos**, Milan (+39 02 2953 1450; asspithekos@tiscali.it; www.pithekos.it). Eco-volunteer organisation.

**La Sabranenque**, Centre International, rue de la Tour de l'Oume, 30290 Saint Victor la Coste, France (+33 04 66 50 05 05; sabranenque.com). French-based organisation uses voluntary labour to restore village and monuments in Altamura (inland from Bari in Southern Italy). The cost of participation is £180 for 3 weeks in July/August.

**WWF Italia**, Servizio Campi, Via Po 25/C, 00198 Rome (+39 06 844971; www.wwf.it/ENG/holiday/listcamps.asp). A few environmental conservation camps, though the emphasis is on holidays. Sample 9-day fire-watching camps in Sicily cost €233.

Volunteers can also join archaeological camps. The national organisation Gruppi Archeologici d'Italia in Rome is the umbrella group for regional archaeological units that coordinate two-week digs (+39 06 3937 6711; segreteria.gruppiarcheologici.org; www.gruppiarcheologici.org). Paying volunteers may join these digs (e.g. €200 for 1 week; €330 for 2 weeks).

# Malta

Although small in area (30km by 15km), Malta has much of interest and is an independent nation state within the European Union. The student and youth travel organisation *NSTS* in Valletta (www.nsts.org) markets English courses in conjunction with sports holidays for young tourists to Malta. NSTS runs a work and study programme, which arranges work experience placements in the hospitality industry in Malta for young English-speaking travellers.

# RUSSIA AND EASTERN EUROPE

With the accession of Bulgaria and Romania to the EU in 2007, the divide between eastern and western Europe has been further eroded. Together with Hungary, Poland, the Czech Republic, Slovakia, Slovenia, Lithuania, Latvia and Estonia, the former Soviet bloc countries are looking to the west and to the future, where the English language dominates. The demand for native speakers to teach English continues strong in both the cities and more farflung corners of this vast region.

During the heady days immediately after the various Communist governments fell (before today's gap year students were born), thousands of young Westerners flocked to Prague, Budapest and Kraków. Many of them supported themselves for short and longer periods by teaching English to a population which clamoured for access to English-language media and culture. Naturally the clamour has subsided and pay for English teachers has dropped, but there is still a demand for native speaker teachers of English at summer camps and in institutes.

## Russia, the Baltic States, other states of the former Soviet Union

### ENGLISH TEACHING

Several English-teaching schemes are described in this chapter suitable for pre- or post-university experiences. Opportunities tend to be in small provincial towns and industrial cities rather than the glamorous capitals. In Russia, the Baltic states (Latvia, Lithuania and Estonia) and the other states of the old Soviet Union, the English teaching situation is more fluid. Native speakers can still arrange some kind of teaching, often on a private basis, but with no guarantee of earning a living wage from it.

#### PLACEMENT ORGANISATIONS
The major chains have multiple franchise schools in the region, particularly Russia, including *International House, EF English First* and *Language Link*. Volunteers are placed by the non-profit organisation *Sharing One Language* or *SOL* (www.sol.org.uk) in state schools in a number of eastern and central European countries, especially Hungary, Slovakia and Romania. Candidates must be graduates, preferably with a recognised TEFL Certificate. Contracts with individual schools are mostly for a complete academic year September to June. All posts include a local salary and free housing.

The youth exchange company *CCUSA* runs a Summer Camp Russia Programme whereby teacher/counsellors from the UK and USA are placed on youth camps in Russia lasting four or eight weeks between mid-June and mid-August. Participants must be between the ages of 18 and 35, have experience working with children and/

or abroad, and have an interest in learning about the Russian language and culture. Camps are widely scattered from Lake Baikal in Siberia to the shores of the Black Sea. The programme fee of £795 includes round-trip travel from London to Moscow, visa, travel, insurance, orientations on arrival and room and board.

Australian **Paul Jones** spent the summer in Russia as a gap within a gap since he was already on a working holiday in the UK to fund trips to Europe and beyond:

> *I worked as a counsellor in a summer camp near the city of Perm. When I first arrived, my heart sank because it looked like a gulag (for which the area around Perm is famous!) but you soon forget the physical conditions, mostly anyway. If I didn't like the food at the start, I definitely learnt to like it by the end and now reminisce about the worst of it! My job, as with American summer camps for kids, was to help lead a group of up to 30 children for their 3 weeks stay at the camp. Because I did not speak the language, I was placed with two other leaders so my services weren't really necessary. However, this region of Russia doesn't exactly get many international visitors so the role I played at camp sometimes felt more like being a rock star! The types of activities the kids did ranged from football, basketball and swimming (the colour of the pool was scary) to singing, dancing and crafts. But while I tried as best I could to lead my group of kids in their daily activities, every single kid in the camp wants a piece of you because you're the foreigner! So a lot of the job is to just be there and share a different culture with the kids (and their parents sometimes), other Russian counsellors and the Camp Director. In return, they also shared their culture. I've actually stayed in contact with a number of the local counsellors. The ones that don't speak English very well make up for it with sign language and friendliness. I found that a few words in Russian go a long way to bridging the culture gap. And if possible take some souvenirs for the kids. Even a pack of cards with the British flag on them provides 52 little gifts.*

*CCUSA* also runs a summer camp in Croatia, where English-speaking counsellors are needed; details from www.campcalifornia.com.

Private language teaching organisations run short-term holiday courses in summer and sometimes winter which require native speakers. The English School of Communication Skills whose Personnel Department is located in the charmless city of Tarnów (+385 14 690 87 49; personnel@escs.pl; escs.pl) hires 100 EFL teachers for five language schools in southern Poland and summer language camps at the Polish seaside. Pay is 25–30 zlotys an hour, 2,200 zlotys a month. ESCS offers its own three-week TEFL training course in September at a cost of $450.

## COURSES AND HOMESTAYS

Ironically the study of Russian has been in sharp decline since Russia abandoned communism and decided to throw in its lot with Western capitalism. Compared to the heady 1960s, few schools and universities offer Russian. The big language agencies such as

*Caledonia, CESA* and *IALC* offer Russian courses in Russia, particularly St Petersburg. *Liden & Denz Language Centres* (see entry) run Russian language courses from casual beginners to advanced academic, and can all arrange a follow-up work experience or volunteering placement.

## VOLUNTEERING

The vast region of eastern Europe is a hive of volunteering activity during the summer, so if a short-term group voluntary project appeals to you at all, contact the main UK workcamp organisations listed in the chapter *Volunteering*, all of which have partners in eastern Europe. Projects vary from excavating the ancient capital of Bulgaria to organising sport for gypsy children in Slovenia. There is also a high proportion of much-needed environmental workcamps.

Many international voluntary schemes are particularly active in the region including the fully funded *European Voluntary Service (EVS)* Programme. Volunteers aged 18–30 are given free travel, food, accommodation and an allowance for the duration of two to 12 months. The programme is delivered in the UK by a range of voluntary agencies such as *EIL-UK* and *ICYE*.

*Kitezh Children's Community* for orphans in Kaluga, 300km south of Moscow, has close links with the *Ecologia Youth Trust* in Scotland (see entry in 'Directory of Volunteering Abroad'). The trust specifically recruits students in their gap year to spend two to three months at Kitezh and provides extensive preparatory information, down to profiles of the resident children. The joining fee is £1,320 for two months, including visa support but not visa fees or airfares to Moscow.

**NATALYA KENNEDY** is among the many volunteers who have found Kitezh a friendly, welcoming and inspiring place to spend some time:

*I came to Kitezh because the three-hour delay of a BA flight from Moscow to London led me to start a conversation with my neighbour who succeeded in instilling in me a curiosity to see the place which obviously meant so much to her. So six months later, just out of school and eager to take on the world, I packed my bag, told my friends they wouldn't hear from me for a while, and set off from Moscow's slushy Tyopli Stan bus station. I didn't have any aims beyond a vague hope that my Russian would improve and that I'd meet some interesting people in a different way of life. The driving force behind daily life in the village is a group of*

> *extremely intelligent, dynamic and enthusiastic young teachers who keep the place buzzing.*
>
> *Living in what is essentially as-near-as-possible-to-the-middle-of-nowhere has its advantages. The beauty of the surrounding countryside is breathtaking. Experiencing the beauty and loneliness of the Russian landscape at first hand is truly awe-inspiring. Of course, life here certainly isn't all sweetness and light. The language barrier is undoubtedly my biggest problem. It makes it difficult for relationships with anyone to progress beyond basic friendliness and curiosity, and I have days when I feel really upset about it. On the positive side, having a limited ability to speak has forced me to explore other means of communication; it's surprising how far you can get with a combination of practical jokes, a limited vocabulary, hugs and smiles. I think that of all the great memories I'll have of this place, the one that stands out is when one of the small children said as we looked out over the frozen lake 'It's as if we've fallen into a magical world.' I don't think I've ever felt happier than I did as I walked back through the snow towards the twinkling lights and smoking chimneys with a child clinging on to each hand. It's the sort of humbling moment which makes you want to do something meaningful with your life.'*

# Romania

The children's homes and special schools of Romania continue to accept voluntary input though not on the scale of a decade ago. *MondoChallenge* has set up programmes for volunteers to work mainly with traditional Hungarian and Csango ethnic groups, teaching and looking after orphans and disadvantaged women and children. *Oyster Worldwide* send volunteers for one to three month placements in orphanages in Brasov (as well as to a nearby bear sanctuary).

A few British charities have recruited volunteers for summer language camps in the past, although *British-Romanian Connections* in Liverpool says that it will not be sending anyone to Piatra Neamt in the summer of 2010; check their Facebook group to see if it will resume the exchange in 2011. *DAD International UK-Romania* (+40 788 473523; www.dad.ro) was advertising for volunteer teachers in the summer of 2009 via www.justjobs4students.co.uk and offering an expenses-paid three or four weeks in various parts of Romania including Transylvania, Moldavia and the Black Sea. Flights are not included.

# Bulgaria

Teaching opportunities in the private sector are still very scarce. A Bulgarian agency of long standing appoints 60–80 native speakers to teach in specialist English language secondary schools for one academic year for which the deadline is the end of May. Details are available from *Teachers for Central and Eastern Europe* (21 V 5 Rakovski Boulevard, Dimitrovgrad 6400; +359 391 24787/27174; tfcee@usa.net; www.tfcee.8m. com). University students, preferably with a TEFL background, are accepted from the USA, UK, Canada and Australia. The weekly teaching load is 19 40-minute classes per four-day week. The salary in Bulgarian levs is equivalent to $200. Benefits include free furnished accommodation, 60 days of paid holiday, paid sick leave and work permit. A summer programme is also available at Black Sea resorts for which the application deadline is 15 June.

# Oyster Worldwide

*Volunteer and have the time of your life*

Have you considered volunteering abroad during your gap year? Or are you thinking:

- I've got no useful skills to offer
- I can't afford to live abroad without a wage
- Anyway, a gap year is supposed to be fun...

Think again.

**Skills:** You really do have something to offer. Your best assets are enthusiasm and initiative. If you also speak fluent English and can think on your feet you'll be a great help teaching kids in the developing world, where speaking English can be their passport out of poverty. You don't need formal training. If you can remember what makes a lesson interesting or boring you'll be on the right tracks. And if you can help out with sport, music or drama too you'll enjoy it even more. Alternatively, maybe you love animals and enjoy being outside? Many conservation projects would love your help. Perhaps you've got a great rapport with kids and are full of ideas for fun things to do? There are orphans, street kids and disabled children around the world who are desperate for someone to take an interest in them.

Oyster Worldwide sends groups of volunteers out to established projects in countries such as **Chile, Tanzania, Brazil, Kenya, Nepal** and **Romania**. You could teach, work in a bear sanctuary or wildlife reserve, help rehabilitate street kids or care for orphaned and disabled children. It's not as daunting as it sounds. You'll be well-prepared at our pre-departure course and have support from our local representative. But you'll also find that you've got lots of hidden talents and strengths just waiting to come out.

**Money:** Perhaps you feel inspired, but can't see how to afford it? Look at it this way. If you spend the first few months of your gap year working in the UK you could earn enough to cover the cost of a 3-6 month placement abroad. Once you're out in the developing world, your living costs will be minimal. You'll probably spend as much in two weeks in Africa as you'd spend on a night out back home. And you'll have a lot more to show for it.

**Fun:** Volunteering is fun - partly because of the things you do and partly because of the people you're with. Our volunteers always say one of the best things about their trip is the close friends they've made with others in the group. You really get to know people quickly when you're doing challenging things together trekking through amazing countryside, riding an elephant or trying out the local bus system. There'll be plenty of laughs, despite the frustrations.

If you'd like to know more about volunteering with Oyster, why not visit our website **www.oysterworldwide.com**, email: **emailus@oysterworldwide.com** or call us on **01892 770771** to find out more.

# SCANDINAVIA

Not every gap year traveller wants to hit the trail to the tropics. The Scandinavian countries of Denmark, Sweden, Finland, Norway and Iceland exercise their own fascination and can be visited as part of an InterRail tour of Europe or separately. One way of getting away from the notoriously high cost of living and of travel in this region is to join one of the organised schemes described in this chapter, for example working on a Norwegian farm or teaching at a Finnish summer school.

The demand for English-speaking au pairs is not vast but remains steady, especially in Denmark, where a certain number of young women over 18 are placed with families for 10–12 months. *Au Pairs International* in Copenhagen (+45 32 841002; www. aupairsinternational.dk) makes placements in Denmark, Norway, Iceland and Sweden as well as worldwide. Weekly pocket money varies, but some families will pay around €100. Another possibility is the *Scandinavian Au-Pair Center* (scandinavian@aupair. se; www.aupair.se), whose website provides contact names, phone numbers and email addresses for its representatives in Helsingborg (Sweden), Oslo (Norway) and Roskilde (Denmark) among others.

## Denmark

Work exists on farms and in factories, offices and hotels: the main problem is persuading an employer to take you on in preference to a Danish speaker. Copenhagen, the commercial and industrial centre of the country, is by far the best place to look for work. It is also the centre of the tourist industry, so in summer it is worth looking for jobs door to door in hotels, restaurants and the Tivoli Amusement Park. Among the largest employers of casual staff in Denmark are newspaper distribution companies. To get a job as an *omdeler* or 'paper boy/girl', contact A/S Bladkompagniet's office in Rødovre (+45 70 20 72 25; bladkompagniet@bladkompagniet.dk) or in Copenhagen (+45 35 27 73 20). Another big hiring company is the morning paper *Morgenavisen Jyllands-Posten* (+45 80 81 80 82; avisbud@jp.dk/cni@daoas.dk). It employs 4,000 people on weekdays and 5,000 on Sundays to deliver all its papers before 6.30am on weekdays and 8am on weekends.

The long-established *WWOOF Denmark* (*VHH*) distributes a list of their approximately 30 member farmers, most of whom speak English. In return for three or four hours of work per day, you get free food and lodging. Always phone, email or write before arriving. The paper list can be obtained only after sending €10/£5/$10/kr50 to Inga Nielsen, Asenvej 35, 9881 Bindslev (+45 98 93 86 07; info@wwoof.dk; wwoof.dk) or you can access it online by sending the same amount to VHH, Horsevadvej 200, 9830 Tårs.

Many young Europeans end up picking strawberries in Denmark in the summer, although earnings are not as attractive as they once were. The *EURES* website (www.seasonalwork.dk) provides a wealth of information about harvest work and invites EU passport holders to apply online. EURES estimates that in 2009, 2,000 foreigners were offered jobs in seasonal harvests in Denmark. Pickers get paid between Kr5.25 and Kr6.50 per kilo and can expect to pick not more than 5kg an hour when they start out. The season lasts from early June to nearly the end of July and applications are processed between April and mid-May. Most employers expect you to bring your own tent and cooking equipment and may charge Kr20–25 for camping. The island of Fyn has been recommended for fruit-picking work, especially the area around Faaborg. But Samsø is where most pickers head in June. The website www.samsobaer.dk/summerjob.html is a central resource for three Samsø farms.

# Finland

At one time the *Centre for International Mobility* (*CIMO*) in Helsinki arranged short-term paid training opportunities for foreign students. However, the Erasmus practical training programme has virtually replaced that and CIMO no longer offers placements to students from EU countries. British students and graduates who want an on-the-job training placement in Finland lasting between one and 18 months in technical subjects should apply to *IAESTE* (www.iaeste.org.uk).

The Nordic School in Russia (+7 812 303 86 96; www.nordicschool.ru) mounts an ambitious series of summer schools at eight different colleges in Finland for Russian children aged 7–17 learning English (age range varies among camps). Native English speakers – from the USA, Canada, Australia and New Zealand as well as the EU – are recruited to implement an intensive programme of conversation lessons, for one to five fortnight-long camps. Teachers are given accommodation and meals plus a wage of €400–€500 at the end of each camp, and also offered transport to another location for those working at consecutive camps.

The University of Helsinki Language Centre offers Finnish courses for foreigners who are not enrolled as students at the University; for details of summer and termly courses, contact Language Services (+358 9 191 23234; www.helsinki.fi/kksc/language.services/eng). Finnish courses for foreigners are also available from the Open University (www.avoin.helsinki.fi) and the Helsinki Summer University (www.kesayliopistohki.fi).

# Norway

*Atlantis Youth Exchange* in Oslo (+47 22 47 71 70; atlantis@atlantis.no/ www.atlantis.no) runs the excellent 'Working Guest Programme' which allows people aged between 18 and 30 of any nationality to spend two to six months in rural Norway (Americans and other non-Europeans may stay for no more than three months). The only requirement is that they speak English. In addition to the farming programme open to all volunteers, placements in family-run tourist accommodation are available to European nationals.

Farm guests receive full board and lodging plus pocket money of at least NOK890 a week (nearly £100) for a maximum of 35 hours of work. The idea is that you participate in the daily life, both work and leisure, of the family: haymaking, weeding, milking, animal-tending, berry-picking, painting, house-cleaning, babysitting, etc. A wardrobe of old, rugged clothes and wellington boots is recommended. Application should be made through partner organisations where available; all are listed on the Atlantis website. British participants can apply through *Twin Work & Volunteer Abroad* in London (0800 80 483 80; www.workandvolunteer.com) whereas North Americans will have to apply directly. Atlantis distributes submitted applications with photos, references, medical certificate, etc. to Norwegian farm families participating in the scheme and then host families that want to offer a placement contact applicants directly to conduct a telephone interview. The registration fees charged by Twin are £550 for two months to £850 for six months.

**Robert Olsen** enjoyed his farm stay so much that he went back to the same family for another summer:

> *The work consisted of picking fruit and weeds (the fruit tasted better). The working day started at 8am and continued till 4pm, when we stopped for the main meal of the day. After that we were free to swim in the sea, borrow a bike to go into town or whatever. I was made to feel very much at home in somebody else's home. The farmer and his daughter were members of a folk dance music band, which was great to listen to. Now and then they entrusted me to look after the house while they went off to play at festivals. Such holidays as these are perhaps the most economical and most memorable possible.*

Atlantis also runs a programme for 200 incoming au pairs who must be aged 18–30 and willing to stay at least six months but preferably 8–12 months. The programme has become so popular that applications are accepted only through partner agencies, and at the moment there is none in the UK. Interested Britons should seek advice from Atlantis since it may be possible to apply through an agency in another country. The pocket money for au pairs in Norway is NOK4000 per month which sounds generous until you realise that it could be taxed at 25%–35% depending on the region. Atlantis can advise on possibilities for minimising tax by obtaining a *frikort*, which entitles you to a personal allowance of at least NOK4,000. Anyone interested in learning Norwegian should find out about the International Summer School offered at the University of Oslo (www.uio.no/iss).

# Sweden

Unfortunately Sweden has no equivalent of Atlantis or CIMO. However, several agencies do make au pair placements in Sweden (see introduction to this chapter). Swedish language courses are available at the *Uppsala International Summer School* (www.uiss.org).

*WWOOF* is now represented in Sweden (www.wwoof.se). In order to obtain the list of 50 WWOOF farms you must pay the membership fee of €15 online. Stiftelsen Stjärnsund (www.frid.nu) is located amongst the forests, lakes and hills of central Sweden. Founded in 1984, the community aims to encourage personal, social and spiritual development in an ecologically sustainable environment. It operates an international working guest programme lasting one week to three months starting throughout the year, but is at its busiest between May and September when most of the community's courses are offered. First-time working guests pay SEK500 for their first week of work and if the arrangement suits both sides it can be continued with a negotiable contribution according to hours worked and length of stay. Enquiries should be made well in advance of a proposed summer visit.

# Iceland

The private employment agency *Ninukot* (PO Box 12015, 132-Reykjavik; +354 561 2700; ninukot@ninukot.is; ninukot.is) originally specialised in agricultural and horticultural jobs throughout Iceland but has branched out to offer jobs in babysitting, fisheries, gardening, horse training and tourism as well. Its welcoming website is in English and holds out the prospect of an easy-to-arrange working holiday in Iceland for EEA nationals.

The majority of vacancies are on farms, looking after animals, working the farm equipment and helping with the household chores, but can be with harvesting and packing produce, training horses or looking after guests on holiday farms. During the summer months from May to September Ninukot offers jobs in small family-owned hotels and restaurants all over Iceland. In other sectors, it is possible to apply all year round. Jobs are open to EEA citizens aged 18–30 with a driver's licence and good English (other languages are a plus). Experience is not essential but makes placement easier. Pay starts at €1,015 a month with a deduction of €12 a day for board and lodging, and terms for flight reimbursement are the same as for au pairs: after completing six months, the family or employer pays for a one-way airfare to Iceland, and return fare after 12 months.

A voluntary organisation called *Worldwide Friends* (*WF*; *Veraldarvinir* in Icelandic; Einarsnes 56, 101 Reykjavík; +354 55 25 214; wf@wf.is; www.wf.is) offers an interesting range of two-week projects (workcamps) which international volunteers can join. Many are concerned with the environment but in others volunteers help prepare for and work during summer festivals in several towns including Heimaey on one of the remote Vestmannaeyjar Islands. The participation fee is €90, €120 or €150 depending on the project and the duration.

# SPAIN AND PORTUGAL

## Spain

At the beginning of the 21st century, the popularity of Spanish studies continues to escalate. It is possible to take short intensive language courses in all the major Spanish cities. Spain has never lost its pre-eminent position as a favourite destination for British holidaymakers, and gap year students are no exception. Many book themselves on cheap packages to the Canaries, Ibiza and the Balearic Islands or any of the Costas as a good place to unwind after exams or after rigorous travels in developing countries. With an explosion in cheap and flexible flights from various UK airports with no-frills airlines, it is now possible to fly very easily to one of many Spanish cities. However, the cost of living is relatively high and opportunities for picking up a job to fund further travels are not as numerous as they were before Spain succumbed to the recession.

The demand for native speakers of English to teach remains strong, but unqualified and inexperienced 18 year olds will have difficulty finding a position during the academic year (with exceptions; see below). They might have more luck at summer language camps. It is always worth checking the English language press in Spanish resorts and cities for the 'situations vacant' columns which sometimes carry adverts for live-in babysitters, bar staff, etc. If you can arrange to visit the Spanish coast in March before most of the budget travellers arrive, you should have a chance of fixing up a job for the season. The resorts then go quiet until late May when the season gets properly underway and there may be jobs available.

### COURSES AND HOMESTAYS

All the major agencies such as *CESA*, *Caledonia*, *Languages Abroad* and *Lanacos* have links with many institutes in Spain, or you can investigate Spanish-only companies such as *Don Quijote* (www.donquijote.org) and *Mester* (www.mester.com). It usually saves money (but not time) to book directly with the school in Spain, as **Annabel Iglehart** from Castle Douglas in Scotland did with Mester (see 'Directory of Language Courses'):

> *I completed my university degree last July and am taking a year (or two) out to gain new skills and participate in interesting activities around the world. I didn't take a year out before I went to university and because of this I think that I am making the most of my opportunities now. As soon as my exams finished I got straight down to organising my year out. I worked for two months in a variety of jobs in Edinburgh and then went to Salamanca, Spain to do a three-month intensive Spanish language course with Mester. The course was fantastic. The classes were fast paced and the teachers excellent. I met loads of people who I am still in touch with now, the social events organised by the school being a lot of fun and there was something for everyone. I lived with a Spanish*

*family for a while and then moved to a flat with other students, something I had arranged before I headed out there. Mester is a company in Spain that provides excellent courses in Spanish, for any number of weeks and in a variety of cities in Spain. I'm afraid I cannot remember exactly how much it cost but it was roughly £1,300 for three months. I had an intensive course (five hours of tuition a day), stayed for three weeks with a Spanish family and the rest in a self-catering flat. The costs are calculated according to the type of course (there are many to choose from) and the class of accommodation. The schools seem to be a lot less busy in winter time (when I was there, September to December) and so this can mean that classes are smaller, but not always. Classes are never more than 10 people I am told.*

Living with a family usually forces you to speak more Spanish from the beginning. Homestays can often lead to longer-lasting friendships and subsequent exchanges arranged on a private basis.

The youth exchange organisation *Relaciones Culturales Internacionales* (Calle Ferraz 82, 28008 Madrid; +34 91 541 71 03; spain@clubrci.es) places native English speakers with families who want to practise their English in exchange for providing room and board; the placement fee is €150 for stays of up to three months, €350 for a year.

The non-profit Instituto Cervantes (www.cervantes.es) is the largest worldwide Spanish teaching organisation, with headquarters in Madrid and a network of centres around the world (comparable to the Alliance Française for French). It also has centres in London and Manchester.

Of course many other things can be studied in Spain apart from language. Learning some of the traditional dances is the aim of some gap year travellers who have the chance to learn Sevillanas, Malagueras, the Pasadoble or even the very difficult Flamenco.

## OPPORTUNITIES FOR PAID WORK

Year out students have successfully found (or created) their own jobs in highly imaginative ways. One of the most striking examples is a 19-year-old student who wrote to the address on a Spanish wine label and was astonished to be invited to act as a guide around their winery for the summer. **Tommy Karske** returned home 'knowing a lot about wine and believing that anything is possible'.

Many yachts are moored along the Costa del Sol and all along the south coast. It might be possible to get work cleaning, painting or even guarding these luxury craft. There are also crewing possibilities for those with no time constraints and outgoing personalities.

Year-round resorts like Tenerife, Gran Canaria, Lanzarote and Ibiza afford a range of casual work as bar staff, DJs, beach party ticket sellers, timeshare salesmen, etc. A good starting point for finding out about seasonal job vacancies in Ibiza, Mallorca and Minorca is www.balearic-jobs.com.

RYA-qualified windsurfing and sailing instructors, BCU-qualified kayak instructors and SPSA-qualified climbing instructors are in demand for the season April/May to September. The largest sailing and windsurfing centre in the Mediterranean hires staff for the season (beginning of May to end of October). Minorca Sailing Holidays (Richmond; recruitment@minorcasailing.co.uk) recruits qualified sailing and windsurfing instructors as well as nannies, reps and other staff for their sailing centre in the Bay of Fornells on the north coast of Minorca. After doing a sailing and windsurfing instructor's course in Sydney Australia with *Flying Fish*, gap year student **Nina Fitton** worked for Minorca Sailing over the summer season before university:

> *It's long hours, low pay and hard work, but the kit available to all us instructors is vast, the social life is good, and it's great fun. I work about 10 hours a day, six days a week, teaching windsurfing and dinghy sailing to all age groups, but generally kids. On my day off and during my free time I can use any of the boats or boards, so my personal sailing has improved loads. Like on the Flying Fish course, all us instructors are about the same age (gap year or students) and all enjoy the same wind-related sports, so I'm having a blast.*

Jobs with British tour companies such as Canvas and Eurocamp can be fixed up months in advance from home. *Siblu Holidays* (siblu.com/contact_us/recruitment) and *TJM Travel* (jobs@tjm.co.uk) need reps and children's staff to work at mobile home/ tent parks and adventure centres from early May to the end of September. Agencies in the major Spanish cities may be able to assist, for example the Easy Way Association (+91 548 86 79; www.easywayspain.com/ingles/employment.htm) in Madrid charges a fee starting at €370 for placing Spanish-speaking or hospitality-trained people in restaurant jobs for a minimum of two months.

Some language schools can arrange work experience placements (mostly unwaged) in Spanish firms. Check out *ONECO Training Agency* in Seville (www.oneco.org) for internships and training.

## ENGLISH TEACHING

The great cities of Madrid and Barcelona act as magnets to thousands of hopeful teachers. Opportunities for untrained native speakers of English have all but disappeared in respectable language academies. However, some determined students have obtained a TEFL Certificate at the beginning of their gap year and gone on to teach.

**SAM JAMES** and his girlfriend Sophie Ellison headed off to Barcelona after A-Levels to do the four-week Trinity Certificate course which they found demanding but passed. Then they did the rounds of the language schools:

'Though tedious, this did work and we doubt we would have found work any other way. Job availability didn't seem that high in Barcelona when we were looking in October and we both accepted our only job offers. (Our age may have put off some employers.) Most schools seem to have recruited in September, so October was a bit of a lean month. I got my job by covering a class at two hours notice for a teacher who had called in sick. When this teacher decided to leave Barcelona, I was interviewed and offered her classes on a permanent basis. I got the job permanently about a fortnight after handing out CVs. Sophie was asked to her first interview after about three weeks of job-hunting. She was selected but then had to wait for several more weeks while her contract was finalised.'

Conventional wisdom says that the beginning of summer is the worst time to travel out to Spain to look for work since schools will be closed and their owners unobtainable. However, Sam handed round his CV again in May (when his hours were cut) and was given some encouragement. He thinks that because so few teachers look for work just six weeks before the end of the academic year, employers are sometimes in need of replacements. With so many no-frills cheap flights on the market, it might be worth a gamble. Sam had to teach a variety of age groups in Barcelona during his gap year and, despite the problems, ended up enjoying it:

'The children I taught were fairly unruly and noisy. The teenagers were, as ever, pretty uninterested in learning, though if one struck on something they enjoyed they would work much better. Activities based on the lyrics of songs seemed to be good. They had a tendency to select answers at random in multiple choice exercises. On the other hand they were only ever loud rather than very rude or disobedient. The young children (8–12) were harder work. They tended to understand selectively, acting confused if they didn't like an instruction. Part of the problem was that the class was far too long (three hours) for children of that age and their concentration and behaviour tended to tail off as the time passed.'

Sam blamed his lack of job security and bitty hours on Barcelona's popularity, 'the result of the great supply of willing teachers here keeping working conditions down and making it hard to exert any lever-age on an employer when one is so easily replaced'. *For this reason other towns may answer your requirements better. There are language academies all along the north coast and a door-to-door job hunt in September might pay off. This is the time when tourists are departing so accommodation may be available at a reasonable rent on a nine-month lease.*

Without a TEFL qualification, the best chance of a teaching job in Spain would be on a summer language camp. Some pay a reasonable wage; others provide little more than free board and accommodation. Try for example TECS Summer Camps in El Puerto de Santa María, Cádiz (+34 956 853000; www.tecs.es/employment) which recruit camp support staff and monitors for at least a month, plus assistant camp monitors and activity teachers for two months. Summer-only positions are available at language camps for children. The *Educational Consortium of Spain* (*TECS*) in El Puerto de Santa María, Cádiz (+34 956 853000; www.tecs.es/employment) hires native English speakers for summer work or for longer-term work in the academy.

It is also possible to arrange an informal exchange of English conversation for a free week in Spain. At least two companies, *Vaughan Town* and *Pueblo Ingles*, offer programmes whereby holiday resorts in Spain are 'stocked' with native English speakers and Spanish clients who want to improve their English. In the case of the former, 17 English native-speaking volunteers participate alongside about the same number of Spanish adults in an intensive six-day 'talk-a-thon' on a one-to-one basis. In exchange for making English conversation, participants receive free room and board, and transport from Madrid. The Pueblo Ingles programme lasts eight days and the average age of participants from all over the world is 40. More information is available from:

**Vaughan Systems**, Madrid (+34 91 748 5950 ext 126; anglos@vaughantown.com; vaughantown.com).

**Pueblo Ingles**, Madrid (+34 91 391 3400; anglos@puebloingles.com; puebloingles.com).

**Catharine Carfoot** went on what amounts to a classic working holiday at the Vaughan Village several summers ago:

*Back in June I took part in an English Language immersion programme in Spain. They want native English speakers (any flavour, although in practice North Americans predominate) to go and talk a lot of English to Spaniards. All people have to do is get themselves to Madrid in time for the pick-up (by the way the cheapest option for getting to Madrid is to fly with Ryanair to Valladolid and then take a bus from there). At the end of the week, you will be delivered back to Madrid, unless you have extraordinary stamina and can manage two (or more) continuous weeks in the programme. It isn't a way to make money, but of course people can and do make friends and contacts both with the other 'Anglos' and with the Spaniards. It's also a week off worrying about food, drink and where to sleep.*

## AU PAIRING AND WORK EXPERIENCE

Au pair links between Spanish agencies and those in the rest of Europe have been increasing partly because Spanish is gaining popularity as a modern foreign language. Young people can often arrange to stay with Spanish families without having to do much domestic or childcare duties by agreeing to help with English tuition. In addition to the British au pair agencies making placements throughout Europe (listed in the *Au Pairing* chapter), you may deal directly with established Spanish agencies. The pocket money for au pairs at present is €55–€75 a week plus €25 per month for transport.

If you deal directly with a Spanish agency, you may have to pay a sizeable placement fee. Here are some of them:

**BEST Programs**, Pozuelo de Alarcón, Madrid (www.bestprograms.org). Au pair placements for Americans and Europeans; fee $1,050 for three months. BEST also organises internships lasting 2 weeks to 6 months in Madrid, Seville, Barcelona and Marbella mainly for North Americans. Paid and unpaid internships are arranged for a fee of €1,680 for 3+ months. All programmes include language course, insurance and a lodging search on request.

**Costa del Sol Au Pair Agency**, Manilva, 29692 (+34 95 289 0484; info@costadel solaupair.com). Located between Marbella and Gibraltar, agency places au pairs in Malaga area, Granada, Estepona, Sotogrande and Gibraltar.

**Easy Way Association**, Madrid (+34 91 548 8679; easywayspain.com). Also makes hotel and restaurant placements.

**GIC Educational Consultants**, Javea (Alicante), (+34 96 646 0410; ecsl@tele fonica.net; gic-idiomas.com/aupair.htm). Au pair placements and live-in language tutors (registration fee €250).

**Globus Idiomas**, C/ Gómez Cortina 5, 2°B, 30005 Murcia (+34 968 295661; globus@ono.com; globusidiomas.com). Member of IAPA. Registration fee €100.

**Instituto Hemingway de Español**, Bilbao (+34 94 416 7901; institutohemingway. com). Accepts most nationalities. Also places interns in local companies, as volunteers and English teachers.

**International Au-Pair & Language Abroad Group**, Marbella (+34 952 90 15 76; languageabroad.info). Member of IAPA. €175 fee for placements of up to 3 months. €320 for up to 1 year.

## VOLUNTEERING

The *Sunseed Trust* (+34 950 525770; sunseedspain@arrakis.es; www.sunseed.org. uk), an arid land recovery trust, has a remote research centre in south-east Spain, near the village of Sorbas in Almeria, where new ways are explored of reclaiming deserts. The centre is run by both full-time volunteers (minimum five weeks) and working visitors who stay two to five weeks and spend half the day working. Weekly charges for part-time volunteers are £65–£118 according to season and for full-time volunteers

£40–£78. Typical work for volunteers might involve germination procedures, forestry trials, hydroponic growing, organic gardening, designing and building solar ovens and stills, and building and maintenance. Living conditions are basic and the cooking is vegetarian. Occasionally workers with a relevant qualification in appropriate technology, etc. are needed who are paid a small stipend.

The *Atlantic Whale Foundation* (www.whalenation.org) is working to protect whales and dolphins in the Canary Islands. Volunteers join the project for four or more weeks and contribute £150 per week. A new database of conservation volunteering opportunities is available on its website.

# Portugal

Portugal is seen by gap year students mainly as a place in which to relax and have fun rather than spend a large part of their gap year. There is a long and vigorous tradition of British people settling in Portugal, and the links between the two countries are strong so, with luck, you might be able to chase up a contact to provide initial accommodation and orientation. If you want to extend your stay, ask members of the expatriate community for help and advice. A good idea is to scan the advertisements in the English language press or place an ad yourself.

If your chosen language is Portuguese, one of the best known language schools is *CIAL Centro de Linguas* in Lisbon, which offers a well-structured series of courses, normally 15 lessons a week for four weeks. Students are billeted in private homes both in Lisbon and Faro.

According to some British backpackers, all you need for a working holiday is to fly to Faro with a tent and hitch a lift to Albufeira where any number of bars and restaurants might hire you for the season. Wages are not high, but accommodation is cheap. If you are aiming a little higher and know some Portuguese, it would be worth contacting the British-Portuguese Chamber of Commerce (*Camara de Comércio Luso-Britanica*) in Lisbon (www.bpcc.pt).

Two summers ago **Richard Ferguson** was astonished at the ease with which he started earning. On the recommendation of someone at home in New Zealand he looked up a contact in Lisbon who helped him to get his first job in a pizzeria:

> *I've been working in Lisbon for almost two months now. My new Portuguese friend and I simply asked the owner of a pizzeria where we were eating and I was told to start to work the next day. I was working six days 11:30 am–4pm then 7pm to closing time for €750 per month plus tips of about €80 a month. All the workers were immigrants and these wages were below par, so after a while I moved on to a rival pizzeria with better pay and conditions. It's an awesome environment – like a family, and I'm living with colleagues in an apartment owned by the owner for next to nothing. I'm loving it and as long as I can resist the temptation to drink every night in the Bairro Alto (upper town), I'll make enough to cover the return ticket to Brazil I've already bought (and then some) by the time I leave in December.*

# SWITZERLAND AND AUSTRIA

## Switzerland

Every winter a small army of gap year students migrates to the Alps to spend the winter season working and skiing at a Swiss or Austrian ski resort. One of the disadvantages of spending any time in Switzerland is the very high cost of living. But of course this goes with high wages which can be earned by people willing to work hard in hotels in the summer season as well as the winter. All legal workers should earn a minimum of SFr3,300/€2,175 a month (gross).

Switzerland is not a member of the European Union. However, a bilateral agreement with the European Union has removed the main obstacles to the free movement of labour. The immigration system is now more in line with the rest of Europe so that EU job-seekers can enter Switzerland for up to three months (extendable) to look for work. If they succeed they must show a contract of employment to the authorities and are then eligible for a short-term residence permit (valid for up to one year and renewable) or a long-term permit (up to five years) depending on the contract.

The Swiss are very *korrect* in regulating employment and foreign workers (including au pairs) will have many deductions made from their earnings. Students staying longer than four weeks must obtain Swiss medical insurance unless they can prove that their cover is as extensive as the Swiss. Few students head for Switzerland to study French or German although it is possible. While it is true that many Swiss and Austrian people speak a dialect of German, language schools teach *Hoch Deutsch*.

## PAID OPPORTUNITIES FOR GAP STUDENTS

### TOURIST INDUSTRY

Provided you have a reasonable CV and a knowledge of languages (preferably German), a speculative job hunt in advance is worthwhile. The *Swiss Hotel Association*'s online recruitment site http://jobs.htr.ch is unlikely to be much use to school leavers; for example a random check in 2009 revealed that there were 460 vacancies being advertised, mostly for German speakers with professional hospitality experience.

Quite a few British travel companies and camping holiday operators are active in Switzerland such as *Canvas* and *Eurocamp*. The *Jobs in the Alps Agency* (www.jobs-in-the-alps.co.uk) places waiters, waitresses, chamber staff, kitchen porters and hall and night porters in Swiss hotels, cafés and restaurants in Swiss resorts, 150 in winter, 50 in summer. The agency is now allied with the online seasonal recruitment specialist Free Radicals.

Most ski tour operators mount big operations in Switzerland, such as *Crystal Holidays* and *Ski Total*. A Swiss company that advertises for resort staff and ski instructors is

*Viamonde* in Anzère (+41 27 398 4882; www.viamonde.com); for the 2009 season it was paying its domestic hotel staff SFr383 per week net in addition to board and lodging.

> **GAPPERS' TIP**
> *The main disadvantage of being hired by a UK company is that the wages will be on a British scale rather than on the much more lucrative Swiss one.*

Swiss hotels are very efficient and tend to be impersonal, since you will be one in an endless stream of seasonal workers from many countries. The very intense attitude to work among the Swiss means that hours are long: a typical working week would consist of at least five nine-hour days working split shifts. Whether humble or palatial, the Swiss hotel or restaurant in which you find a job will probably insist on very high standards of cleanliness and productivity.

A number of ski and snowboard instructor courses are run in Verbier, by *Altitude Futures*, *Base Camp Group*, *New Generation* and the *Ski Academy Switzerland* (see 'Directory of Ski Training Courses').

Sometimes it is necessary to escape the competition from all the other gap year and other job-seekers by moving away from the large ski stations. **Joseph Tame's** surprising tip is to go up as high as possible in the mountains. After being told by virtually every hotel in Grindelwald in mid-September that they had already hired their winter season staff, he despaired and decided to waste his last SFr40 on a trip up the rack railway. At the top he approached the only hotel and couldn't believe it when they asked him when he could start. Although at 18 he had never worked in a hotel before, they were willing to take him on as a trainee waiter, give him full bed and board plus £850 a month. At first he found the job a little boring since there were few guests apart from Japanese groups on whirlwind European tours. But things changed at Christmas and New Year when he had to work three shifts a day, which was rewarded in the end by an increase in pay.

## SUMMER CAMPS

The Swiss organisation *Village Camps* advertises widely to recruit staff over 21 in their multi-activity language summer camp for children in Leysin. They also hire up to 100 ski counsellors and other staff for the winter season. Jobs are available for EFL teachers, sports and activity instructors, nurses and general domestic staff. For jobs with Village Camps, room and board are provided as well as accident and liability insurance and a weekly allowance from €175. Recruitment starts just after the new year; an application pack is available from Village Camps, Recruitment Office, 14 rue de la Morache, 1260 Nyon (+41 22 990 9405; personnel@villagecamps.ch; www.villagecamps.com/personnel).

Another camp operator looking for seasonal summer or winter staff is Les Elfes (CP 174, 1936 Verbier; +41 27 775 35 90; info@leselfes.com; www.leselfes.com). Winter contracts for ski/snowboard instructors and activity staff run from 1 December to 30 April. The company also hires kitchen and domestic staff for its various camps. The *Haut-Lac International Centre* (1669 Les Sciernes; +41 26 928 4200; jobs@haut-lac.com) employs teachers and monitors of any nationality for both their summer and winter camps for teenagers.

## WORK ON FARMS

Young Europeans who are interested in experiencing rural Switzerland may wish to do a stint on a Swiss farm. The *LanddienstZentralstelle* in Winterthur (+41 52 264 00 30; admin@landdienst.ch) runs a programme called Horizon Ferme (*Power deim Bauer* in German) by which farm placements are made for a minimum of three weeks for young people from the old EU countries who know some German or French. Last year about 3,000 young people (including Swiss) were placed through the Landdienst. The scheme is open to European nationals only. Workers are called 'volunteers' and can work for up to two months without a work permit. They must pay a registration fee of SFr40.

In addition to the good farm food and comfortable bed, you will be paid SFr16–20 per day worked. Necessary qualifications for participating in this scheme are that you be between 18 and 25 and that you have a basic grounding in French or German. On these small Swiss farms, English is rarely spoken and many farmers speak a dialect which some find incomprehensible.

Most places in German-speaking Switzerland are available from the beginning of March to the end of October and in the French part from March to June and mid-August to the end of October, though there are a few places in the winter too. The hours are long, the work is hard and much depends on the volunteer's relationship with the family. Most people who have worked on a Swiss farm report that they are treated like one of the family, which means both that they are up by 6am or 7am and working till 9pm alongside the farmer and that they are invited to accompany the family on any excursions, such as the weekly visit to the market to sell the farm-produced cheeses.

*WWOOF Switzerland* (wwoof@gmx.ch; http://zapfig.com/wwoof) keeps a constantly updated list of farmers around the country, currently 45. To obtain the list you must join WWOOF at a cost of SFr20/€15/$21 in cash. Volunteers must apply with a photocopy of their passport and an accompanying letter stating why they want to become unpaid volunteers.

**Joseph Tame** made use of the WWOOF website to fix up a place on a farm in the spring:

*I can honestly say that it has been an absolutely fantastic experience. The hours could be thought fairly long by some (perhaps 35 per week) considering there is no money involved, but I absolutely love the chance to work outside in this land that reminds me so much of the final setting in* The Hobbit. *From our farm your eyes take you down the hillside, over the meadows covered in flowers, down to the vast Lake Luzern below and over to the huge snow-capped mountain Pilatus. It really is paradise here. The family have been so kind, and as I put my heart into learning all that I can about the farm they are only too happy to treat me with generosity. I really feel a part of the family.*

## AU PAIRS

For those interested in a domestic position with a Swiss family there are rules laid down by each Swiss canton which principally apply to non-EU nationals since Europeans can work in Switzerland in any capacity. The regulations were relaxed in 2008, and au pairs/nannies from any country of the world are now able to work in Switzerland, provided they come through one of the handful of authorised agencies (contact details below). Non-EU candidates must be under 26 and can stay as an au pair for one year only. They are required to spend at least three hours a week studying the language. Families usually pay the language school fees or at least make a substantial contribution. The agencies are at pains to remind potential au pairs that Swiss German is very different from the German learned in school, which often causes disappointment and difficulties.

Au pairs in Switzerland work for a maximum of 30 hours per week, plus babysitting once or twice a week. The monthly salary is normally SFr700–800. Rates may be slightly higher for older girls and are generally higher in Geneva than Zürich. In addition, the au pair gets a four or five week paid holiday plus SFr18–20 for days off (to cover food). Au pairs are liable to pay tax and contributions which can mean a deduction of up to a fifth of their wages unless the family is willing to pay or subsidise these costs.

*Pro Filia* (+41 01 361 5331; www.profilia.ch) is a long-established Catholic au pair agency with branches throughout the country: the St Gallen office makes placements in German-speaking families and the Lausanne office in French-speaking households. The agency registration fee is SFr40 plus a fee of SFr290 is to be paid on taking up the placement.

Independent au pair placement agencies include *Perfect Way* in Brugg (+41 56 281 39 12; info@perfectway.ch) which vets all families and distributes a list of other au pairs and their contact details. The agency *Au Pair Link* (part of Wind Connections) in Erlenbach near Zurich (+41 01 915 4104; www.aupairlink.ch) accepts au pairs mainly from Australia and Canada, where it has in-country interviewers.

## VOLUNTEERING

The *Mountain Forest Project* (www.bergwaldprojekt.ch) runs one-week forest conservation projects in the alpine regions of Switzerland and southern Germany. MFP publishes its literature and website in English and is welcoming to foreign volunteers who know some German. It provides hut accommodation, food and accident insurance during one-week education and conservation projects.

# Austria

Like its alpine neighbour, Austria offers seasonal employment to gap year students hoping to save some money and do some skiing. Some knowledge of German will be necessary for most jobs apart from those with UK tour operators. There is no shortage of hotels to which you can apply either for the summer or the winter season. The largest concentration is in the Tyrol though there are also many in the Vorarlberg region in western Austria. The main winter resorts to try are St Anton, Kitzbühel, Mayrhofen, St Johann-im-Pongau which is a popular destination for British holidaymakers creating a demand for English-speaking staff. Wages in hotels and restaurants are lower than in Switzerland, although still reasonable.

The *Deutsch Institut Tirol* in Kitzbühel (www.gap-year.at) offers a 12-week German language course combined with a ski and snowboard instructors' course specially designed for gap year students (see entry in 'Directory of Specialist Gap Year Programmes'). This takes place in the autumn, and the ski instruction is on the glacier at Kaprun.

After spending the first part of her gap year doing a German language course in Dresden, **Rosie Curling** decided she needed to consolidate her new skills by working in a German-speaking environment. She headed for Lech in Austria, where she had a friend, and within 24 hours of arriving she had a job as a *commis* waitress:

> *It would be fair to say that my five months in Austria were a rollercoaster ride of emotions. For the first three weeks I was lonely and homesick, finding the work tough, relations with my colleagues a strain and communication difficult. However, after the Christmas period, I began to make friends and enjoy the wonderful skiing and to realise that the work was a means to an end, namely to have some serious fun. Again I was experiencing a new lifestyle, incredibly relaxed, where the major responsibility of the day was deciding where to ski and then where to après ski. Life assumed an idyllic routine. Get up at 8.50am, be the first on the slopes, ski till 11am, work the lunch shift, a couple more hours skiing, a bit more work in the evening, before hitting the night scene. Despite (or possibly because of) all this it was also an incredibly constructive period. For a start I saved £2,500 (to fund a Trans-Siberian railway trip). My German is now almost fluent, although I speak an Austrian dialect; my skiing has improved from a Grade 4/5 to 3a, but most importantly I have made some life-long friends, mainly Austrians and Swedes.*

Because Austria is a very popular destination for British skiers, jobs abound with UK tour operators, though most are looking for staff over 21. *First Choice Holidays* (020 8541 2223; sla.recruitment@tuiski.com; www.jobsinwinter.co.uk/firstchoice) hires hundreds of people for the winter season. Also go to www.firstchoice4jobs.co.uk to apply for summer employment; in some cases qualifications are not required because staff are given in-house training, but you must be available to stay for the whole season from May to September. *Equity Travel* (www.equity.co.uk/employment) recruit chefs, housekeeping and waiting staff, handymen, night porters, plongeurs and bar staff (EU nationality essential) for its sizeable operation in the Austrian Alps.

# PAID OPPORTUNITIES FOR GAP STUDENTS

## SUMMER WORK

Two Vienna-based organisations that run summer language camps are the similarly named *English for Children* (+41 01 958 1972; englishforchildren.com) and *English for Kids* (01 667 45 79; www.e4kids.co.at) both of which are looking for young monitors and English teachers with experience of working with children and preferably some TEFL background. English for Kids promises a salary from €1,188 per month gross, plus full board and accommodation. Try also the English Camp Company (www.theenglishcampcompany.com) for summer jobs teaching English and supervising activities.

WWOOF Austria is in Stainz (+43 03463 32096; wwoof.welcome@utanet.at; www.wwoof.welcome.at.tf). Membership costs €20/$28 per year, which entitles you to the list of around 130 Austrian organic farmers looking for work-for-keep volunteer helpers.

## AU PAIRS

Austria has a well-developed tradition of au pair placement. According to new regulations that came in to force in 2009, all au pairs must receive €450 per month for working 20 hours per week. Placement agencies include: *Au Pair Austria*, Vermittlungs-agentur in Vienna (+41 01 405 405 0) and Asten (+43 07224 68359; www.aupairaustria.com) which charges a registration fee of €25. Another to try is *Friends Au Pair Vermittlung* (www.aupairvermittlung.at).

# LANGUAGE COURSES AND HOMESTAYS

Deutsch in Graz (+43 316 833 900; www.dig.co.at) can arrange homestays with language courses in Graz and suburbs. The Austrian Education Ministry's organisation *Campus Austria* at the University of Vienna comprises 16 language schools all providing German language training to a high standard. Some courses lead to Goethe Institute qualifications while others lead to the OESD (Austrian diploma for German as a foreign language). Campus Austria publishes a clear pamphlet of the courses on offer and prices, with contact details of its 16 member schools. One of the schools, the ActiLingua Academy (www.actilingua.com) offers some interesting courses including German and Music (in cooperation with the Conservatorium) and German combined with work experience in the Austrian tourism industry for between one and 12 months. Most job opportunities are in Vienna, Salzburg or alpine resorts.

# Part V
# Country guide:
# Worldwide

## AFRICA
## ASIA
## AUSTRALIA AND NEW ZEALAND
## NORTH AMERICA
## LATIN AMERICA

# AFRICA

Like so many gappers, **Angela Clegg** fell in love with Africa (and since she had got married just a month before setting off, she must know a thing or two about falling in love):

> *Africa has something about it, something you instantly fall in love with. The one thing that struck me the most about Tanzania was the local people and their way of life. They are never too busy for you, in fact they had a saying 'poleh poleh in Africa' which means 'slowly slowly in Africa'. To them there is no excuse for a short meet and greet! I honestly thought seeing their lack of resources would devastate me when instead I came back feeling why can't England be like Africa? Why does everyone have so much hostility and no time for each other? I never in a million years thought I would be thinking England should be like Africa.*

Many organisations large and small can assist in setting up a placement in Africa in a Ghanaian orphanage, coaching kids' football in a South African township, assisting a lion project at a Zimbabwean game park or teaching village children in Tanzania.

Conditions can be quite tough and many gap students teaching or working in rural Africa find themselves struggling to cope, whether with the loneliness of life in a rural West African village or with being confronted with the devastation wrought by HIV/AIDS. A certain amount of deprivation is almost inevitable; for example volunteers can seldom afford to shop in the pricey expatriate stores and so will have to be content with the local diet, typically a staple cereal such as millet usually made into a kind of stodgy porridge, plus some cooked greens, tinned fish or meat and fruit. Typically the housing will not have running water or electricity which means that showers consist of a bucket and cup, and toilets are just a hole in the ground. Local customs can come as a shock, for example being treated with something akin to reverence, even though you may feel yourself to be just a naïve school leaver. But the rewards can also be tremendous and any efforts you put in are bound to be appreciated. When **Amelia Cook** started out teaching in a Ghanaian primary school she was bowled over (not just figuratively) by the curiosity of her class:

> *Even our first shaky classes using ideas from our own schools were met with great enthusiasm. Once my class of 45 teenage boys (plus many others who had sneaked in at the back) literally knocked me over in their enthusiasm to see what was in my bag of props for that day's lesson.*

Regional crises also flare up, making volunteering potentially risky. Countries such as Somalia are completely off limits and in recent years conflicts in Kenya, Zimbabwe and Madagascar have resulted the last-minute cancellation of volunteer programmes. Try to research in advance any local issues that may be causing concern. For example news coverage of the Sudan is invariably about the crisis in the Darfur region; however much of the rest of the country is welcoming, safe and friendly, and the long-established *Sudan Volunteer Programme* (SVP) continues its efforts to recruit native English-speaking volunteers to teach English and assist in the effort to restore the use of English as the second official language of Sudan.

The Foreign & Commonwealth Office regularly updates its travel advice for every country in the world and includes risk assessments of current trouble spots. You can contact the Travel Advice Unit by phone on 0845 850 2829 or check the website (www.fco.gov.uk/travel). The warnings need not be taken as gospel (see introductory section on travel warnings for an example, page 37). Often the most useful preparation is to talk to someone who has survived and enjoyed a similar placement in the recent past.

**MATT RIDDELL** was coming to the end of his BTEC National Diploma in Public Services course, when he decided he needed a challenge and fixed up a placement through Travellers:

*'I was motivated to take a gap year by a number of reasons, firstly so that I could do a bit of travelling and see other parts of the world (I had never been further than France before), and I wanted to see other cultures and how they are different to ours, but mostly, I wanted to help others who are in need. On the other hand, there were some issues that I wasn't feeling too good about, for example, I am not the most outgoing person, and I had hardly been away from home before. I wanted to put myself out of my comfort zone and see how I would react and whether or not I could achieve something that later on in life I would be proud to say that I had done.*

*My placement in Zambia was teaching conversational English in a school (Nalituwe Basic School). The school is in a dire state – the ceilings and walls are literally falling down, the majority of the windows are broken, most of the doors are broken. Their light switches were simply a death trap. They just consist of two bare wires hanging out of the wall, and the kids just twist them together. There are not enough desks for the pupils, they sit three to a desk, where two would give them just enough room, some of the desks are broken, and if there are not enough desks, then the pupils who are not sat at a desk either stand throughout the lesson or sit on the windowsill. When I first saw the school, I just felt like breaking down into tears – I was certainly not expecting to see the school like this.*

*During college and the build-up of me going off to Zambia I was fully set on joining the Police Force when I returned. Now, I have realised that there is more to life than just being wrapped up in our own culture, and the feeling of satisfaction that I got from teaching is something that I want to have with me. I am planning on returning to Zambia later on in the year to carry on teaching at the same school, and I am going to look into living out in Zambia as a full-time teacher.'*

Action against the spread of HIV/AIDS in sub-Saharan Africa is a matter of the utmost urgency and a number of agencies are tackling the issue head on, including the well-respected charity *SPW* (*Students Partnership Worldwide*), which sends volunteers to Tanzania, Uganda, South Africa and Zambia.

**Emily Kidson** describes her HIV project in South Africa as tough, since she was thrown in at the deep end and on occasion felt overwhelmed by the magnitude of the task:

*With South Africa as my dream destination the search for a programme was narrowed somewhat and concluded with the aptly named 'Gap Year South Africa Limited'. HIV/AIDS awareness was something I was interested in through studying Geography at A-Level. I attended an HIV conference in my local area in order to get to grips with the basics.*

*The five-week programme incorporated accommodation, some food, airport pick-up, a few activities and daily transportation to the HIV/AIDS awareness programme at Kwa-ford inner city township school. The work proved tougher and less organised than expected, there was poor communication with teachers and the condition of the school left unmentioned for a good reason. Many times we had to think on our feet and just try our best. The children's faces were so expectant but the teachers we were supposed to work with were often absent so it was difficult to know where to start.*

*I do regret not applying for a year's working visa. The opportunities for employment were far greater than expected and a small income would have perhaps prolonged my travels. The highlight has to be doing the highest bungee jump in the world last February 14th at Bloukrans Bridge.*

## SENDING AGENCIES

In addition to SPW, the main year-out agencies such as *Lattitude Global Volunteering* and *Projects Abroad* send volunteers to a range of African countries, primarily South Africa, Ghana, Kenya and Tanzania.

The following organisations also recruit gap year volunteers for Africa, mostly for work in schools and community projects. Most have entries in the 'Directory of Specialist Gap Year Programmes' in the first part of this book.

**Adventure Alternative** (www.adventurealternative.com). One- to three-month programmes for gap year students (among others) in Kenya combining teaching/community work with climbing, trekking, rafting, safaris and independent travel. Participants teach and work in rural or slum schools.

**Africa, Asia & Americas Venture** (www.aventure.co.uk). Places 18–24-year-old volunteers in teaching, sports coaching, community and conservation work experience placements in Kenya, Uganda, Tanzania, Malawi and South Africa, usually for one term. The 2010 participation fee is £3,125 for 4–5 months plus airfares.

**AfricaTrust Networks** (www.africatrust.org.uk). 3- or 6-month residential programmes in Ghana (Cape Coast and Kumasi), Morocco and Cameroon for gap year students and others aged 18–25, to work with needy children and adults.

**Amanzi Travel** (www.amanzitravel.co.uk). Agency in Bristol set up by someone inspired by her own gap year in Africa offering range of mainly short-term volunteering and expedition opportunities in 9 countries.

**Azafady** (www.madagascar.co.uk). 4/8-week Lemur Venture and 10-week Pioneer programmes allow volunteers to work on primate conservation and humanitarian projects at grassroots level in Madagascar. Fundraising target is £1,400/£2,200 for Lemur Venture and £2,000 for Pioneer excluding flights.

**Blue Ventures**, London (www.blueventures.org). Volunteers are needed for at least three weeks to carry out marine research, coral reef conservation and day-to-day management of award-winning marine research programme in South Western Madagascar. Fee for 6 weeks is £2,100 for non-divers; £1,900 for PADI divers.

**KATIE YEWDALL** left Madagascar several years ago, but she says that she still thinks about her time with Blue Ventures on a nearly daily basis:

*I was expecting the beautiful seas, stunning aquatic life, long beaches, quaint huts and friendly, smiling locals (all of which were very much present) but I wasn't expecting quite how much I would learn about myself, what it was like to live another life and, of course, the true meaning of conservation. I thought of myself as someone who was pretty knowledgeable about the natural world and developing countries, but the project in Madagascar was something different altogether. Andavadoaka, where the site is located, is a very typical small African fishing village, with the usual juxtaposition of wooden huts and a couple of 20in televisions (the village 'cinema' where they all loved to gather to watch old kung fu movies!). Being right on the beach, it is obvious how reliant the cash-poor locals are on the marine resources, not only is it an essential food source but marine products are their only source of income. Tragically, the much needed lucrative foreign market may be encouraging the villagers to overexploit their precious resources. They need the ocean for many generations to come but they equally need the money now. I learnt that there is no simple resolution to the problem of conservation.*

*The experience was not free of difficulties; early mornings, boat breakdowns, mundane but necessary cleaning tasks and a lack of chocolate reminded me that I wasn't on a beach holiday, but the feeling part of a research team that was doing valuable work always made up for it. One of the greatest things about the project was opportunity to get as involved as you wanted to be. If you wanted to spend your free time soaking up the sun, you could, but the chance to get further involved with the many research areas was there. The volunteers who threw themselves into the project and didn't wait for the staff to motivate them were the ones who had the most rewarding experience. Chatting to the locals, meeting local people in the village 'bars', and exploring the surroundings made for a very refreshing experience. On the whole, I feel I am a less selfish, more open-minded, motivated and confident person since my return and I would recommend Blue Ventures to anyone.'*

**BUNAC** (www.bunac.org). Runs Work South Africa (up to 12 months), Volunteer South Africa (from 5 weeks) and Volunteer Ghana (2–3 months) programmes. University undergraduates or recent graduates aged 18 or over can have BUNAC's back-up for the duration of their South African working holiday for £720 plus special work permit fee of £40, plus travel and insurance.

**Camps International** (www.campsinternational.com). Gap year placements in rural villages in Kenya and Tanzania (including Zanzibar). Community and wildlife projects followed by trek up Mt Kenya or Kilimanjaro or a scuba diving course.

**Cross-Cultural Solutions** (www.crossculturalsolutions.org). Volunteers work side-by-side with local people in the areas of caregiving, teaching, healthcare and community development to help achieve community-led initiatives. Volunteer opportunities are available in Ghana, Tanzania, South Africa, and Morocco where the one-week Insight Programme is also offered. The programme fee covers lodging and other in-country expenses but not airfares: from £1,449 for 2 weeks to £3,249 for 12 weeks off-peak.

**Dodwell Trust** (www.dodwell-trust.org). Arranges for about 60 volunteers a year to spend 3 weeks to 9 months volunteering in Madagascar.

**Global Vision International (GVI)** (www.gvi.co.uk). Placements from 1–12 months in many countries in Africa including Rwanda, Cameroon and Madagascar.

**The Leap Overseas** (www.theleap.co.uk). Has a variety of volunteering programmes through eastern Africa, which combine working on safari with community and conservation projects. 10-, 6- or 2-week options available based in the Maasai Mara, Okavango Delta, private game reserves, at the beach or on Mt Kilimanjaro. £1,600–£2,900 excluding travel.

**Madventurer** (www.madventurer.com). Madventurer programmes combine overland travel with group projects in rural areas in Uganda, Ghana, Kenya and Tanzania. Most are short-term lasting 2 or 6 weeks.

**MondoChallenge** (www.mondochallenge.co.uk). Volunteer teachers including year-out students but mainly career breakers are sent to projects in three African countries: Tanzania (60 volunteers for projects in Longido, Arusha and Moshi), Gambia and Senegal.

**Operation Wallacea** (www.opwall.com). Marine and forest research projects in Egypt, Madagascar and South Africa from £975. New destination for 2010 Mozambique.

**Quest Overseas** (www.questoverseas.com). 12-week Africa programme with departures from January to April. 6-week voluntary conservation work in Swaziland, community development project in Tanzania, water relief project in Kenya or an orphan community project in Malawi, followed by a 6-week expedition through Mozambique, Botswana and Zambia. £3,900 excluding flights and insurance, plus £850 suggested project donation.

**Reefdoctor.org** (www.reefdoctor.org). Hands-on conservation programme for enthusiastic volunteers to become research assistants for 4, 6, 8 or 12 weeks in Madagascar. Based in Ifaty fishing village, volunteers help to survey the coral reef in the Bay of Ranobe.

**Shumba Experience** (www.shumbaexperience.co.uk) sends gap year students to volunteer on game reserves, veterinary projects, marine placements, wildlife sanctuaries and wildlife research projects, working with conservation professionals in South Africa, Namibia and Botswana.

**Sudan Volunteer Programme** (www.svp-uk.com). Needs volunteers (undergraduates or graduates) to teach English in Sudan for 7 months starting in early September or early January. TEFL certificate and knowledge of Arabic are not required. Volunteers pay for their airfare (from £425) plus initial insurance (£60). Local host institutions pay for living expenses in Sudan; most are in the Khartoum area or in smaller towns in northern Sudan (see first hand account by Chris Milner on page 58).

**Travellers Worldwide** (www.travellersworldwide.com). Teaching placements (English, Maths, Drama, etc.) and Sports Coaching placements in Ghana, Kenya, South Africa and Zambia. Conservation placements with elephants, lions, whales, dolphins, sharks and the other Big Five Game in South Africa, Zimbabwe and Kenya. Professional work experience internships in law, web design, journalism, TV, veterinary, medicine, etc. Placements start from £675 and are available all year round, with flexible start and finish dates.

**VAE Teachers Kenya**, contact addresses in Herefordshire and Gilgil in Kenya (see entry in the 'Directory of Specialist Programmes'; www.vaekenya.co.uk). 6-month gap year placements from January teaching in rural schools in the central highlands of Kenya. No vacancies until 2012.

**Venture Co** (www.ventureco-worldwide.com). Its Kilimanjaro Venture includes time spent at a Swahili language school on the banks of the River Nile in Uganda. The group does 2 aid projects: one in Tanzania working with disadvantaged youngsters south of Lake Victoria, and the other in the foothills of Kilimanjaro helping to conserve the ebony tree. The 2-month expedition takes place in the Great Rift Valley and includes a camel trek, climbing Mt Kenya, the Mountains of the Moon and Kilimanjaro, a safari across the Serengeti and ends on the island of Zanzibar.

**Village Education Project Kilimanjaro** (www.kiliproject.org). Gap year programme that sends a few British students each year to help teach EFL and other subjects in village primary schools in Tanzania for 6–9 months from January. Fee is £3,250.

**Village-To-Village** (www.village-to-village.org.uk). Charity working to reduce poverty in Tanzania which sends volunteers to the Kilimanjaro region to assist on various projects including teaching English in primary schools and orphanages, teacher training as well as construction and sustainable agriculture projects.

**Volunteer Africa** (www.volunteerafrica.org). A UK charity active in Tanzania, working with village projects in the Singida Region of Tanzania and orphanages in Mwanza. Volunteers may join the project for 4, 7 or 10 weeks.

**Volunteer Uganda** (www.volunteeruganda.org/gapyear.html). Newly set-up charity which from February 2010 is recruiting gap year students for 3-month placements starting February and July to live in an enclave in Kirima, Uganda, overlooking the Bwindi impenetrable forest home to 300 mountain gorillas. Gappers will assist in 6 local primary schools that have been built by Volunteer Uganda and its partner charities.

**Zanzigap** (www.zanzigap.com). A new gap specialist that sends young people to teach English and other subjects in secondary schools in Zanzibar. £2,500 fee for 9 months.

**SAMANTHA FULLER** *found the perfect way to end her year out that ticked all the boxes:*

'**A**lthough I was having an amazing time on my year abroad studying in Bordeaux, the itch started again around March and the travelling bug struck. I was due to work in England over the summer before returning to university in Brighton, but I was worried what three months of not speaking any French would do to my level. I had already had a fantastic five months with Projects Abroad in Bolivia during my gap year and a plan started germinating: August, one month, where could I go? And more importantly where could I have an absolutely amazing time while speaking French and getting some teaching experience? MOROCCO!

Projects Abroad is based in Rabat, the capital which is on the coast about a third of the way down. Although Morocco in the summer is very hot, Rabat was a good place to acclimatise as it benefits from the sea breezes and is a little bit cooler (although it was still around 35°C). Rabat itself is a large city, but the majority of volunteers are housed with families who live in the *medina* at its heart. The *medina* is the centre of the old town and is essentially a walled part of the city with meandering (and confusing at first!) side streets and alleys.

I was on a teaching placement in Rabat as I'm considering doing a PGCE after I graduate so I decided this would be the best way to get some actual teaching practice. I was a little worried about how this would go as I literally had no teaching experience, and I won't lie – I did do quite a lot of preparation to start with, but I soon settled into it. I shared classes with another girl, and we all worked at Centre Amal Shabab Takaddoum, a centre which provides internet access, day care for disabled children as well as free language classes in English, German and Spanish. As an English teacher I taught a beginners' class for 1.5 hours in the morning and then a class of upper intermediates from 4pm to 5.30pm. Games like hangman, alphabet races and memory games were always well received.

Overall, I had an amazing time in Morocco. The teaching was at times challenging but the students who turned up to the classes learnt and practised English with native English speakers, which will undoubtedly help them with future studies and job prospects. The Moroccan family

*I lived with were experienced with volunteers and welcomed me into their family. I learnt a lot about Moroccan culture and practices through them. Travelling to different cities at the weekends meant I had a chance to see other parts of Morocco while having a safe base in Rabat.'*

## COURSES AND WORK EXPERIENCE

A few of the main language course organisers can arrange Arabic courses in Morocco, Egypt and the Middle East, for example *Amerispan* (http://study-arabic.amerispan.com). *CESA* offers beginner and more advanced courses in Fez, Morocco for three or six weeks. **Jill Cavanagh** was very happy with the Arabic course that CESA arranged for her in Fez:

*My aim was to gain a basic grounding in Arabic and to learn about Morocco and Islam from being exposed to the culture. I left feeling I had a strong beginning in conversational Arabic. The family I stayed with were very welcoming and supportive. I was invited to join in many family activities and was always offered help with homework, etc. Plus I was fed wonderfully. The downsides are far outweighed by the good aspects of life here. The men aren't that big a deal. Yeah, they hassle you a bit, but you quickly learn how to deal with this, and even though it doesn't go away, you get used to it.*

Other courses of possible interest to year-out students revolve around music and dance. For example it is possible to study drumming at the Academy of Music & Art in Kokrobite not far from Accra in Ghana or on the Senegalese island of Ile de Goree.

*Work Experience International* (WEI, Somerset West, South Africa; +27 (0)21–851 9494; www.gapwork.co.za) arranges unpaid work placements for anyone aged 18–35 in boutique hotels, safari lodges and game reserves in South Africa for at least three months. The pocket money paid and tips earned will not cover the costs of the programme. The fee for three months is £680. Conservation volunteering can also be arranged in Kruger National Park.

Opportunities to do paid work are very limited in Africa although Ghana has a long tradition of welcoming foreign students to participate in its educational and commercial life. Anyone with a diver's certificate might be able to find work at Red Sea resorts like Sharm el Sheikh and Hurghada. If you aren't sufficiently qualified but want to gain the appropriate certificates, the Red Sea is a good place to train. Specialist companies like *Gap Year Diver* (see entry page 390) send gap year students to Egypt. At local dive centres, you can sometimes get free lessons in exchange for filling air tanks for a sub-aqua club.

Vocational placements for aspiring medics and other professionals are arranged by Global Volunteer Projects (www.globalvolunteerprojects.org) in Ghana and Tanzania.

**JONNY STEPHENS** and **RACHAEL BROWN** from Budehaven Community School in Cornwall went in the summer after Year 12 (to avoid delaying entry to medical school) to a hospital placement in Ghana arranged by Global Volunteer Projects. Sixth formers contemplating applying to medicine may want to investigate work placements such as these:

'We figured that if we could get some practical experience of healthcare in a Third World country, this would stand us in really good stead when we started to apply for University places and medical schools. We had both spent time working in hospitals in the UK before we went, and shadowing nurses, GPs, surgeons or consultants, so we were allowed to participate very fully in the life of the Hospital. This was the University of Cape Coast Hospital, a 20-bed unit, with a male and female ward and a small maternity and paediatric unit. We were never idle because we made it very clear that we wanted to be used – some of the girls from other volunteer projects did not fare so well, but, largely because of our experience and our attitude we were always on the wards, rather than doing desk work. We also took our turn on night duty on the wards, which meant you got to do 'vitals' – that is checking patients' blood pressure, pulse, respiratory rate and temperature. The doctors and surgeons were very happy for us to observe operations and to participate in hospital life as fully as was sensible. So we talked to patients, prepped them for operations by shaving them, trolleying them to theatre, staying with them during their op, and taking them back to the ward afterwards. Within hours of going into the hospital on our first day we were allowed to observe a birth by caesarean section, which was a fantastic experience. The two of us were always allowed to follow the doctors on their ward round, and we were encouraged to ask questions and to make comments, so that often we felt that we were being treated as med students, which was strange in some ways, but also very gratifying.'

## GRASSROOTS AND VOLUNTARY ORGANISATIONS

The large majority of volunteers in Africa are trained teachers, doctors, nurses, agricultural and technical specialists who have committed themselves to work with mainstream aid organisations such as *VSO* and *Skillshare Africa* for at least two years.

# Changing Worlds

JAMES PATTERSON remembers his time volunteering in Ghana:

'It was a long journey and heading out on my own was one of the scariest things I had done so far in my life. However arriving in Accra International Airport and meeting my contact, Francis, went smoothly and before long I was on my way to my family house. The journey was not as relaxing as I had hoped as the road was not surfaced and we had a sermon that lasted several hours. However it did start to gear me up for what was to come, and I got my first real shock when I saw a man on the side of the road with no clothes, just standing against a wall crying. We drove straight past and I thought to myself that people must see this all the time and that is why they do not appear to care.

That perhaps gives a bad view of what the people of Ghana were like, yes they were tough and they had to be to survive, but on the other hand I have never been exposed to such a close and intense community spirit. The people really do look out for each other and you see it everyday when someone will help a complete stranger, not because the person has asked for it but because they have noticed that they need help.

My host family was lovely and I instantly felt like part of the family. Once I started working at the school and the orphanage I just got immersed in it all. It was a long day starting at 6am to get to school on time and then finishing at 6pm when all the kids at the orphanage had been fed and were starting to get sleepy, but it was totally worth it.

School was great, the teachers treated me well and I really got into my lessons, making sure math was fun and teaching the kids music before school so they could sing new songs in assembly. We even went on a few school trips to play football and to a dance contest. The orphanage was hard, as I was working with kids ranging from newborn babies to 6 year olds. A lot of them were disabled in some way and everyone's needs were different. Keeping everybody happy all the time was a full time job and I have utmost respect for the women who worked there every day.

It really was an amazing experience and I loved every minute of it. I am not ashamed to say there was a tear in my eye as I left. I will definitely be back to visit all the friends I made. Its a cliché to say the words "life changing experience" but its true in every way and I think the thing I learnt most about in my whole trip was me.'

However openings for unskilled volunteers do exist through smaller charities and indigenous NGOs. It may be possible to offer your services on a voluntary basis to any hospital, school or mission you come across in your travels, though success is not guaranteed. If you have a useful skill and a letter of introduction from a church or family friend, your way will be made smoother.

**Till Bruckner** is a veteran world traveller who has developed a strong preference for fixing up teaching and voluntary placements independently after arrival rather than with the help of an agency:

> *My advice to anyone who wants to volunteer in Africa (or anywhere else) is to go first and volunteer second. That way you can travel until you've found a place you genuinely like and where you think you might be able to make a difference. You can also check out the work and accommodation for yourself before you settle down. If you're willing to work for free, you don't need a nanny to tell you where to go. Just go.*

However, for those who find this prospect daunting (and unless you are a mature and seasoned traveller you probably will), you might like to pursue the middle way which is to make contact with smaller or local organisations in Africa which actively welcome volunteers from abroad. A Cape Town-based agency which offers 'travel work experiences' in a range of countries is *You2Africa* (www.you2africa). The following are listed in alphabetical order by country. Ghana and South Africa have the most highly developed network of projects:

**STAESA** (Students Travel And Exposure South Africa; www.staesa.org). Provides volunteers with work placements in a range of community projects and small-scale industries throughout sub-Saharan Africa. Costs are from $395 for two weeks in Ghana including host family accommodation to $5,000+ for one year in any of the 15 countries in which STAESA has partners.

**ICEYOM (International Centre for Education Youth Orientation and Mobilization)**, c/o Society for Women Empowerment Education & Training (SWEET) Africa, South West Province, Cameroon (iceyom@yahoo.co.uk or rosembone@yahoo.com). Placements for all types of voluntary service including hospitality, conservation, teaching, water and sanitation, community and fundraising throughout Africa, especially Liberia, Ghana, Cameroon and Nigeria. Placement fee €400.

**Ikando** (www.ikando.org). A volunteer and intern recruitment agency based in Accra which deals with education positions lasting up to eight weeks, as well as many others. Volunteers stay in the Ikando house in the centre of Accra and cover their living expenses (£87 per week after their initial fortnight at £481).

**Robbooker Voluntary Organization**, Kumasi, Ghana (www.robborg.org). Service/volunteer projects in Ghana lasting 2–12 weeks or longer. Prices from $350 for 1 month to $950 for 6 months include homestay accommodation with meals.

**RUSO (Rural Upgrade Support Organisation)**, c/o University of Ghana, Accra, Ghana (www.interconnection.org/rap/volunteer_info.html). International volunteers join tree planting, AIDS awareness education, fish farming and other projects especially in the Kome area of Ghana. The cost to volunteers is a $300 registration fee plus $25 per week for stays of 1–3 months or $15 a week if staying 3–6 months.

**WORLDwrite** (www.worldwrite.org.uk). International educational charity that uses documentary film making to investigate global issues. WorldWrite is affiliated with a film academy in Accra, Ghana (www.screenartsghana.org) which takes on occasional foreign volunteers to help organise and market the projects. The Academy is sponsored by IYEP (International Youth Education Program; www.iyep.org), an NGO providing students and young people with intercultural programmes in Ghana, including internships, volunteer positions, semester abroad, high school exchanges and academic placements. Details from Kwame Agyapong in Ghana (+233 24 4998801/233 21 508583; kwamiyep@africaonline.com.gh).

**Inspire Kenya** (www.inspirekenya.com). Range of volunteering opportunities in Kenya. Charity set up by an Englishman.

**Youth for Conservation** (www.youthforconservation.org/volunteers.asp). Opportunities for international volunteers who pay €400 a month to help this Nairobi-based conservation charity.

**Kenya Voluntary & Community Development Project**, *PO Box 554*, Bondo, Kenya (with office in Nairobi International Youth Hostel; www.kvcdp.org). Accept everyone over 18 to work with children, teaching in sustainable agriculture, conservation, etc. in Wagusu/Abimbo village in Bondo District, Nyanza province, Western Kenya. Placement fees from $350 for 2 weeks to $950 for 2 months.

**RIPPLE Africa**, 18 Eden Way, Pages Industrial Park, Leighton Buzzard, Bedfordshire LU7 4TZ (www.rippleafrica.org). A charity working in Malawi, started in 2003 by a British couple, based at Mwaya Beach on the northern shores of Lake Malawi. The charity recruits volunteers to assist in the local nursery, schools, health centre, etc. Variable start dates and lengths of stay. Sample price is £1,350 for 12 weeks which includes accommodation but not local transport or food.

**Soft Power Education**, Jinja, Uganda (+256 774 162541; http://softpowereducation. com). British-registered charity and Ugandan NGO refurbishing government primary schools in Uganda, among other projects. Self-funding volunteers stay for 1 day to 12 months (paying £75 per week).

Some people are apprehensive about living and working close to people living amid such poverty. But the experience is not always negative, as **Simon Preddy** discovered on his gap year:

> *Initially when we first hit our village in Uganda, the kids would come running out of their houses shouting 'mzungo mzungo how are you?' which means 'white man'. By the end of the trip, the kids were running out shouting at white people 'Simone, Kate, how are you?'. Myself and another volunteer called Kate had replaced the word 'mzungo' which really made me feel as though we had truly become a part of the community in those three months.*

*When I think of Africa now, I don't imagine deserts with thin children and no water; I see poverty, but I see immense happiness in that poverty. Ugandans may not have much money, but they have got something much more there than we have here – they have smiles. The bonds of community and family are so much stronger, and it made me wonder what we were missing. In this sense, the best reward from Africa for me was the inspiration to try and find/create those bonds here in the UK. In this sense, Uganda changed my life – I now have a passion for travel, but still have a love for Britain.*

# South Africa

Undaunted by the frightening levels of violent urban crime, many year out and volunteer agencies have programmes in South Africa, the majority of which involve placing volunteers in orphanages or special schools. For paid work it will be necessary to obtain a work permit available to students. *BUNAC*'s Work South Africa programme is run in partnership with the South African Student Travel Services (www.sasts.org.za). The 12-month work permit is available to full-time university students under 30 of any nationality or those who have graduated in the past six months. The programme fee is £720 plus flights, special work permit (currently £40) and insurance. Participants are allowed to take any job they can find. BUNAC warns that finding a job can be tough, though easier in the high season between October and March. BUNAC also runs a series of ambitious volunteer programmes ranging from five weeks (£999) to 33 weeks (£2,699) excluding visa and flights to Cape Town. Departures are year-round. One of the advantages of being attached to a school is that most gap year volunteers are free to travel during school holidays. Many in South Africa choose to do the Garden Route or explore the Cedarberg mountain range. Post-placement travel destinations include Victoria Falls in Zimbabwe, Botswana (with its Okavango Swamps) and Namibia.

**African Conservation Experience** (www.ConservationAfrica.net). Sends people to game and nature reserves in southern Africa where they do conservation work with rangers and conservationists and get first-hand experience of animal and plant conservation. The total cost is £5,220 for 12 weeks including airfares from London (see 'Directory of Specialist Gap Year Programmes' and first-hand account in section on 'Expeditions' below).

**Worldwide Experience** (www.WorldwideExperience.com). Strives to conserve what humans are fast destroying by supporting conservation and community projects through the recruitment of volunteers. Placements South Africa, as well as Kenya and Malawi, might include anything from cheetah tracking to teaching a class of children about conservation.

**Willing Workers in South Africa (WWISA)** (www.wwisa.co.za). A community service volunteer organisation based in The Crags, near Plettenberg Bay. Whatever their age and skills, volunteers work on projects alongside local villagers according to their interests, options and available dates, in the areas for example of schooling

# Worldwide Experience

*One gapper remembers his time in South Africa with Worldwide Experience:*

'I went out to Shamwari Game Reserve with Worldwide Experience for four weeks throughout March, and I have to say, it was one of the best experiences of my life. I got to see, and experience, so much it is hard to talk about just a few occurrences, and I would recommend this placement to anyone.

During my stay we were lucky enough to help with the relocation of five elephants who were being moved to Shamwari's sister reserve; Sanbona, near Cape Town. We woke up early at 4am and got to see the beautiful South African sunrise - quite a sight. When we arrived we pulled up alongside some trucks with massive containers on the back, and they reminded me of Jurassic Park. Elephants are very heavy, so once they were darted the only way to move them into the containers was by using a crane, which was a very odd sight. The tranquilliser only works for so long, so once we got all the elephants in the truck we moved quickly, helping close the doors as speedily as possible - it was very exciting!

The conservation team also got us involved in the darting of a black rhino. We got up early again, but after four hours of searching all over the 25,000 hectares, we could not find him, and we were all in agreement that he was hiding exceptionally well. However, we did manage to locate a mother and baby. All rhinos are ear notched so the rangers can tell them apart and keep track of all of them, so the vets darted the pair of them and got to work. It was really exciting as they wake up pretty quickly and it's quite an adrenaline rush having the rangers call out to you saying "quick she's waking up".

The vets on Shamwari also had to do surgery on two leopards, as they needed monitoring devices used for telemetry implanted, and we got to observe! I cannot think of one minute at Shamwari when I wanted to be somewhere else. From the moment I arrived I had the most incredible time, met amazing people and had so much fun. From rhino monitoring to erosion control, from fishing to watching a lion being darted, everyday presented a fantastic new experience. I enjoyed my time at Shamwari immensely and would go back as soon as possible if I could.'

and education, youth development, business development, healthcare and environmental research. Programmes are geared to the social and economic enhancement of the local rural community of Kurland Village. Prices should be checked on the website:

Volunteer sports coaches, recreation leaders and sports organisers over 20 are placed in rural or urban communities for 6–12 months from January or July. Further details of this programme are available from *SCORE/Sports Coaches' Out-Reach* (see 'Directory of Volunteering Abroad' entry).

**All Out Africa** (www.alloutafrica.com/volunteers). With offices in Swaziland, Mozambique and South Africa, All Out Africa offers a broad range of volunteer programmes in those countries.

# TOURISM

Cape Town is the tourist capital of South Africa including for backpackers, though jobs are harder to find here than elsewhere. Furthermore the job hunt is made much harder by the competition from a large number of Zimbabwean exiles who are willing to accept low wages.

**Roger Blake** made extensive use of South Africa's youth hostels and several times was able to extend his stay by working for his keep:

> There are more than 100 hostels in South Africa, many of which 'employ' backpackers on a casual basis. Within two weeks of arrival I was at a hostel in George on a work-for-keep basis. Through contacts made here I also sold T-shirts at the beach for a small profit and I did a few days at a pizza place for tips only. Then I was offered a job at a hostel in Oudtshoorn (Backpackers Oasis). They gave me free accommodation and 150 rand a week to run the bar and help prepare the ostrich braai (BBQ) that they have every evening. Also I did breakfasts for fellow travellers which was like being self-employed as I bought all the ingredients and kept all the profit. It was a small but worthwhile fortune after six weeks here.

Although Johannesburg is often maligned as a big, bad, city, it is the earning capital of South Africa with better job possibilities than many other places. The areas to head for restaurant and pub work are Sandton and Rosebank and the northern suburbs to which hostels like the Ritz now in Dunkeld West (www.backpackers-ritz.co.za) have moved. The backpackers' travel website backinafrica.com includes a Jobs Offered and Jobs Wanted forum (more of the latter than former).

# CONSERVATION AND WILDLIFE

An increasing number of companies and eco-tourism operations are marketing the South African wilderness to gap year students (and others) as a place to learn skills and see big game. The *African Conservation Trust* (www.projectafrica.com) is a South

African based trust that recruits self-funding volunteers to staff environmental research projects in South African national parks, Malawi, and others.

The *Tembe Elephant Park* in Maputaland in north-east KwaZulu-Natal near the Mozambique border, is home to more than 200 African elephants plus some black rhino, white rhino, buffalo, hippo, lion, leopard and various antelope species. Tembe welcomes gap year volunteers who pay £175 per week. They can participate in lion and leopard monitoring, teaching in local schools and other projects (+27 31 267 0144; www.gap-year-south-africa.org).

The *South African National Foundation for the Conservation of Coastal Birds* (*SANCCOB*) requires volunteers to help with the cleaning and rehabilitation of oil-soaked birds since oil pollution is a major problem in the coastal waters of South Africa. Volunteers must pay a joining fee of R1,000 and fund their own living expenses for at least six weeks (www.sanccob.co.za).

*Wild at Heart* in KwaZulu-Natal (see entry in 'Directory of Volunteering Abroad') offers research opportunities with lions and elephants, equine care and conservation with horses; and hands-on opportunities to work with species such as lions, cheetah and other wild animals at rehabilitation centres in Africa. *Kwa Madwala* Private Game Reserve has a 10-week gap year programme near the Kruger National Park (see entry in 'Directory of Specialist Gap Year Programmes').

**DANIELLE THOMAS** joined Kwa Madwala from January to March, funded by a family legacy and with the money she had saved grape-picking during the vendange earlier in her gap year (see France chapter). Although there was a strong conservation education component, the placement also had elements of an adventure holiday.

*'K wa Madwala is definitely an ideal place for gappers to go. The programme includes learning about the animals and nature but also includes a lot of travelling. It's a very adventurous programme and is very challenging both physically and mentally, as you live in close proximity with 10–20 people for an extended period. It teaches you so much about life and yourself.*

*The days varied a lot and there was no real schedule. Most days we woke up at 6 o'clock so that we could go on a game walk or game drive, before it got too hot. After that we would have some leisure time or we would* have activities planned such as archery, shooting, bush clearing, astronomy lessons, micro lighting, lectures, tree identifications or interaction time with the two domesticated elephants on the Kwa Madwala Game reserve. During the middle of the day we took it quite easy as it was incredibly hot nearing 40°C which made working conditions very tough.

We also learned how to identify 40 different trees. On the reserve, we baited hyenas, did road maintenance, climbed koppies (small hills rising from the African veld), did bush clearing, hikes, had lectures about the animals for instance from a bird expert. We travelled with Kwa Madwala to Mozambique for 5 days to the unspoilt beaches where we did whale-shark diving and relaxed on the beaches and some of us body boarded. Also we went to Sabie, which is an adventure resort where we went abseiling, bridge swinging, tubing, kloofing and caving. Then we spent five days in Kruger National Park which was amazing, there was such an abundance of game. We also did a three-day hike where we also rode wild horses, and another weekend we spent at Badplas where we did various watersports, such as waterskiing, tubing, fishing and rafting. For anyone who loves an adventure, I would highly recommend it.'

Another volunteer placement company is *AVIVA* (*Africa Volunteering & Ventures Abroad*) in Cape Town (www.aviva-sa.com). Its range of placements includes working with AIDS orphans, helping out at an alternative tourist lodge and working in Kruger National Park.

# EXPEDITIONS

The African continent hosts a huge variety of scientific and conservation expeditions and most interests can be accommodated, from measuring the height of waterfalls in Lesotho to tracking warthogs in a Ghanaian national park. If by any chance you know someone doing a PhD on a relevant African subject, you might be able to persuade him or her of your usefulness. But most gap year students will join a more formal expedition, either one organised through a university or the Royal Geographical Society or one set up by an expedition society such as *BSES*.

With *Frontier* (www.frontier.ac.uk) volunteers spend two weeks or more on projects in the forests, savannah and marine habitats and rural villages of Madagascar, Tanzania, Kenya, Cameroon, Ghana, Uganda and Egypt. Projects involve working to save whales and dolphins, tracking lions and building rural schools. Volunteers can get BTEC, TEFL and PADI qualifications on many projects.

## Africatime Travel

LAURA remembers her time volunteering with Africatime Travel:

'I spent five weeks in South Africa, with the Dolphin and Whale Project working as a volunteer. I travelled with Africatime Travel (Hands-on Holidays) and was treated extremely well indeed. My itinerary was met 100% and then some, and my travels were made extremely easy, comfortable, and pleasurable. Africatime Travel is a Tour Company with a personal difference.

From the minute I signed for my Hands-on Holiday all I had to arrange was my international flights and the rest was done for me including: plush accommodation for the lay over; internal flights; taxi transfers to the door of my new house; even my meals were seen to.

At the house I shared an en-suite room with just two other people. Again I was never hungry as my needs were seen to by our lovely cook/housekeeper, who also did our washing and generally looked after us.

Daily activities at the project consisted of: boat trips to watch the whales and seals (weather permitting); collecting mussels and prawns for the fish and turtles at the aquarium; feeding the turtles; beach clean ups; river monitoring; tree planting. I also got the chance to help out at the local leopard and penguin parks. A major part of the program is education. Regular visits to the local township schools to help out and teach them about conservation proves very rewarding.

Opportunities for individual research projects are available and welcomed. These projects can range from looking at whale sounds and recordings to studying a rare, local seahorse.

The day is always broken up, and the activities varied, so there is not much chance of you getting bored. The weekends are your own with plenty of tourist things to do like visiting elephants, skydiving, surfing, sea kayaking, visiting monkey parks, and for the real crazy people, the tallest bungee jump in the world! Or you can simply enjoy the views, do a bit of shopping, or grab ice cream or coffee in town.

The team are great and the programmes ideally suited for someone new to the conservation lifestyle and maybe just wanting to get a feel for the marine based conservation.

My thoroughly enjoyable experience was made very easy and stress free. Africatime are the perfect travel company.'

**EMILY LOGIE** was planning to study for a degree in veterinary medicine and was therefore keen to gain work experience and work with animals during her gap year:

'When I found African Conservation Experience (A.C.E.), I was drawn to the range of projects and how involved I could get with the veterinary side of conservation. So on January 5th 2009 I flew to South Africa to split my time between four A.C.E. conservation projects, each teaching me valuable lessons and introducing me to amazing people from all over the world. I worked as the only volunteer at Hanchi Conservation Project, a game management scheme directed from horseback. My equine veterinary skills were immediately put to the test, tackling tick-related hoof infections and helping a youngster through African horse sickness. On the next phase I hand-reared caracal (African lynx) kittens and was responsible for the care of three mischievous lion cubs.

I spent the next three weeks living in the contrasting world of 'Tuli Conservation Project', an isolated bush camp in the heart of the wilderness of Botswana. Without the safety of South African's reserve fences, electricity or even running water, I learnt to appreciate the simple things in life and racked up my knowledge of the southern hemisphere's star constellations, learnt to recognise hundreds of bird calls, game tracks and the behaviour of elephants in life-threatening situations. Work at Tuli was real conservation, sometimes monitoring game 24 hours at a stretch, forcing me into a love of coffee. Food rationing taught me the hard way that it is possible to live off only avocados, eggs and beef and that a lantern lit shower under the stars is the perfect end to any day.

My last fortnight took me by surprise when I was asked to join a busy game capture team and to promote A.C.E. on international television. Thrown into a world of dangerous physical capture, long-distance trucking and instructions in Afrikaans, I quickly had to find my feet before a Norwegian television crew arrived to film the team's work and follow us and our game movements all over the country. When not on the road I found myself living with the game capture vet. As the only other female and English speaking member of the team I quickly became her trusted assistant and firm friend. I learned to fear nothing, act on instinct and wear the same clothes day after day for the purpose of film editing.

> *From bungee jumping down a waterfall to a well earned chopper flight with one of the country's best capture pilots, no two days were the same and I was taught to expect the unexpected, sleep when the opportunity arises and I realised that nothing in life is perfect apart from nature.'*

When exploring the African bush always take the necessary precautions proffered by locals, rangers and other old hands, to avoid what happened to a round-the-world Australian cyclist (nicknamed Locky) whom **Mark Nash** from Cambridge met on his travels:

*The story goes that in the middle of the night, near Archers Post, a town in Kenya surrounded by national reserves, Locky was woken up by movement outside his tent. Thinking it was someone messing with his bike, he unzipped his tent in a sleepy haze and shouted out to scare away the intruder. I've heard you can scare a lion away if you act fierce enough, well I'm guessing Locky must not have been that fierce, because the lion, startled, immediately jumped on the tent with Locky inside. After a few frantic moments for Locky at the bottom and a few frustrating claws and bites, the lion was confused by the tent 'prey', jumped off, grabbed one of Locky's panniers and disappeared into the bush. Locky decided he should put his tent back together as best he could, glad that it had proved itself lion-proof(ish). He was just crawling in when he heard a noise behind him. Finding no food in the bag, the still-hungry lion had been attracted by noises coming from the tent it thought it had vanquished earlier. In Locky's words: 'I was inside the entrance of the tent facing out shitting myself. The lion was about 5m away, approaching slowly this time. As it walked towards me, I aimed the small can of pepper spray I carried which I had got out after the first attack and, not having used it before, managed to spray the first lot just above my right eye! About 2m away now, my second spray got the lion right in the face. It stopped, shook its head a couple of times, sneezed or something, turned around and left.*

Even more frightening and potentially lethal was the experience of 18-year-old **Grace Forster** whose diving group on Tanzania's Pemba Island near Zanzibar was attacked by machete-wielding bandits who robbed the group of thousands of dollars and put Grace in hospital, though she made a full recovery.

But most trips and expeditions are safe and peaceable including into the deserts of North Africa. Just after A-Levels, **Anna Ling** spent the summer in Morocco living on a daily budget of €4. While she was staying in Marrakesh and Essaouira, she came across a true working holiday opportunity. Tour companies that organise trips into the Sahara ask long-stayers to round up a group of at least eight people and then take you along for free. Anna felt this would have been perfectly possible, since up to half of backpackers join one of these 4–5 day tours (which cost £100) and include a camel ride, food and accommodation. Unfortunately she had to leave to meet a friend in Spain.

# Ticket to Ride

Join **Ticket to Ride** on a gap year surfing adventure and take full advantage of a unique opportunity to combine world-class surf coaching with responsible travel enabling you to put something back into the local community. Depending on the course you choose, there is the chance to become internationally qualified as a Surf Instructor and Beach Lifeguard. (No previous surfing experience is necessary.)

*Ticket to Ride Gap Year Courses Include:*

**TTRide South Africa:** Combine learning to surf with community development in local township whilst training to become internationally qualified as Surf Instructor and Surf Lifesaver.

**TTRide Costa Rica:** Combine learning to surf with learning to speak Spanish whilst helping out at the local school.

**TTRide Mozambique:** Experience the ultimate surf adventure along one of Africa's hidden coastlines (TTRide Mozambique is also recommended as an add on to the TTRide South Africa course).

**TTRide season2season:** Combine a summer surf season with a winter ski/snowboard season and experience the ultimate Ticket to Ride.

**TTRide Volunteer Placements:** Help the Ticket to Ride Foundation with its work to change the lives of young children in South African townships through sport and education.

If you are planning on going straight to university check out **TTRide MiniGaps** for shorter alternatives.

For more information check out www.ttride.co.uk or contact them directly tel: 0208 7888 668; email: info@ttride.co.uk or write to Ticket to Ride Head Office, 263 Putney Bridge Road, London SW15 2PU.

# ASIA

Lumping together places as different as Java and Japan, Hong Kong and Ho Chi Minh City is a dangerous business. The gap year experiences of the student who spends six months in Singapore because her uncle can arrange a job for her in his export business may have almost nothing in common with those of the gap year volunteer who teaches at a village school in Nepal. Different corners of the vast continent of Asia beguile individuals for personal and possibly inexplicable reasons. Perhaps a childhood book, acquaintance or memory has bequeathed a longing to visit a faraway and mysterious place. This may not be the kind of reason which cuts much ice with college admissions tutors but it can be what sparks incredible and memorable experiences.

There are dangers in spending time at a young age in a seriously alien country. This is true of Bolivia, Zambia or even Romania but somehow the culture shock which gap year travellers experience in the Indian subcontinent or in a small industrial Chinese town is especially acute. A novelty-seeking foreigner is not really what a struggling village in Bengal or Borneo most needs. Preconceptions about what benefits you will be able to bring are often proved misguided in the first week. **Andy Green** spent a couple of weeks with a long-established voluntary organisation in India: '*I feel that I was of no help to Indian society whatsoever. Due to differences in climate, food and culture, it is difficult to be productive. I could have paid an Indian a few pounds to do what I did in two weeks. It was, however, an experience I'll never forget.*' In other words, the experience is bound to benefit you, the gap year traveller, but its value to local people may be questionable. That is not to say that a six-month attachment to a school or orphanage will not be valuable for the local community, but its value might lie in unexpected places.

The climate is not a trivial concern. Although **Robert Abblett** had carefully planned his trip to India and had the addresses of organic farms where he intended to work, he had not counted on the debilitating heat and decided to enjoy a holiday instead. This is an alternative worth considering, i.e. to make your fortune at home or in a Western country, whether as an accountancy trainee in England, chambermaid in Switzerland or tomato picker in Australia, in order to finance months of leisurely travel in the developing countries of Asia.

Culture shock and disorientation will be an inevitable part of the process. **Christina Hall** was more amused than frustrated by her first bewildering few weeks in India: '*The main problem lies in the auto-rickshaw drivers; you tell them "I want to go to xyz" and they wobble their heads like dashboard buddies and I assumed this means yes. Often it does, but sometimes it means "Well, I vaguely know that this place is in Chennai. Let's go on an adventure and see if we can find it and I'll try and overcharge you for the privilege of getting lost with me and then I'll drop you off at the street next to where you started."*'

Of course the kinds of adjustment you will need to make will be quite different in the countries of Asia with developed or rapidly developing economies, principally Japan, Taiwan, Korea, China, the Hong Kong Special Administrative Region and Singapore.

Special schemes permit pre- and post-university students to work in some of these countries, mainly as teachers of the English language.

## GAP AGENCIES

Almost all the key gap organisations make placements in a number of Asian countries. India and Thailand are probably the most popular destinations, though opportunities exist throughout the continent. To give a taste of the range of choices, *Travellers* (www. travellersworldwide.com) organises teaching placements (IT, music, maths, arts and crafts, drama) in Brunei, Cambodia, China, India, Sri Lanka, Thailand and Malaysia; hands-on conservation placements working with orangutans, elephants, pandas, monkeys, marine life, etc. in Malaysia, Sri Lanka and Cambodia; professional work experience internships in law, medicine, care, media and journalism in China, India, Sri Lanka and Malaysia; and sports coaching placements in India, Sri Lanka and Malaysia. Asian placements start from £695 and are available all year round with flexible start and finish dates. Some gap-sending organisations specialise in one destination such as *Starfish Venture* for Thailand and *Gap Guru* for India (though the latter has recently expanded its range of countries). Gap Guru offers an interesting range of projects in India such as working at a software company and helping at a crocodile sanctuary.

**IMMA RAMOS** was delighted to win first prize in a gap year essay-writing contest sponsored by Gap Guru, which funded six months of voluntary work in India plus a 10-day travel option:

*I chose to stay in Delhi for a month because I was attracted to the city and also the chance to intern at a charitable children's publishing company which also runs a school for disadvantaged children. Later I spent over a month in Kochi (Kerala) because I wanted to work as a reporter and trainee editor for a national newspaper, and also three months at a school in Chennai attended by many children from fisher folk families who were affected by the tsunami.*

*I love writing about art so I soon took on the role of art critic on the newspaper placement. It was a very exciting internship as I had to be proactive and go to the latest exhibition openings where I interviewed the artists and wrote about the shows. I accompanied the senior photographer on some of his projects too, which was fantastic – we travelled around on his motorbike! I stayed with lovely Indian families who were incredibly welcoming and generous. Whereas in Delhi we usually ate dal, alu gobi, vegetable curry, rice and naan bread, in Kochi the food was very different – dosas and coconut chutneys. I loved it!*

*A few days after arriving in India I went on the Gap Guru Himalayan trip with a fellow volunteer, from Manali to Keylong to Leh. Visiting Buddhist monasteries and passing through awe-inspiring mountainous landscapes was a magical experience. It was such an incredible trip and a great way to start my gap year. After my placement finished I spent a month travelling around Rajasthan with a group and just before taking my flight home from Mumbai, I fulfilled my ambition of seeing the Ajanta and Ellora caves. Travelling and absorbing such diverse cultures was enormously stimulating both visually and intellectually. In my first week I missed home but after a month I didn't want to come back!'*

If you want to spend time in a less well-travelled country of Asia, it will be necessary to sift through the literature of all the relevant organisations to find which ones (if any) offer what you are looking for, for example *Coral Cay Conservation* has projects in the Philippines, *Travellers* in Brunei, *Raleigh* in Sabah-Borneo, *Lattitude* in Vanuatu and Fiji, and *Outreach International* sends people to Cambodia to teach English, computing, art, etc.

## EXPEDITIONS AND CONSERVATION

The mainstream London-based conservation expedition organisers all run projects in Asia. These expeditions are usually open to anyone reasonably fit who can raise the cost of joining (typically £2,500–£3,000; see 'Directory of Specialist Gap Year Programmes' for further details):

**Coral Cay Conservation** (www.coralcay.org). Recruits volunteers to assist with reef and tropical forest surveys in the Philippines and Cambodia to help protect some of the world's most diverse tropical environments. Full training in marine and terrestrial ecology is provided.

**Frontier** (020 7613 2422; www.frontier.ac.uk). Volunteers can spend 4, 8, 10 or 20 weeks on reef diving projects in Fiji (10 weeks from £2,495) or on teaching and many other projects in Cambodia, Thailand, India, Nepal, Mongolia, China and Indonesia; most cost £895 for 4 weeks plus £150 per extra week.

**Global Vision International (GVI)** (www.gvi.co.uk). Placements from 3 weeks to 1 year. Wildlife and community work in Thailand, Laos, Nepal, Sri Lanka, etc. and conservation work including with orangutans in Sumatra and turtles in Vanuatu. Prices from about £995 for 4 weeks.

# Outreach International

LAURA BROWN remembers her time in Mexico at a special needs school and disabled children's centre:

'It is difficult to find the words to describe life in Mexico volunteering with Outreach International. Everyday is like a new adventure full of amazing sights, sounds and feelings. Small cobbled streets unsuitable for cars, stray dogs everywhere, pick up-trucks full to the brim with Mexican men on their way to work, children playing in the streets and restaurants selling the most amazing food.

We were picked up from the airport and taken to stay at a Mexican family's home. Our first week was an experience; we washed outside under the stars and spent a lot of time eating tortillas! The family spent time teaching us Spanish and taking us to the river to swim. Then in the evenings we would listen to Mexican music, dance and drink the family's home brewed tequila. You can't really get more Mexican than that!

I worked at the disabled children's centre. The children receive food, drink, physiotherapy treatment and lots of love. It really is an amazing place run by volunteers and completely reliant on donations. While I was there I helped to set up a new project at a local special needs school. This involved running PE classes for all of the children. They have never had any form of physiotherapy or PE at the school so the staff and children were very grateful for our input. We were usually greeted at the gate with beautiful flowers for our hair and lots of kisses! Resources are so limited that myself and another volunteer went out to buy new equipment ourselves. In England parachutes are used a lot in schools for PE so we made one! The children absolutely loved it and we are so proud to have been able to give them something they can keep and continue to use in the future.

Working life has been good but it is difficult to accept the conditions that the children live in, and the poor access to services. It is very challenging but the rewards gained from making the children laugh, building relationships with them and seeing them improve far outweighs the negatives. In addition I could pass my knowledge onto the members of staff that work at the centres. It made me feel like we were building towards a better future for these children. It really doesn't take a lot to make a small difference, and hopefully enough small differences can make a big change in the future.'

***Gapforce*** (020 7384 3343; www.gapforce.org). Volunteers are sent to assist in panda conservation and teaching placements in China, to work in orphanages in India, conservation projects in Thailand or medical placements in Cambodia. Volunteer researchers can join coral reef surveys in Fiji. Training is given in the UK and in the host country. Gapforce also works in Nepal's Chitwan National Park assisting local people with reforestation, etc. Instruction in Nepali language is given in Kathmandu and there is an opportunity to climb to Everest Base Camp.

***Operation Wallacea*** (01790 763194; www.opwall.com). Volunteer students, divers and naturalists assist with surveys of marine and rainforest habitats on remote islands of south-west Sulawesi in Indonesia. Dive training can be given and land surveys for studying birds and mammals also organised.

***Orangutan Foundation*** (020 7724 2912; www.orangutan.org.uk). Volunteers are based in Kalimantan, Indonesian Borneo and participate in hands-on conservation fieldwork for six weeks. Volunteers must note that there is no direct work with orangutans, although wild and/or rehabilitated orangutans will be in the vicinity where volunteers work.

**SADIE BROWN** wanted to see the world before proceeding to Chichester University to study Performing Arts. She was impressed with the credentials of the Orangutan Foundation, which is a registered charity:

*'The project in Borneo was part of a long-term conservation effort for maintaining the forest, which is currently being destroyed for palm oil plantations, logging and mining, taking with it a lot of the wildlife. We worked with a local NGO who concentrated on educating communities about maintaining their forest, as it would benefit them as well as the wildlife. We worked in a village where, apart from one other person, we were the first Westerners to go there! There, we built a dam in the forest to get the villagers fresh water to drink; we then built them two cesspit toilets in an effort to make their washing more hygienic. From our efforts we hope that if loggers who want to take over their land approach them they will decline the offer.*

*The highlight has to be working with the locals in the village in Borneo – population about 50. It was a one-street village. Their enthusiasm for work and gratitude were so enlightening. Volunteering abroad is such a great experience, which I recommend to travellers, especially if you are looking to do something different with your gap year and to gain valuable experience. It is a totally unique experience, which you will not forget; it is so fulfilling as well, to do something that is making a difference in a developing country, even if it is a very small difference. My experiences on these projects make me want to return to the places I worked in and see all the villagers again.*

*I was also so glad to have the opportunities to see orangutans in Borneo as they are amazing animals and it was truly heartbreaking to see the ones in the care centre, which were injured from having their habitat torn down by humans. I found it hard to deal with emotionally, as they have 97% the same genetics as humans, yet some people believe they just do not deserve any rights. It is a good and bad thing about volunteering, you see the harsh reality, and it's a real eye opener but drives you to help fight against it all.'*

**Raleigh** (020 7183 1270; www.raleighinternational.org) is an established youth and education charity that arranges for 17–24 year olds to take on challenging environmental, community and adventure projects as part of 5- or 10-week programmes. Projects range from the installation of water systems for remote communities to learning about the biodiversity of Malaysia's rainforests. Raleigh also runs expeditions in India, based in Karnataka in the Western Ghats region, one of the world's most bio-diverse hotspots. **Olivia Hayward** describes the community projects she worked on, building 10 composting toilets in the remote village of Hosekerasunda:

*I hate being a tourist, and this definitely wasn't for tourists. It was a wonderful introduction to Indian culture; we lived in their school, ate the food they cooked for us, swam in the reservoir every day, learned some Kannada (the local language) and had a fantastic time.*

**Venture Co Worldwide** (www.ventureco-worldwide.com). Himalayan Venture offers an expedition that lasts 12 weeks and incorporates a 17-day expedition to Everest Base Camp as well as participating in community and conservation projects after undergoing cultural orientation in Delhi. It also offers an Indochina Venture.

# VentureCo Worldwide

Stephanie McCullough remembers her time volunteering in Zambia with VentureCo:

"*You're going to spend a month in a refugee camp? Why?*" asked the lady at Zambian Passport Control, with wide, questioning eyes.

I told her: "*Because it's different to anything I've ever done before...*"

I'd never been to Africa, and prior to the trip I was filled with nervous anticipation. Being a trainee teacher, I knew I could handle spreading a love of books and reading to children, but I worried about what the people of Meheba Refugee Settlement would think of our group of western do-gooders.

Entering Zambia, I watched the country roll by, children running and waving, colourful clothing and the dusty shades of orange and yellow. Meheba defied all my expectations. A vast scrubland, dotted with towering termite hills, it was divided into spacious plots for the refugee families. Although we felt every bit the white strangers, everyone was incredibly friendly, curious and welcoming. They came from all over Africa, and though they possessed little, they did not complain. Each had a story to tell. One man, who taught himself English from a dictionary he carried under his arm, had lived in the camp for 25 years, and hoped to write a book about his experiences. A 13 year-old girl shared her story of pain and violence with me, but ended with her eyes glistening with hope.

During the day, we worked with groups of children in classroom corners or outside in the sun. We shared our favourite childhood books and created hats, masks, stories and drawings. I've never met children more eager to learn. Together we chased the Gingerbread Man, invited the Tiger to tea, and bounced my inflatable globe. Even the teenage boys gathered around to hear the children's stories.

Camp life took some adjustment, with its tents, long-drop toilet, and bucket shower in the trees. We spent the evenings playing games, star-gazing on top of termite hills, watching the local football match, and occasionally battling vast armies of ants. In our spare time we helped build a school kitchen as most of the locals stood by watching. Apparently, TIA (This is Africa).

Travelling with VentureCo and The Book Bus proved an incredibly emotional experience. It hurt to leave, and someday I hope to return. Not for the sunsets or the landscapes, but for the people. Meheba was different to anything I've ever experienced, but it strengthened my feeling that we are all essentially the same. I recommend the experience to everyone.

## CAUTION

So many gap year travellers and other backpackers are wandering around India, Nepal and Thailand that it can be a challenge to get away from them (assuming that is your ambition). Although it is a good idea to try to step off the well-worn path between Goa, Kathmandu and Ko Samui, it may be unwise to stray too far from the beaten track. During his year out, **Joel Emond** from Bristol was travelling alone in north-east China. Unwittingly he wandered out of a national park mentioned in his guidebook and into North Korea where he was instantly arrested and put in jail. The Korean authorities contacted the British Embassy in Beijing to confirm that Joel was not a spy. Unfortunately, they got his name wrong and requested information about Joe Lemond. After several weeks, someone in Beijing twigged and the problem was resolved but not before Joel had gone on hunger strike in protest at the vile diet of rotten cabbages.

One way of exploring Asia in a protected environment is to join an overland tour such as those offered by *Exodus* (www.exodus.co.uk) or *Intrepid Travel* (www.intrepidtravel. com) which runs shorter and longer adventure trips in Asia. After volunteering for an orangutan project in Borneo (see above), **Sadie Brown** joined a 30-day tour (July/August 2009) with *GAP Adventures* through Cambodia, Vietnam and Laos: '*Prior to that I travelled on my own from Singapore to Bangkok, for that I had advice from friends. I think the lowest point of my gap year was the frustration of travelling alone, which is why I was happy to be on the 30-day tour! It took away all those worries. The cost of the tour at first seemed quite steep [currently £869 plus food kitty of $450], but I feel it was all worth it as the transportation, accommodation and tour leader were all brilliant.*'

# TEACHING

Throughout Asia thousands of people of all ages are eager for tuition in English. Native English speakers, whatever their background, are wanted to meet that demand and school leavers can find voluntary placements in a range of countries. It can be a daunting prospect standing in front of a class of eager learners when you are just 18. Most teaching will be of conversational English rather than grammar. Several of the sending agencies insist that you do a short TEFL training course beforehand.

Paid teaching work is available primarily to people who have a university degree. Most commercial language school directors are looking for teachers who are older than 18 and who have finished university. In the case of Korea and Japan, a BA or BSc is virtually essential for obtaining the appropriate visa. Teaching English in Japan is one of the classic jobs for people filling a gap in their lives (see next section).

The situation is different on the Indian sub-continent where very few private English language schools exist. Many gap students find themselves attached to schools, and sometimes with a rather indeterminate role – as **Lizzi Middleton's** story below illustrates it can be just as enriching an experience as teaching English or anything concrete.

**LIZZI MIDDLETON'S** placement in India involved teaching English in a rather unexpected setting.

'N ot quite believing that I was embarking on what was to be the biggest adventure of my life so far, I arrived in Delhi and a few days later caught a 15-hour overnight bus to McLeodganj in north-west India, seat of the Tibetan government in exile and home of His Holiness the Dalai Lama. It was a further hour's hair raising bus journey down into the valley to my placement at the Jamyang Choeling Himalayan Institute for Buddhist women. The nunnery is in a very secluded area of the countryside, set in front of the stunning backdrop of the snow-capped foothills of the Himalayas. It was unbelievably picturesque and was a welcome relief after the madness of Delhi!

Finding out what we were meant to be doing, and where we were meant to be was our first major challenge. Tibetans are notoriously vague – we had been warned about this but it was vague on a level that I've never experienced vague before! This was one of the real cultural differences that I had to adapt to. Having just completed my A-Levels and the careful structuring of time that they had required, and coming from a family where we always let each other know where we are, life at Jamyang Choeling was quite a change. I had to learn to be very easy going, to not mind when a class just didn't turn up or when there was only half a class there.

My classes were loosely organised according to ability but to be honest that didn't mean much. Lessons were fun – I realised soon after I arrived that these women needed their hour with me to be educational but lighthearted. They get up at 5am every day and apart from an hour for lunch and an hour for dinner they don't stop until 10 or 11pm – they're studying Buddhism all day. My first few lessons were pretty diabolical as I tried to find my feet in a completely alien situation. I had no idea of how I was going to learn the names of 90 women, none of whom had any hair and who all wore exactly the same clothes!

So the teaching was the reason that I was there but there were lots of other things to be done at the nunnery too. Cooking for 90+ three times a day is no mean feat and so every day from 10am to noon I cut up vegetables *with a small team of nuns. I found that it was a great time for the nuns to practise the English that they were sometimes too shy to use in front of each other in the classroom, and it was also an opportunity for me to learn some Tibetan and to listen to their stories – often of escape over the Himalayas from Tibet. I made some amazing friends. Together we had a huge amount of fun – riding on the roofs of local buses, swimming in the river, shopping for food for our leaving party, teaching each other national dances (I'm afraid we ended up opting to teach the Macarena), blowing up balloons, and a lot of the time just sitting and chatting about the similarities and most of all the differences between our lives, religions and cultures. It's just amazing to be provided with the opportunity to have a first hand insight into such different perspectives on both every-day things and moral issues. That's definitely something that I'll take from this experience. I've gone from having one penpal from a year nine French lesson who has written to me once in four years to having 90 on the other side of the world who're all desperate to practise their newly learnt language skills!'*

Many other gap year students have found their placements thoroughly rewarding and worthwhile. But some have found themselves attached to schools for privileged children and wonder why they are there. **Rachel Sedley's** main complaint about her placement in Nepal arranged by a commercial gap year agency (now defunct) was that she was teaching in a private school for privileged children when she had been led to believe that she would be contributing her time and labour to more needy children. She suspected that she was there partly to boost the prestige of the school and its head. So anyone with strong views about the kind of school in which they want to work should find out as many details as possible beforehand.

There follows brief descriptions of the situation in the main countries of Asia, together with contact addresses. More detailed information on paid teaching in the countries of Asia is contained in the 2009 edition of *Teaching English Abroad* by Susan Griffith (Vacation-Work/Crimson Publishing, £14.99).

## JAPAN

Japan is an ideal destination for a post-university gap year or two. Thousands of English schools in Tokyo, Osaka and many other Japanese cities are eager to hire *gaijins* (foreigners) to teach. A great many of these are willing to hire native speakers of English with no teaching qualification as long as they have a university degree and preferably some teaching experience. Apart from a few language school chains that advertise and conduct interviews abroad, most schools recruit their teachers within Japan.

Britons, Canadians, Australians and New Zealanders are eligible for a working holiday visa for Japan. British citizens must be aged 18–30. The quota of working holiday visas for Britons was raised from 400 to 1,000 in 2009. Visa holders may accept paid work in Japan for up to 12 months, provided it is incidental to their travels. Applicants must show that they have sufficient financial backing, i.e. savings of £2,500. Note that applications are accepted from April and once the allocation has been filled, no more visas will be granted until April of the following year. Further details are available by ringing 020 7465 6565 or on the embassy webpage (www.uk.emb-japan.go.jp/en/visa/work_hol.html).

Most participants make use of the services of the non-profit Japan Association for Working Holiday Makers (JAWHM; www.jawhm.or.jp) whose principal offices are in Tokyo, Osaka and Fukuoka. A large proportion of the jobs notified to the JAWHM are as English teachers. Note that membership in the Association costs a modest 1,000 yen and you must show your working holiday visa stamp to be eligible for their assistance.

Graduates should investigate the government's flourishing *JET (Japan Exchange & Teaching) Programme*. Anyone with a bachelor's degree in any discipline who is under 39 and from the UK, USA, Ireland, Canada, Australia or New Zealand (plus a number of other countries) is eligible to apply. For British applicants details may be obtained from the JET Desk at the Japanese Embassy (020 7465 6668; www.jet-uk.org). About 200 Britons join the programme each year. Applications in Britain are due by the last Friday in November for one-year contracts beginning late July. The annual salary is 3,600,000 yen (currently equivalent to £24,000/$39,600).

**MARCUS STARLING** spent two fantastic years with JET in Kagoshima, a city in the far south of Japan, which is known as the 'Naples of the East' because of its smoking volcano:

*I* had applied unsuccessfully for my ideal career job on the civil service fast stream, and wanted to gain some more post-university experience and independence before applying again. Having done a very varied gap year before university, I wanted to spend sufficient time in one place to learn a language and make it feel like a second home. I applied for two jobs abroad – one teaching English in a school in China, the other was the JET programme. JET paid far better, was well organised, internationally recognised, and looked to be a good opportunity to learn about the culture and language. I taught at four junior high schools (ages 12–15) on a rota basis, with occasional day visits to primary schools and leading *kids' summer activity programmes. My travel experiences in Japan were unforgettable, particularly visiting some of the sub-tropical small islands off the coast.*

*JET pays for your flight to Japan (and the return flights at the end), so the initial cost is limited to your first month's rent and money you need to equip your new home and settle in. I found I spent £1,000 of my parents' money in the first month, but was able to pay them back within a couple of months by living a modest lifestyle on what seemed a very generous first salary. I should say that Japan isn't actually that expensive a place to live, providing you adapt your tastes (although it is an expensive place to travel). There's something special about Japan, hot spring baths, smoke from the volcano drifting over the bay, politeness and curiosity from people living down the street, small shrines hidden away in forests. Sometimes the curiosity and questions which were so welcome when I was a new visitor became a bit predictable when I had lived there for over a year and knew more of the language and culture – but this was far outweighed by the kindness behind these approaches.'*

A number of the largest language training organisations recruit graduates abroad as well as in Japan. Among the main employers are:

**AEON Corp**, Recruitment office in El Segundo, California (+1 310 662 4706; aeonet. com). Interviews in various American and Canadian cities, plus Sydney and London between February and April. Places 800 native English-speaking teachers with a BA/BSc in their 300+ branch schools in Japan.

**Berlitz** (hr@lc.berlitz.co.jp; http://careers.berlitz.com). More than 1,000 teachers but must be already residing in Japan with a work visa.

**ECC Foreign Language Institute**, with regional offices in Osaka, Tokyo and Nagoya. Recruitment website for job applicants is http://recruiting.ecc.co.jp/index.html. 600 teachers for 150 schools throughout Japan.

**GEOS** (geoscareer.com). Currently interviewing and hiring only in Japan.

**Interac**, Tokyo (+81 03 3234 7840; interac.co.jp/recruit). 1,500 full-time Assistant Language Teachers. Overseas recruitment offices located in USA, Australia, etc.

The most common means of recruitment is online (e.g. via websites such as www. jobseekjapan.com), by word-of-mouth among expat teachers and by advertising your services. The free weekly English language magazine *Metropolis* (www.metropolis.co.jp) has a classified advertisements section which is worth checking for jobs. Another useful free publication is *Tokyo Notice Board* (www.tokyonoticeboard.co.jp). The twice-monthly free electronic newsletter *O-Hayo-Sensei* (which means 'Good Morning Teacher') has pages of teaching positions across Japan at www.ohayosensei.com. Many of these are open only to candidates who are already in Japan. To find private students try www.finda teacher.net which, according to Joseph Tame, really works. Simply enter your details (what you teach, what area of Japan you teach in, how much you charge, etc.), and the students will make contact. Joseph was also impressed with gaijinpot.com when he was looking for bits and pieces of teaching work (the word *gaijin* is Japanese for 'foreigner').

## CHINA

Recruitment of teachers for the People's Republic of China is absolutely booming in the private sector. The internet is a prolific source of possibilities and is expanding all the time. Any web search or a trawl of the major ELT job websites is bound to turn up plenty of contacts, such as www.jobchina.net, which has long lists of jobs, all dated and described in detail. Another to try is www.teach-in-china.cn based in Shenyang City but with vacancies throughout the country.

**PAULA WEALE** was 18 when she went to rural China to teach English in the small town of Li Li with the help of Projects Abroad:

'The countryside was not as green as I imagined and the towns larger yet still distinctively Chinese. Out here, you must contend with the constant stares of curiosity that convince you after a while that you have grown a tail and antlers. You soon get used to these though. The first problem to overcome is the language. The next is the food which is nothing like the Chinese you find at the local take-away. The third is the cold in winter: out here, the thermal vest is my best friend and three pairs of socks. My host family were always willing to help with haggling. In Li Li you could buy most modern comforts in one of the many local supermarkets (except deodorant) and Western brands are available at a price. It can be difficult to decide which bottle is conditioner, and which is shampoo but it's all a trial and error experience in China!

The day of my first lesson was really nerve-racking. I had the first week to watch classes and prepare my own but I'm not a qualified teacher so all I had was my native language. I was amazed at where inspiration would appear from and after initial hiccups the lessons were great and

*I found enthusiasm I never knew I had. The students were very keen to speak with me and improve their English since this is the first time they had seen a Western person. They'd bring in cameras and books for me to sign between classes so it was like being a celebrity in rural China. Make sure to bring pictures from home, as these are immensely popular. There are many weekend opportunities to take a class out to the park or skating in the town.*

*To anyone coming to China I'd say that living in the country is a real adventure. The experience taught me to survive through tough times and how to get on with life when resources were limited. By being a teacher I was able to see life from another culture's perspective which I'd never have managed as a backpacker passing through. I was accepted by the community and looked after by everyone I met really. When in the cities I felt safer than I do in London.'*

*IST Plus* in the UK (020 8939 9057; info@istplus.com; www.istplus.com) runs Teach in China for graduates from the UK while *BUNAC* runs a teach and travel programme which offers a four-week TEFL course, lessons in Mandarin, and placement as a trainee teacher intern. BUNAC's six-month programme costs £1,565, a 12-month programme £1,665.

Foreign-based placement programmes to consider are:

**Amity Foundation**, Jiangsu (www.amityfoundation.org). Christian organisation that recruits people to teach English in China.

**Colorado China Council**, Boulder, Colorado (www.asiacouncil.org). 20–35 teachers per year placed at institutes throughout China. Council fees start at $3,500 (including TEFL training, Chinese course and domestic travel in China).

**Sinoculture**, New Zealand (www.sinoculture.com). Partner of job placement coordinator in Shandong, China (sinoteach@yahoo.com.cn). Provides ongoing opportunities for graduates to teach English in schools and universities throughout China as volunteers. Programme fee from $647 for 2 months to $997 for 9 months plus a $350 application fee.

**WorldTeach**, Harvard University (www.worldteach.org). Non-profit organisation sends volunteers to teach for an academic year in secondary schools or on a summer-only programme in Hunan Province.

With an invitation letter or fax from an official Chinese employer, you will be able to obtain a Z visa (valid in the first instance for three months) or an F visa (business or cultural exchange visa).

## TAIWAN

The country remains a magnet for English teachers of all backgrounds. Hundreds of private language institutes or *buhsibans* continue to teach young children, cram high school students for university entrance examinations and generally service the seemingly insatiable demand for English conversation and English tuition.

Many well-established language schools are prepared to sponsor foreign teachers for a resident visa, provided the teacher has a university degree and is willing to work for at least a year. On arrival check the 'positions vacant' column of the English language *China Post*, although work tends to result from personal referrals more than from advertising.

The following language schools hire on a large scale:

**Hess Educational Organization**, Taipei City (+886 02 2592 3929; hesswork@hess. com.tw). Specialise in teaching children including kindergarten age. 500 native speaking teachers (NSTs) are hired for more than 150 branches. Very structured teaching programme and curriculum.

**International Avenue Consulting Company**, Taichung City (+886 04 2285 5139; www.iacc.com.tw).

**Kojen ELS**, Taipei (+886 2 2581 8511; www.kojenenglish.com). Employs 200–300 teachers at 21 schools, mostly in Taipei but also Kaohsiung and Taichung. Minimum starting wage of NT$580–590 per hour.

## KOREA

Although Korea does not immediately come to mind as a likely destination for British TEFLers, it has been long known in North America as a country which can absorb an enormous number of native speaker teachers, including fresh graduates with no TEFL training or experience. Hundreds of language institutes (*hogwons*) in Seoul, the capital, Pusan (Korea's second city, five hours south of Seoul) and in smaller cities employ native speaker teachers of English. The majority of these are run as businesses, so that making a profit seems to be what motivates many bosses rather than educating people. Certificates and even degrees are in many cases superfluous, though a university degree will be needed in order to obtain the right visa (unless you are an undergraduate willing to undertake a paid teaching internship, for example via *TeachAway* (www. teachaway.com).

*EPIK*, the *English Program in Korea*, is a scheme run by the Ministry of Education, and administered through Korean embassies in the West, mainly in the USA and UK, to place about 2,000 foreign graduates in schools and education offices throughout the country. The annual salary offered is 1.8 to 2.5 million won per month (depending on qualifications) plus accommodation, round trip airfare, visa sponsorship and medical insurance. Current information should be obtained from the EPIK website (http://epik. knue.ac.kr) or by contacting the local Korea government representative, e.g. in the UK the Education Director, Korean Embassy, 60 Buckingham Gate, London SW1E 6AJ (020 7227 5547; education-uk@mofat.go.kr).

In the UK, jobs in Korea can be fixed up in advance through www.huntesl.com, and also through *Flying Cows Consulting* based at Nottingham Trent University (www.flying-cows.com), which is willing to consider anyone with a degree.

After doing a two-week evening course on TESL-teaching in her final term of university, **Jessie Cox** from Canada scoured the job forums at www.eslcafe.com to find some decent recruiters who would not renege on their agreements. Before long she was on her way to provincial Korea:

> *I taught at the only middle school in a small farming town, and the biggest problem I encountered was the extremely low English level of most of the students. Even simple directions were hard for me to give, so we had to spend some time learning simple instructions like 'Open your book to page 22' or 'Repeat after me'. The language barrier also made discipline more of a challenge for me. If the Korean teacher wasn't in the room at the time, I was pretty much limited to 'Stop that' 'No!' and 'Be quiet please'. I was mostly responsible for leading pronunciation and speaking exercises, along with conducting memory tests in which the students had to recite a passage from the text book. The teaching was mostly textbook based. The best feature of working in a state school as the only non-Korean teacher was the chance to be completely immersed in Korean culture in a way that would never be possible as a tourist. The wages at public schools in Korea are quite good and the pay of 1.8 million won per month was more than enough to cover expenses. Although I travelled quite a bit, including to Thailand and Mongolia, I still managed to save about C$10,000 over the year. The biggest reward of my experience in Korea was seeing the world from a different perspective. I was able to climb mountains, visit Buddhist temples, visit the border between North and South Korea, explore ancient palaces, and even eat a live octopus!*

## THAILAND

Thailand is famously welcoming and one of the most popular destinations for gap year travellers and many of the general and specialist placement agencies send volunteers to this country, such as *Volunteer Teacher Thailand*, *Volunthai* and *Gap Year Thailand* (see entries), *JP Education* (www.jpteachers.com) and *Teach-to-Travel* (www.teach-to-travel.com) in Bangkok.

**ALISON WHITE** lived in a small temple in a small Thai town teaching English to monks, a placement arranged by Real Gap. Here she sums up the good and the bad bits:

*I am delighted by:*
- The friendliness of everyone – the smiles and courtesy.
- The beauty of the temple area – set in woods, with buffalo, loads of dogs, and golden Buddha images everywhere.
- The young monks who are so friendly and helpful.
- The old women who can't speak a word of English but always laugh and offer words of wisdom in Thai.
- The children at the school who are so respectful and well behaved.

*My challenges are:*
- Sleeping on a cold hard floor where I get bitten regularly by ants, fleas and mosquitoes.
- Seeing my favourite stray dog and her five young puppies scrounge around for food and affection which is never offered by the locals but warmly received.
- Remaining non-judgmental of the Rayban-wearing chief monk with the mobile phone permanently attached to his ear.

Independent-minded gap year travellers can occasionally pick up casual teaching work in Bangkok but most respectable schools now want their native speaker teachers to have a university degree. The noisy Khao San Road is lined with expat pubs and budget accommodation, many with notice boards offering teaching work and populated with other foreigners (known as *farangs*) well acquainted with the possibilities. They will also be able to warn you of the dubious schools that are known to exploit their teachers and other scams. One of the best all-round sources of information about teaching in Thailand is the website www.ajarn.com with stories and tips as well as many job vacancies (www.teflasia.com/ajarn).

The Thai authorities keep changing the visa goalposts and the situation is hard to fathom. The relevant pages on www.ajarn.com convey the current picture. For those staying for an extended period on a tourist visa, they must leave the country every 15 days (recently reduced from 30) to renew their visa. Some schools will help their teachers to obtain the Thai teacher's licence (for which you need a university degree), work permit and non-immigrant B visa for which you will need multiple documents (including a police clearance from your home country).

**JULIA BOWLER** reflected on the hospitality she had encountered during her three-month teaching stint at Wattharoe School in Rayong Province:

'I took soooooo many photos of the children in lessons, around school, playing, and with me teaching them. My last lessons were spent singing, playing games, and generally getting the kids to recall everything I'd taught them since arriving. Starting to teach feels a lifetime ago, and saying goodbye was a lot harder than I had anticipated.

As this weekend was the last with my Thai family they decided to take me to stay in a Thai-style resort up in Nakhon Nayok, another province of Thailand. When we got back to their home, I made gaeng fang and pla tord for my Thai family (a curry dish and a fried large fish). I think my cooking is getting rather good now with me being confident in a lot of things but I am nervous about making it for people at home in England in case it's too spicy.

Tuesday was my birthday and I was careful not to place too much expectation on it as term had ended. However, I was completely taken aback when they told me that the school was going to hold a party meal for me. I was so surprised and touched at how much effort had gone into it for me. They had cooked all my favourite Thai dishes; presented me with a gorgeous handmade lamp with shells from our local beach and then a van arrived and started unpacking a karaoke system they had hired for the evening. The headmaster made a speech and presented me with a gift of a gold engraved pendant with the King of Thailand on. I even had a handmade cake which said HAPY, BIRTH DAY JULIA in all different colours, and all the teachers sung a very odd version of 'Happy Birthday'. I couldn't stop smiling the whole evening. The teachers have said I am welcome to come back and visit whenever I want. So have my Thai family. I know I will be returning to Thailand – I have fallen in love with it so much.'

**Ashleigh Davey** on the same programme was equally touched by her treatment and proud of what confidence her Thai gap year had given her: '*I left Ireland a little girl from a rural area who had never been farther than a holiday in Spain with my family. And there I was standing in front of 100 people in traditional Thai dress dancing and saying goodbye. Amazing.*'

# Vietnam and Cambodia

The largest growth area in English teaching has been in those countries that were cut off from the West for many years, viz. Vietnam, Cambodia and Laos, where a number of joint venture language schools have been opened employing native speaker teachers. The specialist organisation Teachers for Vietnam places graduates from all English-speaking countries, though its headquarters are in the USA.

*Outreach International* (www.outreachinternational.co.uk) has a long-established programme in Cambodia, a country that tends to be under-represented in the brochures of the main agencies, although *BUNAC* also runs a programme there. Outreach sends volunteers aged 18–22 to work for three or more months with local NGOs, for instance to teach English (which can open a range of employment opportunities for local people), computing or art to landmine victims or to work in a small orphanage or art and craft centre. These placements are suitable for volunteers wishing to pursue a career in overseas development or aid work or genuinely help a damaged and vulnerable section of society. Physiotherapists and older volunteers are needed for some of the projects but others are ideal for younger people.

**LAURA PARKER** described her Outreach International placement in the provincial town of Kratie as an 'absolutely superlative experience':

*The work that Veterans International does is admirable, and working with the staff there was both entertaining and enlightening. The staff are really eager to improve their language skills, and I spent about four hours a day teaching. This focussed on report writing, yet I also found using the English language* Cambodia Daily *newspaper for general language work particularly interesting. It was far more relevant to them than any Eurocentric textbook, and invariably sparked interesting discussions about Cambodian politics, history and scandals.*

*Apart from teaching duties, simply chatting and getting to know the patients, and having them help me practise my Khmer was a rewarding activity. One patient, a 16-year-old girl with polio, had applied for a grant to set up the first beauty parlour in her village. She came back to the centre with all the equipment she'd bought from the market and, within no time, we'd kicked the boys out of the office, and all the girls, patients and staff alike, spent the afternoon, um, 'testing' the merchandise! I think the biggest contrast to a UK working environment was the pace that everything moves at in Cambodia. SLOWLY! It is easy to get used to this, as it's the most sensible way of coping with the heat and humidity, but far less easy to snap out of once back in stressy, constantly-on-the-go Europe!*

*Compared to Phnom Penh, Kratie town is, in my opinion, an infinitely nicer place to spend three to six months (or more!), and I think that if anyone has reservations about being based in the provinces for fear of being too remote or lonely or far from creature comforts, they couldn't be more wrong. Once you've been in town for a week, people realise you're not a passing tourist, and will start to recognise you and take an interest, and just generally want to chat and befriend you. Prices will start dropping for you in the market, and you will soon find it hard to get to and from work without bumping into people you know. I was invited along to all the celebrations and parties, and it really angered me how the guidebooks give barely two pages to the entire province. Not only is it a base for exploring the exciting northeast of Cambodia (think elephant trekking, minority villages, swimming in stunning waterfalls, and a giant crater lake), there is also a multitude of diversions in town itself, from the trivial like getting regular professional manicures costing 12.5 pence, to the active like going swimming in the Mekong every day at sunset. I even made the 20-minute swim across one day, fully clothed of course – Khmer style! The river in Kratie is gorgeous gorgeous gorgeous, and is very clean. Little beats snacking on fresh fruit shakes or sugar cane juice at one of the riverside stalls, watching the sun set (in technicolour) over the Mekong, on your cycle home from work.*

*I certainly had some of the funniest times of my life there. Everything in Kratie is a little bit off the wall (in a very charming way) and 'bizarre' was a word I used daily. From having friends give me Khmer hip hop dance lessons (not dissimilar to the Macarena) to the endless amusement of observing the Khmer can-do attitude to transportation (four piggies on a moto? five people on a push-bike? no problem), life in Kratie never ceased to amuse, and I can guarantee that volunteering there would be both ridiculously fun, and ultimately rewarding, a combination that makes leaving the hardest part of the placement.'*

# Nepal

After a decade-long campaign against Nepal's constitutional monarchy, the Maoist rebels have secured its abolition and formed the government. In June 2008, King Gyanendra and his family quietly moved out of his palace, which has been turned into a museum in 2009. It is now to be hoped that Nepal's political problems will dissipate and the country can concentrate on improving the lives of its people, 100,000 of whom were displaced during the violence.

So once again Nepal is a promising destination for short-term volunteers and casual English teachers. However, people who find voluntary openings in Nepal will be faced with a visa problem. Tourist visas (which can be purchased on arrival for $30 cash) are valid for 60 days and can be extended for $30 a month up to a maximum stay of five months in any one year. Note that a hefty fine or even prison sentence can be imposed on foreigners found overstaying their visas.

A range of organisations makes it possible for self-funding volunteers to teach. Of course living expenses are very low by Western standards, although the fees charged by mediating or gap year organisations such as *i-to-i* and *Africa & Asia Venture* as well as by Nepali agencies (some listed below) can increase the cost significantly. If you want to avoid an agency fee you can make direct contact with schools on arrival. Relevant organisations include:

**Cultural Destination Nepal**, Kathmandu (www.volunteernepal.org.np). Volunteer Nepal, a service work programme. Fee of €650 includes 2-week pre-service orientation and homestay throughout. Placements last 2–4 months starting February, April, June, August and October.

**HELP (Himalayan Education Lifeline Programme)**, Kent (www.help-education.org). Volunteer teachers, nurses and child-carers work in needy schools in Himalayan India (Sikkim, West Bengal, Ladakh and Himachal Pradesh) and Nepal (Kathmandu Valley, Pokhara and Chitwan). Cost includes admin fee of £150 plus donation of £100 (students) or £250 (non-students) plus about £70 per month for accommodation with host families or in school hostel.

**Hope And Home Volunteer Program**, Kathmandu (www.hopenhome.org). Volunteer opportunities in the fields of teaching English as well as community, health and environmental programmes in the Kathmandu Valley, Pokhara, Chitwan and Nawalparasi. Programme fees cover homestay accommodation and food: $250 for 2 weeks, to $800 for 3 months.

**Insight Nepal**, Pokhara (insight@fewanet.com.np; www.insightnepal.org.np). 7-week and 3-month placements for all post A-Level and high-school graduate native speakers of English. Participation fee of $990 for 3 months and $650 for 7 weeks.

**KEEP** (*Kathmandu Environmental Education Project*), Thamel, Kathmandu (+977 01 421 6775; keepnepal.org). Opportunities for volunteers to teach English in trekking villages, government schools, etc. Volunteers stay with a host family and must be self-funding.

**Alliance Nepal** (www.volunteerworkinnepal.org). Prices from €200 for 2 weeks to €650 for 5 months.

**New International Friendship Club**, Maharajgunj, Kathmandu, (www.geocities.com/nifcnepal). 40 English-speaking university graduates placed in schools or colleges.

Volunteer teachers should contribute $100 per month for their keep plus a $150 registration fee. Also runs programme of 15-day workcamps; fee 15,000 Nepalese rupees (€165). Basic Nepalese standard accommodation is provided and Nepali (rice-based) meals.

After **Melissa Evans's** placement in Kenya was cancelled at the last moment, due to the mass violence that broke out after the rigged elections at the beginning of 2008, her gap year agency, *Adventure Alternative*, had to live up to their name and quickly find her an alternative adventure. They arranged for Melissa to fly a month later to Nepal where she taught in a school:

*It was very very rewarding, as the children really thrived off the teaching from a foreign teacher. I found the teaching a challenge as the children struggled with English, and also pronunciation. Sometimes, I found myself unable to understand the children and vice versa. However, familiarity over the three months allowed the language barrier to break down, and conversing with the children was easier by the end of my placement, as I had learned a little Nepali and they had grown used to my pronunciation. Before my gap year I had the ambition of being a teacher. However, after travelling for the first time my ambition changed, and now I aim to found an orphanage.*

# India

Volunteering in India sometimes takes the form of teaching but more often it involves social projects. A wide range of organisations in the UK, in addition to India-specialists such as *Gap Guru*, *Learn Overseas* and *Development in Action*, sends volunteers to teach English or undertake other voluntary work in India. For example *Cross-Cultural Solutions* with offices in the US, UK, Canada and Australia (www.crossculturalsolutions. org) places volunteers in local organisations in the Himalayas and New Delhi (as well as Thailand and China). Among the many projects supported by the UK-based *Development in Action* (entry in 'Directory of Volunteering Abroad'), teaching assignments and social welfare placements are most common. These last for a summer or five months from September.

**CLAIRE MULLINEAUX** returned from India in 2009 after a successful pair of placements through Changing Worlds:

'After a 10-hour flight with British Airways and Sex and the City, we arrived at the smelly, hot and humid Chennai airport. Even at 4.30am there was a sea of excited brown faces awaiting our arrival at *the gate. We had a few days to acclimatise, and see the sights. We found this very interesting and were enthralled by the huge platters of food we were given ranging from bland chutney to 'stupidly spicy orange stuff' (yes that's the technical name!). We drank from coconuts. On the Friday of that week we were all taken to our individual placements.*

*In our orphanage there were 15 houses. Each family had a mother figure and between 7 and 11 children. Some children were blood relatives but every child in the family was treated with the same love and loyalty as each other. I am told a lot of the children were brought there after the tsunami. We taught lower kindergarten on three days a week and upper kindergarten on the other two. We preferred the older ones as they had some idea what we were talking about. The language barrier was quite large so we took to making exotic sounds and shaking our heads in a bobbing manner like the rest of the Indian population. It is a general response meaning yes, no, maybe, and I don't know. It works!*

*We ate dinner in the family homes which was a good time to get to know the families and the Indian style of living. The water only came on for 30 minutes at 6am and sometimes it was late or stopped early (just when we'd shampooed our hair normally) and sometimes it didn't come on at all which was very frustrating. We were filthy by the end of the day and although we had to wash under a cold tap it was very refreshing.*

*After three months I went to the medical placement at Gremaltes Hospital. I will never forget what I learnt in and out of the classroom. I worked mainly in schools, hostels, slums and jails teaching nutrition and personal hygiene. I was involved in CAP programmes (Children's Action for Progress) and activity days at Gremaltes. I helped in several fields: leprosy, HIV/AIDS, TB, diabetes, nutrition, skin infections/diseases, joint diseases including arthritis, eye diseases and fungal infections. I taught post-med students and nurses from all over India and America which was both horrific and hugely rewarding at the same time. I cannot begin to tell you how amazing this experience was. Nobody really understands what it means when they say a gap year changes you. Now I understand.'*

*MondoChallenge* offers rural placements mainly in the district of Darjeeling in the Himalayan foothills and have introduced new programmes in six of the main cities across India.

# Sri Lanka

*Volunteers for Educational Support & Learning* or *VESL* (www.vesl.org; see entry in 'Directory of Volunteering Abroad') is a British charity largely run by volunteers, which provides rural Sri Lankan and other Asian communities with exposure to enthusiastic and creative native English speakers.

**RICHARD NEW** was placed by VESL in a school in Nelliady on the Jaffna Peninsula (in the Tamil north of the country) before communal unrest made the area too dangerous for volunteers. He appreciated the insights he gained that mere travellers never could:

'The north of Sri Lanka is probably the most fascinating place I have ever visited. Having emerged from 20 years of civil war, there is much evidence of the scars of battle. Yet the people were some of the most hospitable and positive that I have ever met. Their welcome was as warm as their climate. From the first day, Dan and I were made to feel part of the community.

Our school was well equipped compared to others on the island, yet resources were still scarce. Regardless of problems, the students were enthusiastic and keen to learn. If I could stop them talking about cricket, developing their spoken English was both challenging and rewarding. I think we made good headway in improving their listening skills especially and even the younger students became better at understanding complex instructions. On the last day I was genuinely moved to see my pupils recite poetry by William Wordsworth at a full school assembly. They were also keen to tell me about their lives and country, so I think that overall they taught me as much as I taught them.

Our home life was equally interesting. Dan and I lived with a family who welcomed us into their lives. Due to the lack of electricity our nightlife tended to end promptly at 8.30. Yet life was not tedious. Dan and I went to a Hindu temple for their annual festival where we were welcomed, fed and blessed. We were special guests at a local football match, and experienced the thrill of a Karavedy local derby. Most interesting was a tour around an Arrack factory (distillery of the local tipple). It showed us the harsh working environment many Sri Lankan labourers must face. Such

> *experiences would be impossible for most travellers to the area. VESL gave me a unique opportunity to understand the culture and people of northern Sri Lanka.'*

*MondoChallenge* (www.mondochallenge.co.uk) arranges mainly three-month teaching placements in Sri Lanka. The teaching takes place in Buddhist temple communities near Kandy.

# VOLUNTEERING

Many young people who have travelled in Asia are dissatisfied with the role of tourist and would like to find a way of making a contribution. It must be stressed that Westerners almost invariably have to make a financial contribution to cover food and accommodation as well as their travel and insurance.

If you have never travelled widely in the developing world you may not be prepared for the scruffiness and level of disorganisation to be found in some places. Not many 18 year olds would be capable of contributing or benefiting much from a long attachment to a grassroots charity in developing regions. A further difficulty with participating in local voluntary projects (of which there are many) is in fixing anything up ahead of time. Occasionally Asian charities have a representative abroad (usually a committed former volunteer) who can send information about voluntary possibilities but this is unusual.

## INDIAN SUBCONTINENT
Here is a selection of indigenous organisations that can sometimes use paying volunteers:

*Mother Teresa's Home for Dying Destitutes*, Kolkata. This and other Homes run by the *Missionaries of Charity* in other Indian cities accept committed volunteers but can offer no accommodation.

*Indian Volunteers for Community Service*, Harrow (www.ivcs.org.uk). Operates the Discover Rural India scheme for anyone over 18. Volunteers start with 3 weeks at Amarpurkashi Polytechnic in Uttar Pradesh learning about development and then join a hands-on project in the region between September and March. The placement fee which includes orientation and training is only £265, while living expenses are £2–£3 a day.

*Dakshinayan* (www.dakshinayan.org). Works with tribal peoples in the hills of Rajmahal and nearby plains. Volunteers join grassroots development projects every month and contribute $300 per month.

*First Light* (www.firstlightindia.org). An NGO running a school in a remote tribal village in West Bengal. A team of international volunteers teaches basic English and sport to the children. The all-in fee to cover living costs is $150 per month.

**SMILE Society** (www.smilengo.org). Kolkata-based organisation that arranges work-camps and internships in teaching, health, rural development, etc. for students from abroad. Volunteers pay no fee but only cover their basic living costs of €100 per week for stays of up to 3 weeks, and €80 for stays of 4–24 weeks.

**Rural Organization on Social Elevation**, (jlverma_rosekanda@hotmail.com; www. rosekanda.org). A community organisation in the Himalayan foothills with the charming acronym *ROSE*, in the state of Uttarakhand places volunteers to work with poor villagers, teaching children, carrying out environmental work and organic farming in this village. Volunteers pay Rs500 a day for board and lodging and a Rs3,500 registration fee.

**Youthreach**, New Delhi (www.youthreachindia.org). Matches volunteers with NGOs working to assist disadvantaged children, women and the environment. Tasks for volunteers include reading to children, teaching academic subjects and art and craft, as well as ones that require special skills or professional training. Volunteers must be self-supporting but pay no fee to participate.

**Bangladesh Work Camps Association**, Dhaka (+880 2 935 8206; www.mybwca. org). Places volunteers in 2-week community development camps between October and March for a fee of $250. Detailed camp information is available in English. *BWCA* can also accommodate foreign volunteers on a medium-term basis (1–3 months) and longer term.

**Samasevaya Sri Lanka**. An established NGO that has been doing useful post-tsunami work, particularly in the Muslim area of Kinniya. The National Secretariat in Talawa (samasev@sltnet.lk) invites volunteers to help in rural locations. Volunteers can be used rather loosely for their educational and development programmes, though it is more akin to a cultural exchange. If the volunteer wants to stay past the initial month of their tourist visa, it is sometimes possible to arrange a renewal. The organisation provides simple accommodation in their office complex in Talawa or with local families. A contribution of about $100 a month is expected for meals.

See entry in 'Directory of Volunteering Abroad' for *Inspire Volunteering* which has programmes in Sri Lanka, for example teaching Buddhist monks.

## SOUTH EAST ASIA AND THE FAR EAST

*Starfish Ventures* (www.starfishvolunteers.co.uk) is a British company that places volunteers of all nationalities in development projects in Thailand, mainly in Surin province, including teaching, dog rescue, school garden construction and turtle conservation.

Volunteers including gap year students are sent out to northern Thailand each year to work in communities of Karen tribespeople. Details of the programme are available from the *Karen Hill Tribes Trust* (see entry in 'Directory of Specialist Gap Year Programmes').

If signing up for a wildlife project locally, make sure you will feel comfortable. Long-time animal lover **Pascale Hunter** visited an elephant sanctuary in Chiang Mai, but felt that the animals were not treated well. Her friend was very shocked when the *mahout* (elephant handler) took out his slingshot, shot a squirrel and stuffed it into his pouch for dinner.

Japan is a famously expensive country in which to travel. One way around it is to join a workcamp. More and more workcamps organisations are being established; links to all of them can be found at www.nvda-asiapacific.org, the Network for Voluntary Development in Asia. Joining a short-term volunteer project can be a good way to visit an exotic place such as Mongolia (contact the *Mongolian Workcamps Exchange*, +976 99131777; mce-mn@magicnet.mn) with partner agencies abroad. The fee for joining a 2-week camp is €160. An NGO in Ulaanbaatar that places international volunteers is the *New Choice Mongolian Volunteer Organization* (011 314577; www.volunteer.org.mn/new/index.html). It arranges short- and long-term placements for volunteers to teach English, renovate buildings, etc. for a fee of $495–$1,950.

Japan and Korea have WWOOF organisations, both of them web based. It costs 5,500 yen (or A$68) to join *WWOOF Japan* (Sapporo; fax 011 780 4908; www.wwoofjapan.com), whose list of member farms has expanded hugely to nearly 350, and 50,000 won ($50) for the Korean list from *WWOOF Korea* (www.koreawwoof.com).

While doing his year abroad of a degree in Japanese at Sheffield University and on previous trips, **Joseph Tame** has had a wonderful time WWOOFing:

> *I spent a few weeks in a beautiful little seaside village on the southern island of Shikoku, working as a volunteer for an organic tangerine cooperative. We would be picked up by local farmers at about 6am, work with them on the tangerine terraces until 11am when the heat got to be too much to bear. One particularly memorable day was when an Australian Wwoofer and I were given the job of picking caterpillars off the leaves of a huge field of organic Japanese potatoes. Over the course of 3 hours we collected two huge sacks of creepy crawlies, but at the end of the day forgot to tie the sacks up – when we returned to the field the following day we found the caterpillars had all escaped and returned to their former homes!*

## PAID WORK AND WORK EXPERIENCE

Few paid jobs are available to gap year students unless they have a contact in Beijing or Singapore, for example, who is able to arrange a business internship. The booming Chinese economy and seeming whole-hearted embracing of Western business means that some Chinese companies do take on American and European staff.

A couple of the gap agencies and a sprinkling of Asian companies focus on matching foreign young people with professional internships for example *Next Step Connections* in China and *Junior Expat* in Indonesia (see entries in 'Directory of Work Experience'). Another company that customises internships in China is B&W (www.bwinternships.com) though these are usually designed for candidates with some professional training.

Internships for people 18–25 are arranged by a company in Colombo called *Volunteer International* (+94 74 720658; www.volunteerinternational.com). They offer a structured programme in the hospitality industry, journalism, business, conservation, teaching and so on. Participants pay £1,495 for three months and £2,395 for six months (plus travel). Some internship placements are available in the Maldives Islands for people who can speak a language in addition to English.

During **JON MCLEOD'S** gap year journalism placement in Shanghai, arranged through Projects Abroad, he had a few bizarre experiences. At one point he was seconded as photographer when Daniel Craig came to town to promote the Bond film. Some of the questions being asked by local journalists made Jon wince, for example about DC's sightseeing itinerary and wardrobe and, bizarrely, who his 'ideal man' might be (a classic example of Chinglish).

'Infamous for its absence of press freedom and until recently relatively shy on the global stage, China is admittedly a curious setting to seek experience and insight into the exposing world of journalism. Sterile though, it is not. Underpinned by dramatic economic growth, there is a buzz and expectancy surrounding the Communist country formerly cloaked in privacy. Especially in its most international city Shanghai.

A three-month internship with That's Shanghai *magazine proved a thrilling, frustrating and ultimately very valuable experience. The most important aspect was the opportunity to write. Writing short rounds-ups on the month's happenings, writing restaurant and bar reviews on a heavy stomach and light head, writing about upcoming music, theatre and opera events, and a sporting feature. The role booted me beyond comfort zones of sport and news into the unknown and perturbing territories of books (an uneasy admission given my placement) and opera (yet to convert). But there is nothing more satisfying than to see your piece in print, nor sometimes more sobering, but actually beneficial, to read an edited copy.

Two months of Chinese lessons had armed me with only the basics; as the novelty wore off the motivation began to haemorrhage and the simplest of phrases were still left hanging awkwardly in the air. Beyond work and*

> the intoxicating lifestyle of Shanghai (I will recover but my bank account won't) trips to Hangzhou, Beijing and Tibet afforded a wonderful insight into more traditional and historical elements of Chinese and Tibetan culture. From the imposing and communistic feel of Tiananmen square to the distinctive colour and vibrancy of Lhasa; all a powerful contrast to the intensely unique and fruitful setting of Shanghai.'

## HOMESTAYS AND COURSES

With China becoming such a global power to be reckoned with, many people with an eye to the future or just an interest in the language, are deciding to study Chinese. Through CESA **Lucy Millett** signed up for a four-week course in Beijing in 2007, in preparation for studying Chinese at university:

> Beijing was great, safe, and cheap and with loads of things to do and see. There were lots of bars and clubs on Sanlitun (the bar street) and plenty of shopping streets, touristy sites, quieter less visited temples and museums. It was horribly dry though, grey and sometimes quite smelly and always noisy which adds to vibrancy. The people are friendly and the place is exciting, I came home craving peace. I loved learning the characters, being able to impress people with simple sentences, looking at the way bits of language linked and clicked together. I found the pinyin [Chinese phonetic alphabet] difficult to pronounce at times though and some of the grammar very tricky.

The **Japan Homestay Service** in Chiba-city (http://home.att.ne.jp/orange/star/homestay) places foreigners with Japanese families for varying charges; the only requirement is 'not to hate Japanese food'. The Hokkaido International Foundation (www.hif.or.jp/en) arranges two-week homestays mainly for foreign students living in Japan and also an intensive eight-week Japanese language and culture programme in the summer which costs $4,450.

**GAPPERS' TIP**
Budding writers under 25 might like to enter the Goi Peace Foundation International Essay Competition for a chance to win a prize of 100,000 yen and a free trip to Japan for the prize ceremony in November; the essay must be no more than 800 words and submitted by the end of June (details on the website www.goipeace.or.jp).

Someone who has always had a fascination with China might consider the range of short or semester-long courses offered in Suzhou near Shanghai by the Boland School (www.boland-china.com/culture) which includes the predictable (Chinese language and cookery) as well as the more obscure (calligraphy, music and martial arts).

**LORNA DAVIDSON'S** choice of gap year activity was different from most, although she achieved her goal of getting fit. Through Real Gap she spent three months at a Martial Arts Academy in China and experienced why 'Kung fu' is Chinese for 'hard work'.

'I hadn't done much exercise before arriving at the academy and after hearing about the extensive training I was worried I wouldn't be able to cope. When I first began my training I didn't know the difference between internal and external martial arts, or even what Shaolin was – it was just something out of 'Crouching Tiger Hidden Dragon' that looked cool! The training is pretty much suited to you and your skill levels. This made it a lot easier to be around people who had been there up to 8 months and were practically flying when I could barely kick above my hip. It's very intense. I stuck it out and ended up loving the training so much, I stayed for an extra month. Sanda classes were hard work as it involved constantly moving, kicking, spinning and ducking. In other classes we learnt different styles of jumping, flipping, cartwheeling, butterfly kicks and other fancy-named twists. Power training involves weight lifting and other physically challenging tasks while power stretching involves your master putting you through excruciating pain for 30 seconds in every body part to make you more flexible. It was my favourite as I always felt very relaxed afterwards and after two months I could quite easily do the splits, which was one of my goals when going there. Every Friday we had to do the mountain. The mountain was the culmination of the week's training when everyone had to run half way up the mountain to some steps which then had to be run up and down four times before we were allowed to go to the bottom to have a shower. When I first arrived I could barely even get up to the steps, but by the end I managed to get up and down four times.

I will never forget my last night when a whole load of my friends (that I had only known for two months) took me out to dinner. We spent the rest of the night roasting marshmallows in my room using chopsticks and candles, and laughing about the great times we had spent together. Even the translators and the dog joined in.'

Dive training is a popular choice for gappers and is offered by (among others) *Personal Overseas Development* on a small island near Koh Samui. **Ross Fairgrieve** enjoyed the POD course on Koh Tao so much that he found himself getting out of bed early in the mornings for the first time since he was seven. He really enjoyed hopping on a moped, sometimes with a local dog on the back, knowing that he had a day of scuba diving and meeting new people from all over the world ahead of him.

**LAUREN SMITH** is another gap year student who fell in love with Koh Tao. She had booked the usual round-the-world itinerary, but her plans changed completely when she got to Thailand. She stayed on Koh Tao for an extra month and decided to return later in her gap year after she had returned home to Shropshire to save more money:

*I wanted to use my gap year before going to Cardiff University to study Journalism, Film and Media, to further my work experience in the film industry as it's a hard industry to break. I came across an underwater videography course on www.thepodsite.com which prompted me to research independent videography courses and found Oceans Below (www.oceansbelow.net) on the Thai island of Koh Tao. I got in contact directly with the company. They were very helpful, but suggested as I had not dived before to look into the opportunities available at Thailand Gap Internships, who offer internships up to and including PADI Divemaster, before I went on to do training and an internship in underwater videography. TGI seemed very personal, adapting the internship to suit the individual and finding the cheapest cost possible.*

*Completing your Divemaster is done in your own time, although you are expected to help with customers, loading and offloading bags and tanks from the boats. Interning in underwater videography is harder work. You're expected to meet the morning boat between 6am and 7am depending on the company. You film Open Water Divers till about 11am, then you have the afternoon to capture and edit all the footage from the morning and burn the completed film to CD. Then after an hour's break you meet the customers from the morning, show them the movie and offer to sell it to them. Your day usually finishes at about 7pm.*

*I felt that the costs of the course were justified. It was an experience of a lifetime, spending five months on one of the most beautiful islands in the world. Not only that but I'm gaining valuable work experience that will help me later in life. Hopefully due to my training in videography it will make finding a job in the industry easier.'*

Alternative dive internships can be investigated such as *Mermaid Dive Centre*'s Learn in Asia instructor training programme in Pattaya, Thailand (www.mermaiddive.com).

# Turkey

Turkey is a wonderful country to travel in with a wealth of important historic sites which you will certainly have heard of, such as Troy and Ephesus. Its economy has strengthened considerably since the Turkish lira lost six zeros against the dollar a few years ago. Turkey is a good choice of destination for fledgling English teachers though few opportunities are available to pre-university gap year students with no TEFL training or experience. Although Istanbul is not the capital, it is the commercial, financial and cultural centre of Turkey, so this is where most of the EFL teaching goes on.

For short-term opportunities, the Education Department of the youth travel and exchange organisation *Genctur* in Galatasaray, Istanbul (www.genctur.com) organises summer camps for children where English, German and French are taught by native speakers who work for seven hours a day in exchange for free board and lodging. Pocket money may also be given according to experience and skills. Applicants must have some experience of working with children.

A *WWOOF* exchange is operated by the Bugday Association in Istanbul (info@tatuta. org; www.bugday.org/eng). At present there are about 70 member farms.

Au pair jobs in Turkey usually involve more tutoring of English than domestic chores. The following agencies make placements in Turkey:

**Anglo Pair Agency**, 40 Wavertree Road, Streatham Hill, London SW2 3SP (020 8674 3605; anglo.pair@btinternet.com). Nannies and au pairs (approximately 100) for summer or academic year. Au pairs earn £50–£65 a week. Agency has office in Istanbul.

**ICEP (International Cultural Exchange Programs)** (icep@icep.org.tr). Au pair in Turkey programme for 3–12 months (www.icep.org.tr/english/aupairturkey.asp). Minimum pocket money $200 a month. Interns with Turkish companies receive accommodation, meals and $150 a month. ICEP also places qualified English teachers who earn $500 a month.

One persistent problem is that it is generally not acceptable for young women to go out alone in the evenings. But Turkish families are usually very generous and allow their live-in child-carers to share in family life on equal terms, even in their free time and on holidays.

The main Aegean resorts of Marmaris, Kusadasi and Bodrum absorb a large number of foreign travellers as workers. Other places firmly on the travellers' trail, such as Antalya on the south coast and Goreme in Cappadocia, are also promising. The best time to look is March or early April. Major Turkish yachting resorts are excellent places to look for work, not just related to boats but in hotels, bars, shops and excursions. A good time to check harbourside notice boards and to ask captains if they need anyone to clean or repair their boats is in the lead-up to the summer season and the Marmaris Boat Show in May.

A Turkish company called *USEH International Training & Education Services* (USEH, Bagdat Cad. 217/14, Ciftehavuzlar, Kadiköy, Istanbul; +90 216 478 3444; www.useh. org) arranges internships mainly in the hospitality industry in Istanbul and the Turkish Republic of Northern Cyprus open to college students of business, marketing, finance, hotel administration, etc.

# The Middle East

Few gap year students are likely to be seriously considering the Middle East at a time when the region is so troubled. With heightened tension between Israelis and Palestinians and an escalation of anti-Western sentiment throughout the region, the taste for travel and employment in the Middle East has been soured and many prospective travellers have (understandably) been put off by fear for their personal security. The Iraq and Afghanistan Wars have undoubtedly destabilised the area and fanned the flames of Islamic distrust of the West. Perhaps young intrepid travellers can play a small part in diminishing the distrust and tension between the two cultures, bringing people together, allowing individuals on both sides to gain some understanding of the complexity of the world's problems.

Many parts of the Middle East remain reasonably calm and untroubled. For example Yemen has a large and interesting expat community and is a good place to consider studying Arabic for example *CALES*. The CALES website (www.y.net.ye/cales) carries some first-hand accounts, including the following by **Isabel Dietrich** from Germany:

> *I studied at CALES for one month. Although it is only a short time, I have learnt a lot there. I want to tell everybody, this is a good school. The teachers are well experienced and the atmosphere is excellent... If you want or need to learn Arabic grammar, you will do so. If you prefer to have more practice of the speaking language they will give you the opportunity to speak a lot to practise the language.*
>
> *It is a good choice to study in Yemen. Here you can experience the real Arabic life, more than in the Arabic countries on the Mediterranean Sea where the Western influence is greater. Yemeni people are friendly and very open to Western people. The school is situated in an authentic building in the old centre of Sana'a and this city is marvellous, a real wonder of architecture. In the souq, close to the school, you can practise the Arabic language all the time.*

## Australia

Picking up casual work to cover all your travelling expenses may not be achievable in the Australia of 2010/11. Partly because of the overwhelming numbers of young foreigners on working holiday visas, it is an employer's rather than a job-seeker's market. The job hunt can be a struggle and optimism needs to be tempered with realism. **Roger Blake** is someone who is willing to turn his hand to anything and has successfully 'blagged' (talked) his way into all manner of jobs around the world. Yet he found Australia an uphill struggle, certainly compared to New Zealand. Although he managed to survive on his occasional earnings, he warns to expect a 'rough ride': '*I have met SO many travellers who are leaving Australia after just 3 months or less of their WHV, thoroughly disgusted with the attitude of employers towards backpackers and the associated struggles of finding an (often lousy) job in the first place. .... But it is not all doom and gloom and I've had fun between troublesome times.*'

On a more positive note first-time visitors to Australia are often surprised by the degree to which that far-off continent is an imitation of Britain. Despite their reputation as 'pommy-bashers', most Australians take for granted a strong link with the UK, and this may be one reason why British travellers are so often welcomed as prospective employees especially off the beaten tourist track. On the other hand, in the areas that backpackers have colonised, such as certain suburbs of Sydney and certain Queensland islands, they are not at all popular since they have a reputation for 'Ibiza'-type behaviour.

## RED TAPE

The number of working holiday visas keeps steadily rising and went from 110,000 in 2006 to 150,000 in 2008. The visa is for people intending to use any money they earn in Australia to supplement their holiday funds. Applicants must be between the ages of 18 and 30 and without children. The rules were recently relaxed to encourage more working holidaymakers to do jobs in country areas. You used to be eligible for a working holiday visa only once but now you can apply for a 12-month extension provided you can prove that you have spent at least three months working in regional Australia, for example fruit-picking, pearling, sheep-shearing or fishing.

Most people apply for a Working Holiday Maker (WHM) visa online, though you can also submit a paper application to any Australian representative outside Australia. When you apply online for an e-WHM visa there is no need to provide proof of funds, nor do you send in your passport. Applying online via the Australian Department of Immigration website (www.immi.gov.au) is normally straightforward and hassle-free and should result in an emailed confirmation inside the promised 48 hours which is sufficient to get you into the country. Your passport isn't physically inspected until you arrive in

Australia when you must take it along to an office of the Department of Immigration and Citizenship to obtain the visa label, avoiding, if possible, the busy downtown Sydney or Melbourne offices where the queues can be discouraging. In either case the fee for the WH visa is A$195 (currently £90).

Visas 2 (www.visas2-australia.co.uk), the Visa Bureau (www.visabureau.com) and Visa First in Dublin (www.visafirst.com) all offer a visa service and typically add £30–£35. All visa information can be checked at www.immi.gov.au or by ringing the Australian Immigration and Citizenship Information line 09065 508 900 (charged at £1 per minute).

## PLACEMENT AGENCIES AND SPECIAL SCHEMES

Naturally, Australia is not included as a destination by those gap year organisations that focus on developing countries. However, the following do make placements downunder, often in boarding schools, doing conservation work or working on outback properties: *Lattitude Global Volunteering* and *Changing Worlds* are two that have quite large programmes in Australia.

**BUNAC**, London EC1 (020 7251 3472; downunder@bunac.org.uk). Offers a Work Australia package.

**CCUSA**, London (www.ccusa.com). Offers a 12-month WorkExperience Downunder programme. US applicants should contact CCUSA in Sausalito.

**Changing Worlds** (01883 340960; www.changingworlds.co.uk). Paid placements in hotels in tourist hotspots, and on farms throughout Queensland, including some with riding opportunities. Voluntary placements in a zoo and on conservation projects. Teaching placement in Melbourne (mainly outdoor education). Pocket money placements last from three to six months. Most groups go out in September, March and July; other departure times available on enquiry.

**IST Plus**, Richmond, Surrey TW9 2SZ (020 8939 9057; info@istplus.com; www.istplus.com) offers the Work and Travel Australia programme.

**Involvement Volunteers Association**, Port Melbourne (+61 03 9646 9392; ivworldwide@volunteering.org.au). Volunteers are placed within a network of voluntary projects around Australia (and worldwide) for up to a year. Package costs A$1,200.

**VisitOz**, Queensland (+61 07 4168 6185; www.visitoz.org) provides a year-round programme for young people with a working holiday visa who wish to live and work in outback and rural Australia for 1 year (see entry at end of 'Directory of Courses').

**Travellers** (01903 502595; www.travellersworldwide.com). Hands-on conservation placements working with kangaroos and dolphins, among others, in wildlife sanctuaries and rehabilitation centres. Challenging volunteer teaching placements with refugees (Australia) or underprivileged children (New Zealand). Professional work experience internships also available in journalism, law, medicine, care, TV, physiotherapy, architecture and others. Placements start from £995 and are available all year round with flexible start and finish dates.

In addition to the gap year specialists, an increasing number of backpacker travel and youth exchange agencies are offering packages that may be of special interest to first-time travellers in their gap year. Some are all-inclusive; others simply give back-up on arrival. Typically, the fee will include airport pick-up, hostel accommodation for the first few nights and a post-arrival orientation which advises on how to obtain a tax-file card, suggestions of employers and so on. Some even guarantee a job. Various perks are thrown in, such as a telephone calling card and maps.

**Travellers Contact Point** (travellers.com.au). Sells working starter packs for Sydney for A$260 including airport pick-up, two nights' hostel accommodation, access to Job Search service, 12-month mail-holding service, etc.

**Downunder Jobs**, Hotel Discovery, 167 Franklin Street, Melbourne (www.downunder jobs.com). Helps people with a working holiday visa to set up work as well as providing a range of other back-up services for a fee of A$330.

**Workstay Australia** (workstay.com.au). Source of working holiday and general travel information for backpackers travelling in Western Australia with links to the job website www.work2excite.com. Workstay runs the Country Pub Barmaid's Programme, by which mainly young women are placed in jobs for 5–12 weeks.

When **Matt Applewhite** chose Australia through a gap year agency, he was not bothered by the fact that Australia was considered a soft option by some of his contemporaries. It didn't always feel like a soft option when he looked at his very full timetable of teaching and supervising, but he ended up having not only a fascinating but a fulfilling year in the Northern Territory:

> As I walked around Kormilda College for the last time, it seemed that every room, every corner had a memory associated with it. A glimpse of the college canoes awakened the vivid memories of Year 8 Outback camps when by day under the blazing sun we noisily splashed around the leafy billabongs and bushwalked through Crocodile Dundee's back yard. A traditional Aboriginal drawing in the library allowed me to reminisce about my trip to the remote community of Peppimenarti and the way in which the welcoming community allowed me to observe the elders silently weaving traditional baskets, watch the village children learn English in the community school and appreciate their cultural traditions, dignity and warmth. I reflected on all the experiences I'd relished and how lucky I'd been to spend time in this place.

# WORK EXPERIENCE

Private employment agencies are very widespread and can be a good potential source of jobs for travellers, especially those with office skills, computer, data processing or financial experience. A surprising number positively encourage UK people on working holidays, often by circulating their details to hostel managers. The offered wages are good too: from A$16 an hour for clerical work up to A$22 for computer work. This might be an ideal route for a student who has done a secretarial or business skills course at the beginning of their year out. Note that in some cases lower youth wages may apply to those under 20.

Two companies that mediate upaid work experience placements in Australia are *Australian Internships* and *Intern Options* (see entries in 'Directory of Work Experience Abroad'). The latter operates out of a London office and has an impressive range of unpaid work experience placements available in Australia and New Zealand; its fixing fee is £800 for internships of any duration.

**HOLLY TATE** hugely enjoyed a 10-week work experience placement in Sydney with Pedestrian TV (www.pedestrian.tv) in 2009. Her internship was in the area of film with duties including video production, online publishing, interview research and conducting interviews:

'When I contacted Intern Options they replied quickly, seemed really helpful and dedicated to finding me an internship that suited me. They gave me a couple of job profiles but on my third I found something that really interested me. I arrived in Sydney at the beginning of January and started straightaway. My internship has been brilliant, and I've really been able to get stuck into the office workload. I generally work a full working week but my bosses are really easy going and if I want to take an afternoon or day off every now and again to go and do stuff in the City they're more than ok with it. The office is really small, everyone gets on well and it's a pretty fun place to work. Since I arrived I've learnt a lot of things, like editing, which I'd never done before. They've included me in lots of production meetings and creative brainstorming sessions for new projects which has been invaluable experience for when I apply for jobs back home.'

Anyone with experience of the horse industry should contact the agency *IEP-UK* in the UK (www.iepuk.com), whose Australian partners are *TEP* trading as *Stablemate Staff Agency* in New South Wales (+61 2 4587 9770; info@tepeople.com.au) and *IRE* (*International Rural Exchange*) in rural Western Australia (+61 08 9064 7411; www. ire.org.au).

Interesting research projects take place throughout Australia and some may be willing to include unpaid staff looking for work experience. For example a research station in northern Queensland operated by the *Australian Tropical Research Foundation* in Cape Tribulation (www.austrop.org.au) welcomes paying volunteers who usually stay two or three weeks, though extensions are possible. Volunteers assist in research and station activities such as radio-tracking bats, counting figs, stomping grass for forest regeneration, constructing buildings, digging holes, and running the Bat House visitor centre. Volunteers are asked to pay US$35 a day to cover food and accommodation.

The *Australian Institute of Marine Science* (*AIMS*) at Cape Ferguson near Townsville (+61 7 4753 4240; www.aims.gov.au) runs a Prospective Visitor Scheme aimed at graduates and undergraduates looking for work experience in marine research; it would be most unusual for a school leaver to be accepted, although anyone with a scuba diving certificate and a keen interest should make contact.

## THE JOB HUNT

The glut of travelling workers is especially bad in Sydney and on the Queensland 'Route' between Sydney and Cairns, whereas Melbourne and Adelaide may offer better prospects. In addition to asking potential employers directly (which is the method used by most successful job-seekers in Australia), the main ways of finding work are via private employment agencies, online advertisements and notice boards especially at backpackers (i.e. hostels).

Some charities are perennial advertisers for paid fundraisers. The most amusing account of earning money this way comes from **Chris Miksovsky**, who was paid an hourly wage (but only a few hours a week) as a street collector in Brisbane:

> *My year in Australia ended with a rather fitting and hilarious job, collecting for the Wilderness Society, a sort of Australian Greenpeace, wearing a koala costume. After a brief interview with the Koala Coordinator ('So, Chris, do you have any experience walking around as a big furry animal?'), I found myself in a busy square wearing a full-body fluffy grey koala suit complete with fake felt claws and droopy oversize ears. Actually it works. Takings per hour were about A$25 on average. For me, probably the best thing was that you learned to not take yourself so seriously.*

The *Wilderness Society* runs a national face-to-face membership campaign called 'Wilderness Defenders' which aims to sign up people to donate by standing order. The charity has so far succeeded in protecting millions of hectares of Australian wilderness. Information about applying is available at www.wilderness.org.au. Hourly earnings average A$15–A$20. In his post-university gap year(s) **Richard Griffiths** worked in Sydney as a charity fundraiser/campaigner for the Wilderness Society, an experience which eventually fed into him becoming a policy adviser on UK climate change.

As mentioned, the dense network of hostels is a goldmine of information. Gappers find employment in the hostels themselves too. **Stephen Psallidas** describes the proliferation of work:

*I've met loads of people working in backpackers' hostels. Typically you work two hours a day in exchange for your bed and a meal. Work may be cleaning, driving the minibus, reception, etc. and is always on an informal basis. I will be jumping on the bandwagon myself soon. I'll be completely shattered from picking tomatoes so I'm going to 'work' in a hostel in Mission Beach, where the owners invited me to work when I stayed there earlier. I'm going to rest up in a beautiful place before continuing my travels, and not spend any of my hard-earned dollars.*

## THE OUTBACK

Most of Australia's area is sparsely populated, scorched land which is known loosely as the outback. Beyond the rich farming and grazing land surrounding the largest cities, there are immense properties supporting thousands of animals and acres of crops. Many of these stations (farms) are so remote that flying is the only practical means of access, though having a vehicle can be a great help in an outback job search.

Your chances of getting a job as a station assistant (jackaroo or jillaroo) will be improved if you have had experience with sheep, riding or any farming or mechanical experience. Several farmers are in the business of giving you that experience before helping you to find outback work, like the one mentioned above in the *VisitOz* scheme.

*JJ Oz* (+61 0428 617 097; ww.jjoz.com.au) offers a choice of five or 12 day courses at Bingara north of Tamworth, New South Wales (NSW); the costs are A$599 and A$1,350. In the same area, the Leconfield Jackaroo and Jillaroo School (Kootingal, NSW 2352; +64 02 6769 4230; www.leconfieldjackaroo.com) runs 11-day outback training course costing A$950 (A$1,050 through agents); on completion successful participants will be guided in the direction of paying jobs.

## CONSERVATION VOLUNTEERING

Several organisations give visitors a chance to experience the Australian countryside or bush. The main not-for-profit conservation organisation in Australia is called, predictably enough, Conservation Volunteers Australia (CVA) and it places volunteers from overseas in its 'Conservation Experience' projects, though the charges are quite steep. Sample projects include tree planting, erosion and salinity control, seed collection from indigenous plants, building and maintaining bush walking tracks, etc. Overseas volunteers are welcome to become involved by booking a four-week or six-week package which include food and accommodation and all project-related transport at a cost of A$1,037 and A$1,500 respectively (which works out at less than A$37 a day for accommodation, food and transport). Further details are available from the National Head Office in Ballarat (+61 03 5330 2600; www.conservationvolunteers.com.au).

**Nicky Stead** was forced to take a gap year at the last minute and hurriedly started researching. The project that caught her eye was doing conservation work in Australia and soon she was saving money for the placement and the flight. She had done a few conservation projects in the Lake District so she knew what she was letting herself in for, and this appealed more than teaching. So she signed up for eight weeks based in Adelaide and had a marvellous time:

> *Going to Australia was the best thing I ever did. Everything worked out as it was meant to. I had no problems at all. We lived in Adelaide but travelled all over South Australia on different projects. We planted trees by a flooded mineshaft, built a fence on the coast of the Great Australian Bight, and weeded on the banks of the huge River Murray. We worked from 8am to 4pm which was not unreasonable, and with a break mid-morning and an hour for lunch it wasn't too strenuous. The fee I'd paid covered food, accommodation (which was often very very basic), transport and training. At the end the estate manager wrote me a great reference.*

More ad hoc opportunities may present themselves and cost considerably less. **Daniele Arena** from Italy stumbled across a project on the coast of Queensland that appealed to him:

> *One of the most amazing experiences I had in Oz was the time I was volunteering at the Turtle Rookery in Mon Repos Beach. We could pitch our tent for free, and gave a small contribution of A$5 a day for food. The work was to patrol the beach waiting for nesting turtles and, when they come in, to tag and measure them and the nest. This goes on between November and March. I was fortunate enough to get this by chance but normally there's quite a few people who want to do it.*

For further information, contact the *Mon Repos Conservation Park* on +61 07 4159 1652.

*WWOOF* is very active in Australia and has a huge supply of unpaid work opportunities. WWOOF Australia headquarters are near Buchan in Victoria (+61 03 5155 0218; www.wwoof.com.au) though their publicity is widely distributed through backpacker haunts. The Australian WWOOF Book contains about 1,500 addresses throughout Australia of organic farmers and hosts looking for short- or long-term voluntary help or to promote cultural exchange. The list is sold with accident insurance at a cost of A$60 within Australia, A$70 for a couple (A$5 extra to cover overseas postage).

A free internet-based exchange of work-for-keep volunteers can be found at www. helpx.net where nearly 600 Australian hosts are listed.

## FRUIT PICKING

Many gap year students fund their travels around Australia by migrating between fruit and vegetable harvests. A short surf of the internet will soon take you to harvesting information since the need is so acute. The *National Harvest Labour Information Service* based in Mildura, Victoria (+61 1800 062 332; nhlis@madec.edu.au; www.jobsearch. gov.au/harvesttrail) is funded by the federal government and therefore free to users. Alternative sources of vacancies are www.harvesthotlineaustralia.com.au and www. goharvest.com.

Although harvesting work is often not hard to *get*, some find it hard to make any money. The apple/pear/grape crates may look quite small at the outset but will soon seem unfillable with mysterious false bottoms. Many eager first-timers do not realise how hard the work will be physically, and give up before their bodies acclimatise. But you should have faith that your speed will increase fairly rapidly and with it your earnings.

## TOURIST INDUSTRY

Casual catering wages both in the cities and in remote areas are reasonably good, for example the award rate for casual waiting staff in New South Wales starts at A$18 an hour, with weekend loadings. Although tipping was traditionally not practised in Australia, it is gradually becoming more common and waiting staff in trendy city establishments can expect to augment their basic wage to some extent.

Standards tend to be fairly high especially in popular tourist haunts, so inexperienced gap year students have little chance of being hired to work in a restaurant or pub. A common practice among restaurant bosses in popular places from Bondi Beach to the Sunshine Coast is to give a job-seeker an hour's trial or a trial shift and decide at the end whether or not to employ them.

**LAURA PANTRY'S** reasons for heading downunder for a gap year instead of doing a PhD as she had intended were different from most. After six months of chemotherapy she decided she wanted to take a year out rather than return to studying. After doing a basic online search she came across one that strongly appealed, a three-month voluntary placement in a Queensland zoo arranged by Changing Places:

*I was determined to incorporate some voluntary work into my gap year even though I knew my chosen destination of Australia wasn't usually a location where voluntary work was offered. The zoo placement was obviously perfect. I then worked various hospitality jobs to fund my travels around the rest of the country. Finding work was never a problem. I had some bar/waitressing experience (the most important factor seemed to be experience) and I wasn't fussy. This led me to jobs from luxury hotels to outback pubs.*

*Working in the zoo was a dream come true. Every day I was genuinely thanked for my help and made to feel valued. The work wasn't all menial. We were entrusted to carry enclosure keys and allowed to work independently once we had proven our reliability. Hospitality jobs varied. Pay was generally good, some agency jobs were dependent on available shifts, other positions like the outback pub jobs were full-time and included food and board on top of a weekly wage.*

*My money was saved until I could afford to go out on another adventure. By working hard I was able to visit Stradbroke Island, the Gold Coast, Sunshine Coast, rainforests and wildlife parks. I was also able to buy a car with friends and drive across the country stopping at Uluru and Kings Canyon, then driving across the Nullarbor to Perth. I stopped to earn more funds then flew to Melbourne to explore the markets and Phillip Island before getting to Sydney for Christmas and New Year. I climbed the Harbour Bridge and sunbathed on Bondi Beach. All in all I did as much as I could time and money permitting.*

*My advice is go out with a list of 10 things you have to do before you come home. If you can do more it'll be a bonus. Incidentally since coming back off my gap year I've decided to retrain as a nurse and am in the final stages of the course. I have been offered a job on the Gold Coast of Australia and am due to move back there in October. So I guess you could say my gap year really did change my life!'*

One tourist area which is not normally inundated with backpacking job-seekers is the stretch of Victorian coast between Dromana and Portsea on the Mornington Peninsula near Melbourne. Although most jobs don't start until after Christmas, the best time to look is late November/early December.

If exploring Australia is your target rather than earning high wages, it is worth trying to exchange your labour for the chance to join an otherwise unaffordable tour. For example camping tour operators in Kakadu and Litchfield Park have been known to do this; try for example Connections Safaris (www.connections.travel).

## DIVING AND WATERSPORTS

One of the larger employers is the dive industry. Non-divers (almost exclusively female) can try to find work as 'hosties' (hostesses) who make beds, clean cabins and generally tidy up. Culinary skills and an ability to speak Japanese would be definite pluses. A non-diver would almost certainly be able to fix up some free dive lessons and thus obtain their basic Open Water Diver qualification while being paid to do so.

Year-out students who have a sailing qualification might find temporary work instructing. To take just one example *Northside Sailing School* at Spit Bridge in the Sydney suburb of Mosman (+61 02 9969 3972; www.northsidesailing.com.au/employment. htm) offers casual instructing work during school holidays to travellers who have experience in teaching dinghy sailing.

*Flying Fish* runs a structured watersports training and recruitment programme in Australia. After yacht, dive, surf and windsurf training, graduates can take advantage of the free careers advice and recruitment service to help find work in the industry for the rest of their gap year. Many trainees who have completed Professional Dive Training with Flying Fish at the Pro Dive Academy in Sydney go on to work at Pro Dive's network of resorts in Australia and the South Pacific. (See entry for Flying Fish in 'Directory of Specialist Gap Year Programmes'.)

**NINA FITTON** spent the beginning of her gap year with Flying Fish in Australia:

'Having been on a number of sailing/windsurfing family holidays, I thought it would be good to improve my personal skills and get the instructor qualifications so that I could work at a holiday centre during the summer of my gap year, and in future uni holidays. So I signed up for the 12-week Sail/Windsurf Instructor Traineeship with Flying Fish in Sydney. Living in Manly was amazing – wonderful weather, fantastic shops, great beach, relaxed lifestyle, excellent nightlife. The first six weeks were spent sailing in Topaz Magno's. We were worked hard, but it was intense and successful training, which improved my sailing loads. One day we went out in 30 knots of wind, and caned it up and down, kite up, crew on the wire, flat out – great fun. I passed my sailing instructor moderation with flying colours – I obviously perform well under pressure!

Moving onto the windsurfing... it's now my favourite hobby. One day I could hardly balance on the board with a 3.5m sail, the next I was planing across the bay, in the harness and footstraps. So much fun! Again, I passed the instructor moderation, so I'm now qualified to teach both sports.

The people on my course, and on all the other Fish courses in Sydney (yachting, diving, surfing) were awesome – a great group who provided endless entertainment. We tended to all go out as one big group, having warmed up for the evening at home, playing 'Beer Pong', building human pyramids, having cake fights. The socials were also always amusing – Bond, Hawaiian, cocktails, barbecues, a real mixture. There were evenings *spent singing karaoke, trolley racing, midnight swimming on famous Manly Beach or in a hotel fountain, at the Sydney Opera House Bar, a mask party.*

*My gap year's been awesome, I can't imagine not having taken a year out. It's changed me as a person, making me so much more confident and giving me skills and hobbies that I wouldn't have achieved if I'd gone straight to uni. I've met loads of great people, and done loads of cool stuff.'*

## SKI RESORTS

Another holiday area to consider is the Australian Alps where ski resorts are expanding and gaining in popularity. Jindabyne (NSW) on the edge of Kosciuszko National Park and Thredbo are the ski job capitals, though Mt Buller, Falls Creek, Baw Baw and Hotham in the state of Victoria are relatively developed ski centres too. The best time to look is a couple of weeks before the season opens, which is usually around the middle of June. Most successful job-seekers use the walk-in-and-ask method, though as everywhere the internet is playing an increasing role. Check out www.ski.com.au/market place/employment.html which has links to the resorts and pertinent email addresses like employment@fallscreek.net or recruitment@thredbo.com.au.

## TRAVELLING FAIRS

Although it is partly a case of being in the right place at the right time, you might find job vacancies at a travelling fair such as the Melbourne Show. To get a job you need to go to the site and walk around asking for work. Some jobs are paid hourly while others pay a percentage of takings; the latter should be accepted only by those with very outgoing personalities who can draw in the punters. Even if you don't land a job before the show opens, it is worth hanging in there in case of last-minute cancellations. You can also get a job dismantling the rides at the end which is very physically demanding work.

**Geertje Korf**, on a gap year between studying archaeology and taking up a career, was at first thrilled to land a job with a travelling fair but it wasn't all as exciting as she had hoped:

*The work itself was good enough, helping to build up the stalls and working on the Laughing Clowns game. But the family I got to work for were not extremely sociable company. As a result, when we left a place and headed for the next I would spend time (about a week) until the next show day wandering lonely around incredibly hot and dusty little country towns where there was absolutely nothing to do while the showmen sat in a little circle drinking beer and not even talking to me.*

Loneliness was not a problem for **Sam Martell** from the Orkneys when he spent a year going round the world after university – and he earned a fair whack for a short burst:

*A girl I met on a tour at Byron Bay got me a job in Brisbane at the Queensland State Fair in the second week of August. I was paid A$10 cash-in-hand working on a bouncy castle rescuing scared kids from the slide and chatting to the mums – it was great. In seven days I clocked up 73½ hours and took home A$735 which meant I could afford the Whitsundays sailing trip.*

## AU PAIRING

The demand for live-in and live-out childcare is enormous in Australia. Applicants are often interviewed a day or two after registering with an agency and start work immediately provided they have a couple of checkable references. Nanny and au pair agencies are very interested in hearing from young women and men with working holiday visas. A number of au pair agencies place European and Asian women with working holiday visas in live-in positions, usually for a minimum of three months. Not all placements require childcare experience. As in America, a driving licence is a valuable asset. As well as long-term posts, holiday positions for the summer (Dec to Feb) and for the ski season (Jul to Sept) are available. Try any of the following:

**Australian Nanny & Au Pair Connection**, Kooyong, Victoria (+61 3 9824 8857; www.australiannannies.info).

**Dial-an-Angel** (+61 1300 721111; administration@dialanangel.com; www.dial-an-angel.com.au). Long-established agency with franchised branches throughout Australia.

**Family Match Au Pairs & Nannies** (+61 2 4363 2500; www.familymatch.com.au). Agency places many working holidaymakers. 25–35 hours per week for pocket money of A$180–$250 plus all live-in expenses.

**People for People**, Brookvale, NSW (+61 2 9971 1393; www.peopleforpeople.com.au). Welcomes working holidaymakers for three-month summer positions.

# New Zealand

Mothers of prospective gap year students have been known to tell their daughters that the only countries they will be allowed to visit are Canada and New Zealand. Mothers always know which countries are safe and friendly, and they don't come any safer or friendlier than New Zealand. These same mothers probably also have a list of expatriate cousins and old school friends who could be relied on in a crisis. New Zealand may be about as far away from Britain as it is possible to get, yet it makes things very easy for young travellers on a budget.

Most year-out students simply travel around New Zealand rather than work or study. Typically, students earn money in Australia to fund a holiday in New Zealand which includes the obligatory bungee jump or other adrenaline sport in Queenstown. Other enterprising gap year students get a working holiday visa for New Zealand (see below) and hunt out their own jobs.

## PLACEMENT ORGANISATIONS

*Lattitude Global Volunteering* has been sending year-out students to boarding schools for many years. Because New Zealanders are so fanatical about sport, schools place a strong emphasis on outdoor activities, and gap year students make ideal helpers. Most of these placements last for a whole year from the end of August, though a few seven-month placements start in February.

*BUNAC* in London (020 7251 3472; downunder@bunac.org.uk) has a Work New Zealand programme that provides a 'Work Exchange Visa' (unique to BUNAC) or ordinary working holiday visa, job assistance from BUNAC's partner organisation IEP and other benefits for a programme fee of £429. You can also buy a package directly from IEP (www.worknewzealand.org.nz).

The *Work Adventures Downunder* programme from CCUSA in London (www.ccusa.com) operates to New Zealand as well as Australia. Fees start at £370 to include initial accommodation and a post-arrival orientation at the partner office in Auckland. Another gap year placement company to operate in New Zealand is Changing Worlds (www.changingworlds.co.uk) which offers 3 or 6-month job placements on the ski slopes or in hotels in Queenstown, or the chance to volunteer on farms or in a school. Unpaid opportunities exist to work in a boat yard with dinghies and yachts. The programme fee including flights is £2,630.

## RED TAPE

Visitors from the UK need no visa to stay for up to six months. Young travellers entering the country may be asked to show an onward ticket and about NZ$1,000 per month of their proposed stay (unless they have pre-paid accommodation or a New Zealand backer who has pledged support in a crisis). In practice, respectable-looking travellers are unlikely to be quizzed at entry.

The UK Working Holiday Scheme was considered so successful in addressing severe labour shortages in seasonal work that the maximum duration was extended recently from one year to two years, and the quota removed. The scheme allows any eligible Briton aged 18–30 to obtain a working holiday visa, allowing her or him to do temporary or full-time jobs in New Zealand. Applicants must have the equivalent of NZ$350 for each month they intend to stay, so if you are applying for the 12-month visa you must show £1,800 and also have enough to cover a return airfare. Participants are permitted to work for up to 12 months of the two-year visa validity, either consecutively or cumulatively. Anyone who has worked for at least three months in horticulture or viticulture can apply to extend their working holiday permit by three months. Information can be obtained from the New Zealand Immigration Service at New Zealand House, Haymarket, London in person, by phone on 09069 100100 (charged at £1 per minute) or via the internet at immigration.govt.nz, an admirably comprehensive and up-to-date site.

Applications for all working holiday schemes can be done online from anywhere in the world. The fee (currently NZ$120/£55) will be payable by credit card at the time of application. Other working holiday schemes (maximum duration one year) are open to Irish, American, Canadian, Dutch, Japanese and many other nationalities, mostly on a reciprocal basis.

## CASUAL WORK

New Zealand is a country where it may be better to take enough money to enjoy travelling, and perhaps supplement your travel fund with some cash-in-hand work, odd jobs or work-for-keep arrangements. Because New Zealand has a limited industrial base, most temporary work is in agriculture and tourism. As in Australia, hostels and campsites are the best sources of information on harvesting jobs (and there is a wealth of budget accommodation throughout New Zealand). Often local farmers co-operate with hostel wardens who collate information about job vacancies or they may circulate notices around youth hostels, for example, 'Orchard Work Available January to March; apply Tauranga Hostel' so always check the hostel board (bearing in mind that some hostels entice job-seekers with a vague promise of local work simply to fill beds). **Ian Fleming** soon realised how valuable hostels could be in his job hunt:

> *During our travels around the North and South Islands, the opportunity to work presented itself on several occasions. While staying in the Kerikeri Youth Hostel, we discovered that the local farmers would regularly come into the hostel to seek employees for the day or longer. (This was in July, which is out-of-season.) My advice to any person looking for farm work would be to get up early as the farmers are often in the hostel by 8.30am.*

Backpackerboard.co.nz has lots of useful job information and tips on budget travel for backpackers in New Zealand. Two recent adverts were offering free accommodation In exchange for gardening and another urgently needed help in clearing a basement for NZ$13 an hour cash-in-hand. Similarly, a website maintained by the Budget Backpackers Hostels group includes job information (www.bbhnet.co.nz/billboard_home.asp). At the time of writing there was a number of hostel vacancies listed among others.

Private agencies are also involved in the working holiday market. New Zealand Job Search (www.stayatbase.com/work) is a specialist job search centre for travellers attached to *BASE Auckland ACB* backpacker hostel (Level 3, 229 Queen Street; +64 0800 462 396; info@nzjs.co.nz). Work starter packs starting from NZ$355 include a 12-month registration with NZ Job Search, job placement service and various perks (one-way airport transfer, orientation session, SIM card, etc.).

*Gap Year NZ* based in Leeds (www.gapyear-newzealand.co.uk) is a commercial website dedicated to helping people take a gap year in New Zealand. The website offers live job listings in various work fields, including fruit picking, hospitality, clerical and adventure tourism, plus general information to help plan a trip. The affiliated *Indie Travel Company* (www.indietravelcompany.com) sells starter packs to New Zealand (and Australia) from £75.

An excellent resource is *Seasonal Jobs NZ* (www.seasonaljobs.co.nz), which provides splendidly full details on current job vacancies.

# RURAL AND CONSERVATION VOLUNTEERING

*WWOOF NZ* (www.wwoof.co.nz) is popular and active, with 830 farms and smallhold-ings on its fix-it-yourself list that welcome volunteers in exchange for food and accom-modation. The list costs £16/US$30/NZ$45.

Another organisation matches working visitors with nearly 200 farmers throughout New Zealand. Farmstays can last from three days to several months. *Farm Helpers in New Zealand* in Palmerston North (www.fhinz.co.nz) charges NZ$25 for their member-ship booklet containing all the addresses. No experience is necessary and between four and six hours of work a day are requested. The coordinator advises that hosts in the Auckland area tend to be oversubscribed, so that it is best to head into the coun-tryside.

Another possibility is the free internet-based exchange of work-for-keep volunteers which can be found at helpx.net where an impressive 725+ hosts in New Zealand are listed. Originally set up by a British backpacker in New Zealand, the scheme is flourish-ing and expanding.

The New Zealand Department of Conservation (DOC) carries out habitat and wild-life management projects throughout New Zealand and publishes a detailed Calendar of Volunteer Opportunities (see www.doc.govt.nz) which lists all sorts of interesting sounding projects from counting bats to maintaining historic buildings and cleaning up remote beaches. Most require a good level of fitness and a contribution to expenses, though not always. The DOC also needs volunteer hut wardens at a variety of locations. Details are available from any office of the Department of Conservation.

**Paul Bagshaw** from Kent spent a thoroughly enjoyable week on an uninhabited island in Marlborough Sound monitoring kiwis, the flightless bird whose numbers have been seriously depleted. An ongoing programme removes them from the mainland to small islands where there are no predators:

> *The object of the exercise was to estimate the number of kiwis on Long Island north of Picton. As the kiwi is nocturnal, we had to work in the small hours. As it's dark, it's impos-sible to count them so we had to spread out and walk up a long slope listening for their high-pitched whistling call. During the day they hide in burrows and foliage so it is very rare to see one. One night, when we heard one rustling around our camp, my girlfriend went outside with a torch and actually managed to see it. She was so excited that she couldn't speak and resorted to wild gesticulations to describe its big feet and long beak.*
>
> *The island has no water source except rainwater which collects in tanks, all very ba-sic. We lived in tents and prepared our own meals from supplies brought over from the mainland. Our one luxury was a portaloo.*

*Conservation Volunteers New Zealand* with an office in Auckland (+64 09 376 7030; www.conservationvolunteers.co.nz) is a not-for-profit organisation operating on both islands, that was set up by Conservation Volunteers Australia not long ago. It oper-ates its own team-based projects which accept overseas volunteers to monitor wildlife, plant trees, maintain tracks and so on. Overseas volunteers can book a four-week or six-week package through CVA's office in Victoria, through agents abroad (see website) or on arrival in Auckland.

The easily confused *New Zealand Trust for Conservation Volunteers* (*NZTCV*) matches both local and international volunteers with conservation projects of all kinds to counteract the loss of native bush and wildlife. Details are available on its website (www.conservationvolunteers.org.nz). NZTCV has created a central database on which individuals can register in order to be put in touch with organisations running conservation projects.

# SKI RESORTS

The last couple of years have seen several New Zealand ski schools beginning to offer instructor training to people from the northern hemisphere. Skiers and riders from all over the world congregate in New Zealand during the northern summer (beginning of July to October). The New Zealand ski schools listed in the 'Directory of Ski Training Courses' operate in several ski centres in the South Island: Craigieburn, Queenstown and Wanaka. Many of New Zealand's ski fields are wonderfully uncrowded compared to Europe. Most courses lead to the NZSIA (New Zealand Ski Instructors Alliance) Levels 1 and 2 exams, qualifications that are recognised around the world; every year graduates from New Zealand's ski schools go on to work in resorts worldwide.

---

**MOTHERS' TIP**
*All the ski schools in New Zealand profess to be ideally suited to gap year students since they provide a safe and friendly English-speaking environment, while being on the other side of the world.*

---

With a passion for snowboarding **Sam Smith** began investigating accommodation options near the slopes in New Zealand. He came across the website of *Snow Trainers* which had everything he wanted: accommodation, season passes, transport and an instructor qualification at the end of it. He started saving:

> *If I went to New Zealand in the months before uni (July–Sept) I would have plenty of time to save up. Situated in Queenstown, the course was spread over 11 weeks with 3 days 'training' a week. It was a perfect balance between working towards becoming an instructor and having your own time to get to get to know the many local bars! The 'training' with the instructors was world class. We all improved our riding more than anyone expected and gained many other skills in the process. As well as making us all instructors, the guys also showed us how to party properly in a town full of travelling gap year students, which got pretty crazy! Doing the instructor course opened many windows for me. I loved the lifestyle so much I put uni on hold and have been snowboarding ever since.*

# NORTH AMERICA

## USA

The spirit of Jack Kerouac is far from dead even though not many gap year students are familiar with his *On the Road* these days. Dubious foreign policy notwithstanding, the lure of America continues strong among young Britons and Europeans, especially at a time when Barack Obama has infected the nation and the world with hope for a better future. The home of so many heroes and of ideas which have shaped the thinking of most people in the West, the USA attracts a wide range of people, including school leavers, who want to experience the reality for themselves. Extended travel around the United States is expensive but various schemes and travel bargains can bring that vast country within reach. It is possible for students to qualify for an Exchange Visitor Programme visa which permits them to enter the USA and work legally. For information about formalities needed for visiting the USA as a tourist, see the *Travel North America* chapter.

## RED TAPE

The non-immigrant visa of most interest is the J-1, which is available to participants of government-authorised programmes, known as Exchange Visitor Programmes and who are permitted to take legal paid employment. Note that some key programmes such as *BUNAC*'s *Work America* are open only to students already in higher education, and therefore students taking a gap year are not eligible.

The J-1 visa entitles the holder to take legal paid employment. You cannot apply for the J-1 without going through a recognised Exchange Visitor Programme such as BUNAC, *IST Plus* or *Camp America*. Only they can issue the document DS-2019 necessary for obtaining a J-1 visa. Participants on an Exchange Visitor Programme can work on a J-1 visa in any job for up to four months between 21 May and 30 October or for the winter season between 21 November and 30 April. After the work period finishes, they are permitted a further 30 days for pure travel in the USA.

Numerous opportunities are available on summer camps and as au pairs (both described below). Some are open only to full-time students, while others accept those between school and university as long as they have a confirmed place at a tertiary institution. Other summer camp programmes are open to non-students over 18 with specific skills.

Apart from the J-1 visa available to people on approved Exchange Visitor Programmes, the other main visa category of interest is the H category, which covers non-immigrant work visas in special circumstances. The H2-B is for temporary or seasonal vacancies that employers have trouble filling with US citizens. For example, the chronic shortage of workers on the ski fields of Colorado means that a certain number of employers can obtain the necessary Labor Certification confirming that there are no qualified American workers available to do the jobs. A petition must be submitted by the employer to the US Citizenship & Immigration Services (USCIS) and there is a strict quota. The maximum duration of the H2-B visa is one year.

By law, all employers must physically examine documents of employees within three working days and complete an I-9 form which verifies the employee's right to work. Employers who are discovered by USCIS to be hiring illegal aliens are subject to huge fines and those caught working illegally run the risk of being deported, prohibited from travelling to the USA for five years and in some cases for good.

# WORK AND TRAVEL PROGRAMMES

A welter of exchange organisations helps candidates from around the world to obtain a J-1 visa.

*BUNAC* (16 Bowling Green Lane, London EC1R 0QH; 020 7251 3472; bunac.org. uk) administers three summer programmes in the USA. The only one open to gap year students is Summer Camp USA, since the other two are restricted to students registered in full-time tertiary education, including final year students. The 'Work America Programme' allows participants to do any summer job they are able to find; the second is 'Summer Camp USA' which is open to anyone over 18 interested in working on a summer camp as a counsellor; the third is 'KAMP' (Kitchen & Maintenance Programme) which is open to students who want to work at a summer camp in a catering and maintenance capacity. All participants must join the BUNAC Club (£5), travel between June and the beginning of October either independently or on a BUNAC flight (for £450), pay the varying programme fees and purchase compulsory insurance (£138).

BUNAC's *Work America* student participants must find their own summer job in the USA, either by using BUNAC's job listings or by waiting to pound the pavements job-hunting on arrival. In addition to the registration fee of £249 for first-time applicants, you must submit a letter from your principal, registrar or tutor on college headed paper showing that you are a full-time degree-level student. You are also required to take at least US$400 in support funds.

In addition to BUNAC, the principal work and travel programmes (as distinct from career-oriented internship programmes described below) are broadly comparable. UK programmes that provide full-time university students with the opportunity to live and work in the USA for a maximum of four months, and charge varying fees, include *CCUSA* (www.ccusa.com), *IST Plus* (www.istplus.com), *Real Gap Company* (www.realgap.co.uk), *Outbreak Adventure Recruitment* (www.outbreak-adventure.co.uk/recruitment), *Global Choices* (www.globalchoices.co.uk) and *Twin Work & Volunteer Abroad* (www.workandvolunteer.com).

## SUMMER CAMPS

Summer camps are uniquely American in atmosphere, even if the idea has spread to Europe. An estimated 8 million American children are sent to 10,000 summer camps each year for a week or more to participate in outdoor activities and sports, arts and crafts and generally have a wholesome experience. The type of camp varies from plush sports camps for the very rich to more or less charitable camps for disabled or underprivileged children, which often tend to be short-staffed. British young people are especially in demand as soccer coaches on summer camps.

It is estimated that summer camps employ nearly a third of a million people. Thousands of 'counsellors' are needed each summer to be in charge of a cabinful of youngsters and to instruct or supervise some activity, from the ordinary (swimming and boating) to the esoteric (puppet-making and ham radio). Several summer camp organisations are authorised to issue J-1 visas, primarily Camp America and BUNAC, but a few smaller ones are also mentioned below.

After camp finishes, counsellors have up to six weeks' free time and usually return on organised flights between late August and the end of September. Some camps are staffed almost entirely by young people from overseas, which can be useful if you are looking for a post-camp travelling companion.

With its Summer Camp USA programme, BUNAC is one of the two biggest counsellor placement organisations in the field, sending several thousand people over 19 (or 18 if expert in something in demand) as counsellors at children's camps. The registration fee of £144 includes camp placement, return flight and land transport to camp and pocket money of US$985–$1,215 (depending on age) for the whole nine-week period. The fact that you do not have to raise the money for the flight is a great attraction for many; the camp which decides to hire you advances the amount from your wages to BUNAC which in turn puts it towards your flight. Interviews, which are compulsory, are held in university towns throughout Britain between November and May.

The other major camp recruitment organisation is Camp America (020 7581 7373; www.campamerica.co.uk), which each summer arranges for up to 9,000 people aged 18 or over, from around the world, to work on children's camps in the USA. Camp America provides a free return flight from London to New York and guidance on applying for a J-1 visa. The camp provides free board and lodging plus pocket money. At the end of your contract, you will be given a lump sum of pocket money which will range from US$575 to US$1,200 depending on your age (as of 1 June), experience and qualifications. Upfront charges include the registration fee of £469 which excludes the US visa fee of £108 and the compulsory police check (£36).

One way to secure a placement early and avoid last-minute uncertainty is to attend one of Camp America's recruitment fairs in various British cities between January and March, which is what **Colin Rothwell** did: '*At the recruitment fair, you could actually meet the camp directors from all over the States and find out more about particular camps. If you are lucky, like me and a thousand others, you can sign a contract on the spot.*'

Summer camps provide more scope for employment than just looking after the kids. BUNAC's Kitchen and Maintenance Programme, otherwise known as *KAMP USA* and Camp America's *Campower* are open only to degree-level students (including final year students) who are given ancillary jobs in the kitchen, laundry or maintenance department, for which they will be advanced their airfare and in some cases paid more than the counsellors.

Other summer camp agencies include *Camp Counselors USA* (www.ccusa.com) and *Camp Leaders in America (CLIA)*, www.campleaders.com.

## INTERNSHIPS AND WORK EXPERIENCE

Internship is the American term for traineeship, providing a chance to get some work experience in your career interest as part of your academic course. These are typically available to undergraduates, recent graduates and young professionals, and are almost always unpaid. Several organisations in the UK are authorised to help candidates find work placements in the USA and obtain a J-1 visa valid for up to 18 months. *IST Plus*, *Realgap*, *Twin UK* and *Global Choices* in the UK (web addresses above) help full-time students and recent graduates to arrange course-related placements in the USA lasting from 3 to 18 months. The placement can take place at any time during your studies, during the summer, as a sandwich year or up to 12 months after graduating. Although you are responsible for finding your own course-related position, the programme organisers supply practical advice on applying for work and a searchable database of internships/work placements. Those who qualify get a J-1 visa. Programme fees differ but may start at £400 for students who can fix up their own training position but rise to more than £2,000 for non-students who want a placement arranged for them. Realgap charges interns £799 for six months, £1,299 for up to 12 months and £1,559 for 18 months, which includes arranging an internship for example in the hotels industry. Wages are paid on a par with US co-workers.

The UK/US Career Development Programme is administered by the *Association for International Practical Training (AIPT)* in Maryland (www.aipt.org). This programme is for people aged 18–35 with relevant qualifications and/or at least one year of work experience in their career field. A separate section of the programme is for full-time students in hospitality and tourism or equine studies. *InterExchange* (www.interexchange.org) and the *Alliance Abroad Group* (http://allianceabroad.com) are both accredited to grant J-1 and H2-B visas to European candidates.

The *Mountbatten Internship Programme* (London EC1; 0845 370 3535; www.mountbatten.org) provides work experience in or near New York City for people aged 21–26. New US regulations stipulate that trainees must have a degree or professional certificate from a post-secondary institute plus a year of relevant work experience to be eligible for the J-1 visa. Placements last one year and provide free accommodation as well as a monthly allowance of about US$1,000. Interns pay a participation fee of £6,000 (2010).

After a consultation with 'Taking Off', a consultancy in Boston, **Elisabeth Weiskittel** fixed up a short internship at the Ocean Mammal Institute (www.oceanmammalinst.com) on the island of Maui in Hawaii in the middle of her gap year. Every January, the woman in charge of the institute takes some of her students and a few interns (often people taking a year off) to Hawaii for 19 days for a fee of US$2,400 (2010):

*The purpose of the institute was to study humpbacked whales and the effects of nearby boats on their behaviour. Our data was intended to support a pending law restricting the use of speedboats and other craft in these small bays where the whales and calves were swimming. One group watched and recorded the whales' behaviour in the morning and had the afternoon off, and the other group watched in the afternoon and had the morning off. I had no problem adjusting to life in Hawaii. Most people were there to get a tan and go to bars, but even if that's not your scene it's still lots of fun in Hawaii. During our last week there was a large conference on environmental issues, which all the interns were invited to attend. Some of the speakers were well-known, and one or two spoke to our group, such as the founder of Greenpeace. When the internship ended, I flew back home to New York for a few days to do my laundry and repack, and then continued my gap year in Italy.*

## CHILDCARE

The au pair placement programme allows thousands of young Europeans with childcare references to work for American families for exactly one year on a J-1 visa. They apply through a small number of sponsoring organisations which must follow the guidelines which govern the programme, so there is not much difference between them. The arrangement differs from au pairing in Europe since the hours are much longer and, if the au pair comes from the UK, there is no language to learn.

The basic requirements are that you be between 18 and 26, speak English, can show at least 200 hours of recent childcare experience, have a clean driving licence and provide a criminal record check. The childcare experience can consist of regular babysitting, helping at a local crèche or school, etc. Anyone wanting to care for a child under two must have 200 hours of experience looking after children under two and must expect the programme interviewers to delve into the experience you claim to have. The majority of candidates are young women though men with relevant experience (e.g. sole care of children under five) may be placed. (It is still not unusual to have just a handful of blokes out of hundreds of au pairs.)

The job entails working up to 45 hours a week (including babysitting) with at least one and a half days off per week plus one complete weekend off a month. Successful applicants receive free return flights from one of many European cities, four-day orientation in New York which covers child safety and development, and support from a community counsellor. The counsellor's role is to advise on any problems and organise meetings with other au pairs in your area. Applicants are required to pay a good faith deposit of US$300–$400 which is returned to them at the end of 12 months but which is forfeited if the terms of the programme are broken.

The fixed amount of pocket money for au pairs is US$176.85 a week which is a reasonable wage on top of room, board and perks. An additional US$500 is paid by the host family to cover the cost of educational courses (three hours a week during term-time) which must be attended as a condition of the visa. Au pairs are at liberty to travel for a month after their contract is over but no visa extension is available beyond that.

As in all au pair–host family relationships, problems do occur and it is not unusual for au pairs to chafe against rules, curfews and expectations in housework, etc. When speaking to your family on the telephone during the application period, ask as many day-to-day questions as possible, and try to establish exactly what will be expected of you, how many nights babysitting at weekends, restrictions on social life, use of the car, how private are the living arrangements, etc. The counsellors and advisers provided by the sending organisations should be able to sort out problems and in extreme cases can find alternative families. Consider carefully the pros and cons of the city you will be going to. **Emma Purcell** was not altogether happy to be sent to Memphis, Tennessee, which she describes as the '*most backward and redneck city in the USA*':

> *I was a very naïve 18-year-old applying to be an au pair for a deferred year before uni-versity. During my eight months so far, I have experienced highs and lows. I have been very lucky with my host family who have made me feel one of the family. I have travelled the USA and Mexico frequently staying in suites and being treated as royalty since my host dad is president of Holiday Inn. On the bad side, I have lost numerous friends who have not had such good luck. One was working 60 hours a week (for no extra pay) with the brattiest children, so she left. Another girl from Australia lasted six months with her neurotic family who yelled at her for not cleaning the toaster daily and for folding the socks wrong. Finally she plucked up the courage to talk to her host parents and their immediate response was to throw her out. A very strong personality is required to be an au pair for a year in the States.*

About half a dozen agencies in the UK send au pairs to the USA, and it is worth com-paring their literature. The *Au Pair in America* programme (see 'Directory of Specialist Gap Year Programmes') is the largest organisation placing in excess of 4,000 young people in au pair and nanny placements throughout the country. It has representa-tives in Europe, South Africa, Australia, etc. and agent/interviewers throughout the UK and worldwide. The programme operates under the auspices of the American Institute for Foreign Study (AIFS) though some of the selection has been devolved to independent au pair agencies such as *Childcare International* in London (www.childint.co.uk).

Other active au pair Exchange Visitor Programmes are smaller but may be able to offer a more personal service and more choice in the destination and family you work for. Try for example *Au Pair Care Inc* in San Francisco (www.aupaircare.com) which is partnered with an agency in Hertfordshire; *EurAupair* (www.euraupair.com) whose UK partner is EurAupair UK in Shropshire (01952 460733; maureen_asseuk@yahoo.co.uk). You can also make direct contact with the US offices of *GoAUPAIR* (www.goaupair.com) and *Au Pair USA* in New York (+1 800 AU PAIRS (28 72477) or +1 212 926 0446; www.aupairusa.org).

## SEASONAL JOBS

Labour demands in summer resorts sometimes reach crisis proportions especially along the eastern seaboard. Dozens of sites may prove useful, though www.coolworks.com and www.jobmonkey.com are especially recommended for seasonal jobs in the tourist industry.

The majority of seasonal jobs will pay the minimum wage of US$7.25 (from July 2009), though some states have legislated a higher wage, e.g. California and Massachusetts (US$8), etc. and five southern states have no minimum wage. Trainee workers aged under 20 may be paid at least the youth minimum of US$4.25 for the first 90 days of their employment. People in jobs that rely on tips earn a pittance since the minimum hourly wage for tipped employees in the US is an appalling US$2.13. These can be checked on the Department of Labor's website (dol.gov/esa/minwage/america.htm).

Live-in jobs are probably preferable, and are often available to British students whose terms allow them to stay beyond Labor Day, the first Monday in September, when most American students go back to 'school' (i.e. university). After working a season at a large resort in Wisconsin, **Timothy Payne** concluded:

> *Without doubt the best jobs in the USA are to be found in the resorts, simply because they pay a reasonable wage as well as providing free food and accommodation. Since many resorts are located in remote spots, it is possible to save most of your wages and tips, and also enjoy free use of the resort's facilities. Whatever job you end up with you should have a good time due to the large number of students working there.*

Popular resorts are often a sure bet, especially if you arrive in April/May (before US students arrive). **Katherine Smith**, who got her J-1 visa through BUNAC, describes the range of jobs she found in Ocean City, a popular seaside resort in Maryland which absorbs a large number of Britons:

> *I decided to spend my summer in Ocean Beach because I knew the job scene would be favourable. I found a job as a waitress in a steak restaurant and another full-time job as a reservations clerk in a hotel by approaching employers on an informal basis and enquiring about possible job vacancies. In my case this was very fruitful and I found two relatively well-paid jobs which I enjoyed very much. Other jobs available included fairground attendant, fastfood sales assistant, lifeguard, kitchen assistant, chambermaid and every other possible type of work associated with a busy oceanside town. Ocean City was packed with foreign workers. As far as I know, none had any trouble finding work; anyone could have obtained half a dozen jobs. Obviously the employers are used to a high turnover of workers, especially if the job is boring. So it's not difficult to walk out of a job on a day's notice and into another one. It really was a great place to spend the summer. I would recommend a holiday resort to anyone wishing to work hard and have a really wild time.*

The Disney International Programs at the Walt Disney World Resort near Orlando in Florida are made up of two programmes: the '*Disney International College Program*' (5–12 months for students and recent graduates) and the one-year '*Cultural Representative Program*'. Participants in both programmes work in front line roles at Disney's theme parks and resorts (+1 407 934 7470; wdw.int.recruiting@disney.com; disney internationalprograms.com). People from the UK and about a dozen other countries are hired to represent the culture, heritage and customs of their countries in a themed pavilion. In the UK, the annual recruiting presentations usually take place in March and October; for details in the UK and Ireland contact Yummy Jobs in London (enquiries@ yummyjobs.com). Any job which involves tips is usually more lucrative than others; wages can be swelled by more than US$100 in a five-hour shift. The gated staff apartments have lots of facilities and a buzzing social life.

After checking out the feedback on the unofficial website for International Program alumni (http://wdwip.com), most of it very enthusiastic, **Catherine Howard** from Cork, Ireland decided to apply to work in Florida. Unfortunately there is no separate Irish pavilion, but she sent an application off to Yummy Jobs anyway for their J-1 Cultural Resort Program and, after she had paid their processing charges of about US$2,000, they found her a front desk position at the Walt Disney World Swan and Dolphin Hotel next to Epcot but not owned by Disney. Interestingly, the literature from the sponsoring organisation in the USA made the training and visa scheme sound far more rigorous a process than it actually was and in the end her interview at the US embassy in Dublin lasted all of 60 seconds.

**CATHERINE HOWARD** had a wonderful 18 months, in spite of sometimes baulking at American business culture:

*I loved my job. Everyone was really nice and helpful, and I did actually enjoy chatting with guests. You are in Disney World after all, so for the most part, guests are usually happy to be there. Sometimes it was difficult to stomach the touchy-feely parts of corporate America. At pre-shift meetings, we would talk about 'core values' and making our guests feel special, and no pre-shift was complete without each of us reciting an example from our own lives where we were made to feel special as well. The Americans did this willingly without irony or self-consciousness, but it wrecked my head. The way I saw it, our time would be better spent fixing the actual problems the hotel had, instead of feeling special, but this attitude got me into trouble with the manager, so my advice would be to smile and suck it up instead! (This was the same manager, mind you, that introduced a directive whereby, if a guest asked us how we were today, we had to reply with a word of three syllables or more, e.g. 'good' was not allowed, but 'wonderful' or 'fantastic' was okay. My favourite was 'homicidal'.)*

*I loved my time in Florida and going there is one of the best decisions I ever made. But my first three months or so were one of the lowest points in my entire life, because I made one crucial mistake: I never learned to drive. I couldn't quite fathom what people meant when they said that in Orlando you couldn't walk anywhere. Not only was I a freak – the only person over the age of 16 in the entire state of Florida who couldn't drive a car – but when it came to finding an apartment, my options were severely limited. Four months in, I learned to drive, bought a car and moved into a much nicer apartment with one of my new best friends.*

*During my 18 months in Orlando, I got to:*
- *See a space shuttle launch from Cape Canaveral – one of my Top 3 Dreams*
- *Spot celebrities. The best one was seeing Steven Tyler in the queue for Pirates of the Caribbean!*
- *Attend a Hallowe'en screening of the* Rocky Horror Show, *in costume.*
- *Watch fireworks every night on my way home from work (and the Seaworld fireworks from my patio every night in the summer)*
- *Go to Mickey's Very Merry Christmas Party at the Magic Kingdom – twice.*
- *Drink and eat my way around Epcot's Food and Wine Festival.*
- *Go to Washington DC, Miami, Mardi Gras in New Orleans, New York at Christmastime, etc.*
- *Wake up to sunshine almost every single morning.*

## SOCCER COACHING

Soccer is gaining huge popularity in North America, including among girls, and demand is strong for young British coaches (now referred to as 'professional trainers') to work on summer coaching schemes. A number of companies recruit players to work regionally or throughout the country including Hawaii:

***Goal-Line Soccer Inc***, Corvallis, Oregon (+1 541 753 5833; info@goal-line.com; www.goal-line.com). Minimum age 21. Mostly in Oregon and Washington. Recruits through BUNAC for July and early August only.

**Major League Soccer Camps**, Connecticut. UK recruitment, Leeds (0113 276 8826; chir.andrew@mlscamps.com; www.mlscamps.com/employment). The best known and largest company, sending out 400–500 coaches for the busy summer season. Package costing £575 includes kit, training, flights from UK, rental car plus gas and insurance expenses, emergency healthcare insurance and a wage of at least US$150 per week. MLSC assists with processing of H2-B visas.

**Soccer Academy Inc**, Manassas, Virginia (www.soccer-academy.com). European-based coaches should apply to Mark Jennings, 38 Shawfield Road, Hadfield, Glossop, Derbyshire SK13 2BJ (07814 390740; markjenco@aol.com).

**UK Elite Soccer**, Cedar Knolls, New Jersey (+1 973 631 9802; jobs@UKElite.com). Offers soccer camps, coaching and programmes in 16 states, mainly on the east coast. Seasonal coaches needed March to November and 70 summer coaches in July to August. Summer coaches earn salary of US$1,400 plus US$4,000 in expenses.

It is more important to be good at working with kids than to be a great football player, though of course it is easier to command the respect of the kids if you can show them good skills and a few tricks. Most companies prefer to hire candidates with a National Coaching Licence, e.g. FA-Level 1 coaching which can be acquired after doing a course lasting 24–40 hours (see www.1st4sportqualifications.com). You are likely also to need an enhanced criminal records bureau check and emergency first aid certificate.

**DOM SAMUELS** was in the last year of his undergraduate programme when he decided to apply for a Summer/Fall coaching role in the USA with MLS Camps.

'After an initial assessment of applicants in Leeds (among other locations), I attended an intensive four-day course at Lilleshall, the National Sports Centre north of Telford, which encompassed various teaching/coaching techniques and forms of assessment. I was told to expect an email and remember well the subject line of that email which read 'Welcome to LA...'. Unbelievable!

Coaching children from the ages of 3 to 19 meant work was varied every day and I got the opportunity to really get to know some of the children. During the fall, coaching wouldn't commence until after school on weekdays and last from 4pm till 9 or 10pm. Summer Camp hours were different, in the morning or all day. One of the most notable days was when, *along with a handful of other coaches, I was sent to coach Hispanic children in downtown LA. Unbeknown to us, it was a heat wave that weekend and we were scheduled to coach from 8am till 3pm. It was 'extra work' but saw us paid for the extra hours, which is always nice in the next pay cheque. However, with the heat wave, not only did the children feel it, but so did we. We were coaching the children on Astro-turf. The rubber base of the turf was melting, and our feet were literally burning as we coached. When we got back to our host's house, we were greeted with two words: 'Beer, Pool'. If you're not a people-person, this job isn't for you.*

*I think the job is glamorised by some... coach in the sunshine, party every weekend, meet great and like-minded lads and ladies, get put up in plush mansions. I connected with many families I stayed with and struggled emotionally to say goodbye. But that's the job. You go into a place, provide a service, get out and do it all again somewhere else. Although many aspects of the job are appealing, the emotional connection that I made with many people is somewhat ignored. I have met and made friends and family for life. Utah and California are homes-from-home for me.*

*The time off we got was rare so I indulged when possible, usually taking a road trip. En route from Vegas to Arizona we saw a sign which said, 'Grand Canyon, 49 miles west ridge' which we assumed would be no more than a couple of hours out of our way, including time out for a few Kodak moments. Not quite. We drove and drove until the road actually ended. We were at the Colorado river. Seven lads, one with a geography degree and a map of the entire US, and we couldn't navigate our way to the biggest hole in the planet. Hilarious!'*

## VOLUNTEERING

*Volunteers for Peace* (www.vfp.org) place hundreds of foreign volunteers on about 35 projects in the USA, ranging from accompanying a group of disabled people on holiday to joining a peace camp in New England; the joining fee is US$300. BUNAC has a Volunteer USA programme in association with American Conservation Experience (ACE) based in Flagstaff, Arizona in which volunteers are deployed in environmental projects, often in areas of outstanding beauty such as the Grand Canyon or Yosemite National Park, for eight to 12 weeks at a cost of £250 plus flights and insurance.

Voluntary opportunities in the USA range from the intensely urban to the decidedly rural. In the former category, you can build houses in deprived areas throughout the USA with *Habitat for Humanity* (www.habitat.org) or work with inner city youth, the homeless, etc. in New York City with the *Winant Clayton Volunteers* (www.winant clayton.org.uk).

The American Hiking Society (AHS) collates volunteer opportunities from around the United States to build, maintain and restore foot trails in America's backcountry. No prior trail work experience is necessary, but volunteers should be able to hike at least 5 miles a day, supply their own backpacking equipment (including tent), pay a US$275 registration fee and arrange transport to and from the work site. Food is provided on some projects. For a schedule of projects, go to www.AmericanHiking.org or ring the Volunteer Vacations department of the AHS on +1 301 565 6714 or +1 800 972 8608.

The ever-growing Student Conservation Association (+1 603 543 1700; www. thesca.org) places anyone 18 or older in conservation and environmental internships in national parks and forests nationwide. If accepted, interns are placed with a land-management agency (National Park Service, US Forest Service) anywhere in the USA for three to six months. Positions range widely, from wildlife management to native plant restoration to wilderness ranger-ing to trail work to fisheries. During the internship, participants work alongside agency employees, basically doing the same work as they do, and gain insight into normally impenetrable organisations. Travel expenses within the USA, housing, training and a weekly stipend are provided.

At a loose end after university, **Emily Sloane** decided to spend some time in the great outdoors:

> *I did a six-month internship in the glacier-covered North Cascades National Park in Washington State. I was a member of the native plant propagation team and spent my season taking care of nursery plants, gathering seeds and swinging pick-mattocks to loosen up restoration sites so that we could re-vegetate them. I had ample time to explore the mountains, picking up some mountaineering equipment and skills, and as an intern was given occasional special privileges, like a spot on an elite botanical expedition for a nearby university and a ride over the mountains in my boss's friend's ultralight glider. My supervisors were lovably insane, leading us in Pilates sessions at the beginning of every workday, screaming out classic rock songs as we planted in the November snow and (per my request) donning wigs for an entire workday as a birthday gift to me. One of my best summers EVER.*

It is also worth trying the *Appalachian Trail Conservancy* based in Harpers Ferry, West Virginia (+1 304 535 6331; crews@appalachiantrail.org), which organises work parties to maintain the Appalachian Trail, lasting one to six weeks. Volunteers receive food, accommodation and insurance. The *Appalachian Mountain Club* (*AMC*) in Gorham New Hampshire (+1 603 466 2721; www.outdoors.org) is one of the oldest outdoor recreation organisations in the country. It operates a system of backcountry hiker huts in the White Mountains of New Hampshire, maintains hundreds of miles of trails and offers environmental education and conservation activities. The AMC hires plenty of

Europeans to work at its base lodge at Pinkham Notch at the foot of Mt Washington, New England's tallest peak (notorious for its horrendous weather). The work there might not itself be terribly exciting – kitchen or housekeeping duties, most likely – but it provides access to a very beautiful area and a community of rugged outdoorsy folks. It might be possible for a foreigner to score a backcountry job although, as these positions are much more competitive, it would be prudent to plan ahead (apply by December for the following summer). The busiest season at the AMC's facilities runs from late May to late August.

# Canada

Canada is one of those countries your mum probably won't mind you visiting for part of your gap year (New Zealand is another). It has what mums like in abundance: low crime rate, prosperity, orderliness, polite and friendly natives and an excellent communication system. On the down side, it is expensive (especially compared with Nepal and Bolivia and all the other countries of which she doesn't probably approve) and bureaucratic (as you will soon discover when you look into obtaining a student Employment Authorization). It is also the country which inspired the writer Saki to say *'Canada is all right, really, but not for the whole weekend'*. However most gap students who choose to work or travel in Canada end up disagreeing strenuously with Saki.

## SPECIAL SCHEMES

The Canadian government administers three similar working holiday programmes for Britons (and other nationalities) and the good news is that gap year students are eligible. Participants must be full-time students with a letter of acceptance from a UK university or recent graduates, but there are also a limited number for non-students too. *BUNAC* has the exclusive right to dispense 12-month Open Employment Authorisation working holiday visas to students and non-students under 31.

Participants of programmes via BUNAC do not require a definite job offer but must prove that they have access to sufficient funds, currently £500. It is also possible for full-time students with a letter of acceptance at a UK university and a concrete job offer from a Canadian employer to apply for the Student General Working Holiday Programme directly to the Canadian High Commission. Participants are permitted to work only for the named employer for the duration of their visa, so it is much less flexible.

The website of the Canadian High Commission in London (www.canada.org.uk) carries the relevant information; the visa information number is 020 7258 6699. Processing of work authorisations can take six weeks and the government fee is C$150 (£90). In addition, the BUNAC programme fee is £200, and insurance currently stands at £123 for three months. Participants can choose to take BUNAC's group travel package or make their own flight arrangements. Places are allocated on a first come, first served basis so early application is advantageous (from December). The great majority of participants go to Canada without a pre-arranged job and spend their first week or two job-hunting.

Participants can choose to take BUNAC's group travel package or make their own return flight arrangements. BUNAC distributes a comprehensive *Work in Canada* handbook, which includes contact details for companies that have employed British students in the past. The majority of jobs are in hotels, and restaurants and shops in and around Toronto and Vancouver, tourist attractions and resorts such as Banff during the winter months.

During the run-up to their A Levels, **Hannah Jones** and her friend Sophie, both 18 and from Maidenhead, began considering the benefits of a gap year abroad. A working holiday would give them a taste of independence and would allow them to make the trip self-funding. So they both enrolled in BUNAC's Canada programme, which gave them access to a flexible Open Work Authorisation allowing them to live and work where they chose, and the security of travelling with a long-established company offering a support network in the country. While researching the different ski resorts in western Canada, they were keen to find an alternative to ever-popular Whistler, which they knew would attract many other gap year job-seekers. Instead they settled on Sun Peaks resort in British Columbia. On arrival at Sun Peaks, the girls booked into the local youth hostel and found jobs within a week. Hannah started working in a ski store where she learnt how to wax and fit rental skis, while Sophie secured a position on the front desk of a hotel. Locating long-term accommodation proved more difficult; after a three-week stint in the youth hostel, a chance conversation on a ski lift provided the girls with an opportunity to house-sit a new five-bedroom home while it was up for sale, an arrangement which lasted five months and made them the envy of their new friends.

*Oyster Worldwide* arranges paid hotel or crèche jobs for students in the Canadian ski resorts of Banff and Whistler plus Mont Tremblant in Quebec. The six-month jobs start in November or late February and cost from £2,245 to £2,545 including airfares. Hotel staff are paid on average C$9 an hour and some will have about C$12 a day deducted for room and board. As with BUNAC, school leavers must have unconditional acceptance from a college or university.

*Gap Year Canada* is a company run by an English expat who pre-organises chalet accommodation and seasonal jobs in and around Banff; the all-in fee of £3,000 includes accommodation (see entry in 'Directory of Specialist Gap Year Programmes').

Several schemes designed for gap year students who want to ski or train to be ski instructors in Canada are described below under the heading Ski Resorts.

# THE JOB HUNT

Those students without a pre-arranged job might find that the job hunt is tougher in Canada than most places. On average BUNACers take at least six or seven days to find a job in Canada. Even Canadian students sometimes find it hard to get summer jobs in the cities. It will be necessary to look presentable, eager to please, positive and cheerful, even if the responses are negative or the employers unhelpful.

# Oyster Worldwide

### Earn a wage and see the world

If you have the chance to take a year off from your studies or work then grab it with both hands. It's a unique opportunity to live a very different sort of life and see what you're made of.

It may be tempting to grab a rucksack and an open ticket and 'go where the mood takes you', but that's quite a hard option. The risk is that you'll drift around hostels having the same types of chat with endless strangers and not making the most of the place you're in. Instead, why not consider living and working somewhere truly different? Yes, working! Not only will it help fund your trip if you can earn a wage, but it also makes sense in many other ways:

- You'll live as a local and get to enjoy real life in a new country
- You'll make good friends among your workmates and housemates
- You'll get new skills and a whole lot of confidence

Oyster Worldwide offers **paid work placements** in **Canada** and **Australia** allowing you to live the life and earn a wage. In Canada you will get guaranteed work and accommodation in some of the best ski resorts in the world. We can arrange hospitality work in The Rockies or French-speaking Tremblant. Alternatively you could work in the Whistler resort crèche, entertaining kids and teaching basic skiing. You'll be expected to work hard but the social life and skiing are second to none. If you prefer a hotter environment, Oyster can help you find paid work in Australia. City-lovers can work in Sydney's restaurants, offices or shops. Alternatively, if you like the idea of being a jackeroo, we'll get you trained up in all the necessary skills and help you find a job in Australia's huge outback.

So, working abroad can be the answer to a great gap year. Just to prove it, here is what some of our travellers have said:

'I had the most amazing time living the Whistler way and getting paid for it! Not only did it help build my confidence and independence; it helped me prepare for times ahead, meeting people at university and living independently... but most fun of all, seeing the look on people's faces when I mention that yes, I am now a qualified ski instructor...brilliant!' (Jenny, Whistler)

'The beach and training farm were great... I worked with a group of other lads spraying non-indigenous trees ... and got to travel up to the salt pans in Burketown and down to the desert at Boulia.' (Rod, Australia outback)

If you'd like to know more about earning money on your gap year with Oyster, why not visit our website **www.oysterworldwide.com**, email: **emailus@oysterworldwide.com** or call us on **01892 770771** to find out more.

Almost all waitressing and shop jobs pay the statutory minimum wage which varies by province, mostly in the range C$8–$10.25, the latter being the rate for Ontario (from 2010). This usually results in an average weekly wage of C$320 while average accommodation costs C$400–$500 a month in a shared house (more in Toronto and Vancouver).

## SKI RESORTS

The past few years have seen an explosion in companies offering programmes to young skiers and snowboarders from the UK taking a year out partly to improve their form or even to train as instructors.

**ROB ASHPOLE** had always wanted to take a year out between school and university, with the main ambition of becoming a ski instructor. He started looking at different companies that offered the training while he was in the first year of sixth form, as a target to aim for at the end of the two years.

'**A**fter results day I went on holiday with my family to Western Canada, and this was vital in helping me to choose a ski instructor training course. We flew into Calgary at the beginning of September and drove to Banff, this allowed me to have a look around the town site of Banff and the different options of accommodation available with the different courses. Hotels in Banff were willing to show us around rooms used for the courses, and the Best Western Siding 29 Lodge, used by the International Academy, stood out as the best of the accommodation I saw. I visited Whistler too – it is an awesome place, but it's a much larger pedestrianised town and didn't have the same intimacy as Banff.

My travels in western Canada confirmed that Banff/Lake Louise was where I wanted to go and, with International Academy, which offered a five week November-December course. I arranged my own insurance for the trip with the British Mountaineering Council (www.thebmc.co.uk), around £250 for a year's snow sports insurance, although the IA offers its own insurance with a winter sports insurance company. There were only five of us on the early winter course, three skiers and two snowboarders. Everyone got on really well.

It was right at the beginning of the ski season, so the area had a limited number of lifts open at the beginning, though this was not a problem as the pistes *at Lake Louise are fairly long, and gradually more runs opened. On the positive side you benefit from quieter slopes, shorter lift and cafeteria queues. Unfortunately on our very first run down, one of the snowboarders fell and broke his arm, which meant that he missed almost all of the training, but he did pass his level 1 Canadian Association of Snowboard Instructors (CASI) qualification.*

*Training provided by the staff at Lake Louise was exceptional, they use a variety of training methods, as well as video analysis, so your overall skiing technique improves rapidly. The training also helps you to discover the vast amount of land covered by the ski area. The mountain offers awesome views over to Chateau Lake Louise Hotel, Lake Louise, Temple Mountain, Valley of the 10 Peaks, Mt Whitehorn, the list is endless! There are so many different parts to the mountain and a great variation in terrain, from awesome powder in Boomerang Bowl to the bumps on Lynx. There is the opportunity to shadow some ski school lessons at Lake Louise which proved to be great help.*

*The test for the level 1 CSIA qualification takes place over four days, focusing for two days on ski improvement and two on ski teaching. Everyone in our group passed, despite that week being incredibly cold, down to –42°C making the area the coldest inhabited place on Earth for that week! Unfortunately the last day of the test was the last full day of the course and the next day, December 19th, we were on the way back to the UK, except for one of our group who had a work visa and managed to get a job working for the ski school at Lake Louise.*

*The experience inspired me to return to get my level 2 CSIA that same winter. I returned from Canada at the end of March 2009, which proved a sad experience as I had had such a great time and made many new friends. I am so glad that I took the opportunity to take a gap year, I had always wanted to be a ski instructor and I achieved what I wanted. I will hopefully be able to return to Lake Louise some time next season so I will be able to take the Canadian Ski Coaches Federation (CSCF) level 1 qualification, as well as see some of the friends that I made there this season.'*

UK-based gap year companies such as *International Academy* and *NONSTOP Ski & Snowboard* tend to run programmes in the well known resorts of Whistler, Banff and Fernie (see entries in the 'Directory of Ski Training Courses'). Other possibilities include *Alltracks Academy* which offers its instructor courses and improvement training camps at Whistler, Revelstoke and Red Mountain. *Ski Le Gap* is active in Québec where it runs one- and three-month programmes during the ski season in the resort of Mont

Tremblant. The course combines ski/snowboard instruction with French conversation lessons plus other activities such as igloo-building, dogsledding and extreme snow-shoeing. The programme is geared to British students and prices are £7,000+ (2010) which includes London-Montréal airfares.

Other companies providing instructor courses include *PowderTrip* with an office in London (08454 900 480; www.powder-trip.com) and which operates in Fernie and Kicking Horse (BC). It is possible to qualify as an instructor in little known resorts such as Mt Washington on Vancouver Island; check out *Section 8 Snowsport Institute* (+1 250 702-SKI8; www.section8ski.com), which offers a 4-week basic training course for C$5,040 and the full 12-week Snow Leadership course for C$11,445 from January 2010. The Canadian Rockies Academy (www.canadianrockiesacademy.com) offers 11-week winter sports programmes in the Marmot Basin near Jasper (north of Banff) for an all-in price of £6,300 (2010) including return flights from London to Calgary; ring 01656 890156 in South Wales for more information.

For those who do not want to embark on the expensive and demanding instructors' courses but still experience a season on the slopes, it is possible to pick up work in Whistler/Blackcomb and the other main resorts like Banff/Lake Louise, provided you have a work permit from BUNAC. Banff is always in desperate need of cheap labour; there are literally thousands of young travellers, mainly Canadian students, Australians, Kiwis and Brits in town. No one seems to struggle to find employment, and as a result many employers are very flexible with hours. Many offer staff accommodation at a heavily subsidised rate, which is incredibly useful since rents in Banff are a killer. It's not unheard of for five people to share a two-bedroom flat to save money.

For Banff, consider *Sunshine Village Resort*, which employs about 400 seasonal staff, with limited basic accommodation provided depending on the position. Its website (www.skibanff.com) has lots of useful information for prospective staff including dates of their annual hiring clinic held at Banff International Hostel in mid-October. You can contact the Human Resources department for more information (on a toll-free number within North America +1 877 WORK SKI (877 967 5754) or +1 403 762 6546 from abroad; jobs@skibanff.com).

Moving west to the Pacific, the Whistler Chamber of Commerce posts employment information at www.whistlerchamber.com. Intrawest is the company that runs the ski operations at Whistler (as well as many other North American ski resorts). The Employment link on the site www.whistlerblackcomb.com gives dates of the annual recruiting fair and allows you to apply online; alternatively you can ring the jobline on +1 604 938 7367. Often there is an exodus of workers after the Christmas rush so it is possible to get a job once the season begins even if you haven't lined anything up at the main hiring time of October/November.

**James Gillespie** spent the winter and summer of his gap year working in Whistler. After taking the beautiful train ride from Vancouver, it soon became clear that getting a place to stay would be a major problem. But soon he had a job as a ticket validator which came with a free ski pass and subsidised accommodation:

*It was an excellent job and, although sometimes mundane, it was often livened up by violent and abusive skiers trying to get on the lift for free. Going there was the best thing I've ever done and I hope to be living there permanently eventually. I came home with a diary full of experiences, a face full of smiles, a bag full of dirty washing and pockets full of... well nothing actually. I was in debt, but it was worth it.*

## SUMMER CAMPS

As in the USA, children's summer camps are very widespread and employ a huge number of camp counsellors and ancillary staff. Unfortunately the big recruitment drives conducted worldwide by Camp America and BUNAC are for American camps only. However, *CCUSA* has recently begun to cooperate with a Canadian company called *NYQUEST* to supply camp staff for Canadian camps (see entry in the 'Directory of Work Experience').

# VOLUNTEERING

Some interesting practical community projects are organised by *Frontiers Foundation* (+1 604 585 6646; frontwest@shaw.ca; www.frontiersfoundation.ca) in low-income communities in Canada, including native communities in isolated northern areas. Volunteers of many nationalities, who must be at least 18 and energetic, work as tutors (e.g. of maths, science, English, music, drama), teaching assistants or recreation workers, along with assisting in First Nations offices. Most projects take place on wilderness camps for native children or in schools in the three northern territories (Yukon, Northwest Territory and Nunavut). Placements last 10 months from September. Some volunteers, preferably with relevant experience, are taken on for at least three months over the summer to help build and renovate housing. All expenses are paid within Canada including domestic travel and medical insurance, plus pocket money of C$50 a week.

According to **Emily Sloane**, watching the rivers break up in the spring was one of the most spectacular things she has ever seen, and her five months with Frontiers Foundation turned out to be one of the best experiences of her life:

*From February to June, I worked as an education volunteer in a Gwich'in village in the Northwest Territories through Frontiers Foundation. The school I worked in desperately needed help and positive energy. I became the teaching assistant in the grade 4–6 classroom, and I think that my presence allowed the overly stressed teacher to relax a bit. And of course, being in the Arctic had its perks. I was able to attend a caribou hunting field trip in the Yukon in March, during which I got up in the middle of the night to use the outhouse in 60 below temperatures. I'd go cross-country skiing after school every day, sometimes with several husky puppies at my heels, and as the days grew longer, my skis were sometimes postponed until 10 or 11 at night. All in all, a thoroughly satisfying experience.*

The organisation can assist with obtaining a work visa for international volunteers, a process which takes between two and five months.

If you are interested in working your way from farm to farm and want to meet Canadians, you might consider volunteering for *WWOOF Canada* (World Wide Opportunities on Organic Farms). You can access all the 800+ host farms at the WWOOF Canada website (www.wwoof.ca) after becoming a member. Membership costs C$45 or C$55 per couple (cash or via PayPal; a printed version costs C$10 extra). All volunteers must have valid tourist visas. Canada permits volunteer work in exchange for accommodation and meals, provided it is not the main object of the trip.

## COURSES

Although culturally hard to distinguish from the USA in some respects, Canada has its French language and culture to guarantee its distinctiveness. Few gap year students think of Canada when considering places to improve their French, but the French-speaking province of Québec has lots of language schools (mostly for English-speaking North Americans). For example the *Point3 Language Centre* (www.point-3.com) and *College Platon* (+1 514 281 1016; www.platocollege.com) both in Montréal offer short intensive courses with homestays. The UK-based language agency *Vis-à-Vis* can place students of French in Canada as well as in France and Belgium. Bear in mind that the Québecois accent is very different from Parisian French and incorporates many more loan words from English.

# Peak Leaders

Eimear Walsh

*EIMEAR WALSH remembers her time on her Peak Leaders course:*

'Before the course I worked as a software developer for an IT company in London. I worked for 7 years in the IT industry and was looking for a break from the office, especially with all the talk of the recession. I did some research online and came across the PL course.

I had a fantastic experience on the PL course. The whole PL team, from the staff in the office to our group leader Ed who met us as soon as we touched down in Canada were all so helpful and friendly. Everything was organised for us over in Banff - our lessons on the hill, evening meals and nights out. We had the best instructors teaching us, and the pass rate for levels 1 and 2 in skiing was an amazing 100%.

I also took part in a backcountry skiing weekend which was a fantastic experience. We also did first aid and avalanche training. Overall I had an amazing time on the course and would recommend it to anyone looking to get qualified or just wanting to have a fun time for a few months.

I had planned on returning to the office but I'm now working as a ski instructor in New Zealand and loving it. Taking the PL course was one of the best decisions I've made. I've gained new skills and made some great friends in Canada.'

# LATIN AMERICA

Two or three decades ago, when everybody was flocking east, few adventurous young travellers from Britain considered South or Central America. Possibly because Britain has few colonial ties with that part of the world, it was less well known than India or South East Asia or Africa. With the recent decline in airfares to the Americas, the situation has changed and thousands of gap year students now head to that great Spanish-speaking continent (including Portuguese-speaking Brazil). They travel independently, go on adventure tours, join a grassroots voluntary organisation or sign up with one of the specialist gap year programmes which combine volunteering in community service or scientific research, language study and active travel.

## PLACEMENT AGENCIES

The project and expedition organisation *Quest Overseas* (www.questoverseas.com) operates a 13-week package from January to April split into three phases: an intensive Spanish language course in Quito or Sucre or Portuguese course in Brazil, followed by a month-long attachment to a voluntary project such as working with deprived children in Peru, conserving Peru's rainforests or working in animal rehabilitation in Bolivia. Finally the longest stint is a 6-week expedition in the Andes which is also available on its own if preferred. The current average cost excluding flights and insurance is £4,000, plus a suggested project donation of £700.

Gap year specialist *Venture Co* (www.ventureco-worldwide.com) combines language course, local aid projects and expeditions on three programmes lasting 4 months in Latin America. *Inca Venture:* Ecuador, Peru, Chile and Bolivia; *Patagonia Venture:* Peru, Bolivia, Chile, Argentina and Tierra del Fuego; and *Aztec Maya Venture:* Mexico, Guatemala, Belize, Honduras, Nicaragua, Costa Rica and Cuba. Programmes start with a two-week intensive Spanish course given in Quito (Ecuador), Cusco (Peru) or Oaxaca (Mexico). Participants then spend four weeks on a local aid project before embarking on an eight or nine week expedition through the Andes.

*Outreach International* has been sending volunteers overseas since 1997 and offers gap year programmes in Ecuador (including the Galápagos), Costa Rica and Mexico. All the projects encourage volunteers to learn the local language and offer good language training. The placements include helping in orphanages, running a Feed the Children programme, organising sea turtle and whale conservation, arts and crafts projects and English teaching in coastal primary schools. There are also projects working with dolphins and volunteering at the premier dance school in Mexico. In Ecuador compassionate volunteers are needed to help run a project for street children and to work at an orphanage. Opportunities are also available to work in the Amazon rainforest. Volunteers live together in an Outreach International house but work in pairs on their project.

**Charlotte Kane** was lucky enough to be sent to the Galpagos by *Outreach International* to teach English:

> *I have just got back to Quito from Galapagos (January 2009). I had the time of my life out there and was absolutely devastated to leave. The family that I stayed with were the nicest people that I have ever met. Teaching at Ingala was great – I had never taught adults before and I really enjoyed it. I think that everyone going to Galapagos will want to see more of San Cristobal than the beaches close to the town, and also some of the other islands as well, because being in Galapagos for that length of time is a once-in-a-lifetime experience. Sometimes we were taken out on boats and did some incredible exploring with the fishermen and other boat owners. This was the best (and free) way of seeing the wildlife. On other occasions we paid for a trip. A four-day tour of the islands cost $400, a day's snorkelling at Kicker Rock is $60, and diving $100. I really didn't mind spending the money, because I wanted to make the very most of my time there.*

*The Leap* has a variety of programmes through South America which combine volunteering in eco-lodges with community and conservation projects. Options are available in Argentina (including riding and polo tuition), Ecuador, Costa Rica and Venezuela. See entries in the 'Directory of Specialist Gap Year Programmes' for other possibilities.

## NON-SPECIALIST PLACEMENT ORGANISATIONS IN THE UK

The following accept gap year students for Latin American projects if they fulfil the requirements (which in several cases include strong Christian commitment) but they do not specialise in placing year-out students:

**Caledonia Languages Abroad** (www.caledonialanguages.co.uk). Language courses for all levels and voluntary work projects starting throughout the year mostly for at least 4 weeks in Costa Rica, Argentina, Bolivia, Ecuador, Peru and (new for 2010) Venezuela. Costs from £65 per week plus a £295 arrangement fee.

**EIL** (www.overseasvolunteering.co.uk) provides volunteering opportunities lasting from 4 to 24 weeks in Argentina, Brazil, Chile, Ecuador and Guatemala, with an average fee of £1,500–£2,000 for 12 weeks.

**ICYE-UK: Inter-Cultural Youth Exchange** (www.icye.org.uk). International exchange organisation that sends volunteers to spend a year abroad and undertake voluntary work placements, for example in drug rehabilitation, protection of street children and ecological projects. Placements available in Bolivia, Brazil, Costa Rica, Ecuador, Honduras, Colombia and Mexico.

**Latin Link STEP Programme** (step@latinlink.org; www.stepteams.org). Self-funded team-based building projects in Argentina, Bolivia, Brazil, Ecuador, Chile, Peru, Costa Rica and Honduras, for committed Christians only. Spring programme runs March to July; summer programme for 4 or 7 weeks.

***MondoChallenge*** (www.mondochallenge.co.uk). Makes volunteer placements in several small mountain village schools in the Monte Grande region of Chile north of Santiago close to La Serena.

***TASK Brasil (Trust for Abandoned Street Kids)***, London SE16 (020 7735 5545; www.taskbrasil.org.uk). Children's charity that looks for volunteers over 21 to work with street children in Rio. Placements cost £1,000 for up to three months, £1,500 for up to six months and £2,500 for up to a year.

## CHILLING IN GUATEMALA

Twenty-year-old **Anna Ling** is not quite sure whether she is on a gap year or not, since her post sixth-form travels are open-ended as she pursues her main interest, writing and performing music. In 2009, she left home in Cambridge and travelled to Lake Atitlán in Guatemala, the perfect place to use as a longer term base. The small villages around the lake are all interconnected by launch boats, and the variety in atmosphere among these villages means that you can choose one that suits. Well-known party town, San Pedro, attracts many foreigners who come to attend one of the many Spanish schools. Rooms are available for 15–35 quetzals (£1–£3). Around eight backpacker bars offer live music, all advertised around the town, as are free film nights at Dinoz, Buddha Bar, etc. Musicians passing through will find many venues happy to swap free drinks for music.

According to Anna, anyone wanting to find bar work in San Pedro will be able to do so without too much effort, needing only to wait a week or so as bar staff are always moving on. In general, the pay is 50Q for an eight-hour shift, though tips can easily double that. Over half the bars are American or English-run, the others French or Spanish, so Spanish is not a necessity, though obviously a knowledge of the language will work in your favour. Street dinners of tacos and a wonderful warm sweet rice milk drink cost around 10Q while 30Q allows you to eat in a restaurant. Most hostels have kitchens of some description, and at the beautiful market up at the top of the hill you can find fresh vegetables and fruit, spices and rice.

San Marcos is not only at the end of the lake, it is at the other end of the spectrum, containing as many holistic and therapy centres as San Pedro has bars. San Marcos' niche crowd veers towards the spiritual, taking advantage of an incredible range of sessions and/or training in alternative healing. San Marcos is almost completely silent, and if you're looking to pamper yourself or to calm your mind after some San Pedro-esque debauchery, it's a tranquil heaven. But it is not a place to live on a budget or make money unless you are a trained therapist of some kind.

**ANNA LING'S** chosen place to settle for a few months from April 2009 was Santa Cruz:

'At Santa Cruz, my current abode, I have found a wonderful in-between place, with yoga lessons and a sauna, balanced with weekly parties and poker nights. I am based at the Iguana Perdida hostel (www. laiguanaperdida.com), the first building near the launch stop. With the daily dinner shared on a long table, guests and workers together, it feels very much like a family. The hostel runs on the basis of voluntary work. I exchange five hours of work a day, six days a week for my bed and three meals a day, on top of various perks like free internet and half-price drinks. Work generally consists of sitting behind the bar, taking orders and chatting to guests. One of my responsibilities is to organise the dressing up clothes for the Saturday night Cross Dressing parties. The hostel almost always has positions opening and the owners ask only that you stay at least two weeks. I personally recommend this relaxed work-for-keep system above getting a paid bar job as wages barely cover living costs. (The cost of staying here for non-working guests is between 25Q and 35Q, plus food is about 75Q a day for cheaper meals.) My shifts start at 7.30am or 1pm, leaving the afternoon or evening free for joyous activities.

The local village is a wonderful place and home to the Amigos (www. amigosdesantacruz.org), a charity that has brought a clinic to the village, along with a paediatrician, dentist, resident doctor and many volunteers who also work in outreach programmes, bringing medical care to the more remote villages. They have also built a library and a school offering free education to all children under 12, and scholarship programmes for older children. They are in the process of building a large new centre for vocational education. They give families water filters and generally help the health and happiness of the village in any way they can. I went up to the village to see Pam, the current brains behind the operation, and within the hour I was teaching an English class. I was soon given a classroom and started an enrichment afternoon with the local kids, doing arts, craft and music projects. The organisation is so well run that anyone willing to give some time will be put to good use, whether in construction, medical or teaching, or any other interests.

*Visas are not a problem at all, neither for work nor volunteering. No one even asks to see a passport. Language is no problem either. Personally I'm trying to live very much on a tight budget and paid language lessons (25Q-50Q per hour) would push me way over my daily price watch. But volunteering at the school has been the best opportunity for learning Spanish I could imagine. I take up a dictionary and the kids speak really slowly and clearly and it has helped so very much.'*

## EXPEDITIONS

*Raleigh International* (www.raleighinternational.org) has been running projects in Costa Rica and Nicaragua since 2001. Volunteers on community projects live and work alongside local families in remote regions to improve the infrastructure. **Lucy Cavoizy** describes the rewarding time she had on expedition to Costa Rica and Nicaragua with Raleigh International:

> *In a small village in Nicaragua we built a system of pipes and filtering tanks to bring drinkable water directly to the families' homes. Seeing the excitement on the family's face when they finally had a tap in their kitchen was one of the highlights. The host country participants helped us know more about the Costa Rican and Nicaraguan community and to interact better with the locals on the projects. Raleigh is definitely a unique experience you shouldn't miss. You get to meet some really good people and have amazing experiences.*

**Coral Cay Conservation** (www.coralcay.org). Runs expeditions in Tobago to survey the coral reefs and establish a database for coastal zone management. This part of the Caribbean is known for its diverse coral reefs and spectacular marine life. A sample 6-week marine project for a dive trainee would cost £1,950; prices exclude flights and insurance.

**Operation Wallacea** (www.opwall.com). Volunteer students, divers and naturalists assist with surveys of marine and forest habitats in Honduras and Peru, and carry out turtle monitoring in Cuba's Guanahacabibes Biosphere Reserve at the extreme western tip of the island.

**Trekforce Worldwide** (www.trekforce.org.uk/expeditions/central_america.htm). Expedition and conservation programmes that suit gap year students (among others) in the rainforests of Central America, concentrating on rainforest conservation, scientific and community projects. Extended programmes of up to 5 months offer a combination of conservation project work, teaching in rural communities, trekking, diving and language courses. Desert and mountain locations planned for the future.

**NADIA DAER** joined a conservation project on the Guyana shield, one of the few pristine rainforests left in the world, with Trekforce (part of Gapforce), after a full and busy gap year of working three jobs to save money followed by four months of travel in Australia and New Zealand:

'I considered many programmes and it took me a long time to find the one that was perfect for me. I had almost given up hope but I received an email from Trekforce about conservation in the Amazon, and it immediately sounded right. I looked into their safety policies and into what the project involved. The projects sounded worthwhile and fun and the location was perfect for me.

I worked with 18 other volunteers on a conservation project in the Iwokrama rainforest reserve where they are trying to establish a successful model of eco-tourism. We contributed by working with a local team of construction workers to build a timber ranger's station on the only road to run through the reserve. It now acts as a vehicle checkpoint so that rangers can try to prevent illegal logging or poaching in the reserve. We started and finished the project in two months of working from around 7.30am to 4pm Monday to Friday. During this time we took 5–10 days out to trek the Iwokrama mountains.

The living conditions were basic; we established our own camp, creating kitchen and eating areas and bathroom facilities from jungle materials and some limited supplies. We slept in hammocks under basha sheets to keep off the rain and washed in the Essequibo river. Roughing it to that degree was really exciting and very empowering, and surprisingly comfortable – inevitably it reminds you how little of what you rely on back home you actually need. Food was basic but nutritious; lots of nuts and raisins, porridge and canned food. Working conditions were good, our team of local construction workers guided us well, and always had medics on site. We all got the chance to try everything and each got a turn as foreman on site for a day. We were there during the rainy season and towards the end of the project we had to take some measures to avoid rising water levels around the camp and work site. It was great fun as it meant we got to construct bridges to cross the streams and ponds that *were forming. We spent part of our weekends in the local village, getting to know the people who lived there, playing football with them, etc. Our Guyanese guides also took us fishing and on nature spotting trips.*

*When our project finished we'd all loved it so much that we wanted to try and get jobs with Trekforce so we could stay out in the jungle. Most of us had jobs or university courses to go back for (I already had my place to study History of Art at Leeds confirmed). However, my time in the rainforest reminded me that a career in wildlife conservation would be fantastic. After university and while already in my first job, I got an email from Trekforce about a job offer, which I applied for and got. I still work for them now so my gap year certainly did influence what I've done since.'*

## COURSES

As mentioned earlier in this book, trends show that increasing numbers of people are learning Spanish. Whereas most prospective learners think of developing their language skills in Spain, more and more are looking to the many Spanish-speaking countries of South and Central America, particularly Ecuador, Chile, Argentina, Mexico and Costa Rica. A number of schools have been working very hard to bring their courses, whether in travellers' survival Spanish or in advanced Spanish, to the attention of potential clients in Europe and North America. Not only are the prices very competitive when compared to courses in Spanish cities, but you are likely to receive a warmer welcome if staying with a family.

Many cultural exchange organisations and Spanish language course providers can advise or even place their 'graduates' in voluntary positions and internships where they will have a chance to immerse themselves in the Spanish language. *Chile Inside* (www.chileinside.cl) in Santiago is an agency that can fix up internships, volunteer placements and working holidays in the tourist industry, the latter for a registration fee of $540 plus varying programme fee according to duration.

**Keri Craig's** successful time in Costa Rica arranged by Caledonia makes it clear why Costa Rica is another favourite destination for people who want to learn Spanish:

*Everyone at the school was friendly and so helpful, whether it was organising extra classes or booking hotels at the weekend. My teacher Gaby was wonderful and my Spanish improved no end having endless gossips with Gaby each afternoon. Considering my Spanish was very basic, I was very pleased with the way it developed so quickly. It was certainly an advantage being so immersed in the culture. The dance classes after school were my particular favourite. Frank and Victor were amazing teachers and soon had us salsa-ing like the locals. My only complaint would be the Thursday night dance class outing – European boys just can't dance like the Latin men!*

Individual language schools often have links with local projects and can arrange for students of Spanish to attach themselves to projects that interest them. Typically **Carisa Fey** started her big trip round South America with a short language course in Quito which led to some voluntary work afterwards teaching knitting to street kids. For example *APF Languages* in Quito (www.apf-languages.com) combine a programme of Spanish tuition with homestays and ecological or humanitarian volunteering. *Jakera* is a youth-oriented company located on the Caribbean coast of Venezuela that offers Spanish language programmes in conjunction with adventure travel and volunteer work experience (www.jakera.com).

Almost any Spanish language school in Guatemala, especially the city of Quetzaltenango, can help arrange a volunteer position. To find links to many of these language schools, visit www.xelapages.com/schools.htm. Casa Xelaju in Quetzaltenango (502 7761 5954; www.casaxelaju.com) runs Spanish courses and refers clients to internships and voluntary work in Guatemala.

Of course many websites link to Spanish course providers; for example www.yo-hablo.com has a useful facility allowing you to search Latin America by topic (e.g. Spanish with voluntary work, or Spanish with scuba) and by country.

## WORK EXPERIENCE

It will not be easy for a school leaver to find paid work or work experience opportunities in South or Central America. Although demand is ubiquitous for English teachers, from dusty towns on the Yucatan Peninsula of Mexico to Punta Arenas at the southern extremity of the continent, south of the Falkland Islands, most of the customers are business people looking for something more professional than what most gap year students can offer in the way of conversation practice. Furthermore, in a land where baseball is a passion and US television enormously popular, American (and also Canadian) job-seekers have an advantage. More detailed information about teaching in Latin America can be found in the 9th edition of *Teaching English Abroad* (2009, £14.99 from bookshops and Crimson Publishing).

It is commonplace for Americans and Britons to move from learning Spanish to teaching English. Independent traveller **Richard Ferguson** has travelled extensively in South America:

> Right now I'm in Buenos Aires. There are heaps of English schools and everyone wants to learn English. I made a few basic signs in Spanish advertising conversational classes, stuck them around Palermo (a wealthier suburb) and sometimes I'll stand on a busy corner and hand out leaflets. I'm charging about 30 pesos an hour and have a few students already so it's a good bet. I think any native speaker can teach here, better with experience and better still with qualifications. Either do as I did, approach some schools or look in the papers in the jobs section. I saw at least 15 in one edition of the Buenos Aires Herald.

English is of course not the only thing that can be taught. The flourishing skiing industry of Chile and Argentina creates some openings for ski instructors. A Scottish firm called *Peak Leaders UK* (see entry page 386) runs snowboard and ski instructor courses in the resort of Bariloche in Argentine Patagonia specifically for gap year and timeout students. The nine-week course (end of July-beginning of October) costs £7,940.

*Travellers* (www.travellersworldwide.com) offers internships in law, medicine, care, business and photography in Argentina, Brazil and Guatemala. Teaching, care and orphanage volunteer placements can be made in Brazil, Argentina, Guatemala and Peru, while sports coaching placements are also available in Brazil. In additional the company offer a range of language and cultural courses, e.g. music and dance (tango, salsa, samba and ballet).

Work experience placements in a number of fields can be arranged by several agencies in Ecuador; see entry for *ELEP* in the 'Directory of Work Experience' or try EcuEVP in Quito (www.ecuevp.com). Argentina is among the most Europeanised countries in Latin America. A cultural exchange organisation, *Grupo de Intercambio Cultural Argentino* (www.gicarg.org), invites paying volunteers and prospective interns from abroad to work in various sectors in Buenos Aires. Assignments last between one and six months and, including accommodation, cost from $1,000 a month. A four-week Spanish language course with GIC is compulsory on the internship programme.

## VOLUNTEERING

Short-term voluntary work projects are scattered over this vast continent, though many of the opportunities are confined to Spanish-speakers. The internet has made it much easier to unearth opportunities for volunteering, whether from one of the mainstream databases such as www.idealist.org, www.traveltree.co.uk or www.wwv.org.uk. One specialist website is www.volunteersouthamerica.net, founded by Steve McElhinney after he had been looking himself for 'grass-roots, zero-cost volunteer work' in Argentina. Finding volunteering opportunities that did not involve paying a large amount of cash to a middle-man or third party was more difficult than he anticipated and he spent dozens of hours trying to track them down. He then posted his findings on the website and now keeps it updated.

A good source of opportunities is on www.volunteeringecuador.org, whose listed projects charge $15 a day to cover living expenses plus a one-off registration fee of $190. In some cases a centralised placement service makes choosing a project much easier, though you will have to pay for the service as in the case of *Volunteer Bolivia* (www.volunteerbolivia.org) located in Cochabamba. It encourages its clients to sign up for a month of Spanish tuition while staying with a local family before becoming a volunteer; a combined language course, homestay and volunteer placement programme costs $1,670 for one month, $2,450 for 12 weeks.

**AFTON BLIGHT** from Michigan signed up with SKIP Peru to volunteer with children in a poor district of Trujillo, which gave her plenty of opportunities to get to know the culture:

'Throughout high school, I investigated various pre-university options. I come from a farming background, which I enjoyed, but I didn't want to limit myself to a career simply because it was within my comfort zone. I also have other interests such as Spanish, carpentry, music, and serving others. I was really undecided about what I wanted to do and I liked volunteering so I worked with Peruvian kids and families for nine months. Living in Peru allowed me time apart from everything I knew. The population of Trujillo is over a million people who walk or ride in taxis everywhere; I come from a small town that has no public transport. Trujillo is on the coast of the Pacific Ocean yet it is very dry with little vegetation, in huge contrast to my home in the States which is surrounded by crop fields and large coniferous trees.

Every morning I worked as an English teacher in two schools in the poor district of Trujillo called El Porvenir. After a good home-cooked lunch and a quick siesta, the other volunteers and I would walk back to the SKIP office to aid kids with their math, history, reading, etc. until around 5pm. El Porvenir is a very dry and sandy area with limited electricity and other luxuries, but SKIP provides necessary amenities for the volunteers and Peruvian families that it supports. As an English teacher there was not a lot of supervision. I was able to teach classes at my own pace with my own material which allowed me to be very creative with my lesson plans and subjects covered. It is a great job for people who are self-motivated, and if I needed materials or help with anything there was always someone willing to step in.

Meanwhile I became close to a native family during my stay in Peru which allowed me to see Peruvian culture from an authentic point of view. Not only did they help me to improve my Spanish speaking skills, but they allowed me to travel, cook, and spend holidays with them. I really enjoyed their companionship during my stay in Peru and we are still in frequent contact. Not only did I learn a ton about Peruvian culture, but I lived with foreigners from around the world who taught me about their beliefs, countries, and lifestyles. The other volunteers also made it apparent to me how much I did not know about my own country and the world.'

For animal lovers the *Inti Wara Yassi* wildlife reserve in Bolivia accepts volunteers to help care for injured animals (www.intiwarayassi.org). On **Rob Harris's** gap year, he was placed here by *Quest Overseas* and divided his time between working in monkey quarantine (feeding, cleaning, looking after newly arrived capuchin monkeys before they were deemed adjusted enough to join the main group in the monkey park) and building the infrastructure of the new park to receive more animals in very remote and basic jungle living conditions.

The relatively new *Flor de la Amazonía Animal Rescue Centre* in Ecuador accepts volunteers through the administrative office in the UK (www.youvolunteer.org), which also sends volunteers to teach and care for children as part of the Arajuno Road Project in Amazonian Ecuador. Both schemes start at an affordable $500 for four weeks.

## TEACHING PLACEMENTS

### ARGENTINA
*Colonias de Inmersión al Idioma (CII)*, Buenos Aires (+54 11 4831 8152; www. ecolonias.com). Recruits language facilitators to work in schools. Participants must have a university degree, speaking knowledge of Spanish and TEFL certificate. TEFL Placement Express fee is $200. Other cultural-cum-teaching programmes available for higher fees but with fewer prerequisites.

*Connecting Schools To The World*, Buenos Aires (+54 11 477 26724; connecting-schools@gmail.com; www.connectingschools.com.ar). Places graduate volunteers from English-speaking countries in different towns from March or July. 1-week ESL training on arrival, homestay with Argentine families, private Spanish tutoring, round trip bus ticket from Buenos Aires to location and 200 pesos monthly stipend are included in the programme fee of $500.

*La Montana Spanish School*, San Carlos de Bariloche, Patagonia (+54 2944 524212; volunteerwork@lamontana.com; www.lamontana.com/volunteer-work). Students who complete a Spanish course, typically lasting 4 weeks, can be placed in rural schools around Patagonia for a month or more. The placement fee is $100.

*Pasantias Argentinas*, Córdoba (+54 351 474 5947; www.pasantias-argentinas. com). Arranges professional internships in Córdoba including English teaching placements. Open to all native English speakers aged 19–35 for a fee of $195 per week. All programmes are combined with intensive Spanish classes.

*Road2Argentina*, Buenos Aires (+54 11 4821 3271; www.road2argentina.com). Places ESL interns for 1 to 6 months, as part of a cultural exchange and language immersion programme. International interns are accepted without relevant training or experience to help in private or public school classrooms. Programme fees start at $975 for one month and include accommodation.

## CHILE

***Programa Inglés Abre Puertas (English Open Doors)***, Ministerio de Educación, Alameda 1146, Sector B, Oficina 204, Santiago – Centro (+56 2 487 5466; voluntarios@mineduc.cl; www.centrodevoluntarios.cl). English immersion courses taught in state schools in small towns and villages throughout Chile. Volunteers receive a small monthly stipend of 85,500 pesos ($150) in addition to free room and board.

***Voluntarios de Esperanza***, Carabineros de Chile 33, Santiago de Chile (+56 2 717 99 37 or in the USA: +1 617 674 2649; info@ve-global.org). Works with partner institutions to place volunteers to work with children, including teaching English. Application process is competitive and no registration fee is charged.

## GRASSROOTS VOLUNTARY ORGANISATIONS

Hundreds of small NGOs and charities, some run by expats, can be found throughout Latin America. As you travel throughout the region you are bound to come across orphanages, environmental projects and so on, some of which may be able to make temporary use of a willing volunteer. The Quaker-run peace and service centre in Mexico City, Casa de los Amigos, has information on a variety of volunteering opportunities throughout Mexico City and Mexico. The Casa also has its own volunteer programme for those who speak Spanish and are able to commit for at least six months to a year, working for peace and social justice. The Casa is at Ignacio Mariscal 132, 06030 Mexico, D.F., Mexico (+52 55 5705 0521; amigos@casadelosamigos.org) and provides simple accommodation starting from 100 pesos ($8) per night.

The *Children of Ecuador* programme based in the coastal town of Bahía de Caráquez is a non-profit organisation created to raise the level of education of Ecuadorian children. Volunteers receive a week of supervised in-class training, and are expected to teach six hours from 7.30am, Monday to Thursday, helped by the class instructor. The cost of a minimum four-week homestay is $1,290, a third of which is donated to the programme. Spanish classes and other extras are provided (www.childrenecuador.org). One of the most acute problems in many South American cities is the number of street children. Working with one of the many charities that are tackling this problem can be both discouraging and rewarding by turns; for example *CENIT* (Spanish acronym for Centre for the Working Girl) in Quito has an entry in the 'Directory of Volunteering Abroad'.

A less stressful opportunity exists in the Nicaraguan countryside at an ecocentre that has been created by British expat Paulette Goudge (see entry for *Mariposa Spanish School & Eco Hotel* page 365). One returning visitor was very impressed with this unique place and thinks that '*Three to 12 months working with Paulette would offer a unique and very special experience for gappers, both to understand about Nicaragua/poverty, learn Spanish and make a very real difference somewhere in an exciting, new and growing project*'.

The Galápagos islands have people as well as animals, and a charity that works to improve education and health facilities for the local populace is Galápagos ICE (www. galapagosice.org).

Two volunteer agencies in Argentina are Insight Argentina (volunteers@help argentina.org) and Buenos Aires Volunteer (bavolunteer.org.ar).

# CONSERVATION

An increasing number of organisations, both indigenous and foreign-sponsored, are in-volved in environmental projects throughout the continent. For opportunities in Ecuador investigate www.my-quito.com/eco-tourism.html.

The *Fundacion Charles Darwin* operates an International Volunteer & Scholarship Program (Charles Darwin Research Station, Casilla Postal 17–01–3891, Quito, Ecuador; vol@fcdarwin.org.ec; www.darwinfoundation.org). Volunteers must be at least second year undergraduates and willing to stay for a minimum of six months. Without relevant scientific skills, international volunteers have to cover all their expenses including air-fares to and from the islands, food and accommodation. To volunteer at the Galápagos National Park, email volunteer@spng.org.ec.

The highest concentration of projects is probably in Costa Rica where the National Parks & Communities Authority runs a voluntary programme *Asociacion de Voluntarios para el Servicio en las Areas Protegidas* (ASVO). To be eligible you must be willing to work for at least 30 days, be able to speak at least minimal Spanish and provide a copy of your passport and a photo. The work may consist of trail maintenance and construc-tion, greeting and informing visitors, beach cleaning, research or generally assisting rangers. There is also a possibility of joining a sea turtle conservation project. Details are available from the San José office (+506 258 4430/223 4260; info@asvocr.org or lmatarrita@asvocr.org; www.asvocr.org). Food and accommodation cost $17 a day in addition to a $30 registration fee.

---

**GAPPERS' TIP**
*One British volunteer has warned that security at the national parks can be lax, allowing the odd confidence trickster to pose as a volunteer and rob money and valuables from the volunteers' dorms.*

---

*BUNAC* has conservation volunteering programmes (among others) in Costa Rica and Peru under the auspices of partner student organisations which provide back-up during the two or three month placements. Students (including gap year students) and recent graduates can participate if they have basic conversational Spanish. The Costa Rica programme fee is currently £1,149/£1,399 excluding flights, while the Peru pro-gramme costs are £1,249/£1,499 for two/three months in Lima, more in Cusco.

The organisation *Rainforest Concern* (020 7229 2093; www.rainforestconcern.org) has rainforest conservation projects in Central and South America (as well as Asia). Volunteers and students who are prepared to work for part of the day can stay at a cloud forest lodge in Ecuador or help with turtle protection projects in Panama and Costa Rica. *Quest Overseas* works with Rainforest Concern by sending volunteers to conservation projects in Ecuador, Bolivia and Chile.

# The Caribbean

The islands of the Caribbean are far too expensive to explore unless you do more than sip rum punch by the beach. Few agencies make placements in the Caribbean. *Greenforce* (part of Gapforce) is one that does, in recruiting fee-paying volunteers for marine projects in the Bahamas. Yet a number of gap year students have managed to spend time in this exotic part of the world by working for their keep, mostly on yachts.

Research opportunities exist as well. See the entry for the *Bimini Biological Field Station* in the 'Directory of Volunteering Abroad'. The Bermuda Institute of Ocean Sciences (St George's GE01, Bermuda; +441 297 1880 ext 206; bios.edu) accepts volunteer science interns to help scientists conduct research for three to six months. Applicants (who are usually upper level undergraduates or recent graduates in relevant subjects) should make personal contact with the faculty member(s) for whom they wish to work (see website). Note that immigration restrictions mean that the station cannot hire foreigners to carry out work other than research.

Cuba's economy is suffering badly, but its music and vibrant culture attract some prospective year-out students. **Nick Mulvey** from Cambridge arranged to spend several months studying guitar with a Cuban musician before starting his university course in World Music at SOAS. *Caledonia Languages Abroad* arranges Spanish courses in Santiago and Havana, and you can add salsa and drumming classes, diving and trekking. But the infrastructure continues to disintegrate and one of two gap year placement organisations have dropped Cuba from their list of destinations.

The *Cuba Solidarity Campaign* (London N4; 020 8800 0155; finance@cuba-solidarity.org.uk) still runs its work/study 'brigade' twice a year in which volunteers undertake agricultural and construction work for 15 days in July and December/January. No specific skills or qualifications are required but applicants must be able to demonstrate a commitment to solidarity work. The cost of the brigade is approximately £975 which covers the full cost of flights, visas, transfers, accommodation and food.

St Eustatius National Parks Foundation in the Netherlands Antilles has a volunteer programme to maintain park trails and a botanical garden, plus participate in a marine turtle monitoring programme organised by the *STENAPA Foundation*, Gallows Bay, St Eustatius (+599 318 2884; statiapark.org). Volunteers from overseas available for one to six months should apply though the British-based www.workingabroad.com. The cost for two months is £990.

# Projects Abroad

**Peter Cooper** spent one month on a community project in Mandeville, Jamaica with Projects Abroad:

'The scenery is ripe with lush rolling hills, nestled with hovels in the yam trees, rivers you can clamber up and beaches that make your heart swell with happiness. What makes Jamaica stand out from the other jewels of the Caribbean is not the cool breeze that compliments the grazing sun, nor the way your presence and work is respected and appreciated, but the unadulterated blend of happening without tourism oozing out of every orifice munching up the atmosphere.

With a civil pride that puts the rest of the free world to shame, you can immerse yourself seamlessly with Jamaican life, and having heard stories from all corners of the island, Mandeville is unquestionably the friendliest place. Around every pub door, every school classroom and every 20 year old Toyota corolla's cab's backseat, there's another story to tell, another experience to feel. And tell your wallet - with the cost of many items on the south coast deceptively low, you may come back some nights thinking you were printing money in your host family's bathroom.

Taking 22 seconds to email Bridgette (Country Director for Projects Abroad Jamaica) was the smartest and most influencing thing I've done in the last 18 years. I've crafted some of the best friendships of my life here with people so incredible I occasionally had to prod their stomachs to check they weren't mythical. I can't recommend Jamaica enough. Scrap the plans for a shop job and get out here and volunteer.

If you'd have told me this January I'd be hanging upside down from the roof of a school with a hammer drill in one hand, a tin of suspicious glue dripping in the other, trying to tell hysterical kids I'll give them a piggy back ride once I'd finished THIS pipe, I'd have probably have laughed.

In a market full of Jimmy-screechers (" devious young squires") we were told was the best patois translation), I can safely say Projects Abroad have their heart where it counts, and we've made a difference here that will outlive countless lifetimes and ultimately changed lives in ways I could never have dreamed possible.'

**LIZZIE WALKER** like many of her friends at school, burnt herself out during A Levels, and taking a gap year before proceeding to UCL seemed a very good idea:

'When I was eight I had decided I wanted to be a marine biologist, so a marine expedition really would be like living a childhood dream. I soon found a number of organisations that arrange for people to work abroad, study the reefs, and learn to scuba dive. It hadn't ever occurred to me that I could do something along those lines until it appeared on my Google screen, and goes to show that there really is so much out there to suit anyone. Initially I booked myself on an expedition to go to Madagascar, conducting coral reef surveys and working with the local people. When this fell through due to the political situation in the country I was absolutely gutted. But after searching around a little more, I came across Coral Cay, a conservation group that offers marine expeditions to the Philippines and Tobago. Tobago really appealed to me, and I signed up straightaway. Tobago is English speaking, and really easy to get to, which reassured me as I hadn't felt too confident about travelling for the first time through Madagascar, as a single British female. The fact that I was able to fit in a six-night stay in a New York hostel on my way here was just the icing on the cake.

I'm writing this from Tobago. The expedition site is right on the beach, and every night I fall asleep to the sound of the sea. I'm surrounded by people from totally different backgrounds, but who share a love for the ocean and scuba diving. It can be hard at times – we're living in close quarters and work long, hard days, but we also have a fantastic team – and great Saturday night parties! I'll be gaining qualifications in scuba diving, marine science and first aid that are going to be much more use to me than my GCSEs ever were. I have another 11 weeks left in Tobago and I know I'm going to love every second of it. I can't say I ever thought living on a beach in paradise was a realistic dream, but here I am living it – and it doesn't get much better than this.'

# APPENDIX

## CONTACT DETAILS OF ORGANISATIONS

***Accenture Horizons School Sponsorship Scheme***, 60 Queen Victoria Street, London EC4N 4TW (0500 100189; ukgraduates@accenture.com; UKI_people line_HR@accenture.com; https://microsite.accenture.com/UK_graduate_joiners/ Where_will_I_fit_in/Internships_and_placements/Pages/Horizons.aspx).

***Adventure Alternative***, PO Box 14, Portstewart, Northern Ireland BT55 7WS (02870 831258; office@adventurealternative.com; www.adventurealternative.com).

***Africa, Asia and Americas Venture***, 10 Market Place, Devizes, Wiltshire SN10 1HT (01380 729009; av@aventure.co.uk; www.aventure.co.uk).

***African Conservation Experience***, Unit 1, Manor Farm, Churchend Lane, Charfield, Wotton-Under-Edge, Gloucester GL12 8LJ (0845 5200 888; info@Conservation Africa.net; www.ConservationAfrica.net).

***African Impact***, 6 Carlton Close, Noordhoek, Cape Town 7985, South Africa (+27 21 7854319; 0800 5200926 (UK toll-free); 0877 2532899 (USA toll-free); sarah@ africanencounter.org; www.africanimpact.com).

***AfricaTrust Networks***, Africatrust Chambers, PO Box 551, Portsmouth, Hants PO5 1ZN (02392 730987; info@africatrust.org.uk; www.africatrust.org.uk).

***Agriventure***, International Agricultural Exchange Association (IAEA), Speedwell Farm Bungalow, Nettle Bank, Wisbech, Cambridgeshire PE14 0SA (01945 450999; uk@ agriventure.com; www.agriventure.net).

***AIESEC UK***, International Association for Students of Economics and Management, 29–31 Cowper Street, 2nd Floor, London EC2A 4AT (020 7549 1800; national@ uk.aiesec.org; www.aiesec.co.uk).

***Alltracks Academy***, 3 Egbert Road, Winchester, Hampshire SO23 7ED (01962 864203; info@alltracksacademy.com; www.alltracksacademy.com).

***Amanzi Travel***, 4 College Road, Westbury on Trym, Bristol, BS9 3EJ (0117 904 1924; info@amanzitravel.co.uk; www.amanzitravel.co.uk).

***AmeriSpan***, PO Box 58129, Philadelphia, PA 19103, USA (+1 800 879 6640 or 020 8123 6086 (UK); info@amerispan.com; www.amerispan.com).

***Archaeology Abroad***, 31–34 Gordon Square, London WC1H 0PY (020 8537 0849; arch.abroad@ucl.ac.uk; www.britarch.ac.uk/archabroad).

***Art History Abroad***, The Red House, 1 Lambseth Street, Eye, Suffolk IP23 7AG (01379 871800; info@arthistoryabroad.com; www.arthistoryabroad.com).

***Atlantis Youth Exchange***, Rådhusgt 4, 0151 Oslo, Norway (+47 22 47 71 70; atlantis@atlantis.no; www.atlantis.no).

***Au Pair in America***, 37 Queen's Gate, London SW7 5HR (020 7581 7322; info@ aupairamerica.co.uk; www.aupairamerica.co.uk).

***Azafady***, Studio 7, 1A Beethoven Street, London W10 4LG (020 8960 6629; mark@ azafady.org; www.madagascar.co.uk).

**Base Camp Group**, Unit 30, Baseline Business Studios, Whitchurch Road, London W11 4AT (020 7243 6222; contact@basecampgroup.com; www.basecampgroup.com).

**BBC**, Work Experience Placements (www.bbc.co.uk/workexperience).

**Blue Ventures**, Unit 2D, 22–24 Highbury Grove, Islington, London N5 2EA (020 3176 0548; enquiries@blueventures.org; www.blueventures.org).

**Brathay Exploration Group**, Brathay Hall, Ambleside, Cumbria LA22 0HP (01539 433942; admin@brathayexploration.org.uk; www.brathayexploration.org.uk).

**British Council**, 10 Spring Gardens, London SW1A 2BN (020 7389 4596; www.britishcouncil.org).

**British Institute of Florence**, Piazza Strozzi 2, 50123, Florence Italy (+39 055 2677 8200; info@britishinstitute.it; www.britishinstitute.it).

**BTCV (British Trust for Conservation Volunteers)**, Sedum House, Mallard Way, Potteric Carr, Doncaster DN4 8DB (01302 388883; information@btcv.org.uk/ http://shop.btcv.org.uk).

**BSES Expeditions**, Royal Geographical Society, 1 Kensington Gore, London SW7 2AR (020 7591 3141; info@bses.org.uk; www.bses.org.uk).

**BUNAC**, 16 Bowling Green Lane, London EC1R 0QH (020 7251 3472; enquiries@bunac.org.uk; www.bunac.org).

**Cactus Language Training**, 4 Clarence House, 30–31 North Street, Brighton BN1 1EB (0845 130 4775; info@cactuslanguagetraining.com; www.cactuslanguagetraining.com).

**Caledonia Languages Abroad**, The Clockhouse, 72 Newhaven Road, Edinburgh EH6 5QG (0131 621 7721/2; courses@caledonialanguages.co.uk; www.caledonialanguages.co.uk).

**Camp America**, 37a Queen's Gate, London SW7 5HR (020 7581 7373; enquiries@campamerica.co.uk; www.campamerica.co.uk).

**Camp Counselors USA (CCUSA)**, Devon House, 171/177 Great Portland Street, London W1W 5PQ (020 7637 0779; info@ccusa.co.uk; www.ccusa.com). *Scottish office*: 39 Sherwood Terrace, Bonnyrigg, EH19 3NB (0131 454 1687; Scotland@ccusa.co.uk).

**Camps International**, Unit 1, Kingfisher Park, Headlands Business Park, Salisbury Road, Blashford, Ringwood, Hants. BH24 3NX (01425 485390; info@campsinternational.com; www.campsinternational.com).

**Canvas Holidays**, East Port House, 12 East Port, Dunfermline, Fife KY12 7JG (01383 629012; www.canvasholidaysrecruitment.com).

**CESA Languages Abroad**, CESA House, Pennance Road, Lanner, Cornwall TR16 5TQ (01209 211800; info@cesalanguages.com; www.cesalanguages.com).

**Chalet Academy**, Broomlea, Lingfield Road, East Grinstead, West Sussex, RH19 2EJ (020 3287 6839; info@chaletacademy.com; www.chaletacademy.com).

**Challenges Worldwide**, 13 Hamilton Place, Edinburgh EH3 5BA (0845 2000342; info@challengesworldwide.com; www.challengesworldwide.com).

**Changing Worlds**, 11 Doctors Lane, Chaldon, Surrey CR3 5AE (01883 340960; ask@ changingworlds.co.uk; www.changingworlds.co.uk).

**Community Service Volunteers**, see *CSV*.

**Concordia**, 19 North Street, Portslade, Brighton, Sussex BN41 1DH (01273 422218; info@concordiavolunteers.org.uk; www.concordiavolunteers.org.uk).

**Connect Youth**, Youth in Action programme, British Council, 10 Spring Gardens, London SW1A 2BN (020 7389 4030; connectyouth.enquiries@britishcouncil.org; www.britishcouncil.org/connectyouth).

**Conservation Volunteers Australia (CVA)**, National Head Office, Box 423, Ballarat, Victoria, Australia 3353 (+61 03 5330 2600; www.conservationvolunteers.com. au).

**Coral Cay Conservation**, Elizabeth House, 39 York Road, London SE1 7NJ (020 7620 1411; info@coralcay.org; www.coralcay.org).

**Council for British Archaeology**, St Mary's House, 66 Bootham, York YO30 7BZ (01904 671417; info@britarch.ac.uk; www.britarch.ac.uk).

**Cross-Cultural Solutions**, UK Office: Tower Point 44, North Road, Brighton BN1 1YR (0845 458 2781/2; infouk@crossculturalsolutions.org; www.crosscultural solutions.org).

**CSV – Community Service Volunteers**, 5th Floor, Scala House, 36 Holloway Circus, Queensway, Birmingham B1 1EQ (0800 374991; volunteer@csv.org.uk; www.csv. org.uk).

**Deloitte**, Stonecutter Court, 1 Stonecutter Street, London EC4A 4TR (020 7303 7019; vconisbee@deloitte.co.uk; www.deloitte.co.uk/scholars).

**Development in Action**, 78 York Street, London W1H 1DP (07813 395957; info@ developmentinaction.org; www.developmentinaction.org).

**Disneyland Paris**, Service du Recrutement-Casting, BP 110, 77777 Marne-la-Vallée Cedex 4, France (http://disneylandparis-casting.com).

**Disney World, EPCOT Center**, for recruitment see *Yummy Jobs*.

**Dodwell Trust**, 16 Lanark Mansions, Pennard Road, London W12 8DT (020 8740 6302; dodwell@madagascar.freeserve.co.uk; www.dodwell-trust.org).

**Don Quijote**, 2–4 Stoneleigh Park Road, Epsom, Surrey KT19 0QT (020 8786 8081; uk@donquijote.org; www.donquijote.org).

**Earthwatch Institute (Europe)**, Mayfield House, 265 Banbury Road, Oxford OX2 7HT (01865 318838/1; info@earthwatch.org.uk; www.earthwatch.org/europe).

**Ecologia Youth Trust**, The Park, Forres, Moray, Scotland IV36 3TD (01309 690995; info@ecologia.org.uk; www.ecologia.org.uk).

**EIL UK: Experiment in International Living**, Elphick House, 287 Worcester Road, Malvern, Worcs. WR14 1AB (0800 018 4015/ 01684 562577; info@eiluk.org; www.eiluk.org).

**Eurocamp Holidays**, see *Holidaybreak Camping*.

**European Commission, Bureau des Stages**, 200 Rue de la Loi, 1049 Brussels, Belgium (02–299 23 39; http://ec.europa.eu/stages/index_en.htm).

**European Voluntary Service**, see *Connect Youth*. (www.britishcouncil.org/connect youth-programmes-evs.htm).

**Flying Fish**, 25 Union Road, Cowes, Isle of Wight PO31 7TW (0871 250 2500; mail@ flyingfishonline.com; www.flyingfishonline.com).

**Frontier**, 50–52 Rivington Street, London EC2A 3QP (020 7613 2422; info@frontier. ac.uk; www.frontier.ac.uk).

**Gap Enterprise Consultants**, East Manor Barn, Fringford, Oxfordshire OX27 8DG (01869 278346; johnvessey@gapenterprise.co.uk; www.gapenterprise.co.uk).

**Gapforce**, 530 Fulham Road, London SW6 5NR (020 7384 3343; info@gapforce.org; www.gapforce.org).

**Gap Guru**, Futuresense, Town Hall, Market Place, Newbury, Berkshire RG14 5AA (0800 032 3350 or 01635 45556; info@gapguru.com; www.gapguru.com).

**gapwork.com** (0113 274 0252; info@gapwork.com; www.gapwork.com).

**Gap Year Canada Incorporated**, Box 4955, Banff, Alberta, Canada T1L 1G2 (020 7096 1632 (UK); +1 403 762 3625 (Canada); info@GapYearCanada.com; www. GapYearCanada.com).

**Gap Year Diver**, Tyte Court, Farbury End, Great Rollright, Oxon OX7 5RS (0845 257 3292; info@gapyeardiver.com; www.gapyeardiver.com).

**Gap Year NZ**, Unit C4 Evans Business Park, Burley Rd, Leeds LS4 2PU (08456 525357; info@gapyear-newzealand.co.uk; www.gapyear-newzealand.co.uk).

**Gap Year South Africa**, PO Box 592, Cambridge CB1 0ES (020 8144 2423; info@ gapyearsouthafrica.com; www.GapYearSouthAfrica.com).

**Gap Year Thailand**, 1 Vernon Avenue, Rugby, CV22 5HL (01788 552617/07899 887276; david@gapyearthailand.org.uk; www.gapyearthailand.org.uk).

**Global Choices**, 420 Omega Works, 4 Roach Road, London E3 2LX (020 8533 2777; info@globalchoices.co.uk; www.globalchoices.co.uk).

**Globalteer**, Globalteer House, TheaChamrat Road, Wat Bo Village, Salakamroeuk Commune, Siem Reap, Cambodia (+855 63761802; volunteer.camkids@globalteer. org; www.globalteer.org).

**Global Vision International (GVI)**, 3 High Street, St Albans, Herts AL3 4ED (01727 250250; info@gviworld.com; www.gvi.co.uk). *USA:* 252 Newbury Street, Number 4, Boston, MA 02116 (+1 888 653 6028; www.gviusa.com).

**Global Volunteer Projects**, 7–15 Pink Lane, Newcastle upon Tyne NE1 5DW (0191 222 0404; info@globalvolunteerprojects.org; www.globalvolunteerprojects.org).

**Goethe Institut**, 50 Princes Gate, London SW7 2PH (020 7596 4000; german@ london.goethe.org).

**Go Gap Sport**, Swell Surf Camp, Cabarete, Dominican Republic (+1 809 571 0562; info@gogapsport.com/ http://gogapsport.com).

**Holidaybreak Camping**, Hartford Manor, Greenbank Lane, Northwich, Cheshire CW8 1HW (01606 787522; overseas_recruit@holidaybreak.co.uk; www.holidaybreak jobs.com).

***IAESTE UK***, International Association for the Exchange of Students for Technical Experience, British Council, 10 Spring Gardens, London SW1A 2BN (020 7389 4774/4771; iaeste@britishcouncil.org; www.iaeste.org.uk).

***IALC (International Association of Language Centres)***, Lombard House, 12/17 Upper Bridge Street, Canterbury CT1 2NF (01227 769007; info@ialc.org; www.ialc.org).

***IBM UK***, PO Box 41, North Harbour, Portsmouth PO6 3AU (023 92 564104; ibmstudent@uk.ibm.com; www.05.ibm.com/employment/uk/futures).

***ICYE-UK: Inter-Cultural Youth Exchange UK***, Latin American House, Kingsgate Place, London NW6 4TA (020 7681 0983; info@icye.org.uk; www.icye.org.uk).

***Inspire Volunteering***, 28 Chatsworth Drive, Market Harborough, Leicestershire LE16 8BS (07773 874545; sales@inspirekenya.com; www.inspirevolunteering.com).

***InterExchange Inc***, 161 Sixth Avenue, New York, New York 10013, USA (+1 212 924 0446; info@interexchange.org; www.interexchange.org).

***International Academy***, Sophia House, 28 Cathedral Road, Cardiff CF11 9LJ (029 2066 0200; info@international-academy.com; www.international-academy.com).

***Intern Options***, 159–161 Temple Chambers, 3–7 Temple Avenue, London EC4Y 0DA (020 7353 7699; info@internoptions.com; www.internoptions.com).

***Involvement Volunteers***, PO Box 218, Port Melbourne, Victoria 3207, Australia (+ 61 3 9646 9392; ivworldwide@volunteering.org.au; www.volunteering.org.au).

***IST Plus***, Rosedale House, Rosedale Road, Richmond, Surrey TW9 2SZ (020 8939 9057; info@istplus.com; www.istplus.com).

***i-to-i***, Woodside House, 261 Low Lane, Horsforth, Leeds LS18 5NY (0800 011 1156; info@i-to-i.com; www.i-to-i.com).

***IVS-GB – International Voluntary Service***, Thorn House, 5 Rose Street, Edinburgh EH2 2PR (0131 243 2745; info@ivsgb.org; www.ivsgb.org).

***JET (Japan Exchange & Teaching) Programme***, c/o JET Desk, Japanese Embassy, 101–104 Piccadilly, London W1J 7JT (020 7465 6668; info@jet-uk.org; www.jet-uk.org).

***Jobs in the Alps*** (info@jobs-in-the-alps.com; www.jobs-in-the-alps.com).

***John Hall Venice Course***, 9 Smeaton Road, London SW18 5JJ (info@johnhallvenice.com; www.johnhallvenice.co.uk).

***JST Youth Leadership @ Sea Scheme***, Jubilee Sailing Trust, Hazel Road, Woolston, Southampton SO19 7GB (023 8044 9108; sales@jst.org.uk; www.jst.org.uk).

***Karen Hilltribes Trust***, Midgley House, Heslington, York YO10 5DX (01904 411891; penelope@karenhilltribes.org.uk; www.karenhilltribes.org.uk).

***Keycamp Holidays***, Overseas Recruitment Department, see *Holidaybreak Camping*.

***Kibbutz Program Center***, Volunteer Department, 6 Frishman Street, Cnr. Hayarkon Street, Tel Aviv 61030, Israel (+972 03 524 6154/6; kpc@volunteer.co.il; www.kibbutz.org.il/volunteers).

**Kwa Madwala**, PO Box 192, Hectorspruit 1330, South Africa (+27 82 779 2153/255 4105; UK contact: 01590 688014; info@kwamadwala.co.uk; www.kwamadwala. net/www.kwamadwalagapyear.co.za).

**LANACOS**, High Streeet, Wrotham, Sevenoaks, Kent TN15 7AH (01732 456543; languages@lanacos.com; www.lanacos.com).

**Landdienst-Zentralstelle/Service Agricole**, Central Office for Voluntary Farm Work, Archstr. 2, Case Postale 2050, 8401 Winterthur, Switzerland (+41 52 264 00 30; admin@landdienst.ch).

**Language Courses Abroad**, 67–71 Ashby Road, Loughborough, Leicestershire LE11 3AA (01509 211612; info@languagesabroad.co.uk; www.languagesabroad. co.uk).

**Lattitude Global Volunteering**, 44 Queen's Road, Reading, RG1 4BB (0118 959 4914; Volunteer@lattitude.org.uk; www.lattitude.org.uk).

**The Leap Overseas**, 121 High Street, Marlborough, Wiltshire SN8 1LZ (01672 519922; info@theleap.co.uk; www.theleap.co.uk).

**Leonardo Programme**, ECOTEC Research & Consulting, Haines House, 28–34 Albert Street, Birmingham B4 7UD (0845 199 2929; leonardo@ecotec.com; www. leonardo.org.uk).

**Madventurer**, The Old Smithy, Corbridge, Northumberland NE45 5QD (0845 121 1996; tribe@madventurer.com; www.madventurer.com).

**Mark Warner** (08717 033955; www.markwarner-recruitment.co.uk).

**MondoChallenge**, Town Hall, Market Place, Newbury, Berkshire RG14 2QD (01635 45556; info@mondochallenge.co.uk; www.mondochallenge.co.uk).

**Mountbatten Programmes**, Michael House, Fifth Floor, 35–37 Chiswell Street, London, EC1Y 4SE (0845 370 3535; info-uk@mountbatten.org; www.mount batten.org).

**natives.co.uk**, 263 Putney Bridge Road, London SW15 2PU (020 8788 4271; www. natives.co.uk).

**New York Film Academy**, 100 E 17th Street, New York, New York 10003, USA (+1 212 674 4300; film@nyfa.com; www.nyfa.com).

**NONSTOP Adventure**, Unit 3B, Plough Brewery, 516 Wandsworth Road, London SW8 3JX (0845 365 1525; info@nonstopadventure.com; www.nonstopadventure. com).

**Oasis UK**, 75 Westminster Bridge Road, London SE1 7HS (020 7921 4200; enquiries@ oasisuk.org; globalprojects@oasisuk.org; www.oasisuk.org).

**Objective Gap Safety**, Bragborough Lodge Farm, Braunston, Daventry, Northants NN11 7HA (01788 899029; office@objectiveteam.com; www.objectivegapyear. com).

**Operation Wallacea**, Wallace House, Old Bolingbroke, Near Spilsby, Lincolnshire PE23 4EX (01790 763194; info@opwall.com; www.opwall.com).

**Orangutan Foundation**, 7 Kent Terrace, London, NW1 4RP (020 7724 2912; info@ orangutan.org.uk; www.orangutan.org.uk).

**Outreach International**, Bartletts Farm, Hayes Road, Compton Dundon, Somerset TA11 6PF (01458 274957; gap@Outreachinternational.co.uk; www.outreach international.co.uk).

**Oxford Media and Business School**, 5 Cambridge Terrace, Oxford OX1 1UP (01865 240963; courses@oxfordbusiness.co.uk; www.oxfordbusiness.co.uk).

**Oyster Worldwide**, Hodore Farm, Hartfield, East Sussex TN7 4AR (01892 770771; roger@oysterworldwide.com; www.oysterworldwide.com).

**Peak Leaders UK**, Mansfield, Strathmiglo, Fife KY14 7QE, Scotland (01337 860079; info@peakleaders.com; www.peakleaders.com).

**Platform2**, 35 Lower Marsh, London SE1 7RL (020 7523 2258; plaform2@myplat form2.com; www.myplatform2.com).

**POD (Personal Overseas Development)**, Linden Cottage, The Burgage, Prestbury, Cheltenham, Gloucestershire GL52 3DJ (01242 250901; info@thepodsite.co.uk; www.thepodsite.co.uk).

**Prague Film School**, Pstrossova 19, Prague 1, 110 00 Czech Republic (+420 257534013; info@filmstudies.cz; www.filmstudies.cz).

**Projects Abroad**, Aldsworth Parade, Goring, West Sussex BN12 4TX (01903 708300; info@projects-abroad.co.uk; www.projects-abroad.co.uk).

**Project Trust**, Hebridean Centre, Ballyhough, Isle of Coll, Argyll PA78 6TE (01879 230444; info@projecttrust.org.uk; www.projecttrust.org.uk).

**Quest Business Training**, 5 Grosvenor Gardens, London SW1W 0BD (020 7233 5957; info@questcollege.co.uk; www.questcollege.co.uk).

**Quest Overseas**, 15A Cambridge Grove, Hove, East Sussex BN3 3ED (01273 777206; info@questoverseas.com; www.questoverseas.com).

**Raleigh**, 207 Waterloo Road, London SE1 8XD (020 7183 1270; info@raleigh.org.uk; www.raleighinternational.org).

**Real Gap**, 1 Meadow Road, Tunbridge Wells, Kent TN1 2YG (01892 516164; info@ realgap.co.uk; www.realgap.co.uk).

**Safetrek**, East Culme, Cullompton, Devon EX15 1NX (01884 839704; info@safetrek. co.uk; www.safetrek.co.uk).

**SCORE International/Sports Coaches' OutReach**, 3rd Floor, Burleigh House, 25 Bar-rack Street, Cape Town, South Africa (+27 21 461 0466; info@score.org.za or info. nl@score.org.za; www.score.org.za; www.scorefoundation.nl (Dutch website)).

**Shumba Experience**, 95 Ditchling Road, Brighton, Sussex BN1 4ST (0845 257 3205; info@shumbaexperience.co.uk; www.shumbaexperience.co.uk).

**S.I.B.S.**, Beech House, Commercial Road, Uffculme, Devon EX15 3EB (01884 841330; trish@sibs.co.uk; www.sibs.co.uk).

**Ski Le Gap**, 220 Wheeler Street, Mont Tremblant, Quebec J8E 1V3, Canada (+1 819 429 6599 or freephone from UK 0800 328 0345; info@skilegap.com; www. skilegap.com).

**Snowcrazy**, La Rosière, France (01342 302910 (UK); +33 4 79 09 14 86 (France); laura@snowcrazy.co.uk; www.snowcrazy.co.uk/www.chaletcookerycourse.co.uk).

**Snowskool**, 37–39 Southgate Street, Winchester, Hampshire, SO23 9EH (0871 223 0060; team@sportskool.co.uk; www.sportskool.co.uk).

**SPW – Students Partnership Worldwide**, 7 Tufton Street, London SW1P 3QB (020 7808 1783/4; info@spw.org; www.spw.org).

**STA Travel** (0871 230 0040; www.statravel.co.uk).

**STEP (Shell Technology Enterprise Programme)**, 14 Bridgford Road, West Bridgford, Nottingham NG2 6AB (0870 036 5450; enquiries@shellstep.org.uk; www.shellstep.org.uk).

**Sudan Volunteer Programme**, 34 Estelle Road, London NW3 2JY (020 7485 8619; david@svp-uk.com; www.svp-uk.com).

**Tall Ships Youth Trust**, 2A The Hard, Portsmouth, Hants. PO1 3PT (02398 322055; info@tallships.org; www.tallships.org).

**Tante Marie School of Cookery**, Woodham House, Carlton Road, Woking, Surrey GU21 4HF (01483 726957; info@tantemarie.co.uk; www.tantemarie.co.uk).

**Tearfund**, 100 Church Road, Teddington, Middlesex TW11 8QE (020 8943 7777; transform@tearfund.org; www.tearfund.org/Transform/Youth+and+student).

**Ticket to Ride – Gap Year Surfing Adventures**, 263 Putney Bridge Road, London SW15 2PU (020 8788 8668; info@ttride.co.uk; www.ttride.co.uk).

**Travellers Worldwide**, 2A Caravelle House, 17/19 Goring Road, Worthing, West Sussex BN12 4AP (01903 502595; info@travellersworldwide.com; www.travellers worldwide.com).

**Travel to Teach**, Cll 5 De Mayo 505, Jalatlaco Esq. Noche Triste, Oaxaca De Juarez, Oaxaca, Mexico C.P. 68080 (+52 951 5132365; mobile: +52 12281259242; info@travel-to-teach.org; www.travel-to-teach.org).

**Tutors Worldwide**, Gaufron Villa, Gaufron, Near Rhayader, Powys LD6 5PB (01597 810 861; 07768 19143 (mobile) ; r.finney@xtra.co.nz; www.tutorsworldwide.org).

**Twin Work and Volunteer Abroad**, 67–71 Lewisham High Street, Lewisham, London SE13 5JX (0800 804 8380; workandvolunteer@twinuk.com; www.workand volunteer.com).

**UKSA The Maritime Academy**, West Cowes, Isle of Wight PO31 7PQ (01983 294941; info@uksa.org; www.uksa.org).

**Ultimate Gap Year**, 5 Beaumont Crescent, London W14 9LX (020 7386 9101; info@ ultimategapyear.co.uk; www.ultimategapyear.co.uk).

**UNA Exchange**, United Nations Association, Temple of Peace, Cathays Park, Cardiff CF10 3AP, Wales (029 2022 3088; info@unaexchange.org; www.unaexchange.org).

**VAE Teachers Kenya**, Bell Lane Cottage, Pudleston, Near Leominster, Herefordshire HR6 0RE (01568 750329/ fax 01568 750636; vaekenya@googlemail.com; www.vaekenya.co.uk).

**Venture Co Worldwide**, The Ironyard, 64–66 The Market Place, Warwick CV34 4SD (01926 411122; mail@ventureco-worldwide.com; www.ventureco-worldwide.com/www.ventureco.org).

***Village Africa***, 126 Hambledon Road, Waterlooville, Hants. PO7 6XA (01242 250901; info@villageafrica.org.uk; www.villageafrica.org.uk).

***Village Camps***, Recruitment Office, 14 rue de la Morache, 1260 Nyon, Switzerland (+41 22 990 9405; personnel@villagecamps.ch; www.villagecamps.com).

***Village-to-Village***, Callmate House, 1 Wilton Street, Bradford BD5 0AX (01274 397830; enquiries@village-to-village.org.uk; www.village-to-village.org.uk).

***Vis à Vis***, 2–4 Stoneleigh Park Road, Epsom KT19 0QT (020 8786 8021; info@visavis.org; www.visavis.org).

***VisitOz Scheme***, Springbrook Farm, 8921 Burnett Highway, Goomeri, 4601 Queensland, Australia (+61 7 4168 6185; info@visitoz.org; www.visitoz.org). UK Contacts: Will and Julia Taunton-Burnet, Oxford (07966 528644; will@visitoz.org).

***Volunteer Action for Peace (VAP)***, 16 Overhill Road, East Dulwich, London SE22 0PH (0844 209 0927; action@vap.org.uk; www.vap.org.uk).

***Volunteer Adventures***, 915 S. Colorado Boulevard, Denver, Colorado 80246, USA (toll-free in North America: 866 574 8606; toll-free in the UK: 0808 120 7613; volunteer@volunteeradventures.com; www.volunteeradventures.com).

***Volunteers for Peace***, 1034 Tiffany Road, Belmont, Vermont 05730, USA (+1 802 259–2759; vfp@vfp.org; www.vfp.org).

***Volunteer Uganda***, gapyear@volunteeruganda.org/www.volunteeruganda.org/gap year.html.

***Wild at Heart***, Suite 8, Corporate Park, 11 Sinembe Crescent, La Lucia Ridge, Umhlanga Rocks, 4320 Kwa-Zulu Natal, South Africa (+27 31 566 5264; info@wah.co.za.; www.wah.co.za).

***Wind, Sand & Stars***, PO Box 4322, Bath BA1 2BU (01225 320 839; info@windsand stars.co.uk; www.windsandstars.co.uk).

***Winston Churchill Memorial Trust***, 15 Queen's Gate Terrace, London SW7 5PR (020 7584 9315; office@wcmt.org.uk; www.wcmt.org.uk).

***Worldwide Experience***, The Oak Suite, Guardian House, Borough Road, Godalming, Surrey GU7 2AE (01483 860560; info@WorldwideExperience.com; www.World wideExperience.com).

***Worldwide Volunteering for Young People*** (www.wwv.org.uk).

***WWOOF (World Wide Opportunities on Organic Farms)***, PO Box 2154, Winslow, Buckingham MK18 3WS (www.wwoof.org.uk for WWOOF UK; www.wwoof.org/ www.wwoofinternational.org).

***Year for God***, Holmsted Manor, Staplefield Road, Cuckfield, West Sussex RH17 5JF (01444 440229; yfg@holmsted.org.uk; www.yearforgod.co.uk).

***Year in Industry***, University of Southampton, Southampton SO17 1BJ (02380 597061; info@yini.org.uk; www.yini.org.uk).

***Year Out Drama Company***, Stratford-upon-Avon College, Alcester Road, Stratford-upon-Avon, Warwickshire CV37 9QR (01789 266245; yearoutdrama@stratford.ac.uk; www.yearoutdrama.com).

**Year Out Group**, Queensfield, 28 Kings Road, Easterton, Wiltshire SN10 4PX (01380 816696; info@yearoutgroup.org; www.yearoutgroup.org).

**Yomps**, 10 Woodland Way, Brighton, East Sussex BN1 8BA (0845 006 1435; info@yomps.co.uk; www.yomps.co.uk).

**Young Explorers' Trust**, at the Royal Geographical Society, 1 Kensington Gore, London SW7 2AR (01623 861027; info@theyet.org; www.theyet.org).

**Youth for Development**, 317 Putney Bridge Road, London SW15 2PN (020 8780 7500; yfd@vso.org.uk; www.vso.org.uk/youth).

**Youth Hostels Association**, Trevelyan House, Dimple Road, Matlock, Derbyshire DE4 3YH (01629 592700; www.yha.org.uk).

**Yummy Jobs**, 120 High Street, Epping, Essex CM16 4AG (01992 579 999; enquiries@yummyjobs.com; www.yummyjobs.com).

**Zanzigap**, 18 Melrose Road, Sheffield S3 9DN (0114 249 1661; enquiries@zanzigap.com; www.zanzigap.com).